Java
First Contact

Java:
First Contact

COURSE
TECHNOLOGY

Roger Garside
John Mariani

Java: First Contact is published by Course Technology.

Copyright © 1998 by Course Technology — I(T)P°

Course Technology
One Main Street
Cambridge, MA 02142

ITP Europe
Berkshire House 168-173
High Holborn
London WCIV 7AA
England

Nelson ITP, Australia
102 Dodds Street
South Melbourne, 3205
Victoria, Australia

ITP Nelson Canada
1120 Birchmount Road
Scarborough, Ontario
Canada M1K 5G4

International Thomson Editores
Seneca, 53
Colonia Polanco
11560 Mexico D.F. Mexico

ITP GmbH
Königswinterer Strasse 418
53227 Bonn
Germany

ITP Asia
60 Albert Street, #15-01
Albert Complex
Singapore 189969

ITP Japan
Hirakawacho Kyowa Building, 3F
2-2-1 Hirakawacho
Chiyoda-ku, Tokyo 102
Japan

Disclaimer
Course Technology reserves the right to revise this publication and make changes from time to time in its content
without notice.

ISBN 1-85032-316-X

Printed in Canada

3 4 5 6 7 8 9 WC 02 01 00 99 98

Special thanks to these members of the International Thomson Computer Press team from Course Technology:

Publisher/Vice President
Jim DeWolf

Director of Acquisitions & Development
Robert Kern

Marketing Manager
Christine Nagle

Projects Director
Vivienne Toye

Manufacturing Managers
Elizabeth Martinez
Sandra Sabathy

Production Manager
Jaimie Livingston

Creative Services Manager
Diane Lennox

Project Editor
Amy Hayworth

Copy Editor
Judy Flynn

Technical Reviewer
Daniel I. Joshi

Desktop Publisher
Caroline McKenzie

Proofreader
Jessica Ryan

Indexer
Dick Evans

Interior Designer
Patrick Berry

Cover Illustrator
Leigh Salmon

Editorial Assistants
Becky Steele
Christine Cleveland

About the Authors

Roger Garside and **John Mariani** are Senior Lecturers in the Computing Department of Lancaster University. They developed this book while teaching their first-year students.

Acknowledgments

We would like to thank Professors Doug Shepherd and Ian Sommerville of our department for supporting our efforts with this book. We introduced Java as our first-year teaching language in October 1996, one of the first UK universities to do so. We would also like to thank Richard Cardoe for his assistance in developing course material during the summer of 1996, and Pete Sawyer for his cover concept. We would especially like to thank our first-year students during the academic year 1996–97 for acting as willing guinea-pigs for the draft versions of this book and the exercises. Finally, we would like to thank our long-suffering wives for putting up with us during the long process of producing this book.

—R.G.G.
—J.A.M.

Dedication

To Tessa, la migliore fabbra, and to Dan and Beth—R.G.G.

To Louise, and her own personal inheritance hierarchy: Moira, Elisabeth, Louis, Vera, and Thomas—J.A.M.

Contents

Part 2   Writing Objects

Part 6   Appendices

Preface

This is a book about programming in the Java programming language. It is intended for people who have no previous programming experience, so it is unlike many other Java programming books that appear to have been written by experts for experts. It was written from scratch, and not based on previous C or C++ text books by the same authors. This also makes it different from many other books—this book was developed for a specific purpose, and is not an evolution from an earlier book, which means it's well-suited for a first-year undergraduate programming course.

The authors have between them taught the first-year programming course at Lancaster University for over ten years, first in Pascal, then in Ada, and, since 1996–97, in Java, one of the first British universities to do so. This book is based on our first year's experience of teaching the language to a cohort of some 150 students. One author has experience in object-oriented software development and database management systems from Objective-C to C++ and ONTOS to POET. The other has written a number of text books on natural language processing and computer architecture.

Java is a very exciting development in the field of programming languages. We briefly explore some of the history of Java in our first chapter, but for now suffice it to say that it is very much a language of the 1990s and capable of taking us into the next millenium. Part of the "buzz" around Java is because it's the language of the World Wide Web (itself a major aspect of modern and future computing), but a significant feature of the language is that it's object-oriented. This means that we can think of systems as being composed of a number of objects that provide and request services from each other in order to accomplish an overall task. The object model can be applied from the early stages of system requirements and design, and carried through to coding, testing, and maintenance.

Rather than avoid or delay object-orientation, we have decided to make objects our departure point. We "grasp the nettle" and present our study of Java in terms of objects from the very start, rather than begin as a conventional programming text and graft on objects at a later point.

We believe that Java is an elegant language, with an extensive class library that supports the programming of graphical interfaces and use of computer networks. Therefore, we believe that it's a good language with which to introduce the concepts of computing, and it's rewarding in that the programmer is quickly able to write significant pieces of code.

The book consists of five parts:

- In Part 1 of the book, we concentrate on using objects. Here, objects are supplied either from the standard Java library of classes or from example classes of our own creation. The programmer writes applications that call upon the services of these pre-existing objects and interprets the results.

- In Part 2, we change emphasis and look at what is required in order to write (and use) objects of our own.

- In Part 3, we explore a major concept in object models, that of inheritance, and how we can apply it in Java. This part also covers two areas of Java which rely heavily on inheritance: the use of exceptions for dealing with error conditions in programs, and the Abstract Window Toolkit (AWT), which supports the creation of graphical user interfaces.

- In Part 4, we examine more advanced features of Java, such as the input/output facilities, and how applets — applications which can be executed over the World Wide Web — can be written. We also examine how common data structures can be realized in Java, introducing ideas about the use of pointers and linked data structures.

- In Part 5, we look at object-oriented design and show how we can identify objects from the requirements of a system and move forward through design and onto coding. This section is supported by examining the development of a system from start to finish.

We cover all the major parts of the language except multithreading, which we introduce only briefly in Chapter 21. In a book of this size, it is of course possible to cover only a small part of the extensive facilities provided by Java, so we introduce only a few of the main classes of the AWT, and we consider access to networks only in terms of the communication between an applet and its originating computer. Some of the sections are marked as optional on a first reading. We see Java as having a future as a good general-purpose programming language, rather than as just a vehicle for Web programming. Therefore, we spend most of the book discussing normal application programs, discussing how applets can be written to be executed over the Web only in Chapter 20.

The book contains many examples and exercises to illustrate the principles discussed; all example programs are also available through a Web site (see Appendix A). A laboratory manual is available for this book.

A number of new environments are becoming available for developing Java programs. This book describes version 1.1.1 of Java, and the development environment it describes is the basic JDK (Java Development Kit) from Sun MicroSystems. The examples have all been tested under the UNIX operating system.

We believe that Java is an exciting new development both in programming language design and in the development of the World Wide Web as a global information resource. We hope you will enjoy this introduction to the world of Java programming!

RGG & JAM
Lancaster
May 1997

Using Objects

CHAPTER 1

Programming & the Java Language

1.1   Programs & Programming

Most of us use computers and computer programs nearly every day of our lives. When we want to write something, we start up a word processing program such as Word or WordPerfect. When we have to do some calculations, we use a spreadsheet program such as Excel. Increasingly, if we want to find some up-to-date information, we turn to a browser such as Netscape Navigator or Microsoft Internet Explorer to search the World Wide Web. These are all examples of computer *programs*, written by a programmer (or more likely, a team of programmers) for our use.

A computer itself has no intelligence. As we shall see, all it can do is follow a rather detailed set of instructions. So a program is simply a detailed set of instructions in a suitable format that tells the computer how to carry out a task. For example, for a word processing program, it has to be specified how the computer is to deal with text typed in by the user, how to format the text as a series of lines of characters, how to change the format according to instructions from the user, how to check the spelling of each word against a dictionary of valid words, how to pass the text to a printer to produce a printed version, and so on.

Nowadays there are computer programs in places we might not expect. A modern washing machine contains one or more small computers, or *processors*, which control the sequence of operations carried out by the machine according to the instructions of the user and the state of the wash (is the machine full of water? is it at the right temperature? has the user specified a long spin cycle? and so on). Similarly, in a car there will be several processors to control the ignition system according to the state of the engine, to check that the seat belts are being used correctly, and so on. Each of the processors in these *embedded systems* will be following a program, or set of instructions, specifying in detail how the system should react to any particular combination of input information sensed by the processor.

The programs we have discussed so far are called *application* programs; that is, there is some particular task that we want carried out, and the program is designed to deal with it, perhaps (as in the word processing and spreadsheet examples) in collaboration with the user. However, there are other programs which do not directly carry out an application task but instead make it easier for an application program to do so. One such program is the *operating system* in the computer (such as Windows 95 or UNIX). This program organizes and manages the resources of the computer system as instructed by the user. For example, we can, by typing in a sequence of characters as a command to the operating system, or by clicking on an icon representing a particular program, request that a word processing program be run. We can request that the resultant file (a letter, a report) be passed to a suitable printer, and the operating system will organize the queue of files waiting to be printed. Or we can store the resultant file in a *filing system* so that we can retrieve it by name for use at a later time, and we can organize our various files in a way that enables us to find them easily the next time we need them.

This book is about learning to write programs. That is, we must learn to specify how to carry out a task in a clear step-by-step procedure, in sufficient detail, and in an appropriate format so that the computer can understand and carry out the task. We want to organize this programming task in such a way that the task will be correctly carried out, and the program will make a suitable response if the information supplied to it is invalid in some way (even if the response is simply to display an error message for the user). And we want to organize the program so that it is as straightforward as possible in the event that modifications become necessary because we want to extend or revise how the task is to be carried out.

In order to write a program, or set of instructions, for a computer to carry out, we have to write in a language the computer can understand, a *programming language*. Over the years, a vast number of programming languages have been designed for different types of programming tasks. They have incorporated different ideas of how a programming language should be organized to make it as easy as possible to write a program with few errors (or "bugs") in it.

In this book, we use *Java* as the programming language. Java was released by Sun Microsystems in 1995. There has been a lot of interest in Java because of its ability to deliver programs across the World Wide Web, but we use Java in this book because we think it is also a clear and elegant programming language, suitable as a first language for teaching programming.

1.2   Algorithms

If we are going to carry out any step-by-step procedure, we must have a clear and unambiguous specification of the steps needed. This clear specification, called an *algorithm*, doesn't have to be written in a programming language; it could be in some form of English or in some other more formal language. The problem with using English (or any other natural language) is its ambiguity, so we may turn to more formal languages to be more precise.

Here is an example of part of an algorithm for calculating the date Easter falls on in a given year. The algorithm is in the 17th-century language of the Church of England Book of Common Prayer. Actually, it is an algorithm for working out the position of the sun in a 19-year period called the "saros cycle," because this information is needed by the Easter Day calculation:

```
To find the Golden Number, or Prime, add One to the Year of our Lord, and then
divide by 19; the Remainder, if any, is the Golden Number; but if nothing
remaineth, then 19 is the Golden Number.
```

Here is the beginning of another algorithm, written in the formal language of knitting patterns:

```
SLEEVES

Size 4 mm (8) needles.
Working in St. St.
Pick up 70 (76, 82, 88, 102, 108, 114, 118) Sts. around armhole edge.
Work 10 (10, 10, 10, 12, 2, 0, 0) rows in St. St.
Next Row K.2. K.2. Tog. T.B.L. K. to last 4 Sts. K.2 Tog. K.2
```

And Figure 1-1 is part of a third algorithm, expressed in an even more formal language.

Figure 1-1: An algorithm expressed in the formal language of music.

What are the requirements for an algorithm which specifies how a programming task is to be carried out?

The steps of the algorithm must be *precise* and *unambiguous*—we must know, at least in principle, how we would specify each step in the programming language we are using.

We also need to be precise about what type of input data is required by our algorithm. In the Easter Day algorithm, a single piece of data is required, the year for which we want to find the date of Easter, but the algorithm states that it is valid only for years `from the present time till the year 2199 inclusive`.

The algorithm must be *correct*—we must know that if we set the algorithm going with suitable data, it will eventually finish its calculation and deliver a result which is appropriate for the given input data.

The algorithm should be *efficient*. For programs that are run rarely or that do not require much calculation, efficiency is not very important. But many programs become useful only if they can deliver a result in a time short enough to be useful (tomorrow's weather forecast is useful only if we can calculate what it is before tomorrow) and in a space (amount of memory) small enough to fit into the computer that is to carry out the task. So for most algorithms, we will be interested in how much time and space are needed (for a particular amount of input data).

When we code the algorithm in a programming language, the preceding factors are still important, and some further factors become relevant.

A new issue becomes important when we consider correctness. We need to have the program check that the input data is valid for the task to be performed. If it is not valid, we need to ensure that the program displays clear and unambiguous error messages explaining what is wrong with the input data and exactly what the program has done about it—it could abandon the task for this set of data, or it could try to adjust the values in some way to obtain a valid set of input data.

We need to consider the *maintainability* of the program. Inevitably, errors (bugs) will be found in the program and will need to be corrected; changes will occur in the outside world which require corresponding changes to the program; and there may be a desire to extend the tasks carried out by the program. It is difficult enough making changes to a program that we last worked on several months or years ago, but the changes may have to be made by a different programmer (the original programmer may have moved to another job, or at least to a different programming task). All this requires us to organize the structure of our program as clearly as possible. It needs to be obvious what parts of the program need to be modified for any particular change in the task. And we need to be assured that, as far as possible, changes to one part of a program do not affect other parts. A major issue of programming language design has been how to split up a program into its constituent parts so that a modification to one part affects all other parts as little as possible.

1.3 High-level Languages & Programs

High-level programming languages have been in use since the early 1950s. Most computer languages, from early examples like Fortran and Algol to more recent languages like C and Ada, have been imperative or procedural. A computer program in a language of this type consists of:

- A collection of *variables* (of named areas or "pigeon-holes" in the computer), each of which at any stage contains a certain value (a number, a character, a string of characters, and so on).

- A collection of *statements* which change the values of these variables. The new value (which will replace the previous value of this variable) could be a fixed value specified in the program. Or it could be a value computed from values held in other variables. These statements will be interspersed with tests on values held in variables to decide in what order the statements of the program are to be executed (and consequently what the final result of the program will be).

A programming language of this style is called an *imperative* language, since the basic operation is an order to change the value in a variable to a suitable new value. This style of programming is based on the style of the underlying hardware of the computer or "machine code" (see Section 1.5), but with a clearer syntax for specifying how new values are to be calculated and how tests are to affect the ordering of statements.

Early experience in the difficulties of writing programs revealed that it was important to be able to divide up a program into a number of practically independent pieces, so that the programmer could concentrate on writing one piece at a time. A typical piece would be a program in miniature, consisting of a sequence of statements to assign values to variables, with tests applied to the values of variables already read in or calculated. Such a subdivision of a program is usually called a *procedure*. Since imperative languages generally rely on some form of procedure as the basic building block of a program, they are often also called *procedural* languages.

Consider the following problem. Someone has given us a list of all the salaries at the place we work, and we want to know the largest salary (actually we probably would also like to know who receives it, but let us keep the problem simple). There are several hundred employees so we need some sort of systematic way of going about it (that is, we need an algorithm). Written in an imperative style, we could have a procedure, called, let's say, maxList, which, given a list of numbers stored in a variable called list, proceeds as follows:

```
1 We assume that the number of salaries in list is stored in a
     variable called count.
2 Copy the first salary in list to a variable called max
3 Set a variable i to the number 2
4 Copy the ith salary in list to a variable called current
5 if the number in current is greater than that in max
6    copy the number in current into max
7 add 1 to the number in i
8 if the number in i is not greater than the number in count, repeat
     from step 4
9 print the number in max
```

In this imperative programming example, we have several variables—pigeonholes—that each have a name and hold a value. Some, such as count and current, can hold only a single value (here it is a whole number or integer, but in another program it might be a number with a decimal part, or a character). The value in count does not change (i.e., it is a *constant*) in this piece of code, while the value in current probably changes several times. The variable list holds a whole collection of items, all of the same type (i.e., whole numbers)—when we look at Java programs, we will see variables referring to collections of simpler items, where they are not necessarily all the same type. In some of the statements we specify an actual value—2 in statement 3, and 1 in statement 7—these are called *literals*.

Each of the statements either calculates a new value to be stored in a variable based on other values already available or (as with statement number 8) specifies a test to decide which of two actions is to occur (proceed to step 9, or repeat from step 4).

We assume in the preceding program that, if we have a variable i containing a number, we can easily extract (or change) the ith element of list. This is a common operation in imperative languages and uses a mechanism called an *array*, which we discuss in Chapter 9.

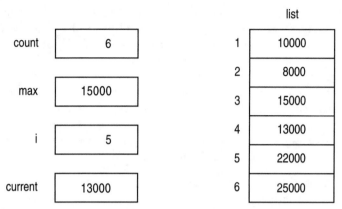

Figure 1-2: Variables in the maxlist procedure.

Figure 1-2 shows the situation just after the computer has checked the fourth salary in the list and is about to return to step 4 with the variable i set to 5.

Note that we have to be careful with this program. It assumes that there are at least *two* salaries in the list. We could easily revise the algorithm so that it still works correctly with a list consisting of a single salary. But if there are no salaries in the list, the correct action for the program to take is not clear. Perhaps the program should check for this situation and stop after printing an error message.

We have here a program written in a *high-level* language. A computer cannot directly understand a program written in this form. As we shall see, a computer executes a much more basic type of language called *machine code*. But the computer can come to the rescue and translate the program written in the high-level language into an equivalent program in machine code. Such a translation program is called a *compiler*, and we would need one for the particular high-level language in which our program is written and for the particular computer and machine code on which we want our program to run (as shown in Figure 1-3).

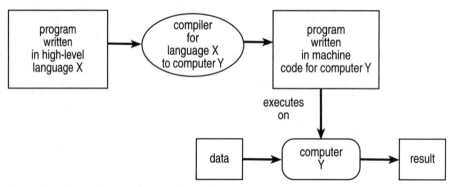

Figure 1-3: Compiling and executing a program.

A more recent style of programming language uses *object-oriented programming*, which is based on this imperative or procedural style. Since Java is an object-oriented language, the features of this style of programming language are discussed in detail in the next chapter.

1.4   A Simple Computer

In order to motivate some of the discussion later in this book, we need to have a basic idea of how a computer works. The most important distinction to be made is between the software and the hardware.

The *software* is the set of programs which tell the computer how to carry out any particular task. One important piece of software is the operating system: this program automatically starts to run when the computer is switched on. It responds to user commands—to run some piece of application software, for example, such as a word processing program, a Web browser, or a Java program. When the application program finishes, control is returned to the operating system, which awaits the user's next command.

The *hardware* is the basic electronics of the computer itself and its associated peripheral or input/output equipment. The latter would usually include a keyboard and display, disk storage (perhaps of various types), a printer, and some form of connection to a local or wide-area network (as shown in Figure 1-4).

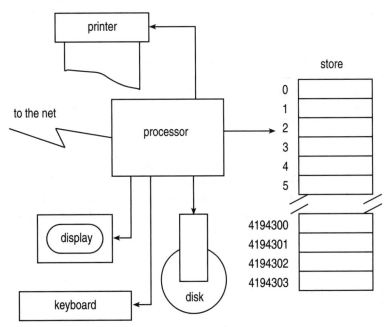

Figure 1-4: The parts of a simple computer.

The computer itself is divided into a *processor* and a *store*. Ultimately, everything is controlled by the processor, which has a repertoire of operations it can carry out. It can, for example:

- Add two numbers together.

- Test to see if one number is the same as another.

- Request the next character to be read in from a particular input device (such as from the keyboard or from a particular location on a disk).

- Request that a character be written to a particular output device (causing it to be displayed on the screen or printed by the printer).

The store consists of a number of store *locations* which hold the data (the numbers or characters) upon which the operations take place. The store locations are all the same size, usually a *byte* of 8 binary *bits*, which is capable of holding 256 different values, each representing a character in the ASCII character set or a number in the range −128 to +127. In order to access an individual location in the store, we must have some unique way of referring to it. Since the store is a long sequence of locations, we simply use the position in this sequence as the *address* of this location, in a range from 0 to, say, 4,194,303 (for a 4-megabyte store).

Since a byte is rather small, we use a group of adjacent bytes to hold a larger item of data. Thus the designer of the computer might decide that a group of four adjacent bytes could be treated as a *word*, capable of holding an integer in the range from −2,147,483,648 to +2,147,483,647. We specify a particular word by the address of its first byte (i.e., the byte with the lowest address). For example, Figure 1-5 illustrates a word at address 1024 holding the number 1512345.

1024	1025	1026	1027
00000000	00010111	00010011	10011001

Figure 1-5: Four adjacent bytes holding the value 1512345.

A *program* consists of a set of instructions to be carried out by a computer in order to complete some task. An *instruction* is a specification of an operation to be carried out together with the address of the data which is to be used for the operation. A basic insight from the early days of computing is that such an instruction can be considered as just a set of numeric values and can therefore also be stored in a sequence of bytes in the store.

1.5 Machine Code (optional)

Let us consider a concrete example. We assume a very simple computer, with a store of only 65,536 bytes (numbered with addresses from 0 to 65,535). An instruction consists of three bytes:

■ The first byte specifies the operation to be carried out. One byte gives us 256 different possibilities, but we are going to use only a small number of different operations in this simple computer, as listed in Table 1-1.

Value	Function
0	load
1	add
2	subtract
3	multiply
4	divide
5	store
6	...

Table 1-1: Operations for a simple computer.

■ The second and third byte, taken together, represent a value in the range 0 to 65,535. So these two bytes give the address of a store location whose contents are to be used in the specified operation.

Most arithmetic operations, such as add and subtract, require *two* pieces of data. One is to be found in the store location specified in the instruction; the other is in a special location in the processor called the *accumulator*. In order to get a calculation started, we have a *load* operation to bring a value into this accumulator; and when the calculation is finished, we can use the *store* operation to put the result in a specified location.

Let us assume that we never need to perform arithmetic on values outside the range –32768 to +32767. Then the accumulator needs to be 16 bits long (equivalent to two bytes), and we need to assume that an instruction specifies the store address of a location containing a number by giving the address of the lower of the two bytes making it up.

Suppose that, in an electricity billing program, we want to perform the calculation:

(unitsConsumed * pencePerUnit) + standingCharge

with the values unitsConsumed, pencePerUnit, and standingCharge in locations:

```
unitsConsumed    123-4
pencePerUnit     125-6
standingCharge   127-8
```

The result (totalCharge) is to go in location 129-30. To keep things simple, we assume all values are held as whole numbers of pence. This calculation would be accomplished by the fragment of a program shown in Figure 1-6; the fragment starts at location 1005.

Figure 1-6: Part of an electricity billing program.

The way this program of instructions is carried out is as follows. The processor contains another register, the *program counter*, which always holds the address in store of the *next* instruction to be executed. The basic *instruction cycle* of the processor is to carry out repeatedly the following sequence of steps:

1. Copy to the processor the instruction in the store starting at the address given by the program counter (in this computer, occupying the addressed byte and the next two bytes).

2. Update the program counter so that it refers to the next instruction (in this computer, the program counter is updated by adding three).

3. Execute the instruction that has been copied from the store. This may involve reading from or writing to a store location, at the address specified in the instruction.

4. And repeat.

If the program counter starts by containing the value 1005, then by the time it contains the value 1017 (and is ready to execute the next instruction after our code fragment), the instructions will have evaluated the value 2618 * 3 + 827 and stored the result (8681) in the two bytes at locations 129-30. We can imagine that the instructions before location 1005 calculated the unitsConsumed from the two most recent meter readings, and the instructions from location 1017 onward print a bill containing the total charge (in location 129-30) together with the customer reference number, which we assume is the number 16812 stored in locations 121-2. In a real billing program, of course, there will be a lot more information associated with the customer—the name and address, the current and previous meter readings, and so on.

There are major difficulties in trying to write a program in what is called a machine code and that is broken down into such a detailed set of steps that correspond to the requirements of this particular computer. But we can enlist the help of the computer itself. As discussed in Section 1.3, we can design a high-level programming language which is easier to use than machine code and have a program called a compiler to translate it into the machine code to be executed. In a high-level language, the preceding calculation could be written in a much clearer form, such as:

```
totalCharge = unitsConsumed * pencePerUnit + standingCharge ;
```

We can design the language so that the programmer's intentions are more explicitly declared in a program, and the compiler can cross-check to make sure the program and the programmer's intentions match. For instance, if we declare that a certain store location in a program holds a character, then some operations that our program tries to perform on it are likely to be valid (for example, displaying it on the screen or testing it against another character), but others are not (for example, adding 3.7 to it). The ability to do as much checking as possible of the validity of a particular operation on a particular piece of data is called *type checking*. If our programming language specifies what type of data each variable can hold, the type checking can be done during the compilation process (i.e., at *compile-time*) rather than when the program is running with test data or, even worse, when the program is in use (i.e., at *run time*). This is a powerful factor in reducing the cost of developing and maintaining a program if it is written in a high-level language.

Let us return to the electricity billing program. We had a set of store locations (starting at address 121) which held the data corresponding to some particular customer (in fact, customer number 16812), and we had a piece of code to perform the billing calculation—the fragment we looked at started at location 1005, and the code to print the bill presumably started at location 1017. If we wished to calculate the electricity bill for a number of different customers, then we might have the details of each customer in a separate area of the store, together with a table containing the addresses of these areas, as shown in Figure 1-7.

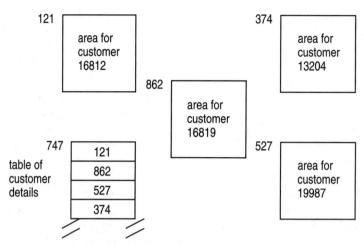

Figure 1-7: Sets of data for different customers.

The billing program would have to be modified slightly so that each time we execute it the instructions refer to the appropriate set of locations for the customer currently being dealt with. The machine code of a modern computer has facilities enabling the programmer to establish the address of a particular piece of data, if it is given the address of the store area containing it (and if all the areas of store have the same layout). For example, the units consumed by customer 19987 will be two bytes on from the beginning of the area allocated to this customer— that is, 529-30.

The point of this illustration is to make clear that a store location can contain any one of several different types of information:

- It may contain a *value*, such as the number of units consumed by customer 16812 (i.e., 2618) in bytes 123-4.

- It may contain an *instruction*, such as the multiply instruction in bytes 1008-1010.

- It may contain an *address*, such as the address 121 of the store area containing details for customer 16812 in bytes 747-8. We call this address a *reference*. Since we are usually not concerned with the exact address of a store area, our diagrams will usually show such a reference as a pointer from the location containing the reference to the area of store referred to, as shown in Figure 1-8.

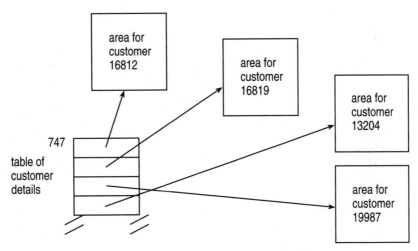

Figure 1-8: Sets of data for different customers—version 2.

It will be important when studying Java programs to be clear when a store location contains a value (like 2618) and when it contains a reference (like the address of the area associated with customer 16812). The store areas we have considered in this example contained only values (customer reference number, units consumed, etc.). But they could also (or instead) have contained instructions. We could have had a table specifying that the instructions for calculating the units consumed starts at, say, location 996; the instructions for calculating the total charge starts at location 1005; the instructions for printing the bill start at location 1017; and so on. Or the area could have contained a further reference, perhaps the address of the customer, a string of characters located somewhere else in the store.

1.6   Files & the Filing System

Useful information (the text of a letter, the text of a high-level language program, the machine code version of this program, data to be read in by a program, data produced by a program, and so on) is held in *files* in the *filing system* on a computer. We briefly review the terminology of filing systems in this section. If you are familiar with the terminology, you can skip to the next section.

Files may be grouped together into *directories* (called *folders* on some systems). Since a directory is like a file, we can further group directories (and other files if we wish) into other directories. Thus the complete filing system looks like a tree (growing downward, as is usual in Computer Science) starting at a particular directory called the *root* of the filing system. Figure 1-9 shows an example.

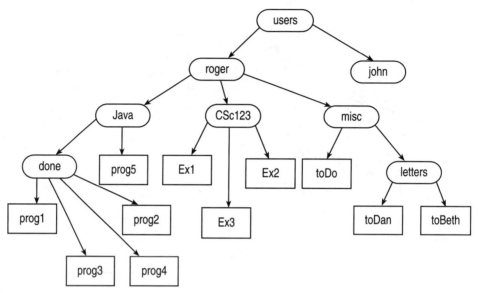

Figure 1-9: An example of a filing system.

When we start to use a computer (when we switch on or log in), we will be placed at some position within this tree, the *current directory*, and there will be facilities for making some other directory the current directory.

If we want to refer to a file in the current directory, we simply specify its name. Thus, if the current directory is roger, we specify the file misc (which happens to be a directory) by simply quoting its name. If we want to access a file in some other directory, we have to specify a *path name*, which gives the sequence of directories from the current directory or from the root directory to the file in question. On a UNIX system, we could specify the file toBeth (assuming the current directory is still roger) as:

misc/letters/toBeth

or we could specify it as a path from the root directory as:

/users/roger/misc/letters/toBeth

Here the initial / character indicates that we are starting from the root directory (an *absolute* path name) rather than from the current directory (a *relative* path name). On other systems, we would do something similar. On an MS-DOS-based system, we would specify the same file (assuming our current directory is roger) as:

misc\letters\toBeth

where the separator between one filename and the next is the character \ instead of /.

1.7   The World Wide Web

There has been a phenomenal growth in the World Wide Web as a source of information and entertainment since the first sites and browsers became available in 1991. There is, of course, a lot of hype over what can be achieved with the Web, but it clearly has great potential for making available, at a locally accessible computer, up-to-date information or interesting entertainment from all over the world.

The Web, illustrated in Figure 1-10, is based on a set of standard formats for data of various types, together with computer software which can access data if it is in one of these standard formats and on a computer connected into the *Internet*. The Internet is a network of computers (originally in Europe and North America, but now in almost every country in the world). It probably makes no sense to ask how many computers are connected to the Internet since it would be out of date immediately, but it must be tens of millions. The Internet is based on a set of communication protocols, a set of standard formats for forwarding data from one computer to another and getting a reply back.

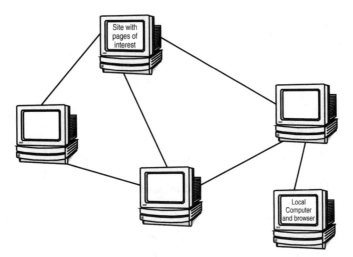

Figure 1-10: Diagram of part of the World Wide Web.

We access the information on the Web with a program called a *browser*, such as Netscape Navigator or Microsoft Internet Explorer. The information making up the World Wide Web is held as a number of *pages*, which contain the information itself together with formatting information written in a language called *HyperText Markup Language (HTML)*. The browser displays the page, laid out according to the HTML instructions (which pieces of text are headings, where to display images, and so on), as shown in Figure 1-11.

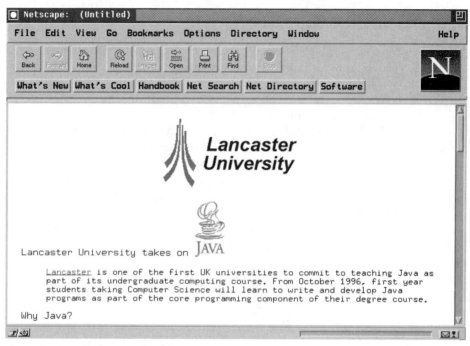

Figure 1-11: A Web page displayed in a browser.

The HTML instructions can indicate a *link* to another page (for example, the underlined word <u>Lancaster</u> on the page in Figure 1-11). If we click on text marked in this way, the browser fetches a page specified by the HTML instructions and displays it. In this case, it would bring up a page describing general features about Lancaster University. This page is what is usually called the University's *home page*.

Until recently, pages in HTML were essentially passive objects. We could read the text and look at the images displayed; we could click on a reference and display a new page; we could fill in a form and pass it back to the originator of a page; we could send an e-mail message to a specified address. Until recently, that was all.

With the advent of Java, things have changed. Now a page can contain a reference to a Java program, or *applet*. If the browser is *Java-aware*, it brings a copy of the program from the originating Web site to the local computer, where the browser is running, and executes the program as part of the page is being displayed. The Java program can create moving images within the page; it can collect information from the user, perform some sort of calculation, and display the results; it can extract information from the Web, filter it in some way according to the user's instructions, and display it locally. The applet could play a game with the user; it could animate some subject of educational interest (for example, it could show how planetary orbits would be affected by a change in the force of gravity); it could extract stock information selected by the user and display it in various useful ways.

There are two issues which need to be dealt with before applets can be routinely downloaded from the Web and run on your own local computer:

- One issue is *security*. Downloading a program from a remote Web site and running it on our machine seems like an invitation for computer viruses to destroy our hard disk or to copy all our private data files back to the originating Web site. The Java language and system have been designed to cope with this threat. An applet which is downloaded from a remote site by a Web browser is in fact very restricted in what it can do—it cannot access files on our disks, and the only access it has to the Web is to its originating site (but it can, of course, interact with a program at the originating site to access information at other locations).

- A second issue is *platform independence*. Our local computer might be a PC, a Macintosh, or a UNIX system, and each of these platforms has a different machine code. Does the writer of the applet have to supply a version of the applet for each such machine code, and how does the browser make sure it picks the right version? In the next section, we look at the Java solution to this question.

1.8   The Java Programming Language

The background of Java is in the C and C++ programming languages. C was an imperative language designed in the early 1970s; it became well-known as the language in which the UNIX operating system was written, and by the early 1980s, it was perhaps the most popular language among software developers and researchers. It is characterized by what its supporters would call its flexibility in allowing the programmer to mix variables of different types (numbers, addresses, characters, etc.). Its detractors would call this a dangerous lack of rigor because it does not carry out as much type checking as possible at compile time (and consequently leaving bugs to be discovered at run time, when they are much more dangerous in their effects and more expensive to put right).

By the early 1980s, it had become clear that C was an extremely popular language among programmers and that object-oriented programming was an influential way of organizing the task of writing software. The result was the C++ programming language, which is essentially the C language (with a few changes) with the features of object-oriented programming added onto it. This language has in its turn became very popular. But C++ is a large language to learn, containing nearly all the features of C together with a full set of features for object-oriented programming. Some people felt that a new and more radical departure was called for.

In 1990–91, the Java language was designed by a team from Sun Microsystems lead by James Gosling (although the language was at the time called Oak). The designers started with the basic syntax of C and C++, but they did not feel constrained to include all the features of these languages. Their aim was to create a small language, which was parsimonious in features. But they decided that it should be object-oriented. The language was first intended for use in "information appliances" such as cellular phones. By 1993, it had become clear to Sun that the language (now called Java) could be used to provide animation and interaction on the World

Wide Web, which was rapidly becoming popular at that time. Java caught the popular imagination in 1995 with the announcement that the next version of the popular Netscape Navigator browser would be able to download and run Java applets. And the rest is history (or about to become so).

Let us now return to the problem of platform independence of Java applets downloaded across the Web. We want to be able to download a Java applet to our local machine and execute it there; and we want to be able to do this whatever our local machine is (a PC, a Macintosh, or a UNIX system, each with its own idiosyncratic machine code). As shown in Figure 1-12, we could compile the program for each of the main platforms and try to ensure that the most appropriate copy is downloaded, but this requires a potentially large number of different copies every time we recompile.

Figure 1-12: Compiling for different platforms—the problem.

Alternatively, as shown in Figure 1-13, we could download the Java source text, compile it locally into the appropriate machine code for our local platform, and then execute it; but this requires an extra step for the user and the presence of a suitable Java compiler and associated software. It also requires the developers of the program to be prepared to make available the source text (which may be commercially valuable) to anyone who wants to use it.

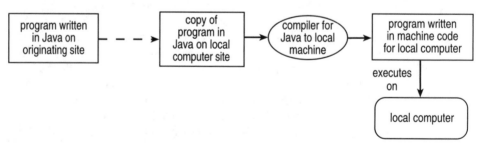

Figure 1-13: Compiling for different platforms—downloading the source program.

The solution, illustrated in Figure 1-14, arrived at by the Java developers was to compile the Java source code, not into some particular machine code, but into a machine code (*bytecodes*) for a hypothetical machine, and this is what is downloaded to the local machine.

But the bytecodes are not the native machine-code of the local computer, so how do they get executed? We have to have a program in the local machine (called an *interpreter*) which reads the bytecodes, interprets what operations have to be carried out on what data, and then carries them out. It turns out that it is easier to write an interpreter for the Java bytecodes than it is to write a compiler for the Java source code. As long as we have a bytecode interpreter on our local machine, we can download a Java program and execute it.

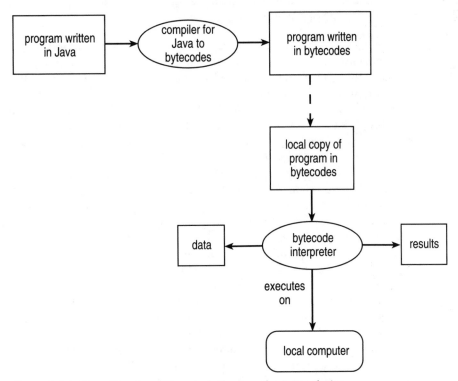

Figure 1-14: Compiling for different platforms—the Java solution.

How do we obtain a bytecode interpreter? Most Web browsers nowadays are *Java-aware*; they contain an interpreter, so when they read an HTML page containing a reference to a Java applet, they can download the bytecodes and execute the applet while they are displaying the page.

The Java programs we have discussed in this section are all *applets*; that is, they are designed to be downloaded and run from within a Web browser. With most programming languages, we write programs that are not run from within a browser; they are typically run as isolated programs, invoked by specifying the name of the program at the command-line interface or by clicking on a program icon in a graphical user interface (GUI). It is possible to write programs of this type in Java; the Java term for a program not run from within a browser is called an *application.** We concentrate on writing Java applications for most of this book, starting with a simple application in Section 1.10. By Chapter 20, we will have introduced sufficient concepts of the Java language to be able to return to the writing of *applets*.

1.9   Getting Started With Java

In order to learn to use the Java language, you need access to a Java compiler, which converts a file containing the text of a Java program into a file of bytecodes, and the bytecode interpreter, which enables you actually to run the Java program you have written. Sun Microsystems provides a version of these two programs, together with some other useful programs, in something called the *Java Development Kit (JDK)*, which is available for various computers such as PCs (running Windows 95), Macintoshes, and UNIX systems. The JDK can be obtained from various sources, including over the Internet. Details on how to obtain it are given in Appendix A.

In this book, we assume that you are using the JDK on a PC or a UNIX system. This is the environment we describe, for example, when we explain how to compile and run a Java program in the next section. This book describes the 1.1 version of Java.

The user interface to the JDK is fairly primitive; we have to type a command string to carry out each step while developing a Java program. There are a number of other Java development environments which provide a more sophisticated, integrated environment in which to do the development. If you are using one of these environments, then you should substitute the appropriate procedure for compiling and running a Java program.

One very important resource provided by the JDK is what is called the *application programming interface*, or *API*, which gives details of all the classes provided by Sun Microsystems for the Java language. It is important to have access to the API when writing a program, because it allows you to check all the details of the classes you are using. You need to use a browser to access this documentation. Details of the API are also given in Appendix A.

In this book, we make use of a number of classes to illustrate features of Java or to provide simple access to some of Java's more sophisticated features (such as input/output). Versions of these classes and the accompanying documentation, or API, are available from the Course Technology Web site. See Appendix A for more information.

We illustrate programming concepts with examples of code fragments or complete programs. The relevant portion of the code, and sometimes the complete program, is printed in the appropriate part of the book. But complete versions of all programs discussed in this book are given on the Course Technology Web site (see Appendix A).

---

*Java applications and applets are both application programs in the sense mentioned in Section 1.1, in that they carry out a particular task we want carried out.

1.10 A First Java Program

In this section, we demonstrate a very simple Java program to illustrate the basic format of a program and to introduce the procedure to compile and run it. It is common in books on programming in the C tradition to start with a program to display the message "Hello, World" on the terminal screen. This is a slightly unusual program, as it requires no input from the user (or anywhere else) when it runs—every time it boringly does the same thing.

This first Java example is an *application* rather than an *applet*; it is executed by quoting its name at the command prompt rather than from an HTML page being accessed by a Web browser.

Java source code must be in a file whose name ends in the characters .java; this first program is in a file called Hello.java. It is important for you to be aware that the case of the individual letters (capital or lowercase) is significant in the Java language. Java makes a distinction between the characters Hello and the characters hello. You will unfortunately find that peculiar things happen if you use the wrong case in writing a Java program—it is important to get into the habit of checking the case of everything you write in Java, and it will soon become second nature. You have been warned!

Here are the contents of the file Hello.java:

```
/**
*
* demonstration of the simplest Java application program
*
* Written by: Roger Garside
*
* First Written: 12/June/96
*
* Last Rewritten: 4/July/96
*
*/

public class Hello
   {

   /**
   *
   * main
   *
   */

   public static void main(String[] args)
      {
      System.out.println("Hello, World") ;
      } // end of method main

   } // end of class Hello
```

The program commences with some text between the characters /* and */. This is one way of marking the beginning and end of a *comment* in Java. Comments are ignored by the Java system and so can be used to insert "signposts" in the code to enable a human reader to follow the structure of the program. Each separate file of Java code should have a header comment giving details of the status of the code, along the lines illustrated here.

Everything in a Java program has to be part of a *class*. In the next chapter, we will explain exactly what a class is, but in this program the line:

```
public class Hello
```

introduces or *defines* a class called Hello (not hello). The word public is what is called an *access modifier*; it specifies the circumstances in which the class can be accessed—this class is publicly accessible. It is a rule in Java that if there is a public class in a file (and there cannot be more than one public class per file), the name of the public class (Hello in this case) must be the same as the first part of the name of the file (that is, up to the full stop).

The contents of the class Hello starts at the { character immediately after the class statement and finishes with the } character at the end of the program. To make it easy to match up the curly brackets, we have put a comment after the } character—this uses the other way of introducing comments in Java, with the characters // (the comment finishes at the end of the line).

The class Hello contains only one thing, a *method* (that is, a piece of code to carry out some task) called main. This method is introduced by the *method header* line:

```
public static void main(String[] args)
```

Again, we will explain later what the words public static void and (String[] args) tell us about the method main. For the moment, simply assume that this is what is required to get things off the ground. The *body* of the main method (that is, the specification of its detailed steps) starts at the { character immediately after the method header line and finishes with the } character on the second to the last line of the program—again we have used a comment to make this clear.

The braces { and } are used to delimit the beginnings and ends of classes and methods and of various other things in the Java language. It is easy to insert one too many or one too few of these braces. In order to help a human reader understand how the braces match up, it is usual to *indent* each pair of braces a fixed number of characters further to the right than the braces that enclose them. In the programs associated with this book, we indent successive pairs of braces by *four* characters.

When you look at Java programs written by other people, you will find that there are in existence a number of alternative conventions for laying out the pairs of braces. In this book, we use a simple convention that requires the beginning and ending braces and all the enclosed lines of text, to be lined up vertically. It also needs to be pointed out that these indentation conventions are used *solely* to guide the human reader of a program; the Java system itself makes no use of the convention. But it *is* important, as the programs you write become larger, to get into the habit of laying out your programs according to a convention that makes the program's structure clear. You will be amazed at how unfamiliar a program looks if you come back to it several months after first writing it!

The contents, or *body*, of a method consists of one or more *statements*. Each statement in Java must end with a semicolon (;). This allows a long statement to spread over several lines. In this program, there is only one statement:

```
System.out.println("Hello, World") ;
```

The Java system provides a number of mechanisms for the output of results from a program, and output to the user's terminal is associated with an *object* called `System.out`. Like the terms *class* and *method*, we will explain the term *object* in the next chapter. This statement invokes or *calls* a method called `println` belonging to the `System.out` object, and this `println` method outputs a value to the screen.

The value to be output is supplied as an *argument* or *parameter* to the method and is specified in parentheses (...) after the method name. In this example, the argument we supply is a fixed character string, what we call a character string literal. We write a character string literal by putting the characters between double-quote characters:

```
"Hello, World"
```

Later we will see arguments which are not literals—the string we want to print will have been constructed from other strings or read in from the user or from a file.

The procedure for compiling and running a Java program (using the JDK environment, on a UNIX system or the MS-DOS window under Windows 95 on a PC) is as follows:

1. Create the Java source code as a file (here called `Hello.java`) using a suitable editor.

2. Compile the source code with the command `javac` followed by the name of the file to be compiled:

   ```
   javac Hello.java
   ```

   If there are no compilation errors, a new file `Hello.class` is created.

3. Run the resulting program with the command:

   ```
   java Hello
   ```

This causes the Java bytecode interpreter `java` to be executed. It first looks for a file called `Hello.class`. If it finds the file, it looks in it for a method called `main` and executes it. It starts at the first statement, executes it, and goes on to the next. In our simple program, there is only one statement, a call of the `println` method of the `System.out` object, with the argument `"Hello World"`. This results in the text being displayed on the screen, so you should see:

```
Hello, World
```

displayed at your terminal. After the message has been displayed, the program terminates.

If there is a grammatical error in your program, the compiler will display an error message together with an indication of where it thought the error occurred. Try deleting the ; character from the end of the statement:

```
System.out.println("Hello, World")
```

Then rerun the compiler with this file. You will get an error message indicating that it expects the ; character.

Now delete the / character at the end of the first comment in the original file, and recompile the program. Can you explain what has happened?

1.11   The print & println Methods

Actually, the `println` method does two things:

- First it prints the string we have specified (here `"Hello, World"`).

- Then it prepares to output the next piece of information by positioning itself at the beginning of the next line.

We can see how this works if we replace the single statement with:

```
System.out.println("Hello,") ;
System.out.println("World") ;
```

Now the first `println` writes the string `"Hello,"` and positions itself at the beginning of the next line. Then the second `println` writes `"World"` on this new line (and moves to the beginning of the next line).

There is another, slightly different output method called `print`. This displays a string, but it does not move to the next line. If we replace the *first* `println` with `print`:

```
System.out.print("Hello,") ;
System.out.println("World") ;
```

we get `"Hello,World"` all on one line. Notice that no space has been left between `"Hello,"` and `"World"`. The `print` and `println` methods output *exactly* what we specify. If we want a gap between the words, we must insert it explicitly:

```
System.out.print("Hello, ") ;
System.out.println("World") ;
```

What happens if you replace the second `println` with `print`? If you do this, you will find that nothing gets output to the screen. What has happened is that the Java system always displays a complete line at a time. If you write a series of `print` calls, the system saves up (or *buffers*) the characters to be output, waiting for more characters to be added to the line for display or waiting until a call of `println` tells it that the end of the line has been reached and the line can be displayed. If the `println` method is never called, the line is never displayed.

There is, in fact, another way to make Java output the characters in the buffer to the screen without waiting for a call of `println` to move on to the next line. This is with the method `flush`:

```
System.out.print("Hello, World") ;
System.out.flush() ;
System.out.println("Look, we are still on the same line!") ;
```

Unlike the `print` and `println` methods, the `flush` method does not need any argument. But notice that we still have to put in the parentheses.

1.12   How This Book Is Arranged

It is important when using an object-oriented language like Java that you are completely familiar with the way objects are used in the language. We have therefore designed this book so that it starts off by introducing the basic concepts of setting up and manipulating objects in the language. The other concepts you require for programming in Java can then be introduced using these basic object-oriented ideas.

The book is divided into five parts:

- The first part (Chapters 1 to 6) introduces the basic concepts of setting up and using classes and objects; we then build on these basic concepts to introduce the procedures for adjusting the flow of control from one statement to another by using the selection and repetition mechanisms provided by Java. Not everything in Java is in fact an object, so we conclude this first part with a discussion of the basic data types provided by Java, such as characters and numbers.

- The classes and objects manipulated in the first part have already been written for you— they are either part of the basic language provided by Sun, or they have been provided by the authors of this book. In the second part of the book (Chapters 7 to 11), we have a look at how these classes were originally set up and allow you to create classes of your own. The first such classes are quite simple, but the later chapters of this part introduce more complex features we might wish to use in our classes.

- There is a very important concept in object-oriented programming called *inheritance*, which allows us to create classes by reusing classes written by someone else, rather than always having to start again from scratch. The concept of inheritance is introduced in the third part of this book (Chapters 12 to 16). This part concludes with a discussion of the Abstract Window Toolkit (AWT), which enables you to design and create graphical interfaces to your programs.

- In the fourth part (Chapters 17 to 21), we introduce further features of the Java programming language, leading up to a discussion (in Chapter 20) of how to create Java applets that can be downloaded from the Web and run by a browser.

- The final part (Chapters 22 to 25) introduces the ideas of object-oriented *design*, discussing the question of how to take a specification of a task to be carried out and design and implement a set of classes which carry out the task.

Each chapter ends with a list of key points summarizing the main concepts introduced in the chapter and a selection of exercises. Programming is a practical craft, and the only way to learn it is to do it. We encourage you to try out the exercises in each chapter.

1.13 Key Points in Chapter 1

- An *algorithm* embodies a set of steps or instructions to be followed to reach a goal. An algorithm should be clear and unambiguous. It could be specified in a natural language (such as English) or in some other more formal (and usually specialized) language or notation.

- A *program* is a version of an algorithm that can be executed on a computer. A program in an *imperative* style consists of a number of *variables* with values and a sequence of *statements* to compute new values for some of the variables. Computer *software* includes *application* programs to carry out particular tasks and an *operating system* to manage the resources of the computer. A program in a high-level language has to be translated by a *compiler* into machine code before it can be executed on a computer.

- Computer *hardware* is the electronics of the computer and consists of a *processor* and *store* together with associated peripheral or input/output equipment. The store consists of a collection of *locations*, each usually a *byte* (eight binary bits) in size and with a unique *address*. A group of adjacent bytes could be used to represent a larger unit, or *word*. The store contains data *values*, *instructions* specifying an operation to be carried out by the processor, or addresses of (*references* to) other areas of the store.

- A computer's filing system consists of a set of *files* grouped into *directories* or *folders*. A file can be specified by a *path name*, starting from the *current directory* (a *relative* path name) or from the *root* directory (an *absolute* path name).

- The *World Wide Web* is a global information resource made up of *pages* of data held at different sites across the world. A page contains some information and some formatting instructions and *links* to other pages specified in a language called *HTML*. These pages can be viewed with a *browser*, which can follow links from one page to another.

- *Java* is a new programming language. Programs in Java are compiled into an intermediate form called *bytecodes*, which are executed by a program called an *interpreter*. A browser can contain such an interpreter, which enables a Java *applet* to be downloaded from a site on the World Wide Web and executed on our local computer, whatever type of machine it is. Alternatively, we can write and run a program on our local computer without using a browser; such a Java program is called an *application*.

- A Java program consists of a *class* containing one or more *methods*, which are made up of a *header* and a series of *statements*, each terminated with a semicolon. *Comments*, which are ignored by the Java compiler, start with the characters `/*` and finish with the characters `*/`, or they start with the characters `//` and finish at the end of the line. Extra blank lines and *indentation* should be used to make the program structure clear. The `print` and `println` methods of the `System.out` object can be used to output messages to the computer screen.

- A Java program resides in a file with the name `Something.java`. It can be compiled using the JDK command `javac`, which produces a file `Something.class`. This can then be run with the JDK command `java`.

1.14 Exercises

1. Have a look at some examples of algorithms in everyday life. Some places to look are:

   - The recipes in a cook book.

   - The instructions for some piece of equipment (for example, the instructions for programming your video recorder to record a TV program).

   - The constructions in a geometry book.

   To what extent do these algorithms meet the criteria set out in Section 1.2? What sort of notation do they use to specify the algorithm? If they use English, how precise and unambiguous is it?

2. Try to specify a precise algorithm for checking the spelling of all the words in a piece of text, such as the text of this question. A dictionary would be likely to contain the word *word* but not *words*, since it will assume you know how to deal with this—does your algorithm know how to deal with this? Will it work with *boxes* and *tries*?

3. In a spreadsheet, each cell can contain a number or a formula to calculate a value for this cell from the values in other cells. The formulae can include any of the usual arithmetic operations. Sketch out an algorithm which a spreadsheet program could use to recalculate all the values after the user has changed a few of the numbers or formulae. You need to consider in what order the formulae are to be evaluated. What would happen if the formulae in two cells each referred to the value in the other cell? Is this question a clear statement of what is required from your algorithm, or have you had to make assumptions about what the question means?

4. Carry out the program given in Section 1.3 to find the largest in a list of salaries, for each of the following lists of salaries:

   10000, 8000, 15000, 13000, 22000, 25000

   10000, 8000, 15000, 13000, 15000

   10000

5. Consider an office worker sitting at a desk with an IN and an OUT tray and a filing cabinet containing information which needs to be referred to from time to time. Compare this worker with the hardware of the computer system described in Section 1.4, and map the components of the office (including the worker) onto the components of the computer system. What corresponds to the software of the computer system? What would correspond to the Net connection?

6. Use a browser to visit some sites on the World Wide Web which contain applets, and try running some of the applets which look interesting:

   - The Web site for this book contains an applet `HelloApplet`. This is a very simple applet corresponding to the "Hello, World" program we met in Section 1.10. Have a look at the HTML page (`HelloApplet.html`) to see how it refers to the applet, and have a look at the code (in `HelloApplet.java`) to see how it differs from `Hello.java`. More details in Chapter 20.

■ The Gamelan site (the URL is given in Appendix A) is a source for a number of interesting applets—explore the resources there.

7. Compile and run the "Hello, World" program given in Section 1.10.

■ Make some changes to the code and try recompiling it, trying to understand what sort of error the compiler is indicating. For example, delete the semicolon at the end of the print statement. Or delete the / character at the end of the first comment. Or change the name of the class from Hello to Hello1 (without changing the filename).

■ Try making the changes to the print statement given in Section 1.11, and observe the changes.

■ Change the print statement to:

```
System.out.println("Hello, " + args[0]) ;
```

Recompile the program, and run the program with:

```
java Hello Mary
```

Try it again with Mary changed to Bill, and then changed to your first name. Then try running it again with:

```
java Hello
```

CHAPTER 2

Object Orientation

2.1   Introduction: Objects & Classes

Object orientation (or OO) is a technique that has pervaded all aspects of computer science over the past decade or so. Object-oriented ways of thinking have been applied to software system design, operating systems, programming languages, and database systems, to name but a few areas on which this recent technology has had an impact. In this chapter, we will introduce some of the basic concepts of object orientation.

One of the main claims made for object orientation is that it is a natural way of thinking about things. In the world we live in, we are surrounded by *objects*. Once a problem has been clearly stated, it should be possible to identify an object involved in the problem and the actions we can perform on that object as well as the actions it may ask of us and other objects. Moreover, an object has some kind of *state* that dictates its actions in response to requests. Consider a radio receiver, which has as part of its state the frequency to which it is currently tuned and also its waveband—for example, AM/FM. Actions that we can perform on the radio are to tune in to another broadcasting station and change the waveband.

Let's try to clarify what we mean by using an example. If we consider a CD player as an object, we can list the actions we can ask the CD player to undertake. This is a very simple undertaking, as we only need to look at the control panel of the CD player in order to find out what it can do. The control panel (as shown in Figure 2-1) forms the "user interface" to the CD player object.

We can:

- Play
- Pause
- Seek a particular track
- Fast forward
- Fast reverse
- Eject the CD

Notice also that the CD player has some state. For example, does it currently contain a CD? The answer to that question has an impact on how the player responds to user requests; if we ask it to play while it does not contain a disk, it will simply do nothing or it may flash an indicator light.

Figure 2-1: CD player control and display panel.

The control panel of a CD player has more than just ways for the user to express their desires; it also has some *readouts*, which give the user information about its state—which track is currently playing, for example, and how many minutes we are into the track.

Notice that the control panel reveals only the information that the user is directly interested in. In no sense do we need to know how the CD player actually works, that it contains a laser, what the current intensity of the laser is, and so on. The CD player is an example of a "black box" mechanism; most of the details of how it works are hidden from the user.

The CD player object illustrates some valuable features of object orientation:

- The idea that an object provides a set of operations that the user may invoke. These operations are known as *methods*.

- An object has an internal *state*. Some of that state may be available to the user, either directly or through the use of methods.

- An object is a black box. Some of its internal state is hidden from the user. Moreover, how the methods actually work is also hidden, as is how they manipulate the internal state.

So far, we have discussed a single CD player. However, as you know, there are millions of such players throughout the world. CD players of the same make and model will have exactly the same functionality; but even with players of different makes and models, they will all provide the same basic, core functionality—that of allowing the user to insert a CD and play it!

In object-orientation terminology, we can therefore identify a *class* of CD players. In this class, we can specify the operations (or actions, or methods) we expect each CD player to provide and list the state it will maintain. At this point, when we discuss the state of a CD player, we are talking in a general sense about the kind of state all CD players will maintain—for example, the number of the current track being played. Obviously, here we are not considering a single instance of a CD player, so we do not need to think of a single value for the state; rather, we need to consider the kind or type of value that would be sensible. For example, a character value would not be sensible, as CD tracks are numbered. Floating point values (decimal fractions) are also unsuitable. Clearly, integers (whole numbers) are best. We can even go so far as to say that positive, nonzero integers are exactly what we want. To summarize, we are talking about state in a general sense and how it will apply to all CD players rather than the actual state (or particular value) of an individual CD player.

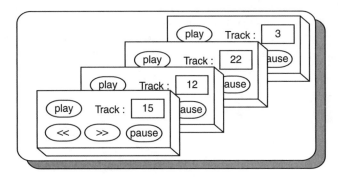

Figure 2-2: Instances of the class of CD players.

Specific, individual CD players are *instances* of the *class* of CD players (see Figure 2-2). They all share the same operations, but they will usually have states that are different from each other. For two distinct players, asking them to play the first track may result in different tunes being played because each CD player contains a different disk. Moreover, even if they contain the same CD, asking to play the next track may result in different music because they may currently be at different positions within the CD. In general, an object is, in fact, an instance of a class. In this case, an individual CD player object is a single instance of the CD player class.

We have, till now, considered only a single type of object—a CD player. We can use the concept of objects to model quite complicated real-world systems that consist of many different kinds of objects and many instances thereof. Consider, for example, a university. A university (among other things) typically consists of a number of academic departments. These departments in turn consist of a number of staff members. A department offers a number of courses. Each course is taken by a number of students.

From this very simple textual description, we can already identify a number of classes of objects:

- University
- Academic department
- Member of staff
- Course
- Student

We can move forward and identify the state of each class and a set of operations (or methods). From these class definitions, we can generate as many instances as we require; for example, a student "object" for each student we have on a course.

Indeed, we can use these classes to represent as many universities as we like.

2.2   Software Objects

Let's move on to a software object. We wish to represent information about a person. The kind of information we wish to model will, of course, depend on the application (what we want to use the information for), but for now we will consider some basic data about people. A person has a name, a gender, and an age. We can represent this as a class specification, as shown in Figure 2-3.

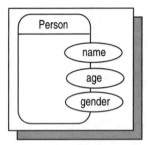

Figure 2-3: Class specification of Person.

We have introduced three simple *attributes*. These attributes make up the state of a Person object. If we wish to have a person object to represent fred, we can declare this as shown in Figure 2-4.

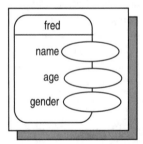

Figure 2-4 : A Person instance called fred.

We can set the values of these attributes directly by placing values within them, as shown in Figure 2-5.

However, in this case, the attributes of a Person object are all visible to the user and are not hidden at all. It is often desirable to make the attributes hidden and to provide methods that allow access. This means that direct access is no longer possible and the methods can contain code that allows checks to be made on the access. For example, when setting someone's age, it is not sensible to allow negative numbers or numbers greater than, say, 150. By forcing access to an attribute through a method, we can control the setting of the attribute's value.

Moreover, some of the state of the object may never be accessible by the user, although the methods make use of them.

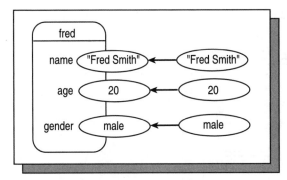

Figure 2-5: Setting the attributes of fred.

Let's make all the attributes of the person object hidden from the user (see Figure 2-6).

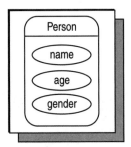

Figure 2-6: Revised class specification of Person.

We can now provide a group of get and set methods (see Figure 2-7).

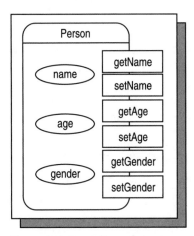

Figure 2-7: Providing methods to access the hidden attributes of Person.

In Figure 2-8, we see a newly declared instance of Person, fred. The values of the attributes are unknown.

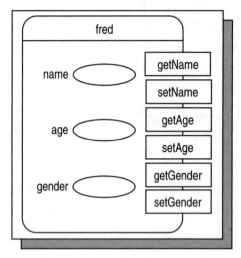

Figure 2-8: An instance fred of the revised Person class.

We can set the values of the attributes using the set methods (Figure 2-9).

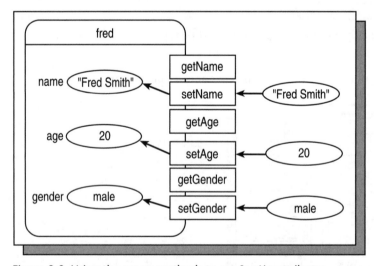

Figure 2-9: Using the access methods to set fred's attributes.

Similarly, we can extract the values using the get methods (Figure 2-10).

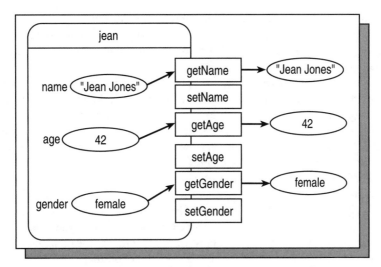

Figure 2-10: Using the access methods to get `jean`'s attributes.

An object-oriented program consists of a set of object definitions (such as `Person`) and instances of actual objects (such as `fred` and `jean`). A Java program (an application) contains a *main* method that initiates the program. The methods of an object are invoked by requests from other objects. For the moment, however, we return to our study of a single object.

2.3 More About Single Objects

As we have said, a single object consists of two main parts: its state, which can be defined as a set of *attributes*, some or all of which may be hidden from the user, and its *methods*, which access and manipulate the state of the object. Broadly speaking, the state is the data of the object and the methods are the code or processing part of the object.

Even at this rudimentary level, the object meets some important criteria for *software engineering*. Software engineering was the response to the "software crisis," identified in the late 60s. Basically, software engineering acknowledges the fact that if we are building a bridge across a river, we cannot use the same techniques we would to place a plank over a stream. Software systems are now among the most complicated artifacts made by humans; we cannot expect the same approach we might use to write a 20-line program to scale up to those millions of lines of code used to implement a complex system.

Early efforts concentrated on the design and coding of software. One of the oldest problem-solving approaches is to "divide and conquer"; if the problem we face is just too large, then we should split it up into a set of subproblems. We can repeat this process as often as required; if a subproblem is still too big, split it into a set of sub-subproblems and so on.

We should end up with a set of subproblems that are "directly" solvable. It was realized that the software systems that are intended to solve our original problem should mirror this structure. A program can be subdivided up into a set of subprograms. For the moment, we can think of subprograms as analogous to methods.

It was also realized that sets of useful subprograms could be grouped together in a construct that is neither a program nor a subprogram; this construct is known as a *module*.

For decades, the concept of a module has been a major part of software engineering. A module is a software black box. It provides a set of subprograms that can be invoked by users of the box. The state of the box is encapsulated within it and is only accessible through its *interface* to the outside world. Does this sound familiar? It should!

One of the most important concepts supported by the module is that of *information hiding*. When a module provides a service, the user is interested only in the results of that service, not in how it is actually provided or realized. The actual implementation of how the service is realized—both its code and its internal, hidden state—is completely invisible to the user. Like the CD player, we don't need to know how it works in order to use it. We don't have to understand the complex electronics and mechanics behind the control panel if we want to hear some music. The impact for the *service provider* is equally great. If we discover a better way to implement the same service, we can freely change the insides of the black box, and as long as the user interface does not change, this has no impact on the user (other than hopefully to improve the service).

The simple object we have introduced in this chapter is very similar to a module; the methods are the subprograms that manipulate the state of an object.

An object then encapsulates both data (internal state) and operations (methods). How do we ask an object to carry out an operation? We simply issue a request to an object.

The code that realizes a method will make use of data from two sources:

- The actual state of the object. No part of the internal state of the object is hidden from the object itself, so a method can freely access all of the state information.

- Data provided along with the request. These are referred to as *arguments* or parameters.

For example, when we want to set someone's age, we issue the following request shown in Figure 2-11.

Figure 2-11: Sending a request to an object.

In this diagram, we see bill as the name of the object; it is the destination of our request. Our request, in this case, consists of two parts: it has the name of the method we wish the object to carry out, together with some data that the object will need in order to carry out our request (see Figure 2-12). In this case, it is the actual age that we want bill to have.

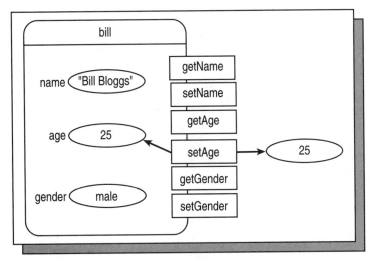

Figure 2-12: Setting `bill`'s age attribute.

Note that we are not reading any of the state of the person; all we are doing is setting the value of the age attribute to that of the value supplied when we call the `setAge` method. In this extremely simple example, we are writing to one attribute of the state. The `setAge` method does not make use of any of the current state of the person.

Now let us make a request to extract information from an object (see Figure 2-13).

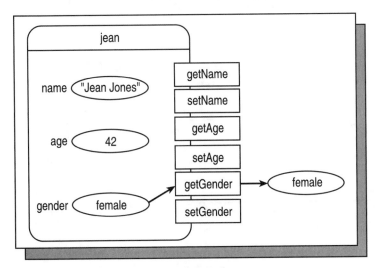

Figure 2-13: Getting `jean`'s gender attribute.

Here, our request has no associated parameters. We are simply reading the value of one of the object's attributes. We are accessing the state, but only for the sake of returning it.

Let's take an example where we *do* make use of the state of the object. Consider a video cassette recorder (VCR) as an object like our CD player. One functionality that a VCR possesses that a CD player does not is that of recording; it is also possible to "program" the VCR to record at a given time for a given period. We do this by specifying a start and stop time and a TV channel.

The VCR object stores, as part of its state, the current date and time. When we issue the request to start "programming the timer," the object accesses this state and presents it to the user—it may even use this to give an initial value to the proposed start time.

Back to software: consider a software object representing a personal telephone book, with lists of our friends' and colleagues' names and their telephone numbers. We can sketch this as follows as shown in Figure 2-14.

Figure 2-14: A telephone directory object.

The state of the object includes the actual telephone index. To access a number, we issue a request that includes the person's name (see Figure 2-15). The object returns the data we require.

Figure 2-15: Making a request of the object.

Notice that we, as users of myTelephoneDirectory, need not know or care how the internal state of the object is structured and stored; all that matters is that we know how to get a telephone number back out of the object.

2.4   An Object-Oriented Program

An object-oriented program, then, is made up of sets of class definitions (for example, the Person class) and object declarations (for example, fred). Java applications have a main method that starts the ball rolling. Thereafter, objects may *call methods* of other objects, and they in turn can *request services* from further objects. Notice that these are two ways of describing the same thing.

One way of thinking about this is to visualize each object individually within an object space. If an object is inactive, it is simply waiting to receive a request from a fellow object in the space. We can say that the objects communicate by passing messages from one to the other. A message consists of three parts:

- Its destination. Which object is it addressed to?

- The service it requires. If the destination is fred, what method do we want to invoke?

- The message arguments. Is there any additional information the receiving object needs to know in order to carry out the service properly; for example, the telephone directory getNumber method needs a subscriber name.

The reply to a message usually consists of the result of the request. If we ask the fred object to execute getAge, then we will get back a number that represents fred's age in years.

In many object-oriented languages, there is exactly one active object. The currently active object is the one that is executing a method body. If in the course of this execution, we call a method of another object, then control switches to that other object and thereafter it is the currently active object. When a method finishes execution, control returns to the calling object.

In a world where the use of computers linked by communications networks is ever increasing, it is useful to have a model where there can be many active objects at the same time. Indeed, even on single processor machines, it is possible to have multiple active objects. Java supports this approach, but it is largely beyond the scope of this book. Nevertheless, we introduce the concept in Chapter 21.

2.5   Types

When we declare a class in Java, it consists of a set of attributes and a set of methods. If we think of attributes as entities in a data space, we can visualize the contents of an object as shown in Figure 2-16.

Let's say we are modeling a person. This graphical definition shows us only that a person has four attributes. We cannot uniquely select and use one because there is no way to specify which one we want. One technique for differentiating among a set of entities is to give each entity a unique name. As we are modeling a person, the four attributes could have the names shown in Figure 2-17.

Figure 2-16: Four attributes contained within an object.

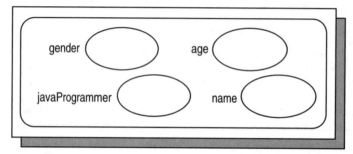

Figure 2-17: Four named attributes contained within an object.

Naming can be an issue of great importance, particularly where the maintenance of software is concerned. For example, if we used names such as x1, x2, x3, and x4 (instead of the names in Figure 2-17), it means that someone reading our class definition really has no idea what each attribute is intended to represent. In a sense, we have almost returned to the first situation (in Figure 2-16) where there are no names. Yes, we can specify each individual attribute, but they all seem to be exactly the same; we have no indication of the underlying semantics or meaning of each attribute. What does it represent? How is it intended to be used?

It is very important to give attributes (and classes and objects, for that matter) meaningful names. This increases the readability and understandability of our software, both for ourselves and for others. Where we are producing classes that others will use, this is particularly crucial.

Looking at our set of named attributes, are there still any problems? Well, for one thing, all the attributes look exactly the same. Is this sensible? Surely some attribute that will store the value of a person's age should look different from one that will store a person's name.

The issue we are raising here is one of *type*. Different attributes will store different kinds (or types) of data. For example, a person's age will be an integer value. Normally, when we discuss someone's age, we give it in terms of whole years. We do not normally talk about someone being 24.523 years old, so we would not expect to use floating point numbers to represent someone's age. Also, we would not write that someone was *twenty-four*, so we would not use characters to store information about someone's age.

Similarly, a person's name cannot be represented as an integer or a floating point number, but rather as a sequence (or string) of characters.

The Java programming language provides a set of basic types. They can be used to specify the type of some attributes. The basic types include:

```
boolean, char, byte, short, int, long, float and double
```

We will explore these types in more detail later in this book. For the moment, we will concentrate on the `boolean` and `int` types. Boolean attributes can store only one of two possible values—true or false. We shall see later how Booleans can be used to control the flow of a program; for now, however, we examine their suitability for modeling one attribute of a person.

There are aspects of people that can be considered to be true or false. For example, `wearsGlasses` could be true or false. Similarly, `hasDegree` or `javaProgrammer` can be true or false. Either you have a degree, or you do not; either you have programmed in Java or you have not.

We have already discussed how we can use integers (or Java's `int`s) to represent a person's age. We can also use integers to encode information; for example, we can represent a person's gender by deciding to represent male by the value 1 and female by the value 2. We will see later how we can declare constant values in order to associate meaningful names (MALE and FE-MALE) with our choice of encoded values (1 and 2).

In our graphical representation of a class declaration, we choose to represent Booleans, integers, doubles, and characters (Java's `char`s) as follows:

int   double   boolean   char

A person's name cannot be represented as one of these basic types. A name is made up of a sequence or a string of characters. For now, we shall represent a string graphically as follows:

string

We are now in a position to return to our definition of a `Person` class and use the graphical type specifications, as in Figure 2-18.

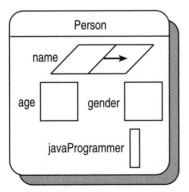

Figure 2-18: Person class definition showing named and typed attributes.

2.6   Classes & Instances Revisited

We have spoken about classes and instances. Let's revise these concepts here. We can think of a *class* as an abstraction over a group of entities. Rather than discuss individuals, we can talk about a class. We can say, by and large, people have two eyes. This is a lot simpler than having to name every individual person in the world and say that they each have two eyes. Once we have this kind of abstraction, we can think, reason, and talk about the group as a whole, and this can make life much easier for us.

This allows us to identify a number of attributes that group members will possess. People normally have a name, an age, and a gender. We can think of the class as a blueprint for the individual instances we will create.

Once we have reasoned in this manner, we can create a class definition for people in general. We have done so in this chapter and called it `Person`. We can also think of the class definition as a template for individual objects in that class. Once we create instances of the class, we know they will have a name, age, and gender by looking at the template, and we know what methods they possess.

Consider another example: we might want to model the concept of a house as a class. Again, by and large, houses have a fixed location, details of which are captured as the address of the house. Such an address usually consists of a number, street, and town. Further attributes could be the type of house it is (bungalow, detached, semi-detached, etc.) and the date of construction of the house.

Without considering the type of each attribute, we can model our class definition graphically as shown in Figure 2-19.

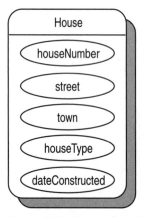

Figure 2-19: House class definition.

Later, it becomes necessary to model the concept of a (family) home. A home has, among its attributes, the name of the family who lives there and the date they moved in. It also has all the attributes of a house, as a physical location. It seems silly to have to define a `Home` class from scratch, ignoring the existence of a `House` class. It would be nice to have a mechanism that allows us to define a Home class in terms of the House class; basically saying that a Home is the same as a House except for these additional details. We can see this in Figure 2-20.

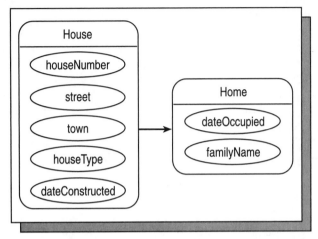

Figure 2-20: Defining the Home class with the help of the House class.

Object orientation has a mechanism, called *inheritance,* to define one class in terms of modifications to another class; we will begin to look at this mechanism in Chapter 12. This means we can introduce a new class, such as Home, which we do not need to define from scratch; instead, we base our new class on an existing one, such as House. We only need to specify the differences between Home and House.

We can think of a factory that processes our requests to create new instances of a class. The factory receives our request, which includes the name of the class. The factory generates new instances of the class. Such a factory, for the Person class, is shown in Figure 2-21.

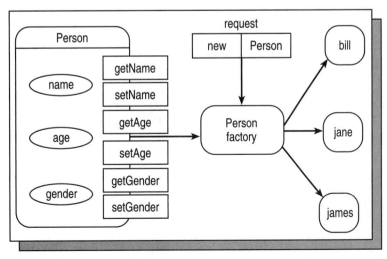

Figure 2-21: The Person factory.

Here, we have a class "template" that we use to create individual instances of people. However, it is also possible to describe a class as a set of individual objects that possess the same attributes and methods. Theoretically, this means we have examined a group of objects, extracted a set of common features, and used it to form a new abstraction. It would be as if we knew nothing about people in general but had a number of specimens to examine. After this process, we might know that bill, jane, and james all have two eyes, a name, an age, and a gender. From this, we might formulate a new class definition and call it Person.

In Java programs, we will always proceed from the class definition to create a set of instances. Because all the Person instances are manufactured using the same Person definition, they will all automatically have a set of common features. So we can see that all Person objects form part of the group that makes up the Person class.

So, in this book (and elsewhere), the term *class* has at least two meanings. It is the class definition itself and the group of instances that belong to that class (see Figure 2-22).

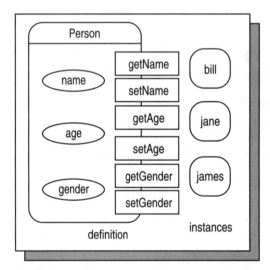

Figure 2-22: Class as a definition and a collection of instances.

However, once we have a group of people, and we need to manipulate the state of those people, we can't generally treat them as a group. We have to move from the abstract to the concrete individual. For example, reasoning about people as a group does not help us update Fred's age. We have to identify the single object that represents Fred and send it a request that will update his age.

2.7 Key Points in Chapter 2

We can think of the real world as consisting of *objects*.

Objects provide a set of operations or *methods* for the user. They maintain internal *state*, which is either:

- Directly accessible to the user
- Accessible indirectly through the methods
- Completely hidden

An object's state is defined by a set of *attributes*. Attributes have both a distinguishing name and a *type*.

Objects support the concept of *information hiding*.

Objects can *call* or *invoke* methods (or request services) from other objects. We can think of this in terms of *message passing*.

A *class* can be thought of in two ways:

- As a template that describes objects in the class in a general way. It lists the names and types of attributes/methods that objects in the class possess. The actual values of attributes are held in individual objects.
- As a collection of all the objects, or *instances*, belonging to the class.

2.8 Exercises

1. Think of an everyday, real-world object that you use—it could be a household appliance, a tool, a vehicle, and so on. Model it as a software object by:
   a) Identifying operations that you can invoke.
   b) Identifying state information that it maintains and list these as attributes.

2. Imagine that you have a collection of Person objects. Outline an algorithm that would allow you to calculate the average age of the people in your collection. How would you access the age of an individual?

CHAPTER 3

Declaring Objects & Calling Methods

3.1 Introduction

In Chapter 2, you were introduced to the idea of object-oriented programming. A program consists of a number of *objects*, each of a certain *class*, and the action carried out by the program is a series of calls or invocations of the *methods* of one object by the methods of another. The remainder of the book shows you how this is actually done in the Java language. To start with, in Chapters 3 through 6, we are going to assume that someone has already written all the classes that we need, and we are simply going to declare objects from these classes and call methods associated with them. Some of the classes are part of the standard Java environment (we have already met an object, System.out, of this type in Chapter 1), and some have been specially written for this book. Starting in Chapter 7, we will begin to show you how to "open up the box" and create simple classes of your own.

All of the programs we write until Chapter 20 are going to be *applications* rather than *applets*. Applications are executed directly by the Java bytecode interpreter java. In Chapter 20 we will see how a browser executes an applet when it finds a reference to the applet in a page it is displaying. An application contains a main method, which is started by the bytecode interpreter to set the action of the program in motion. The structure of the program is going to look like this:

```
/**
 *
 * brief description of the program
 *
 * Written by: author
 *
 * First Written: date
 *
```

```
 * Last Rewritten: date
 *
 **/

public class ClassName
  {

/**
 *
 * main
 *
 **/

public static void main(String[] args)
  {

  body of the main method

  } // end of main method

  } // end of class ClassName
```

The program starts with a comment giving a short description of what it does, who wrote it, and when it was written (in particular when it was last modified). This could be expanded to give further information about the program—for instance, how to use the program, what input and output it requires, a history of the changes made to the program, and so on. When we show you a program in this book, we often omit these comments to save space, but you will see that we include them in all the programs on the Web site that accompanies this book (see Appendix A). Similarly, all your programs should start with a comment giving all this information.

The rest of the program consists of a class definition. This contains a method called main, and the body of this method contains statements that set up suitable objects and manipulate them.

It is a convention in Java that class names start with a capital letter and have a capital letter marking each new word in the class name. The classes of our demonstration programs will all have names of the form Chapter3n1 (the first program discussed in Chapter 3) or Chapter15n5, and they will always be in a file with a corresponding name ending in the characters .java (for example, Chapter3n1.java). The Java compiler insists on this correspondence, as you will see if you change the class or filename. When we compile the program, we will get a new file with a name such as Chapter3n1.class.

3.2   The Class Person

The first class of objects we are going to introduce is called Person. It represents a few simple facts about a person—a surname, a (single) forename, an age, and a gender, as shown in Figure 3-1.

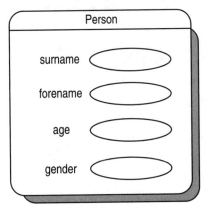

Figure 3-1: The class *Person*.

This class has a number of methods to allow us to set up objects of this class, to extract the various facts held about a particular person, and to specify the facts about a person in the first place. This class is not built into the standard Java environment; we have supplied it as part of this book. We have also supplied documentation to tell you everything you need to know about objects of this class; and this is made available on the Web site that accompanies this book (see Appendix A).

If we look at this documentation with a browser, it lists all of the classes provided to accompany the book; see Figure 3-2. At the moment, we are interested only in the Person class, so we can click on the reference to this class in the list to look at its documentation. The documentation tells us mainly about the methods available for the Person class—what they are, what they do, what their arguments are, what value (if any) they return, and so on. But it does not tell us what the internals of the objects are—that should be of no concern when we are using an object from the class. Of course in this case, we *will* in fact start to show you the internals of the Person class in Chapter 7.

The documentation for the Person class is similar to the documentation for the standard Java classes and methods, which is called the Java application programming interface (API), which we will be discussing later.

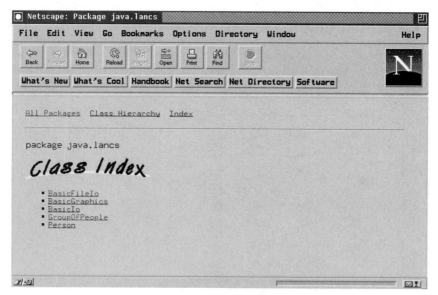

Figure 3-2: Accessing the class documentation with a browser.

3.3   A Program to Manipulate a Person

In this first simple program, we are going to:

- Set up two objects of type Person.
- Set the attributes of the objects to suitable values.
- Display the attributes of the objects to prove that they have the values we have set.

Here is the Java program, a main method in a class called Chapter3n1 in a file called Chapter3n1.java:

```
import java.lancs.* ;

public class Chapter3n1
  {

  public static void main(String[] args)
    {
    // step 1 - declare two "Person" variables
    Person person1 = new Person() ;
    Person person2 = new Person() ;

    // step 2 - set the attributes of "person1"
    person1.setForename("John") ;
```

```
        person1.setSurname("Smith") ;
        person1.setAge(24) ;

        // step 3 - set the attributes of "person2"
        person2.setForename("Peter") ;
        person2.setSurname("Wright") ;
        person2.setAge(19) ;

        // step 4 - display the attributes of "person2"
        System.out.print("the second person is ") ;
        System.out.print(person2.getForename()) ;
        System.out.print(" ") ;
        System.out.print(person2.getSurname()) ;
        System.out.print(" (") ;
        System.out.print(person2.getAge()) ;
        System.out.println(")") ;

        // step 5 - leave a blank line
        System.out.println() ;

        // step 6 - display the attributes of "person1"
        System.out.print("the first person is ") ;
        System.out.print(person1.getForename()) ;
        System.out.print(" ") ;
        System.out.print(person1.getSurname()) ;
        System.out.print(" (") ;
        System.out.print(person1.getAge()) ;
        System.out.println(")") ;
        } // end of method main

    } // end of class Chapter3n1
```

In the next sections we look at the parts of this program one by one.

3.4   The import Statement

We are going to set up a number of objects of the class Person, which has been written specially for this book. How does the compiler know where to find information about this class? In Java, a group of related classes can be collected together into a larger unit called a *package*. All the classes supplied for this book, including the Person class, are collected together into a package called java.lancs. The Java compiler is given some information called the CLASSPATH (technically an "environment variable") that gives it a sequence of places in the computer's filing system in which to look for the class information it requires; more details of CLASSPATH are given in section 8.8. As long as the compiler can find the classes it requires in one of the places specified, it will be able to compile our program. The full name of the Person class is java.lancs.Person (i.e., package name-dot-class name), and we could use this full name every time we want to refer to the class. But there is a shortcut, which is the `import` statement that begins our program:

```
import java.lancs.* ;
```

This tells the compiler to expect the following program to contain references to *any* of the classes found in the package, `java.lancs`. Furthermore, we do not have to specify the full class name; `Person` is sufficient.

If we wanted to refer (as in this program) only to the `Person` class in the `java.lancs` package, we could write:

```
import java.lancs.Person ;
```

but there is no penalty overhead for importing all the `java.lancs` classes (later we are going to use other classes from this package). Incidentally, if you make a mistake in typing this line (which must be the first line in your program, except for comments), the Java compiler is likely to find a cascade of further errors on every line containing a reference to an object of one of the imported classes. Simply correct the `import` statement and recompile the program.

You will have noticed that this program (and indeed the "Hello, World" program in Chapter 1) refers to an object, `System.out`, but does not have a corresponding `import` line. The `System.out` object is in a standard package called `java.lang`. But since the things provided in this package would be needed in almost any program, the Java compiler acts as if each Java file starts with:

```
import java.lang.* ;
```

so we can refer to `System.out` rather than `java.lang.System.out` even though we have not written an `import` statement for the package.

3.5 Declaring Objects

We first need to set up an instance of the `Person` class, and we do this by declaring a *variable* of type `Person`. This is done with the statement:

```
Person person1 = new Person() ;
```

Let us look at this statement in detail.

The first part (up to the = symbol) declares a *local* variable of type `Person`; that is, a pigeon-hole of a certain shape. Furthermore it specifies that we have decided to call this variable `person1`. We say that the *scope* of the variable `person1` is *local*, which means that the variable is part of the `main` method and is not visible to other parts of the program outside this method—we will discuss the scope of variables in more detail later.

This statement declares that this variable is of type `Person`, so the compiler can check to see that it is used only in ways that match the specification of objects of this class. Note that this checking is done at *compile time*, so errors are found as soon as possible and we don't have to wait until the program is run with test data to catch the error. The danger of leaving it until *run time* to catch errors is that we may not catch them during the testing phase if our test data is not comprehensive enough. So it would be possible for some parts of the program to be visited for the first time only when the program is in use, which could cause major problems.

We have decided that this variable should be named person1. The Java rules for an *identifier* allow any sequence of upper- and lowercase letters and digits, together with the character _. An identifier must start with a letter, and it must not be the same as any of the Java *reserved* words such as class, public, and so on (a full list of Java reserved words is given in Appendix C). Thus all the following are valid identifiers:

```
person1
ClassOne
THIS_IS_A_RATHER_LONG_IDENTIFIER
thisIsAnotherRatherLongIdentifier
```

and the following are not:

```
this-is-an-identifier      (contains the character '-')
1st_person                 (starts with a digit)
```

It is important to give your identifiers meaningful names to help the reader understand the usage of variables in your programs. It would be unhelpful to the reader (although perfectly acceptable to the Java compiler) for your variables to be called x1, x2, x3, and so on. The Java convention for variables like this is that an identifier should be made up of a sequence of words with the first letter of each word (except the first) capitalized, thus:

```
testResult
```

Remember that case is important in Java—thisResult and thisresult (and ThisResult) are all names of *different* variables, although it would be rather trying to the person reading the program to use more than one of them in a single program!

So far we have set aside an area of the store of the computer, named it person1, and specified that it can be used *only* to refer to objects of type Person. But what does the area that we have set aside actually hold? The part of the statement to the right of the = symbol tells us:

```
Person person1 = new Person() ;
```

The characters Person() in fact refer to a *method*, and this is signified by the brackets ( ). A call of a method consists of its name followed by its arguments in brackets. You have to insert a pair of brackets even if (as here) there are no arguments. Since this method call appears after the Java reserved word new, it is a special type of method, called a *constructor* method—the fact that it is a constructor method is also revealed by the fact that the method name is the same as the name of the class with which it is associated, namely Person.

An object is likely to be a large and complex thing, with a number of attributes and methods. It will take up an area that possibly consists of quite a large number of bytes or words. What the constructor method does is create a new *instance* of the specified class; that is, it works like the instance factory at the end of Chapter 2. When we get to write the definition of a class of objects for ourselves in Chapters 7 and 8, we will be writing constructor methods for this class—as we will see then, we can specify an initial value for each of the attributes of the object when we set it up. For the moment, we simply check the documentation for this constructor method for the Person class (see Figure 3-3), and this reveals that the forename and surname are each initialized to the string of characters `"NONE"`, the age is initialized to the number zero, and the gender is initialized to a special value `UNKNOWN` (more about this later).

```
Person

  public Person()

       Creates an instance of the Person class with default values (forename =
       "NONE", surname = "NONE", age = 0, gender = UNKNOWN)
```

Figure 3-3: Documentation for the Person constructor method.

Thus the expression `new Person()` constructs a new instance of the `Person` class and initializes the attributes of this instance as specified by the constructor method. But the aim of the statement is that we shall be able to refer to this instance of the `Person` class by the name `person1`. What happens is that the constructor method passes back a *reference* to the store area (actually the address of the beginning of the area) holding this new instance. This reference is stored in the location named `person1`. A diagram of what has happened is shown in Figure 3-4.

Notice the form of this first statement:

```
Person person1 = new Person() ;
```

The part to the left of the = symbol sets up a location in the computer's memory that is capable of holding a reference to (the address of) an instance of the `Person` class. The part to the right of the = symbol sets up a `Person` instance with suitable initial values and passes back a reference to the instance. We can interpret `new Person()` as an expression that (among other things) returns a value that is a reference to a `Person` instance, just the right sort of thing to be stored in the location `person1`.

The = symbol is the *assignment* or "becomes" operator, indicating that the value generated by the expression to the right of the symbol should be stored in the location specified to its left (replacing whatever value might have been there before). Thus the = symbol in Java (and in other languages derived from C) does *not* test for equality of the things on either side of it—it is an indication that a value is to be assigned to a variable.

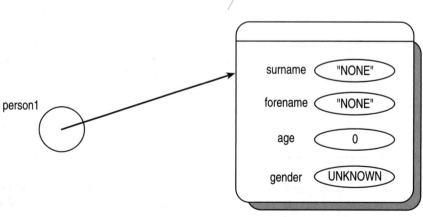

Figure 3-4: The result of declaring the object person1.

The second statement:

```
Person person2 = new Person() ;
```

similarly uses the constructor method `Person()` to generate a new, different instance of `Person`, initializes its attributes, and stores the reference in a new local `Person` variable called `person2`. The situation is therefore now what is shown in Figure 3-5.

Finally, note the line preceding the declaration statements, which begins with the characters `//`. This is the second way to write a comment in Java, mentioned in Chapter 1—the comment extends from the `//` characters to the end of the line. If we are writing a comment that consists of a single line—here we are indicating the aim of each set of following program statements—then this form of the comment is appropriate. If we are writing a more extended comment, then it is more appropriate to use the `/* ... */` form.

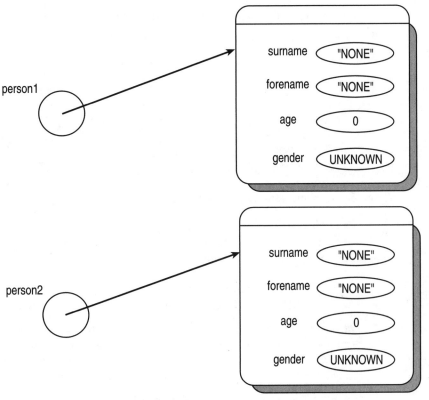

Figure 3-5: The result of declaring the objects person1 and person2.

3.6   Using Methods to Set the Attributes of Objects

We have set up some `Person` objects, and their attributes have the default values provided by the constructor method. Now we want to be able to set the attributes to more interesting values. For this we are going to call some methods associated with the `Person` class. When we examine the documentation for `Person`, we see that there are a number of methods with which we can change the attributes of an object—it is a standard convention in Java (although not always adhered to) for what are called "mutator" methods, which we can use to change the values of one or more of an object's attributes, to have names starting with the characters `set`.

In order to call a method, we need to know four things:

- The name of the object to which the method is to be applied.

- The name of the method.

- Any argument values required by the method to carry out its task.

- What to do with any information passed back by the method.

We can look at the documentation for the method (see Figure 3-6) to find out what it requires in the way of arguments and return values.

```
 setForename

    public void setForename(String f)

        set the forename attribute of the person
        Parameters:
            f - the forename of the person
```

Figure 3-6: Documentation for the setForename method.

If we wish to set the forename attribute of the object `person1` to the string `"John"`, then the four pieces of information are as follows:

- The name of the object to which the method is to be applied is `person1`.

- The name of the method (taken from the documentation) is `setForename`.

- The setForename method needs to know what value the forename should be given, so there is a single argument to the method. Java insists (quite rightly) on knowing what type of thing the argument is—the document specifies that the single argument is of type String (note the capital S); that is, a string of zero or more characters.

- It is possible (as we shall see shortly) for a method to pass back a "return" value. This is not required for the `setForename` method—the documentation indicates this with the reserved word `void` immediately before the name of the method. We have already met this reserved word in Chapter 1, where it indicates that the `main` method (like the `setForename` method) does not pass back any value when its execution terminates.

A method call has the format:

- Name of object
- Dot
- Name of method
- Left parenthesis
- Zero or more arguments, separated by commas if there are more than one
- Right parenthesis

Thus, to set the forename attribute of the `person1` object to `"John"`, we write the statement:

```
person1.setForename("John") ;
```

There is no value passed back by this method, so the call is a statement in its own right (terminated with the ; character). The method requires a single `String` argument, and we have supplied an appropriate value for this string (enclosed in double-quote characters). The specification of an actual string value, enclosed in double-quote characters, is called a character string *literal.*

We set the surname of `person1` in a similar way, with the `setSurname` method (which similarly requires a character string argument):

```
person1.setSurname("Smith") ;
```

Now we want to set the age attribute of the `person1` object to, say, 24. This is a number rather than a string of characters. We consult the documentation, shown in Figure 3-7, for the `setAge` method.

```
● setAge
     public void setAge(int a)

         set the age attribute of the person
       Parameters:
             a - the age of the person
```

Figure 3-7: Documentation for the setAge method.

We see that the `setAge` method requires a single argument of type `int` (note the lack of an initial capital). This means the age is going to be an integer or whole number like 14 or 52—the designers of this class have decided that ages are stored as whole numbers (of years) and not numbers with a decimal part like 14.6 or 52.95. We supply the argument to `setAge` as a numeric *literal*—notice that there are no quote characters:

```
person1.setAge(24) ;
```

So the situation is now what is shown in Figure 3-8.

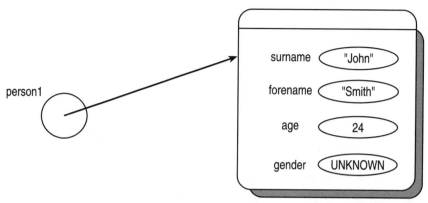

Figure 3-8: The person1 object after initialization.

We have laid out the statements that make up the body of the `main` method one after the other in a sequence, each on a separate line. When we have a number of statements in a program, there is an implicit question:

```
when we have finished executing one statement,
what shall we do next?
```

This program illustrates the simplest way of answering this question—when we have finished one statement, we go on to the next in sequence. We can imagine one of those bouncing balls that guides the audience in singing the choruses in a pantomime by bouncing from one statement to the next in sequence. The way the ball bounces from one statement to the next is called the *flow of control*, and the different ways control can flow from one statement to the next are called *control structures*. The simplest control structure is thus *sequencing* from one statement to the one that follows it next in the program text:

```
• first we set up the person1 object
• then we set up the person2 object
• then we set the forename attribute of person1
• then we set the surname attribute of person1
• then we set the age attribute of person1
• and so on
```

Notice that the order of some of these statements is forced on us by the logic of the situation—we have to set up the `person1` object before we can set its surname or age. But we could have set up the surname, forename, and age of the `person1` object in any order.

There are a number of other control structures—we introduce the two other main ones in Chapter 4 *(selection)* and Chapter 5 *(repetition)* and a further one in Chapter 15 *(throwing and catching exceptions)*. There are other possible control structures, but they lead to programs that are exceptionally difficult to design and correct, and we do not discuss them in this book.

Note that there is only one flow of control in a program here; there is only one bouncing ball. It is possible to write Java programs with more than one flow of control (more than one bouncing ball, a red one for the left half of the audience and a blue one for the right half of the audience). In Java, these multiple flows of control are called *threads*; we briefly discuss threads in Chapter 21, but a full treatment is beyond the scope of this book.

3.7 Using Methods to Extract Object Attributes

Having set the attributes of the objects `person1` and `person2`, we now want to extract the attributes and output them to the screen. For this we have a collection of *selector* methods—the Java convention is that generally their names start with the characters `get`. For example, the method `getForename` extracts the value of the forename attribute for the specified object.

The `getForename` method is going to pass back the forename, a string of characters, and we are then going to display this string on the screen. But we know how to display strings; we use the statement:

```
System.out.print( ... ) ;
```

and we put the string we want printed in place of the dots. Note that we want to write the forename and surname on the *same* line (with a space in between), so we want `print` rather than `println`.

```
● getForename
    public String getForename()
        returns the forename attribute of the person
    Returns:
            the forename attribute of the person
```

Figure 3-9: Documentation for the getForename method.

If we now look at the documentation for the `getForename` method (see Figure 3-9), we see that it has the word `String` just before the method name (where `setForename` had the word `void`). This means that the method passes back a string of characters as its *return value*. Anywhere in a program we expect to see a `String`, we could insert a method that returns a `String`. We know that the `print` method requires a `String` as its argument, so we can insert as its argument any method that returns a `String`. So we write:

```
System.out.print( person2.getForename() ) ;
```

If we check the documentation for `getForename`, we see that it requires no arguments. But we still have to write the brackets that would enclose the argument if there had been one.

How does this work? When the Java system reaches this statement, it decides that it must call the `print` method of the `System.out` object, and this method requires a single argument of type `String`. But the argument provided is a method call that returns a value of type `String`. The method `getForename` associated with the object `person2` is therefore called, and it returns a `String`, in this case `"Peter"`. We can imagine this returned value as replacing the call of the `getForename` method, so the effect is as if the statement had been:

```
System.out.print( "Peter" ) ;
```

So the string "Peter" is displayed at the terminal (or it will be, after any further print calls followed by a println call).

We now want to output the surname associated with the person2 object, so we write:

```
System.out.print(person2.getSurname()) ;
```

We want a gap of one blank character between the forename and surname, so we want to write a character string literal consisting of a single character:

```
System.out.print(" ") ;
```

This statement goes in between the printing of the forename and the printing of the surname because we want the correct sequence:

- First we print the forename.
- Then we print the space.
- Then we print the surname.

Now we want to print the age of the person2 object. We extract this attribute with the getAge method, which we see from the documentation (see Figure 3-10) has a return value of type int—that is, it will return a whole number. We have println and print methods for displaying strings; what can we do with an integer? The Java system also supplies methods to display integers; they are called println and print, depending on whether we want to position ourselves at the beginning of the next line after printing the number or not. So we can display the age with:

```
System.out.print(person2.getAge()) ;
```

```
● getAge

    public int getAge()

       returns the age attribute of the person
    Returns:
          the age attribute of the person
```

Figure 3-10: Documentation for the getAge method.

The Java system knows the type of any argument passed to the print method, so it can work out the appropriate action to take.

Notice how the number is displayed—it takes up as much space as is required by the size of the value (including a leading minus sign, if necessary). If we want to leave a gap, we must do so explicitly.

To complete the display of information, we have added further calls of print and println to output an introductory string "the second person is " (notice the additional space at the end—try leaving it out), to put brackets round the age, and to leave a space between the surname and the age.

We could have used another version of the `print` method to output the gap between the forename and surname. The method call:

```
System.out.print(" ") ;
```

outputs a string literal, a string one character long consisting of a space character. Alternatively we could have written:

```
System.out.print(' ') ;
```

(note that the double-quote marks have been replaced by single-quote marks). Now we are passing a single character literal, a space character, rather than a string of characters that happens to be one character long. And the appropriate version of `print`, the one for dealing with individual characters, will be invoked. Of course, in this case, it makes little difference which we use. But later we will have to be clear whether we are talking of *characters* or of *strings of characters* (which might happen to be only one character long). If we want to specify a single character literal, we must put it between single quote marks; if we want to specify a `String` literal, we must put it between double-quote marks.

After we have displayed the details of the `person2` object, we display the details of the `person1` object with a similar sequence of calls of the `print` and `println` methods. The statement:

```
System.out.println() ;
```

is used to output nothing and to go to the beginning of the next line. This inserts a blank line between the details of the two `Person` objects. Another version of `println`!

So far, each separate element (string, character, number) that we want to output requires a separate call of `print` or `println`. But things are not as bad as that. We can join together two strings, or a string and a character, with the *concatenate* operator + and pass this longer string as an argument. So:

```
System.out.println(person1.getForename() + ' ' +
                   person2.getSurname()) ;
```

passes as argument to the `println` method a string consisting of the forename attribute of `person1`, then a space, and then the surname attribute of `person2`.

You can even mix strings and integers, and the concatenate operator is clever enough to cope. For example we could write:

```
System.out.println("the first person is " +
           person1.getForename() + ' ' +
           person1.getSurname() + " (" +
           person1.getAge() + ')') ;
```

We have spread out the statement over several lines, to make it easy to follow.

Here the concatenate operator understands that the `getAge` method returns a number rather than a string, so it converts it to a string for concatenating with other parts of the expression.*

When we have extracted the value of an attribute from an instance, the only use we have yet made of it is to output it to the screen. But we could use it anywhere in a program that requires a value of that type. Suppose we wanted to set up `Person` instances for two sisters; we could write:

```
Person person1 = new Person() ;
person1.setForename("Mary") ;
person1.setSurname("Smith") ;
person1.setAge(23) ;

Person person2 = new Person() ;
person2.setForename("Susan") ;
person2.setSurname(person1.getSurname()) ;
```

The `setSurname` method requires a `String` as argument, and the `getSurname` method returns a `String`, so the final statement extracts the surname attribute from `person1` and sets the surname attribute of `person2` to this value. Similarly, if these sisters are twins, we could set the age attribute of `person2` from the age attribute of `person1`:

```
person2.setAge(person1.getAge()) ;
```

If Susan were two years older than Mary, we could set the ages accordingly:

```
person2.setAge(person1.getAge() + 2) ;
```

This extracts the age attribute from `person1`, adds 2 to it, and then sets the age attribute for `person2` with the resulting value.

3.8   Using Constants in Java

We have discussed setting and extracting the forename and surname attributes, which are `String`s, and the age attribute, which is an `int`, or integer. What about the gender attribute? This can be any one of three things—female, male, or unknown.

How should we model this attribute? In some programming languages, there are facilities for specifying what are called *enumerated types*, whereby we can specify that a particular attribute can take on any one of a set of values that we can list or enumerate. So here we would specify that the gender attribute can take on any one of the values female, male, and unknown. We would not need to worry exactly what sort of thing such an attribute was, as the programming language would automatically police its use and ensure that only these three values are available for it.

---

*However, the concatenate operator does not always give you the result you expect; for example, with a character and an integer. If you write:

```
System.out.println('X' + 3) ;
```

(expecting it to convert the integer to a character string and output "X3"), it in fact converts the character to its Unicode value (see Chapter 6), which it adds to the integer 3, and the resulting integer is what is output. Try it.

The Java language does not provide enumerated types. Instead we have to use attributes of type int to model the gender type. We would allocate integer values to the three possible values (perhaps 1 for male, 2 for female, and 99 for unknown) and then use these values to keep track of the gender.

But this is not a very good idea, as it is easy to forget which integer we have decided to allocate to which value. It would perhaps not be too difficult in this case, where we have only three possible values to worry about, but we might have four card suits, or a dozen or more colors, or a hundred places, to remember. What Java allows us to do is to specify names for the different values, so we can use the names and not try to remember the values to which they correspond.

In the Person class, we have defined the names FEMALE, MALE, and UNKNOWN for the three values the gender attribute can take on (see the documentation in Figure 3-11). These are *constants*, and it is a convention in Java (though it is not always adhered to) to give the names all in capitals.

So if we want to set the gender of the person1 object to female, we would write the statement:

```
person1.setGender(Person.FEMALE) ;
```

```
Variable Index

• FEMALE
      Constant - female gender
• MALE
      Constant - male gender
• UNKNOWN
      Constant - unknown gender
```

Figure 3-11: Documentation for the Person constants.

Notice that Java requires us to include the name of the class the constant belongs to; that is, class name-dot-constant name, or here, Person.FEMALE. If we consult the documentation for the setGender method, we will see that its argument is an int, but the method checks the value passed to it and will not accept any but the values allocated to FEMALE, MALE, and UNKNOWN.

If we extract the value of the gender attribute, it will of course be an int. So if we write:

```
System.out.println("the gender of the first person is " +
                        person1.getGender()) ;
```

the program might output:

```
the gender of the first person is 2
```

In the next chapter, we will see techniques that enable us to create more meaningful messages from attributes with a limited range of values. In the meantime, the Person class has an extra method, getGenderString, which passes back a String version of the gender attribute:

```
System.out.println("the gender of the first person is " +
                        person1.getGenderString()) ;
```

which would output:

```
the gender of the first person is female
```

It is good programming practice not to make use of a knowledge of what numerical value is associated with a particular conceptual value in such types of attributes. If you want to refer to a particular value, you should use the constant provided. This will make your program much easier for others to follow.

3.9   Using Objects & Methods

We have introduced a class `Person` of objects with attributes forename, surname, age, and gender. Why bother? A primary reason for doing this is that all the information relating to one instance of this class is held together in one place and can be referred to as a single entity. If we have two instances of the class, the information for one is held completely separate from the other. In the example program earlier in this chapter, the changes to the attributes of `person1` have no effect on `person2`.

A further reason is that we can arrange to validate any changes we attempt to make to the attributes of an object before accepting them. For instance, the `setAge` method has been designed to accept only ages in a certain range. What this range should be is, of course, a design issue—should the upper limit be 100 years, or 120 years, or perhaps 150 years if we live in Georgia? Suppose we write the statement:

```
person1.setAge(155) ;
```

The `setAge` method checks the argument and discovers it is outside the valid range. What does it do about this? The method is designed to bring the program to a halt with a suitable error message. Similarly, the methods that the forename and surname bring the program to a halt if we give them an argument string that is zero characters long. Try:

```
person1.setForename("") ;
```

At the moment, these methods have no option but to halt the program. Later we will see a more refined way of dealing with situations like this, with what are called *exceptions*.

If we are writing a program and we wish to ensure that it supplies only valid arguments to any method it calls, we might wish to check that the argument lies in a suitable range before we call the `setAge` method. But to do this, we need to have access to information about what this range actually is, so the `Person` class provides a method called `getUpperAgeLimit`, which returns the upper limit of the age range (an `int`).

There is a peculiarity about this method. Up to now, all the methods belonging to the `Person` class are associated with a particular instance of this class. It makes no sense to try to extract the age attribute without having a `Person` instance of which it is an attribute. It makes no sense to set a surname attribute without a `Person` instance whose attribute is to be set. All these methods are therefore called *instance* methods, as they must be associated with a particular instance of the class—they are invoked with the syntax "instance variable-dot-method name (arguments)".

But it makes perfectly good sense to find out the upper age limit of the Person class without there being any instances of the Person class about. This method is therefore called a *class* method, as it is properly associated with the class rather than any instance of the class. A class method is sometimes called a *static* method in Java, because all such methods have the word static in their headers, as we can see from the documentation in Figure 3-12.

```
getUpperAgeLimit

    public static int getUpperAgeLimit()

        returns the upper limit for a valid age
    Returns:
            the upper limit for a valid age
```

Figure 3-12: Documentation for the getUpperAgeLimit method.

A class or static method is invoked with the syntax "class name-dot-method name (arguments)". So:

```
System.out.println("the upper age limit is " + Person.getUpperAgeLimit()) ;
```

would output:

```
the upper age limit is 150
```

In the next chapter, we will learn how to make use of the value returned by the getUpperAgeLimit method to check a number to see if it is a valid age.

3.10   A Variety of Methods

We have a number of methods in the Person class with which we can set individual attributes of an object. But it makes sense to be able to set the forename and surname at the same time. The method setFullName (note the capitalization) allows us to do this. If we examine the documentation for this method (see Figure 3-13), we see it has two arguments, both of type String, the first being the forename and the second the surname.

```
setFullName

    public void setFullName(String f,
                            String s)

        set the full name of the person in one operation
    Parameters:
            f - the forename of the person
            s - the surname of the person
```

Figure 3-13: Documentation for the setFullName method.

We can invoke this method with a statement such as:

```
person1.setFullName("Bill", "Watson") ;
```

The method does not return any value (it is a `void` method) so it is called, like the other `set` methods, as a statement. The two arguments are written in between the argument parentheses and separated by a comma. We must ensure that the arguments are in the right order—first the forename, then the surname—because the method uses the position in the list to work out which argument is which.

In some methods, the arguments might be of different types (for example, if we were to set the surname and the age in a single method, one argument would be a `String` and the other an `int`), and the Java compiler would then complain if the types of the expected (or *formal*) arguments did not match up with the types of the argument values we supplied (the *actual* arguments). So if we had a method `setSurnameAndAge(String, int)` and we called it with `person1.setSurnameAndAge(25, "Smith")`, then the compiler would be looking for a method `setSurnameAndAge(int, String)`, which it would not be able to find. But here both arguments are of type `String`—it would be rather difficult to make the method check that the forename passed to it (for instance) was or was not a legitimate one (how could you construct a list of all and only the names that could be valid forenames?).

So far, the methods you have seen have either been constructor methods, or they have set or extracted one or more of an instance's attributes. But a method could do a more substantial task than this. It is difficult to give good examples for the `Person` class—we will see examples with other classes later—but it does have two methods that are slightly different from the patterns seen so far:

- The method `increaseAge` takes the number of years specified as the integer argument and adds it to the age attribute of the object associated with the method:

```
System.out.println("The age is " + person1.getAge()) ;
person1.increaseAge(4) ;
System.out.println("The age is " + person1.getAge()) ;
```

would output:

```
The age is 24
The age is 28
```

- The method `formalTitle` returns a string that is a formal title for the person and is constructed from one of the strings `"Mr"` and `"Ms"` (according to the gender attribute), the first initial of the forename, and the surname:

```
person1.setForename("Bill") ;
person1.setSurname("Sowerbuts") ;
person1.setGender(Person.MALE) ;
System.out.println("Dear " + person1.formalTitle() + ',') ;
System.out.println("I am writing to you ... ") ;
```

would output:

```
Dear Mr B. Sowerbuts,
I am writing to you ...
```

3.11   Constructors Revisited

We created a Person object with a statement like this:

```
Person person1 = new Person() ;
```

This called the constructor method Person() to create and initialize a new object. The documentation for the constructor method tells us that the attributes are set to suitable values ("NONE" for the names, zero for the age, UNKNOWN for the gender).

But it is possible to have several different constructors for the Person object, initializing the object in various ways. If we again consult the documentation (see Figure 3-14), we will see that there is a second constructor. This allows us to initialize the object to specific values for the forename, surname, age, and gender. Thus we could write:

```
Person person3 = new Person("Bill", "Watson", 45, Person.MALE) ;
```

This would have the result shown in Figure 3-15.

```
⌐ Person

   public Person(String f,
                 String s,
                 int a,
                 int g)

      Creates an instance of the Person class with specified attribute values
      Parameters:
           f - forename of the person
           s - surname of the person
           a - age of the person
           g - gender of the person
```

Figure 3-14: Documentation for a Person constructor with several arguments.

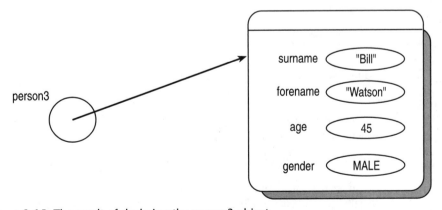

Figure 3-15: The result of declaring the person3 object.

We now have two versions of the constructor for Person, one with no arguments and one with four (and, of course, both with the name Person). This is an example of something called *overloading*, where we have several methods with the same name but differentiated by the number and types of the arguments. All constructors for Person instances have the name Person, and the Java system picks out the right version by checking the number and type of the actual arguments supplied (here, two Strings and two ints) against the formal arguments provided for each constructor method.

In Java, you can declare an object variable without initializing an object for it to refer to:

```
Person person4 ;
```

What is happening here? The variable person4 contains some unknown value (see Figure 3-16).

Figure 3-16: The result of declaring person4 without calling a constructor.

If we do not want to create an object for the variable person4 to refer to when we declare it, it would be safer to set person4 to the special value null to make it clear that this is deliberate and that the variable person4 does not refer to a Person instance at present:

```
Person person4 = null ;
```

This has the result shown in Figure 3-17.

Figure 3-17: The result of declaring person4 and setting it to null.

Later we could make person4 refer to an instance of the Person class with new and a constructor method:

```
person4 = new Person("Henrietta", "Lime", 21, Person.FEMALE) ;
```

Notice that there is no Person at the beginning of this statement—the variable person4 has already been declared as a local variable in the main method; it already exists as an identifiable named location in the store and does not need to be redeclared. It simply needs to be assigned a value (to replace the value null) by using the assignment ("becomes") operator to store in it a reference to a new instance of the Person class. The result is shown in Figure 3-18.

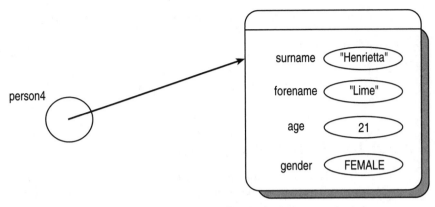

Figure 3-18: The result of assigning a new Person instance to person4.

Suppose we had declared an object variable and initialized it to null and then neglected to create a Person object for it to refer to. If we then invoke a method associated with this variable, we will get an exception NullPointerException. Of course, if we tried to write this statement and we had *not* declared the person4 variable earlier, the compiler would complain, since in Java all variables must be declared before use.

Finally, suppose we write the following:

```
Person person4 = new Person("Henrietta", "Lime", 21, Person.FEMALE) ;
Person person5 = person4 ;
```

We know that the first statement declares a Person variable called person4 and makes it refer to a new instance of the Person object with the specified attributes. The second statement also declares a Person variable, this time called person5. We assign to it the value contained in the variable person4, namely the reference to the new object instance, so person4 and person5 refer to the same object (see Figure 3-19).

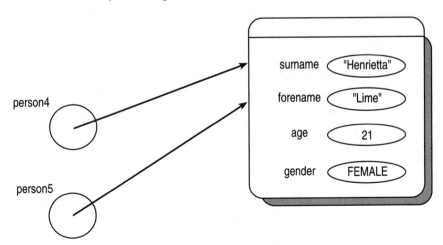

Figure 3-19: Two variables referring to the same object.

We can set an attribute via one variable and retrieve it via the other:

```
person4.setSurname("Williams") ;
System.out.println(person5.getSurname()) ;
```

So we can see that the two variables refer to the same instance.

3.12   Input to a Program (optional)

In the programs we have written so far, there is no scope for the program to seek information from outside. If we want to change the effect of a program, we have to revise the Java source text with an editor, recompile it, and then run it again. This is of course inappropriate in most cases (and impossible if the user of the program knows nothing about Java). In the next chapter, we will start to introduce mechanisms for the program to seek information from the outside world—initially from the user at the keyboard and later from files on disk.

For the present, for those who are interested, we reveal a simple way to pass small amounts of information to a program without recompiling it. This is by means of *command-line parameters*. When we call for a Java program to be executed with the Java bytecode interpreter `java`, we can write a number of strings on the same line after the name of the file we want executed, thus:

```
java Chapter3n2 Fred Smith
```

In the header line for the `main` method, we have seen the characters (`String[] args`) after the method name. This specifies that `args` is where to find these command-line parameters (actually it is an *array* of `Strings`, as we shall see in Chapter 9). The first parameter (`Fred` in this example) is referred to as `args[0]`—counting in Java (as in C and C++) usually starts at zero rather than one; the second parameter (`Smith` in this example) is referred to as `args[1]`; and so on.

Suppose we want to set the forename and surname of object `person1` to the first and second command-line parameters. This could be done with the statement:

```
person1.setFullName(args[0], args[1]) ;
```

We have to be careful that there *are* two command-line parameters. If there are not, we will get an `ArrayIndexOutOfBoundsException` exception—try it. The value `args.length` tells you how many command-line parameters there are. The statement:

```
System.out.println("No of parameters is " + args.length) ;
```

would display:

```
No of parameters is 2
```

in this example. After the next chapter, you will be able to use a selection statement to check that there are enough command-line parameters before making use of them.

3.13   Key Points in Chapter 3

- To declare and create a new object, we write:

  `<object class> <object identifier> = new <object class> () ;`

  For example:

  `Car fiatUno = new Car() ;`

  We can now refer to the object by its identifier (here `fiatUno`).

- The expression to the right of the assignment symbol—here `new Car()`—is an example of a special type of method call, a *constructor* method. A constructor method creates a new object of the required class (in this case `Car`) and returns a reference to the object (which, in this case, is stored in the variable called `fiatUno`).

- Identifiers must obey the following rules:

  - Must start with a letter.

  - Can be any sequence of upper- and lowercase letters, digits, and the underscore character _.

  - Must not be the same as any of the Java reserved words.

- It is important to use meaningful identifiers.

- To call a method, we must know the following four things:

  - The name of the object to which the method is to be applied.

  - The name of the method.

  - Any arguments required by the method.

  - What to do with any information passed back by the method.

- We can identify two common types of methods:

  - *Mutators,* which allow us to change the values of attributes—by convention the names of mutator methods start with set.

  - *Selectors,* which allow us to obtain the values of attributes—by convention the names of selector methods start with `get`.

- To call a method, we write:

  `<object identifier> . <method name> ( <argument values> )`

  Even if there are no argument values, the parentheses are still required. If there are two or more argument value, they are separated by commas.

  If a method returns no value, the method call would be written as a statement:

  `<object identifier> . <method name> ( <argument values> ) ;`

If a method returns a value, then the method call would be written in a place inside a statement where you would expect a value of this type (for example, as an argument to a print method):

```
System.out.print( <object identifier> . <method name>
    (<argument values>) ) ;
```

- It is possible to *overload* method names; that is, to have two or more methods with the same name. However, they must be differentiated by the number and types of the arguments they have. One common use of overloading is to have several different constructor methods for the same class.

- If we have an attribute that can take only a certain range of values, we may have a set of constants that name these values. We refer to such a constant with the notation:

```
<class name> . <CONSTANT name>
```

- Most methods are *instance* methods because they are associated with a particular instance of the class. But *class* or *static* methods are possible; they are not associated with a particular instance, but with the whole class. To call a class method, we write:

```
<class name> . <method name> ( <argument values> )
```

- Two or more strings can be joined together with the concatenation operator +. If we concatenate a number with a string, it is converted to a string first.

3.14   Exercises

1. Write a Java program called `FirstExercise` that:

   a) Sets up an instance of the `Person` class.

   b) Sets the name, age, and gender attributes of this instance to your name, age, and gender (using the appropriate `set` mutator methods).

   c) Outputs the attributes of this instance (using the appropriate `get` selector methods, and the `print` and `println` methods) in the form:

   ```
   this person is John Smith (21, male)
   ```

2. Modify your program for exercise 1 as follows:

   a) Output the information in the form:

   ```
   Smith, John is 21 years old
   ```

   b) Use the `formalTitle` method (and other methods, as required) to output the information in the form:

   ```
   Mr J. Smith is 21 years old
   ```

   c) Use the `increaseAge` method with an argument of 10, and then output the information again using the `formalTitle` and other methods.

3. Write a Java program to:

a) Set up a `Person` instance for Peter Booth, a male aged 30, and output a line giving the values of all the attributes.

b) Set up a second `Person` instance for Gail Turner, a female aged 28, and output a line giving the values of all the attributes.

c) Since Peter and Gail are getting married, write a statement that makes Gail's surname the same as Peter's, and output the new values of the attributes for both instances.

4. There is a `Card` class in the `java.lancs` package that models the basic facts about a playing card, its suit, and value. Have a look at the documentation supplied—note that the `Card` constructor method (with no arguments) chooses a random card and sets its suit and value and that there are `get` methods for returning suit and value as strings and as integers.

Write a program that sets up two `Card` instances and prints out their values; for example:

```
The first card is the four of hearts
The second card is the queen of clubs
```

5. The `Date` and `GregorianCalendar` classes are part of the standard Java API, in the `java.util` package. They provide a way of holding and manipulating date and time information.

The documentation of these two classes in the Sun API (see Appendix A) is quite difficult to follow, as you have also to consult the documentation for the class `Calendar` (in the same package) for some of the methods and constants required. (The class `Calendar` is, in fact, an abstract class from which `GregorianCalendar` is derived; you will find out what these terms mean in Chapter 14). A synopsis of what you need to know for the simple use of dates and times is:

a) the constructor method `Date()` sets up a `Date` instance initialised to the current date and time:

```
Date myDate = new Date() ;
```

b) there are several calendars in use round the world. In most of the Western world the Gregorian calendar is in use, and has been since (usually) some time in the 18th century. We next have to specify that we are using the Gregorian calendar, and that we are going to interpret our `Date` instance according to this calendar:

```
GregorianCalendar myCalendar = new GregorianCalendar() ;
myCalendar.setTime(myDate) ;
```

c) we can then extract the attributes we are interested in with the `get` method—this requires an argument which is a constant from the `Calendar` class to specify which attribute we are interested in. For example, to get the day of the month (an integer in the range 1 to 31) we could write:

```
int myDayOfMonth = myCalendar.get(Calendar.DAY_OF_MONTH) ;
```

Other useful constants in the `Calendar` class are `HOUR_OF_DAY` (in the 24-hour clock—i.e., in the range 0 to 23), `MINUTE` (in the range 0 to 59), `MONTH` (which gives an integer in the range 0 to 11, instead of 1 to 12—note this), and `YEAR`.

Write a program to obtain the current date and time, and then display them in the format:

```
The time (sponsored by Java) is 11:47 on 20/2/1997
```

Note: you will need the line:

```
import java.util.* ;
```

near the top of your program, so you can access the classes you need in the `java.util` package.

6. `BasicGraphics` is another class provided as part of the `java.lancs` package to enable you to display a window on the computer screen containing shapes of different kinds, sizes, positions, and colors. In Chapter 16, you will learn details of how to write your own programs to draw shapes like these (and others) using a part of the Java language called the Abstract Window Toolkit.

The `BasicGraphics` class draws an area 600 units (or *pixels*) wide by 400 units high, with the origin (0, 0) at the top left-hand corner of the area. We have supplied documentation for this class—you need to look up information on the `BasicGraphics` constructor method, the methods `setShape`, `setDimensions`, and `setColour` to specify what you want drawn, and the method `draw` to display the window on your computer screen.

a) Write a program to set up a `BasicGraphics` instance, specify a single red square centered at (200, 200) with side 60, and display it.

b) Write a program to set up a `BasicGraphics` instance, specify a red square centered at (200, 200) with side 60 and a blue circle centered at (400, 200) with diameter 80, and display them.

c) Write a program to declare two `BasicGraphics` instances, specify a red square centered at (200, 200) with side 60 in the first and a blue circle centered at (400, 200) with diameter 80 in the second, and display them both.

Experiment with rearranging the order of the statements of your program.

d) Write a program to declare a `BasicGraphics` instance, specify two red equilateral triangles centered at (200, 200) with sides 100 and 150, and display them.

e) Experiment with the other facilities provided by the BasicGraphics class.

Note ▪

(1) The argument for the `setShape` method is one of a set of constants provided by the BasicGraphics class—`BasicGraphics.RECTANGLE` for rectangles (including squares), `BasicGraphics.OVAL` for ovals (including circles), `BasicGraphics.TRIANGLE`, and so on.

(2) There are four arguments to the `setDimensions` method—the first two give the X- and Y-coordinates of the top left-hand corner, and the next two are the width and height of a rectangle drawn around the shape we are displaying.

(3) The argument for the `setColour` method is one of the colors provided by the standard class `Color` in the package `java.awt`—`Color.red`, `Color.blue`, `Color.green`, `Color.yellow`, and so on. You will need to import the `java.awt` package into your programs.

CHAPTER 4

Selecting Among Alternatives

4.1 Reading Values From the Keyboard

In this chapter, we begin by considering how to read in values for attributes. This involves us in thinking further about different sorts of *variables,* a concept that we introduced in the previous chapter. We then embark on a study of Java's selection statements—the `if` statement and the `switch` statement.

In the previous chapter, we wrote a program that:

- Set up some local variables for `Person` instances.

- Set the attributes of these instances to suitable values.

- Output the values of the instance attributes so that we could check them.

The values we used as attributes were all "built into" the program. If we wanted to set an attribute to a different value, we would revise the program with an editor, then recompile it, and finally run it again—a rather laborious process. What we would prefer to do is to have the program request a suitable attribute value from the user, and then use the value that the user types in.

Java provides a number of powerful facilities for reading values from the keyboard or from a file in the filing system. The problem is that these facilities (in a package called `java.io`) are rather difficult to use when you are starting to write programs. We have provided a set of simplified ways to allow the user to type a value at the keyboard and have it read and used by the program. These facilities are collected together as a class called `BasicIo`, and this class is held in the same `java.lancs` package that holds the `Person` class we used in the previous chapter. If we want to use any of the `BasicIo` facilities, we must have the appropriate `import` statement at the beginning of our program:

```
import java.lancs.* ;
```

If our program wants the user to type in a value, it must output a message saying so. For this task, the `BasicIo` class provides a method called `prompt`, which takes a single argument that is the message to be output. This is a *class* or *static* method, so we have to precede it with the name of the class:

```
BasicIo.prompt("please type the surname of the first person ") ;
```

Now the user types in a string of characters and presses the Return key. In order for the program to read in this string, the `BasicIo` class has a method `readString`. This method has no arguments, but returns the string typed in by the user at the keyboard.

Where shall we put the string returned by this method? What we want to do is set up a named location to hold the string until we are ready to make use of it, in the same way we have locations (or local *variables*) to hold the `Person` instances. In Java, we can set up a variable called `string1` to hold a string of characters `"This is a string of characters"`:

```
String string1 = "This is a string of characters" ;
```

The first word in this statement, `String`, specifies the sort of thing we can store in this variable. The type `String` is provided by the Java language to hold strings of zero or more characters. Notice that it is spelled with a capital S because it is in fact a class provided by the Java language (see section 6.7) Next comes the name of the variable, then the "becomes" symbol, and finally the value (the string of characters) that we want stored. This is illustrated in Figure 4-1.

Figure 4-1: Assigning a string value to a string variable.

Similarly, we can set up a variable called `surname` that can hold a string typed in by the user:

```
String surname = BasicIo.readString() ;
```

The part after the = symbol reads the character string typed by the user at the keyboard (using the class method `readString` in the `BasicIo` class) and returns this string to be stored in the variable `surname`.

Whenever we want to refer to the string that has been typed in, we give the name of the variable `surname` holding it. For example, we could set the surname attribute of the `person1` instance with:

```
person1.setSurname(surname) ;
```

We can now read a string from the user for the surname and forename attributes. What about the age attribute? This is not a string of characters but a number; actually it is an integer—that is, a whole number with no fractional part. There is a method `readInteger` in the `BasicIo` class to read such a value typed in at the keyboard. But we must store it in a different type of variable:

```
int age = BasicIo.readInteger() ;
```

Here we have declared a local variable called age that is the right shape to hold an integer or whole number. Notice that in Java it is spelled int with a small *i*, and it is one of the basic data types provided by Java as a building block for all the rest. We can use the value held in this variable to set the age attribute of the person2 instance:

```
person2.setAge(age) ;
```

Here is a complete program (a) to prompt the user for a string, to read it in, and then to output it again for confirmation, and then (b) to prompt the user for an integer, to read it in, and then to output it again for confirmation:

```
import java.lancs.* ;

public class Chapter4n1
    {
    public static void main(String[] args) throws Exception
        {
        // read in and output a String
        BasicIo.prompt("please type in a string ") ;
        String string1 = BasicIo.readString() ;
        System.out.println("the string you typed was **" + string1 +
                            "**") ;

        System.out.println() ;

        // read in and output an integer
        BasicIo.prompt("please type in an integer ") ;
        int intValue = BasicIo.readInteger() ;
        System.out.println("the integer you typed was " + intValue) ;
        } // end of method main
    } // end of class Chapter4n1
```

If we compile and run this program, we will have a dialog like the following (where the user input is in bold):

```
please type in a string Hello Everyone
the string you typed was **Hello Everyone**

please type in an integer 6
the integer you typed was 6
```

Suppose that, in response to the second message, we typed something that Java couldn't interpret as an integer. In this case, the readInteger method "throws up its hands in horror, and abandons its task"—in Java language it "*throws an exception*":

```
please type in an integer abc
java.io.IOException: invalid integer
```

```
at java.lancs.BasicIo.readInteger(BasicIo.java:56)
at Chapter4n1.main(Chapter4n1.java:17)
```

Here the Java system is telling us that it has abandoned our program because of an exception called IOException, and it occurred at line 17 of the file Chapter4n1.java. At the moment, there is nothing we can do about this exception; later (in Chapter 15) we will learn how to have our program catch the exception so that it can do something about it.

The Java system always wants to know when an exception might be thrown. All the read methods in the BasicIo class can throw exceptions, so we have to tell the Java system that our main method is not going to catch any of these exceptions but simply allow them to stop our program. That is why we have written:

```
... throws Exception
```

at the end of the header line for our main method. We need to do this whenever the main method contains any calls of these BasicIo methods.

4.2 More on Integer Variables

As we have seen, variables can refer to instances of objects, or they can refer to more basic types—we have met only the one basic type, int, so far, but there will be others shortly. For now, we will concentrate on basic types, using int as an example. We can declare a local variable called total that can store an integer value:

```
int total ;
```

Graphically, the result of this is shown in Figure 4-2.

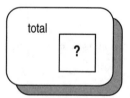

Figure 4-2: An integer variable called total.

We have set aside an area in the computer that is the right size for an integer value and called it total. We have not set it to any particular value.

It is possible to initialize a variable by giving it a value when we declare it. For example, we could have instead declared the variable total:

```
int total = 4 ;
```

The result is given in Figure 4-3.

Figure 4-3: Initializing total to the value 4.

We can change the value of total anywhere within the method in which it is declared (that is why we have called it a *local* variable, as it is local to the body of the main method and cannot be accessed from outside the method). We can write:

```
total = 6 ;
```

This is an example of the *assignment* statement, which we first met in Chapter 3. We have assigned the value 6 to the variable total. It is because of the fact that we can change or vary the value of a variable that they are so called. In algebraic or arithmetic terms, we are using an equal sign here as the assignment operator. It may look like an equal sign, but it can be read as "becomes." In other words, "the value of total becomes 6."

So, we have integer variables that can be visualized as "integer-shaped" boxes. Into these boxes we can place integer shaped values, as shown in Figure 4-4.

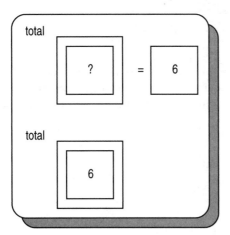

Figure 4-4: Assigning the value 6 to total.

We can assign the value of an integer variable to another integer variable; we do this by taking the value contained in one box and placing a copy of it in another box (leaving the original unchanged). So, for example:

```
int final ;
final = total ;
```

The result is given in Figure 4-5.

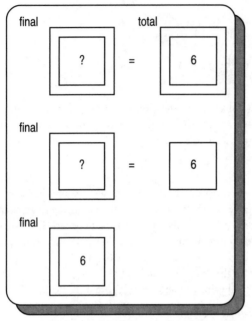

Figure 4-5: Assigning the contents of `total` to `final`.

It is possible to form integer *expressions*; these are expressions that can involve integer variables and values combined using arithmetic operators. An integer expression is one that, once evaluated, results in a single integer value. This value can then, of course, be assigned to an integer variable. For example:

```
int x ;
int y = 6 ;
x = y + 4 ;
```

The result is given in Figure 4-6.

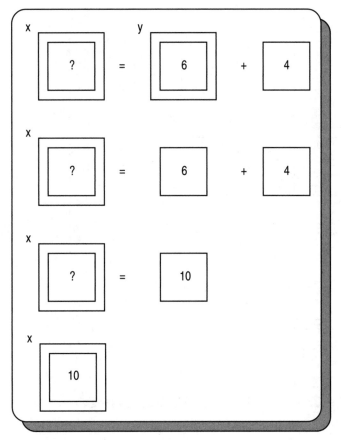

Figure 4-6: Evaluating an expression involving y and assigning the result to x.

Finally, it is possible to have an assignment statement such as:

```
total = total + 2;
```

If we look at this algebraically, it makes no sense at all. Remember, however, we read the = sign as "becomes," so this statement should be read "the value of total becomes the value of total plus two." We explore this graphically in Figure 4-7.

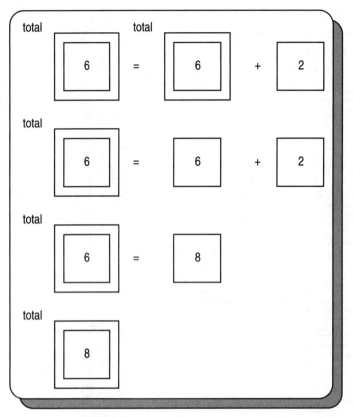

Figure 4-7: Assigning the value of an expression involving `total` to `total`.

So the statement makes perfect sense; make the value of `total` 2 more than its previous value.

4.3 Type Checking

Java is what is called a *strongly typed* language. This means that whenever we try to assign a value of type X, we can only do so to a variable of type X. So, for example, a successful assignment would be:

```
int final = 4 ;
```

Consider the following:

```
int final = someValue ;
```

This may or may not be valid (or legal). We can tell only by finding out how `someValue` was declared. If it was declared to be of type `int`, then this assignment will be all right. If it was declared as some other type, then we will have problems. The Java compiler will generate an error, and we will have to fix it before we can continue.

If we consider our graphical version, it should be obvious why any attempt to place a value of one type into a variable of another will fail; they are simply the wrong shape:

```
int total = 'c' ;
```

We are trying to store a value that is a character in a variable that is the right shape only for an integer, as shown in Figure 4-8.

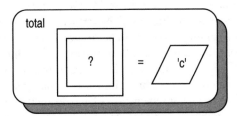

Figure 4-8: Trying to assign a character-shaped value to an integer-shaped box.

As we have seen, this kind of checking also occurs when inputting information. If we are using the `readInteger` method, and the user types letters instead of digits, we will get a run-time error (an exception) unless we, the programmers, take steps to handle such an error.

4.4 Making Decisions

In the course of an average day, we make thousands of commonplace decisions.
This evening, shall I:

- a) Stay in and study programming?
- b) Go out?

These two decisions can lead to others:

- a-1) Write solutions to the exercises at the end of this chapter, which I can type in and try out when I next have access to a computer?
- a-2) Read over the last chapter?
- b-1) Go to the pub?
- b-2) Go to the movies?
- b-3) Go to the sports center?

As humans, we base our decisions on feelings and information. We might go to the movies if the film showing is one we want to see. In order to make that decision, we need to know what movie is on this evening. Computers make decisions based only on information:

- If it is 10:30 A.M. and a weekday, it is coffee time!

- If it is coffee time and I am not busy, I will take a break and have a coffee!

Computers use binary arithmetic and manipulation. We can base our programs' decisions on a binary value of TRUE or FALSE. There are certain kinds of statements that we can make in English that are either true or false; there is no other interpretation of them. For example, if someone asks if it is raining, then we can only say (factually) "Yes" or "No." So the statement, "It is raining," will be true if it is raining and false otherwise. We can venture an opinion, "No, it isn't raining now, but it looks like it is clouding over." Nevertheless, although we think it might rain later, the statement, "It is raining," is still false, until such time as it starts raining.

It is this kind of factual statement (based on available information) that allows us to write programs that have a more complex flow of control. In the programs we have written so far, statements are executed one after the other, in the order in which we have placed them. It is often useful to be able to decide to do one set of statements rather than another set. Also, as we shall see in the next chapter, we will wish to repeat a set of statements over and over again.

The "flow of control" through the programs we have written so far can be visualized as a straight line, linking each statement to the next, as shown in Figure 4-9.

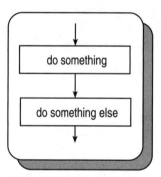

Figure 4-9: Sequential action.

Using selection statements in a program leads to a more complicated diagram. We shall use a rather old-fashioned technique, flowcharting, to illustrate the flow of control when using selection.

In most programming languages, the selection statement begins with an if keyword. This is followed by an expression that can only ever be either true or false. Such expressions are known as *Boolean* expressions. Boolean expressions, when evaluated, have a value of TRUE or FALSE, just as arithmetic expressions have an arithmetic value. We shall look at Boolean expressions in more detail later in this chapter. Depending on the result of the Boolean expression, we can choose to do one of two sets of actions:

- If the Boolean expression is TRUE, then do this.
- Otherwise, do that.

Associated with some Boolean value, then, we can have two actions—"do this" and "do that." We chose which action to carry out depending on whether the value is TRUE or FALSE. If it is TRUE, we carry out the "do this" action; if it is FALSE, we carry out the "do that" action. This is illustrated by the flowchart in Figure 4-10.

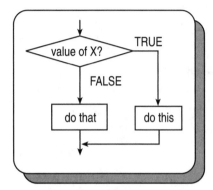

Figure 4-10: Choosing to do this or do that.

Let us examine the syntax of the diagram in Figure 4-10. In the diamond box, we place the Boolean expression. Now, instead of a single line, we have two alternative lines emanating from the diamond "decision" box. The two lines are labeled TRUE and FALSE to indicate which path we should follow depending on the value of the Boolean expression within the decision box.

One line leads to a box containing one or more statements ("do this"), and the other line leads to a different box ("do that") containing a different set of instructions. Finally, note that once the selection statement is completed, the two different lines join up and we are back to our simple, sequential flow of control.

Notice that the "do that" action might be to do nothing!

- If (I feel like a coffee), then get one; otherwise do nothing.
- If (X is true), then do this; otherwise do nothing.

We can simply omit the "otherwise do nothing" part of the statement, as illustrated by the flowchart in Figure 4-11.

Being limited to two choices may seem restrictive, but any multiway decision can be broken down into a sequence of binary decisions:

"If the animal is an elephant, put it in the elephant enclosure, or else if it is a tiger, put it in the tiger cage, or else if it is a shark, put it in the shark tank."

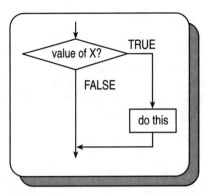

Figure 4-11: Choosing to do this or do nothing.

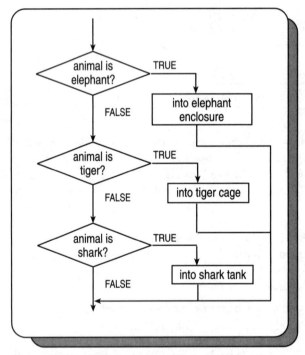

Figure 4-12: Making a choice of three actions.

This is illustrated by the flowchart in Figure 4-12. Notice we may make one, two, or three choices, but we carry out only one of the actions. (We certainly wouldn't want to put an elephant in the elephant enclosure and then put it in the shark tank!)

We can try to clarify the textual representation of our conditional statement by using indentation:

```
if (animal is elephant) then
    put in elephant enclosure
else if (animal is tiger) then
    put in tiger cage
else if (animal is shark) then
    put in shark tank
```

4.5   Selection Statements in Java

We now return to our use of the `Person` class. Let us suppose we wish to classify the current person according to his or her age. A simple program might examine the value of a person's age and, depending on that value, tell us if the person is an adult:

```
if (person1.getAge() > 18)
    {
    System.out.print(person1.getForename() + ' ' +
person1.getSurname()) ;
    System.out.print(" is an adult") ;
    System.out.println() ;
    }
```

Notice that the `if` keyword is followed by a Boolean expression in parentheses. Either a person is older than 18 or they are not. The only possible outcome of this question is true or false. If the expression evaluates to true, then we execute the set of statements contained in the curly brackets.

This might be suitable in some situations, but notice that if the person is younger than 18, this program prints nothing. It might be useful if we made some other statement about the classification the person's age places them in if they are not an adult:

```
System.out.print(person1.getForename() + ' ' +
person1.getSurname()) ;
System.out.print(" is ") ;
if (person1.getAge() > 18)
    System.out.print("an adult") ;
else
    System.out.print("a minor") ;
System.out.println() ;
```

Notice that here we have a simple statement following the Boolean expression. It becomes even more important that we use indentation sensibly so that we can see the flow of control through this sequence of statements. Moreover, we introduce a further keyword, `else`. This allows us to specify the second path emanating from the decision box. We can show the preceding sequence diagrammatically (see Figure 4-13).

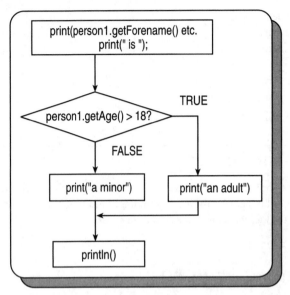

Figure 4-13: Deciding if a Person is an adult or a minor.

If the person is older than 18, we will execute the statement that prints out that the person is an adult. Otherwise, we will execute the statement that prints out that the person is a minor.

4.5.1 Statements

In this section, we consider the grammar and construction of a statement. We can identify two kinds of statement: *single* (or simple) and *compound*. An example of a single statement could be an assignment statement:

```
x = 4 ;
```

A compound statement is a sequence of statements enclosed in curly brackets:

```
{
x = 4 ;
System.out.println("about to do something with x");
y = x * 2 ;
}
```

A statement can be either a single statement or a compound statement; both are grammatically correct. This means that wherever we expect a statement to appear, we can have a single statement or a compound statement.

If we then say that the general structure of an if statement is:

```
if (Boolean expression) statement else statement
```

then where we have *statement,* we could have a single or a compound statement. Consider the following example:

```
if (age >= 60)
   System.out.print(person1.getSurname()) ;
   System.out.println(" is an old age pensioner") ;
```

What we intend to happen is that if age is greater than or equal to 60, then we output the person's surname and a suitable message. However, despite our indentation, the statement following our Boolean expression is a single one. This means that regardless of the result of the test, we will always output the message "is an old age pensioner". If we flowchart this if statement (see Figure 4-14), it should be clear what is happening.

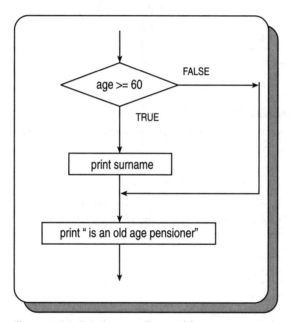

Figure 4-14: Printing out "is an old age pensioner" every time.

We must use the curly brackets (also known as *braces*) to create a compound statement:

```
if (age >= 60)
   {
   System.out.print(person1.getSurname()) ;
   System.out.println("is an old age pensioner") ;
   }
```

Now if we flowchart this statement (see Figure 4-15), we can see that it behaves as expected.

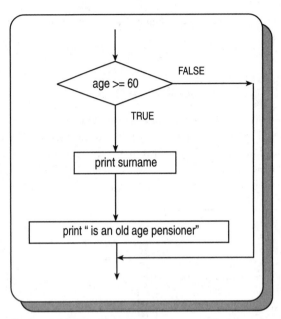

Figure 4-15: Printing out the surname of old age pensioners with suitable message.

4.5.2 Relational Operators & Boolean Expressions

Boolean expressions can be formed using the *relational operators*. They allow us to compare one value with another value of the same type. The relational operators are listed in Table 4-1.

Operator	Description
==	equal to
!=	not equal to
<	less than
<=	less than or equal to
>	greater than
>=	greater than or equal to

Table 4-1: Relational operators.

We have already been using a couple of these operators—namely, "greater than" and "greater than or equal"—when we've been comparing the value of a person's age with the integer constants 18 and 60. This was OK because both values are integers. We can also compare other values of the same types—for example, two characters. However, we cannot compare two values of different types—for example, an integer and a character—as this does not make sense.

An important point to note is the use of == (two equal signs in a row) to denote equality. The equal sign (=) is already being used in Java to denote the assignment operator, so we cannot use it again here as the relational equality operator. It is very important not to get these operators mixed up! It can cause some problems at compile time.

As we saw earlier in our example concerning animals and the dilemma facing the zookeepers as to which enclosure the animals belong in, sometimes we need to make a multiway decision. Concerning a person's age, we can classify it with a finer granularity than just adult and minor. For example, we can have four categories: child, teenager, adult, and pensioner. We can lay this out as a table:

Condition based on age	Classification
less than 13	child
greater than or equal to 13 and less than 18	teenager
greater than or equal to 18 and less than 60	adult
greater than or equal to 60	pensioner

Table 4-2: Conditions and classifications.

We can implement this as a sequence of if-else statements as follows :

```
System.out.print(person1.getForename() + ' ' +
person1.getSurname()) ;
System.out.print(" is ") ;
if (person1.getAge() < 13)
   System.out.print("a child") ;
else if (person1.getAge() < 18)
   System.out.print("a teenager") ;
else if (person1.getAge() < 60)
   System.out.print("an adult") ;
else
   System.out.print("a pensioner") ;
System.out.println() ;
```

This is illustrated by the flowchart in Figure 4-16.

Consider now the following. At present, and for a few years more, deciding whether someone is a pensioner in the United Kingdom involves more information that just the person's age. This is because until early in the next century, women are allowed to retire at 60 and men at 65.

As we saw in Chapter 3, the Person class provides us with a gender attribute and a set of integer constants—namely MALE, FEMALE, and UNKNOWN. As class users, we do not need to know what integer values these constants have; we simply use the semantics that they represent—namely, the possible information we may have regarding a person's gender:

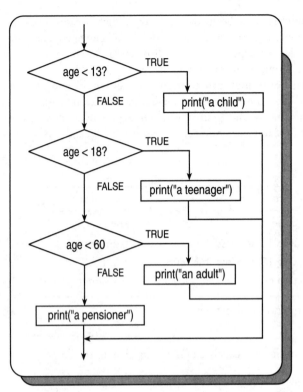

Figure 4-16: Four classifications based on a person's age.

```
System.out.print(person1.getForename() + ' ' +
person1.getSurname()) ;
System.out.print(" is ") ;
if (person1.getAge() < 13)
   System.out.print("a child") ;
else if (person1.getAge() < 18)
   System.out.print("a teenager") ;
else if (person1.getGender() == Person.FEMALE)
   {
   if (person1.getAge() < 60)
      System.out.print("an adult") ;
   else
      System.out.print("a pensioner") ;
   }
else
   {
   if (person1.getAge() < 65)
      System.out.print("an adult") ;
```

```
   else
      System.out.print("a pensioner") ;
   }
System.out.println() ;
```

Figure 4-17 is a flowchart of the last two parts of this multiway decision.

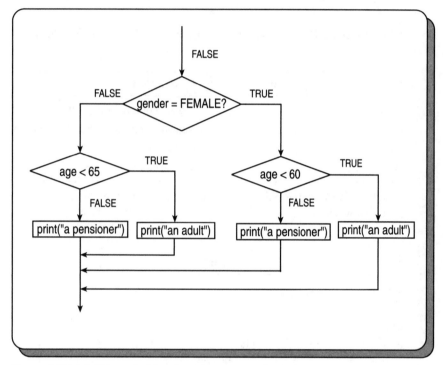

Figure 4-17: Multiway decision based on age and gender.

4.6   The boolean Type

In addition to having Boolean expressions as the result of statements containing relational operations, we can have variables of type `boolean` in Java. So, for example, we can have the following :

```
boolean myBool = true ;
```

This is similar to having an integer variable and giving it an integer value. As you know, integer variables can also be given the value of an integer expression:

```
int x = 4 +(9 * 20) / y ;
```

Similarly, a variable of type `boolean` can be assigned the result of a Boolean expression:

`myBool = (person1.getAge() > 18) ;`

Depending on the value of a person's age, `myBool` will be given the value true or false. We can construct more complicated Boolean expressions by using the set of *logical operators*.

In Java, the logical operators in Table 4-3 may be used with Boolean expressions.

Table 4-3: Logical operators that may be used with Boolean expressions.

Name	Symbol	Description
AND	&	logical conjunction (both)
OR	|	logical disjunction (one or the other or both)
NOT	!	logical negation
EQUALS	==	equivalence

Tables 4-4 through 4-7 define the operators AND, OR, NOT, and EQUALS (here *b* and *d* are Boolean values).

b	d	b AND d
false	false	false
false	true	false
true	false	false
true	true	true

Table 4-4: The AND operator.

b	d	b OR d
false	false	false
false	true	true
true	false	true
true	true	true

Table 4-5: The OR operator.

b	NOT b
false	true
true	false

Table 4-6: The NOT operator.

b	d	b EQUALS d
false	false	true
false	true	false
true	false	false
true	true	true

Table 4-7: The EQUALS operator.

The tables are known as *truth tables*. Because there are only two possible values for a Boolean, it is possible to write down all possible combinations of two Booleans and the result of the operation. (Imagine doing this for integers and the plus operation!)

For the results of an AND to be true, *both* operands must be true. For the result of an OR to be true, *any* of the operands must be true.

There is a formal algebra (Boolean algebra) built up around these operators and the values of the operands.

Now that we have introduced the logical operators, we can take a second look at the problem of male and female pensioners. If we wish to examine a person and decide if they are a pensioner, we can have the following selection statement:

```
boolean isPensioner = false ;
if (person1.getGender() == Person.FEMALE)
   {
   if (person1.getAge() >= 60)
      isPensioner = true ;
   }
else
   {
   if (person1.getAge() >= 65)
      isPensioner = true ;
   }
```

Here we see the nested if statements executed depending on whether a person is male or female. Notice how we make the initial assumption that the person is not a pensioner and subsequently check for "pensioner-hood."

In this particular example, we can use the logical operators to combine the Boolean expression from the outer if statement with the inner if statement and thus remove the need for a nested if statement:

```
boolean isPensioner = false ;
if (
      (
        (person1.getGender() == Person.FEMALE)
        &
        (person1.getAge() >= 60)
      )
      |
      (person1.getAge() >= 65)
    )
    isPensioner = true ;
```

We have indented the parentheses in the preceding example to highlight the structure of the Boolean expression; we can, of course, write it more compactly as follows:

```
boolean isPensioner = false ;
if (((person1.getGender() == Person.FEMALE) &
      (person1.getAge() >= 60)) |
    (person1.getAge() >= 65))
    isPensioner = true ;
```

In this Boolean expression, we have put parentheses around each individual part. It is possible to leave out some of the parentheses, but we have to be careful that the priority, or *precedence,* of the logical operators does not affect the final result of the expression. The three logical operators we have introduced have the priorities shown in Table 4-8 (in Chapter 6 we will see a fuller version of this table, including other operators).

Priority	Operator	Description
high	!	NOT
medium	&	AND
low			OR

Table 4-8: Precedence for the logical operators.

Those operators with a higher priority are executed first so that, for instance, AND operators are evaluated before OR operators.

In our expression that tests for pensioners, we want to make sure that we test for females over 60 before we test for anybody over 65. The expression that tests for females over 60 links two simpler expressions with an AND operator. We can see from the priority table (Table 4-8) that AND is executed before OR; therefore we will indeed test for females over 60 before we OR that result with the test for anyone over 65.

In this particular case, then, we do not need to put the "females over 60" expression in parentheses and can write the overall expression as follows:

```
boolean isPensioner = false ;
if ((person1.getGender() == Person.FEMALE) &
    (person1.getAge() >= 60) |
    (person1.getAge() >= 65))
    isPensioner = true ;
```

While the additional parentheses are not actually necessary—the operator priorities ensure that the expressions are evaluated in the order we require—they do add to the readability of the expression and reflect the programmer's intention explicitly. In a moment, we will look at an example of an expression where the parentheses do affect the outcome.

Let's take our pensioner expression as a worked example of how Boolean expressions are evaluated. Consider Joan, age 18, and Bill, age 72 (see Table 4-9).

	Joan	Bill
gender = FEMALE	true	false
age >= 60	false	true
(gender = FEMALE) AND (age >=60)	false	false
age >= 65	false	true
((gender = FEMALE) AND (age >= 60)) OR (age >= 65)	false	true

Table 4-9: Joan, Bill, and the value of the Boolean expressions.

In the first and second rows, we evaluate the two simple Boolean expressions contained within the larger AND expression.

In the third row, we evaluate the AND. We can do this by looking at the AND truth table presented earlier, or we can remember the rule that AND results in true only if both the operands are true. In the previous two examples, one of the operands is false, so we know immediately that the result of the AND is false.

In the fourth row, we evaluate the last simple Boolean expression that we must OR with the result of the AND.

Finally, in the fifth row, we OR the results shown in rows three and four. Again, we can do this by referring to the OR truth table, or we can remember the rule that the result of an OR is true if either of the operands are true.

Returning to operator priority and the use of parentheses, consider the following expression:

```
switch4 = ( ! ( switch1 | switch2 ) ) & switch3 ;
```

If we evaluate this for a particular set of values for the Boolean variables, we get the results shown in Table 4-10.

switch1	true
switch2	true
switch3	true
switch1 OR switch2	true
NOT (switch1 OR switch2)	false
NOT (switch1 OR switch2) AND switch3	false

Table 4-10: Evaluating the Boolean expression.

Now let us take the brackets out completely:

```
switch4 = ! switch1 | switch2 & switch3 ;
```

If we evaluate the expression for the same values, we arrive at Table 4-11.

switch1	true
switch2	true
switch3	true
NOT switch1	false
switch2 AND switch3	true
NOT switch1 OR switch2 AND switch3	true

Table 4-11: Evaluating the Boolean expression without brackets.

From the tables, you can see how the operations are being executed in a different order because of operator precedence, and in this case, arrive at a different result.

Consider the pensioner example again. We are checking the value of a Boolean expression. If it is true, we set the value of Boolean variable to true. If it is false, we leave it false. In this particular case, there is no need for the if statement at all! We can do all the work with the Boolean expression itself and an assignment statement, as follows:

```
boolean isPensioner = (((person1.getGender() == Person.FEMALE) &
                        (person1.getAge() >= 60)) |
                        (person1.getAge() >= 65)) ;
```

In addition to the & and | forms of the AND and OR operators, there are the && and ||
forms. These are known as *short-circuit* versions of the AND and OR operators and they function as follows.

If we inspect the AND truth table, we will find that in order for "b AND d" to be TRUE,
both *b* and *d* must be TRUE. As soon as either *b* or *d* is FALSE, then we know the overall result
of "b and d" must also be FALSE. If *b* or *d* are Boolean expressions, once we have evaluated *b* to
FALSE, there is clearly no need to go on and evaluate *d*; regardless of whether *d* is TRUE or
FALSE, the result of "b AND d" must be FALSE.

Similarly, the OR truth table shows us that in order for "b OR d" to be FALSE, both *b* and
d must be FALSE. As soon as either *b* or *d* is TRUE, the result of "b OR d" must also be TRUE.

In Java, we can use the short-circuit AND (&&) and OR (||) operators to avoid the needless
evaluation of the second Boolean expression:

```
switch4 = ! switch1 || switch2 && switch3 ;
```

4.7 The Switch Statement

It is clear that it is possible to split a multiway decision into a series of binary decisions. However, it is sometimes possible to replace a sequence of if statements with a switch statement.
The switch statement more directly models the multiway decision, making life easier for both
the programmer and the maintainer: it is easier to read and understand something that more
accurately captures the semantics of what is being done.

Let's begin with a simple example. Suppose that grades denoted by letters of the alphabet
have been assigned to students. However, for the purposes of deciding whether a student should
progress to the next year of study, these grades need to be converted into points that are then
added together. If the result is greater than some nominal threshold, the student is allowed to
proceed. We can achieve the transformation from grade to points using the following switch
statement:

```
char grade = ...
...
int points = 0;
switch (grade)
   {
   case 'A' :
     points = 3;
     break;
   case 'B' :
     points = 2;
     break;
   case 'C' :
     points = 1;
     break;
   };
```

The `switch` keyword is followed by an expression or variable name in parentheses. The value of the expression or variable must belong to an *ordinal* type. An ordinal type is one whose values form an ordered list and differ in complete steps. For example, `int` is an example of an ordinal type, as its values range from the smallest integer to the largest in steps of one. The `char` type is also an ordinal type, but the `double` and `String` types are not.

Following the *controlling expression* (in this example, `grade`), we have a list of *case* statements. The value of the controlling expression is compared with each case label. When we find a match, the statements associated with the matching label are executed. If `grade` was equal to 'B', then the statements `points = 2` and `break` would be executed.

The `break` statement transfers control to the statement following the `switch` statement. If we omit the `break` statement, then it would mean we execute all the case statements following the one we matched `grade` with. We will see examples of this later.

Compare this with the `if` statement that would achieve the same effect:

```
int grade = ...
...
int points = 0;
if (grade == 'A')
   points = 3;
else if (grade == 'B')
   points = 2;
else if (grade == 'C')
   points = 1;
```

Actually, this doesn't look too bad. However, consider a statement with 20-odd decision points.

Consider now an application where we represent the months of the year as twelve integer constants JAN to DEC. We need to be able to obtain the number of days in the current month. We could use the following `switch` statement as an almost direct realization of the rhyme:

```
30 days hath September,
April, June and November,
All the rest have 31,
Except February, which has 28 days clear,
And 29 in each leap year.

int month = ...
...
switch (month)
   {
   case SEP : case APR : case JUN : case NOV :
      days = 30;
      break;
   case FEB : // assume not a leap year, for the present
      days = 28;
      break;
```

```
default :
  days = 31;
  break;
};
```

In this example, we have introduced the `default` case statement. Clearly, a controlling expression can potentially return any value from the ordinal type. For example, `month` here is an `int` and could contain any integer value in the range (for our example to work correctly, they should really be in the range JAN to DEC, but that's another story). Rather than provide a case statement for every possible value of `month` (a rather tedious and boring task), we can use the "catch-all" `default` statement instead. In our example, if `month` does not contain SEP, APR, JUN, NOV, or FEB, we assume it contains either one of the other valid months or some other integer, and we set the value of `days` to 31.

The `default` statement matches any value of the controlling expression that is not listed as part of any of the other case labels.

Consider writing the 30-days option as an `if` statement.

```
if ((month == SEP) || (month == APR) ||
   (month == JUN) || (month == SEP))
   ...
```

This example illustrates a number of important points about the `switch` statement. It may appear as if we have only listed the 4 options for 30 days, but this is purely a matter of layout. If we view the overall `switch` statement as follows :

```
switch (month)
  {
  case SEP :
    // empty statement
  case APR :
    // empty statement
  case JUN :
    // empty statement
  case NOV :
    days = 30;
    break;
  case FEB : // assume not a leap year, for the present
    days = 28;
    break;
  default :
    days = 31;
    break;
  } ;
```

we can see that we have five identified cases plus the sixth `default` case (more about this in a moment). Once we have entered a case, we execute *all* subsequent statements until we encounter the end of the overall `switch` statement or a `break` statement. If the month was APR, then we would "execute" the empty statement associated with the APR case, continue on to the empty statement associated with JUN, execute the "days = 30" assignment statement associated with NOV, reach the break statement, and exit from the switch statement.

So, if the month is SEP, APR, or JUN, we will enter at the appropriate case statement but end up executing the code associated with NOV. This is as it should be. Notice if the month is NOV, we execute only the single assignment statement and leave. We do not continue on to the FEB case.

If there were no break statements in this example, the value of the days variable would always end up being that of the last case statement. In this example, that is the default statement, and therefore, days would always have the value 31.

Consider now a pay rise being granted to employees and managers. Employees are to receive a 10 percent raise, as are managers. However, before this raise is applied, managers are also to receive a 50 pounds increase. One way of achieving this would be:

```
if (status == MANAGER)
   {
   salary = salary + 50 ;
   }
if ((status == EMPLOYEE) || (status == MANAGER))
   {
   salary = salary + ((salary / 100) * 10) ;
   }
```

Taking advantage of our ability to execute consecutive case statements, we can handle this as a switch statement:

```
switch (status)
   {
   case MANAGER :
      salary = salary + 50;
   case EMPLOYEE :
      salary = salary + ((salary / 100) * 10);
      break;
   default :
      // do something appropriate
   }
```

Now, if status is MANAGER, not only do we get our 50 pound raise, but we "fall through" to the EMPLOYEE statement and get our 10 percent increase on top of that.

What would happen if we placed a break statement at the end of the MANAGER case? Would our manager be very pleased about this mistake? The use and non-use of break statements has to be very carefully handled; it can be a source of errors that are quite difficult to spot.

Let us return to our "days of the month" example. The original rhyme has a nice "get out clause;" it covers 4 of the months that all have 30 days, handles the odd-ball February, and then simply says "all the rest have 31." If we wanted to be pedantic about things, we could have:

```
switch (month)
  {
  case SEP : case APR : case JUN : case NOV :
    days = 30;
    break;
  case FEB : // assume not a leap year, for the present
    days = 28;
    break;
  case JAN : case MAR : case MAY : case JUL :
  case AUG : case OCT : case DEC :
    days = 31;
    break;
  } ;
```

If we cannot know for sure that only "valid" month values will be given to this switch statement, then we need to be pedantic (or careful) in order to catch and handle any invalid attempt to use the switch:

```
switch (month)
  {
  case SEP : case APR : case JUN : case NOV :
    days = 30;
    break;
  case FEB : // assume not a leap year, for the present
    days = 28;
    break;
  case JAN : case MAR : case MAY : case JUL :
  case AUG : case OCT : case DEC :
    days = 31;
    break;
  default :
    System.out.print("illegal month!");
  };
```

Imagine now a very rudimentary integer calculator implemented as a Java program. The user types in an operand, followed by an operator (one of the characters +, −, *, /), followed by a final operand. The operands are read with the readInteger method, and the operator, which is a single character, is read with the readCharacter method. The operator is applied to the operands and the result is output. We can use the switch statement to help realize this program:

```
BasicIo.prompt("type the first operand: ") ;
int operand1 = BasicIo.readInteger() ;
BasicIo.prompt("type an operator (+, -, * or /): ") ;
char operator = BasicIo.readCharacter() ;
BasicIo.prompt("type the second operand: ") ;
```

```
int operand2 = BasicIo.readInteger() ;
switch (operator)
  {
  case '+' :
    result = operand1 + operand2 ;
    break;
  case '-' :
    result = operand1 - operand2 ;
    break;
  case '*' :
    result = operand1 * operand2 ;
    break;
  case '/' :
    result = operand1 / operand2 ;
    break;
  default :
    System.out.print("illegal operator") ;
  } ;
System.out.println("the result is " + result) ;
```

The statement that follows a case specifier can be a complex one. This means we can use if statements in conjunction with switch statements (and vice versa). To complete our implementation of the "days of the month" example, we need to tackle the problem of February. This is not just a simple value; it depends on whether the year involved is a leap year or not. We need to know the year, and we need a Boolean expression that tells us if it is a leap year or not:

```
case FEB :
  days = 28;
  if (year % 4 == 0) days = days + 1;
  break;
```

The expression year % 4 means "calculate the remainder from dividing year by 4." This is not a full leap-year calculation, because a century year is a leap year only if it is divisible by 400—so 2000 is a leap year, but 1900 is not. Can you rewrite this expression to do the full calculation?

4.8   Testing a New Class

When developing a new class, or using an existing one, it is often useful to be able to test the class as thoroughly as possible before issuing it or using it in a real application. One technique for doing this is to develop a *test harness* or *driver program*. As we have seen, the object orientation of Java allows us to build software with a strict, enforced interface. Users of a class have access to a list of available methods. We can use this as the basis of our interactive test harness.

A person using the test harness can select which method they want to test; the harness then prompts for the arguments for the method, calls the method under test, and outputs any return value. The following is a test harness for the Person class, which tests the getting and setting of forename, surname, age, and gender using a switch statement to select which method is to be called. We obviously want to try out a *sequence* of method calls, so we have used a loop or repetition statement—the while (continueLoop) statement (this will be explained in the next chapter):

```
import java.lancs.* ;

public class Chapter4n2
    {
    public static void main(String[] args) throws Exception
        {
        Person myPerson = new Person() ;
        boolean continueLoop = true ;

        while (continueLoop)
            {
            // get the command (a character)
            BasicIo.prompt("type a single command character: ") ;
            char command = BasicIo.readCharacter() ;

            int age = 0 ;
            String response = null ;

            // call the appropriate method
            switch (command)
                {
                case 'a' : // set forename
                    BasicIo.prompt("type a forename: ") ;
                    response = BasicIo.readString() ;
                    myPerson.setForename(response) ;
                    break ;

                case 'b' : // set surname
                    BasicIo.prompt("type a surname: ") ;
                    response = BasicIo.readString() ;
                    myPerson.setSurname(response) ;
                    break ;

                case 'c' : // set age
                    BasicIo.prompt("type an age: ") ;
                    age = BasicIo.readInteger() ;
                    myPerson.setAge(age) ;
                    break ;

                case 'd' : // set gender
                    BasicIo.prompt("type a gender: ") ;
```

```
        response = BasicIo.readString() ;
        if (response.equals("male"))
          myPerson.setGender(Person.MALE) ;
        else if (response.equals("female"))
          myPerson.setGender(Person.FEMALE) ;
        else
          myPerson.setGender(Person.UNKNOWN) ;
        break ;

    case 'e' : // get forename
        System.out.print("forename is ") ;
        System.out.println(myPerson.getForename()) ;
        break ;

    case 'f' : // get surname
        System.out.print("surname is ") ;
        System.out.println(myPerson.getSurname()) ;
        break ;

    case 'g' : // get age
        System.out.print("age is ") ;
        System.out.println(myPerson.getAge()) ;
        break ;

    case 'h' : // get gender
        System.out.print("gender is ") ;
        switch (myPerson.getGender())
          {
          case Person.MALE :
            System.out.println("male") ;
            break ;
          case Person.FEMALE :
            System.out.println("female") ;
            break ;
          default :
            System.out.println("unknown") ;
          }
        break ;

    case '?' : // print 'help' information
        System.out.println("a : set forename") ;
        System.out.println("b : set surname") ;
        System.out.println("c : set age") ;
        System.out.println("d : set gender") ;
        System.out.println("e : get forename") ;
        System.out.println("f : get surname") ;
        System.out.println("g : get age") ;
```

```
            System.out.println("h : get gender") ;
            System.out.println("? : output this message") ;
            System.out.println("s : stop the program") ;
            break ;

         case 's' : // stop the program
            continueLoop = false ;
            break ;

         default :
            System.out.println("illegal command") ;
         }
      }
   } // end of method main
 } // end of class Chapter4n2
```

Notice how the gender attribute was handled. The argument to the `setGender` method is an integer, and the `Person` class provides the constants `MALE`, `FEMALE`, and `UNKNOWN`. We don't want the user to have to remember the values of these constants, so we allow the user to type in one of the strings `"male"` and `"female"` (any other string is treated as an `UNKNOWN` value). So we need to test the input string (response) to see if it is the string `"male"`—if so, we set the gender attribute to the `MALE` constant:

```
if (response.equals("male"))
   myPerson.setGender(Person.MALE) ;
...
```

We cannot compare strings with the == relational operator. Instead, Java provides an `equals` method that returns the value TRUE if the argument string is the same as the string to which the method is applied; it returns the value FALSE otherwise. If the string was not `"male"`, we need to test for the string `"female"`:

```
else if (response.equals("female"))
   myPerson.setGender(Person.FEMALE) ;
...
```

If this also fails, we set the value accordingly:

```
else
   myPerson.setGender(Person.UNKNOWN) ;
```

It would be nice if the user could type `"Male"` or `"MALE"` as well as `"male"`, so we could write:

```
if ((response.equals("male")) ||
    (response.equals("Male")) ||
    (response.equals("MALE")))
   myPerson.setGender(Person.MALE) ;
...
```

Alternatively, we could convert the `response` string all to lowercase before doing any tests. We will see how to do this in Chapter 6.

When outputting the gender, we want to output a string rather that an integer. We use a `switch` statement to convert from one to the other (instead of the `getGenderString` method provided).

4.9   Key Points in Chapter 4

- A program that allowed only a linear progression through a sequence of statements would be very limited in its functionality. A program needs to be able to decide which of two or more sets of actions needs to be carried out based on the current circumstances.

- An `if` statement has the form:

```
if (BOOLEAN EXPRESSION)
    FIRST SET OF STATEMENTS
else
    SECOND SET OF STATEMENTS
```

- If the BOOLEAN EXPRESSION evaluates to true, the FIRST SET OF STATEMENTS is executed; otherwise the SECOND SET OF STATEMENTS is executed. If there is more than one statement in FIRST/SECOND SET OF STATEMENTS, they must be enclosed in curly brackets.

- The `else` and the SECOND SET OF STATEMENTS can be omitted.

- `if` statements can be written in sequence, or nested, to allow more complex tests.

- We can compare two values with a set of relational operators ==, !=, <, <=, >, and >=. The relational operator == means test for equality; != means test for nonequality.

- Boolean variables and expressions can take on only the values true and false.

- We can combine Boolean values with the Boolean operators AND (&), OR (|), and NOT (!).

- The operators && and || are short-circuit versions of & and | respectively. They do not evaluate the second operand if the value of the result can be deduced from the value of the first operand.

- Java also provides a `switch` statement that has the form:

```
switch (EXPRESSION)
    {
    case FIRST_VALUE:
        FIRST SET OF STATEMENTS ;
        break ;
    case SECOND_VALUE :
        SECOND SET OF STATEMENTS ;
        break ;
    ...
```

```
        default :
            FINAL SET OF STATEMENTS ;
        } ;
```

- If the break is omitted, execution "falls through" to the next set of statements. If the EXPRESSION does not match FIRST_VALUE, or SECOND_VALUE, and so on, the FINAL SET OF STATEMENTS for the default case is executed. The default case may be omitted.

4.10 Exercises

1. Write a program that sets up a `Person` instance with suitable attributes and then prints out the person's name (forename followed by surname) followed by `is a man` or `is a woman` as appropriate.

   Modify the program so that it prints out the name followed by:

   ```
   is a girl
   is a boy
   is a woman
   is a man
   ```

   as appropriate (a boy or girl is defined as aged 17 or less).

2. Write a program that sets up two `Person` instances with suitable attributes, finds the elder, and prints out the name of the elder, followed by `is older than` followed by the name of the younger.

   Modify your program to check for the two age attributes being the same, and print out a suitable message in this case.

3. Modify your answer to exercise 3.1 to prompt the user to type in a forename, surname, age, and gender. Then set the attributes of a `Person` instance to these values and print them out.

   Make use of the `getUpperAgeLimit` method to test that the age typed in by the user is a valid one. If it is not valid, output an error message and stop the program with a call of the `System.exit` method:

   ```
   System.exit(1) ;
   ```

   This is a method (in the `java.lang` package) that causes our program to stop immediately. The argument is a status code—it should be zero if everything worked satisfactorily, nonzero if (as here) the program terminated with some sort of error condition.

4. In exercise 3.4, two cards are selected at random and displayed. Assuming that the first card selected is for the computer and the second for the user, print out who wins according to the value on the cards.

   Modify your program so that ace counts as higher than king.

5. In a card game, the user selects a card value and suit, and then the computer does the same. If the computer selected a red card (hearts or diamonds), the highest value wins, but if the computer selected a black card (spades or clubs), the lowest value wins. Aces always count as high.

   Write a program to prompt the user for their card selection and store the result as a Card instance. The computer then selects a card at random, decides who is the winner, and outputs what the cards were and the result of the game.

6. Modify your answer to exercise 3.5 to print today's date and time in the form:

   `The time (sponsored by Java) is 11:47 on 20th 2 1997`

   Using the switch statement to put the correct suffix on the end of the number of the day within the month—for example 1st, 2nd, 3rd, 4th, and so on.

   Further modify the program to print the name of the month instead of the number:

   `The time (sponsored by Java) is 11:47 on 20th February 1997`

7. Modify your answer to exercise 3.6 to prompt the user to type in the name of a shape (one of the strings "square", "circle", or "triangle") and the dimensions and color of the shape, and then draw the specified shape on the screen using the BasicGraphics class. You should check the input from the user for validity, stopping the program with a suitable error message if the data is not valid.

CHAPTER 5

Repetition

5.1   Repetition as a Basic Control Structure

So far we have met two *control structures*—two ways in which we can answer the question, "After I have finished this statement, what shall I do next?" We met basic *sequencing* in Chapter 3 and *selection* in Chapter 4. In this chapter, we discuss the remaining major control structure—"After we have finished this statement, perhaps we should *repeat* it."

Let's look at an example from cooking. The instructions for a recipe for Christmas pudding say, "Add three tablespoons of brandy to the mixture, mixing well after each spoonful." We can write this in a more formal way as follows:

```
do the preceding step
do the following three times
   add a tablespoonful of brandy to the mixture
   mix well
do the next step
```

This is an example of a *repetition statement* or *loop*. The *body* of the loop, that is, the statements:

```
   add a tablespoonful of brandy to the mixture
   mix well
```

are to be repeated a certain number of times (in this case, three times). Notice that we have *indented* the body of the loop to make clear to the reader which statements form part of the body and which do not. Notice also that in this loop, we know how many times we are going to go around the loop (three times) *before* we start the loop.

In this example, we do the same thing on each iteration of the loop. Another recipe contains the instructions, "Add the next three ingredients, stirring well after each one" (where the next three ingredients are orange juice, olive oil, and cider vinegar). So the loop written out formally looks something like:

```
do the preceding step
do the following three times
   add the ith ingredient to the mixture
   mix well
do the next step
```

Here we assume that we are counting the iterations 1, 2, 3, and that *i* indicates the number of the iteration we are currently performing.

Another recipe contains the instruction, "Whisk the egg whites until they stand in soft peaks." We write this formally as:

```
do the preceding step
repeat
    whisk the egg whites for a bit
    look at the result
until the result forms soft peaks
do the next step
```

Again we have a body:

```
    whisk the egg whites for a bit
    look at the result
```

which we indent for clarity. We are going to repeat this a number of times, but we do not know before we start how many times we are going to repeat it. We perform the iteration and then do a test to decide whether to do it again or whether we can terminate the loop and proceed with the next step.

There is a problem with the loop in the preceding example. Occasionally, when I attempt to follow this recipe, I cannot seem to reach the soft peaks stage—instead the egg whites eventually separate, and I know the only option is to throw this mixture away and start again. There are two ways of taking account of this possibility in the instructions:

- We could have a more elaborate test—"until the result forms soft peaks or the result has separated." The next step after the loop would have to check what happened and take two different actions depending on which of the two possibilities caused us to terminate the loop.

- Alternatively, we could decide that the mixture separating is an error condition (it certainly is) and that it occurs rarely (yes, that too). We could test for the separation of the mixture inside the loop and, if it separates, *throw* an error *exception*. If we do nothing about the exception, it would cause the whole recipe to be abandoned with an error message. A more sophisticated cookery program would *catch* the exception somewhere and take appropriate action—perhaps restarting the recipe at a suitable point after clearing up the mess.

Let us now turn to programming. We want to be able to carry out a set of statements a number of times. Sometimes we know before we start how many times we are going to perform the iteration, and sometimes we have to do a test on each iteration to decide whether or not we require another. Most computer languages provide two different mechanisms for efficiently carrying out these two different types of repetition.

Java, following the example of C and C++, has two different repetition statements, `for` and `while`. As with most other computer languages, the Java `while` statement provides a repetition structure that performs a test on each iteration. But the `for` statement in Java provides a rather more powerful repetition structure than the basic "do this a fixed number of times" mechanism of the first example and is more powerful than the version of `for` provided by most other programming languages. In this chapter, we will introduce only a simple version of Java's `for` statement.

Consider again the egg white whisking example. We whisked for a bit and then tested to see if we had done enough; if not, we had a second iteration—whisk, test, and so on. So the test is done at the *end* of the iteration. We always do at least one iteration before the first test.

But suppose miraculously the egg whites started out forming soft peaks (maybe my wife has already done the whisking for me). Then to ensure I do not waste any effort, I would need to do the test at the *beginning* of each iteration. If I am lucky, I may perform *no* iterations of the loop.

In writing loops that involve a test on each iteration, we will have to decide whether the test goes at the beginning of the loop (this is by far the most common form), at the end, or perhaps somewhere in the middle of the loop. In this final case, we carry out part of the iteration, which puts us in a position to decide whether we require no further iterations (in which case we leave the loop and go to the step after the loop), or we complete this iteration and then at least commence the next iteration.

Finally, consider the following loop found on a shampoo bottle:

```
wet the hair
apply a generous amount of the shampoo and work in
rinse with clean water
repeat
```

This is an *infinite* loop—we will never get out of the loop (unless the bottle becoming empty generates an exception)! Furthermore, how can we "wet the hair" on the second and subsequent iterations? The loop would be more carefully written as follows:

```
wet the hair
do the following twice
    apply a generous amount of the shampoo and work in
    rinse with clean water
```

Luckily we (unlike a computer program) are able to do what it means rather than what it says.

5. 2   Looping a Predetermined Number of Times—The for Statement

We begin with the case where we know before we begin the looping how many iterations there are going to be. The basic idea is that we have a counter, or *control variable,* that keeps track of how many times we have been around the loop and stops the repetition when the counter has recorded that we have iterated the appropriate number of times. The control variable is going to take on a *range* of values; so, if we want to repeat a loop ten times:

- We could start the control variable at the value one.

- At the end of each iteration we could add one to the value of the control variable.

- We could keep testing the control variable, stopping when it reaches the value 10.

Or perhaps we stop when we have reached the value 11? It is very easy in writing loops to make an "out-by-one" error; in a loop where we want to go around 10 times, we go around 9 or 11 times by mistake. We have to be careful where we add 1 to the control variable in relation to where we test the value of the control variable.

In order to perform this type of loop, where we know before entering the loop how many iterations there are going to be, and where we are going to count a control variable through a range of values, Java provides the for statement. This takes the form:

```
for ( INITIALIZATION ; TESTING ; MODIFICATION )
    LOOP BODY
```

This specifies a loop with the structure shown in Figure 5-1.

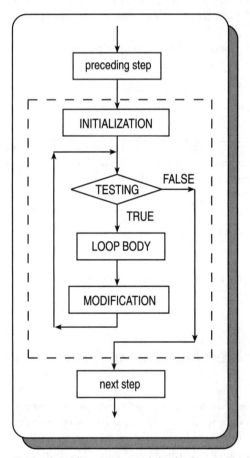

Figure 5-1: The structure of the for loop.

Before we start the loop, we carry out the INITIALIZATION. Then we have the statements executed on each iteration of the loop. We carry out the TESTING at the beginning of each iteration to decide whether to proceed with this iteration. If we proceed, we next carry out the LOOP BODY, and finally we carry out the MODIFICATION at the end of each iteration.

For a simple version of the for statement, we are going to use a *control variable* to ensure that we execute the LOOP BODY 10 times. In the INITIALIZATION section, we need to declare a suitable control variable and set it to its initial value. For example:

```
int i = 0
```

declares an int variable called i and assigns it the initial value zero. It is usual in Java, for reasons that will become clear later, to start counting at zero (rather than one). Since we have declared the variable i as part of the for statement, it is available for use only inside the body of the for loop.

In the MODIFICATION section, we specify what has to be done to the control variable at the *end* of each iteration. We write:

```
i++
```

This is an incrementation statement that takes the value in the variable i, adds one to it, and restores it in the variable.

Finally we have the TESTING section. This is a Boolean expression that is evaluated at the *beginning* of each iteration. As long as the expression evaluates to true, we proceed with the iteration; when it evaluates to false, the loop is terminated and we proceed to the next statement. We want to execute the loop 10 times, so our TESTING section is:

```
i < 10
```

What shall we do on each iteration? For this first example, we are simply going to display the current value of the control variable in the *body* of the loop so that we can see that it is taking on the correct sequence of values. Here is the code:

```
System.out.println("Before the beginning of the loop") ;
for (int i = 0 ; i < 10 ; i++)
   System.out.println(i) ;
System.out.println("After the end of the loop") ;
```

Figure 5-2 shows a diagram of the loop, and this is what happens:

- The text Before the beginning of the loop is displayed.
- The variable i is declared and initialized to the value 0.
- We start the first iteration.
    - The Boolean expression i < 10 is evaluated (i has the value 0).
    - This gives the value true, so we proceed with this iteration.
    - We execute the body of the loop—display the current value of i, which is 0.
    - We increment the control variable i, so its value is now 1.

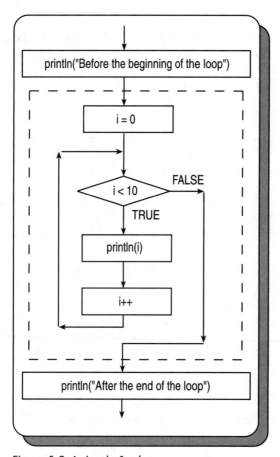

Figure 5-2: A simple for loop.

- We start the next iteration.
    - The Boolean expression i < 10 is evaluated (i has the value 1).
    - This gives the value true, so we proceed with this iteration.
    - We execute the body of the loop—display the current value of i, which is 1.
    - We increment the control variable i, so its value is now 2.
- We start the next iteration.
    - The Boolean expression i < 10 is evaluated (i has the value 2).
    - This gives the value true, so we proceed with this iteration.
    - We execute the body of the loop—display the current value of i, which is 2.
    - We increment the control variable i, so its value is now 3.
    - And so on.

- We start the next iteration.
  - The Boolean expression i < 10 is evaluated (i has the value 8).
  - This gives the value true, so we proceed with this iteration.
  - We execute the body of the loop—display the current value of i, which is 8.
  - We increment the control variable i, so its value is now 9.
- We start the next iteration.
  - The Boolean expression i < 10 is evaluated (i has the value 9).
  - This gives the value true, so we proceed with this iteration.
  - We execute the body of the loop—display the current value of i, which is 9.
  - We increment the control variable i, so its value is now 10.
- We start the next iteration.
  - The Boolean expression i < 10 is evaluated (i has the value 10).
  - This gives the value false, so we terminate the loop.
- The text After the end of the loop is displayed.

The loop has been executed with the control variable i having the successive values 0, 1, 2, 3, 4, 5, 6, 7, 8, and 9. So the loop was executed 10 times.

We are now going to rewrite our loop slightly because we want to display a table of numbers together with their squares. Here is the code:

```
System.out.println("Table of Squares") ;
for (int i = 0 ; i < 10 ; i++)
    {
    System.out.print("the square of " + i) ;
    System.out.println(" is " + (i * i)) ;
    }
System.out.println("**end of table**") ;
```

The body of the loop now consists of *two* statements (although we could have written it as one if we had made more use of the concatenate operator +). But the body of a for loop (like each of the branches of an if statement) must be a *single* statement. The solution is the same as it is for the if statement—if we want the loop body to consist of more than a single statement, we must make it into a *compound* statement by enclosing the sequence of statements in curly brackets { ... }.

Notice that we have *indented* the body of the loop in both of the preceding examples to make it clear to the reader which statements are part of the loop and which are not. The Java compiler makes no use of the indentation. If we forgot to insert the curly brackets around the two statements, the compiler would ignore the indentation and assume that only the first statement was part of the loop and the second statement follows the loop.

Some programmers advocate *always* inserting the curly brackets, even for loops with bodies that are only one statement long—the argument is that inserting the brackets around the loop body is a good practice to get into, and it makes things easier (and less likely to cause an error) if we have to insert more statements into the loop body later.

The INITIALIZATION, TESTING, and MODIFICATION sections of the for statement can, in Java, be more complex than the example we have given. However, it is good programming practice to limit them to initializing, testing, and incrementing a single, simple control variable.

Another simple example would allow us to start the control value at a value typed in by the user and count it down toward zero. We are going to prompt the user for a string and then output the characters of the string one per line in reverse order. If we have a String, we can use the length method to find out how many characters there are in it, and we can extract the individual characters of the string with the charAt method (the characters are numbered from zero to one less than the length of the string). Here is the code:

```
BasicIo.prompt("type a string") ;
String response = BasicIo.readString() ;

for (int i = response.length() - 1 ; i >= 0 ; i--)
    System.out.println(response.charAt(i)) ;
```

First we prompt the user and store in the variable response the string typed in.

In the for loop, we initialize the control variable to a value one less than the length of the string, that is response.length -1. We test for i being greater than or equal to zero. The MODIFICATION section i—means "take the value of the variable i, reduce its value by one, and restore it as the new value of i." Before you run the program, check how many iterations there will be with a string of length 7 (such as welcome). The loop will be executed for control variable values of 6, 5, 4, 3, 2, 1, and 0, so the loop is actually executed 7 times, and this is what we want the program to do.

What would happen if the string had no characters; that is, the user immediately presses Return at the prompt? The variable i gets set to -1, so on the first iteration, the test i >= 0 fails immediately, and *no* iterations will be performed. The program simply skips the loop and moves on to the next statement.

5.3 Looping an Indeterminate Number of Times—The while Statement

We use the Java for statement when we want to repeat a loop a predetermined number of times. We use the Java while statement where we do not know before entering the loop how many iterations we are going to perform; on each iteration we perform a test to decide whether or not to perform another iteration. The while statement takes the form:

```
while ( BOOLEAN EXPRESSION )
    LOOP BODY
```

The structure of the *while* statement is shown in Figure 5-3.

Figure 5-3: The structure of the `while` loop.

We start by evaluating the BOOLEAN EXPRESSION. If it is TRUE, then we execute LOOP BODY for a first iteration and then reevaluate the BOOLEAN EXPRESSION for a second time; if it is still TRUE, then we execute LOOP BODY for a second iteration and then reevaluate BOOLEAN EXPRESSION for a third time; and so on. When the BOOLEAN EXPRESSION evaluates to FALSE, no more iterations are performed, and control proceeds to the statement following the loop. Notice that there is no INITIALIZATION or MODIFICA-TION section as there was with the `for` statement. Any INITIALIZATION must be done in the "preceding step." Any MODIFICATION must be done as part of the LOOP BODY (presumably at the end).

Suppose we have a class `GroupOfPeople` that holds information about a group of individuals; for the present, our `GroupOfPeople` instance is going to hold simply a collection of people's surnames. When we set up an instance of this class, it will contain no surnames, and we can always find out how many surnames are held with a `getCount` method (which returns an integer). We can add a surname with an `addSurname` method; this requires a single `String` argument, the new surname we wish to add to the collection.

We are going to write a program that allows the user to type in a sequence of surnames, and we are going to store them in a `GroupOfPeople` instance that we have declared. How will the program know when there are no more surnames to be stored? We are going to instruct the user to press Return when there are no more surnames, so the program will recognize a zero-length surname as the end of the list. Since the program starts executing the loop without knowing how many iterations there are going to be, we use a `while` statement. Here is the code:

```
GroupOfPeople computing = new GroupOfPeople() ;
String s ;

System.out.println("Type a surname followed by 'return'") ;
System.out.println("(type 'return' if there are no more surnames)") ;
s = BasicIo.readString() ;
while (s.length() != 0)
    {
    computing.addSurname(s) ;
    System.out.println("inserted surname " + s) ;

    System.out.println("Type a surname followed by 'return'") ;
    System.out.println("(type 'return' if there are no more surnames)") ;
    s = BasicIo.readString() ;
    }
System.out.print("There are " + computing.getCount()) ;
System.out.println(" people in the group") ;
```

We declare an object of type `GroupOfPeople` called `computing` and a `String` called `s`. We prompt the user for the first surname, and read it into the variable `s` with the method `readString`.

In the loop, we test for a string of length zero. If the string `s` that we have read in is of length zero, we terminate the loop immediately. If the string is not of zero length, it is a valid surname, so we insert it in the `computing` object with the method `addSurname` and tell the user that we have done so. Now we need to prompt for the *next* surname, which is the remainder of *this* iteration. The body of a `while` must be a single statement; since we want a sequence of statements to be executed on each iteration, we put curly brackets { .. } round the sequence in the usual way.

Suppose the user types in the surnames `Smith`, `Jones`, and `Williams`. What happens is as follows:

- The computer prompts for the first surname, and the user types `Smith` into the String `s`.
- On the first iteration:
    - The string `s` is not of length zero, so we proceed with the body of the iteration.
    - The string `Smith` is inserted in `computing`, and the user told as such.
    - The computer prompts for the next surname, and the user types `Jones`.
- On the next iteration:
    - The string `s` is not of length zero, so we proceed with the body of the iteration.
    - The string `Jones` is inserted in `computing`, and the user told as such.
    - The computer prompts for the next surname, and the user types `Williams`.

- On the next iteration:
  - The string s is not of length zero, so we proceed with the body of the iteration.
  - The string Williams is inserted in computing, and the user told as such.
  - The computer prompts for the next surname, and the user presses Return (that is, s is set to an empty string).
- On the next iteration:
  - The string s is of length zero, so the loop terminates.

As usual, if the first string we typed in was of length zero, then *no* iterations of the loop would be performed.

We can now print the surnames we have stored. The getSurname method takes an integer argument, say i, and returns surname number i. The numbering system is the order in which the surnames were added, starting at zero. Since we now know how many surnames there are (the getCount method tells us), we can use a for loop:

```
for (int i = 0 ; i < computing.getCount() ; i++)
    {
    System.out.print("The " + (i + 1) + "th surname is ") ;
    System.out.println(computing.getSurname(i))
    }
```

One flaw in the preceding code is that the computer displays 1th instead of 1st, 2th instead of 2nd, and so on. Can you fix this?

5.4   Stopping in the Middle of an Iteration

If we return to the code we used to read in the surnames, you will have noticed that we read the *next* surname in at the end of *this* iteration. Furthermore, we have written out the statements twice to prompt the user and read in the surname—before the loop for the first surname and at the end of the loop body for all the rest. Many programmers try to avoid writing the same code more than once—this may be because of laziness, but it is also because, if we decide to change a piece of code, it is more difficult to get it right if there are several different places where it has to be changed.

How can we arrange to have the prompting and reading done at one place in the program? The problem is that the looping test has to come at the beginning of the loop. If we could put the test somewhere in the middle of the loop, then we could write everything only once. We can do that with a version of the break statement; in Chapter 4, we used it to break out at the end of the individual cases of the switch statement, and here we use it to break out of the middle of a loop. Here's how:

```
GroupOfPeople computing = new GroupOfPeople() ;
String s ;
```

```
while (true)
  {
  System.out.println("Type a surname followed by 'return'") ;
  System.out.println("(type 'return' when there are no more surnames)") ;
  s = BasicIo.readString() ;

  if (s.length() == 0)
    break ;

  computing.addSurname(s) ;
  System.out.println("inserted surname " + s) ;
  }

System.out.print("There are " + computing.getCount()) ;
System.out.println(" people in the group") ;
```

The BOOLEAN EXPRESSION in this loop is true, which of course always evaluates to TRUE; so in principle, we will go around the loop forever. Inside the loop, we prompt the user and read in the string s. Then we test the length of the string; if it is of length zero, we execute the break statement. This takes us out of the loop immediately, and the next statement executed is the first one after the loop. If the length of the string is not zero, we proceed to the statement following the if statement, insert the string s in the computing object and tell the user so. Then we start the next iteration.

Notice that we had to invert the test—the BOOLEAN EXPRESSION in the while in the original program tested for nonzero length; with the break statement, we are testing for zero length.

The layout of this new looping structure is shown in Figure 5-4.

Suppose, as before, the user types in the surnames Smith, Jones, and Williams. What happens is as follows:

- On the first iteration:
    - The computer prompts for a surname, and the user types Smith.
    - The string s is not of length zero, so we proceed with the rest of this iteration.
    - The string Smith is inserted in computing, and the user told as such.
- On the next iteration:
    - The computer prompts for the next surname, and the user types Jones.
    - The string s is not of length zero, so we proceed with the rest of this iteration.
    - The string Jones is inserted in computing, and the user told as such.
- On the next iteration:
    - The computer prompts for the next surname, and the user types Williams.
    - The string s is not of length zero, so we proceed with the rest of this iteration.
    - The string Williams is inserted in computing, and the user told as such.

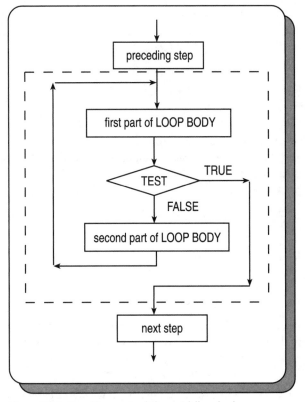

Figure 5-4: Breaking out of the middle of a loop.

- On the next iteration:
  - The computer prompts for the next surname, and the user presses Return (that is, s is set to an empty string).
  - The string s is of length zero, so the break is executed and the loop terminates.

As usual, if the first string we typed in was of length zero, then only the first half of the first iteration would be performed.

5.5   For Loops & While Loops

It has probably not escaped your attention that we don't really need both the `for` and the `while` mechanism.

Suppose we have a `for` loop like this:

```
for (int i = 0 ; i < n ; i++)
  BODY OF LOOP ;
```

Then we could have written this as a `while` loop:

```
int i = 0 ;
while (i < n)
  {
  BODY OF LOOP ;
  i++ ;
  }
```

One advantage of the `for` loop is that it collects together all the parts of the loop. If the LOOP BODY is lengthy, then the `i++` statement is a long way from the `i < n` test, and it may not be easy to see the structure of what is going on.

Similarly, if we have a `while` loop:

```
while (s.length( ) != 0)
  BODY OF LOOP ;
```

then we could write this as a `for` loop:

```
for ( ; s.length( ) != 0 ; )
  BODY OF LOOP ;
```

where the INITIALIZATION and MODIFICATION sections are empty (or we could insert something unrelated to the test, although this would be very poor programming style).

However, it makes your programs easier to follow if you use `for` and `while` in different programming situations. We recommend the following rules:

- If the number of times the loop is to be executed is known before entering the loop, then use a `for` loop. More generally, if the situation is such that you are processing your way through a *complete* set of data that is set up before entering the loop and expect to reach the end, then a `for` is appropriate—we will see examples of this more general situation in Chapter 17.

- If we do not know when we start the loop how many times we will execute it, use a `while` loop. More generally, if we are processing through a set of data, but expect that we might stop before reaching the end of the data, then it is appropriate to use a `while`. For example, if we are searching a set of data for a particular value and find it, we will not look at the remainder of the data—so a `while` is appropriate.

5.6 Nested Loops

The body of a loop can contain any statement, so it is possible for a loop to contain another loop, as shown in Figure 5-5. This is called a *nested* loop. For each iteration of the *outer* loop there will be zero or more iterations of the *inner* loop.

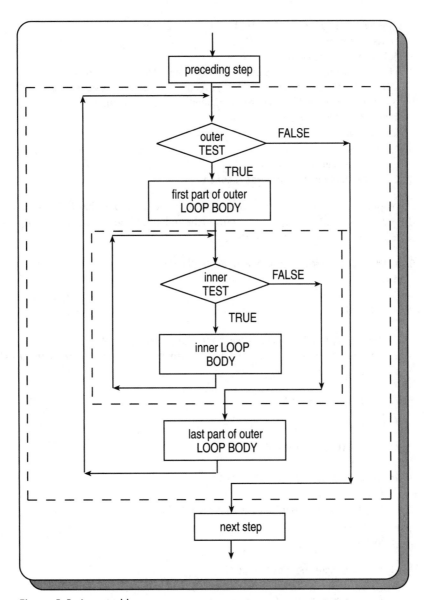

Figure 5-5: A nested loop.

Suppose we are reading in surnames as before and want to store a surname only if we have not already stored it. So we are going to test each new surname against all the surnames that have already been read and stored, and this requires a nested loop. The program will have this structure:

```
set up the "GroupOfPeople" instance and String
   prompt the user
   get the next surname
   if the string length is zero, then leave the outer loop
   start at the beginning of the list of surnames stored so far
      look for a match with each stored surname in turn
   if we found no match
      add the surname
   otherwise
      print an error message
output the number of surnames stored
```

Notice in this sketch of the solution, and in the Java code that follows, that we have indented the body of the inner loop within the indented body of the outer loop to clarify the structure of the program. Here is the code:

```
GroupOfPeople computing = new GroupOfPeople() ;
String s ;

while (true)
   {
   System.out.println("Type a surname followed by 'return'") ;
   System.out.println("(type 'return' when there are no more surnames)") ;
   s = BasicIo.readString() ;

   if (s.length() == 0)
      break ;

   // explanation starts HERE
   int i = 0 ;
   while (i < computing.getCount())
      {
      if (s.equals(computing.getSurname(i)))
         break ;
      i++ ;
      }
   if (i == computing.getCount())
      {
      // search did not find a match
      computing.addSurname(s) ;
      System.out.println("inserted surname " + s) ;
      }
   else
      {
      // search did find a match
      System.out.println("WARNING: surname " + s + " duplicated") ;
```

```
        System.out.println("not added to the list") ;
    }
// explanation finishes HERE
}
```

```
System.out.print("There are " + computing.getCount()) ;
System.out.println(" people in the group") ;
```

Here's how the inner loop works. Remember that we are checking whether the surname the user has just typed in is already stored in the `computing` object. We start at the comment `explanation starts HERE`:

- We declare an integer variable `i` and initialize it to zero. This is a control variable for the `while` statement that follows it. We have decided that it should be a `while` statement because stopping before we look at *all* the stored surnames is a distinct possibility.

- On each iteration of the inner loop, we test `i` against the number of surnames stored in `computing`. If it is the first iteration of the outer loop, then there will be no surnames in the `computing` object, so the `getCount` method returns zero, and no iterations of the inner loop will be performed.

- If there is at least one surname in the `computing` object, this BOOLEAN EXPRESSION will succeed, and we will check the string `s` against the first surname held in the `computing` object, that is the one returned by `computing.getSurname(i)` with `i` set to zero. The `String` method `equals` tests its `String` argument against the `String` with which the method is associated (here `s`), and returns TRUE if they are equal (i.e., the same length, with the same characters) and FALSE otherwise.

- If the strings match, we execute the `break` statement. This always breaks out of the *innermost* loop that contains it. So we break out of the surname-matching loop but not the outer loop that reads in a surname on each iteration. The `break` in fact sends us to the `if` statement immediately after the inner loop.

- If the strings did not match, the variable `i` is incremented and we prepare to start the next iteration of the inner loop.

- If there are at least two surnames stored, we will enter the second iteration of the inner loop and test the string `s` against the next surname stored (that one associated with the value one for the argument to the `getSurname` method), and so on.

- Eventually we will leave the inner loop, either because we have run out of surnames to look at (so we didn't find a match) or because we have broken out of the loop early (because we *did* find a match). We need to distinguish between these two cases, and this is what the `if` statement does.

If we broke out of the inner loop early, the control variable `i` will be set to the value at which `s` matched a surname in `computing`. We know that there are `computing.getCount()` surnames in this object, and they are therefore numbered from 0 up to `computing.getCount() - 1`. So in this case, `i` will have a value in the range 0 to `computing.getCount() - 1`.

If we did *not* break out of the inner loop, we must have looked at the final surname, and this would have had the number `computing.getCount()` - 1. Since the `equals` method returned FALSE, we did not break out of the loop. Instead we incremented the control variable i and prepared to start the next iteration of the loop with i set to `computing.getCount()`. The BOOLEAN EXPRESSION of the inner loop would have evaluated to FALSE, so we would not have started a further iteration. We would have stopped with i holding the value `computing.getCount()`.

Thus, if there were 7 stored surnames, i would have had a value of 7 if no match had been found and a value in the range 0 to 6 if a match had been found.

- So the `if` statement checks the final value of the control variable i against the value returned by `computing.getCount()`. If they are equal, the search failed to find a match, and we can add the surname to the `computing` object and tell the user so. Note that we inserted comments to remind us which was which of the two branches of the `if` statement—it is easy to get the two branches mixed up.

- If the BOOLEAN EXPRESSION in the `if` statement evaluates to FALSE, we must have broken out of the loop early, so the new surname is a duplicate of one already stored. We want to tell the user so and not add the surname to the list. Note that the error message tells the user that there was a duplicate, what the surname was that was duplicated, and what the program has done about it (i.e., that the surname was ignored and not added to the list). It might be important in certain circumstances also to display the position at which we found the duplicate (i.e., the value of i), but we have not done so here.

In order to see exactly what is going on, we can add statements to output some information as we traverse the inner loop:

```
// explanation starts HERE
int i = 0 ;
System.out.println("TEST: starting inner loop: count=" +
                                               computing.getCount()) ;
while (i < computing.getCount())
    {
    System.out.print("TEST: start inner iteration: i=" + i) ;
    if (s.equals(computing.getSurname(i)))
        break ;
    i++ ;
    System.out.print("TEST: finish inner iteration: i=" + i) ;
    }
System.out.print("TEST: leaving inner loop: i=" + i) ;
if (i == computing.getCount())
    {
    // search did not find a match
    computing.addSurname(s) ;
    System.out.print("inserted surname " + s) ;
    }
else
```

```
        {
        // search did find a match
        System.out.println("WARNING: surname " + s + " duplicated") ;
        System.out.println("not added to the list") ;
        }
    // explanation finishes HERE
```

Now try running the program with different sets of surnames, some with duplicates and some without. And make sure you are quite certain you can explain *all* the values that get printed out by these test statements. In particular, convince yourself that the program works properly (a) on the first iteration, when there are no surnames to match against and (b) when a pair of duplicates occurs together, so that we find the match on the *last* iteration of the inner loop.

5.7   Boolean Expressions for Loops

In the last example we wrote the inner loop like this:

```
int i = 0 ;
while (i < computing.getCount())
    {
    if (s.equals(computing.getSurname(i)))
        break ;
    i++ ;
    }
if (i == computing.getCount())
    ...
```

There are several different ways of writing this loop. Another alternative is:

```
int i = 0 ;
while ((i < computing.getCount()) &&
        (!s.equals(computing.getSurname(i))))
    i++ ;
if (i == computing.getCount())
    ...
```

Look carefully at the BOOLEAN EXPRESSION here. It says continue with another iteration if *both* of two things are true:

- The control variable i has not yet reached the end of the list of surnames (that is, it is a valid argument for the getSurname method).

- The new surname s is not equal to the surname in the list at position i.

If both these things are true, we can go around the loop another time and increment the variable i with the statement i++. If either of the tests fail, we must terminate the loop. As before, the value of i tells us whether we found a match or not.

To see how this works, we insert output statements as before, and try some test data:

```
int i = 0 ;
System.out.println("TEST: starting inner loop: count=" +
                                        computing.getCount()) ;
while ((i < computing.getCount()) &&
       (!s.equals(computing.getSurname(i))))
   {
   System.out.print("TEST: start inner iteration: i=" + i) ;
   i++ ;
   System.out.print("TEST: finish inner iteration: i=" + i) ;
   }
System.out.print("TEST: leaving inner loop: i=" + i) ;
if (i == computing.getCount())
   ...
```

Note that when we inserted the output statements in the loop, we had to insert curly brackets { ... } around the loop body. We did not need these when the loop body was a single statement.

Notice that we have written the operator && instead of the normal AND operator &. There is a subtlety about this BOOLEAN EXPRESSION of which you need to be aware. In the purely logical meaning of the AND operation, we can evaluate both operands of the AND and then work out the value of the AND. Suppose we try that here, when we have reached the final iteration and i has reached the value computing.getCount(). The left-hand operand of the AND operation has the value FALSE. But what about the right-hand operand, which contains the expression computing.getSurname(i)? This is not valid since there is no surname with this number. It may be that the programmer who wrote the GroupOfPeople class has been kind enough to ensure that an invalid argument still causes a valid response. But in general, this cannot be relied on.

So we have replaced the & operator with the && operator, which is sometimes called a short-circuit operator. If its first operand evaluates to FALSE, then it knows that the result of the && operation must be false and does not evaluate the second operand. So, in fact, this expression is always valid—if the first expression decides that there is no surname, the second expression is not evaluated, and the correct result of FALSE is returned.*

A third way of writing this loop avoids the break statement and has a clearer test after the loop. Here is the code:

```
int i = 0 ;
boolean duplicateFound = false ;
while ((i < computing.getCount()) && (!duplicateFound))
   {
   if (s.equals(computing.getSurname(i)))
     duplicateFound = true ;
```

---

*Unlike Java, some programming languages (for example, Pascal) do not have a short-circuit version of the AND operation, and this form of the loop would not be possible.

```
    i++ ;
    }
if (!duplicateFound)
    . . .
```

We have declared a `boolean` variable to record whether we have found a duplicate, and before entering the loop, we have initialized it to `false`. The body of the loop sets the Boolean variable to `true` when it finds a match. The loop terminates because either (a) we have tried all the elements in the list or (b) the Boolean variable has been set to `true` on the previous iteration (because we found a match). The `if` statement following the loop can then test the Boolean variable to decide whether or not a duplicate was found.

5.8   Testing at the End of the Loop—The do Loop

We have looked at loops where the test is at the beginning of the iteration (the `for` statement and the `while` statement without a `break`), and we have looked at loops where the test is in the middle of the iteration (the `while` statement with the `break`). Java provides another form of repetition statement with the test at the end (so the loop is always executed at least once). It looks like this:

```
do
    LOOP BODY
while ( BOOLEAN EXPRESSION ) ;
```

and has the structure shown in Figure 5-6.

The LOOP BODY is executed once, and the BOOLEAN EXPRESSION is then evaluated. If it is TRUE, then the iteration and test is repeated. If it evaluates to FALSE, the loop terminates and the statement following the loop is executed. Of course, if the LOOP BODY is more than one statement long, we need to insert curly brackets { . . . } as usual.

Suppose we have a program to work out the square of a number specified by the user. If we run the program, we presumably have at least one number for which we want the program to calculate a square, so we know we want to do the calculation at least once. But we might want to do it more than once. So, after calculating a square, we can ask the user if they want another calculation.

In our loop we will accept a number from the user and calculate its square. Then we will ask the user if they want to do any further calculation; if so, we repeat the loop. We will always execute the loop at least once, and we test the user's response at the *end* of the loop to see if another iteration is in order. So the `do...while` statement is the one to use:

```
String response ;

do
    {
    BasicIo.prompt("type a number ") ;
    int n = BasicIo.readInteger() ;
```

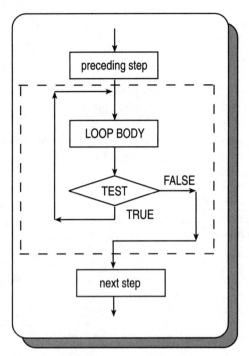

Figure 5-6: The structure of the do loop.

```
   System.out.print("the value of " + n) ;
   System.out.println(" squared is " + (n * n)) ;
   BasicIo.prompt("calculate more numbers (y or n)? ") ;
   response = BasicIo.readString() ;
   }
while (response.charAt(0) == 'y') ;
```

The loop is repeated as long as the user types in a string whose first letter is `'y'`. A slightly better version would allow the user to type in a String starting `'y'` or `'Y'`, making use of the `String` method `toLowerCase` to convert the user response to lowercase before doing the test. There would still be problems if the user typed in a line containing no characters—we can fix that as well:

```
String response ;

do
   {
   System.out.print("the value of " + n) ;
   int n = BasicIo.readInteger() ;
   System.out.println("the value of " + n) ;
   System.out.println(" squared is " (n * n)) ;
```

```
    BasicIo.prompt("calculate more numbers (y or n)? ") ;
    response = BasicIo.readString().toLowerCase() ;
    }
while ((response.length() > 0) && (response.charAt(0) == 'y')) ;
```

This form of loop, with the test at the end, is less common than the for and the while with a test at the beginning.

5.9   Other Java Loop Features

The break statement always (a) terminates the current iteration immediately and then (b) terminates the loop. There is also a continue statement, which also terminates the current iteration immediately but then proceeds to start the next iteration. A typical use of this might have a loop something like the following:

```
while (BOOLEAN EXPRESSION1)
    {
    STATEMENTS1 ;
    if (BOOLEAN EXPRESSION2)
        continue ;
    STATEMENTS2 ;
    }
```

This could have been written without the continue, as follows:

```
while (BOOLEAN EXPRESSION1)
    {
    STATEMENTS1 ;
    if (!BOOLEAN EXPRESSION2)
        {
        STATEMENTS2 ;
        }
    }
```

The advantage of the version with continue is that it allows the STATEMENTS2 to be written with less indentation than the version without.

Finally, Java has an additional form of the break statement, called the *labeled* break. The normal (unlabeled) form of break leaves the *innermost* loop; that is, the first looping statement that you encounter if you work back from the break statement. Sometimes you may want to break out of a number of nested loops. Code that includes a labeled break would look something like this:

```
loopLabel : while ...
    {
    ...
```

```
while ...
   {
   ...
   if ( BOOLEAN EXPRESSION )
     break loopLabel ;
   ...
   }
...
}
NEXT STATEMENT ;
```

If BOOLEAN EXPRESSION evaluates to TRUE, the *labeled* break statement takes us out of both loops to the statement NEXT STATEMENT; that is, it goes to the first statement after the end of the loop labeled loopLabel.

5.10   Key Points in Chapter 5

- We often need to be able to repeat a group of statements several times, and Java provides a number of "looping" statements to allow us to do so. The main ones are the for statement and the while statement.

- We use the for statement when we know before we start how many times we are going to repeat the loop. It has the form:

```
for (INITIALIZATION ; TESTING ; MODIFICATION)
   LOOP BODY
```

A typical loop, to be executed n times with a control variable i set to 0, 1, 2, 3, ... up to n - 1, would be:

```
for (int i = 0 ; i < n ; i++)
   LOOP BODY
```

- We use the while loop when we do not know beforehand how many iterations are going to be required. It has the form:

```
while (BOOLEAN EXPRESSION)
   LOOP BODY
```

Each iteration starts with a test of the BOOLEAN EXPRESSION. If it is TRUE, it does one more iteration. If it is FALSE, it does no more iterations but proceeds to the statement after the loop.

If the BOOLEAN EXPRESSION evaluates to FALSE when the loop is entered for the first time, then no iterations are performed.

- The break statement allows us to break out from inside a loop and proceed immediately to the statement after the loop. This allows us to have the loop test in the middle of the body of the loop.

- It is possible to "nest" one loop inside another.
- In a BOOLEAN EXPRESSION for a loop, it is often important to use the short-circuit operator && so that only the valid operands are evaluated.
- There is another repetition statement with the test at the end. This has the form:

```
do
    LOOP BODY
while (BOOLEAN EXPRESSION) ;
```

5.11   Exercises

1. Rewrite this program from Section 5.2 earlier in this chapter:

```
System.out.println("Table of Squares") ;
for (int i = 0 ; i < 10 ; i++)
    {
    System.out.print("the square of " + i) ;
    System.out.println(" is " + (i * i)) ;
    }
System.out.println("**end of table**") ;
```

so that it outputs the cube of each number from 0 to 9 as well as the square, making sure that it outputs suitable accompanying text.

Modify the program so that it deals with the numbers from 1 to 25 instead of 0 to 9.

2. Rewrite this part of the program from Section 5.3 earlier in this chapter:

```
for (int i = 0 ; i < computing.getCount() ; i++)
    {
    System.out.print("The " + (i + 1) + "th surname is ") ;
    System.out.println(computing.getSurname(i)) ;
    }
```

so that it outputs the correct letters after each number (1st, 2nd, 3rd, 4th, and so on).

3. Use the Card class to implement a simple card game between the computer and the user. The computer chooses 5 cards for the user. If their total value comes to 21 or less, the user has won; if their total value comes to more than 21, the computer has won.

The program should choose each card in turn, reveal to the user what it is, and inform the user of the total value of cards chosen so far.

Modify the program so that after each card has been chosen, the user can specify whether to draw the next card or whether to "stick" with the cards chosen.

Note ▪

The Card constructor with no arguments, which chooses a card at random, is arranged so that it never chooses the same card twice. When we want the random drawing of cards from the deck to start again (that is, we are allowed to pick a card that we have picked before), we call the restart method.

4. Write programs that use a for statement and the BasicGraphics class to draw:

   a) A sequence of 10 red squares, each 20 units wider and higher than the previous one but all with the same top left-hand corner.

   b) A sequence of 10 green squares all the same size and with successive top left-hand corners 20 units further along the X- and Y-axes.

   c) A sequence of 10 blue circles, all with their centers at the same place but with the diameter decreasing successively by 20 units.

5. Modify your answer to exercise 4.7 so that the user can specify a number of different shapes to be drawn. When the user has finished specifying a shape, the program should ask if the user wants to specify another shape. If so, it should prompt the user for details of the next shape. Finally, the program should display all the shapes specified.

6. Modify your answer to exercise 5.5 so that the information is read in from a file in the filing system. The file should be created using an editor and might look like this:

```
square
200
200
60
red
circle
300
350
40
yellow
EndOfFile
```

The program should terminate when it reads a shape EndOfFile from the file.

Note

For this you need the `BasicFileIo` class (in the `java.lancs` package). To read from a file called `shapes.data`, you call the constructor `BasicGraphics` with two arguments—(a) the constant `BasicFileIo.INPUT`, and (b) the name of the file. For example:

```
BasicFileIo fileIn = new BasicFileIo(BasicFileIo.INPUT,
"shapes.data") ;
```

Then you can read a complete line from the file as a string:

```
String s = fileIn.readString() ;
```

or you can read in a complete line from the file as an integer:

```
int n = fileIn.readInteger() ;
```

A set of methods for reading from a file are provided similar to the read methods in the `BasicIo` class. When you have finished reading from the file, you should close it with:

```
fileIn.closeFile() ;
```

7. Use the facilities of the `BasicGraphics` class to draw two octaves of a piano keyboard, as in Figure 5-7.

Figure 5-7: A piano keyboard.

Try to use looping and selection statements as much use as possible in this program.

CHAPTER 6

Basic Java Data Types

6.1 Objects & Basic Data Types

In some object-oriented languages, *all* the data elements of a program are objects; that is, all the variables in a program refer to objects of one type or another. In Java, many elements are objects, but for efficiency there are a few types of elements that are not, and these form the basic blocks out of which we can build objects. We have already met the int and boolean types in Chapters 4 and 5. In this chapter, we review these and Java's other six basic data types, and we recap the differences between variables of these types and variables that refer to objects. We also discuss the String type, which in fact *is* a class of objects, in this chapter.

There are a number of differences between the way we handle objects in Java and the way we handle these basic data types.

6.1.1 *Declaration*

We declare a variable that refers to a object with a statement such as:

```
Person person1 = new Person("John", "Smith", 55, Person.MALE) ;
```

This creates a variable, a location in the computer called person1, capable of holding a *reference* to an instance of the class Person. In this case, it actually refers to an instance of a Person object whose attributes have been initialized to suitable values by the constructor method Person(...). The result is shown in Figure 6-1.

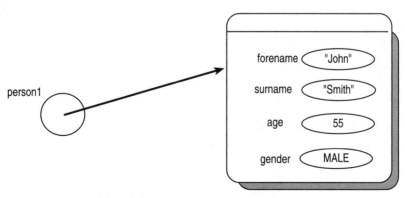

Figure 6-1: A variable referring to a Person instance.

If we do not invoke a constructor method, we should set the value of the variable `person1` to the special value `null`:

```
Person person2 = null ;
```

indicating that the variable does not at present refer to a specific instance. The result is shown in Figure 6-2.

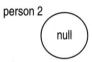

Figure 6-2: A `Person` variable initialized with `null`.

Later we could set up an instance and have the variable `person2` refer to it:

```
person2 = new Person("Jane", "Black", 35, Person.FEMALE) ;
```

Notice that there is no `Person` at the beginning of this line—we are not declaring a variable `person2` since it already exists; we are simply making it refer to a new object. The result is shown in Figure 6-3.

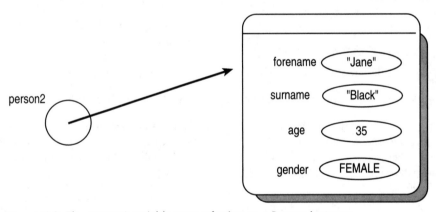

Figure 6-3: The `person2` variable now referring to a `Person` instance.

We declare a variable of one of the basic types with a statement such as:

```
int countOfMembers = 4 ;
```

This creates a variable, a location in the computer called `countOfMembers`, which is capable of holding an integer *value*. In this case we have initialized the variable to hold the value 4, as shown in Figure 6-4.

countOfMembers

Figure 6-4: An initialized `int` variable.

We could have left the variable uninitialized, in which case the variable would contain an unknown value. It is usually best to initialize each variable to a suitable value when declaring it.

6.1.2   *Setting a Value*

We set a value for one of the attributes of an object by invoking a suitable method associated with the object. This will be a *mutator* method, often with a name starting with `set`. For example:

```
person1.setSurname("Jones") ;
```

This method changes the value of the surname attribute of the `person1` object to the string `"Jones"`. Whatever previous value this attribute had (whether initialized by a constructor method or changed by an earlier call of a mutator method) will be overwritten and lost (see Figure 6-5).

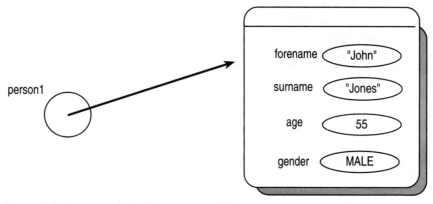

Figure 6-5: A new value for the surname attribute.

In this case, no other attributes of the `person1` object have been changed. But in principle, a method could be written that changes some other attribute or attributes as a side effect of its task—for example, if there was another attribute recording the number of characters in the surname (perhaps so that it can be displayed neatly), then this attribute would also be changed by the `setSurname` method. We have also seen the `setFullName` method, which explicitly sets two attribute values.

The value of a basic data type is changed by the assignment statement. This has the form:

```
nameOfBasicVariable = EXPRESSION ;
```

The EXPRESSION is evaluated, and the result becomes the value of the variable named to the left of the = sign. The previous value of the variable is lost. Thus, suppose we had declared `firstValue` and `secondValue` as integer variables and set them to initial values specified by the user:

```
BasicIo.prompt("type the first value ") ;
int firstValue = BasicIo.readInteger() ;
BasicIo.prompt("type the second value ") ;
int secondValue = BasicIo.readInteger() ;
```

The result of these statements might be as shown in Figure 6-6.

Figure 6-6: Two `int` variables initialized.

We could set the value of `secondValue` to be twice the value of `firstValue` with:

```
secondValue = 2 * firstValue ;
```

The symbol ∗ is the multiplication operator. The multiplication operator cannot be omitted as it can in many mathematical formulae (where for instance 2 r means 2 times   times r); it must always be written explicitly in Java.

After execution of this assignment statement, the value of `secondValue` will be set to twice the value of `firstValue` and lose its original value, as shown in Figure 6-7. The value of `firstValue` is unchanged.

Figure 6-7: The result of an assignment to `secondValue`.

Note that the assignment symbol is the character =, which we distinguish from the equality relational operator, which is the symbol == in Java. Some people are confused by statements such as :

```
x = x + 1 ;
```

This does not assert that the value of x is equal to a value one larger than itself. It is an assignment statement that specifies that one should be added to the value in x. As we have already seen, we could instead write this:

```
x++ ;
```

Note that we wrote the assignment statement:

```
secondValue = 2 * firstValue ;
```

There is no `int` at the beginning of the statement. In this case, we are not declaring a new variable because the variable `secondValue` already exists—we are simply assigning it a new value.

6.1.3   Obtaining a Value

We extract the value of one of the attributes of an object by calling a suitable method associated with the object. This will be a *selector* method, often with a name starting with `get`. For example:

```
person1.getAge()
```

extracts the age attribute of the object instance `person1`, an integer. Since this method call returns a value, the call is not a statement but an expression and must appear in a position where an expression is appropriate. It could appear as the argument of a suitable method call (such as `System.out.println`) since this is a position where an expression is valid:

```
System.out.println(person1.getAge()) ;
```

Another place where an expression is valid is the right-hand side of an assignment statement. So (if the variable `thisAge` has not yet been declared) we could write:

```
int thisAge = person1.getAge() ;
```

The variable `thisAge` now contains the value of the age attribute of the `person1` object and is now ready for further manipulation. Or we could write:

```
thisAge = person1.getAge() - 4 ;
```

which sets the (preexisting) variable `thisAge` to a value four less than the age attribute of `person1`.

We access the value of a variable of a basic type by simply quoting the variable name. Thus, in the statement:

```
secondValue = 2 * firstValue ;
```

we extracted the value of the integer variable `firstValue` by quoting the variable name (and then multiplied the value by two before storing it as the value of the variable `secondValue`).

6.1.4   Arguments to Methods

Each of the arguments of a method can be an expression. So it can be:

- A constant value or `literal` such as 44 or `"Smith"`:

  ```
  person1.setSurname("Smith") ;
  person1.setAge(44) ;
  person1.setGender(Person.FEMALE) ;
  ```

- The name of a variable of a suitable basic type or `String`, in which case the value of the variable is passed to the method:

```
BasicIo.prompt("type in a string ") ;
String surname = BasicIo.readString() ;
int ageValue = 27 ;
int female = Person.FEMALE ;

person1.setSurname(surname) ;
person1.setAge(ageValue) ;
person1.setGender(female) ;
```

Notice that since we are passing the *value* of the variable to the method, there is no way that the method can get at the variable and change its value.

- A method that returns a value of a suitable type:

```
person1.setSurname(person2.getSurname()) ;
person1.setAge(person2.getAge()) ;
person1.setGender(person2.getGender()) ;
```

- Any suitable combination of the above.

```
person1.setSurname(person2.getSurname() + "son") ;
person1.setAge((person2.getAge() + person3.getAge())/2) ;
```

Here the first line sets the surname of `person1` to that of `person2` with `"son"` added on the end. The second line sets the age of `person1` to the average of the ages of `person2` and `person3`.

6.2   The int Data Type

A variable of the `int` data type can hold an integer, a whole number without fractions or decimal places, in the range:
−2,147,483,648 to +2,147,483,647

In many programming languages, different versions of the language on different computers (or even on the same computer) have different definitions of the range of the basic integer type, although the better languages have mechanisms that allow the program to find out what the range is and take action accordingly. But a result of Java's insistence on platform independence is that each of the various numerical types has a fixed range on all platforms. So we can assume that an `int` can hold the above range of values whatever machine our program runs on.

The usual arithmetic operations of addition (+), subtraction (−), multiplication (*), and division (/) are available between integers. As we have already mentioned, the multiplication operator * must not be omitted as is sometimes done in mathematics but must be written explicitly. Some examples are:

```
int x1 = 4, x2 = 6, x3 = 7, x4 = 9 ;
```

```
int result = x1 + x2 ;        // result has the value 10
result = x2 - x3 ;            // result now has the value -1
result = x3 * x4 ;            // result now has the value 63
```

The division operation between integers is what is called *integer division*; any fractional part is thrown away. There is an *integer remainder* or *modulus* operation (%), which returns the fractional part that the integer divide throws away. This is illustrated by the code:

```
int x5 = 21, x6 = 4 ;
result = x5 / x6 ;            // result now has the value 5
result = x5 % x6 ;            // result now has the value 1
x5 = -21 ;
x6 = 4 ;
result = x5 / x6 ;            // result now has the value -5
result = x5 % x6 ;            // result now has the value -1
```

Investigate what happens if x6 is negative or if both x5 and x6 are negative.

A very common operation is to add one to, or subtract one from, a variable. Instead of writing:

```
counter = counter + 1 ;
```

you can use a special notation Java has for this, the incrementation operator ++. If the integer variable counter contains the value 5, then after the statement:

```
counter++ ;
```

it will contain the value 6.

Similarly, there is a decrementation operator, --, which reduces the value of the variable by one:

```
counter-- ;
```

Another fairly common operation for which Java provides a special notation is to add a constant (other than one) to the value of a variable. For example, instead of writing:

```
taxablePay = taxablePay + 125 ;
```

in Java we can write the more concise form:

```
taxablePay += 125 ;
```

Similarly, instead of:

```
x1 = x1 - 3 ;
x2 = x2 * 4 ;
x3 = x3 / 5 ;
x4 = x4 % 6 ;
```

we can write, respectively:

```
x1 -= 3 ;
x2 *= 4 ;
x3 /= 5 ;
x4 %= 6 ;
```

Tip ▪

The += operator is probably the most useful of these four.

Our `GroupOfPeople` class allows us to store the age for each member as well as a surname. We could work out the average age with the following code:

```
int num = computing.getCount() ;
int sum = 0 ;
for (int i = 0 ; i < num ; i++)
    sum += computing.getAge(i) ;
System.out.println("The average age is " + (sum / num)) ;
```

We declare and initialize two integer variables, num for the total number of individuals in this group and sum to total up all the ages. Note that it is very important to initialize sum to zero—we cannot assume that Java will do it. We then add successive ages to sum, using a for loop and the += operator. Finally, we calculate the average by dividing sum by num. Since the argument to a method can be an expression, we give the expression sum / num as the argument to println. Since the operands are integers, this is *integer* division; we will have a result truncated to the next lower integer.

Consider now a piece of code to calculate the perimeter of a field whose dimensions are supplied by the user. Here is the code:

```
BasicIo.prompt("type the field length in feet: ") ;
int length = BasicIo.readInteger() ;
BasicIo("type the field breadth in feet: ") ;
int breadth = BasicIo.readInteger() ;
System.out.print("the perimeter of a field " +length+ " feet by ") ;
System.out.print(breadth + " feet is ") ;
System.out.print(2 * length + breadth) ;
System.out.println(" feet") ;
```

Before you run this program, what should the result be for a length of 4 feet and a breadth of 5 feet? What do you get when you run the program with these values? Why are they different?

The reason for the error is what is called *precedence*, which decides the order in which the operations in an expression are carried out. The basic rule in Java is the same as that in most other programming languages and in mathematics. First all multiplication and division are carried out from left to right, and then all additions and subtractions are carried out, again from left to right. So in this case, the multiplication 2 * length is carried out first, and then breadth is added to the result. If we want to change the order in which operations are carried out, we must insert brackets. So the erroneous line should be rewritten:

```
System.out.print(2 * (length + breadth)) ;
```

The relational operators (==, !=, <=, <, etc.) and Boolean operators (!, &, |, &&, and ||) were introduced in Chapter 4. In this section, we have mentioned a number of arithmetic operators (+, -, /, *, %, ++, --, +=, -=, *=, /=, and %=). The precedence for all these operators is given in Table 6-1 (Java has a number of other operators that we have omitted from this table).

Precedence Level	Operators
Level 1	unary + unary - ++ — !
Level 2	* / %
Level 3	+ -
Level 4	< <= > >=
Level 5	== !=
Level 6	&
Level 7		
Level 8	&&
Level 9	||
Level 10	= += -= *= /= %=

Table 6-1: A (partial) list of Java operators and their precedence level.

In an expression containing no brackets, operators at a lower-numbered level are performed before operators at a high-numbered level. Operators at the same level are performed from left to right through the expression, except for operators at level 1 and 10, which are performed from right to left through the expression. If an expression contains brackets, these rules are applied to the contents of each pair of brackets in turn, starting with the innermost set of brackets.

Unary + and – are the operators appearing in +4 and -x, to be contrasted with the binary versions of these operators in x + 4 and 5 - x. Thus the expression - 4 - - 5 means (- 4) - (- 5).

Here are some of the consequences of these rules:

- 2 * length + breadth means (2 * length) + breadth.
- a * b / c * d means (((a * b) / c) * d) rather than (a * b) / (c * d), which is what one might expect from the mathematical convention.
- a + 2 > b means (a + 2) > b.
- a > b && a < c means (a > b) && (a < c).
- a < b < c means (a < b) < c; the expression in brackets evaluates to a Boolean, so this is an invalid expression—we would have to write (a < b) && (b < c).

It is difficult to remember the full precedence ordering of a language's operators (and in fact the full precedence table in Java contains over forty operators), especially as another language's ordering will be not quite the same. It is always in order to insert brackets even if the precedence ordering does not strictly require them. You should always insert sufficient brackets to make it clear to yourself and the average reader what the order of the operations will be.

6.3   Other Whole Number Data Types in Java (optional)

The Java int data type occupies four 8-bit bytes of storage to hold a value. Java provides three other basic data types that, like int, hold whole numbers but occupy different amounts of storage and therefore have different ranges of values. They are as listed in Table 6-20:

Data type	Storage	Range of values
int	4 bytes	–2,147,483,648 to +2,147,483,647
byte	1 byte	–128 to +127
short	2 bytes	–32,768 to +32,767
long	8 bytes	–9,223,372,036,854,775,808 to +9,223,372,036,854,775,807

Table 6-2: Whole number data types in Java.

The long data type is provided for situations where the range of the int data type is too small. The byte and short data types are provided for situations where we need to save space in storing large numbers of integer values, each with a smaller range than int. In this book, we will be using only the int data type for values that are whole numbers.

As we said in Chapter 4, Java is generally what is called a *strongly typed* language; that is, it is very careful not to allow the programmer to inadvertently mix values of one type with values of another type. For example, Java will not allow you to store a boolean value in an int variable. It would be possible for Java to apply these strong typing rules to the various whole number data types. It could, for example, refuse to add together a short and a long value. In some other programming languages, a programmer explicitly has to specify that some sort of conversion of the short value to a long value is to take place before such an addition is allowed to go ahead. But this would make it rather difficult to work with the different whole number data types, so Java relaxes the rules in this area. Java always allows a value with a smaller potential range to be stored in a variable with a larger range. So the following assignments are valid:

```
byte byteValue = 12 ;
short shortValue = byteValue ;
int intValue = shortValue ;
long longValue = intValue ;
```

In each case, we are taking a value from a variable with a smaller potential range and storing it in a variable with a larger potential range, and this is guaranteed not to cause a problem. For example, in the second line, we are taking a value that must be in the range –128 to +127 and storing it in a variable capable of holding a value in the range –32,768 to +32,767.

Similarly, in an expression that involves variables of different whole number types, values of a type with a limited range are "promoted" to have the larger range. So, for example, in adding a short and a long value, the short value is automatically converted to a long value before the addition:

```
longValue = shortValue + longValue ;
```

But suppose we want to store a value with a larger potential range in a variable with a smaller range—for example, a value of type short in a variable of type byte:

```
byteValue = shortValue ;
```

There could be a problem with this statement if the actual value to be stored is outside the range of the variable in which it is to be stored. So the compiler would reject this statement as it stands and require the programmer to indicate that a statement of this type is not an error but an intended part of the program. We do this by specifying explicitly that a type conversion is required to convert a value with a larger potential range to one with a smaller range. This is done with a *cast*—we specify the required type in brackets before the value or expression:

```
byteValue = (byte) shortValue ;
```

The cast here says, "The expression on the right potentially gives a value in the short range (32,768 to +32,767), and I want to store the value in a variable that is of type byte and can therefore accept only a value in the range –128 to +127; but this is all right because I am expecting the actual value of the expression to lie within the smaller range." The compiler will arrange for the value to be suitably converted from one type to the other.

Using casts (because we are storing values with a wider range in variables with a narrower range), all the following statements are possible:

```
long longValue = 12L ;
int intValue = (int) longValue ;
short shortValue = (short) intValue ;
byte byteValue = (byte) shortValue ;
```

Note that we can specify a long integer literal value with the letter L as a suffix.

6.4   Floating-point Data Types

The int data type always holds *whole* numbers. If we want to hold numbers with a fractional part like 3.7 and –123.45, then there is a separate basic data type called float. The name comes from the term *floating-point*, which refers to the format in which such numbers are held. A floating-point number is stored in such a way as to preserve as much precision (i.e., as many significant decimal places) as possible. For more details about the floating-point representation, see, for example, *Computer Systems: Architecture, Organization, and Programming* by Arthur B. MacCabe (Irwin 1993), Chapter 8.

A value in the Java `float` data type occupies 4 bytes and holds about 7 significant decimal digits. Since 7 significant decimal places is often insufficient for a typical calculation, Java provides another floating-point type called `double`. A value in this format occupies 8 bytes, and holds about 15 significant decimal digits. We will use `double` for all floating-point calculations in this book. The type `float` is available if we need to save space in storing large numbers of floating-point values and are prepared to lose some precision.

We can specify a floating-point value in either of two ways:

- For small values, in the normal way—for example `3.7`, `-123.45`.

- In *scientific notation* where a power of 10 can be specified. In Java, the power of 10 is written after the letter *e*. So the value `123.456e3` represents 123.456 times "ten to the power 3," or 123456.0, and `123.456e-3` represents 123.456 times "ten to the power -3," or 0.123456.

A literal value in either of these two formats is assumed to be a `double` value, with the appropriate amount of precision, unless it has the letter `f` or `F` following it, which specifies that it is a `float` value, which is therefore stored to lower precision. Thus, `1.2` is a `double` value (we could write it `1.2d` or `1.2D` if we want), and `1.2f` or `1.2F` is a `float` value. So we can write:

```
double doubleValue = 1.2 ;
doubleValue = 2.4f ;        // promoted to larger precision
float floatValue = 3.6f ;
floatValue = (float) 4.8 ;  // need to cast to smaller precision
```

In the first line, we are storing a `double` value in a `double` variable, and in the third line, we are storing a `float` value in a `float` variable, so these statements present no problems.

In the second line we are storing a `float` value with a low precision (a smaller number of significant digits) in a `double` variable with higher precision (a larger number of significant digits), so Java allows us to do this.

In the final line, we are storing a value with a larger number of significant digits (since we do not specify the type after the value, it is a `double` value) in a variable capable of holding only a smaller number of significant digits, and Java requires the programmer to indicate with a cast that they intend the possible loss of precision.

For the floating-point data types, all the arithmetic operators are provided—addition (+), subtraction (-), multiplication (*), and division (/). Division between floating-point values is the normal one. So the expression `21.0 / 4.0` applies the division operator to two floating-point (actually `double`) values, so the result is 5.25. Here is a simple example of a floating-point calculation:

```
BasicIo.prompt("type the radius: ") ;
double radius = BasicIo.readDouble() ;
double circumference = 2 * Math.PI * radius ;
System.out.print("a circle of radius " + radius) ;
System.out.println(" has circumference " + circumference) ;
```

There is a `double` constant `PI` (3.14159...) provided in the `Math` class in the `java.lang` package (there is also the constant `E`, for 2.71828...). So we can refer to it with `Math.PI`—we do not need an import statement for this package.

There is no exponentiation operator in Java, but there is a method `pow` in the `Math` class. The expression `Math.pow(5.0, 3.0)` represents the first argument (5.0) raised to the power of the second argument (3.0), giving 125.0. The `Math` class contains methods for a number of other useful functions, such as logarithms and the trigonometric functions.

The integer and floating-point data types are *different* types, but the strong typing rules of Java are again relaxed here. We can store an integer value in a floating point variable:

```
int intValue = 3 ;
double doubleValue = intValue ;          // stores 3.0
```

and we can mix integer and floating-point values and variables in an expression:

```
BasicIo.prompt("type the radius ") ;
int radius = BasicIo.readInteger() ;
double circumference = 2 * Math.PI * radius ;
System.out.print("a circle of radius " + radius) ;
System.out.println(" has circumference " + circumference) ;
```

Storing a floating-point value in an integer variable is potentially dangerous since some precision may be lost. Java therefore requires the programmer's attentions to be marked explicitly with a cast:

```
doubleValue = 1.9 ;
intValue = (int) doubleValue ;           // stores 1
```

The fractional part of the floating-point number (if any) will be ignored; that is, the floating-point value will be *truncated* to an integer (1) before it is stored in the integer variable. Of course, the value stored in the variable `doubleValue` is not changed.

There is a method `round` (in the `Math` class) to convert a double value to an integer value by rounding:

```
intValue = (int) Math.round(doubleValue) ; // stores 2
```

The version of `round` that takes a `double` argument actually returns a `long` value, so we have to cast it to an `int`.

6.5   The boolean Data Type

We first met the `boolean` data type in Chapter 4. A variable of this type can hold only one of two values, `true` and `false`. In some languages (including C and C++) numerical values can be treated as Boolean values—for example, zero representing false and any nonzero value representing true. This is not possible in Java.

We can assign a value to a `boolean` variable with an assignment statement, but the expression on the right-hand side of the = sign must be a Boolean expression:

```
boolean found = true ;
boolean variableInRange = (intValue > 20) && (intValue < 40) ;
```

Notice the second assignment. If the value of the (integer) variable `intValue` lies in the range 21 to 39, then the Boolean expression evaluates to `true`, and this value is assigned to `variableInRange`. If the value of `intValue` is 20 or less, or 40 or more, then the value `false` is assigned to `variableInRange`. It is not necessary to use an `if` statement to set the variable to `true` or `false` in cases like this.

Variables of type `boolean` can be used as the BOOLEAN EXPRESSION in an `if` or `while` statement. For example, we could write:

```
if (variableInRange)
   ...
```

Notice how the test works. If the value of `variableInRange` is `true`, then the first (or only) branch of the `if` statement will be executed. If the value is `false`, then the `else` branch (if any) is executed. It is unnecessary to write:

```
if (variableInRange == true)
   ...
```

Similarly, to carry out a sequence of statements if a `boolean` variable is false (in this case, for example, if the variable is out of the range) we can use the NOT operator (!) and write:

```
if (!variableInRange)
   ...
```

6.6   The char Data Type

A variable of type `char` holds a single character. There is not much we can do with a single character other than set it to a value or test its value. We are usually more concerned with strings of one or more characters, discussed in the next section.

There are a large number of different character sets in use on different computers. Probably the best known is the ASCII (American Standard Code for Information Interchange) character set, and you may already be familiar with it because it is the one used on many PCs. Java uses an international standard called the *Unicode* character set. A Unicode character occupies 2 bytes of storage, so there is room for up to 65536 different characters, which is sufficient to cover a large number of different scripts from around the world.

Although Java uses Unicode internally, a Java program is able to manipulate ASCII characters because the input and output methods can translate between ASCII and Unicode where necessary. So an input method such as `readString` can read ASCII characters from the keyboard or a file and turn them immediately into Unicode for internal processing. An output method such as `print` can take the internal Unicode characters and output them as ASCII characters to the screen or to a file.

Unicode character literal values in a Java program are written between single quotation marks:

```
char charValue = 'b' ;

if ((thisCharacter == 'a') || (thisCharacter == 'A'))
   ...

while (nextCharacter != '.')
   ...
```

There are some special characters that cannot be represented in this way. Instead, they are represented by an *escape sequence*, that is, the *escape character* \ followed by a letter to denote the particular special character. The most useful are listed in Table 6-3.

Special character	Meaning
\t	tab
\n	newline character
\'	single-quote character
\"	double-quote character
\\	backslash (i.e., the character \ itself)

Table 6-3: Special escape sequences in Java.

So we could check to see if a character is a space or a tab character:

```
if ((thisCharacter == ' ') || (thisCharacter == '\t'))
   ...
```

It is also possible to specify a character by quoting its number within the Unicode character set. The numbering system runs from 0 to 65535, but it must be specified in hexadecimal following the prefix \u, so it runs from \u0000 to \uFFFF. The printable ASCII characters occupy the beginning of this numbering sequence, from \u0020 to \u007E, and are listed in Appendix D. Since, for example, the Unicode character 'E' is allocated the (decimal) number 69, we could specify this character in either of two ways:

```
char thisCharacter = 'E' ;
```

or

```
char thisCharacter = '\u0045' ;              \\ i.e. decimal 69 or 'E'
```

In this book, we do not really need to consider the differences between Unicode and ASCII, and the printable ASCII subset of Unicode is all we will use. We will specify character literals by writing the character itself in single quotes or by using one of the escape sequences listed previously in Table 6-3.

6.7 The String Class

The `String` data type is not a basic data type. It is, in fact, a *class* like `Person`. However, the `String` class is fundamental to the Java language, and it has a number of features that we do not find in other classes, so we discuss it in this chapter. Remember the spelling is `String`, not `string`.

A `String` is a sequence of zero or more characters from the Unicode character set. We can declare a string variable s1:

```
String s1 = "Tweedle" ;
```

The result is shown in Figure 6-8. You can see from this example that, although a `String` is an object, it is initialized by specifying a literal constant rather than by calling a constructor method with `new`. A `String` literal is written between *double*-quote characters.

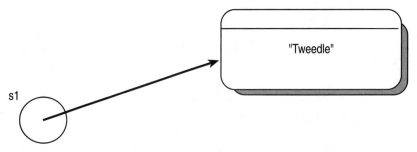

Figure 6-8: Declaration of a `String` variable.

We can declare some more `String` variables:

```
String s2 = "dum" ;
String s3 = s1 + s2 ;            // i.e. "Tweedledum"
String s4 = s1 + ' ' + s2 ;      // i.e. "Tweedle dum"
String s5 = "He said \"Go Home\"." ;
String s6 = "First Line\nSecond Line" ;
```

The declarations of the variables s3 and s4 show the use of the concatenation operator + to join strings, or strings and characters, together. If you want a space to separate the two strings you are joining, you must explicitly insert one.

The double-quote character marks the end of a string. In order to have a double-quote character in the string, you must write it as an escape sequence, as illustrated by the declaration of the variable s5. In order to set up a string that will print over two lines, you can write a newline character as an escape sequence, as illustrated by the declaration of s6.

```
String s7 = "   " ;       // i.e. three spaces
String s8 = "" ;          // i.e. the empty String
String s9 ;               // i.e. no String at all
```

Finally, notice the difference between the strings referred to by the variables s7, s8, and s9; they are shown in Figure 6-9. Variable s7 refers to a string of a certain number of spaces (in this case, three). Variable s8 refers to an empty string, a string that is zero characters long. But variable s9 does not refer to a string at all at present—we should really have written:

```
String s9 = null ;            // i.e. no String at all.
```

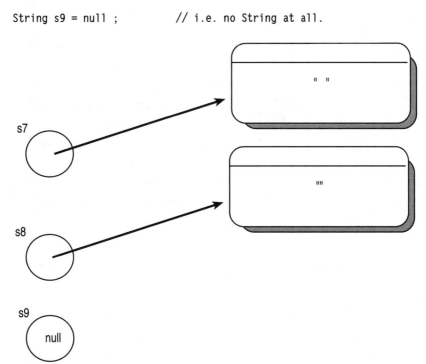

Figure 6-9: Some more String declarations.

We can find out how long a string is by using the method length( )—do not forget the parentheses (we will see in Chapter 9 that arrays use a reserved word length *without* parentheses, but here we are referring to a method, so we do need the parentheses). So s1.length( ) is 7, s2.length( ) is 3, and s3.length( ) is 10. Similarly, s7.length( ) is 3, and s8.length( ) is 0. But s9.length( ) is invalid as s9 does not at present refer to an object—a call of this method would cause a NullPointerException.

We could change the String that one of these variables refers to in an assignment statement thus:

```
s2 = "dedee" ;
s3 = s1 + s2 ;               // i.e. "Tweedlededee"
```

Figure 6-10 shows what the three String variables look like before executing these assignment statements. Figure 6-11 shows what the three String variables look like after executing the assignment statements.

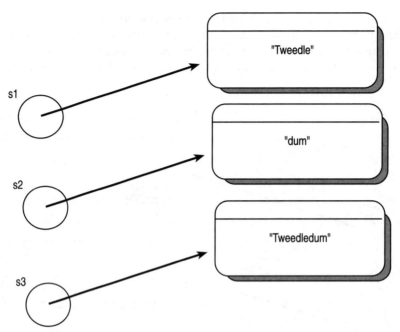

Figure 6-10: Variables s1, s2, and s3 before the assignments.

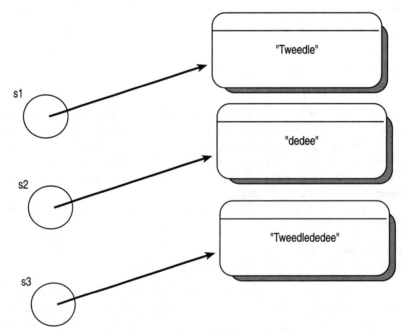

Figure 6-11: Variables s1, s2, and s3 after the assignments.

We still have the three variables, but s2 and s3 now point to different (in this case longer) strings. What happened to the old strings? When each of the assignments takes place, the Java system does the following:

- Allocates a new area of a sufficient size from the store area set aside for strings.

- Writes the new string into this new area—for the first assignment, this is "dedee".

- Puts a reference to this area into the variable—for the first example this is s2.

- Now no variable refers to the area containing the string "dum". In due course, the Java system will recognize that this string area is unused and return it to the pool for later use. This process, called *garbage collection*, is completely automatic in Java.

In Java Strings are said to be immutable; that is, once a String has been set up, it is never changed. Every time we modify a String, even if we just want to change one character, the Java system in fact makes a new one and throws the old one away. If we are making a lot of changes to a string (perhaps we are constructing it one character at a time), this may be a bit inefficient. In Chapter 21, we discuss another way of holding a string of characters, called a StringBuffer, which is more efficient if we are making a lot of modifications. But for now the String class provides the facilities we need.

6.8   Methods for the String Class

We have already introduced the length method for the String class, which gave us the number of characters in a string. Some other useful methods in this class are:

- charAt(...) returns the character at a specified position in a string (the first character is at position zero). Thus s1.charAt(4) returns the 'd' of "Tweedle":

```
s1 = "Tweedle" ;
char aCharacter = s1.charAt(4) ;              // stores 'd'
```

- substring(...) returns a new String containing the substring starting and finishing at specified positions in the string. The first argument is the position of the first character of the substring. The second argument specifies a position just after the last character of the substring. Thus s1.substring(1, 4) returns the substring from position 1 to position 3 of s1, namely "wee".

  There is a second version of the substring method with a single argument, the starting position of the substring. The substring extends to the end of the string. So s1.substring(4) returns "dle":

```
s1 = "Tweedle" ;
System.out.println(s1.substring(1, 4)) ;      // outputs "wee"
System.out.println(s1.substring(4)) ;         // outputs "dle"
```

- Since a String is an object and not a basic type, you should not compare Strings with the relational operator ==. Instead you should use the String method equals(...).

This method compares the String with which the method is associated with the String provided as the argument to the method. Each character at each position in the two Strings must match. Characters in different cases do not match with this method—so, for example, 'a' and 'A' are *different* characters. So s1.equals("Tweedle") returns true, s1.equals("tweedle") returns false, and s3.equals(s4) also returns false:

```
if (s1.equals("tweedle"))
    ...

if (s1.equals(s4))
    ...
```

Other useful String methods for comparison include: equalsIgnoreCase(...). This works like the equals method but ignores the case of the individual characters. With this method, 'a' and 'A' are treated as the *same* character.

- So s1.equalsIgnoreCase("tweedle") returns true.

- startsWith(...) and endsWith(...) match the argument String against the beginning or the end of the String with which the method is associated. So s1.startsWith("Twee") returns true, and s1.endsWith("dlE") returns false.

- indexOf(...) returns the position of the first (i.e., the leftmost) occurrence of the argument String in the String with which the method is associated. Thus s1.indexOf("ee") returns 2 (remember the character positions are numbered from 0 upward). If there is no occurrence of the argument String, the method returns −1. It is the leftmost occurrence that is returned:

```
String s3 = "Tweedledee" ;
System.out.println(s3.indexOf("ee")) ;        // outputs 2
```

There is also a method lastIndexOf(...) to return the position of the last (i.e., the rightmost) occurrence of the argument String in the String with which the method is associated:

```
String s3 = "Tweedledee" ;
System.out.println(s3.lastIndexOf("ee")) ;    // outputs 8
```

- The method trim( ) returns the String with all leading and trailing spaces and tab characters removed, toLowerCase() returns the String with all uppercase characters converted to lowercase, and toUpperCase() returns the String with all lowercase characters converted to uppercase. Consider the statements:

```
BasicIo.prompt("type in a string ") ;
String response = BasicIo.readString().trim().toLowerCase() ;
```

If the user types in a string, this converts it to a standard form in the variable response, with all leading and trailing tabs and spaces removed and all alphabetic characters converted to lowercase.

- replace(...) replaces all occurrences of the first character argument with the second character argument. So s1.replace('e', 'o') returns "Twoodlo". The statement:

```
BasicIo.prompt("type in a string ") ;
String response =
BasicIo.readString().trim().toLowerCase().replace('\t', ' ') ;
```

ensures that any tab characters are converted to space characters.

Full details of all these (and other) methods can be found in the documentation for the String class in the java.lang package.

6.9   Wrapper Classes (optional)

In some object-oriented languages (for example, Smalltalk), everything is an object. For efficiency, Java makes a distinction between objects and the basic data types discussed in this chapter. But occasionally we need to be able to treat a basic type as an object. What Java does is to have one special class of objects associated with each basic data type. These are called *wrapper* classes (they "wrap up" the basic data types as objects), and they are listed in Table 6-2.
Table 6-2: Wrapper classes.

Basic Type	Wrapper class
boolean	Boolean
char	Character
byte	Byte
short	Short
int	Integer
long	Long
float	Float
double	Double

We use the basic types most of the time because operations are more efficient on such types. We can create an instance of a wrapper object by calling a constructor method with a value of the basic type as argument. So:

```
int iBasic = 42 ;
Integer iWrapper = new Integer(iBasic) ;
```

declares an instance of the Integer wrapper class with the value 42.

Each wrapper class has an appropriately named method for extracting a basic value from the wrapper class. So:

```
int iNewValue = iWrapper.intValue() ;
```

extracts the value 42 from the iWrapper object and stores it in the (basic) int variable iNewValue.

We have seen a number of useful methods associated with the String class—for example, to force a string to all uppercase or all lowercase or to trim off leading and trailing spaces. There are a number of similar tasks we might like to be able to carry out for the basic data types—for example, to force an individual character to upper- or lowercase. But these basic types are, by definition, not objects, so they cannot have associated methods to carry out these useful tasks. The wrapper classes are a suitable place to put methods like this.

Most of these methods are *class* or *static* methods—that is, they are associated with the class rather than an instance of that class. To call them, you specify the name of the *class* and then add a dot as usual followed by the method name and arguments.

Useful methods from the Character class include:

- toLowerCase(...) and toUpperCase(...) to change, respectively, a lowercase letter (passed as the argument) to uppercase (the returned value) and an uppercase letter to lowercase (other characters are left unchanged). So:

```
char firstChar = 'A' ;
char secondChar = Character.toLowerCase(firstChar) ;
```

puts the value 'a' in the character variable secondChar (the value of firstChar is, of course, unchanged).

- isLetter(...), isDigit(...), isLowerCase(...), isUpperCase(...), isWhitespace(...). These are all *class* methods that take a char argument and return a boolean value indicating whether or not the character argument is in the set of characters specified in the name of the method. For example:

```
Character.isDigit(response)
```

returns true if response is a digit character in the range 0 to 9 and false otherwise.

```
Character.isLowerCase(response)
```

returns true if response is a lowercase letter in the range 'a' to 'z' and false otherwise.

```
Character.isWhitespace(response)
```

returns true if response is one of the white space characters, namely the space, tab, and newline characters and two less common ones (form feed and carriage return) and false otherwise.

The Integer class contains the useful (class or static) method parseInt. This method takes a String argument and returns the corresponding int value. So:

```
String stringValue = "123" ;
int intValue = Integer.parseInt(stringValue) ;
```

puts the value 123 in intValue. If the String argument is not a valid integer, we get a NumberFormatException exception.

We can convert an int value to a String with the (class or static) toString method. So:

```
int intValue = 456 ;
String newStringValue = Integer.toString(intValue) ;
```

puts the value "456" in newStringValue.

Both `parseInt` and `toString` have versions that allow the programmer to specify a radix other than 10 for the string of digits.

6.10   Key Points in Chapter 6

- Java provides a number of *basic data types*. The main ones are `int`, `double`, `boolean`, and `char`.

  Variables of these types are declared as follows:

  `<name of basic type> <name of variable> = <initial value> ;`

  A variable of one of these types can be assigned a new value with an assignment statement:

  `<name of variable> = <expression> ;`

- The `int` type can store a whole number value in the range:
  −2,147,483,648 to +2,147,483,647

  Operations that can be performed on integer values include addition (+), subtraction (−), multiplication (*), integer division (/), and remainder (%).

  The order in which operations are carried out in an expression depends on the *precedence* of the operators (see Table 6-1).

- The `double` type can store a number with a fractional part with about 15 decimal places of accuracy. Operations that can be performed on these values include addition (+), subtraction (−), multiplication (*), and division (/).

- In an expression with both `int` and `double` values, an `int` value is automatically converted to a `double` value where necessary.

  If a `double` needs to be converted to an `int` value, the programmer must indicate this with a *cast*; the `double` value will be *truncated* to an `int` value.

  `<int variable> = (int) <double expression> ;`

- Strings of characters are held as instances of the `String` class. We can set up a `String` variable with a particular value:

  `String stringName = "This is a String" ;`

  We can set this `String` variable to a different value:

  `stringName = "This is a different String" ;`

  The `String` class provides the `length` method to return the length of the string, `charAt` to return a particular character (numbered from zero), `toUpperCase` and `toLowerCase`, and so on. Comparisons between strings should be done with the `equals` method, not with the `==` operator.

- There is a wrapper class corresponding to each basic data type. The `Character` and `Integer` classes contain some useful (static or class) methods.

6.11   Exercises

1. Write a program to prompt the user to input an amount in ounces and return the amount in grams (1 ounce = 28 grams).

   Modify the program so that the user can type in a number of ounces to be converted to grams or a number of pints to be converted to liters (1 pint = 0.568 liters).

   Modify the program so that the user can do a sequence of metric conversions.

2. Write a program to prompt the user to type in an amount in pence. Your program should then work out the least number of the following coins needed for this amount of money:

   £1, 50p, 10p, 1p

   For example, the least number of coins for 195 pence is:

   1 x 1 pound, 1 x 50 pence, 4 x 10 pence, 5 x 1 pence

Note ▪

A pound is 100 pence.

Note ▪

There will be a significant amount of repetition in parts of your solution as you have not yet learned how to use an array to store the different coin values. This is why you have not been asked to handle all possible denominations of British notes and coins.

3. Write a program to read in a string of characters from the user, and output the characters one per line on the screen (see the example at the end of Section 5.2).

   Modify the program so that all vowels are output in uppercase and all consonants in lowercase, so the string "Hello" would appear as:

   h
   E
   l
   l
   o

4. Write a program to read in a string of characters typed by the user and test if it is palindromic. That is, test whether the string reads the same in both directions. The matching of the characters should ignore the case, so the word "Madam" is considered to be palindromic.

   Modify the program so that the user can type in a sequence of strings and have the program indicate for each one whether it is palindromic or not.

5. Write a program that takes two strings and tests whether or not the first string is contained within the second. For example, the string "pen" is contained within the string "independent".

Modify the program so that it reports the starting position of the first string within the second, if it is so contained.

Modify the program so that it always looks for the shorter string within the larger, whatever order they are typed in.

6. You have been invited to participate in a game show where you could win a free star prize. When you play, you are asked to choose one box from three. Only one of the boxes contains a prize; the other two boxes contain lemons. When you have chosen your box, but before you open it, the game show host will open one of the two remaining boxes and show you a lemon. At this point you have three possible strategies:
a) Keep the box you chose initially and open it.
b) Take the remaining box, which the game show host did not open.
c) Flip a coin to decide whether to open the box you originally chose or the remaining box, which the game show host did not open.

When you play the game, which of the three strategies should you adopt? Write a Java program to help you decide. The program should simulate playing the game a large number of times (to be specified by the user) with each of the three strategies to see which one offers you the best chance of winning. You may be surprised at the result.

Note

Java provides the Random class (in the `java.util` package) to generate random numbers. You can declare:

```
static Random rand = new Random() ;
```

and then the following method returns a random integer in the (inclusive) range 1 to the value of the argument supplied:

```
public static int random(int n)
    {
    return (int) (1 + (Math.abs(rand.nextInt()) % n)) ;
    } // end of method random
```

Writing
Objects

CHAPTER 7

A Simple Class

7.1 Introduction

Object-oriented programming provides us with a mechanism—the object itself—that supports a number of important concepts in software engineering. As the software artifacts we build become ever more complex, we need much more control over the structure and use of their components. One of the crucial features of objects is that they can be gathered together under the general concept of *encapsulation*, long heralded as a vital feature for modern software components.

Encapsulation has an impact on a number of areas. It gives us a structuring mechanism whereby we can gather together, in one place, logically related program elements. It also, for example, makes it possible to:

- Gather together a number of related functions in one module.
- Group both the code and the data it manipulates.

Over and above this useful grouping mechanism that allows us to structure our components (and the systems we build from them) in a logical and sensible fashion, we can also use the module concept to support *information hiding*. Essentially, the users of the modules have information about them on a "need-to-know" basis. If we have a geometry module that supports shapes and functions that operate on those shapes—for example, circles and radii and perimeters—we do not need to know how the function that calculates radii works; we only need to know how to call it.

The module should also be self-contained. It should contain everything it needs in order to function appropriately. The module user should not need to declare additional data or provide additional code in the program in order to support the module.

The classic example of a module that contains a data structure and related state information is the stack. A stack is a data structure that supports a LIFO (Last In First Out) queue. We shall find out more about stacks later in the book. For the moment, all you need to know about a stack is that we can add data to it and get data back from it. However, the stack is organized in such a way that the last item added will be the first one back. Two essential operations for stack users are *push*, to add a data item to the stack, and *pop*, to get a data item back from the stack.

The point is that users of the stack only need to understand the general LIFO concept and what the push and pop operators do. They do not have to know how the operators work nor the nitty-gritty details of how the stack is implemented. This kind of information hiding makes the module easier to use. Also, the fact that the module is self-contained means that there is generally no need to provide additional code or data structures to make the module work.

Encapsulation is also beneficial for the module provider. If the module provider decides there is a more efficient way to implement the stack—either through a new data structure or algorithm for the operators—these changes can be made with impunity as long as they do not have an impact on the appearance and behavior of the module as far as the users are concerned.

Most, if not all, of the data within a module is hidden from the user. The only way we can access hidden data is through the methods the module provides. For example, if we model a person's age as a visible integer, we can do anything to that age that we could do to an integer. This includes assigning it a negative value. As far as people's ages are concerned, this action is semantically incorrect. If we hide the person's age within a module, however, and provide a method setAge, then the module provider can check to make sure that the value provided by the user is semantically valid; that is, greater than 0 and less than 150 (say). We shall see later in this chapter how this can be done. This is a simple example of how module providers can ensure that objects can only be manipulated in valid, sensible ways.

In this chapter, we shall consider three types of people involved in writing and using elements of a Java program. The first is the *class provider*; this is the person (or team) responsible for the definition and implementation of the class. This is the person who identifies and defines the attributes and the methods of the class and whether they should be hidden (private) or available to the class user (public).

The second is the *class user*; this is the person who takes the classes provided and uses them to write a Java program. This is the role we have adopted thus far in the book. We shall see how we can use classes to write other classes later in this book.

The final type of person is the *end user*; this is the person who takes the Java program we have written and executes it, either as an application or as an applet accessed over the Web. He or she interacts with our program as it executes and may be prompted to provide data via the keyboard and/or some graphical input artifact (for example, a menu).

As we have already seen from the perspective of class users, classes support the encapsulation mechanism. In this chapter, we shall switch hats and start to look at objects from the viewpoint of the class provider. We shall progress by continuing to use the Person class as our example.

Each class should provide some documentation aimed at the class user. This documentation should detail the publicly available aspects of the class; this may include constants, attributes, and methods. The information provided should be enough to allow the class user to successfully employ the class as part of his or her application(s).

The following is a list of the methods available for the user of the person class:

```
public Person()
public Person(String f, String s, int a, int g)
public String getForename()
public String getSurname()
public int getAge()
public int getGender()
public String getGenderString()
public void setForename(String f)
```

```
public void setSurname(String s)
public void setAge(int a)
public void setGender(int g)
public void increaseAge(int n)
public void setFullName(String f, String s)
public static int getUpperAgeLimit()
public String formalTitle()
public String toString()
```

Notice the group of get and set methods. These allow us to get and set the values of the person's forename, surname, age, and gender. We can extract or change these values, but only indirectly, through the provided methods. We can thus assume that this information—the state of a person—is encapsulated within the object.

Note the provision of the toString method. Many classes, such as those contained in the Java libraries, provide this method. Its intention is to provide a representation of the object in a String, which can then be printed. For example, if we have an instance of the Person class called bill, we can obtain the String representation as follows:

```
bill.toString()
```

We could use this in conjunction with the System.out.println method:

```
System.out.println("the person is " + bill.toString());
```

However, for reasons that will be presented in Chapter 14, we can omit the call to toString in these particular circumstances because System.out.println is clever enough to apply the method on our behalf to a variable that is not of type String.

Notice also the getUpperAgeLimit method that is declared as static. We will examine what this means in Section 8.6.

How do we declare and use an object of this class? The class provider gives us at least one *constructor* method. We can tell which methods are constructors as they have the same name as the class, here Person. We can also tell it is a constructor as it does not have a return type specified. We can see earlier in this chapter that we have two constructor methods in the Person class. One has no arguments, and the other has four. The way to use the constructors is in conjunction with the keyword new:

```
Person aPerson = new Person();
aPerson.setForename("James");
aPerson.setSurname("Kirk");
aPerson.setAge(34);
aPerson.setGender(Person.MALE);
```

Once we have created the new person, we can use any of the methods provided. Here, we are using the four set methods to give aPerson some state. We are setting the four values or attributes encapsulated within the object. Alternatively, we could use the second constructor:

```
Person aPerson = new Person("James", "Kirk", 34, Person.MALE);
```

This second constructor takes four parameters, which map onto the four attributes (forename, surname, age, and gender). For the fourth parameter, we use one of the gender constants provided by the `Person` class.

On the birthday of aPerson, we need to increment the age by one. We can do this using the `getAge` and `setAge` methods:

```
int temp = aPerson.getAge();
temp = temp + 1;
aPerson.setAge(temp);
```

However, looking back at the list of methods provided, we can see there is an `increaseAge` method. We can use this as follows:

```
aPerson.increaseAge(1);
```

7.2 Providing the Person Class

It is time at last to swap hats and examine the `Person` class as a class provider. We begin by looking at a skeleton declaration of this class:

```
public class Person
   {

   // Person class constants

   public static final int UNKNOWN = 99 ;
   public static final int MALE = 1 ;
   public static final int FEMALE = 2 ;

   private static final int UPPER_AGE = 150;

   // Person instance fields

   private String forename ;
   private String surname ;
   private int age ;
   private int gender ;

   // Person Constructors

   public Person() { ... body removed ...    }
   public Person(String f, String s, int a, int g) { ... }

   // selector methods for Person instance fields
```

```
public String getForename() { ... }
public String getSurname() { ... }
public int getAge() { ... }
public int getGender() { ... }
public String getGenderString() { ... }

// methods for setting Person instance fields

public void setForename(String f) { ... }
public void setSurname(String s) { ... }
public void setAge(int a) { ... }
public void setGender(int g) { ... }


public void increaseAge(int n) { ... }
public void setFullName(String f, String s) { ... }
public static int getUpperAgeLimit() { ... }
public String formalTitle() { ... }
public String toString() { ... }
} // end of Person class
```

Let's look at the head of the class:

```
public class Person
    {
    // Person class constants

    public static final int UNKNOWN = 99 ;
    public static final int MALE = 1 ;
    public static final int FEMALE = 2 ;

    private static final int UPPER_AGE = 150;

    // Person instance fields

    private String forename ;
    private String surname ;
    private int age ;
    private int gender ;
```

It starts with the keywords public and class followed by the name of the class, here Person. It is followed by the body of the class, enclosed in curly brackets. Next we have a group of three public and one private class constants. These will be discussed in more detail in the next chapter (section 8.3). Suffice it to say the first three classes are intended to model the possible values of a person's gender: either it is male or female, or else we simply do not have access to that information yet.

Next we have a set of variables that store the state of a `Person` object, one for each attribute: a person, as we are modeling one, has a forename, a surname, an age, and a gender. As you can see, these are of type `int` or `String`. In the class body, they are declared much as local variables have been declared in the `main` method, the type to which they belong followed by the name of the variable. The major difference here is that they are encapsulated within the class body. We make them hidden by prefacing their declaration with the keyword `private`. The user of the class cannot directly reference them. These variables are known as *instance variables* or *attributes*.

Notice, however, that all attributes, regardless of whether they have been declared as `public` or `private`, are accessible to all methods contained within the same class.

Let's explore this further. If we had the following class definition:

```
public class Car
    {

    private String carName;
    public int mileage;

    // methods

    } // end of class "Car"
```

then a class user can try to write:

```
Car aCar = new Car();
aCar.mileage = 10000;              // legal
System.out.print(aCar.carName);    // illegal
```

When an instance variable is declared as `public`, then we can access it directly as part of the object with the notation "instance name-dot-attribute name." So we can directly assign an integer value to aCar's mileage. There is no need for a `get` or `set` method. However, when we try to directly access a `private` attribute (like carName), this will not work. Attributes should usually be private.

The `Car` class specification does not actually contain two instance variables called `carName` and `mileage`; it contains only their specifications. We cannot say, for example:

```
Car.mileage = 100;
```

Object instances of the `Car` class have their own distinct copies of the two instance variables (see Figure 7-1). They have the same name and form, but we can access them only through the object that contains them:

```
Car bCar = new Car();
bCar.mileage = 105;
```

We use the name of the object to select which set of instance variables we wish to use.

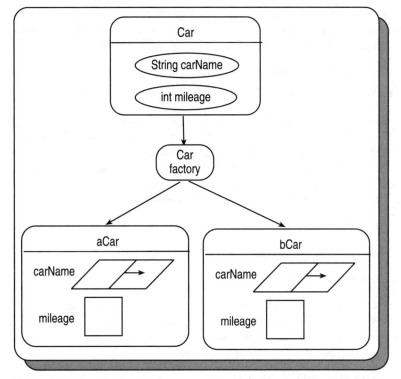

Figure 7-1: The relationship between class definition and instances.

7.3   Methods for the Person Class

Returning to the `Person` class, next we have two constructor methods; these will be discussed in more detail in the next chapter. Finally, we have a set of methods used to extract or insert information or to generally manipulate the values contained in the instance variables. It is this set of methods that we will now examine in more detail.

The general form of a method header is:

```
public-or-private return-value-type name parameters-in-parenthesis
```

This is followed by the code, contained in curly brackets, that implements the method. This is known as the *body* of the method.

Just as for the instance variables we have seen so far, the keyword `public` indicates that the method is available to the class user. The class user can thus call the method. It is possible to have `private` methods. The `private` methods can be called by the other methods in the class, but no method outside the body of the class can call a private method. They are hidden from the user but will be of great importance in implementing the public methods the user can call. In other words, they can only be called indirectly by the user. We shall discuss this further later.

The "return-value-type" specifies:

- Whether the method returns a value or not.
- What type the value will have.

The keyword `void` specifies that no value will be returned. In the current implementation of the `Person` class, none of the `set` methods return a value, and thus all feature the `void` keyword. We will look at an example of a `set` method shortly.

On the other hand, we can see methods that do return a value, such as `getAge`. Because the instance variable `age` has type `int`, when we return this as the result of a method, we are returning a value of type `int`. Hence the `getAge` header looks like:

```
public int getAge()
```

When the user calls `getAge`, it can be written as follows:

```
int oneAge = aPerson.getAge();
```

As ever, we need an integer variable in order to hold an integer value.

Now to examine the actual bodies of our methods. They contain code just like the code we have seen so far in this book. Let's begin with the simplest kind of method, one that returns the otherwise hidden value of an instance variable:

```
public int getAge()
   {
   return age ;
   }
```

Here, the body of the method consists of a single statement. It uses the keyword `return` to prefix the value it is going to return as the result of the user calling this method. Because the instance variable `age` has the type `int`, then the "return-value-type" specifier in the method header must also be `int`. Consider the following:

```
public String getSurname()
   {
   return surname ;
   }
```

Similarly, where the instance variable `surname` has type `String`, so the "return-value-type" specifier is `String`.

So far, we have considered methods that return a value, those belonging to the hidden instance variables—these are the so-called `get` methods. Let us now examine methods that allow us to change the value of the hidden instance variables—the `set` methods:

```
public void setAge(int a)
   {
   age = a ;
   }
```

Here we see a *formal parameter*, a of type int. When class users call this method, they will provide a corresponding *actual parameter*, a value of type int:

```
aPerson.setAge(uAge);
```

The formal parameter a takes the value of the actual parameter (in this case, uAge). In the body of the method, we have an assignment statement that assigns the value of a to the attribute age. We have taken the value provided by the class user as an actual parameter, copied it into the formal parameter, and assigned it to the attribute. This has the desired effect. We shall describe this whole process in more detail in the next section.

Notice that the types of the formal parameters of the set methods must match the types of the instance variables. So setAge has a parameter of type int to match that of the age instance variable, and setForename has a parameter of type String to match that of the forename instance variable.

However, as we discussed earlier, we can do a bit more in the set methods to try to ensure that only sensible (semantically valid) values can be passed into the instance variables. In this case, we might say that ages must be in the range 0 to 150. We can enhance the setAge method using a selection statement as follows:

```
public void setAge(int a)
   {
   if ((a < 0) || (a > UPPER_AGE))
   {
   System.out.println("bad age in 'setAge'") ;
   System.exit(1) ;
   }
   else
   age = a ;
   } // end of method setAge
```

Here we are making the entire application program shut down in response to a bad age value.

We can, of course, do something similar with most of the set methods; consider setForename:

```
public void setForename(String f)
   {
   if (f.length() < 1)
       {
       System.out.println("bad forename in 'setForename'") ;
       System.exit(1) ;
       }
   else
       forename = f ;
   } // end of method setForename
```

Here we are saying that the smallest forename we will find acceptable has at least one letter in it.

7.4 Actual & Formal Parameters

To understand what is actually happening when we call a method, we need to explain some terminology—that of *actual* and *formal* parameters. To make matters worse, we will have to swap hats quite quickly between class user and class provider.

We will take the setAge method as our first example. Let's say that the class user has written some code that allows the end user to type in someone's age. This is stored in an integer variable before it is used as the actual parameter to the setAge method:

```
Person aPerson = new Person() ;
BasicIo.prompt("Type in the person's age ");
int uAge = BasicIo.readInteger();
aPerson.setAge(uAge);
```

The actual parameter, then, is whatever variable or value we provide when we call the method. In this case, it is the integer variable uAge. It could have just as easily been a single integer value (e.g., 5) or an integer expression that results in a single integer value.

For that matter, it could even have been a call to a method that returns a single integer value. Let's say we have brother and sister who are twins. Once we have set one's age, we can use that information to set the other's:

```
boy.setAge(girl.getAge());
```

On the other hand, if they are not twins, and we know the boy is a year older than the girl, we could have:

```
int uAge = girl.getAge() ;
boy.setAge(uAge+1) ;
```

or

```
boy.setAge(girl.getAge()+1);
```

Now let's put on our class provider hat and look again at the declaration of setAge:

```
public void setAge(int a)
```

Here again we see that it is a method called setAge, that doesn't return a value, and is available to the class user. Inside the round brackets is the *formal* parameter. We see that it is named a and is of type int. It is the type of formal parameter that dictates the type of actual parameter. This is why a call of setAge can only have a single integer variable or value as its actual parameter.

Note also that we can see there is only one formal parameter. Of course, it is possible to have as many as necessary for the method to carry out its work. Because there is only one in this case, calls of setAge can only have one actual parameter; any more or less would be illegal:

```
aPerson.setAge(5);          // legal
aPerson.setAge();           // illegal -- no parameters
aPerson.setAge(uAge, 6, 9); // illegal -- three parameters instead
                            // of one
aPerson.setAge("fred");     // illegal -- one parameter, but wrong
                            // type
```

So, by examining the formal parameters of a method, we can learn a lot about how we can call the method; specifically, what types of the parameters we can have and how many.

Where we have many formal parameters, we have to be careful that the types of the actual and formal parameters match up. For example, we could extend our Car class with engine capacity modeled as an integer, registration number as a string, and road worthiness as a Boolean. We could have a method that allows the class user to set up these instance variables as follows:

```
public void setup(String regNo, int engCap, boolean onRoad)
```

When we call this method, we must ensure that the first parameter is a String, the second an int, and the third a boolean. Any other ordering and we will have an illegal situation:

```
aCar.setup("D54VBV", 999, true);    // legal
aCar.setup(999, true, "D54VBV");    // illegal
```

So the ordering of formal and actual parameters is important.

Let's return to setAge. We are calling it with an actual parameter of uAge:

```
aPerson.setAge(uAge);
```

Whatever the contents of that integer variable are (for the sake of this example, let's say it is 21), we want to set the value of the instance variable age to the value contained in the actual parameter. If we look at the body of setAge, there is no reference at all to uAge, only to the formal parameter a. How does the value of uAge end up in the formal parameter a? It is through the *calling process* that this occurs.

Before a method is called, its formal parameters do not exist. If the body of the method contains any declarations of variables, those variables also do not exist. When a method is called, the formal parameters and the variables come into existence so they can be used by the instructions contained in the method body as they are executed. When a method is finished, the formal parameters and the variables again cease to exist.

The variables contained within the body of a method are said to be *local* variables. This is because they can be referenced (and accessed) only by the instructions contained in the method body.

When the formal parameters come into existence, the values of the actual parameters are copied into the formal parameters. It is as if an assignment statement had taken place. In our example, this would be:

```
a = uAge;
```

Let's look at this diagrammatically. Before the method is called, and no one is using the aPerson object, it appears as shown in Figure 7-2.

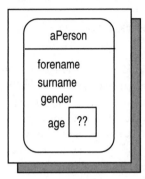

Figure 7-2: The aPerson Object.

We can see the four instance variables, forename, surname, gender, and age. Because age is the one that most interests us, we have shown it here as a labeled box. It contains an integer value, denoted by ?? because we neither know nor care what value it currently has. We want to replace it with the value stored in uAge.

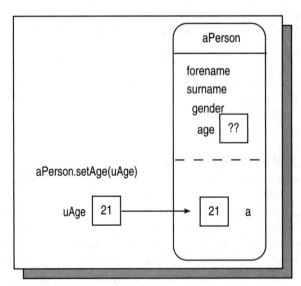

Figure 7-3: Calling setAge.

When we call setAge with the actual parameter uAge, the temporary existence of the formal parameter a begins. We show the temporary data in the lower half of the aPerson object in

Figure 7-3. The formal parameter a is given the same value as the actual parameter uAge. In this way, we can say that the value 21 is being passed *into* the object.

To complete the process, the method body is now executed and the value 21 is passed from a into the instance variable age (see Figure 7-4).

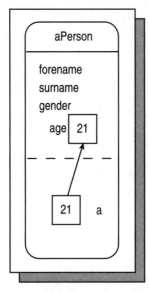

Figure 7-4: Executing setAge.

Finally, when setAge terminates, any temporary variables (formal parameters and local variables) cease to exist. This leaves us with aPerson after the method has been executed (see Figure 7-5).

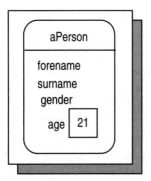

Figure 7-5: Post setAge.

7.5   Modes of Parameter Passing

In this section, we return again to the mechanism of passing a parameter where the type of the parameter is one of the basic types (`boolean`, `int`, etc.) or a `String`. By this, we mean the process of taking a value from the actual parameter and "passing it into" the formal parameter.

We can pass values only in one direction, from the actual parameter to the formal parameter. Any changes we make to the formal parameter have no effect on the actual parameter. Suppose we have a class `Dog` with a method `setAge`:

```
class Dog
    {
    private int age, dogAge;

    public void setAge (int a)
        {
1.      age = a;
2.      a = a * 7; // map onto dog years
3.      dogAge = a;
        }
    } // end of class Dog
```

We call this `setAge` method as follows:

```
int mda = 2;
myDog.setAge(mda);
```

Before we call the method, we have the situation shown in Figure 7-6.

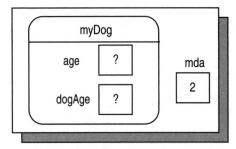

Figure 7-6: Before the method call.

When we call the method, the value of the actual parameter is copied into the formal parameter (see Figure 7-7).

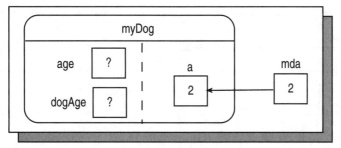

Figure 7-7: Creating the formal parameter and copying the actual parameter into it.

From this point on, the actual parameter is no longer relevant to the execution of the method. Line one of the method sets the **age** attribute to the value of the formal parameter (see Figure 7-8).

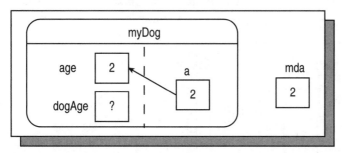

Figure 7-8: Assigning the formal parameter to the attribute.

Line two multiplies the formal parameter by 7. Notice that this has no effect on the actual parameter (Figure 7-9).

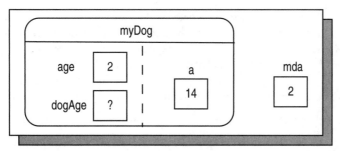

Figure 7-9: After multiplying the formal parameter.

Line three sets the value of the dogAge attribute to that of the formal parameter (Figure 7-10).

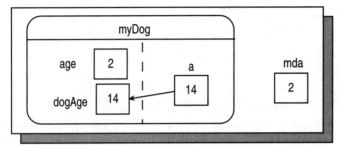

Figure 7-10: Assigning the formal parameter to the attribute.

The method concludes, the formal parameter disappears, and as we can see in Figure 7-11, the attribute values have been set as we would expect, and the actual parameter remains unaltered.

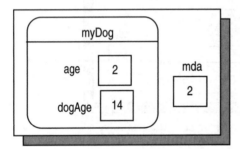

Figure 7-11: After the method call.

Traditionally, this is known as *call by value*; values are passed *into* the formal parameter. Some languages support *call by value returned*, whereby values are passed out of the formal parameter back into the actual parameter. If this were the case in Java, the diagram in Figure 7-10 would have an arrow leading from a to mda, and mda would contain the value 14.

It is not possible in Java to use actual parameters of the basic types to pass values back out of the method. The only way methods can pass values back to the calling program is if the method has a return value. In Chapter 10, we will examine the use of objects as parameters.

7.6   Return Values

As we have seen, some methods return a value. For example, any get method will normally return a value of the same type as the attribute it is associated with. We usually do this by returning the value of the attribute itself.

However, as we have seen in connection with variables, we can assign an integer value on the right-hand side of an assignment statement to an integer variable on the left-hand side. The integer value may be a literal integer value or taken from another integer variable, or it may be the result of an integer expression.

Similarly, the value returned from a method may be a literal, the contents of a variable, or the result of an expression.

In our `Dog` class, we chose to store the value that represented a dog's age in dog years. However, as we store the age in normal years, we could always calculate the dog years version of the age whenever it was requested.

We could provide the following method:

```
public int getAgeInDogYears()
  {
  return age * 7;
  }
```

Here we can see that following the `return` keyword, we have an expression involving an integer literal (the number seven) and an integer attribute. This integer expression evaluates to produce a single integer value, which we return as the result of the method call.

7.7   Lexical Conventions Within a Class

It is often useful to have conventions for the textual representation of elements within a class. By this we mean ways of varying the appearance of text to impart information to the reader so they can tell at a glance whether the word they are looking at is a class name or an attribute name.

The main techniques we explore here involve the use of capitalization and "visible" spaces. When we want to give something a name that involves two (or more) words, we cannot use actual spaces as the name of something; in Java it has to be a continuous string of characters (with no spaces). There are two main techniques for handling this problem—using capital letters to represent the start of the next word in the sequence or using the underscore character to represent the space. So the name *dog age* can be represented as `dogAge` or `dog_age`. We will adopt the former convention for the names of attributes, variables, instances, and methods.

To differentiate the name of a class, we use a capital first letter. So the person class is `Person`. Other class names you have already met are `GroupOfPeople` and `BasicIo`.

Finally, we wish to distinguish constant names from all others; we have chosen to represent these as all capital letters. Of course, our visible space solution will not work under these circumstances, so we resort to the use of the underscore character. So *VAT rate* is represented as `VAT_RATE`.

These are the conventions we have tried to apply throughout this book. We make no particular claim for them; the important point is that you should decide on the conventions you will use and stick with them.

7.8   Key Points in Chapter 7

- *Encapsulation* is an important aspect of modern software engineering. It allows us to collect together data and instructions that manipulate that data in one place to protect the data and instructions if required and to present a strict interface to the end user. Java classes allow us to use encapsulation.

- We can identify three types of people by their relationship to Java software:

  - A *class provider*, who writes the class definition.

  - A *class user*, who uses the class and instances thereof to implement an application.

  - An *end user*, who uses a Java application.

- It is possible to provide different constructors for the same class (see Chapter 8). We use constructors to create new instances of a class.

- A class definition contains:

  - Class constants (such as MALE, FEMALE, etc.)

  - Instance variables or attributes (such as name, gender, etc.)

  - Methods

  We shall generally refer to these contents as *elements* of the class.

- The contents of a class definition can be specified as `public` or `private`. This relates to the visibility (or availability) of the element. Private elements are available only within the class (to the class provider), and public elements are generally accessible (to the class provider and class user).

- Methods consist of sets of instructions that manipulate the data contained within the instance. A method has two parts—a header and a body.

- The general form of a method header is:
  "public-or-private return-value-type name parameters-in-parenthesis"

- Like any element of a class, we can make a method public or private.

- A method may return a value as part of its function. We specify the type of value it returns. If the method does not return a value, we specify the return type of the method as `void`.

- The body of a method consists of a set of Java statements. If the method returns a value, it must contain at least one `return` statement.

- The *formal parameters* of a method appear in the method header and will be referred to in the method body. Formal parameters form a run-time link to *the actual parameters*, which are the values or variables used when the method was called. We use parameters to pass data into the method.

7.9 Exercises

1. Complete the definition of the Dog class. Provide a suitable driver application to test your class.

2. a) Extend the Person class so that it has a new instance variable, maritalStatus.
   b) A person can be single, married, divorced, or widowed. Since class constants are not introduced until Section 8.3, you'll have to use the integers, say 1, 2, 3, and 4, for the four possible values of this attribute.
   c) Add new get and set methods to deal with the marital status. Make sure the set method semantically validates the value being passed into the object.
   d) A person is eligible to marry if they are above or on the age of consent (say, 18) and are not married. Write a method, eligible, which returns true if the person can be married, false otherwise.
   e) Write a driver program that uses your extended Person class and allows you to fully test your new code.

3. We saw earlier that the Person.setAge method simply abandons the execution of the application if an age that is out of range is provided as a parameter. This might seem a bit excessive, and there are a number of approaches we can take to make this a friendlier method. One thing we can do is change the method so it returns a Boolean value that indicates whether the class user's attempt to set the person's age was successful or not. Let's say we return true if the attempt succeeded, false otherwise.

   Rewrite the setAge method to reflect this, and provide a driver application that checks the return status of the operation. For example, we could provide a loop that repeatedly asks the end user to provide an age until a valid age is supplied.

Exercises 4 onward require you to implement a class and to provide an appropriate driver application. These drivers should be interactive and prompt the end user to select a command and provide the necessary arguments. They should consist of a main loop which continuously prompts the user for a command, interprets the command, and calls the appropriate methods. You should include commands that:

   a) Allow the end user to find out what commands are available.

   b) Terminate the application gracefully.

4. Write a class called Distance that maintains two attributes that represent the distance in miles and kilometers. Provide suitable get, set, and toString methods. Write an appropriate driver application to test this class:
   [1 mile = 1.609 Km]

5. Write a class called Rectangle that maintains two attributes to represent the length and breadth of a rectangle. Provide suitable get, set, and toString methods plus two methods that return the perimeter and area of the rectangle. Write an appropriate driver application to test this class.

6. Write a class called Journey that maintains statistics about a journey undertaken by a car. At the beginning of a journey, a car's odometer reads S kilometers and the fuel tank is full. After the journey, the reading is F kilometers and it takes L liters to fill the tank. The Journey class should maintain the above data and provide a method that returns the fuel consumption in liters per 100 km. Declare the class with appropriate methods; use more meaningful attribute names than S, F, and L. Write an appropriate driver application to test this class.

7. In the last three exercises, we assume the values provided by the end user will all be non-negative. Alter the class set methods to ensure valid values have been provided; they should return a boolean result: TRUE if valid, FALSE if otherwise. Update your driver applications to check this result and take appropriate action.

CHAPTER 8

More on the Simple Class

8.1   Constructor Methods

You will recall from earlier chapters how we can declare and initialize objects in our programs. Continuing our use of the `Person` class, we begin by declaring a variable of type `Person`:

```
Person aPerson;
```

We can then use a class *constructor method* to set up the actual `Person` instance. In essence, the `aPerson` declared above is a reference to an instance we have yet to create. When we provide a class, if we do not provide a constructor method, Java provides a default one. However, we can provide as many constructor methods as required. The simplest kind of constructor method is one that takes no parameters (the default constructor provided by Java has this form). So, for example, in our class definition we can have:

```
public Person()
   {
   // do nothing
   }
```

This is pretty much what Java's default constructor would look like, but we will see in a moment how we can usefully extend the functionality of our own constructor. To use the constructor, we write the following statement:

```
Person aPerson = new Person();
```

Notice that the name of the constructor method is always the name of the class. We do not need to specify the type of a return value. All this does is set up the space for the actual object's attributes or instance variables. So in this case we have a new instance, as shown in Figure 8-1.

There is something important to note about declaring any kind of variable in this way, be it a simple basic type (like `int`) or an object type (like `Person`). We have simply allocated the space for the object, we have said nothing about what value might currently occupy that space. This is an example of an *uninitialized* variable.

Why might this cause problems? Well, for example, an integer variable might be intended to contain the current heading (in degrees) of a rocket. Let's declare it as follows:

```
int heading;
```

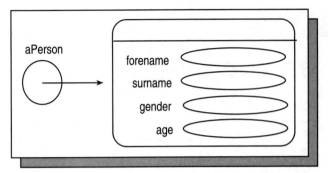

Figure 8-1: A new instance.

Let's assume 0 degrees is to the left, 90 up, 180 to the right, and 270 down (see Figure 8-2).

Figure 8-2: Points of the compass.

Now, we need to update that heading due to new information. Let's say we assume the rocket is heading straight up (90 degrees) and we want it to shift 10 degrees to the right. The `change` variable contains the value 10.

```
heading = heading + change;
```

What can we say about the new value of `heading`? Before the assignment, `heading` will contain some integer value, but it may not be 90. It could be, say, 260. Adding 10 to this and then interpreting it as the direction we should be heading in gives us 270 degrees, straight down.

It is important to note that the Java language system initializes attributes (but not local variables) on our behalf if we forget to do so. The default values are listed in Table 8-1.

boolean	char	byte	short	int	long	float	double
false	\u0000	0	0	0	0	0.0	0.0

Table 8-1: Default values.

However, it may be that we have more sensible initial values. For example, our enumerated integer attribute, gender, would be initialized to 0 (zero). However, this value has no meaning. We should always initialize an integer attribute that is modeling gender to UNKNOWN.

Equally important, when you move on to other programming languages, you have no guarantee that they will behave like Java. They may or may not initialize variables for you, so we believe it is important that you get into the habit of initializing your own variables sensibly and not be lazy and leave it to the system.

Constructor methods give us a powerful mechanism for avoiding the uninitialized attribute problem. We, the class providers, can ensure that sensible initial values are given to the attribute when the class user chooses not to allocate them themselves. So, we can extend our declaration of the constructor method as follows:

```
public Person()
    {
    forename = "NONE" ;
    surname = "NONE" ;
    age = 0 ;
    gender = UNKNOWN ;
    }
```

Now, when a user calls this particular method, we create the instance shown in Figure 8-3.

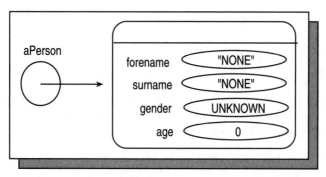

Figure 8-3: An instance with default values.

In our method, we have tried to ensure that sensible, interpretable values have been given to the attributes of the object rather than truly unknown and unpredictable values.

Now that the class user has created the object, he or she can use the other methods provided to manipulate the contents of the object. So, if the class user now wants to represent a person called James Kirk, we can issue the following instructions:

```
aPerson.setForename("James");
aPerson.setSurname("Kirk");
aPerson.setAge(34);
aPerson.setGender(Person.MALE);
```

This would now give us an object like that shown in Figure 8-4.

Figure 8-4: An initialized instance.

However, it may be that the class user knows these details when he or she creates the object, and would like to set these values at the same time. We can do this by having a constructor method with parameters. For example:

```
public Person(String f, String s, int a, int g)
    {
    forename = f ;
    surname = s ;
    age = a ;
    gender = g ;
    }
```

Here, the class provider has included a method, also called Person, but this time with four parameters. The formal parameters f, s, a, and g are intended to represent the forename, surname, age, and gender of the person. Now we can say:

```
Person bPerson = new Person ("James", "Kirk", 34, Person.MALE);
```

The result of this is identical to Figure 8-4.

8.2   Overloading

It is important to note that we haven't replaced the original, parameterless constructor; instead we have added a new one with four parameters. Both these methods have exactly the same name (Person). How can this be? Won't the compiler and language system complain that we have used the same name twice? Try declaring two attributes or two local variables with the same name and see what happens!

The situation with methods is somewhat different. A method can be said to have a *signature*. The signature of a method is the number, type, and ordering of its formal parameters. Let's take a couple of examples in Table 8-2.

method name	formal parameters
getForename	none
setForename	String
getAge	none
setAge	int

Table 8-2: Examples of signatures.

Now, let's look at our `Person` constructors in Table 8-3.

method name	formal parameters
Person	none
Person	String, String, int, int

Table 8-3: Signatures for the Person constructors.

In order for us to have a true "name clash," the signatures of two methods must match in every respect. Here, we can see that the two methods have the same name; however, they differ in their list of formal parameters. This means there is enough distinction between the two methods that the compiler and the language system can treat them as being, indeed, two different methods.

As far as the compiler is concerned, when it processes our `Person` class definition, these two constructor definitions offer no problem whatsoever:

```
public Person( ) // constructor one
    {
    forename = "NONE" ;
    surname = "NONE" ;
    age = 0 ;
    gender = UNKNOWN ;
    }

public Person(String f, String s, int a, int g)     // constructor two
    {
    forename = f ;
    surname = s ;
    age = a ;
    gender = g ;
    }
```

What happens for the class user, though?

```
Person aPerson, bPerson;
aPerson = new Person();
bPerson = new Person("James" , "Kirk", 34, Person.MALE);
```

How does the compiler know which version of the constructor to call for aPerson and bPerson? Again, it turns to the signature information. When we call a constructor for aPerson, it can see that it has no actual parameters. This matches the signature for the first constructor, and that is the one we shall call.

For bPerson, we can see the constructor call has four actual parameters, and the types are in the order (String, String, int, int). This matches the signature for the second constructor.

This concept of having methods with the same name but different signatures is generally available for all types of methods.

For example, we could have two methods called increaseAge. Their signatures and behaviors are given in Table 8-4.

method name	formal parameters	behavior
increaseAge	int	adds the value of the parameter to the age attribute
increaseAge	none	adds 1 to the age attribute

Table 8-4: Signatures and behaviors for increaseAge.

The new variant of increaseAge is shown here:

```
public void increaseAge()
    {
    age = age+1;
    }
```

We can call the two versions as follows:

```
aPerson.increaseAge(10);    // adds 10 to the age of aPerson
aPerson.increaseAge();      // adds 1 to the age of aPerson
```

The general term for this mechanism is *overloading*. It is called this because we are using the same name but in different circumstances, and thence we are overloading the name.

8.3   Class Constants

As we have already seen, it is often desirable to have some named *constant* values that we can use (either as a class provider or a class user) when dealing with an object. In our Person example, we want to model a person's gender in a more meaningful, semantic way. Although in Java we can use an integer to store a person's gender, we don't want to use simple integer values (1, 2,

99) to represent the gender. Such values are completely meaningless. The use of constants gives us a simple mechanism for naming these values sensibly, in a way that someone reading our code can understand. Thence, in our `Person` class, we declare the following constants:

```
// Person class constants
```

```
public static final int UNKNOWN = 99 ;
public static final int MALE = 1 ;
public static final int FEMALE = 2 ;
```

Thereafter, whenever we wish to reference someone's gender, we can use the terms `UNKNOWN`, `MALE`, and `FEMALE` rather than 1, 2, or 99.

We can, of course, use other kinds of constants. For example, a class that calculates the price of consumer goods needs to include information on VAT (value-added tax). VAT is a rate that is subject to change only at budget times, so here again it is useful to model this as a constant between budgets. For this example, we will assume VAT is set at 10 percent:

```
public static final double VAT_RATE = 10.0;
```

What this means is that throughout the class and the program that uses it, we can refer to `VAT_RATE` rather than its actual value. Why is this useful?

Imagine the situation where you have used the VAT rate extensively throughout your program. The budget is announced and the rate has changed. Now you must search through your program and change the rate wherever it occurs. Moreover, you have to be sure that the value as it occurs in any instruction is actually the VAT rate and not "just" the actual value (here, 10.0).

If you have used a class constant, however, no such difficulties arise. You have only to change the constant definition and recompile your program. We have already encountered a class constant in the `Person` class, namely `UPPER_AGE`, which was declared as private.

To declare a class constant, the general form is:

```
static final <type> <constant name> = <value>;
```

The keyword `static` indicates that this constant belongs to the class rather than every individual instance. For example (as shown in Figure 8-5):

```
public class Car
  {

  private String carName;
  public int mileage;

  public static final int TOP_SPEED = 150;

  // methods
  } // end of class "Car"
```

As we said in the previous chapter, we represent constants by using all capital letters and use the underscore character as a visible space between words.

Figure 8-5: Car class and instances.

The static keyword also means that we can access the value of TOP_SPEED without declaring any instances of the class:

```
System.out.println("The top speed is " + Car.TOP_SPEED);
```

We access the value via the class name, not an instance.

The keyword `final` means this constant is the final value this "variable" can have. It also happens to be its first as well!

One benefit of Java's approach is that a constant is strongly typed; in our example, TOP_SPEED is an integer-shaped box and can be used everywhere an ordinary integer can be used (except, of course, on the left-hand side of an assignment statement).

In Java 1.1., we can initially declare constants without a value, as follows :

```
static final int NUMBER_OF_WHEELS;
```

Before we can use this constant, however, we must unambiguously assign it a value.

Constants must be declared at class level; you cannot have constant declarations within a method body.

8.4   Class Variables

Just as we can have class constants, it is possible to declare class *variables*. For example, we may wish to keep a count of how many Car objects have been made. It seems natural to keep this count with the Car class. This would be declared and initialized as follows, in the body of the class (see Figure 8-6):

```
public static int carCount = 0;
```

Figure 8-6: The Car class with constant and variable and two instances.

Now, our constructor method(s) must remember to increment this count every time they are called:

```
public Car()
    {
    // initialise instance variables to appropriate values
    carCount++;
    }
```

To find out how many Car instances have been created at any time, we can write the following:

```
System.out.println("Number of cars is " + Car.carCount);
```

8.5   Private Methods

The methods we have seen so far have all been declared as public. This means they can be accessed and used by any class user. However, it is also possible to declare methods as private. This means they are hidden from the class user. Of what possible use can private methods be?

Private methods are unavailable (directly) to the class user; however, the class provider may use them to support the public methods. What do we mean by this? Well, for example, whenever we set the age attribute of a person, it is possible (as we have seen) and useful to ensure that we only set that attribute to a sensible value. Thence we have the setAge method as follows:

```
public void setAge(int a)
   {
   if ((a < 0) || (a > UPPER_AGE))
      {
      System.out.println("bad age in 'setAge'") ;
      System.exit(1) ;
      }
   else
      age = a ;
   } // end of method setAge
```

However, we can set the age of a person in more than one method; for example, we can set it in one or more of our constructor methods. If we want to make sure the age is valid, we would have to repeat the preceding if statement everywhere we set the age. One possibility is to encapsulate the testing code in a private method:

```
private boolean validAge(int a)
   {
   return ((a >= 0) && (a <= UPPER_AGE));
   }
```

Now we can rewrite the setAge method as follows:

```
public void setAge(int a)
   {
   if (! validAge(a))
      {
      System.out.println("bad age in 'setAge'") ;
      System.exit(1) ;
      }
   else
      age = a ;
   } // end of method setAge
```

And we can revise the second constructor method:

```
public Person(String f, String s, int a, int g)
   {
   forename = f ;
   surname = s ;
   if (validAge(a))
      age = a ;
   else
      age = AGE_UNKNOWN;
   gender = g ;
   }
```

Here we are simply setting a default value (which we would need to declare) to the incorrectly valued age.

In our next example, we model temperature as a class. This class has two private instance variables, celsius and fahr, to hold the temperature in Celsius and Fahrenheit, respectively. We have the normal get and set methods associated with these variables. However, we have decided that these two variables should be kept in step. That is to say, whatever the temperature in celsius is, the fahr variable will contain the matching value in Fahrenheit and vice versa.

In order to achieve this, we have provided two private methods to take care of the conversion: celsiusToFahr and fahrToCelsius:

```
public class Temperature
    {
    private double celsius, fahr;

    //    Temperature Constructor

    public Temperature ()
        {
        setCelsius(0.0);
        celsiusToFahr();
        }

    // selector methods for Temperature instance fields

    public double getCelsius() { return celsius ; }

    public double getFahr() { return fahr ; }

    private void celsiusToFahr()
        {
        fahr = (double) (1.8 * celsius + 32);
        }

    public void setCelsius(double c)
        {
        celsius = c;
        celsiusToFahr();
        }

    private void fahrToCelsius()
        {
        celsius = (double) (5.0 * (fahr - 32.0) / 9.0);
        }

    public void setFahr(double f)
        {
        fahr = f ;
        fahrToCelsius();
        }

    } // end of class Temperature
```

Notice that when we call setCelsius, we not only set the value of celsius, but we also use the celsiusToFahr method to convert the value into Fahrenheit and to set the value of fahr. We do the same within setFahr.

If you are familiar with spreadsheets, you can think of celsius and fahr as two cells in the sheet. They are linked with each other through the formulae contained in the two private conversion methods. Whenever a user directly updates one of these cells, the other is also updated according to the formula. The same thing is happening here.

Both the conversion formulae and the methods that use them are hidden from the class user. In our main program, if we want to convert one temperature scale to the other, all we have to do is set one and then get the other:

```
public static void main(String [] args)
   {
   Temperature aTemp = new Temperature();

   aTemp.setFahr(104.3);
   System.out.print("Celsius = " + aTemp.getCelsius() +
           " Fahr = " + aTemp.getFahr());
   System.out.println();
   } // end of main
```

So this, then, is the usage of private methods: to support the functionality of the public ones. In some cases, it may be arguable whether a method should be private rather than public. But initially, this is essentially a design decision and one that may change once the class is in general use.

Often when we write the main class that drives an application, within that class, as well as within the main method, we will need "helper" methods. These methods are acting as private methods that assist the main method. We will see examples of them later in the book.

8.6   Class or Static Methods

It is possible to declare methods as static; just as with constants, this means they belong to the class rather than to an instance. For example, if the Car class TOP_SPEED static constant had been declared as private, we would be unable to access it directly. We would need a get method. As TOP_SPEED belongs to the class, however, the getTopSpeed method should also belong to the class rather than to instances of that class:

```
public class Car
   {
   private String carName;
   public int mileage;

   private static final int TOP_SPEED = 150;
```

```
public static int getTopSpeed()
  {
  return TOP_SPEED;
  }

// other methods
} // end of Car class
```
So we can write:

```
System.out.println("top speed is " + Car.getTopSpeed());
```

The Person class provides similar functionality with the static method getUpperAgeLimit.

If we examine some of the Java system-supplied classes, we can find some static (or class) methods. For example, java.lang.Math is a class that is never intended to have any instances. Instead, it gathers together some constants and methods that can be used, in general, in association with ints, doubles, longs, and floats as parameters and/or return values. For example, a method that takes two ints as parameters and returns the smaller of the two can be called as follows:

```
int smaller = Math.min(x, y);
```

The java.lang.Integer wrapper class (see section 6.9, "Wrapper Classes") provides a toString method. This method takes an int value and converts it into a String. We can call this as follows:

```
int x = 21;
...
String xStr = Integer.toString(x);
```

This is an example of a method where it is not clear where else this method could be placed. There is no int class, as int is a primitive type. It belongs to Integer, but it does not operate on instances of Integers; it operates on ints.

It is often difficult to decide whether a method should be implemented as an ordinary instance method or as a class method. We shall see an example later in this chapter.

8.7   Revisiting the Main Class

It is time to again consider the main class of any Java application. While we can envisage our object instances as floating within an object space and exchanging messages as requests to other objects to execute methods on our behalf, there is clearly the need for some initial event to set the ball rolling. In Java, that event is the main class. It is here that initial objects can be created and requests made of them.

The main class is the class that is specified when we run the Java interpreter, which on most systems is called simply java. To execute a class (say User.class) we type the following:

```
java User
```

In order for our application to execute, the named class *must* contain a class method called main. This can be declared as follows:

```
public static void main(String[] args)
```

On some systems, it may be possible to omit the formal parameter:

```
public static void main()
```

The args parameter allows us to provide run-time arguments when we execute the Java interpreter. (By the way, the actual name of the String array is arbitrary; we do not need to use the name args, but it is one that is often used by convention). As a simple example of this, consider a Java application that prints out the run-time arguments, each on its own line:

```
public class Arguments
    {

    public static void main(String[] args)
      {
      for (int i = 0; i < args.length; i++)
          System.out.println(args[i]);
      }

    } // end of class Arguments
```

The parameter to the main method in our example is String[] args. This is an array of String objects. We will study arrays in more detail in Chapter 9. For the moment, suffice it to say that we can access each individual String in this array by using an index. In the for loop in the body of the main method, the variable i will index each individual element and allow us to treat each one like a single String (for example, we can print it out).

Further, the attribute length of the array lets us find out how many elements are present in args. This will, of course, be the number of run-time arguments we provide when we execute the application.

To execute the application, we type:

```
java Arguments one two three
```

and the results are:

```
one
two
three
```

Returning to our Temperature class; we can write an application that takes temperatures in Celsius from the command line and prints out the equivalent temperature in Fahrenheit:

```
class Temperature
    {
    private double celsius, fahr;
```

```
// as before plus a new method ..

public String toString()
{
   return celsius + " degrees celsius " +
      fahr + " degrees Fahrenheit";
}


} // end of Temperature
```

We have added a new toString method. This produces a String that contains the temperature in Celsius and Fahrenheit with some explanatory text:

```
public class Chapter8n1
   {

   public static void main(String[] args)
      {
      String strCel;
      Double convert = new Double(0.0);
      double cel;
      boolean valid;
      Temperature temperature = new Temperature();

      for (int i = 0; i < args.length; i++)
         {
         valid = true;
         strCel = args[i];

         try {
            convert = Double.valueOf(strCel);
            }
         catch (NumberFormatException e)
            {
System.out.println("parameter provided [" + strCel + "] not in double format");
            valid = false;
            }

         if (valid)
            {
            cel = convert.doubleValue();
            temperature.setCelsius(cel);
            System.out.println(temperature);
            }
         }
      }
   } // end of class Chapter8n1
```

If we type:

```
java Chapter8n1 12.1 gur 34.1
```

the results are:

```
12.1 degrees celsius 53.78 degrees Fahrenheit
parameter provided [gur] not in double format
34.1 degrees celsius 93.38 degrees Fahrenheit
```

Notice that when we call `System.out.println(temperature)`, it in turn calls `toString` in order to obtain a printable text version of the temperature object. This is why we provided a `toString` method, so that we could use `println` in this way.

The command line could also include *flags*. Following the conventions of the UNIX operating system, we could have a flag `-c` that specifies that the temperature is to be considered in celsius and a flag `-f` for Fahrenheit:

```
public class Chapter8n2
    {

    public static void main(String[] args)
        {
        String flag, strCel;
        Double myDouble= new Double(0.0);
        double temp;
        boolean valid = true;
        Temperature temperature = new Temperature();
        char flagChar;

        // have we got two arguments?
        if (args.length != 2)
            {
System.out.println("incorrect number of arguments : 2 expected");
            System.exit(1);
            }

        // does the first argument look like a flag?
        flag = args[0];
        if (flag.charAt(0) != '-')
            {
            System.out.println("first argument not a flag");
            System.exit(1);
            }

        // ok it's a flag but is it valid?
        flagChar = flag.charAt(1);
```

```
        switch (flagChar)
          {
          case 'f' :
          case 'c' :
            break;
          default :
   System.out.println("unknown flag [" + flagChar + "] used");
            System.exit(1);
          }

        strCel = args[1];
        try  {
          myDouble = Double.valueOf(strCel);
          }
        catch (NumberFormatException e)
          {
          System.out.println("parameter provided [" +
            strCel + "] not in double format");
          valid = false;
          }

        if (valid)
          {
          temp = myDouble.doubleValue();
          switch (flagChar)
            {
            case 'f' :
              temperature.setFahr(temp);
              break;
            case 'c' :
              temperature.setCelsius(temp);
            }
          System.out.println(temperature);
          }
        }// end of main method

    } // end of class Chapter8n2
```

If we type:

```
java Chapter8n2 -f 93.38
```

the result is:

```
34.1 degrees celsius 93.38 degrees Fahrenheit
```

If we type:

```
java Chapter8n2 -c 12.1
```

the result is:

```
12.1 degrees celsius 53.78 degrees Fahrenheit
```

The class that contains the `main` method is not intended to have any instances. It is the "main program" of our application. Hence, the `main` method is declared as `static`, as a class method. Clearly, the Java interpreter sets out by executing the `main` method of the named class; in our example, `Chapter8n2.main`.

The `main` method is thus no different than other class methods; they are methods that can be executed whether or not instances of the class exist.

Just as the normal classes can, the main class can contain class variables and declarations of methods. The methods can only be called in the `main` method of the main class and can manipulate the class variables of the main class. The relationship between the `main` method and private methods within the same class is very close to the relationship between the main program and the first-level subprograms in the traditional world.

In our approach to the `main` method and the main class, we have tried not to deviate too far from the traditional world. However, we stress this has been only an approach (and attempt to simplify the treatment) and not a requirement in Java. Any concrete classes can provide a main method; this means we can run such individual classes without the need for driver applications. This can be a very useful debugging technique.

8.8   Packages & Directories

In this section, we review the use of *packages* in the Java programming environment. Classes can be grouped together into packages. They are related very closely to the underlying file and directory structure of the operating system supporting the Java programming environment, which we reviewed in section 1.6, "Files & the Filing System."

The source text for a Java class is contained in a file. It is possible to have more than one Java class source in a single file, but if so, only one of the classes can be declared as public. It is perhaps more usual to have a single class source in a single file. Whatever the situation, the single public class must have the same name as the file. The file, however, additionally has the extension `.java`.

Therefore, the `Temperature` class should be contained in a file called `Temperature.java`. When the source is compiled successfully, the Java bytecode is contained in a single `.class` file. The results of compiling a valid Temperature class will be contained in `Temperature.class`. Where a source file contains more than one class definition, there will be multiple `.class` files, one for each class defined.

Suppose now that John wishes to collect together the classes he has developed into a package called `johnsClasses`. He can do this by creating a directory called `johnsClasses` in his `john` directory and placing there the compiled Java bytecode for the classes in question. For the sake of example, assume that John has written the `Temperature` class and wishes it to be part of the `johnsClasses` package. The file `Temperature.class` must be stored in the directory `johnsClasses`. One way to do this is to put the file `Temperature.java` in the `johnsClasses` directory, go to this directory, and then compile the file with the `javac` command.

In addition to doing this, he would have to edit the source file so that the first line of text in the file reads:

```
package johnsClasses;
```

This tells the compiler the name of the package that the class belongs to. Note also that the declaration of the class `Temperature` has to be public:

```
public class Temperature
```

Now suppose that John has, in the directory `john`, a file called `Tdrive.java` containing Java source code that uses the class `Temperature`. In order for the compiler to find the `Temperature` class, we add the following `import` directive at the beginning of `Tdrive.java`:

```
import johnsClasses.* ;
```

This tells the compiler that this code will need to access one or more classes to be found in the `johnsClasses` directory. The situation is shown in Figure 8-7.

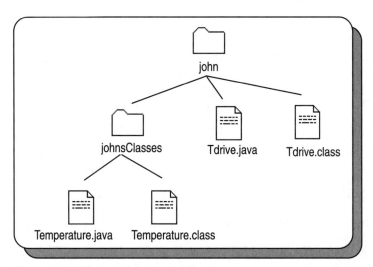

Figure 8-7: John's directories and files.

The Java system knows that the bytecode for the `Temperature` class is in a file called `Temperature.class` and (since this class is in the package `johnsClasses`) that this file will be in a directory called `johnsClasses`. How does it know where this directory is?

The operating systems under which Java can be used have a number of environment variables, which can be set by the user or contained in files that are executed when the user logs in. By setting the environment variable `CLASSPATH` to the path name of the directory containing our package, we can allow the Java interpreter to find our user classes.

For example, in UNIX we would execute the command:

```
setenv CLASSPATH .:/usr/local/classes
```

This tells the Java system to look for any classes it needs in the current directory (called .) or in the directory /usr/local/classes. So the Java system looks in the current directory john, where it finds the directory johnsClasses, which it is looking for.

What if we wish to share the classes written by our colleagues? For example, John wishes to use Roger's Car class, which is in a package called rogersClasses, in order to write a simple program Tcuser.java that uses both cars and temperatures. The situation looks like Figure 8-8.

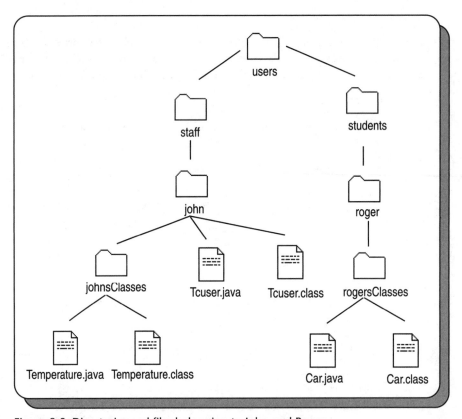

Figure 8-8: Directories and files belonging to John and Roger.

Since the class he wants is in the rogerClasses package, John adds the following import line to his Tcuser.java source file:

```
import rogersClasses.* ;
```

Now the Java system will be expecting to find a directory called rogersClasses containing a file Car.class, and the CLASSPATH environment variable tells it that the rogersClasses directory should be either in the current directory john or in /usr/local/classes. Since the file is in neither directory, we need to modify the CLASSPATH variable. How we would do this depends on what operating system we are using; for example, in UNIX we would use the `setenv` (set environment variable) command:

```
setenv CLASSPATH .:/usr/local/classes:/users/students/roger
```

This tells the Java system that a further place to look for the `rogersClasses` directory is in `/users/students/roger`, and this time the search will be successful.

If a class does not contain a package statement, then it is part of an unnamed default package, which is usually the directory the class was compiled in. This is useful for small text programs or development and is probably the situation you will be in.

The Java API (application programming interface) provides a set of standard classes, grouped together in 22 packages. The ones we discuss in this book are listed in Table 8-5.

Package Name	Contents
java.applet	Classes for implementing applets (see Chapter 20)
java.awt	Classes for graphics, text, windows, and GUIs (see Chapter 16)
java.awt.event*	Classes for GUI button, mouse actions, etc. (see Chapter 16)
java.io	Classes for input and output (see Chapter 19)
java.lang	Classes for the core language
java.net	Classes for networking (see Chapters 19 and 20)
java.util	Classes for useful data types (see Chapter 21)

Table 8-5: The Java API.

Your Java environment is usually set up to ensure that these packages are visible to the Java system when needed by having their (known) location included in your CLASSPATH environment variable.

8.8.1 *The import Statement*

It is worth noting that the `import` statement does not actually import code from other places; it simply tells the compiler where the other code can be found (in conjunction with the CLASSPATH environment variable and the underlying file system).

You can have as many `import` statements as you like; they must appear before any class definitions and after the optional *package* statement at the start of the file.

We examine two forms of the statement:

   a) import package.class;

   b) import package.*;

---

* This package is new in Java version 1.1.

Form (a) allows the class in the package to be referred to by its class name only.

```
import java.util.Hashtable;
```

lets us use `Hashtable` instead of `java.util.Hashtable`.

The second form (b) means that *all* classes within a package are accessible by class name only. For example, if `johnsClasses` contained `Car.class` and `Temperature.class`, then to refer to these classes by name only we need:

```
import johnsClasses.*;
```

It should be noted that where a "." (dot) seperator appears, this is like a "/" (slash) seperator in a UNIX file name, denoting a subdirectory. Any classes contained in a subdirectory to an imported directory (such as `johnsClasses`) will not be imported. We can see an example of this in the Java API itself.

```
import java.awt.*;   //does not import classes in
                     // java.awt.event so another
                     //import is needed:
import java.awt.event.*;
```

8.9   Scope & Visibility

In this section, we consider the visibility and accessibility of attributes, variables, and methods. We have already discussed issues of hidden attributes and methods; here we give a general treatment to the various circumstances and properties of "hiding" things.

We begin by considering a class that contains some attributes and methods. We first consider only availability of attributes and methods within the class (*intraclass*). We will turn to *interclass* (availability among classes) later in this section. Within the class, all attributes and methods are visible to everything else, even if they have been specified as "private"; the private specification only holds for interclass visibility.

8.9.1   *Intraclass Visibility*

The range over which something is visible is called its *scope*. So for example, in the `Temperature` class, the attributes `celsius` and `fahr` have the entire class as their scope. Any method within the class can access and use these attributes. The same holds for the methods; any method within `Temperature` can call any of the others.

Moreover, in Java, the textual organization of attributes and methods does not affect their visibility. In some programming languages, things have to be declared before they are used (i.e., earlier in the file); in essence, their scope ranges from their point of declaration to the end of the programming unit. This is not so in Java; items declared at the end of a class still have the entire class as their scope.

On a software engineering note, this is not necessarily a good thing. An important aide to understandability and readability (and thence to reuse and maintenance) is that items within a programming unit are organized in a sensible manner. It would probably help us understand a class more easily if the attributes are at the start of the class rather than the end of it, even though Java does not require this. Just because we can get away with something does not mean we should do it! This is a situation where good programming practice is not enforced by the language syntax.

So far we have dealt with attributes (instance variables) and methods. However, methods themselves contain declarations of formal parameters and of local variables. Local variables are so called because they are local to the body of the method. Unlike attributes within a class, which can be accessed anywhere within the class, local variables exist only within the method body. Their *scope* is limited to the method in which they are declared.

For example, consider the following piece of code:

```
public class Chapter8n3a
   {

   void method1()
      {
      int year;
      // code
      }

   void method2()
      {
      int y = year+ 1;
      // code
      }

   } // end of class Chapter8n3a
```

Here we assume there are no attributes called year in the class that contains these two methods.

When we try to access year (which is the local variable belonging to method1) in method2, we will get a compile-time error. This is because year does not exist as far as method2 is concerned. The scope of year is only within method1.

What happens if we use the same name for a local variable as we do for an attribute? Consider the following code:

```
public class Chapter8n3b
   {

   int year = 1;// attribute

   void method1()
      {
      int year;
      year = 4;
```

```
    System.out.println("method1 year = " + year);
    }

void method2()
    {
    method1();
    System.out.println("method2 year = " + year);
    }
} // end of class Chapter8n3b
```

If we call method2, this would print out the following:

```
method1 year = 4
method2 year = 1
```

This is because the year referred to within method1 is the local variable declared within the method. When control returns to method2, the year referred to is the instance variable. It is the local variable that has its value set to 4; the instance variable is unaffected.

What we say is happening here is that there is a *hole* in the scope of the year instance variable. This hole is exactly the same size as the scope of the year local variable. This is obviously something that we must be wary of. In Table 8-6, we see the scope of the instance variable year, and how a hole can be made in the scope by a local variable of the same name.

Scope of Year Attribute	Value	Scope of Year Local Variable	Value	Code
•	1			int year = 1;
•	1			
		•		void method1()
		•		{
		•	0	int year;
		•	4	year = 4;
		•	4	System.out.println("method1 year = " + year);
		•		}
•	1			
•	1			void method2()
•	1			{
•	1			method1();
•	1			System.out.println("method2 year = " + year);
•	1			}

Table 8-6: The scope of the year attribute and the year local variable.

Another way to punch a hole into the scope of an instance variable is to have a formal parameter with the same name:

```
class OurDate
  {
  int day, month, year;

  void incrementYear(int year)
    {
    year = year + 1;
    }
  } // end of class OurDate
```

The year that is incremented will be the formal parameter year, not the instance variable year. Notice that the actual parameter will remain unaltered. Sometimes, however, you might have a valid reason for using the same names:

```
void setYear (int year)
  {
  year = year;
  }
```

Whatever this strange-looking method does, it does not do what we expect or want it to do. We want this method to take the values of the formal parameter and pass it into the corresponding attribute. One option is to change the name of the formal parameter:

```
void setYear (int y)
  {
  year = y;
  }
```

A further option is to distinguish between the names—to specify that on the left-hand side of the assignment we mean the attributes belonging to the instance of the class rather than the formal parameters appearing on the right-hand side of the assignment. We can use the . (dot) notation to do this. We have already seen how we can specify a (public) constant within a class as follows:

```
System.out.println("top speed is " + Car.TOP_SPEED);
```

We can do the same to access a public instance variable, as follows:

```
System.out.println("current mileage is " + aCar.mileage);
```

We could place the name of the instance on the left-hand side, followed by a dot, followed by the attribute name. The problem here is that, as class providers, we cannot possibly know the name of the instance! Only the class users will know this at some point in the future.

8.9.2   Use of this

Java provides a keyword, `this`, which stands for the current instance of the class that is calling this method. This means that class providers can write the following:

```
void setYear (int year)
   {
   this.year = year;
   }
```

so that, when as class users we have the following code:

```
christmas.setYear(97);
```

everywhere we have `this` appearing in `setYear`, it is as if we had `christmas`. We can think of `this` as a kind of implicit parameter to the methods.

8.9.3   Interclass Visibility

There are four levels of access permission; here we list them from least to most restrictive: `public`, `protected`, default (package visibility), and `private`.

The `protected` permission relates to subclasses, so we delay discussion of this access level until Chapter 12.

A class either has the access modifier `public` or none (which specifies the default level). When we apply the `public` modifier to a class, it means it is visible everywhere. The default package visibility means the class is visible only to other classes in the same package.

A method or constant or attribute can be `public`, `default`, or `private`. When they are public, they are visible everywhere. If they are default, they are visible within their own class and to other classes in the same package. If they are private, they can be accessed only within their own class.

Normally, classes and constants are public, attributes are private, and methods are either public or private. This is because classes are usually intended as "building blocks" for an application and wouldn't be of much use if they were private. Constants are usually public because they are intended for use by class and/or instance users; for example, a class that contains useful mathematical constants would normally make them publicly available. Attributes, as they represent the state of an object, are normally subject to information hiding and are thus private. Finally, methods that are public are provided to allow the class user to manipulate instances of the class, with private methods being used to support the implementation of the public methods.

8.10   Key Points in Chapter 8

- *Constructors* allocate sufficient space for an object instance. It is often useful to make the constructor sensibly initialize the attributes of the instance.

■ It is possible to have multiple versions of any method (including constructors) as long as their signatures differ. This is called *overloading*.

■ Elements in a class definition can belong to the class rather than to instances of the class. This is denoted by the keyword `static`. We can use static elements even if no instances of the class exist. The `static` keyword is useful for the following:

   ■ Defining constants applicable to all instances (for example, `MALE`, `FEMALE`, etc.).

   ■ Maintaining data about the collection of instances rather than individual instances (for example, `carCount`).

   ■ Collecting together methods where there is no associated object (for example, a maths library).

■ `Private` methods are accessible only to the class provider. They are usually used to support the functionality of other (private or public) methods within the class.

■ The *main* method is a class method that is the first one (in an application) executed by the Java interpreter.

■ *Packages* are constructs that allow us to group classes together. Classes are kept in individual files; files are kept in directories, and we can treat directories as a package.

■ To tell the system which package (if any) a class belongs to, we use the `package statement`.

■ To use the classes contained in packages, we use the `import statement`.

■ The concept of *scope* relates to the visibility of attributes, variables, and methods. Within a class, scope is closely related to the idea of *global* and *local* variables. For example, a variable declared anywhere in a class definition, except within a method, is said to be *global* to that class. It can be referred to in any statement, anywhere in the class. If a variable is declared within a method (as a variable or formal parameter), it is *local* to that method. We can refer to it only within the method body.

■ However, holes in scope can arise due to:

   ■ Local variables in method bodies

   ■ Formal parameters to methods

■ For class users, scope is defined by the four levels of access permission. At this point in our study of Java, these collapse onto the three levels shown in Table 8-7.

private	visible only within own class
(default)	visible within own class and other classes in the same package
public	visible everywhere

Table 8-7 : Access permissions.

8.11   Exercises

1. Provide a class `MonthManager` that provides the following facilities:

   a) Static constants `JAN`, `FEB`, ... `DEC`, starting from 1.

   b) Static conversion methods that take the following styles of month names:

   `"JAN"`, `"Jan"`, `"January"`

   and return the appropriate constant.

   c) A static conversion method that takes a constant and returns a string containing the full name of the month.

      Provide a driver application to test your class.

2. Develop your `Rectangle` class from Chapter 7 to include:

   a) A parameterless constructor that nevertheless initializes the length and breadth attributes to zero.

   b) A constructor that takes two parameters to initialize the length and breadth of the rectangle.

3. We need to represent the manufacturer of a car as a constant. The manufacturers we are concerned with include BIGNOLI, NAVARRO, BENFORD, and PRINZ.

      Develop the `Car` class so that it includes:

   a) Constants to represent the four manufacturers

   b) An attribute that stores the manufacturer of the car

      We also wish to represent the particular model of a car; the models we are concerned with are shown in Table 8-8.

      We need a method that will convert a car manufacturer constant and the car model attribute into a string. For example, if the manufacturer is Bignoli and the model is Flash, then this method should return "Bignoli Flash". This method should be defined as private and called `toName`.

Manufacturer	Model	Engine Capacity
Benford	Hawkeye	999
Benford	Scarlet	1100
Bignoli	Flash	1200
Bignoli	Quicksilver	1250
Navarro	Angel	999
Navarro	Beast	1000
Prinz	Aqua	1150
Prinz	Supreme	1300

Table 8-8: Car data.

c) A `toString` method that returns the manufacturer, the model, and the engine capacity of the car. It should of course make use of the private method `toName`.

We also need method(s) that allow the end user to type in data about a particular car as text and to convert this information into the appropriate internal representation using the above car manufacturer constants.

d) `encodeManufacturer` should take the `String` version of the data and return the appropriate constant (if it is known).

- Provide suitable constructors to initialize the contents of a Car instance.
- Provide a suitable driver application to test your development of the Car class.

4. Continuing our work on the Car class, provide a method that allows us to compare two Car instances. It should return:

- −1 if the first Car is less powerful than the second
- 0 if they have the same engine capacity
- 1 if the first Car is more powerful than the second

5. In this exercise, we need to create two classes as follows:

a) A `Cooker` class, which defines an oven for cooking food.

b) A `Dish` class, which defines some food we wish to cook.

Each instance of these classes maintains the current temperature of itself.

When we place a `Dish` in the `Cooker`, we specify how long (in seconds) we want the `Dish` to be cooked. We assume that for every second the `Dish` remains in the oven, its temperature increases by (cooker temperature - dish temperature) / 10. Obviously, the dish can only ever become as hot as the cooker.

Specify and implement the necessary methods and attributes to support an application that allows the end-user to:

- Input the current temperature of a dish
- Input the current temperature of the oven
- Input how long the dish is to remain in the oven

The application responds by displaying the temperature of the dish when the time expires.

Notice that the current temperature of the `Dish` should be updated appropriately during (and after) its time in the `Cooker`.

6. a) Write a class `Videotape` to model the details of an individual recording of a TV program on a videotape. The attributes should be:

- classification—at least film, comedy, education, other
- title
- playing time

b) Write a driver program to allow the user to test your `Videotape` class.

CHAPTER 9

Arrays

9.1 Collections of Elements

So far, we have been dealing mostly with variables that refer to individual elements: a single integer, a single string of characters, a single instance of the Person class. If we needed more than one element of the same type, then we have simply declared several elements all of the same type, each with its own name.

But we often want to be able to refer to large numbers of elements all of the same type; a collection of integers to hold a number of salaries, let's say, or a collection of strings to hold a number of lines making up a page. We could of course declare a number of individual elements:

```
int firstSalary ;
int secondSalary ;
int thirdSalary ;
```

and so on.

However, this takes a lot of writing, and we have to make a decision at the time we write the program how many of these salary elements we are going to need. Furthermore, we would have difficulty processing these elements because we have to write a separate statement to process each element. What we need is some systematic way of naming the elements so that we can process them inside a loop, referring to successive elements in successive iterations of the loop.

Java provides a mechanism called an *array* to hold a collection of elements all of the same type. If, for example, we want to hold a collection of 10 integers, we declare:

```
int[] salaries = new int[10] ;
```

This creates a programming element called salaries. It is of type int[], which is pronounced "array of int"—the characters [] appended to a type indicate an array of that type. The reserved word new introduces a constructor for the array, and we need to specify how many elements there are going to be in the array—here there will be 10.

This array declaration is rather like the declaration of an object variable. What in fact happens is that the variable salaries contains a reference to an area of store containing a set of elements of the type specified. This is shown in Figure 9-1.

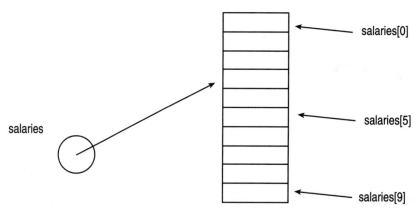

Figure 9-1: An array of ten `ints`.

We refer to an individual element of this array by writing the name of the array (here `sala-ries`) followed by the number of the element, the *index*, in square brackets. In Java, following the convention of C and C++, the numbering of the elements of an array starts at zero. So the first element of this array is `salaries[0]` and the last is `salaries[9]`; they are of type `int`, of course. It is important to remember that the index of the last element is one less that the number of elements we have declared.

If we have an `int` variable `i`, then we can refer to the `i`th element of the array with `salaries[i]`. As long as `i` takes one of the values in the range 0 to 9, the appropriate element of the array is accessed. If `i` has a value outside this range, then an attempt to access the array will cause the exception `ArrayIndexOutOfBoundsException` to be thrown.

So far, we have set up this array `salaries` so that it is capable of holding 10 integers, but we have not yet set them to any particular value. We could set them in a `for` loop:

```
for (int i = 0 ; i < salaries.length ; i++)
    salaries[i] = i * 10000 ;
```

We can find out the number of elements in the array `salaries` by writing `salaries.length`. Of course, in this case we could have written `i < 10`. But if we later decided that the length of the array should be, say, 20, we would then have to go through the program changing all the 10s that referred to the length of this array, and remembering not to change all the 10s that refer to something else. So it is better to use the `length` attribute of the array where we can. Notice that we do not put brackets after `length`; it is not a method like the `length()` method of the `String` class.

This is a typical loop for processing an array. We start with the index set to zero, and the last iteration is with the index set to one less than the length of the array.

There is an alternative way to initialize an array in Java, by using a *literal array expression*. The language allows us to write the initial values for an array as a sequence of expressions separated by commas and surrounded by curly brackets. So we could have declared and initialized the `salaries` array as follows:

```
int[] salaries = {0, 10000, 20000, 30000, 40000,
    50000, 60000, 70000, 80000, 90000} ;
```

The declaration is able to calculate how many array elements there should be (here 10, numbered from 0 up as before).

When we used the for loop to initialize the array, it was perhaps unusual to be able to calculate the value in the array from the index; why would we need to store all the values? A more typical array initialization would be one where there is no systematic way of going from the index value to the contents of an element, such as an array of the number of days in each month:

```
int[] daysInMonth = {31, 28, 31, 30, 31, 30,
    31, 31, 30, 31, 30, 31} ;
```

An alternative way of assigning values to the salaries array might be to read them in from the user:

```
int noOfSalaries = 0 ;
int[] salaries = new int[10] ;
while (true)
  {
  System.out.println("Type the " + noOfSalaries +"th salary") ;
  System.out.println("\ttype zero after the final salary") ;
  int response = BasicIO.readInteger() ;
  if (response == 0)
     break ;
  if (noOfSalaries == salaries.length)
     {
     System.out.println("ERROR: too many salaries")
     System.out.println("salary " + response + " ignored") ;
     break ;
     }
  salaries[noOfSalaries] = response ;
  noOfSalaries++ ;
  }
```

We prompt the user for a salary value and read it into the integer variable response. If the value is zero, we can leave the loop with a break statement. We keep track of how many salaries we have read in with the variable noOfSalaries. We check that we have not read in too many salaries with the test:

```
if (noOfSalaries == salaries.length)
  ...
```

Is this the correct form of the test? If we failed to perform this test, we would be storing an element into the array with index value salaries.length. But we know that the index values must lie in the range zero to one less than the length of the array. So the test is in the correct form.

If the number of salaries is not too large, we can store the new value in the next array element and then increment the count of salary values we have seen. After we leave the loop, we have to remember that for the rest of the program, the valid salaries have index values in the range zero to noOfSalaries − 1. To print them out we could write a for loop:

```
for (int i = 0 ; i < noOfSalaries ; i++)
    System.out.println(salaries[i]) ;
```

9.2   Arrays of Objects

So far we have declared arrays of a basic data type, int. But we can also declare arrays of objects. For example, we could declare an array of one hundred Person objects as follows:

```
Person[] personGroup = new Person[100] ;
```

What does this do? It sets up a variable (of type "array of Person," written Person[]) and this refers to a block of one hundred elements of type Person (numbered from zero to one less than personGroup.length). This is shown in Figure 9-2.

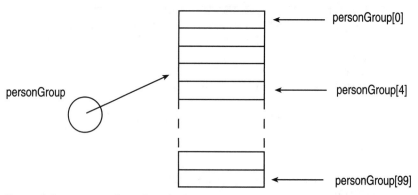

Figure 9-2: An array of one hundred Person instances.

But just like the integer array, the Person elements in this array have not yet been initialized; they do not refer to instances of the Person class. If we try to set one of the attributes of, say, personGroup[0], we get a NullPointerException. We could again initialize the array elements in a for loop using a constructor method:

```
for (int i = 0 ; i < personGroup.length ; i++)
    personGroup[i] = new Person() ;
```

This sets up each element of the array to refer to an instance of the Person class, as shown in Figure 9-3. Each of these objects has been set up with whatever initial values are provided by the Person constructor method with no arguments (namely strings "NONE" for the names, zero age, and UNKNOWN for the gender—see the documentation for the Person class).

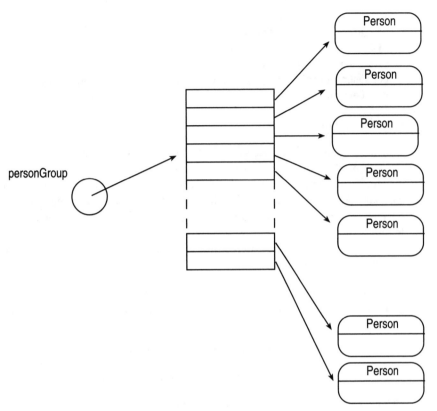

Figure 9-3: An initialized array of `Person`s.

Alternatively, we could read the values in. This time we will read them in from a file:

```
Person[] personGroup = new Person[100] ;
BasicFileIo file = new BasicFileIo(BasicFileIo.INPUT,
                "person.data") ;
int noOfPersons = 0 ;
while (true)
   {
   String fore = file.readString() ;
   if (fore == null)
      break ;
   String sur = file.readString() ;
   int age = file.readInteger() ;
   String x = file.readString() ;
   int gender ;
   if (x.equalsIgnoreCase("MALE"))
      gender = Person.MALE ;
```

```
    if (x.equalsIgnoreCase("FEMALE"))
       gender = Person.FEMALE ;
    else
       gender = Person.UNKNOWN ;
    personGroup[noOfPersons] = new Person(fore, sur, age, gender) ;
    noOfPersons++ ;
    }
file.closeFile() ;
```

This program reads a succession of values of forename, surname, age, and gender. When it has a set of values, it creates a new instance of the `Person` class initialized with the values just read in. In the case of the gender, a string of characters read in has to be converted to an integer constant. When the program reaches the end of the file, the `readString` method returns a `null` reference rather than a `String`, and the program tests for this `null` reference to terminate the loop.

We can extract an attribute of one of the array elements by writing something like `personGroup[i].getSurname()`:

- First we specify the array name—so we have something of type "array of `Person`".
- Then we specify the index value in square brackets—this gives us something of type `Person`.
- Then we apply the method name and any arguments.

We could display all the surnames we have read into the array with:

```
for (int i = 0 ; i < noOfPersons ; i++)
    System.out.println(personGroup[i].getSurname()) ;
```

Java provides another way to hold a collection of elements all of the same type, a *Vector*. We will discuss this other mechanism further in Chapter 21.

9.3 Searching an Array

Suppose we have read a set of personal details into the array `personGroup`. We now read a surname into a `String` variable `surname` and wish to find all the personal details relating to this surname. Here is some code to carry out this task:

```
int i = 0 ;
while ((i < noOfPersons) &&
                (!personGroup[i].getSurname().equals(surname)))
    i++ ;
```

We use a `while` loop because there are two possible outcomes: (a) we search right through the loop and do not find what we are looking for; or (b) part of the way through the loop we find a matching surname. Since we may stop early, we do not use a `for` loop.

We have a control variable i initialized to zero, which we increment as long as (a) this value is a legitimate index into the personGroup array, and (b) the surname of the Person instance at this index value does not match the surname we are looking for. This latter test is done by extracting the surname from the ith array element (with personGroup[i].getSurname()) and then using the equals method from the String class to compare it to the variable surname—hence:

```
personGroup[i].getSurname().equals(surname)
```

Finally the Boolean value required is the opposite of this, so we add the NOT operator !.

When we leave the loop, the control variable i will be set either to the value noOfPersons, indicating that the surname we sought was not among those held, or it will be a value in the range 0 to noOfPersons – 1, indicating that we have found a match at that index position in the array.

It could be that there are several Person instances with this surname—what would happen in this case? It is obvious that the loop would find the *first* such Person instance. If for some reason we wanted to find the *last* such Person instance, we could search backward through the loop, starting the index variable at noOfPersons – 1 and stopping when i reaches the value –1; we need to check the Person at offset 0, as this could be a match.

If we want to know whether there are multiple matches, we could write:

```
int matchIndex = -1 ;
int noOfMatches = 0 ;
for (int i = 0 ; i < noOfPersons ; i++)
   if (personGroup[i].getSurname().equals(surname))
     {
     matchIndex = i ;
     noOfMatches++ ;
     }
```

We have to traverse the whole of the array now to make sure we have counted all the matches, so we use a for loop. When we find a matching surname, we remember where it occurred in matchIndex. This is the index of the *last* match, because that was the easiest to write—how would you modify the code so that it remembered the *first* match? The number of matches will be in noOfMatches (a value of zero, meaning there were no matches, of course).

If we wanted to have a list of *all* the matches, then we could store each index value in a new array of matches when we find it. Try writing this version.

Let us return to the original code for searching the array, where we stop as soon as we find the first match. How efficient is this algorithm? The amount of time required to run the program will be proportional to the number of times around the loop, so the number of iterations is a good measure of how much time the program will take. If there is a matching surname at index value i in the array, then we must go around the loop i + 1 times. If the surname is not in the array, we will loop at each surname in the array, which means personGroup.length() iterations. So in the worst case (when there is no match), for an array of n elements, we require n iterations, or an amount of time proportional to n. We say that this linear search is an $O(n)$ algorithm, pronounced "order n algorithm." If we double the size of the array, we double the amount of work to be done (in the worst case).

Suppose now that we *sorted* the array on the surnames; that is, we rearranged the elements in the array so that the `Person` instance at index value zero had the alphabetically earliest surname and the `Person` instance at index value `noOfPersons` − 1 had the alphabetically latest surname. We will see later how to do this rearrangement—let us for the moment just assume that it has been done. We can rewrite the searching algorithm to stop the search as soon as we find ourselves starting to look at surnames alphabetically later than the one we want because we then know that later ones are higher still and therefore could not match:

```
int i = 0 ;
boolean matchSurname= false ;
while (i < noOfPersons)
   {
   int result = personGroup[i].getSurname().compareTo(surname) ;
   if (result == 0)
      {
      matchSurname = true ;
      break ;
      }
   else if (result > 0)
      break ;
   }
```

The method `compareTo` compares the `String` to which it is applied with the `String` argument (like the `equals` method), but the return value is an integer representing three possibilities:

- The value zero if the two `Strings` match.

- A value less than zero if the instance's `String` is alphabetically earlier than the argument `String`.

- A value greater than zero if the instance's `String` is alphabetically later than the argument `String`.

If we are in an iteration where we find that the surname at this position in the array is later than the one we are looking for, we know that there is no point in looking further, and we can break out of the loop. Similarly, if we find a match, we can also break out, but we need to set the boolean variable `matchSurname` to `true`.

How good is this algorithm? If we find a match at index value i, we need i + 1 iterations, as before. If we don't find a match, then we generally no longer need to search all the way through the array. Sometimes we will be lucky and decide at the first array position that the surname we are looking for is not in the array; sometimes we will be unlucky and decide only at the last array position. On average, we are likely to have to search about halfway through the array. So we have improved the searching. In fact, we still call this an *O(n)* algorithm because it still requires time proportional to the size of the array *n*. If we double the size of the array, the amount of time required is approximately doubled. It is just that the proportionality constant is smaller.

One way to improve the average performance (though not the worst-case performance) might be to find out which are the values most commonly sought, put them at the beginning of the array, and then use the original linear search. If some surnames are much more commonly searched for than others, this would improve the *average* searching time. If, for example, this is a list of all my e-mail aliases, it is certainly true that there is a small number of aliases I use several times a day and others I use once a month or less. So this is a case where ordering by frequency of access might pay off.

9.4 Binary Search

A more general alternative is to make better use of the fact that we have put the array into alphabetical surname order. We can use a technique called *binary search*, which works as follows:

- First we look at the array element at (or near) the middle of the array. If this is the element we want, then we have finished. If it is not the element we want, we at least now know (because the array is ordered) whether the element is in the first half of the array or in the second half (if it is there at all).

- We now look at the middle element of the appropriate half. Again, we may find what we want. But if not, we now know which quarter (if any) the element is in.

- We look at the middle element of the appropriate quarter, and continue on looking at the middle element of smaller and smaller sections of the array.

- We stop when we have either found what we want or the section of the array we are looking in has dwindled to nothing.

Here is the code for binary search of an ordered array:

```
int i = -1 ;
int j = noOfPersons;
int k = 0 ;
boolean matchSurname = false ;
while ((i + 1 < j) && (!matchSurname))
   {
   k = (i + j) / 2 ;
   int result = personGroup[k].getSurname().compareTo(surname) ;
   if (result == 0)
     matchSurname = true ;
   else if (result < 0)
      i = k ;
   else // i.e. result > 0
      j = k ;
   }
```

On each iteration, the section to be searched is from just after the value i to just before the value j. We initialize these values before the first iteration to include all the elements in the array, and we test on each iteration to find out if the section we are searching has shrunk to contain no elements. We set the variable k to point to the middle element of the section, using integer divide to get a valid index value, and we compare the surname at this position with the surname we are searching for, using the `compareTo` method and putting the result of the comparison in the variable `result`.

If `result` is zero, we have a match and can terminate the search; k now holds the index value for the matching surname in the array. If it is less than zero, then the element we want must be in the second half of the section we have just searched, so we change the value of the variable i, which indicates the bottom of the section to be searched. If it is greater than zero, then the element we want must be in the first half of the section we have just searched, so we change the value of the variable j, which indicates the top of the section to be searched.

How well does this work? It can easily be shown that binary search of an array of n elements takes something like "logarithm of n to base 2" iterations. Thus, binary search of an array of 1,024 elements would take no more than 10 iterations (where with linear search, we would expect to need something like 500 iterations, on average). So we say binary search is an $O(\log n)$ algorithm.

Two further points need to be made about searching:

- If there are several elements in the array with the same surname, we cannot be sure with a binary search which one it will find. It will not necessarily be the first or last, or any predictable position. It will depend on the positioning of the surnames with respect to the binary subdivision of the array.

- When we are searching for a surname, our search will be efficient, as we have rearranged the array to make it so. But if we now want to search for a particular forename or a particular age, we are back with the $O(n)$ linear search because the array cannot be ordered on these attributes and the surname too.

9.5   Sorting an Array

We now need to consider how to *sort* the array; that is, to rearrange it so that it is in alphabetical order by surname in order to search it efficiently. There are a large number of algorithms for sorting arrays; there are in fact whole books on the subject—a definitive but rather dated one is Donald Knuth's *Art of Computer Programming, Volume 3, Sorting and Searching* (Addison Wesley 1973); see also Chapter 2 of Sara Baase's *Computer Algorithms* (Addison Wesley 1988). We are going to demonstrate only one of these algorithms and set another as an exercise.

The first sorting algorithm is called an *insertion* sort. Suppose we have already put some of the array in order; elements 0 to i - 1 are in order, and elements i to noOfPersons - 1 are still to be sorted. We can take the element at position i, find out where it should go within the elements 0 to i - 1, and then insert it. Then we repeat this with element i + 1. Here is the code:

```
for (int i = 1 ; i < noOfPersons; i++)
  {
  int j = i ;
  String s = personGroup[i].getSurname() ;
  Person p = personGroup[i] ;
  while ((j > 0) &&
                  (personGroup[j - 1].getSurname().compareTo(s) > 0))
    {
    personGroup[j] = personGroup[j - 1] ;
    j-- ;
    }
  personGroup[j] = p ;
  }
```

On each iteration of the *outer* loop we put the ith array element in its correct location within the sorted array of elements 0 to i (inclusive). Since an array consisting of a single element can be considered to be already sorted, we do not need to perform an iteration for i set to 0 to position the 0th element in the sorted array consisting only of the 0th element. So we start with i set to 1, and finish with i set to noOfPerson − 1.

We are going to move the element at position i to position j, so the inner loop needs to find the correct value of j. We start with j set to the value of i, since it may be that the ith element is already in the right place. We then scan down through the elements that are already sorted, making a gap at the appropriate place for the ith element. If the element at position j − 1 has a surname alphabetically later than that at position i, we move the element at position j − 1 up one and then decrement j by one so that there is a gap at position j. We go on doing this until we find an element that should appear *before* the element at position i or until we have scanned right to the beginning of the array (i.e., the ith element should be at position 0).

Since we are shuffling the elements up through the array, we need first to clear out the element at position i to a temporary Person variable p. We also make a copy (in the String variable s) of the surname of the original ith element, to make the comparison statement a bit shorter.

Let us now watch how the sort works. Suppose there are four elements in the array, and initially they have surnames in the order Smith, Jones, Thomas, Matthews. The initial situation is shown in Figure 9-4. Initially we assume that the section of the array consisting only of element 0 (i.e., the Person with the surname Smith) is in the correct order, as indicated by the thick line drawn across the array below this element.

We start the first iteration of the outer loop, with i set to 1 and consequently with j set to 1 and s set to Jones. Finally we copy the value in the array element at position 1 to the variable p, so that p refers to the object instance containing the surname Jones. We have what is shown in Figure 9-5.

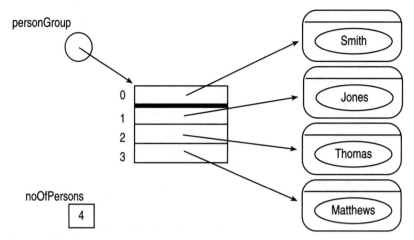

Figure 9-4: The original unsorted array.

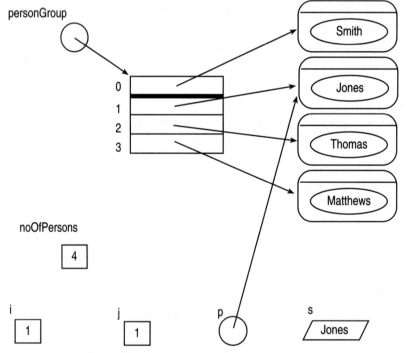

Figure 9-5: Beginning the first iteration of the inner loop.

We start executing the inner loop. We test that j is greater than 0 (which is true) and that personGroup[j - 1].getSurname() (which is Smith) is alphabetically later than s (which is Jones), and this is also true. So we perform an iteration of the inner loop, making the element at position j refer to the same object instance as that at position j - 1 (with the statement personGroup[j] = personGroup[j - 1]) and decreasing the value of j by 1. Figure 9-6 shows what we end up with.

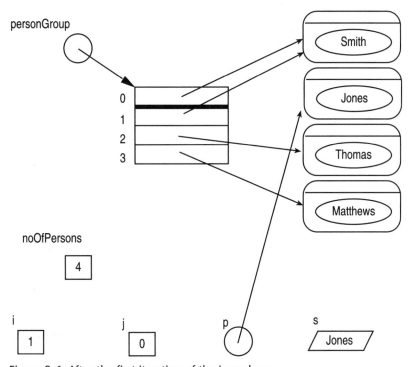

Figure 9-6: After the first iteration of the inner loop.

The variable j now has the value 0, so we do not perform any more iterations of the inner loop. So we execute the statement:

```
personGroup[j] = p ;
```

which makes the jth element of the array (i.e., the one at position 0) refer to the object instance with surname Jones. So we have what is shown in Figure 9-7. The section of the array personGroup[0 .. 1] is now in order, as indicated by the thick line.

We commence the next iteration of the outer loop, with i set to 2, j to 2, s to Thomas, and p referring to the object instance with surname Thomas. Figure 9-8 shows the result.

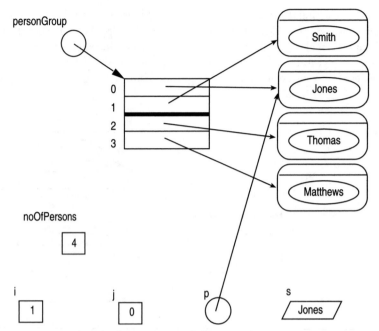

Figure 9-7: After the first iteration of the outer loop.

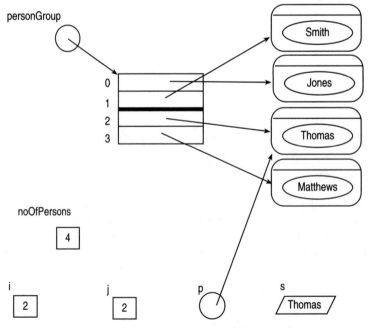

Figure 9-8: Beginning the second iteration of the outer loop.

We prepare to reenter the inner loop. The value of j is greater than 0, but the method compareTo as applied to the value of personGroup[j - 1].getSurname() (namely Smith) and the value of s (namely Thomas) returns a negative value. So the iteration test fails, and we perform no iterations of the inner loop.

So we copy back the reference to the Thomas instance into the jth element (i.e., that at position 2), leaving what is shown in Figure 9-9.

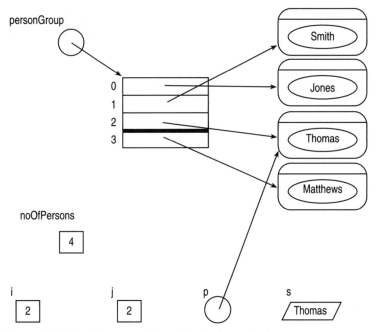

Figure 9-9: After the second iteration of the outer loop.

In other words, nothing has changed, except that we now know that the sorted section of the array is personGroup[0 .. 2]. We could have arranged not to do the copying of the references in this case since it is unnecessary, but it probably makes the code more difficult to follow, with little improvement in efficiency (remember we are copying references to objects, not the objects themselves), so we leave the code as it is.

We are now ready for the next (and last) iteration of the outer loop, with i set to 3. If you follow the code step by step, you will find that the two surnames Thomas and Smith will be shifted up one position and Matthews shifted into position 1, leaving what you see in Figure 9-10. The algorithm terminates, and the array section personGroup[0 .. 3], which is the whole of the relevant portion of the array, is now sorted.

How much effort does this insertion sorting algorithm take? We go around the outer loop noOfPersons - 1 times. How many times do we go around the inner loop? In the worst case (when the array to be sorted is exactly in the wrong order—in decreasing alphabetical order in this case), we have to go through the whole sorted array each time. So we have one inner loop

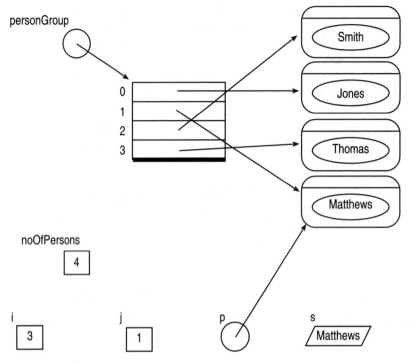

Figure 9-10: The final sorted array.

iteration for i set to 2, two for i set to 3, and so on. So in the worst case, this is 1 + 2 + 3 ... + noOfPersons − 2. If there are n elements in the array, this comes to n(n–1)/2. So insertion sort is an $O(n^2)$ algorithm, pronounced "order n squared."

This is not the best we can do. There are sorting algorithms that are O(n log n); that is, of order "n times log n to base 2." This is considerably better—if n is 1024, n^2 is a million and n log n is 10,000, so it is a factor of 100 better for this value of n.

What happens if we have two elements with the same surname? We have carefully written our sorting algorithm so that it is *stable*; that is, if two array elements have the same sorting field, they are left in the same order as in the original array. Check that you understand how this algorithm ensures this stability. With some other sorting algorithms, it is less easy to ensure stability.

9.6   Arrays as Arguments

So far our program consists of a single main method to read in the values for the array, to sort it into alphabetical order by surname, and then to search it for a succession of surnames typed in by the user. It would be better to organize our program into a simpler main method, which calls separate private methods (readArray, sortArray, and searchArray) to carry out these three steps.

Here is the sortArray method:

```
private static void sortArray(Person[] array, int arrayLength)
   {
   for (int i = 1 ; i < arrayLength ; i++)
      {
      int j = i ;
      String s = array[i].getSurname() ;
      Person p = array[i] ;
      while ((j > 0) &&
                     (array[j - 1].getSurname().compareTo(s) > 0))
         {
         array[j] = array[j - 1] ;
         j-- ;
         }
      array[j] = p ;
      }
   } // end of method sortArray
```

There are two arguments to this method. The first is the array to be sorted (of type Person[]—that is, an array of Person instances), and the second is the number of elements to be sorted (of type int).

In the main method, we declare the array and a count of how many people we have read into the array:

```
int MAX_NO_OF_PERSONS = 100 ;
Person[] personGroup = new Person[MAX_NO_OF_PERSONS] ;
int noOfPersons = 0 ;
```

We read the data into the array, setting noOfPersons while we do it, and then we sort the array:

```
sortArray(personGroup, noOfPersons) ;
```

While this method is being executed, the situation looks like what you see in Figure 9-11.

In the main method, there are an array variable personGroup and an int variable noOfPersons, which are passed as actual arguments to the sortArray method, corresponding to its formal arguments array and arrayLength, respectively. We know how int arguments are passed—the value of the actual argument noOfPersons, let's say 7, is copied into the formal argument arrayLength for use inside the method. With an array argument, a *reference* is passed across, so we can refer to individual elements of the array from inside the sortArray method—for example, array[0] or array[arrayLength - 1].

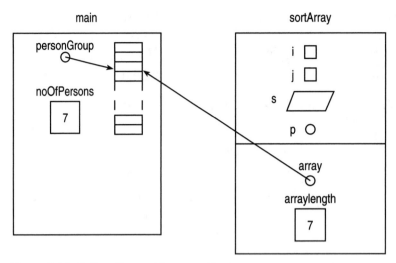

Figure 9-11: Calling the sortArray method.

Since only the value of an int argument is passed to the method, a change to the formal argument arrayLength will not affect the actual argument noOfPersons. But since a *reference* to the array has been passed across, any modifications to the array from inside the sortArray method using the formal argument array will affect the actual array personGroup in the main method—in particular, the elements of the array will be rearranged into sorted order.

We have a problem with the readArray method since we need to pass back *two* pieces of information—the array with the values copied into it and how many elements were inserted. We can pass the array as an argument, as before, but we have to pass the count of elements as a return value:

```
private static int readArray(String name, Person[] array)
                  throws IOException
  {
  BasicFileIo file = new BasicFileIo(BasicFileIo.INPUT, name) ;
  int arrayLength = 0 ;

  while (true)
    {
    String fore = file.readString() ;
    if (fore == null)
       break ;
    if (arrayLength == array.length)
      {
      System.out.println("ERROR: too many people") ;
      System.exit(1) ;
      }
```

```
      String sur = file.readString() ;
      int age = file.readInteger() ;
      String x = file.readString() ;
      int gender ;
      if (x.equalsIgnoreCase("MALE"))
         gender = Person.MALE ;
      else if (x.equalsIgnoreCase("FEMALE"))
         gender = Person.FEMALE ;
      else
         gender = Person.UNKNOWN ;
      array[arrayLength] = new Person(fore, sur, age, gender) ;
      arrayLength++ ;
      }

   file.closeFile() ;
   return arrayLength ;
   } // end of method readArray
```

We call this method as follows:

```
BasicIo.prompt("type file name ") ;
String fileName = BasicIo.readString() ;
noOfPersons = readArray(fileName, personGroup) ;
System.out.println("read " + noOfPersons + " elements from file "
                   + fileName) ;
```

You will recall that the main method usually has a single formal argument args:

```
public static void main(String[] args)
```

It is now clear that this is an array of Strings, the "command line arguments" passed to the program when it begins to run. Thus, if we run a Java application program with:

```
java JavaProgram now is the hour
```

in the main method args.length is 4, args[0] is "now" and args[3] is "hour".

9.7 Multi-dimensional Arrays

So far we have discussed *one-dimensional* arrays; that is, a single sequence of elements all of the same type. We can introduce *two-dimensional* arrays to represent matrices from mathematics, boards from games like chess, computer display screens, and so on. In all these cases there are two dimensions or index values, usually called the *row* and the *column*, and a particular element is specified by its row and column number. As before, all elements of the array must be of the same type.

We are going to illustrate two-dimensional arrays by starting to create a class to represent a game of noughts-and-crosses (tic-tac-toe). A typical board, with three rows and three columns, is shown in Figure 9-12.

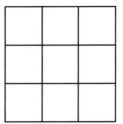

Figure 9-12: A board for a game of noughts-and-crosses.

The squares of the board need to contain only a blank, a nought, or a cross, so we declare some constants:

```
public static final int BLANK = 0 ;
public static final int NOUGHT = 1 ;
public static final int CROSS = 2 ;
```

and then we declare a two-dimensional array `board`:

```
private int[][] board = new int[3][3] ;
```

The variable array `board` is of type `int[][]`, pronounced "array of array of int." Unlike some programming languages, in Java we cannot directly create a two-dimensional array; we have created a one-dimensional array of one-dimensional arrays. Figure 9-13 shows what is created.

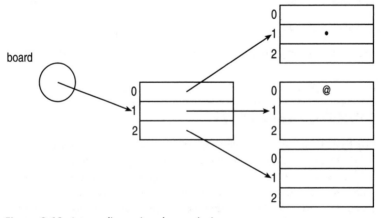

Figure 9-13: A two-dimensional array in Java.

We refer to an individual element with an extension to the notation for single dimensional arrays. The element at row zero, column one (indicated with a blob • in Figure 9-13) is board[0][1]. Notice that the first declared dimension is also the one specified first when referring to an individual element. The element board[1][0] is the one with the @ symbol in the figure.

We can initialize an empty board, before starting to play a game, using a nested loop:

```
for (int i = 0 ; i < 3 ; i++)
    for (int j = 0 ; j < 3 ; j++)
        board[i][j] = BLANK ;
```

Alternatively, Java allows us to initialize a multidimensional array by listing the values in an extension of the literal array expression notation provided for a single-dimensioned array:

```
private int[][] board = {{BLANK, BLANK, BLANK},
        {BLANK, BLANK, BLANK},
        {BLANK, BLANK, BLANK}} ;
```

The outermost pair of { } encloses the whole initialization expression, and each inner pair of { } encloses a row; the row expressions, like the expressions for the individual elements of the row, are separated by commas. The compiler can deduce from this expression that there are three rows in the array (numbered 0 to 2), and each has three elements (numbered 0 to 2). In this situation, we want to set all the elements to the same value, but we could set some of the elements to different values:

```
private int[][] board = {{CROSS, BLANK, BLANK},
        {BLANK, CROSS, BLANK},
        {BLANK, BLANK, CROSS}} ;
```

The result of this statement is shown in Figure 9-14.

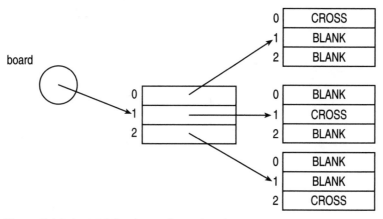

Figure 9-14: An initialized two-dimensional array.

We could test for a win on the diagonal from top left to bottom right with the test:

```
if ((board[0][0] == board[1][1]) && (board[1][1] == board[2][2]))
    ...
```

Actually, there is something wrong with this code as a test for a winning move. Our first attempt to write a program to play this game had the preceding code, and we were surprised to find it was claiming a victory before any moves had been made. The code has to be rewritten to ensure that the contents of the three positions is either a NOUGHT or a CROSS (that is, not a BLANK)—for example:

```
if ((board[0][0] == board[1][1]) &&
        (board[1][1] == board[2][2]) &&
        (board[0][0] != BLANK))
    ...
```

This was a square array with the same number of rows and columns. We can of course declare rectangular arrays. For example, to declare an array rainfall to hold a double value for the rainfall for each month of a period of 10 years, we could write:

```
double[][] rainfall = new double[10][12] ;
```

The result of this is shown in Figure 9-15.

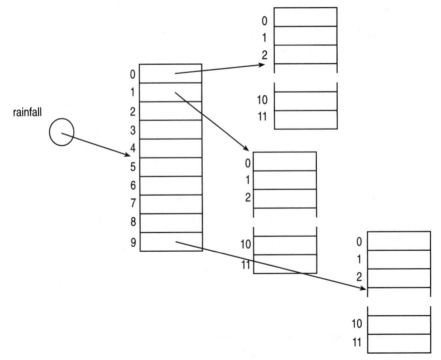

Figure 9-15: A rectangular two-dimensional array in Java.

The first index is for the 10 years, say 1990 to 1999, represented by index values 0 to 9, and the second is for the months—notice that the latter take the range 0 to 11 rather than 1 to 12. The value for, say, June 1996 would be `rainfall[6][5]`.

We can declare arrays with more than two dimensions, although three dimensions are probably the most we are likely to find useful. A array for rainfall figures for each month of a 10-year period for each of 20 locations could be declared as:

```
double[][][] rainfall = new double[10][12][20] ;
```

The value for, say, June 1996 for location 15 (numbered 0 to 19) would be `rainfall[6][5][15]`.

We are going to have difficulty remembering which location is which, so we could declare a set of constants to give a location name to each of the 20 index values for the third index.

If we take the `length` of the rainfall array (with `rainfall.length`), we get the length of the array of row references, which here is 10. Applying it to one of the row arrays (with, say, `rainfall[0].length`) gives 12. The expression `rainfall[0][0].length` gives 20.

9.8   Nonrectangular Arrays (optional)

In Java, it is possible to have arrays that are not in fact rectangular. Suppose we wanted an array to hold Pascal's triangle, which looks like this:

```
        1 1
       1 2 1
      1 3 3 1
     1 4 6 4 1
   1 5 10 10 5 1
```

Each row starts and finishes with the value 1, and the remaining values are the sum of the two values above it—so the first 3 in the third row is 1 + 2 from the row above it. We could hold this in a normal rectangular array (and waste some space), but in Java we could also use a triangular array. We first declare a two-dimensional array with the second dimension unspecified:

```
int[][] pascal = new int[10][] ;
```

Figure 9-16 shows what this code creates.

The elements of this array are of type `int[]`—they can refer to an array of integers but do not yet do so. We can set up an array of the correct size and put its reference into the appropriate place in the array we have declared:

```
for (int i = 0 ; i < pascal.length ; i++)
  {
  pascal[i] = new int[i + 2] ;
  pascal[i][0] = 1 ;
  pascal[i][i + 1] = 1 ;
```

```
for (int j = 0 ; j < i ; j++)
    pascal[i][j + 1] = pascal[i - 1][j] +
            pascal[i - 1][j + 1] ;
}
```

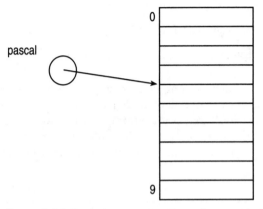

Figure 9-16: Declaring a non-rectangular array in Java—step 1.

The first line in the body of the loop generates an array of i + 2 integers and stores a reference to it, as the ith row, in pascal[i]. The second and third lines fill in the first and last values, and the for loop in the final line fills in the rest of the values in the row. Figure 9-17 shows what the array now looks like.

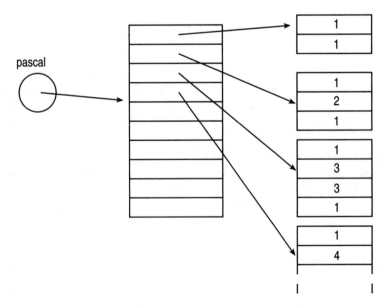

Figure 9-17: Declaring a non-rectangular array in Java—step 2.

The elements of the array can be accessed in the usual way. So pascal[3][2] has the value 6. Accessing the element pascal[0][2] would cause an exception to be thrown. Here is some code to print the array:

```
for(int i = 0 ; i < pascal.length ; i++)
   {
   for(int j = 0; j < pascal[i].length ; j++)
      System.out.print(" " + pascal[i][j]) ;
   System.out.println() ;
   }
```

9.9 Key Points in Chapter 9

- It is often necessary to maintain, manipulate, and process collections of data. We use the Java *array* mechanism to support this.

- A typical declaration of an array would be:

  ```
  int[] years = new years[5] ;
  ```

  This declares an array of integers called years with five elements.

- To access an individual element of an array, we use an *index*. An index is an integer value that uniquely identifies a position within an array.

- The years array has five elements, indexed by the values 0 to 4. The expression year.length gives us the value 5. An individual element (say years[3]) can be treated exactly the same as a single integer variable.

- We can initialize the contents of an array when we declare it:

  ```
  int[] years = {1957, 1962, 1969, 1974, 1978} ;
  ```

- Just as we can have arrays of the basic data types (such as ints), we can also have arrays of objects.

- Arrays and loops are made for each other. We use loops to sequentially process each element of an array.

- We can sort and search the contents of an array. The algorithms we can apply to searching are closely related to the ordering of the array elements. For example, if an array of objects including a search attribute (for example, the surname) are in random order, then to search for all occurrences of a surname, we must sequentially examine all surnames.

  If the array is sorted in alphabetical order by surname, however, we can use the binary search algorithm and significantly reduce the number of elements we must examine.

- It is possible to declare, initialize, and use multidimensional arrays:

  ```
  int[][] matrix = new int[2][2] ;
  ```

The logical view of this (directly supported in some languages) would be :

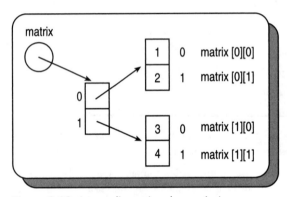

matrix[0][0] = 1

matrix[0][1] = 2

matrix[1][0] = 3

matrix[1][1] = 4

The actual implementation in Java, however, is that of an array whose elements are further arrays; this is shown in Figure 9-18.

Figure 9-18: A two-dimensional array in Java.

9.10   Exercises

1. Rewrite the code in Section 9.3 to find *all* the Person instances with a matching surname, not just the first or last. You should set up an array for the matching index values, together with an integer variable noOfMatches.

2. Write a method evaluateHand with one argument, an array of five Card instances that models a hand in the game of poker. Your program should return an indication of the value of the hand, which could be full house (three of a kind plus a pair), three of a kind, two pairs, a pair, or none of these.

    Write a program to test your method.

    Expand your method to test for *all* the possible winning combinations of a poker hand.

3. Here is a second way of sorting an array (called a *bubblesort*—can you see why?):

Go through the array, looking at each adjacent pair of elements in turn—if they are in the wrong order, interchange them, and then go on to look at the next pair. If any changes were made, repeat the process. Figure 9-19 shows the first pass through an unsorted array.

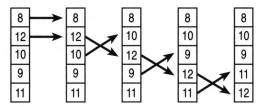

Figure 9-19: The first pass of a bubblesort.

Figure 9-20 shows the second pass of the bubblesort.

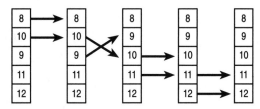

Figure 9-20: The second pass of the bubbblesort.

As Figure 9-21 shows, on the third pass we would make no changes (and so realize that we don't need any more passes).

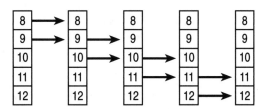

Figure 9-21: The third (and final) pass of the bubblesort.

Write a method which uses this sorting algorithm to replace the version of `sortArray` given in Section 9.5.

4. In Section 9.7 we declared an array `board` to represent a position in the game of noughts-and-crosses. Write a method:

```
boolean winForSomeone(int[][] board)
```

that, given a position board in noughts-and-crosses, returns TRUE if it is a win for one of the two players (that is, there is a row that is horizontal, vertical, or diagonal of either noughts or crosses). Otherwise it should return FALSE.

5. Write a class `Sentence` that provides the following functionality:
a) Reads in and stores a sentence from the keyboard (using the `readString` method in `BasicIo`). The sentence becomes part of the hidden state of the class.
b) On request, returns the next word from the sentence, with an indication when there are no more words.

You should supply the following methods:

`void getSentence( )`

This reads in a sentence from the keyboard and stores it within the body of the instance in a suitable data structure (for example, a `String`).

`String nextWord( )`

This extracts the next word in sequence from the sentence, and returns it.

`boolean hasMoreWords( )`

This returns TRUE if there are still words left in the sentence, FALSE otherwise.

Write a suitable driver application; for example, one that allows the end user to type in a sentence and prints out the sentence, one word per line.

Be careful to define certain elements of the `Sentence` class as private (for example, most if not all of the state of an instance and any methods you may write to support the functionality of the three public methods listed).

6. Write an application to store and update changes to a set of monthly unemployment figures for a particular year for a small urban area. Your application should allow the user to enter numbers of jobs gained or lost (a negative number indicates jobs lost) during any month.

With each iteration through a loop, the user selects one of three choices:
a) To enter the number of jobs gained or lost for a particular event (e.g., a factory opening or closing) and the month in which the event occurred. For example, to indicate that 27 jobs have been created by the opening of a new factory in August, the user types:

`August 27`

b) To calculate statistics for the data entered so far. Note that we are interested only in the overall trend in employment for each month:
  i. The net change in unemployment over the year; that is, the sum of each month's figures.
  ii. The month(s) during which most jobs were lost; that is, the month(s) with the smallest value.
  iii. The month(s) during which fewest jobs were lost; the month(s) with the largest value.
c) To quit.

You don't know the number of unemployed at the start of the year so you need to store the *change* in unemployment for each month.

Your objective is to implement this application by providing a class EmploymentStatistics that maintains the monthly unemployment figures and provides methods that support the needs of the application (adding new information and producing the three statistics; the latter methods might be called netChange, worstMonth, and bestMonth).

If the user loads up the following information:

August 27; February -6; March 120; April 62; May -90; June 21; May 30; July 82; October 100; August -4; September 22; December 43; October -20; September 15; October 40

this should result in the net results for the year given in Table 9-1.

Month	Net Jobs
January	0
February	-6
March	120
April	62
May	-90+30 = -60
June	21
July	82
August	27 - 4 = 23
September	22+15 = 37
October	100-20 + 40 = 120
November	0
December	43

Table 9-1: Net results for each month.

Thus, in response to requests of type :
  b i: The total number of jobs for the year: 442
  b ii: The month(s) with the smallest value: May
  b iii: The month(s) with the largest value: March, October

Remember to provide a suitable initializing constructor for the class.

7. A millionaire has a car collection. S/he wants to have an application that calculates the average power of the collection. Using the Car class, write an application that allows the end user to input data about a set of cars and that produces the average power of the collection. You may assume there will be no more than 10 cars in a collection.

8. a) Define a class to hold the information for a university timetable slot (course number, course title, lecturer, and location).

b) Write a file, `timetable.data`, containing timetable information for a computer science course in the format:

```
day
time
course number
course title
lecturer
location
```

For example:

```
Fri
9
CSc112
Programming in Java
Roger Garside
GF1
```

c) Write a program that reads in the timetable data from the file `timetable.data` and stores it in an array of timetable slot objects of the type you have declared. You can assume that there is no more than one teaching event at a time, and each event is one hour long.

Display the details of a timetable slot given a user request from the terminal specifying a day and time. A suitable response should be given if there is no teaching at the time specified.

d) Write a method to display a list of all the timetable slots for a lecturer, specified as the single `String` argument to the method. The slots should be displayed in chronological order, and a suitable message should be displayed if there are no slots for the specified lecturer. Use this to allow a user of your program to list the timetable slots for a lecturer specified by the user at the terminal.

How would you modify your program if there could be more than one teaching event at a time?

9. Magic squares are squares that contain numbers arranged in such a way that all the rows and columns add up to the same number.

Examples of magic squares of size n=3 and n=5 are shown in Figure 9-22.

15	8	1	24	17
16	14	7	5	23
22	20	13	6	4
3	21	19	12	10
9	2	25	18	11

6	1	8
7	5	3
2	9	4

Figure 9-22: Magic squares.

An algorithm exists to determine where numbers should be placed so that rows and columns will add up to the same number. The algorithm works for *odd n only* and is as follows (for a square of size n):

(1) Start with k set to 1 and insert this value in the top center square.

(2) Repeat the following steps until (a multiple of) n numbers are in place.
Add one to k.
Move left one square and up one square* and insert the number k.

(3) Add one to k.

(4) Move down one square from the last number you placed and insert the number k.

(5) Go back to step 2 until all squares are filled.

Write a program to implement this magic square algorithm. Your program should prompt the user for the required size (n) and then, assuming n is valid, it should print out a magic square of that size. To check that your square is in fact magic, calculate and print out the sum of each row, column, and diagonal and confirm that they are all identical.

Note ∎

For practical reasons, when running your program, n should not be too big!

---

* This algorithm assumes that rows and columns *wrap-around*—if a move is off the top of the square, start again at the bottom; similarly, if a move is off the left of the square, start again at the right (see Figure 9-22).

CHAPTER 10

Objects Within Objects

10.1 Introduction

So far, the classes we have written have contained a set of instance variables that were all examples of the basic types (`boolean`, `char`, `byte`, `short`, `int`, `long`, `float`, and `double`). We have also used the type `String`; as we know, `String` is not a basic type or even an array. `String` is an example of a system-provided class, so we can say it is an *object* type.

What this means is that an instance variable of one object can, in fact, be a reference to a further object. In our `Person` class, the forename and surname instance variables are references to two `String` objects. Just as `String` is a class, so we can use any classes—system-provided or written by ourselves—in the same way. Part of the state of an object, then, can be modeled by a further object.

This phenomenon is familiar to those working with databases and is known as the *parts-explosion* situation. If we model a car as an object, then there may be certain attributes of that car that we can handle with basic types. For example, the number of wheels a car has can be stored as an integer value. In Java, the name of the car must be stored in a `String` object, so here we have already left the basic types behind. However, there are other parts of the car, such as the engine, which in turn is made up of other complex parts, such as the carburetor, and so on.

So you can see how we can start off with a single conceptual object such as a car, but when we begin to explore the components that make up that object, we find that they too must be modeled as objects rather than basic types. This is what we mean by a parts explosion.

As our main Java example, we are going to again consider the `Person` class. So far we have modeled a person's name (as `String`s) and their age and gender (as `int`s). Our application now requires that we know the date of birth of a person. A date can be thought of as a triple of integers; one for the day of the month, one for the month, and finally one for the year. We could model this directly within the `Person` class as three separate instance variables, all of type `int`. However, this is not very satisfying for a number of reasons.

First of all, as we have said, classes are a way of collecting together data that logically belongs together and the methods that operate on that data. Second, classes are a way of modeling real-world entities more directly. The concept of a date is a real-world entity. It feels more natural to declare a class `Date` that has these three integers as its state, and thereafter we can provide a number of methods that operate on dates. This also makes the `Date` class available to any other applications that require them—for example, an electronic diary or calendar. Other classes may have dates analogous to a person's birth date; for example, the date a car rolled off the assembly line.

If we went ahead with our initial plan of including the three integers within Person itself, we would be greatly reducing the possibilities of reusing the Date concept and methods elsewhere.

In fact, the Date class is so useful, it is actually a system-provided class in the package java.util. However, that class does not provide quite the facilities we are going to require for manipulating dates. We are therefore going to write our own class, OurDate, to represent people's birth dates.

10.2   Writing the OurDate Class

We have decided to model the actual date as a set of three integers, one for day of the month, one for the month, and one for the year. These will be the instance variables of the class. We have also provided a constructor that expects all three values to be specified when an instance of OurDate is created. Last, we have a group of set and get methods that allow us to inspect the state of a OurDate instance:

```java
public class OurDate
   {
   private int dayOfMonth, month, year ;

   public OurDate(int y, int m, int d)
      {
      dayOfMonth = d;
      month = m;
      year = y;
      }

   public int getDayOfMonth()
      {
      return dayOfMonth ;
      }

   public int getMonth()
      {
      return month ;
      }

   public int getYear()
      {
      return year ;
      }

   public void setDayOfMonth(int d)
      {
      dayOfMonth = d;
```

```
        }

    public void setMonth(int m)
      {
      month = m ;
      }

    public void setYear(int y)
      {
      year = y;
      }


    } // end of class OurDate
```

The set methods that operate on the day and month should contain checks to ensure that only valid integers are being used; for example, the month should lie between 1 and 12.

10.3   Using the OurDate Class

We update the Person class with the following instance variable and methods:

```
    private OurDate dateOfBirth;      // new instance variable

    public void setDateOfBirth(OurDate d)
      {
      dateOfBirth = d;
      }

    public OurDate getDateOfBirth()
      {
      return dateOfBirth;
      }
```

The treatment is the same as for the age or gender attributes. However, notice that we are here using an object rather than a basic type.

In our main class, we add a method called displayPerson as follows:

```
private static void displayPerson(Person person)
   {
   System.out.print(person.getForename()) ;
   System.out.print(' ') ;
   System.out.print(person.getSurname()) ;
   System.out.print(' ') ;
   System.out.print(person.getAge() + " ") ;
   OurDate tDate = person.getDateOfBirth();
```

```
System.out.print(tDate.getDayOfMonth() + "/" +
   tDate.getMonth() + "/" + tDate.getYear());
} // end of displayPerson
```

Here, we are using an instance as the formal parameter to a method. We will discuss this further in the next section.

In order to gain access to the information about the person's date of birth, we have a local variable, tDate, which is of type OurDate. We use the getDateOfBirth method associated with the Person class to return a reference to the OurDate object contained within the Person object.

Once we have that reference, we can call the OurDate methods directly on the referenced OurDate object. So in the statement:

```
System.out.print(tDate.getDayOfMonth() + "/" +
   tDate.getMonth() + "/" + tDate.getYear());
```

we can quite happily apply getDayOfMonth, getMonth, and getYear to the instance tDate.

Here is an example from our main class:

```
static void main (String[] args)
   {
   Person aPerson = new Person("James", "Kirk", 32, Person.MALE) ;

   // set up a Person's age

   OurDate birthday = new OurDate(1957, 3, 8);
   aPerson.setDateOfBirth(birthday);

   displayPerson(aPerson) ;
   System.out.println();
   } // end of main
```

Notice that here again we have a "temporary" object, in this case birthday. We first use the OurDate constructor to set up a suitable instance of the class. Then we use its setDateOfBirth method to set the dateOfBirth attribute of the Person instance to refer to the birthday instance. Diagrammatically, we have something like what you see in Figure 10-1.

The result of running this code is as follows:

```
James Kirk 32 8/3/1957
```

10.4 Objects as Parameters

We have an application in mind. We wish to provide a program that allows the end user to enter his or her date of birth; the application then calculates and displays the following:

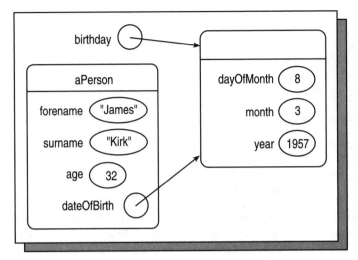

Figure 10-1: A single OurDate object with two references.

- The actual day of the week on which the end user was born.
- The appropriate line of the following nursery rhyme:

    Monday's child is fair of face,
    Tuesday's child is full of grace,
    Wednesday's child is full of woe,
    Thursday's child has far to go,
    Friday's child is loving and giving,
    Saturday's child works hard for a living,
    Sunday's child is fair and wise and good and gay.

- The astrological sign the end user was born under.
- The length of life of the end user so far.

In order to calculate the length of life so far, we have to define a kind of "subtraction" operator that takes two OurDates as operands and returns the elapsed time as an integer number of days.

In an object-oriented fashion, we can look at the idea of sending an OurDate object a subtract request with an OurDate as parameter. The destination object subtracts the parameter object from itself and returns an integer result:

```
class OurDate
  {
  // declarations
```

```
    public int subtract (OurDate operand)
       {
       // body
       } // end of method subtract

    } // end of class OurDate
```

This could be used as follows:

```
int lifeLength;
OurDate aDate, bDate;
// code
lifeLength = aDate.subtract(bDate);
```

It is purely a matter of taste, but it seems more natural to model "subtraction" as a dyadic operator between two operands rather than a monadic operation where the second operator is a parameter. If this is the preferred option, we can model this as a class method:

```
class OurDate
   {
   // declarations

    public static int subtract (OurDate oper1, OurDate oper2)
       {
       // body
       } // end of method subtract

    } // end of class OurDate
```

This version could be applied as shown here:

```
int lifeLength;
OurDate aDate, bDate;
// code
lifeLength = OurDate.subtract(aDate, bDate);
```

A possible implementation of this subtract method is:

```
/* contained as private methods in the OurDate class are the following :

    dayOfTheYear : this operates on the attributes of OurDate to calculate
    which day of the year the current OurDate lands on, in the range 1 to 365

    leapyear : this operates on the "year" attribute and
    returns true if the current OurDate lies
    within a leap year, false otherwise.
*/


static int subtract(OurDate low, OurDate high)
/*
```

```
    given two "OurDates" (where 'low' < 'high') this subtracts (high - low)
    and returns the result as an integer (of days)
*/
  {
  int lowdoty, highdoty, lowyear,
    highyear, i, days, daysleft;

  days = 0;
  lowdoty = low.dayOfTheYear();
  highdoty = high.dayOfTheYear();
  if (low.year == high.year)
     {
     days = highdoty - lowdoty;
     return(days);
     }
  lowyear = low.year+1;
  highyear = high.year-1;
  for (i = lowyear; i <= highyear; i++)
     {
     days = days + 365;
     if (leapyear(i) == true) days++;
     }
  daysleft = 365-lowdoty;
  if (leapyear(low.year) == true) daysleft++;
  days = days + highdoty + daysleft;
  return(days);
  } // end of method subtract
```

Note that we can directly access the private attributes of aDate and bDate. This is because the body of subtract is declared within the OurDate class itself; all things are visible within the body of the class.

Let's say we cannot change the OurDate class but we are users of the class. We decide that we need a method that will print the date in a standard format; for some reason, the class providers have not supplied this method. We can write a method in our main program of the form:

```
static void displayOurDate (OurDate d)
   {
   // body of method
   }
```

Here we have a method, outside of the class of object it takes as parameter, which has an object instance as parameter. We can, as ever, use the get and set methods to access the attributes of an instance. So the body of the method might be:

```
{
System.out.print(d.getDayOfMonth() + "/" + d.getMonth() +
   "/" + d.getYear());
}
```

10.5 Multiple References to the Same Object

We need to address a possible danger. If, in our main class, we continue to use `birthday` as follows:

```
birthday.setMonth(6);
displayPerson(aPerson);
System.out.println() ;
```

what do you think the results of this second `displayPerson` call are?

```
James Kirk 32 8/6/1957
```

This is because we can think of this `OurDate` instance as having two distinct references to it. It doesn't matter which one we use to update it, either `birthday` or `aPerson.dateOfBirth`. We may not be able to access `aPerson.dateOfBirth` directly as it is a private instance variable, but we can get a reference to it (yet another one!) through the `getDateOfBirth` method. When we say:

```
birthday.setMonth(6);
```

the situation becomes what is shown in Figure 10-2; the value of the `month` attribute of `birth-day` is set to 6, as we would expect. We mustn't forget the true picture, shown in Figure 10-3, that the month of James Kirk's birthday is now 6.

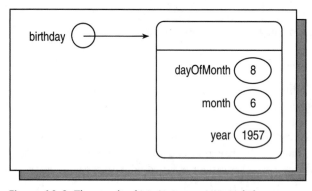

Figure 10-2: The result of `birthday.setMonth(6)`.

There are a number of problems with this scenario; one is that one of the references may go "out of scope" and disappear. For example, if "birthday" happened to be a local variable or a formal parameter, once the method that contains it terminates, the local variable or formal parameter will vanish. This means the associated object cannot be reached through that reference anymore, but as long as there are others, the object will continue to exist. This isn't a problem, really, as long as there are other references.

The other thing to note is that sometimes updating an object via different references may be a desirable behavior. On the other hand, sometimes it may not! If we want the `dateOfBirth` attribute of aPerson to be a totally independent object with no other references to it, we have to make what is called a *deep copy* of the birthday object.

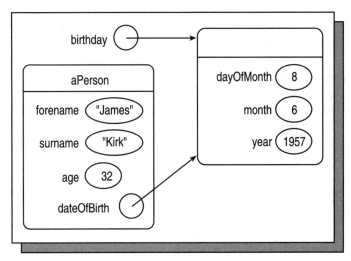

Figure 10-3: Remember this single object has two references.

What we have done so far in the setDateOfBirth method is to make a *shallow copy* of birthday. This simply means we have taken a copy of the object reference. What we need to do now is a deep copy where we actually create a brand new object, but make sure all its instance variables are the same as the original.

In order to achieve this, we have added a copy method to the OurDate class as follows:

```
public OurDate copy ()
    {
    OurDate t;
    t = new OurDate();
    t.dayOfMonth = dayOfMonth;
    t.month = month;
    t.year = year;
    return t;
    } // end of method copy
```

This is used in a revised version of the setDateOfBirth method of Person as follows:

```
public void setDateOfBirth(OurDate d)
    {
    dateOfBirth = d.copy();
    }
```

Figure 10-4 shows what happens when setDateOfBirth is called with the actual parameter birthday .

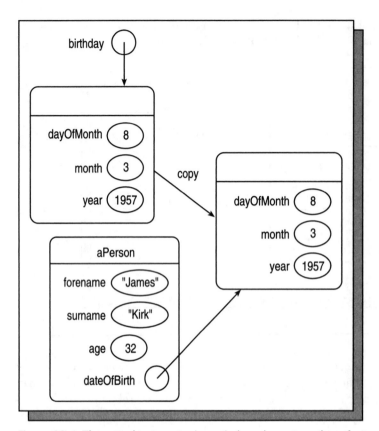

Figure 10-4: The actual parameter is copied, and we store the reference to the copy in
`aPerson.dateOfBirth`.

Now if we change the month of the date object referenced by `birthday`, we have the situation
shown in Figure 10-5. The `aPerson.dateOfBirth` object no longer references the same object as
`birthday`. So the `aPerson.dateOfBirth` object's month attribute remains as it was before.

Another way to try to avoid the problem of a "floating reference" is not to have an intermediate object reference. In essence, the only reason `birthday` exists is to allow us to set up an
`OurDate` object, which we then pass into the `Person` object `aPerson`. We can create the `OurDate`
object we need without `birthday` as follows:

```
aPerson.setDateOfBirth(new OurDate(1957,3,8));
```

As before, the call of `new OurDate` creates an `OurDate` instance, but instead of placing its
reference in an intermediate variable, instead we pass it directly as a parameter to the `Person`
method, `setDateOfBirth`. In a sense, we have an "anonymous" reference because we never
name it. Because it is anonymous, we cannot, now in our `main` method, directly access the
`OurDate` instance.

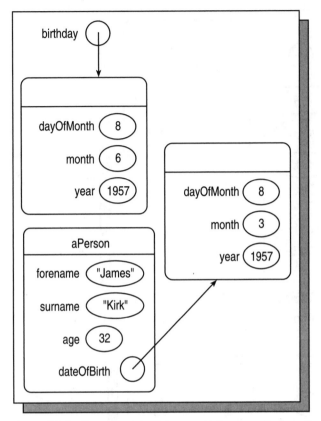

Figure 10-5: Changing `birthday.month` has no effect on the copy `aPerson.dateOfBirth`.

10.6   Objects as Parameters & Return Values: Call by Reference

Let's continue our study of object references, with particular regard to how they are used with methods—as parameters and as the returned result. First of all, let's consider them as parameters. We have already seen a method that takes an object as a parameter: namely, `setDateOfBirth` in class `Person`. Let's begin with our original version, which used a shallow copy. This sets the value of the `OurDate` object reference to that of the object in the parameter. Let's examine what happens, step by step:

- Figure 10-6 shows the temporary creation of the formal parameter `d`, which is given the same object reference as `birthday`.

- In Figure 10-7, the body of `setDateOfBirth` has executed, and `dateOfBirth` has been assigned the same reference as the formal parameter `d`.

- Figure 10-8 shows the situation after `setDateOfBirth` has completed execution, and the temporary formal parameter `d` has vanished.

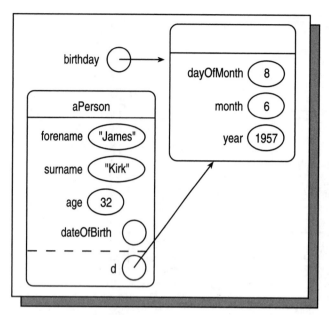

Figure 10-6: Formal and actual parameter to `setDateOfBirth`.

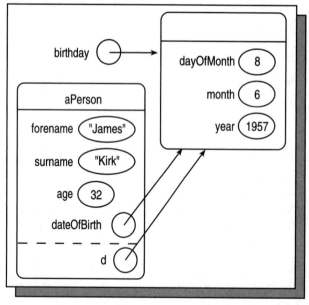

Figure 10-7: Setting the value of the `dateOfBirth` attribute.

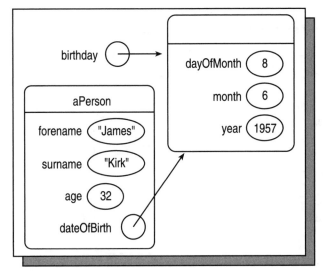

Figure 10-8: After the method has finished.

We now consider objects as return values; more correctly, these are return references. Take the `getDateOfBirth` method of class `Person`. This returns the reference that it stores in the `dateOfBirth` attribute:

```
OurDate someBirthday = null;
someBirthday = aPerson.getDateOfBirth();
```

Figure 10-9 shows what we have before the method is called.

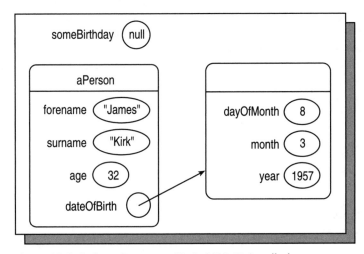

Figure 10-9: Before aPerson.getDateOfBirth is called.

After the method has been called, the reference that was in the `dateOfBirth` attribute of `aPerson` is also in the `someBirthday` object reference, as shown in Figure 10-10.

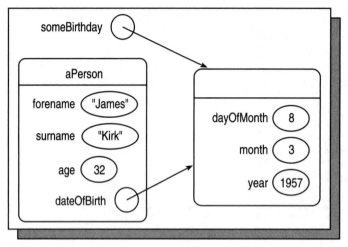

Figure 10-10: After `aPerson.getDateOfBirth` has been called.

Again, we have the situation where there is a single physical object but two references; two ways of accessing the methods associated with that object.

10.6.1   *Changing the Contents of the Formal & Actual Parameters*

It should be noted that when we change the contents of an object acting as a parameter, we also change the contents as far as the actual parameter is concerned. This should be obvious, for as we have already seen in connection with a person's birth date object, there is only one object but more than one reference to it. This is in marked contrast to the situation with the basic types and `Strings`, as discussed in Section 7.5.

We can access and update the attributes of an object parameter if the suitable `get` and `set` methods are available. Consider the following method belonging to a main class acting as a client of the `OurDate` class:

```
static void incrementMonth(OurDate d)
    {
    int month = d.getMonth();
    month = month + 1;
    if (month > OurDate.DEC)
        {
        System.out.println("oops!");
        System.exit(0);
        }
    d.setMonth(month);
    } // end of method incrementMonth
```

In the preceding code, we assume the class provider has declared 12 static integer constants to represent the months of the year.

How does this work? When we call incrementMonth, the formal parameter(s) and local variable(s) come into existence.

```
incrementMonth(today);
```

The formal parameter d is given the same value as the actual parameter today. As today is an object reference, this means that today and d both refer to exactly the same object, as shown in Figure 10-11.

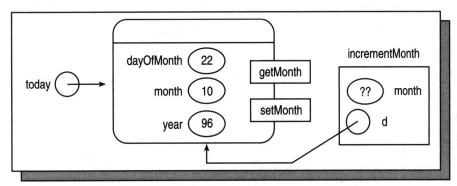

Figure 10-11: After calling incrementMonth, the formal parameter and local variable are created.

When we execute getMonth on the OurDate object d, the value 10 is returned and placed in the local variable, month, as we can see in Figure 10-12.

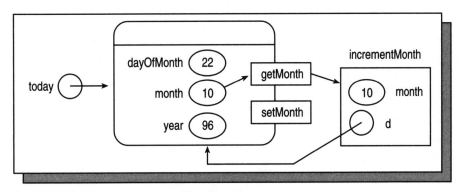

Figure 10-12: Setting the value of local variable month.

The incrementMonth method now adds one to the value of the month variable. Finally, this value is passed into the OurDate object referenced by d, using the setMonth method, as in Figure 10-13.

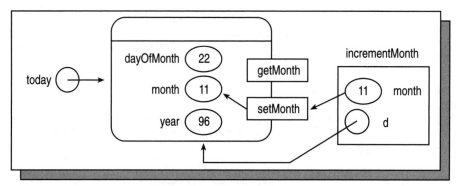

Figure 10-13: Putting back the incremented month value.

Finally, when incrementMonth terminates, we are left with the situation shown in Figure 10-14.

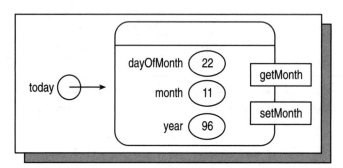

Figure 10-14: After the call of incrementMonth.

As a further example, consider a Marriage class that models the fact that two people are married. As attributes, it contains two Person objects, husband and wife. Traditionally in the Western countries, a wife takes on her husband's surname. When we create a Marriage object, we change the wife's surname to that of her husband. In the following code, we show the Marriage class:

```
public class Marriage
    {

    private Person husband, wife ;
```

```
      public Marriage(Person h, Person w)
         {
         w.setSurname(h.getSurname());

         husband = h ;
         wife = w ;
         }

      public String toString()
         {
         return (husband + " and " + wife);
         }

      } // end of class Marriage
```

And now, the main class that uses the `Marriage` class:

```
class Chapter10n1
   {
   public static void main(String[] args)
      {
      Person hus, wife;
      Marriage wedding;

      hus = new Person("Bill", "Jones", 35, Person.MALE);
      wife = new Person("Jenny", "Smith", 32, Person.FEMALE);

      System.out.println("husband is " + hus +
         " and wife is " + wife);
      wedding = new Marriage(hus, wife);
      System.out.println("wedding : " + wedding);
      System.out.println("husband is " + hus +
         " and wife is " + wife);
      } // end of method main

   } // end of class Chapter10n1
```

The result of executing this program follows :

```
husband is Bill Jones and wife is Jenny Smith
wedding : Bill Jones and Jenny Jones
husband is Bill Jones and wife is Jenny Jones
```

We can see that while the formal parameter `w` was used in the body of the `Marriage` constructor, the surname of the actual parameter `wife` was also changed. This is because the object references named `w` and `wife` are both referring to exactly the same object.

10.7 Hiding References to Other Objects

Just as in earlier examples we have seen objects provide services to the main class, here we can see that a server class, namely Person, can act as a client to a further server, namely OurDate. However, this is not the whole story. The main class has also had to declare and use objects of class OurDate in order to set up the birthday object before it could be passed into a person object.

It would, of course, be possible to organize matters so that the OurDate class was not known by the main class at all. This could be done by adding a method to the Person class as follows:

```
void setDateOfBirth(int y, int m, int d)
  {
  dateOfBirth = new OurDate(y, m, d);
  }
```

Getting back someone's date of birth, without using the OurDate class, is slightly trickier. Our current getDateOfBirth returns an object of type OurDate. Now, however, we are proposing that this is not allowed. We are left with the position that we return the individual components of OurDate; namely the three integers that represent the day, month, and year. It is not possible to write a method that returns three values; we can only ever return a single value of a basic type or an object reference.

Here, we have ruled out the possibility of returning an object reference of type OurDate. The alternatives are:

- Have three get methods that return the day, month, and year, respectively.
- Introduce a new class expressly for the purpose of allowing these three values to be returned in an object reference.

The latter seems a bit strange as we would be duplicating the OurDate effort. Let's take the first approach:

```
static int getDayDateOfBirth()
  {
  return dateOfBirth.getDayOfMonth();
  }

static int getMonthDateOfBirth()
  {
  return dateOfBirth.getMonth();
  }

static int getYearDateOfBirth()
  {
  return dateOfBirth.getYear();
  }
```

Now we have a `Person` class that completely hides the fact from its clients that it is using the `OurDate` class.

It feels as if there is more effort involved in ensuring this level of information hiding; however, as always, there are certain advantages to information hiding. If the `OurDate` class changes, this will have an impact on all classes that use it. By insulating clients of `Person`, we limit the amount of potential damage due to the `OurDate` changes. We will only have to update `Person` to take account of these changes, but all clients of `Person` should not see any effects (unless, of course, the changes to `OurDate` are so extreme that they change the `Person` class itself).

In effect, what we have done is to "pass calls on." Instead of the user of `Person` obtaining an object reference to `Person.dateOfBirth` and then directly executing methods on that reference, we are making a request to `Person`, who then passes the calls on (internally) to `Person.dateOfBirth`. We will discusses these issues again in Chapter 25.

10.8   Key Points in Chapter 10

- Objects may contain references to further objects. For example, a `Person`'s date of birth could be modeled as an `OurDate` object.

- We can pass object references into and out of objects using `get` and `set` methods.

- If we provide a `get` method for an object that is part of another object's state, we must take care! If we simply hand back a reference to someone's date of birth, what we have made is a *shallow copy* of the date of birth object. If we change the contents of the date of birth object via either reference, we may not get the results we were hoping for. This is generally true for any situation where we have more than one reference to the same object.

  If this is not the desired effect, we must make a *deep copy*, that is, create a new object of the same type and copy each individual attribute of the old object to the new object. This means we have two different references to two different objects.

  The problem is, if we have a shallow copy but believe we have a deep copy, then if we change our copy and find the original has also changed, we don't get the effect we were after.

- When we pass an object reference into a method, effectively what we have done is set up the formal parameter as a shallow copy of the actual parameter. This means if we change the attributes of the object via the formal parameter (the "copy") then we are of course changing the attributes of the actual parameter (the "original"). In general, this would be the desired effect.

- It may not be desirable to provide `set` and `get` methods that use object references directly as this has an impact on information hiding. For now, remember that a client of `Person` must now also be a client of `OurDate`, if they wish to use the date of birth attribute of `Person`. If `OurDate` changes, not only will this have an impact on `Person` (which is a direct client of `OurDate`), but also on clients of `Person` (who are now, perforce, also direct clients of OurDate). If Person's use of OurDate is completely hidden from the client of Person, then any "knock-on" effects of OurDate's alteration rest solely with Person and not the client of Person.

10.9   Exercises

1. In this chapter, we updated the Person class to store a person's date of birth as an instance of the OurDate class. This means it is a bit redundant to store the person's age because we can always calculate it by taking today's date and subtracting the person's date of birth from it.

   Update the Person class so that:

   a) It no longer holds a person's age as an attribute.

   b) It no longer provides a setAge method.

   c) The getAge method calculates the person's age and returns the result.

2. We need to model the concept of a family. For our needs, a family will consist of:

   a) A father and a mother

   b) A number of children (no more than 10)

   We can model these individual elements as instances of the Person class. Implement the Family class and provide appropriate methods for setting the elements of the class. Don't forget to provide suitable initialization constructors and a toString method.

   We would suggest that you add children to the family one at a time.

   Provide a suitable driver application to test your Family class.

3. We now need to be able to calculate the average age of the children in a family. Provide an averageAge method for your Family class; update your application to allow for testing of this method.

4. Families can consist of a single parent. We want to be able to model this in our Family class. Extend the class and, of course, the application as required to test your work.

5. In this exercise, we want to model two different classes. The first is a CD disk, which has the following attributes:

   - Name of recording artist(s)

   - Name of album

   - A track listing

   The second is a CD player. We can load up the CD player with any of our CD disks, and we can select a track to be "played." So among the methods are:

   - Load with a CD disk

   - Select track

   - Eject CD disk

When we select a track, the CD player should display the name of the artist(s), the name of the album, and the name of the track. If the track number we provide is nonexistent (negative or zero, or greater than the last track number), we should get an appropriate warning. If we try to select a track and the CD player is currently empty, again we should be warned. We can eject disks and load others as required.

Write an application to test both these classes.

6. We want to be able to model the state of the board during a game of draughts or checkers. For this problem, we will need to model the `board` (as a two-dimensional array of `squares`); squares can be empty or can contain a `piece`. A `piece`, in turn, has a color, and for the sake of redundancy, also contains its current location on the board.

Implement the three classes. Write a test application that:

a) Sets up the starting state of the board.

b) Allows the players to specify a move.

c) Checks if the move is valid.

d) If the move is valid, makes the move, updates the piece(s) involved, updates the board, and displays the board to the player(s).

CHAPTER 11

Putting Objects to Work

11.1 A Task Organizer Program

In this chapter, we are going to put to work the concepts and techniques we have learned so far about programming in Java. We are going to design and implement a program to carry out a simple task; as a by-product of this, we will be led to implement a useful sort of object that we will use in later chapters in this book.

The program we are going to write is a very simple system to keep track of all the different tasks we need to remember to carry out. A list might look something like the following:

```
Mow the lawn.
Complete programming assignment.
Look at recipes for party on Saturday.
Read the next chapter of the book on Java.
```

And so on.

If you are anything like us, this list will be extremely long, containing things that we must do today and things that we might do if there were any free time available. So we would like to assign each task a priority. This is going to be an integer in the range 1 to 4, with lower numbers being higher priorities—1 means URGENT, 2 means HIGH, 3 means MEDIUM, and 4 means LOW. So our list might now look like this:

```
2 Mow the lawn.
1 Complete programming assignment.
4 Look at recipes for party on Saturday.
4 Read the next chapter of the book on Java.
```

And so on.

We are going to have an application program constantly running on our computer that allows us access to this list. We will want to add new tasks to the list when we are committed to doing them, and we remove items from the list when they are complete. When we start the program up at the beginning of the day, we will read the current version of the list from a file on the disk. At the end of the day, before we switch the computer off, we will make an up-to-date copy of the list in a file so we can reload it tomorrow.

We are going to keep things extremely simple. One important restriction will be that we only ever remove from the list the item with the highest priority.

11.2 A Priority Queue Class

When we think about this programming task, we can see that the list of tasks is a bit like a queue. We add new tasks to the queue, and we remove the task at the front of the queue. But this is not the normal sort of queue, where things are always added to the back of the queue and removed from the front of the queue in the same order that they are added to the back (what is called a *First In First Out* or *FIFO* queue). Instead, an item is added to the queue at a position corresponding to how its priority matches the priority of the items already in the queue. This is a *priority queue* (see Figure 11-1).

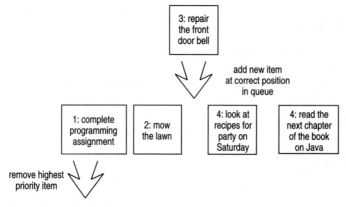

Figure 11-1: A priority queue.

Now it may be that a priority queue could be a useful feature in other programs we have to write. We are therefore going to consider writing a new class, PriorityQueue, to provide this useful type of data structure. For our task organizer, which has only four levels of priority, we could have kept four separate queues, one for each priority level. But since we have decided to write a more generally useful class, we are going to allow *any* integer as the priority number, with low values being higher priorities, and we are going to have a single queue, with the priority stored away along with the other information.

We need to start by deciding what methods such a class should have. We have already mentioned two of them:

- We need to be able to add a task to the queue in the correct position, bearing in mind its priority.

- And we need to be able to remove the item at the front of the queue (the highest priority item) because we have completed this task.

Thinking about the task further, we see the need for the following further methods:

- We suggested that we only remove an item from the queue once we have completed it. So we need to be able to look at the first item in the queue without removing it. In fact, we might like to be able to look at any or all the items in the queue, but we are going to simplify things by allowing only the first item, the item with the highest priority, to be viewed.

- Since we are not going to be allowed to look at any item but the first, it might be useful to be able to know how many items there are in the queue. We might also like to have a method to tell us whether or not there is anything at all in the queue before we try to look at it. Depending on how we implement the queue, there might be circumstances in which the queue could be completely full, so it would be useful to have a way to find this out if we are trying to add a further item.

- We are going to need a constructor method to set up a new, empty queue. We may also need a method to take a preexisting queue and to set it back to empty.

If we think about the methods to remove an item from the queue, or to look at the item at the front of the queue, we will see that *two* items of information must be passed back—a specification of the task that is to be carried out (a String) and the priority (an int), as we probably need to know how important the task is. So we are going to create a subsidiary class QueueElement, which contains these two items of information—an instance of this class will be what the "remove" and "look at first item" methods return. It also makes sense for the "insertion" method to have such an object as its single argument, although we could have provided two arguments, the task (a String) and the priority (an int).

The QueueElement class will need a constructor method to set up an object with a specified task, and there will need to be methods to extract (and possibly to set) the two attributes:

```
public class QueueElement
   {
   private int priority ;
   private String data ;

   public QueueElement()
      {
      priority = 0 ;
      data = "" ;
      } // end of constructor method

   public QueueElement(int p, String d)
      {
      priority = p ;
      data = d ;
      } // end of constructor method

   public void setPriority(int p)
      {
      priority = p ;
      } // end of method setPriority

   public void setData(String d)
      {
      data = d ;
      } // end of method setData
```

```
public int getPriority()
   {
   return priority ;
   } // end of method getPriority

public String getData()
   {
   return data ;
   } // end of method getData

} // end of class QueueElement
```

This class needs to be `public`, because an application using the `PriorityQueue` class will also need access to this class. So we will put it in a separate file, `QueueElement.java`.

A suitable set of methods for our `PriorityQueue` class is the following:

- A constructor method for this class:

  ```
  public PriorityQueue()
  ```

- An initializer method, which resets the instance to empty:

  ```
  public void initialize()
  ```

- A method for inserting an item in the queue at the correct point. This needs one argument of type `QueueElement`, containing the information (task and priority) to add to the queue:

  ```
  public void insert(QueueElement d)
  ```

- A method to remove the item with highest priority from the queue. This method has no arguments, but returns a `QueueElement`:

  ```
  public QueueElement remove()
  ```

- A method to provide information about the highest priority item without removing it from the queue. Like the `remove` method, this has no arguments but returns a `QueueElement`:

  ```
  public QueueElement first()
  ```

- A method to return how many items there are in the queue, an integer:

  ```
  public int length()
  ```

- Two Boolean methods to tell us if the queue is empty and if it is full. We will discuss later whether the latter method is the best way to deal with the possibility of queue overflow:

  ```
  public boolean isEmpty()
  ```

  ```
  public boolean isFull()
  ```

The overall structure of our code is going to be:

```
public class PriorityQueue
   {
   ... constants and instance variables ...
```

```
public PriorityQueue()
   {
   ...
   } // end of constructor method

public void initialize()
   {
   ...
   } // end of method initialize

public void insert(QueueElement d)
   {
   ...
   } // end of method insert

public QueueElement remove()
   {
   ...
   } // end of method remove

public QueueElement first()
   {
   ...
   } // end of method first

public int length()
   {
   ...
   } // end of method length

public boolean isFull()
   {
   ...
   } // end of method isFull

public boolean isEmpty()
   {
   ...
   } // end of method isEmpty

} // end of class PriorityQueue
```

This code will be in a file PriorityQueue.java. Complete versions of the code for this example are given on the Web site associated with this book.

11.3   Implementing a Priority Queue With an Array

How are we going to implement a priority queue? We are going to need to store a collection of items, each of which looks much the same—a priority (`int`) and the data (a `String`) making up a `QueueElement`. So it is natural to think of using arrays for this (we will see an alternative way of storing this queue, as a *linked list*, in Chapter 17).

We need to have an array of `QueueElements` for the items in the queue and an integer variable to remember how many items there are in the queue. So we declare:

```
private QueueElement[] buffer = new
        QueueElement[MAX_BUFFER_SIZE] ;
private int queueLength ;
```

It is not clear how big the array should be for this queue, so we are going to declare a constant:

```
private static final int MAX_BUFFER_SIZE = 100 ;
```

It will be easy to change the value of this constant once if we need to rather than go through the program looking for all the places where we need to change the value. An alternative implementation might be to allow the user to specify the maximum size of the queue as an argument for the constructor method.

The constructor method is obvious:

```
public priorityQueue()
    {
    queueLength = 0 ;
    } // end of constructor method
```
and the `initialize` method is similar:
```
public void initialize()
    {
    queueLength = 0 ;
    } // end of method initialize
```

The `length` and Boolean functions are also easy:

```
public int length()
    {
    return queueLength ;
    } // end of method length

public boolean isEmpty()
    {
    return queueLength == 0 ;
    } // end of method isEmpty

public boolean isFull()
    {
    return queueLength == MAX_BUFFER_SIZE ;
    } // end of method isFull
```

Notice that we return the Boolean value, which is the result of evaluating a Boolean expression (for example queueLength == 0); we do not need to write:

```
if (queueLength == 0)
   return true ;
else
   return false ;
```

There are several ways of using the array to hold the queue items. We are always going to insert a new item at its correct place in the array according to its priority. And we are going to have the items stored in descending order of priority with the first item (the item with the highest priority) in array position zero. When we remove this first item we are going to shuffle all the other items along one, with the item in position one going into position zero, that in position two going into position one, and so on. There are a number of alternative ways to store the information in the array, which we discuss in the next section.

Figure 11-2 shows a typical example of a priority queue according to this way of doing it.

buffer

highest priority item	next highest priority item	next highest priority item	next highest priority item	lowest priority item					
0	1	2	3	4	5	6	7	8	9

queueLength

5

Figure 11-2: Holding items in descending order of priority.

With this design, the first method is easy:

```
public QueueElement first()
   {
   if (isEmpty())
      {
      System.out.println("queue underflow") ;
      System.exit(1) ;
      }
   return buffer[0] ;
   } // end of method first
```

We first use our isEmpty method to check that the queue is not empty. We should always do this—we should not rely on the programmer who uses our package (it might be ourselves!) to remember to check before calling this method. If the queue is empty, we abandon the program with an error message (which is probably too terse) and a call of the System.exit method. A better solution would probably be to throw an exception (we will learn how to do this in Chapter 15).

The remove method is similar but needs to do the shuffle down:

```
public QueueElement remove()
   {
   // check for empty queue
   if (isEmpty())
      {
      System.out.println("queue underflow") ;
      System.exit(1) ;
      }

   // remember the first item
   QueueElement temp = buffer[0] ;

   // shuffle everything else up
   for (int i = 0 ; i < queueLength - 1 ; i++)
      buffer[i] = buffer[i + 1] ;

   // adjust the length
   queueLength-- ;

   // return the first item
   return temp ;
   } // end of method remove
```

There are several ways to write the shuffling loop—another is:

```
for (int i = 1 ; i < queueLength ; i++)
   buffer[i - 1] = buffer[i] ;
```

We chose the first way because it seemed to be clearer what the range of the index variable i should be. The elements of the queue *after* the removal are in locations zero to queueLength--1.

Finally, we have to write the most complicated method, the insert method, which we have been putting off for as long as possible. Here it is:

```
public void insert(QueueElement d)
   {
   // check that the queue is not full
   if (isFull())
      {
      System.out.println("queue overflow") ;
      System.exit(1) ;
      }
```

```
// search for the correct insertion position "i"
int i = 0 ;
while ((i < queueLength) &&
       (buffer[i].getPriority() <= d.getPriority()))
   i++ ;

// shuffle the data up (if necessary)
for (int j = queueLength ; j > i ; j--)
   buffer[j] = buffer[j - 1] ;

// insert the item
buffer[i] = d ;

// adjust queue length
queueLength++ ;
} // end of method insert
```

We first check that the queue is not full.

We then scan through the array leaving the variable i pointing to the place the new item should go, according to its priority. We continue to scan until either (a) we reach the end of the queue or (b) we meet a queue element with a priority value larger (that is, with a lower priority) than the one we are adding. The test on the priorities is "less than or equal" (<=) rather than "less than" (<) so if we have several items with the same priority, they will be inserted in the order they were added to the queue (that is, the queue is FIFO within priority).

If the queue is empty, or the new item has a lower priority value than all the items already in the queue, we will be adding the item in the first free space after any items already in the queue. But otherwise we have to shuffle up the items from position i (inclusive) to the end of the array. The next loop does this.

Finally we insert the data and priority in the appropriate place in the array and update the queue length.

Actually, there is a problem with this implementation, and it relates to the issue of *shallow* and *deep* copying, raised in the previous chapter. We have inserted the new item in the queue with an assignment statement:

```
buffer[i] = d ;
```

This causes the ith element of the array buffer to refer to the formal argument, the object d; that is, it refers to the actual argument of the insert method. Suppose we do the following:

```
PriorityQueue q = new PriorityQueue() ;
QueueElement temp = new QueueElement(1, "first item") ;
q.insert(temp) ;
```

Then, since we copied a *reference* to temp into buffer[0], the situation is shown in Figure 11-3.

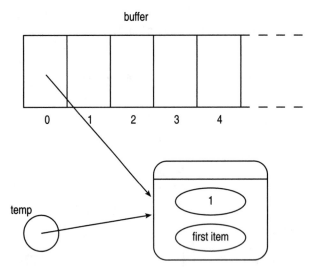

Figure 11-3: An object with a reference from the priority queue.

If we now attempt to insert a new element in the queue with the following code, it will not work:

```
temp.setPriority(2) ;
temp.setData("second item") ;
q.insert(temp) ;
```

What is happening is that the insert method copies only a reference (that is, we are doing a shallow copy, and we will change the element occupying the first location in the queue). This is presumably not what we want. The situation is in fact what you see in Figure 11-4.

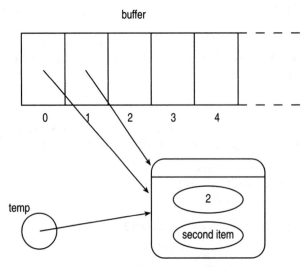

Figure 11-4: A single object with two references from the priority queue.

We need make a deep copy of the element we are inserting in the queue, so the correct form of the assignment statement in the insert method is:

```
buffer[i] = new QueueElement(d.getPriority(), d.getData()) ;
```

We generate a new object instance for buffer[i] to refer to and use the constructor method to set its attributes from those of the instance d.

There is a similar problem with the first method. We have written:

```
return buffer[0] ;
```

Suppose we call this method as follows:

```
QueueElement x = q.first() ;
x.setPriority(5) ;
```

We would now find that the first element in the queue has had its priority changed to 5. We should have taken a copy of the element in the first method:

```
return new QueueElement(buffer[0].getPriority(),
buffer[0].getData()) ;
```

The remove method does not have this problem, since the object is actually removed from the queue. So once we have returned from the method, the only reference to the object is in the actual argument.

11.4 Alternative Implementations of PriorityQueue (optional)

The array implementation in the previous section involves inserting a new element at the correct position in the queue (which may involve shuffling element references about) and doing more shuffling when the highest priority element is removed. An alternative implementation would store the elements in reverse order, with the lowest priority element in position zero in the buffer and with increasing priority as we move through the array, as shown in Figure 11-5.

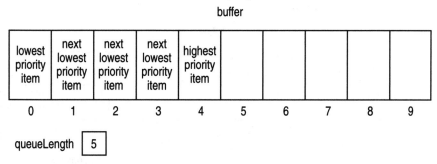

Figure 11-5: Holding items in ascending order of priority.

The highest priority item (the "first" or "front" item) is at location `queueLength-1`. This means that we can remove this item without any shuffling; the shuffling is always done on input.

Suppose we want to revert to the original scenario of having priority decreasing as we move up through the array. We are forced to do any shuffling required by the `insert` method because we are committed to keeping the elements in priority order. But we can avoid the shuffling in the `remove` by using what is called a *circular buffer*, where an item stays in the same array location while it is in the queue. In a simple first-in-first-out queue, we could use a similar circular buffer to eliminate all shuffling.

The idea is that when we remove the first queue item from array location zero, we simply remember that the new first element in the queue is now at array location one, and so on (see Figure 11-6). We would declare instance variables for this implementation as follows:

```
private QueueElement[] buffer = new
QueueElement[MAX_BUFFER_SIZE] ;
int firstPointer, lastPointer ;
```

buffer

		highest priority item	next highest priority item	next highest priority item	next highest priority item	lowest priority item			

0   1   2↑   3   4   5   6↑   7   8   9

firstpointer   lastpointer

Figure 11-6: Using a circular buffer.

Of course, what happens now is that, as items are added to and removed from the queue, the queue data migrates up through the array (see Figure 11-7). We simply have to assume that the last location of the array is followed by the first element, which is where the term *circular buffer* comes from.

buffer

next highest priority item	lowest priority item						highest priority item	next highest priority item	next highest priority item

0   ↑1   2   3   4   5   6   7↑   8   9

lastpointer   firstpointer

Figure

11-7: A circular buffer where `lastPointer` is behind `firstPointer`.

This is easy to program—you have to ensure that the lastPointer never catches up with the firstPointer. It is best to retain the variable queueLength to make it easy to test for this condition.

A more radical alternative would be not to store the elements in priority order, but simply to insert each one in the next free location in the array. Then we would extract the highest priority item by scanning through the array looking for it when required.

11.5   Testing the PriorityQueue Class

We have written our PriorityQueue class, and we now need to make sure that it works. We may have already written the program that is going to make use of this class, in which case we might hope that running the program with the new class will iron out any bugs. But this is not a good way to proceed:

- It may actually be very difficult to make the program systematically try out all the different ways of calling the methods of the new class because it depends on the particular ways the program uses the PriorityQueue methods for particular sets of data.

- If the results are not what we expect, the problem could be in the PriorityQueue class code, or it could be in the code of the program using it.

- Finally, in this case we have not in fact yet written the program code for the overall task.

So we are going to write a simple driver program that we can use to exercise our PriorityQueue class. Here it is:

```
public static void main(String[] args) throws IOException
    {
    int priority ;
    String data ;
    String response ;
    boolean continueLoop = true ;
    PriorityQueue q = new PriorityQueue() ;
    QueueElement temp = new QueueElement() ;

    while (continueLoop)
        {
        displayMenu() ;
        response = BasicIo.readString().toLowerCase() ;
        if (response.length() == 0)
            response = "x" ;

        switch (response.charAt(0))
            {
            case '1' :
                q.initialize() ;
                System.out.println("queue initialized:") ;
                break ;
```

```
case '2' :
  BasicIo.prompt("priority? ") ;
  priority = BasicIo.readInteger() ;
  BasicIo.prompt("string to insert? ") ;
  data = BasicIo.readString() ;
  temp.setPriority(priority) ;
  temp.setData(data) ;
  q.insert(temp) ;
  System.out.print("'" + data) ;
System.out.print("' inserted in queue with priority ") ;
  System.out.println(priority) ;
  break ;
case '3' :
  temp = q.first() ;
  System.out.print("'" + temp.getData()) ;
System.out.print("' at head of queue with priority ") ;
  System.out.println(temp.getPriority()) ;
  break ;
case '4' :
  temp = q.remove() ;
  System.out.print("'" + temp.getData()) ;
System.out.print("' removed from queue with priority ") ;
  System.out.println(temp.getPriority()) ;
  break ;
case '5' :
  System.out.print("there are " + q.length()) ;
  System.out.println(" items in the queue") ;
  break ;
case '6' :
  System.out.print("the queue is ") ;
  if (!q.isFull())
    System.out.print("not ") ;
  System.out.println("full") ;
  break ;
case '7' :
  System.out.print("the queue is ") ;
  if (!q.isEmpty())
    System.out.print("not ") ;
  System.out.println("empty") ;
  break ;
case '8' :
  while (true)
    {
    BasicIo.prompt("priority (0 to terminate)? ") ;
    priority = BasicIo.readInteger() ;
    if (priority == 0)
      break ;
```

```
                    BasicIo.prompt("string to insert? ") ;
                    data = BasicIo.readString() ;
                    temp.setPriority(priority) ;
                    temp.setData(data) ;
                    q.insert(temp) ;
                    }
                break ;
            case '9' :
                while (!q.isEmpty())
                    {
                    temp = q.remove() ;
                    System.out.print("'" + temp.getData()) ;
                    System.out.print("'with priority ") ;
                    System.out.println(temp.getPriority()) ;
                    }
                System.out.println("**end of queue**") ;
                break ;
            case 'a' :
                q.print() ;
                break ;
            case 'q' :
                continueLoop = false ;
                break ;
            default :
                System.out.println("invalid response") ;
                break ;
            }
        if (continueLoop)
            {
            BasicIo.prompt("press RETURN to continue ") ;
            response = BasicIo.readString() ;
            }
        }
    System.out.println("program terminating") ;
    } // end of method main

private static void displayMenu()
    {
    System.out.println() ;
    System.out.println("Options to Exercise the Priority Queue") ;
    System.out.println() ;
    System.out.println("1 : initialize") ;
    System.out.println("2 : insert") ;
    System.out.println("3 : first") ;
    System.out.println("4 : remove") ;
    System.out.println("5 : length") ;
    System.out.println("6 : is full") ;
```

```
        System.out.println("7 : is empty") ;
        System.out.println() ;
        System.out.println("8 : multiple item insert") ;
        System.out.println("9 : scan and empty queue") ;
        System.out.println("a : print queue contents") ;
        System.out.println() ;
        System.out.println("q : quit") ;
        } // end of method displayMenu

private void print()
    {
    System.out.println("the queue is (highest priority first)") ;
    for (int i = 0 ; i < queueLength ; i++)
        {
        System.out.print(i) ;
        System.out.print(": priority = " + buffer[i].getPriority()) ;
        System.out.print(": data = '" + buffer[i].getData()) ;
        System.out.println("'") ;
        }
    } // end of method print
```

Notice that we have written this driver program as the `main` method in the `PriorityQueue` class. The idea is that it is part of the class, allowing us to test it whenever necessary—for example, if we add new methods, or make a change to a method. If we call this class with:

`java PriorityQueue`

the `main` method is called in the usual way. It sets up an instance of the `PriorityQueue` class, and then the user can exercise this with the commands provided, which invoke the various methods with suitable data provided by the user, afterward indicating what the result of the call was.

A test of the `PriorityQueue` class should include at least the following:

- Some straightforward tests to determine that a sequence of inserts followed by a sequence of removes returns the correct values in the correct order.

- A test of inserting a sequence of values, removing some of them, then inserting some more, and finally removing all of them, at all times returning the correct values in the correct order.

- Tests to determine that insertions into an empty queue, at the beginning of a queue, at the end of a queue, and in the middle all give the right results.

- Tests to determine that insertion of multiple items with the same priority all give the same results.

- Tests to determine that while the preceding sequences are being performed, the methods `first`, `isEmpty`, and `length` return the correct results, and that `remove` and `first` work correctly on an empty queue.

- A test of reinitializing a `PriorityQueue` and then seeing that insertion, removal, and the other method calls still work.

■ A test of the isFull method and what happens if you try to insert an item into a full queue. Notice that a special command has been provided in the driver program to allow these capacity tests to be done with reasonable ease.

11.6 Using the PriorityQueue Class

We can now return to our original "task organizer" program. The basic structure of the program is:

■ When the program starts up, set up a PriorityQueue instance, open the file of tasks, and read them into the queue using the insert method.

■ Manipulate the queue using insert to add new tasks, first to look at the highest priority task (the next one to be carried out), and remove to remove it when completed.

■ When the program closes down, reopen the file of tasks on disk and copy the current set of tasks from the queue (with remove) to the file.

The code for a simple version of this program is as follows:

```
import java.lancs.* ;

public class TaskOrganizer
    {
    public static void main(String[] args) throws Exception
        {
        PriorityQueue p = new PriorityQueue() ;
        QueueElement temp = new QueueElement() ;

        BasicIo.prompt("type name of file containing tasks ") ;
        String fileName = BasicIo.readString() ;
        BasicFileIo fileIn = new
            BasicFileIo(BasicFileIo.INPUT, fileName) ;
        while (true)
            {
            int priority = fileIn.readInteger() ;
            if (priority == 0)
                break ;
            String task = fileIn.readString() ;
            temp.setPriority(priority) ;
            temp.setData(task) ;
            p.insert(temp) ;
            }
        fileIn.closeFile() ;
        System.out.println("there are " + p.length() + " tasks") ;
```

```
int priority ;
String data ;
String response ;
boolean continueLoop = true ;

while (continueLoop)
    {
    displayMenu() ;

    response = BasicIo.readString().toLowerCase() ;
    if (response.length() == 0)
        response = "x" ;

    switch (response.charAt(0))
        {
        case 'a' :
            BasicIo.prompt("task to add ") ;
            data = BasicIo.readString() ;
            BasicIo.prompt("priority? ") ;
            priority = BasicIo.readInteger() ;
            temp.setPriority(priority) ;
            temp.setData(data) ;
            p.insert(temp) ;
            break ;

        case 'f' :
            temp = p.first() ;
            System.out.print("'" + temp.getData()) ;
        System.out.print("' at head of list with priority ") ;
            System.out.println(temp.getPriority()) ;
            break ;

        case 'r' :
            temp = p.remove() ;
            System.out.print("'" + temp.getData()) ;
    System.out.print("' removed from list with priority ") ;
            System.out.println(temp.getPriority()) ;
            break ;

        case 'q' :
            continueLoop = false ;
            break ;

        default :
            System.out.println("invalid response") ;
            break ;
        }
```

```
        if (continueLoop)
          {
          BasicIo.prompt("press RETURN to continue ") ;
          response = BasicIo.readString() ;
          }
        }

    BasicFileIo fileOut = new
       BasicFileIo(BasicFileIo.OUTPUT, fileName) ;
    while (!p.isEmpty())
       {
       temp = p.remove() ;
       fileOut.println(temp.getPriority()) ;
       fileOut.println(temp.getData()) ;
       }
    fileOut.println(0) ;
    fileOut.closeFile() ;
    } // end of method main

 private static void displayMenu()
    {
    System.out.println() ;
    System.out.println("Options to Manipulate Task List") ;
    System.out.println() ;
    System.out.println("a : add new task") ;
    System.out.println("f : look at first task") ;
    System.out.println("r : remove first task") ;
    System.out.println() ;
    System.out.println("q : quit") ;
    } // end of method displayMenu

 } // end of class TaskOrganizer
```

11.7 Outstanding Issues

In writing our TaskOrganizer program and its PriorityQueue class, a number of issues arise, which we will revisit in the remainder of the book.

When we created our PriorityQueue class, we did the job in two stages. First we decided what operations we would like to be able to carry out on objects of this type. Second, we decided how we would implement objects of this type. We decided to use arrays for the moment, despite that fact that it forced us to consider issues like the maximum size of a queue and how best to do the shuffling around of items (which might be quite costly in time if the queue was very long).

Later (in Chapter 17), we will see that there is an alternative way of implementing a priority queue. We can build a priority queue class that provides the same set of methods as the one described in this chapter, except, we will use a linked list structure instead of an array. We will no longer have to consider the maximum queue size, and we will no longer have to do the shuffling around of items. But the cost is that the concepts and coding involved are slightly more complicated, and we have to take extra care with the implementation.

As far as we are concerned, a priority queue is defined in terms of what operations are allowed—in other words, what method calls we can make. We are free to choose whatever implementation we like; we can start off with a simple but inefficient implementation and later return to the task of making a more complex but more efficient version of the queue. We have used the object-oriented nature of Java to ensure that a programmer who uses the class cannot make use of any knowledge about how the class is actually implemented, since it is all encapsulated inside the class. This is the basic idea of *information hiding*, which we have met in several places in this book.

When we define a type of programming element and specify what type of operations can be performed on it, we call this a *data type*. For example, Java's basic data type `int` is defined in terms of what values it can take on and what operations can be performed on values of this type—all the arithmetic operations, for example, but not Boolean AND or string concatenate. Similarly, our priority queue is defined in terms of what values it can take on (a collection of strings of characters with associated priority values) and what operations can be performed on it—insert, remove, and so on. We call this an *abstract data type*. It is abstract because we define the operations but not how they are to be implemented.

This priority queue is actually a priority queue of strings of characters. We might wish to store along with our task definition some further information, such as an estimate of how long it will take or what other resources are needed to complete it. We could collect all this information together as a new class (perhaps called `TaskDetails`). So we would now like our priority queue to be a priority queue of `TaskDetails` objects.

Some programming languages allow us to define a priority queue of some incompletely specified object. We could then use this partially specified abstract data type to generate a completely specified priority queue by indicating what the basic queue item is to be. This concept is sometimes called *genericity*. We specify a priority queue in terms of a "generic" ELE-MENT, and then we have a mechanism to say, "take the generic priority queue, and make it into a specific type of priority queue where the ELEMENT is actually a `String`, or a `TaskDetails` instance, or whatever."

Java handles this genericity requirement in a different way. We first have to introduce the concept of inheritance and the inheritance hierarchy of objects in the next three chapters before we can explore this.

If we attempt to extract an item from an empty queue or insert an item in a full queue, we have set the methods up to display an error message and stop the program (using the `System.exit` method). This is fairly drastic, and it would be better to throw an exception to allow the program using the `PriorityQueue` class to attempt to recover if possible. To tell the full story of how to manipulate exceptions again requires an understanding of inheritance, so we will return to the topic of exceptions and exception handling in Chapter 15.

11.8   Key Points in Chapter 11

- If we write a class to model some concept, we can put a `main` method inside the class to provide a test harness.

- Whenever we modify the class, we should use the test harness to do a full check on the facilities provided by the class.

- An *abstract data type* is a class of objects with a range of facilities provided by a set of methods, where the behavior of the class is defined in terms of the behavior of the methods and not in terms of how they are implemented.

11.9   Exercises

1. Add the following methods to the `PriorityQueue` class:

   (a) A second `insert` method, where the information to be inserted into the queue is passed as two arguments, the task (a `String`), and the priority (an `int`):

   ```
   public void insert(String task, int priority)
   ```

   (b) Methods `getTopData` and `getTopPriority` to return, respectively, the data and the priority of the element in the queue with the highest priority:

   ```
   public String getTopData()
   public int getTopPriority()
   ```

   Modify the test harness, and fully test your new methods.

2. Reimplement the `PriorityQueue` using the alternative array implementations discussed in section 11.4. Fully test your new versions. Is one implementation in particular simpler to program than the others, and (if so) why?

3. Define a class `BookDetails` to hold information about books—the title, the author's name, and the year of publication.

   Implement a simple First In First Out (FIFO) queue, where the element removed is the element added to the queue longest ago, to hold a queue of `BookDetails` instances.

   You should provide a similar set of methods to the `PriorityQueue` class, and you can use any of the array implementations discussed in this chapter.

   Write a program to allow you to test your implementation.

Advanced
Objects

Introduction to Inheritance

12.1 Motivation

Inheritance is a very important part of the object model. Unfortunately, it is also one of the more complex aspects of the model. It is crucial that you gain a thorough understanding of the concept in order to make full use of the mechanism. We begin by examining the concept in connection with data modeling; for the moment, we will ignore programming features such as methods.

12.1.1 Data Modeling

As we have already seen, a class can be viewed as a set of objects that share common features. This means we can have the universal set of all objects in our universe, and, by examining all of them, we can identify subsets. Membership of a subset will be dictated by the features (or attributes) of each object. For example, we could have subsets for males and females; membership would be based on the value of an object's "gender" attribute.

As a side issue, we hope you can envisage how set membership could be automated using selection statements and Boolean conditions. It is worth noting, however, that it is possible to form sets that cannot be automatically formed because they are based on subjective assessment of an object's features. For example, if we have a set of books, and we wish to form a subset of good books, then membership of this latter set must be based on a personal assessment.

In a programming language like Java, set membership is automatic. When we declare an object of type `Person`, we know it will have a group of features in common with all other instances of type `Person`, hence it is a member of that set (or class).

However, just as we start with the universal set of all objects and can form various subsets of that set, it should be obvious that we can repeat this procedure as often as we like. For example, we can examine a subset and decide that it, too, can form the basis for subsequent subsets. Indeed, there may be so many possible subsets that it becomes difficult to decide which sets to use. Obviously, in programming terms, we can use the application requirements to help us choose.

Regardless, let's continue with our general model with the initial set "object". Now, we may choose to have subsets for people and animals. We can look at people and say we want to have young people and old people. We can look at young people and say we want to have school pupils, toddlers, undergraduates, and so on, as shown in Figure 12-1.

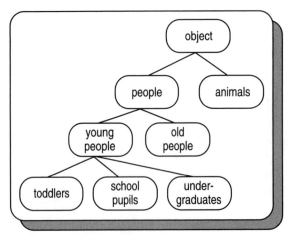

Figure 12-1: A generalization/specialization tree.

What exactly are we doing as we move away from the root of the tree and out toward the leaves? We are moving from the most general concept—the object—to a set of much more specialized ones—toddlers, pupils, undergraduates. In data modeling terms, we are using the concepts of *generalization* and *specialization*.

Specialization means that we examine the features of a set and identify a group of objects that share one or more additional features that others within the set do not possess. For example, in the set of young people, we may find that some of them have a feature that they are registered for a degree at a university. Clearly, this is a feature that not all young people have (e.g., toddlers, pupils, etc.). So we form a new subset, undergraduates, and make all relevant objects members of this subset.

Generalization means we are examining the features of a number of sets and identifying a group of features common to members of all those sets. We should use this conclusion to generate a new "superset" that the involved sets become subsets of. For example, consider an academic set of publications. These may be the sets books, journal papers, and conference papers, as shown in Figure 12-2.

We can see that all three groups share a set of features; that is, author name and title. We can thus form a new set, publications, and make the three existing sets subsets of this new set, as shown in Figure 12-3.

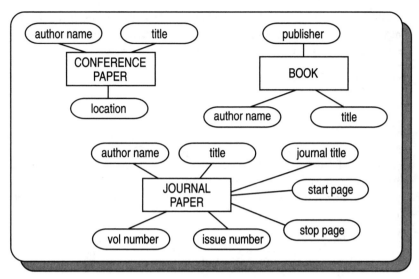

Figure 12-2: Three separate sets.

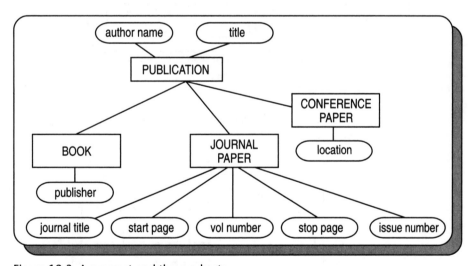

Figure 12-3: A superset and three subsets.

Let's pause for a moment and see what it means for an object to be a member of a subset. Let's declare some objects in a Java-style syntax.

```
Publication p1;
Book b1, b2, b3;
JournalPaper j1, j2;
ConfPaper c1, c2;
```

Object b1 has been directly declared of type Book; this means it is a member of the set of Books. However, because Book is a subset of Publication, this means it is also a member of the set of Publications. If we write this in set notation, we have:

```
Books = {b1, b2, b3}
JournalPapers = {j1, j2}
ConfPapers = {c1, c2}
Publications = {p1, b1, b2, b3, j1, j2, c1, c2}
```

Although object c1 was not declared as type Publication, because it is of type ConfPaper, it shares a set of features with all Publication objects—namely "author name" and "title." It is therefore a member of the set of Publications.

We can draw a diagram to represent the relation between sets and subsets as a tree (see Figure 12-4).

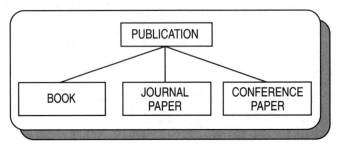

Figure 12-4: Sets and subsets as a tree.

We can also use standard Venn diagrams to represent the relationship between elements of sets and subsets (see Figure 12-5).

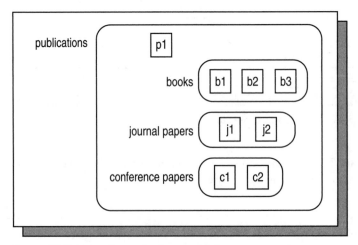

Figure 12-5: Venn diagram of set and subsets.

In a Java-like syntax, how might we represent the declarations of these four sets? We may proceed as we have up until now:

```
class Publication
   {
   String authorName, title;
   }

class JournalPaper
   {
   String authorName, title;

   String journalTitle;
   int startPage, stopPage, volNumber, issueNumber;
   }

class ConfPaper
   {
   String authorName, title;

   String location;
   }

class Book
   {
   String authorName, title;

   String publisher;
   }
```

Now, this may reproduce some of the effects we desire, but it is seriously lacking in a number of areas:

- We haven't captured the information that Book is a subset of Publication. By inspecting the attributes or features, we can deduce this, but we shouldn't have to. It should be clearly indicated. This is a matter of unclear semantics.

- On a pragmatic level, what happens if we realize Publication should have an additional attribute (such as "date of publication")? Now we must remember to add it to all of the subsets as well, and, as noted earlier, we have no easy or quick way of finding all those subsets.

- On a linguistic level, when we declare an instance of Book, it will only be a member of the set of Books. There is no way of knowing that it is also a member of the set of Publications.

Java provides us with a keyword, extends, which allows us to overcome these three problems. Now we can write our declarations as follows:

```
class Publication
   {
   String authorName, title;
   }

class JournalPaper extends Publication
   {
   String journalTitle;
   int startPage, stopPage, volNumber, issueNumber;
   }

class ConfPaper extends Publication
   {
   String location;
   }

class Book extends Publication
   {
   String publisher;
   }
```

Notice that something interesting has happened: Now, when we declare Book, we do not need to repeat the declarations of the attributes contained in Publication. An instance of Book has the attributes directly associated with the declaration of Book (namely publisher), but it also automatically has those associated with the class it extends (namely, those of Publication—authorName and paperTitle). Book is said to *inherit* the features of Publication.

There is quite a bit of loose terminology in the area of inheritance. As we have seen, a new class may extend an existing class. In our example, Book *extends* Publication. Book is a specialization of Publication. We can describe the participants in an "extending" relationship in various ways, as shown in Table 12-1.

existing class	new class
superclass	subclass
base	derived
parent	child

Table 12-1: Participants in an extending relationship.

It can get pretty confusing, so we will usually refer to superclasses and subclasses in the remainder of this book.

12.1.2 Programming

We have considered the impact of inheritance on data modeling. In this section, we turn our attention to software. Inheritance gives us a mechanism for extending an existing class. This is a powerful way of adapting an existing class that provides most—if not all—the functionality we need without having to rewrite the existing class.

For example, consider the work we did earlier in the book using the OurDate class (Chapter 10). As we have said, there is already a system-provided class called Date. However, we used OurDate as an example, and it contains three methods that Date does not—most importantly, subtract, which allows us to subtract one date from another to return an integer result that is the number of days elapsed between the two dates.

If we started again without OurDate and wanted to use the system Date, it would provide most of the functionality we require—but not the subtract method. In a non-object-oriented system, how would we adapt the Date module to provide this new functionality? It could prove to be rather awkward.

In Java, we can use the inheritance mechanism. We declare a new class, Date2, which extends the existing class Date. As we have seen earlier, when we declare a subclass, we do not need to repeat the declarations of the attributes and methods of the superclass. All we have to specify is the difference between the subclass and the superclass. In this case, the difference is the subtract method, and the two methods that directly support it, dayOfTheYear and leapyear.

Moving from a base class to a derived class is the *specialization* process. We are adding more detail and more functionality as we move from the superclass to the subclass. In this example, we have added more functionality.

It should be seen that inheritance is a powerful mechanism for supporting software reuse. Developing Date2 by extending Date means that:

- We can use all the existing public methods and attributes of Date in implementing Date2.

- The "information hiding" principle, so important in software engineering and modular construction, is upheld. We may never need to know how the Date methods are implemented in order to provide the extended functionality of Date2.

We are, in the truest sense, building on existing work rather than tearing it all down and starting again.

We can also apply the generalization approach. There may already exist a number of classes that provide similar functionality. We can identify a new superclass that we can use to factor out the common code from the existing classes.

For example, if we were developing classes for Java's AWT (Abstract Window Toolkit, see Chapter 16), we could imagine independently developing (test) classes for Panels, Frames, and Dialogs. We would quickly find that we were carrying out the same kinds of operations on these basic graphical constructs; for example, adding other graphical components (such as buttons, labels, and text fields) and managing these components.

As a result, we might identify that our three graphical classes are, in fact, all types of containers for other components. We could then introduce a new class, Container, which would bring together the necessary shared methods and act as a superclass to Panels, Frames, and Dialogs.

The bonuses here include:

- There is a single place where the common code resides. Previously, the same (or similar) code would be in a number of different classes. If a modification is made in one class, how can we ensure it is updated everywhere?

- Chances are that the common code will represent a useful "abstract" concept that can now be reused in other specializations. If we hadn't factored it out, it might have stayed hidden, "buried" within the other classes.

12.2   What's the Difference?

As we indicated earlier, one way of figuring out what we need in the derived class is thinking about what the difference is between the existing base class and the proposed derived class.

In terms of data modeling, if we already have a `Person` class and now need to represent an `Employee` class, we need to think about the difference between people in general and someone who has a job. If we look at the `Person` class, we find out that people have a name, an age, and a gender. So do employees, as we would expect. What does an employee have that a person doesn't? Employees have a salary and a tax code. So we can define an `Employee` class as follows:

```
class Employee extends Person
   {
   double salary;
   String taxCode;
   }
```

All we have to declare are the differences between a `Person` and an `Employee`. The similarities are taken care of by inheritance:

```
Employee - Person = {salary, taxCode }
```

This holds for methods as well as attributes. What we define in our derived class are the additional attributes and methods that make up the difference.

The difference between `Date` and `Date2` are the methods `subtract`, `dayOfTheYear`, and `leapyear`:

```
Date2 - Date = {subtract, dayOfTheYear, leapyear}
```

So we have seen how we can supply additional methods.

12.3   Overriding Inherited Methods

It is also possible to replace existing methods (which we inherit from the base class) by ones that are more suited to the derived class. For example, we can define a class to represent a square, and subsequently define a subclass rectangle. With geometric shapes such as these, it is often useful to provide methods such as area and perimeter.

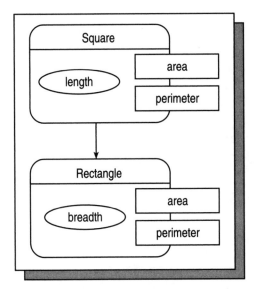

Figure 12-6: The Square and Rectangle classes.

From the diagram in Figure 12-6, we can see that Square has one attribute, length. Rectangle provides one attribute, breadth, and inherits length from Square. Square has two methods, area and perimeter. The algorithms for calculating the area and perimeter of a square use the length of the square as shown in Table 12-2.

area	length * length
perimeter	length * 4

Table 12-2 : Algorithms for area and perimeter of a square.

The definition of the Square class is as follows:

```
class Square
   {
   protected int length ;
```

```
public Square()
   {
   length = 0;
   }

public Square(int 1)
   {
   length = 1 ;
   }

public int getLength()
   {
   return length;
   }

public int area()
   {
   return length * length;
   }

public int perimeter()
   {
   return length * 4;
   }

} // end of class Square
```

The length attribute has been declared as protected; we shall discuss what this means later. Rectangle also has two methods with the same name. However, the algorithms use more than the length attribute; they have to use both the length and the breadth as shown in Table 12-3.

area	length * breadth
perimeter	(length + breadth) * 2

Table 12-3 : Algorithms for area and perimeter of a rectangle.

It would be quite inappropriate for instances of Rectangle to use the area and perimeter methods provided by the superclass. We wish to override or replace the Square methods with new, more suitable ones for the Rectangle. We simply do this by redefining them in the Rectangle class:

```
class Rectangle extends Square
   {
```

```
private int breadth ;

public Rectangle()
   {
   length = 0;
   breadth = 0;
   }

public Rectangle(int 1, int b)
   {
   length = 1 ;
   breadth = b;
   }

public int getBreadth()
   {
   return breadth;
   }

public int area()
   {
   return length * breadth;
   }

public int perimeter()
   {
   return (length + breadth) * 2;
   }

} // end of class Rectangle
```

Table 12-4 summarizes what is provided by Square and what is inherited, added, or overridden by Rectangle:

Square	length		getLength		area	perimeter
Rectangle	inherited	breadth	inherited	getBreadth	overridden	overridden

Table 12-4: Methods and attributes of Square and Rectangle.

Those of you in the know about geometric figures will realize that it is unusual to consider Rectangle as a specialization of Square rather than vice versa. In our defense, we have done it this way because it is a good example (!), and we revisit the situation later.

To end this section, we present a small test program of the `Square` and `Rectangle` classes:

```
class Chapter12n1
  {
  public static void main(String[] args)
    {
    Square s1 = new Square(5);
    Rectangle r1 = new Rectangle (4,2);
    System.out.println("square of side " + s1.getLength() +
       " has area "+s1.area()+
       " and perimeter "+ s1.perimeter());
    System.out.println("rectangle of length " +
    r1.getLength() +
       " and breadth " + r1.getBreadth() +
       " has area "+ r1.area()+
       " and perimeter "+ r1.perimeter());
    } // end of main
  } // end of class Chapter12n1
```

The appropriate method is called in each case. For example, when the compiler processes the method call:

```
r1.area()
```

it knows the type of `r1` from the declarations at the start of the `main` method; it knows that `r1` is a `Rectangle`. When it encounters the call of `area`, therefore, it knows to call the `area` method that belongs to the `Rectangle` class.

On the other hand, when we call:

```
r1.getLength()
```

we know that the `Rectangle` class does not directly possess a method called `getLength`. However, through inheritance, we know that a `Rectangle` is also a `Square`, and the `Square` class does have a `getLength` method. We will therefore call the `getLength` method belonging to the `Square` class.

12.4 Access Rights & Subclasses

Now that we have introduced the concept of subclasses, we need to revisit the access rights we introduced in Chapter 8, section 8.9.3. We spoke about the four levels of access permission: public, protected, default, and private. The two ends of the spectrum, public and private, remain as before. The issue of subclasses does not affect them. When a method or variable is *public*, it can be accessed anywhere. When a method or variable is *private*, it can only be accessed from within the class in which it is declared.

In `Rectangle`, we wish to represent both the length and the breadth of a rectangle. `Square` already contains an instance variable, `length`, which we wish to use by inheritance. However, if in `Square` we had defined the variable `length` as private, there is no way in which we could inherit and use it directly in `Rectangle`. We could, of course, still access it with the `getLength` method.

One solution might be to make `length` public; however, this means it is generally accessible and not hidden in any way. This means we could interfere directly with the value of this instance variable by simply writing a value into it (using an assignment statement, from any part of the program which contained an reference to the object). This completely circumvents the read-only access we intended by making `length` private and providing a `getLength` method

What we desire is to keep `length` hidden from general use but available to any subclasses of `Square`. We do this by using the `protected` level. A `protected` method or attribute is visible within its own class and subclasses and also to any classes within the same package. This is why in `Rectangle` we can quite happily use the inherited instance variable `length` in conjunction with our own new attribute, `breadth`.

Now that we have introduced both packages and subclasses, we can summarize the access levels in Table 12-5, based on (Flanagan 1997).

situation	public	protected	default	private
Accessible to subclass from same package?	yes	yes	yes	no
Accessible to non-subclass in same package?	yes	yes	yes	no
Accessible to subclass from different package?	yes	yes	no	no
Accessible to non-subclass from different package?	yes	no	no	no
Inherited by subclass in same package?	yes	yes	yes	no
Inherited by subclass in different package?	yes	yes	no	no

Table 12-5 : Access levels.

Consider the situation where B is a subclass of A and B contains a reference to an instance of A. *Protected* attributes are inherited by subclasses and can be accessed in instances of those subclasses. However, subclass B cannot access these attributes in instances of A.

To illustrate a possible use of the `private` access level between superclass and subclass, we revisit our `Square` and `Rectangle` example. Originally, we had `Square` as the superclass and `Rectangle` as the subclass. However, in set theory, we can think of `Rectangle` as the superclass of `Square`. A square is a special example of a rectangle. The set of all squares is a subset of all rectangles.

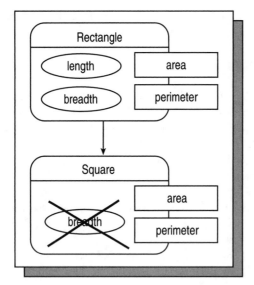

Figure 12-7: Rectangle as superclass of Square.

If we model this in Java, we can see (as before) that the subclass overrides the superclass methods (see Figure 12-7). The Square subclass does not want to add any new attributes but only inherit from Rectangle. Further, it does not want all the attributes from Rectangle, only length.

We have already seen how to block inheritance of attributes; in Rectangle, we declare breadth as private. This means that no other class, including any subclasses, may directly access this attribute.

12.5   Airline Reservations: An Example

In the following example (Barnes 1996), we consider the different kinds of airline reservations. The basic type of reservation maintains a date of travel, a flight number, and a seat number. There is a more expensive style of reservation, a "nice" reservation, that allows us to specify the kind of seat we want (aisle or window) and the kind of meal we want (green for vegetarians, white for fish or fowl, and red for meat). Finally, if we can afford it, we can make a "posh" reservation so that a limousine can meet us at the airport and take us to our final destination.

The *inheritance hierarchy* (see Figure 12-8) shows the superclass/subclass relationship as a hierarchy. A hierarchy is an example of a very common data structure in computing; an inverted tree. It is inverted because the root of the tree is normally at the top of the diagram (in this example, Reservation) and the leaves of the tree appear at the bottom of the diagram (here BasicReservation and PoshReservation). We can recognize the leaves because they are nodes (such as Reservation, BasicReservation, NiceReservation, and PoshReservation) that are not linked to any further nodes.

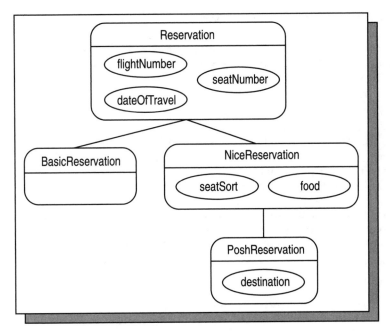

Figure 12-8: The reservation inheritance hierarchy.

In the diagram in Figure 12-8, we have additional information in the form of the attributes defined by different classes (and subclasses).

As before, we can define the subclasses in terms of what they offer that is different from their superclass. We can see that a reservation offers a flight number, date of travel, and a seat number. There is no difference between a basic reservation and a reservation, so the new subclass has no additional attributes. The difference between a posh reservation and a nice reservation is the limousine, so the additional attribute specifies a destination:

```
BasicReservation - Reservation = { }
NiceReservation - Reservation = {seatSort, food}
PoshReservation - NiceReservation = {destination}
```

Let's look at the Java declarations necessary to capture our data model:

```
class Reservation
   {
   private int flightNumber;
   private OurDate dateOfTravel;
   private int seatNumber;
   } // end of class Reservation

class BasicReservation extends Reservation
   {
   } // end of class BasicReservation
```

```
class NiceReservation extends Reservation
    {
    public static final int AISLE = 1, WINDOW = 2;
    public static final int GREEN = 1, WHITE = 2, RED = 3;
    private int seatSort;
    private int food;
    } // end of class NiceReservation
```

```
class PoshReservation extends NiceReservation
    {
    private String destination;
    } // end of class PoshReservation
```

In our example application, we want to provide an interactive system that a travel agent can use to enter the details (excluding the date of travel, in order to simplify the example) of a customer's reservation. In order to do this, each class provides a read method. Without regard for the inheritance of methods, one way of doing this would be to provide a method that reads all the attributes of each class. For example:

```
class PoshReservation extends NiceReservation
    {
    ......

    public void readPr() throws IOException
        {
        BasicIo.prompt("Flight number? :");
        flightNumber = BasicIo.readInteger();
        BasicIo.prompt("Seat number? :");
        seatNumber = BasicIo.readInteger();
BasicIo.prompt("kind of food? 1 (green), 2 (white), 3 (red) :");
        food = BasicIo.readInteger();
        BasicIo.prompt("kind of seat? 1 (aisle), 2 (window) :");
        seatSort = BasicIo.readInteger();
        BasicIo.prompt("Destination address?:");
        destination = BasicIo.readString();
        } // end of method readPr

    .......
    } // end of class PoshReservation
```

Let's look at the read method for NiceReservation:

```
class NiceReservation extends Reservation
    {
    ......
```

```
public void readNr() throws IOException
   {
   BasicIo.prompt("Flight number? :");
   flightNumber = BasicIo.readInteger();
   BasicIo.prompt("Seat number? :");
   seatNumber = BasicIo.readInteger();
   BasicIo.prompt("kind of food? 1 (green), 2 (white), 3 (red) :");
   food = BasicIo.readInteger();
   BasicIo.prompt("kind of seat? 1 (aisle), 2 (window) :");
   seatSort = BasicIo.readInteger();
   } // end of method readNr


.......
} // end of class NiceReservation
```

Finally, the read method for Reservation:

```
class Reservation
   {
   ......

   public void readRes() throws IOException
      {
      BasicIo.prompt("Flight number? :");
      flightNumber = BasicIo.readInteger();
      BasicIo.prompt("Seat number? :");
      seatNumber = BasicIo.readInteger();
      } // end of method readRes


.......
} // end of class Reservation
```

The problem we have here is that while we are using inheritance of attributes, we are not using inheritance of methods! Look at the code duplication between the read methods of NiceReservation and PoshReservation; there is only one line of difference. PoshReservation needs the extra line in order to prompt for, and read in, the value of the destination attribute. This is logical, as destination is the difference between PoshReservation and NiceReservation.

What we should be doing here is allowing each class to take responsibility for reading its own set of attributes. If readPr can assume that readNr is reading the attributes it supplies, then readPr can call readNr before reading its own attributes. Similarly, readNr depends on readRes to read the attributes provided by Reservation.

Table 12-6 summarizes the attributes and the method responsible for reading those attributes.

Reservation	NiceReservation	PoshReservation	responsibility
flightNumber			readRes
seatNumber			readRes
	seatSort		readNr
	food		readNr
		destination	readPr

Table 12-6 : Attributes and methods responsible for reading those attributes.

Unsurprisingly, the responsibility lies with the class that provided the attribute(s) in the first place.

Let's look at the revised set of read methods for each class:

```java
class Reservation
    {
    ........

    public void readRes() throws IOException
        {
        BasicIo.prompt("Flight number? :");
        flightNumber = BasicIo.readInteger();
        BasicIo.prompt("Seat number? :");
        seatNumber = BasicIo.readInteger();
        } // end of method readRes


    .........
    } // end of class Reservation

class NiceReservation extends Reservation
    {
    .........

    public void readNr() throws IOException
        {
        readRes();
        BasicIo.prompt("kind of food? 1 (green), 2 (white), 3 (red) :");
        food = BasicIo.readInteger();
        BasicIo.prompt("kind of seat? 1 (aisle), 2 (window) :");
        seatSort = BasicIo.readInteger();
        } // end of method readNr


    .................
    } // end of class NiceReservation
```

```
class PoshReservation extends NiceReservation
   {
   ..............

   public void readPr() throws IOException
      {
      readNr();
      BasicIo.prompt("Destination address?:");
      destination = BasicIo.readString();
      } // end of method readPr


   ................
   } // end of class PoshReservation
```

So we now have a situation where each class has its own `read` method, each with a unique name. We shall soon see that it is possible, and useful, for each `read` method to have the same name!

12.6   Key Points in Chapter 12

- A class can be viewed as a set of objects that share common features.

- From the set of all objects, we can identify subsets.

- In Java, set membership is automatic. When we declare an instance of type `Person`, we know it has a group of features in common with all other instances of type `Person`, hence it is a member of that set (or class).

- As we examine a set (for example, people) we can identify subsets (such as young people and old people). In turn, we can identify subsets of young people (toddlers, school pupils, undergraduates).

- As we move from sets to increasingly more detailed subsets, we are moving from general concepts to more specialized ones. This is known as *specialization*. If we examine several sets and identify common features that we can represent as a subset, we are moving from specialized concepts to a more general one. This is known as *generalization*.

- We can represent the relationship between sets and subsets as an inverted tree.

- In Java, when we introduce a new subclass of an existing class, we use the keyword ex-tends.

- When declaring a new subclass, we need only to specify the elements (attributes, method) that are different. For example, if `Employee` is to be subclass of `Person`, we need to ask ourselves what the difference is between a `Person` and an `Employee`—what does an employee have that a person doesn't?
    We do not need to specify again the elements of the `Person` class; the `Employee` class is said to *inherit* the elements of its superclass.

- It is possible to replace existing (inherited) methods with more appropriate ones in the inheriting class; this is known as *overriding*.

- Now that we have introduced the subclass concept, the four access levels supported by Java for element visibility are now distinct and are summarized in Table 12-7.

public	visible to everyone
protected	visible to all classes in the same package and to all subclasses
default	visible to all classes and subclasses in the same package
private	visible only within same class

Table 12-7 : Access levels.

12.7 Exercises

1. Figure 12-9 shows an inheritance hierarchy linking together classes that describe vehicles that operate on land.

   a) Set up the LandVehicles hierarchy as a set of Java classes.

   b) Provide appropriate get and set methods.

   c) Create instances of a car, a truck, and a bicycle.

   d) Write a simple driver application to illustrate your classes.

2. In an earlier exercise, we chose to model parents as part of a family. We now intend to model Parent as a subclass of Person. A Parent is different from a Person in that they have one or more children. A Parent may also have a spouse or a partner.

   Declare a class Parent according to the description in the previous paragraph. As always, remember appropriate initialization constructor(s) should be provided. Provide a driver application.

   As you did for the prior example, provide an averageAge method that operates on the children.

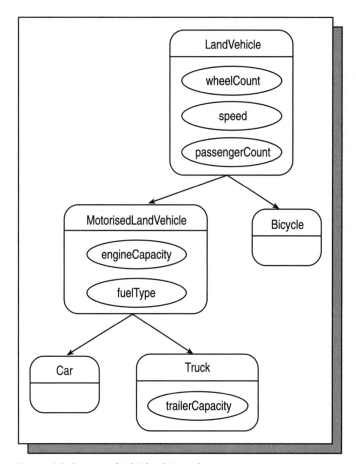

Figure 12-9: A LandVehicles hierarchy.

3. a) Write a class, Circle, that has one attribute, radius, and a method, space, which returns the area of the circle. The formula for calculating the area of a circle is r^2, where r is the radius. Provide additional methods as required and a driver application.

b) Write a class, Sphere, as a subclass of Circle. It also has one attribute, radius, and a method, space, which returns the volume of the sphere. The formula for calculating the volume of a sphere is $4/3$ r^3, where r is the radius. Provide additional methods as required and a driver application.

c) Vary the access permissions to the inherited radius attribute and note the effects on the Sphere subclass.

4. a) Write a class, Time, which holds the time in hours and minutes. Provide suitable get and set methods along with a toString method. Write a driver application. Make the attributes protected.

b) We now discover we need a method earlier to compare two Time instances to find out if one is earlier in the day than the other. Pretend that the Time class is a library class and that we do not have access to the source. We must extend the functionality by inheritance. Do so, creating a new class Time2, and update your driver application.

c) Change the attribute access levels of Time from protected to private. How does this affect your Time2 class? Update it accordingly.

12.8   References

Barnes, John. 1996. *Programming in Ada 95*. Reading, Mass: Addison-Wesley.
Flanagan, David. 1997. *Java in a nutshell*. 2nd Edition. Sebastopol, CA: O'Reilly & Associates.

CHAPTER 13

Class & Method Polymorphism

13.1 Person & Student: An Example

In this section, we revisit our Person example and show how it can be used as the base class for a new class, Student.

In this simple example, the difference between a Person and a Student is that a Student is enrolled in some major subject. The Student class inherits all the attributes of the Person class and adds a new attribute, major:

```
class Student extends Person
   {
   private String major ;

   public Student()
      {
      super(); // call constructor of Person

      major = "UNKNOWN";
      }

   public Student(String f, String s, int a, int g, String m)
      {
      super(f, s, a, g); // call constructor of Person
      major = m;
      }

   public String getMajor()
      {
      return major ;
      }

   public void setMajor(String m)
      {
      major = m ;
      }
```

```
public String toString()
   {
   return super.toString() + " " + major;
   } // end of toString


} // end of class Student
```

13.2   Constructor Methods & Inheritance

We have already seen how classes provide one or more constructor methods. We can use the constructor methods to ensure that new instances of a class have meaningful "default" values set up in their attributes. What impact does inheritance have on constructor methods? Consider our example of Person and Student. Person provides a constructor, so too does Student. How can we insure that when we initialize a Student we also initialize those attributes it inherits from Person?

Here we introduce the keyword super and show how it can be used in conjunction with constructor methods.

When we declare an instance of Student:

```
Student fred = new Student();
```

we are calling one of the constructors provided by the Student class. We expect this to set aside space for the attributes and to perhaps initialize them to meaningful default values. Student only has one directly defined attribute—major. But what about the inherited attributes (the ones from the Person class)? How are they to be initialized? If we look at the Student class, we find:

```
public Student()
   {
   super() ;
   major = "UNKNOWN" ;
   }
```

We see that, as usual, the attribute of Student is being given a suitable initial value. But the first line of the method body is the one of interest. Here it appears as if we are calling a method called super. What we are actually doing is calling the constructor of the base class, namely Person.

The terminology is derived from the idea of a superclass and a subclass. Here, Student is the subclass, and Person is the superclass. We are calling the constructor belonging to the super-class, hence super.

There are two rules about this use of super:

- It can be used in this way only in a constructor method.
- If it appears in the constructor method at all, it must be the very first statement within the constructor method, even before variable declarations.

Notice again the use of super, in our version of a constructor, which allows the user to specify the initial values for some of the attributes:

```
public Student(String f, String s, int a, int g, String m)
    {
    super(f, s, a, g);
    major = m;
    }
```

Again, the call to super appears as the very first statement in the body of the constructor.

13.2.1   Constructor Chaining

The Java language system guarantees that whenever an instance of a class is created, the class's constructor method is called. However, it also guarantees that the constructor is called whenever an instance of any subclass is created. This means that when we create an instance of class Student, not only is the Student constructor called, so too is the Person constructor.

In order to meet this guarantee, Java must ensure that every constructor method of a subclass calls one of the constructors of its superclass. In our Student example, we have provided a super call in both our constructors; Java can check that we have done so and know that the guarantee is being upheld.

Our Student constructors call different versions of the overloaded Person constructor methods, as indicated by the parameters.

If we are lazy and do not include the super call, Java will implicitly insert a call to super( ). So, for example:

```
public Student()
    {
    // super() ;
    // we've omitted the call but it is implicitly put in by Java
    major = "UNKNOWN" ;
    }
```

Being lazy doesn't always pay off:

```
public Student(String f, String s, int a, int g, String m)
    {
    // super(f, s, a,g) ;
    // we've omitted the call so Java calls "super()" for us
    major = m ;
    }
```

In this case, Java calls the parameterless version of the constructor. We might as well have not bothered supplying the formal parameters f, s, a, and g for all the use they are going to be. Try it out for yourselves!

13.3 Multiple Levels of Inheritance: The Inheritance Hierarchy

It is, of course, possible to have multiple levels of inheritance. The hierarchies we have seen so far in the book typically have two; at most, they have three levels. Theoretically at least, we can have as many as we like. In this section, we present two examples of multilevel hierarchies (shown in Figures 13-1 and 13-2). If you examine some of the Java libraries, you will find many more.

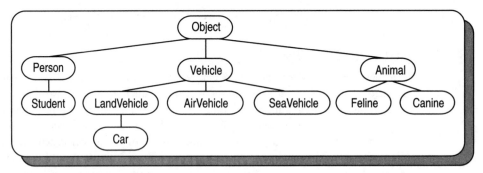

Figure 13-1: An inheritance hierarchy.

In our first example, we introduce the Object class as the root of the tree. We shall examine the Object class in more detail in the next section. In the example, it acts as superclass to Person, Vehicle, and Animal. You can see that we further subclass Person to Student, Vehicle to LandVehicle, AirVehicle, and SeaVehicle, and Animal to Feline and Canine. Finally, at our lowest level (two nodes removed from the root), we have LandVehicle as superclass to Car. In this example, we have concentrated on classes and ignored methods and attributes.

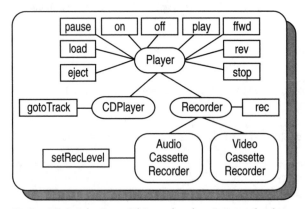

Figure 13-2: Inheritance hierarchy showing methods.

In our second example, we returned to the CD Player introduced in Chapter 2. This time, however, we position it in a possible hierarchy that relates various home entertainment systems that play prerecorded CDs or audio/video cassettes and also offer the possibility of recording. Here we include methods, and it should be noted that it is possible to capture quite a large amount of commonality between CD players, audio cassette records, and video cassette recorders (VCRs).

This hierarchy has only three levels, but is a graphic example of how inheritance allows us to capture commonality and to apply generalization to existing (physical) objects to produce a specialization hierarchy.

It is possible to prevent any further inheritance. As class providers, we may decide that it is not sensible to have any further subclasses of Car; there are no more vehicles that are specializations of Car. We require a mechanism to prevent further extends. We reuse the keyword, final.

When we declare a class that is to have no subclass extensions, we include final in the declaration:

```
final class Car ....
```

13.4 The Class Object

As you have seen, the superclass/subclass relationship forms an inheritance hierarchy. For instance, in the airline reservations example, we formed an inheritance hierarchy with Reservation as the root and its subclasses as nodes further down the tree.

This seems logical when we examine the declarations of the Reservation subclasses; they each include an extends statement that names their superclass. The Reservation class declaration itself does not include such a statement. We have seen several examples similar to this one; for instance, the Person and Student superclass and subclass.

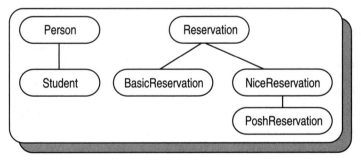

Figure 13-3: Two inheritance hierarchies.

However, in Java, there is an implicit root to the overall inheritance hierarchy. We can use this to bring together the two separate subtrees shown in Figure 13-3. Where a class is defined without an extends statement, it is as if one is inserted on that class's behalf. Every such class is a subclass of the system java.lang.Object class (see Figure 13-4).

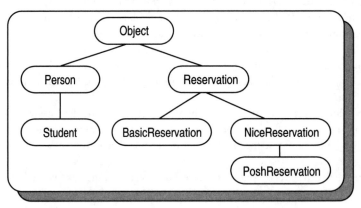

Figure 13-4: A single inheritance hierarchy.

For illustration purposes it is possible to explicitly insert the extends Object statement. So for example, public class Person extends Object or public class Reservation extends Object is the same as public class Person or public class Reservation.

Object is the only Java class that does not have a superclass. Also, notice that any class may call (or override) the methods provided by the Object class. This is, of course, due to the inheritance mechanism. All classes we declare can be considered subclasses of the Object class.

One method that the Object class provides is toString. You may have noticed in some of our class definitions that we have been overriding toString to provide our own version. The basic toString provided by Object when applied to an instance returns a String in the format:

```
<class which instance belongs to>@<numerical value>
```

The numerical value need not concern us here; it relates to the low-level representation of the instance. So, for example, if we have an instance of Student and we have not overridden the toString method in the Student class definition (or in any of its superclasses), we would have a result similar to the following:

```
Student@123456
```

Overriding toString allows us to specialize the method to suit the needs of the specific class and ourselves; we can provide a more meaningful representation of the instance and its contents.

The toString method is of further interest because the method System.out.print makes use of it. Because toString is declared as part of the Object class, System.out.print can safely make the assumption that every object in a Java program has access to that method. It can safely invoke the method without raising an exception or causing an error.

When we override it to provide a more meaningful mapping from the instance to a String, it is our overriding toString method (see Figure 13-5) that System.out.print will call. This is why in some of our example test programs we are able to include statements like:

```
NiceReservation nr1 ....
System.out.print("Nice Reservation is " + nr1);
```

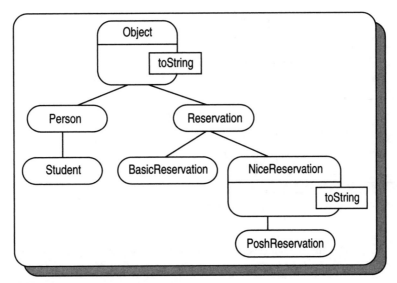

Figure 13-5: Overriding `toString`.

`System.out.print` knows that `nr1` is a reference to an object and thence calls `toString` on it. If this was not the case, we would have to convert it explicitly:

```
System.out.print("Nice Reservation is " + nr1.toString());
```

13.5 Polymorphism

Polymorphism is a powerful mechanism that is exploited fully in object-oriented systems. Essentially, what it means is there are a number of different classes of objects that will respond to the same request. We return to our example of `Person` and `Student`.

We can describe instances of a class as being members of the set of instances of that class. For example:

```
Person p1, p2;
```

Instances `p1` and `p2` are members of the set (of instances) of `Person` (see Figure 13-6). Also:

```
Student s1, s2;
```

Instances `s1` and `s2` are members of the set `Student` (see Figure 13-7).

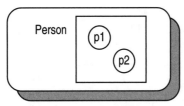

Figure 13-6: A Venn diagram showing two instances of Person.

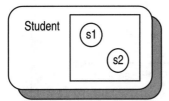

Figure 13-7: A Venn diagram showing two instances of Student.

Because Student is a subclass of Person, however, we can say that the set of instances of Student is a subset of the Person set (see Figure 13-8).

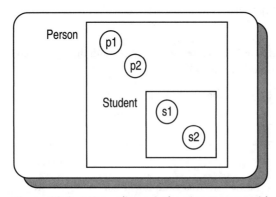

Figure 13-8: A Venn diagram showing Person with the Student subset.

In other words, s1 is a member of the set of students but is also a member of the set of (simple) persons. So, s1 is a Person as well as a Student.

An instance of Student, in addition to having those methods and attributes directly associated with Student, also (via inheritance) possesses those associated with Person (see Figure 13-9).

So, just as we expect a Person to have the four attributes forename, surname, age, and gender, and the associated get and set methods, we can expect a Student to have them as well.

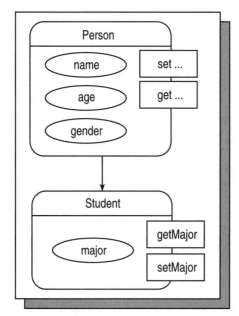

Figure 13-9: Person and its subclass, Student.

We can apply setAge to an instance of Student just as we can to an instance of Person. Everything a Person possesses and the methods it can respond to are shared by a Student:

```
Person p1;
Student s1;
.....
p1.setAge(40); // applying a Person method to a Person
s1.setAge(18); // applying a Person method to a Student
```

Everywhere we expect a Person instance, we can use a Student instance:

```
p1 = s1;
p1.setGender(Person.MALE);
```

This is because an object that is a member of the class Student is, by inheritance, also a member of the class Person.

Consider the following procedure:

```
void printPersonName (Person ppn)
  {
  System.out.println("A person's name is " + ppn.getSurname());
  }
```

We can call this with an actual parameter of type `Person` or `Student`:

```
printPersonName(p1);
printPersonName(s1);
```

The general rule is that everywhere an instance of a class is expected, we can use an instance of any of its subclasses (or sub-subclasses, etc.). This is a precise example of polymorphic behavior.

Notice, however, that we cannot go in the opposite direction:

```
s1 = (Student) p1; // illegal
```

First of all, in order to avoid a compile-time error, we must explicitly cast the type of the object on the right-hand side (`Person`) into that of the type of the object on the left-hand side (`Student`).

Second, however, while this statement compiles, at run time it generates an exception, namely `java.lang.ClassCastException`.

Consider the following:

```
void printStudentMajor (Student psm)
  {
  System.out.println("A student's major is " + psm.getMajor());
  }
```

```
printStudentMajor(s1);     // OK
printStudentMajor(p1);     // illegal
```

The second attempt to call the method with a `Person` actual parameter generates a compile-time error; this is because the compiler cannot find a method called `printStudentMajor` that expects a `Person` actual parameter.

While these attempts generate different types of errors, the fundamental problem they alert us to is the same. While `Person` and `Student` share some behavior (that of `Person`), they do not share all of each other's behavior (that of `Student`). While a `Student` can behave the same as a `Person`, the opposite is not true. `Student` has an additional attribute and two extra methods; a `Person` instance cannot handle a `getMajor` method call.

In brief, an object that is a member of a subclass shares all the behavior of the superclass. An object that is a member of a superclass does not share all the behavior of the subclass.

13.6 Polymorphism & Heterogeneous Collections

The situation we wish to explore is that of a heterogeneous collection of objects. To start our examination, we return to our Reservation example. It is possible to imagine a set of reservations to be processed at a travel agent. If, for example, we wish to simply print out and view the different reservations, this means we need to traverse the collection in some way, examine each Reservation in turn, and print each one out.

As we shall see, we can model collections in a number of ways: as an array or as a linked list (see Chapters 11 and 17). We will use the array here. In our simple test program, we will set up an array of four reservations; a basic one, two nice ones, and the last one, a posh:

```
Reservation[] collection = new Reservation[4];

BasicReservation br = new BasicReservation();
br.set(12,23);
collection[0] = br;

NiceReservation nr1 = new NiceReservation();
nr1.set(34, 45, NiceReservation.AISLE, NiceReservation.GREEN);
collection[1] = nr1;

NiceReservation nr2 = new NiceReservation();
nr2.set(45, 56, NiceReservation.WINDOW, NiceReservation.RED);
collection[2] = nr2;

PoshReservation pr = new PoshReservation();
pr.set(67, 78, NiceReservation.AISLE,
   NiceReservation.WHITE, "Motherwell");
collection[3] = pr;
```

We begin by declaring an array called collection; each element is of type Reservation. Then we declare four variables: one of type BasicReservation, two of type NiceReservation, and one of type PoshReservation. Since we last examined these classes, we have added a new method to each of them. It is called set, and we use it to set all the attributes of the class to which it belongs. After setting up these instances appropriately, we assign them to the collection array.

Here are some points to notice: Polymorphism has already come into play in our example. Just as we saw earlier, it is possible to use an instance of a subclass where the superclass is expected. As each element of the collection array is of type Reservation, we can assign objects of class Reservation or any of its subclasses. This is why we can successfully assign objects of class BasicReservation, NiceReservation, or even PoshReservation (a sub-subclass of Reservation) to the elements of the collection array.

We have created a heterogeneous collection of objects (see Figure 13-10); not all the objects in the collection have the same type (see Figure 13-11).

When we declare a heterogeneous collection of objects, we need to find at least one common superclass. As we saw earlier in this chapter, we are guaranteed to find such a superclass—namely, Object! It is a question of finding the lowest class in the inheritance hierarchy that our heterogeneous collection has in common.

If we wish to make a collection that will contain references to instances of BasicReservation, PoshReservation, and NiceReservation, we can make the collection of type Reservation. There is no need to go "all the way back" to the Object root. On the other hand, if we want references to instances of PoshReservation and Students, we must make the collection of type Object, as this is the only superclass the instances will have in common.

Figure 13-10: A heterogeneous collection of Reservations.

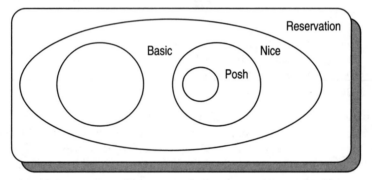

Figure 13-11: A Venn diagram showing subsets of Reservations.

Our next problem is to process the contents of `collection` and to print out each element of the array. Here is a skeleton of the code we need to produce:

```
for (int i = 0; i < 4; i++)
  {
  /* print out the contents of the ith element
    of the collection array */
  System.out.println();    // print a new line to
                           // separate the elements
  }
```

The problem we are now faced with is how to implement the actions detailed in the first comment. Clearly, we wish to delegate responsibility for how an object is to print itself to the object itself. This means that for each class from `Reservation` down, we need to implement a method to do this.

If we chose not to take advantage of polymorphism, we may have implemented the methods correctly but given them different names in each class. For example:

class	method name
Reservation	printRes
NiceReservation	printNr
PoshReservation	printPr

If we do this, we are introducing a further problem. When we wish to print `collection[i]`, which method should we call? Should it be:

```
collection[i].printRes()
collection[i].printNr()
```

or

```
collection[i].printPr()
```

The method we call depends on the type of the object indicated by `collection[i]`. To pursue this approach further, we would need some way of finding out the type of the object at run time and attempt to use this to direct a `switch` statement to call the appropriate method. This is actually possible, as we will see in Chapter 21. However, as we have seen in the `Person` and `Student` example, calling a method on an inappropriate object can lead to a compile- or run-time error.

The fact of the matter is that we can arrange things so that the problem of which method to call is left to the language system. We do this by exploiting polymorphism. In this case, we just rename all the print methods to simply `print`.

This leads us to the final solution, which is as follows:

```
for (int i = 0; i < 4; i++)
   {
   collection[i].print();
   System.out.println();
   }
```

13.6.1 *Dynamic Method Binding (Late Binding)*

When we are processing a collection of Reservations and we invoke the `print` method (as in our example in the previous section), how do we know which version of the `print` method to call? After all, there are three such methods, one for each `Reservation` class.

When we use a superclass reference (an element of the `Reservation` collection array) to refer to a subclass object and invoke the `print` method, the program selects the correct subclass `print` method dynamically (at run time). This is known as *dynamic method binding*.

While the compiler doesn't know which subclass a superclass reference is referring to, the Java interpreter does. In our example, it knows which `Reservation` collection array elements are `Basic`, `Nice`, and `Posh` and can thus ensure the correct `print` method is called.

Instead of the programmer doing the work, we leave it to the system to work out the class of the reference and which method to call. Imagine that we introduce yet another kind of reservation to our hierarchy (say SuperReservation). An instance of SuperReservation could be an element of our collection. As long as we give SuperReservation a method called print, the solution as shown earlier should not need altering and will work as is. If we were doing the work with an if statement, we would have to add a new arm to the statement that handled SuperReservations.

While dynamic method binding is fast, it is not as fast as invoking a method directly. Wherever there is no possibility of overriding, we can use direct method invocation. Methods declared as static, private, and/or final cannot be overridden, and thus we do not need to use dynamic method binding.

13.7 Calling Overridden Methods

We will now continue with our airline reservations example; in the previous chapter, each class provided its own read method:

class	"read" method
Reservation	readRes()
NiceReservation	readNr()
PoshReservation	readPr()

However, using different names like this raises the same problems for a heterogeneous collection of different types of reservations as did the different print method names earlier in this chapter.

Imagine that we want to process a collection of reservations and read in the values for each one. The skeleton code is remarkably similar to that for our printing of the collection:

```
for (int i = 0; i < 4; i++)
    {
    // read in the contents of the ith element
    // of the collection array
    System.out.println(); // print a new line to separate the reads
    }
```

To tackle this, we wish to give every "read" method the same name, read!

```
for (int i = 0; i < 4; i++)
  {
  collection[i].read();
  System.out.println();
  }
```

We have decided to call the method responsible for reading the attributes of an instance read. We have done this in each class so that we have overloaded the name. Just as we saw in Chapter 12, we have overridden the superclass method in our Square and Rectangle classes. Whenever we have an instance of a reservation (be it basic, nice, or posh), we always know how to invoke the appropriate read method; it is just called read in every case.

However, this leaves us with a problem: how do we call the read method of the superclass? If in PoshReservation.read we simply said:

```
public void read()
  {
  read(); // used to be "nrRead()"
  BasicIo.prompt("Destination address?:");
  destination = BasicIo.readString();
  } // end of method read
```

this would be an unintentional (and completely useless) use of a technique called *recursion* (see Chapter 18). Essentially, PoshReservation.read would call itself; this call would then call itself again; this third call would call PoshReservation.read again; and so on into infinity.

Fortunately, the super keyword comes to the rescue. We can use this keyword to indicate the superclass. In order for PoshReservation.read to call NiceReservation.read, we prefix the call of NiceReservation.read with super. The final version of PoshReservation.read looks like the following:

```
public void read()
  {
  super.read(); // call read method belonging to
  // superclass -  in this case
  // NiceReservation.read
  BasicIo.prompt("Destination address?:");
  destination = BasicIo.readString();
  } // end of method read
```

Notice that super is being used in two different ways—as super and super(). In the former case, it is acting like a class reference. We use it to access a method belonging to our superclass and apply it to ourselves. It is a bit like using this, which acts as an instance reference to ourselves. When we use super, we use it to reference the superclass of the class that we are an instance of. We can then supply the name of a method belonging to that superclass, usually one which we have overridden. This means we can override a method but still have access to that method should we require to.

In the latter case, it is a method call to a constructor belonging again to our superclass.

13.8 Methods in Derived Classes

We have discussed in earlier chapters the importance of information hiding in modern software engineering. Information hiding allows us to think of modules or classes as black boxes; we know how they behave, what messages or requests they can process, and what kinds of results they return. We use the black boxes on a "need to know" basis. This means we do not need to know exactly how they work, only what they do. This reduces the level of complexity in using the black box. Further, as long as the interface and behavior remain unchanged, the box provider can make any changes they wish as to how the box provides its services.

The issue we wish to raise at this point is what impact does information hiding have on inheritance? If we program by extending (or refining) existing classes (by adding attributes and methods), is there any way we can extend the functionality and behavior of an existing method without knowing how the original method works?

Until now, we have used methods in derived classes in one of two ways. First, we have used them as additional methods, intended to extend the functionality of the base class.

Second, we use them as refinements of existing classes—for example, the read method in PoshReservation. In general, this new read method has the same basic functionality as the read method in the NiceReservation class, the base class. We can still access this functionality using the super.read notation to call the read method in class NiceReservation. However, we are free to provide additional code that refines the existing code and makes the new read method more suitable for the PoshReservation class.

The airline reservations classes contain a number of examples of refinement. The methods read, print, and set are all defined in terms of their corresponding superclass method. We have already seen the read methods; let us now look at the set methods and how they refine their superclass method by adding more functionality without changing the inherited behavior:

```
//set method in class Reservation ...
public void set (int fn, int sn)
    {
    flightNumber = fn;
    seatNumber = sn;
    }

//set method in class NiceReservation ..
public void set (int fn, int sn, int st, int f)
    {
    super.set(fn,sn);
    seatSort = st;
    food = f;
    }

//set method in class PoshReservation ..
public void set(int fn, int sn, int st, int f, String d)
    {
    super.set(fn, sn, st, f);
    destination = d;
    }
```

A further example might be as follows. We have the class Manager as subclass of Employee. There is a method (increment) used to calculate an employee's annual increment. Managers are entitled to the same increment with a bonus based on their department's productivity. As before, we can define the class Manager by the difference between it and the class Employee. From the details given so far, the difference is:

- An attribute to denote their department's productivity (deptProd).

- An overriding version of increment.

We can thus define the new version of increment as follows:

```
double increment()
  {
  double res = super.increment();
  res = res + deptProd * 0.1;
  return res;
  }
```

We can see that we do not need to know how an employee's increment is calculated nor what attributes are used. All we need to know is how a manager's additional bonus is calculated. If, at some future point, the way an employee's increment is calculated is changed, this will have no impact on the Manager's increment method; we will automatically inherit (and use) the revised version. The principle of information hiding is being maintained through the inheritance mechanism.

As a final example, consider the Student class, which inherits from Person. If we want to produce a toString method for Student, which will simply want to provide details from the Person class plus the major attribute from Student, why should we have to write a completely new toString method from scratch? Instead, we want to use Person.toString and simply append the major details. We can do this using the super keyword as follows:

```
public String toString()
  {
  return super.toString() + " " + major;
  }
```

13.9   Key Points in Chapter 13

- Whenever an instance of a class is created, the class's constructor method is called. It is also called whenever an instance of any subclass is created.

- We can explicitly ensure the superclass constructor is called by including a class to super( ). We can only use super in this way in a constructor method, and it must be the very first statement.

- If we do not include a call to super( ), Java automatically inserts one. Notice that it always calls the parameterless version (this may not be the one that we want).

- It is possible to have multiple levels of inheritance and create an inheritance hierarchy.

- Class providers may wish to block inheritance. We can prevent inheritance of elements by specifying `private` access to those elements. If we don't want to have any subclasses at all, we can declare our class as `final`. Note also, if you do not want to have an attribute or method overridden, you can declare them as `final` as well.

- *Polymorphism* means instances of different classes can respond to the same request. For example, if `Student` is a subclass of `Person`, every place we expect a `Person` object, we can use a `Student` object. This is because a `Student` object has inherited all the elements of a `Person` object and can thus handle any `Person` method call.

  Notice that we cannot expect polymorphism from subclass to superclass.

- Because of polymorphism, we can set up and process heterogeneous collections of objects. We can have an array of `Reservations` that contains `BasicReservations`, `NiceReservations`, and `PoshReservations`. If each class provides a method (of the same name and signature), we can execute this method on each element of the array.

- It is useful to be able to call an overridden method (often within the method that overrides it). We can again use the `super` keyword to refer to our superclass. This means we can extend the functionality of an inherited method without understanding how it is implemented.

- Inheritance allows us to extend the functionality of inherited methods without compromising information hiding. We can override the inherited method (but still call it within the overriding method using `super`) and add the additional code, which refines the functionality (this sounds like the last key point!).

- There is an implicit root to Java's inheritance hierarchy. Any class declared without an `extends` statement is automatically a subclass of the system `Object` class.

13.10 Exercises

1. Zeller's congruence is a formula for determining the day of the week on which a calendar date falls. It works for any U.K. date since 1752 when the Gregorian calendar was introduced in England. The formula is as follows:

   W = (k + [(2.6*m) - 0.2] - (2*C) + Y + [Y/4] + [C/4]) mod 7

   Where:

   - Expressions in [] give rounded-down integer results.

   - k is the day (1 to 31).

   - m is the month. This is slightly peculiar in that 1 = March, ...10 = December, 11 = January, 12 = February with January and February being treated as months of the *preceding* year. See Y.

- C is the century. So 1992 has C = 19.

- Y is the year. So March '92–Feb '93 have Y = 92, while Jan and Feb '92 have Y = 91. See m.

- W is the weekday where 0 = Sunday and 6 = Saturday.

Write a program that repeatedly prompts the user for dates and returns the corresponding weekday for each. So if the user types:

16 October 1992

The answer returned is:

Friday

We propose that you tackle this problem by:

a) Extending the OurDate class to include a method that calculates the day of the week.

b) The new subclass should include a String attribute that stores the result of the method.

c) Whenever a method is called to set the date, you should call the Zellers method to similarly update the String attribute.

Remember to make elements of the class private if they should be!

2. a) Write a class called House to hold details of the location (street number, street name, town) and (if known) the year of construction and the property tax.

b) Write a derived class Home with additional instance fields for the name of the occupying family and the date they moved in. You should use the OurDate class from the java.lancs package.

Note the following:

There should be two constructor methods:

```
public Home (int house, String street, String town, String family,
Date movedIn)
```

and

```
public Home (int house, String street, String town, int
yearConstructed, char taxBand, String family, Date movedIn)
```

These should make use of the super keyword where appropriate.

There should be the usual methods to set and extract the values of the new instance fields:

```
setFamily
getFamily
setDateMovedIn
getDateMovedIn
```

There should be a printDetails method that calls the printDetails method provided by the House class to display the address of the house and then displays the text has been occupied by SOMEONE since DATE, with suitable values inserted.

3. Write a program that contains an array of Houses:

```
House[] collection = new House[100] ;
```

The user inserts elements in this array as follows: The program prompts the user for the number, street, and town and (if the user wishes) a family name and date of moving in. The program should then create an instance of the appropriate class (House or Home) and store it as the next element of the array collection.

Finally the program should scan through the array collection calling the printDetails method for each element. Check that Java correctly calls the appropriate version of this method in each case.

4. Continuing our development of the Time class from Chapter 12, it is now found that we need to maintain the time to an accuracy of seconds. Assume now that Time and Time2 are both library classes. Create a Time3 class that allows us to keep hours, minutes, and seconds and provides new versions of toString and earlier. As usual, provide a suitable driver application to test your methods.

5. Consider again the problems of modeling objects within a university. We have undergraduate students, postgraduate students, and staff members. You should decide what attributes and methods instances of each of these classes could possess and develop an inheritance hierarchy (with the Person class as its base). Declare a heterogeneous collection of university objects and write an application that prints out each element of the collection.

6. Write a program to read two text files with names specified by the user at the terminal. The program should match each line of one file with the corresponding line of the other and display a list of the lines that do not match together with a count of the total number of mismatching lines.

Two lines match if they differ only in (a) the number of leading or trailing spaces or tab characters, (b) the case (upper- or lower-) of the letters, or (c) one line contains multiple spaces or tab marks at a position where the other has a different number of spaces or tabs (but not zero).

Thus:

```
____The____Cat____Sat____ON____The____Mat____
```

matches:

```
the_cat_sat_on_the_mat
```

where the character _ represents a space or tab.

Implement this program by deriving a class from BasicFileIo and adding a method:

```
public String getCanonicalLine( )
```

to read a text line from a file and return it in canonical form.

Initially this method could simply be the readString method from the BasicFileIo class while you write the matching program to use it. Then rewrite the method to (a) strip out leading and trailing spaces from the line read before returning it, (b) force all letters to lowercase, (c) replace a sequence of two or more spaces by one space, and finally (d) deal with the tab character in the same way you deal with space.

Note ■

Canonical means "in a standard form." The getCanonicalLine method returns a line transcribed into a form standardized with respect to case of letters and the presence of *white space* (like spaces and tab characters).

Note ■

The match is line by line. You do not have to deal with lines inserted into, or deleted from, one of the files (this is a much more difficult problem).

Test the program by trying it on a file containing a suitable program text (perhaps the very same program you've just written!).

CHAPTER 14

Abstract Classes & Interfaces

14.1 Abstract Classes

In this section, we introduce the concept of an *abstract class*. The classes we have seen so far are all examples of *concrete* classes. A concrete class can be defined as one that has direct instances. For example, the Person class provides the template for a number of Person objects. Similarly, we can have instances of Employees or Students. An abstract class is one that does not have such direct instances. It is provided only to have other classes derived from it (some of which eventually will have instances). In this section, our main example of an abstract class is the Solid class. We would therefore never write in a Java program:

```
Solid aSolid = new Solid();
```

In one sense, we are returning to the issues of data modeling and sets of objects. In a generalization exercise, we can identify a whole host of geometrical solids, such as cuboids, spheres, and cylinders. These three entities have some features in common; for example, they all have an enclosed volume and a surface area. We should thus identify a common superclass that possesses these features, and the three subclasses should inherit from the superclass, which we will call Solid (see Figure 14-1).

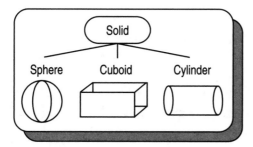

Figure 14-1: Solid and its subclasses.

Next, we need to decide whether these features (volume and surface area) should be modeled as attributes or methods. Clearly we would want the object to calculate its own surface area and volume rather than the user, who would then provide these values through a set method. So we want them to be methods.

How are we to implement these methods? It is at this point that we run into problems. The algorithm for calculating the surface area of a cuboid is quite different from that for the area of a sphere. We give these algorithms in Table 14-1:

object	attributes	surface area	volume
cuboid	length, breadth, height	2 * ((length * breadth) + (length * height) + (breadth * height))	length * breadth * height
cylinder	radius, height	2 * ((* radius * radius) + (* radius * height))	* radius * radius * height
sphere	radius	4 * * radius * radius	4/3 * * radius * radius * radius

Table14-1: Algorithms for cuboids, cylinders, and spheres.

Notice that the algorithms make reference to features that the solids do not all have in common. For example, a sphere and a cylinder have a radius. A sphere has no height of side, which a cuboid and cylinder do. These features belong only to the specific class; they do not belong to the shared superclass Solid.

How then can we specify these algorithms as methods within the Solid class? They need access to instance variables that do not belong in Solid.

We can say that Solid is an abstract class. It specifies two abstract methods, called surfaceArea and volume, that have no arguments and return a double. We can define this as follows:

```
public abstract class Solid
    {
    public abstract double surfaceArea();
    public abstract double volume();
    }
```

Note that we do not provide the method bodies—simply because we are quite unable to do so! You should be able to understand now why we cannot have direct instances of Solid; how would we interpret the following?

```
Solid aSolid = new Solid();
double res = aSolid.surfaceArea();  // meaningless
```

We can now begin to define the subclasses, Sphere, Cuboid, and Cylinder, as follows:

```
class Sphere extends Solid
    {

    private double radius;
```

```
        public Sphere()
           {
           radius = 0.0;
           }

        public Sphere(double r)
           {
           radius = r ;
           }

        public double volume()
           {
           return 4.0/3.0 * Math.PI * radius * radius * radius;
           }

        public double surfaceArea()
           {
           return 4 * Math.PI * radius * radius;
           }

        public String toString()
           {
           return "Sphere radius "+ radius +" volume "+ volume()
              + " surface area "+ surfaceArea();
           }

        } // end of class Sphere

class Cuboid extends Solid
    {

    private double height, breadth, length ;

        public Cuboid()
           {
           length = 0.0;
           breadth = 0.0;
           height = 0.0;
           }

        public Cuboid(double l, double b, double h)
           {
           length = l ;
           breadth = b;
           height = h;
           }
```

```java
    public double volume()
       {
       return length * breadth * height;
       }

    public double surfaceArea()
       {
       return (2 * length * breadth) + (2 * length * height)
          + (2 * breadth * height);
       }

    public String toString()
       {
       return "Cuboid length "+ length +
          " breadth "+ breadth +
          " height "+ height +
          " surface area "+ surfaceArea()+
          " volume "+ volume();
       }

    } // end of class Cuboid

class Cylinder extends Solid
    {

    private double height, radius;

    public Cylinder()
       {
       radius = 0.0;
       height = 0.0;
       }

    public Cylinder(double r, double h)
       {
       radius = r;
       height = h;
       }

    public double volume()
       {
       return Math.PI * radius * radius * height;
       }

    public double surfaceArea()
       {
```

```
    return (2 * Math.PI * radius * radius) +
        (2 * Math.PI * radius * height);
    }

public String toString()
    {
    return "Cylinder height "+ height +" radius "+ radius +
        " surface area "+ surfaceArea()+
        " volume "+ volume();
    }

} // end of class Cylinder
```

Note that now these subclasses contain the instance variables they need in order to implement the algorithms as methods.

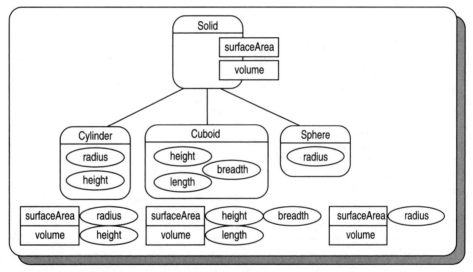

Figure 14-2: The inheritance hierarchy for solids, showing the features added at each level and the final set of features for the concrete classes.

At this point, you may be wondering why bother with the Solid class at all? It hasn't saved us any work since we still had to define the methods for each subclass. We didn't inherit any concrete methods or attributes from it at all.

Well, as you have already seen, it is useful to have generalization and specialization in data modeling. The Solid class allows us to state that there is a general thing called Solid, of which Sphere, Cuboid, and Cylinder are but three specializations. It allows us to state that every shape has common features, namely a surface area and a volume. The compiler will check that the eventual concrete class has the named methods and appropriate argument and return value type. We shall see in a moment how polymorphism allows us to have some practical advantages from abstract classes as well.

It is the responsibility of a derived class to provide a physical implementation of an abstract method. As we have seen, the inheritance tree can be several levels deep. It may be several levels before we can make every aspect of an abstract class concrete. In this case, as long as a derived class contains an abstract method, then that class is itself abstract. It is only when all methods have been given a body that the method becomes concrete and we can set up instances of the class.

In the diagram in Figure 14-2, we show the inheritance hierarchy for the Solid class and its immediate subclasses. We show the attributes and methods defined at each level and finally summarize the set of methods and attributes available to instances of the subclasses.

14.2 Polymorphism

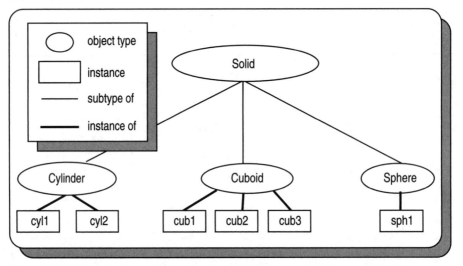

Figure 14-3: The inheritance hierarchy showing instances of the concrete classes.

In Figure 14-3, we show the hierarchy, but this time we show the object instances of the subclasses. It is these instances that will expect the methods and attributes shown at the bottom of Figure 14-2.

In the diagram in Figure 14-4, we consider classes as collections or sets of object instances. The sph1 instance of Sphere is directly a member of the set of spheres but also a member of the set of Solids. Finally, in Figure 14-5 we show set membership in a traditional Venn diagram.

In the Venn diagram, we can see how objects that have been directly declared as instances of the concrete classes are also members of the superclass. Through polymorphism, anywhere we expect a Solid, we can also use a Cuboid, Cylinder, or Sphere. For example:

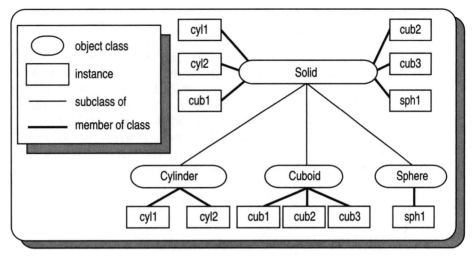

Figure 14-4: Showing the class membership of the object instances.

Figure 14-5: Showing the class memberships as a Venn diagram.

```
Solid aSolid; // valid declaration. Note we haven't
              // used a constructor.

Sphere aSphere = new Sphere (4.0);
aSolid = aSphere;
System.out.println(aSolid.volume());
```

We can use the aSolid variable more directly:

```
Solid aSolid = new Sphere (4.0);
System.out.println(aSolid.volume());
```

Just as we saw in the previous chapter, we can set up a collection of different classes where the classes share a common superclass. We used an array of type Reservation to store elements of the different subclasses of Reservation (BasicReservation, NiceReservation, and PoshReservation). In that example, Reservation was not an abstract class; it contained two attributes (flightNumber and seatNumber) and matching get and set methods.

Even though Solid is an abstract class, we can do exactly the same kind of thing. In this example, we build an array of class Solid with different elements (Sphere, Cuboid, and Cylinder) and calculate their total volume (see Figure 14-6):

Figure 14-6: A heterogeneous collection of solids.

```
Solid[] collection = new Solid[4];

Sphere s1 = new Sphere(4);
collection[0] = s1;

Cuboid c1 = new Cuboid(2,3,4);
collection[1] = c1;

Cylinder cyl = new Cylinder(4,2);
collection[2] = cyl;

Sphere s2 = new Sphere(3);
collection[3] = s2;

double totalVolume = 0.0;
```

```
for (int i = 0; i < 4; i++)
        {
        totalVolume = totalVolume +
          collection[i].volume();
        }
System.out.println("total volume = "+ totalVolume);
```

As described in section 13.6.1, the system uses dynamic method binding at run time to select the version of the volume method associated with the appropriate class.

14.3   Interfaces

You may have noticed in all our examples that a subclass can have only a single immediate superclass. Student has Person, BasicReservation has Reservation, and so on. This restriction means that the graph that represents the superclass-subclass relationship is a hierarchy, that is a tree with a single root—hence inheritance *hierarchy*.

Some systems allow multiple superclasses; for example, the class ToyTruck may inherit from Toy and Truck. The class NuclearSubmarine may inherit from NuclearPoweredVehicle and Submarine. In such systems, the superclass-subclass graph is a network or lattice—hence inheritance *lattice*.

Java allows only *single* inheritance, as opposed to *multiple* inheritance. This restriction means we can inherit functionality and data only from a single superclass. In an attempt to alleviate this limitation, Java supports the concept of *interfaces*.

Polymorphism says that a set of objects have a common set of methods or behaviors; this means we can (for example) find out the volume of a set of objects that were declared as members of different classes (although they share a common "root" class). This means that it might be useful if we can expect instances of different classes to provide common methods. If we do not provide these specifications through inheritance, how then are we to implement polymorphism?

Interfaces are like abstract classes in that they define a set of methods (or behaviors) that a class can be expected to provide. They can also provide a set of constants (i.e., implicitly modified with *public, static,* and *final*). They do not define attributes, however.

If we return to our example of Players, we can identify video cassette recorders (VCRs) in the hierarchy. One very common use of VCRs is to record programs at a given day and time. We need to include a set of methods (and attributes) that allow us to program the VCR. However, elsewhere in our home entertainment hierarchy (see Figure 14-7) we may find a satellite receiver. This is also programmable. Is there any way we can capture the fact that these two pieces of equipment share the same behavior?

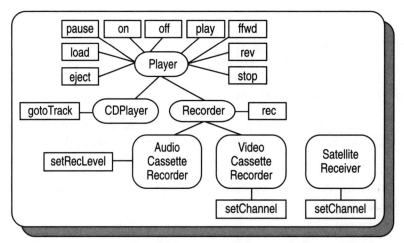

Figure 14-7: A hierarchy of home entertainment.

If Java supported multiple inheritance, we could introduce a new class, ProgrammableTimer, and have VideoCassetteRecorder and SatelliteReciever inherit from it, as shown in Figure 14-8.

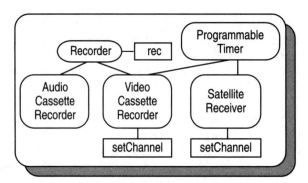

Figure 14-8: A lattice of home entertainment.

However, this is not possible in Java. Instead, we define an interface, Programmable, which specifies the (abstract) methods that a programmable VCR or satellite receiver would need (see Figure 14-9):

```
public interface Programmable
    {
    void setCurrentTime(int day, month, hour, minute);
    void setChannel(int channel);
    void setStart(int day, hour, minute);
    void setStop(int day, hour, minute);
    } // end of interface Programmable
```

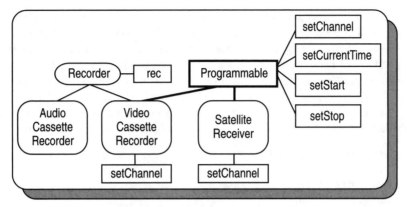

Figure 14-9: Interfaces as well as classes.

The interface provides a set of specifications of methods; it does not provide any code that we can reuse or extend. It is the responsibility of the class to implement the methods (just as it is with abstract methods). An interface is a guarantee, enforced by the compiler, that certain methods will appear with certain names, arguments, and return values.

Notice that we have not provided any access (`public`, `private`) or status (`static`, `final`, `abstract`) modifiers to our method specifiers in the interface. This is because all methods given in an interface are implicitly `public` and `abstract`, so there is no need to explicitly state this in our specification.

Let us illustrate the concept with the help of an example, shown in Figure 14-10.

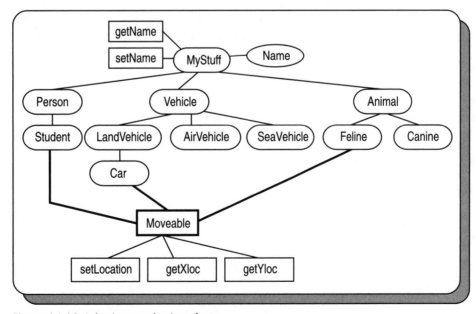

Figure 14-10: Inheritance plus interfaces.

Here we have an inheritance hierarchy linking a number of disparate kinds of real-world objects. We have decided, quite early on, that all the objects of interest to us will have a name. We have captured this by placing a `name` attribute and associated `get` and `set` methods in the `MyStuff` class. Later on, we decide that some classes will be `Moveable`; that is, they will be able to move from one position to another on a two-dimensional plane. We now need to represent this by a pair of Cartesian coordinates and associated `get` and `set` methods.

As we have already seen, we cannot do this by means of multiple inheritance. We must use the Java `interface` mechanism. We provide the following interface definition:

```
public interface Moveable
    {
    void setLocation(int x, int y);
    int getXLocation();
    int getYLocation();
    } // end of interface Moveable
```

Note that we store this in a file called `Moveable.java` and compile it as usual. This produces a file called `Moveable.class`.

We now identify the classes that we wish to make moveable; these are `Student`, `Car`, and `Feline`. We change their class definition to include the fact that they are going to implement the `Moveable` interface as follows:

```
class Student extends Person implements Moveable ...
class Car extends LandVehicle implements Moveable ...
class Feline extends Animal implements Moveable ...
```

At this point, the class providers of `Student`, `Car`, and `Feline` must implement the three methods listed in the `Moveable` interface specification. We cannot inherit any code or attributes from the interface; this may mean we have to introduce completely new attributes and the associated code. In this example, each class may use exactly the same code, as follows:

```
// implementing Moveable interface methods

private int x, y;

public void setLocation(int x1, int y1)
    {
    x = x1;
    y = y1;
    }

public int getXLocation()
    {
    return x;
    }
```

```
public int getYLocation()
   {
   return y;
   }
```

This is very similar to inheriting from an abstract class. Polymorphism is supported now as all Moveable classes can respond to requests for setLocation, getXLocation, and getYLocation.
   Let us now examine an example that uses our Moveable classes:

```
class Chapter14n1
   {
   public static void main(String[] args)
      {
      MyStuff[] collection = new MyStuff[3];
      Moveable[] moveCol = new Moveable[3];

      Student stud = new Student();
      stud.setName("James T. Kirk");
      stud.setLocation(0,0);
      collection[0] = stud;
      moveCol[0] = stud;

      Car aCar = new Car();
      aCar.setName("Fiat Uno");
      aCar.setLocation(1,1);
      collection[1] = aCar;
      moveCol[1] = aCar;

      Feline aCheetah = new Feline();
      aCheetah.setName("The Flash");
      aCheetah.setLocation(2,2);
      collection[2] = aCheetah;
      moveCol[2] = aCheetah;

      // access object directly

      System.out.println("Name of aCar is " +
         aCar.getName() + " Current location is " +
         aCar.getXLocation() + " " + aCar.getYLocation());
      System.out.println();

      for (int i = 0; i < 3; i++)
         {
         System.out.println("Name of "+ i +
            "th element is "
            + collection[i].getName());
```

```
        System.out.println("Current location is " +
            moveCol[i].getXLocation() +
            " " + moveCol[i].getYLocation());
        System.out.println();
        }
    } // end of method main

} // end of class Chapter14n1
```

As before, we set up a collection of objects. Here, we set up two exact duplicates; however, one is of class MyStuff and the other of interface Moveable.

Notice, however, that when we use a single object directly (aCar), we do not need to refer to it via two different references, be it MyStuff or Moveable. We know what class aCar belongs to, and we know it can respond to its own methods, the methods it inherited, and the methods it implemented to conform to the Moveable interface. We can thus apply these methods directly.

When we come to processing the elements of the heterogeneous collections, however, we must take care to apply the methods to the appropriate collection. The MyStuff array elements only expect method invocations that the MyStuff class can handle—hence, getName. If we try to say:

```
collection[i].getYloc()
```

this will result in a compile-time error. This is why we must have a Moveable collection, so that the compiler understands we are calling a Moveable interface method.

Unlike classes, where we can only extend a single class, it is possible to implement multiple interfaces. We may want to make our Moveable objects have a graphical representation, and we may want those representations to be placed at X,Y screen locations. We could define our classes as follows:

```
public class Car extends Land implements Moveable, Drawable ...
```

Finally, just as classes can have subclasses, interfaces can have sub-interfaces. A sub-interface inherits all the abstract methods and constants of its super-interface and may add new ones of its own. Again, we have the ability to handle multiple interfaces in that an interface can extend more than one interface.

```
public interface Transformable extends Scalable,
        Rotatable, Reflectable { ...
public interface DrawingObject extends Drawable,
        Transformable { ..
public class Solid implements DrawingObject { ...
```

14.4   Key Points in Chapter 14

- A *concrete* class is one that we expect to have direct instances. An *abstract* class will not; it exists only to have other (abstract or concrete) classes derived from it.

- Abstract classes can contain abstract methods; these are methods that do not (and often cannot) exist within the abstract class but we expect subclasses to override them by providing implementations of the method.

- Abstract classes support the polymorphism concept. For example, an abstract class `Shape` could have a number of concrete subclasses such as `Triangle`, `Rectangle`, and `Circle`. We can now set up a heterogeneous collection of triangles, rectangles, and circles as an array of Shapes. If `Shape` has an abstract method, `area`, then we expect the subclasses to provide implementations of that method suitable for their own geometry. Thereafter, the `Shape` subclasses will respond to the same method request(s).

- Any class with at least one `abstract` method must be declared abstract.

- Java only supports inheritance from a single superclass—hence inheritance *hierarchy* rather than *lattice* or network.

  Some systems support multiple inheritance—hence `ToyTruck` inheriting from `Toy` and `Truck`.

  What if we identify two sets of behavior? For example, what if we find out the volume of objects from different classes? How do we support polymorphism under these circumstances if multiple inheritance is not allowed? Java's answer to this is the *interface*.

- Interfaces are like abstract classes because they define a set of methods they expect a class to provide. They also provide sets of constants, but *not* attributes. Unlike abstract classes, interfaces can contain no concrete code.

- We can thus use inheritance and interfaces to model the following situation. We have a home entertainment system hierarchy and find a VCR and satellite receiver, both of which are programmable. We can't make these subclasses of a `ProgrammableDevice` superclass because VCR is already a subclass of `Recorder`. Instead we define a `Programmable` interface and specify that VCR and satellite receiver both `implement` that interface. The onus is on the class provider to implement the methods specified in the interface.

- We can have collections of objects that are polymorphic because they all implement a common interface and can thus respond to requests for the interface methods.

14.5 Exercises

1. We have a number of classes to represent institutions. The Institution class is abstract and has two concrete subclasses, Educational and Commercial. These three classes are shown in Figure 14-11. An Institution has a value associated with it. However, for the Educational class, this is calculated as follows:

```
assets = number of students * fees - running costs
```

For the Commercial class, we have:

```
profits = gains - losses
```

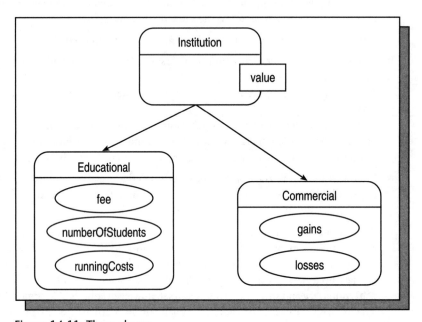

Figure 14-11: Three classes.

a) Model the hierarchy as a collection of Java classes with appropriate method and attribute definitions as required.

b) Create a heterogeneous collection of educational and commercial instances.

c) Provide a driver application that allows us to find out:

The total value of our collection

The names of the institutes with the highest and lowest values

2. Figure 14-12 shows a portion of a classification hierarchy for the natural world.

   a) Show how we can use interfaces to specify the following:

   ■ Bats and sparrows can fly (a possible method might be `maximumTimeInFlight`).

   ■ Humans, rats, and bats are carnivorous (a possible method might be `huntingRadius`).

   b) Realize the relevant portions of the hierarchy and interfaces in Java.

   c) Provide a driver application to test your classes and interfaces.

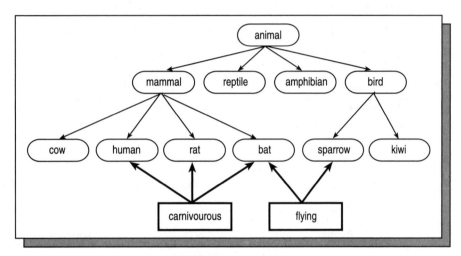

Figure 14-12: Inheritance and interfaces.

3. We have three different classes:

Person, Car, and (Household) Appliance.

We wish to provide a method that allows us to get a String containing a summary of the instance (rather than a perhaps too detailed toString). For Person, we may wish to get the title and surname of the person; for a Car, just the make and model; for an Appliance, the manufacturer and item.

There are two different approaches. We can have Car, Person, and Appliance all inherit from a shared abstract class (call it MyObject) that has the method specifier getSummary. We then implement it in the three subclasses, as shown in Figure 14-13.

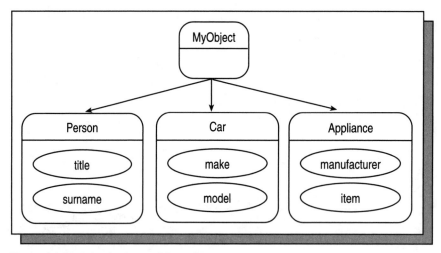

Figure 14-13: Inheritance and four classes.

If we are unable to reorganize the inheritance hierarchy, we can provide an interface summarizable with, again, the method specifier getSummary (as shown in Figure 14-14).

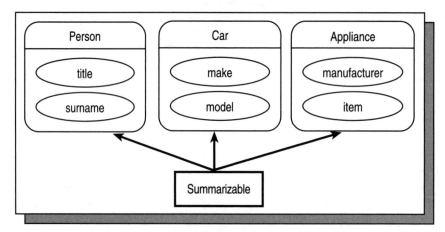

Figure 14-14: Three classes and an interface.

a) Implement both the solutions.

b) For both cases, create a heterogeneous collection of instances of the three classes.

c) For both cases, provide a driver application to test your classes and interfaces.

4. We wish to model a game of chess. As in exercise 10.6, we will again wish to model the board, the squares, and the pieces. However, we want to make use of abstract classes. We will have an abstract class, ChessPiece, that provides a concrete method and attributes to represent a piece's location but also provides the abstract method isMoveLegal. We will have a number of concrete classes inheriting from ChessPiece (such as Pawn, Rook, Knight, etc.), and their responsibility is to provide a concrete implementation of isMoveLegal for their own characteristics.

As in exercise 10.6, we want to set up the board for the start of the game and allow player(s) to specify moves that are checked for legality before the move is made.

CHAPTER 15

Throwing & Catching Exceptions

15.1 Introduction

One of the problems with writing a program is to make sure that it is *robust*. That is, when something unexpected happens (for example, an invalid piece of data has been typed in by the user, or an access to the Internet has failed), we have to ensure that the program can detect what has happened and do something about it. The program could modify the processing as appropriate in light of what has happened, or it could perhaps retry the operation (for example, reaccess the Internet), or it could at least close down the program in a "safe" way with a suitable error message.

If we are going to test for and then cope with a large number of special situations, our program may end up as a spaghetti of code, most of which is there to handle one of a large number of possible special situations, none of which occur very frequently. A common system would be for each method to pass back a special indication of any failure and for the calling method to detect this and pass it back in its turn. Such a system may make it difficult to write the code that handles the standard, common situations in a well-structured way. What we need is a mechanism that allows each special condition to be checked for at the point where it could occur. But when the condition does occur, we want control to be passed automatically to a section of code at a suitable location (which may be at some distance from where the condition was detected) for the appropriate action to be taken.

The mechanism supplied for this in the Java language is the *exception*. An exception is an indication that some special condition has occurred; as we will see, it is in fact an instance of a class derived from the `java.lang.Exception` *class*. The piece of code that detects that the condition has occurred creates an exception of the appropriate type; it is said to *throw* the exception. Somewhere else in the program there may be a piece of code that is able to deal with the condition, some sort of error handler. We can arrange for the code to *catch* the exception and then deal with it. Since there may be several error handlers in the program, there needs to be a scheme by which an exception is caught only by a handler that can deal with it. If the handler cannot deal with it, then the exception will be passed on for another handler to deal with it. If no handler is found, the program will be brought to a halt with a suitable error message (see Figure 15-1).

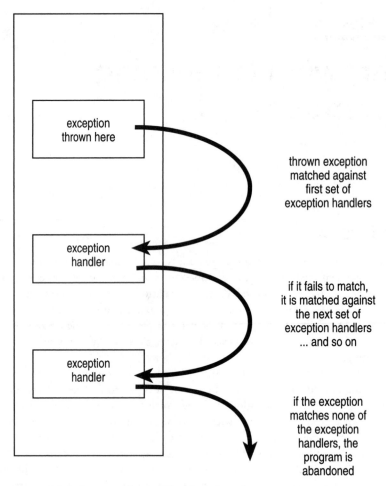

Figure 15-1: An exception looking for a handler.

We have in fact already met the concept of an exception. When we are using the BasicIo or BasicFileIo classes, various things can go wrong. For example, when the program is trying to read an integer with the readInteger method, the user could type the string "two", or we could try to write to a file that is read-only. In situations like these, the methods of these classes throw an exception from a class called IOException (derived from the Exception class). In the code we have written so far, we have made no attempt to catch and do anything about these exceptions; we have simply allowed the program to be abandoned. But we have already found that Java insists on strict accounting for exceptions. If we have a method that calls other methods that may throw exceptions, and our method is not going to do anything about them, then as far as Java is concerned, our method is responsible for possibly throwing an exception. We have to report this in our method header with a throws clause.

So, whenever we write a method that calls any of the `BasicIo` or `BasicFileIo` methods, we have to indicate that our method may throw an `IOException`:

```
public static void main(String[] args) throws IOException
   {
   ...
```

In Chapter 11, we implemented a `PriorityQueue` class. We are going to discuss exceptions in terms of this class. You will recall that if we attempt to extract an item from an empty queue or insert an item in a full queue, we have set the methods up to stop the program (using the `System.exit` method). This is fairly drastic, and it would be better to throw an exception to allow the program using the class to attempt to recover if possible. We need to do three things:

- We need to define the exceptions that we might need to throw.

- We need to throw an exception at an appropriate point.

- We need to set up handler code at appropriate places and make it catch the appropriate exception or exceptions.

15.2 Defining a New Exception

First we have to decide what exceptions we want to throw. Sometimes we want to throw an exception that has already been defined in the standard Java language. For example, as was mentioned in the previous section, we have written all the methods of the `BasicIo` and `BasicFileIo` classes so that they throw the standard exception `IOException`.

At other times we will want to define our own new class of exceptions. This is a new class that inherits from one of the standard Java exceptions. In the case of the `PriorityQueue` class, we want to define a new class of exception called `QueueEmptyException`, to be thrown when either of the methods `first` or `remove` is called on to access the "first" element in an empty queue.

It should be noted that it is considered poor programming practice to throw and catch generic exceptions. Increased granularity (by defining more specific exceptions) always gives the class user and end user more information about what went wrong.

We define this exception by extending one of the standard Java exception classes (or one of the exception classes that we have defined earlier):

```
public class QueueEmptyException extends Exception
   {
   ...
   } // end of class QueueEmptyException
```

This is going to be a public class (because we will want to refer to it in other programs where we are coding exception handlers), so it will be in a separate file, `QueueEmptyException.java`.

What do we need to put in our new class? We normally need to provide only a pair of constructor methods, a default one and one with a single `String` argument. The `String` argument can give more information about the exception than is available from its name. For example, if we were throwing an exception because an argument to a method was invalid, we might want the string to include information about the particular argument value that caused the problem.

The body of these constructors simply calls the appropriate constructor of the base class, either implicitly or explicitly:

```
public QueueEmptyException()
   {
   } // end of constructor method

public QueueEmptyException(String message)
   {
   super(message) ;
   } // end of constructor method
```

15.3   Throwing an Exception

When a program detects a condition that requires that an exception is reported, it creates an instance of that exception (using the appropriate constructor method) and *throws* it. So in the remove method, we test for there being nothing to remove. If so, we create and throw an instance of the QueueEmptyException exception:

```
if (isEmpty())
   throw new QueueEmptyException() ;
```

or:

```
if (isEmpty())
   throw new QueueEmptyException("'remove' from empty queue") ;
```

The Java system requires the programmer to inform it of what exceptions could be thrown by each method. So the header line of the remove method becomes:

```
public QueueElement remove() throws QueueEmptyException
```

If the throw statement is reached, the flow of control does not proceed any further through the code of the method, nor does it return to the method that called it. Instead, the Java system searches for an exception handler that is able to handle this type of exception. If it does not find one, it will terminate the program with a suitable error message.

Similarly, we insert a throw statement in the first method (and a throws clause in its header):

```
public QueueElement first() throws QueueEmptyException
   {
   if (isEmpty())
      throw new QueueEmptyException("'first' on empty queue") ;
```

In the `insert` method, we need to throw a `QueueFullException` (with a `throws` clause in its header):

```
public void insert(QueueElement d) throws QueueFullException
  {
  if (isFull())
    throw new QueueFullException("'insert' in full queue") ;
```

Of course, we need to define this `QueueFullException` class first, as we did with the `QueueEmptyException` class.

If we compile the `PriorityQueue.java` file now, we will find a further problem. We left in the class a `main` method for testing purposes. This calls all three of our modified methods, which means that exceptions may be thrown that `main` does nothing about. So we have to modify the header:

```
public static void main(String[] args) throws IOException,
                QueueFullException,
        QueueEmptyException
```

Because we call `BasicIo` methods, we are already reporting that instances of `IOException` may be thrown.

15.4 Catching an Exception

If we now try our new version of the `PriorityQueue` with the `main` method that we left for testing purposes, we find that attempting to remove from an empty queue causes the program to be abandoned with a suitable error message:

```
QueueEmptyException: 'remove' from empty queue
    at PriorityQueue.remove(PriorityQueue.java:111)
    at PriorityQueue.main(PriorityQueue.java:226)
```

if we used the `QueueEmptyException` constructor with an argument, or:

```
QueueEmptyException:
    at PriorityQueue.remove(PriorityQueue.java:111)
    at PriorityQueue.main(PriorityQueue.java:226)
```

if we used the `QueueEmptyException` constructor without an argument.

But now we want to catch these exceptions in the main method so that we can continue with the testing. If we wish to deal with some or all of the exceptions in a certain sequence of code, we have to make it into a `try` block:

```
try {
   SEQUENCE OF STATEMENTS WHERE WE WISH TO CATCH EXCEPTIONS
   }
catch (EXCEPTION-CLASS-1 variable name)
   {
   CODE TO DEAL WITH EXCEPTIONS OF THE SPECIFIED CLASS
   }
catch (EXCEPTION-CLASS-2 variable name)
   {
   CODE TO DEAL WITH EXCEPTIONS OF THE SPECIFIED CLASS
   }
catch (EXCEPTION-CLASS-3 variable name)
   {
   CODE TO DEAL WITH EXCEPTIONS OF THE SPECIFIED CLASS
   }
```

The basic idea is that if an exception is thrown in the try block, it is tested against each of the catch clauses in turn, starting at the first one. The first matching catch clause is executed, and then control passes to the code immediately after the last catch clause. That is, only one of the catch clauses is executed, the first one that matches, and then the program continues from after the try-catch code (see Figure 15-2).

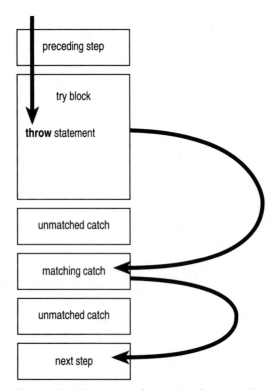

Figure 15-2: Sequence of execution for a caught exception.

If none of the catch clauses matches the exception that has been thrown, the Java system has still not caught the exception, and it will look for an enclosing try clause so that it can try to match the exception against each of its catch statements in turn (see Figure 15-3).

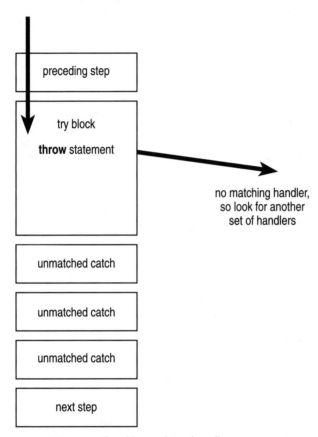

Figure 15-3: No "local" matching handler.

Of course, if no exception is thrown, control proceeds to the end of the try block, ignores all the catch clauses, and proceeds with the code after the last catch clause (see Figure 15-4).

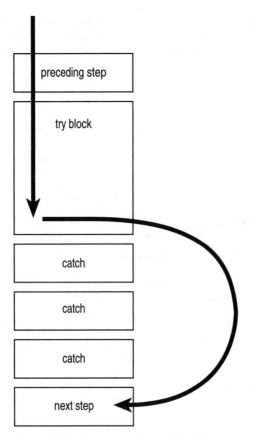

Figure 15-4: Sequence of execution if no exception is thrown.

So we take the loop in the main method of the `PriorityQueue` class:

```
while (continueLoop)
    {
    displayMenu() ;
    ...
    switch (response.charAt(0))
        {
        case '1' :
        ...
```

code that includes calls of insert (which may throw QueueFullException) and first and remove (which may throw QueueEmptyException)

```
        ...
        default :
            System.out.println("invalid response") ;
```

```
      break ;
    } // end of switch

  if (continueLoop)
    {
    BasicIo.prompt("press RETURN to continue") ;
    response = Basicio.readString() ;
    } // end of if
  } // end of loop
```

and we insert a try block in it, to catch the exceptions for the "queue full" and "queue empty" conditions:

```
while (continueLoop)
  {
  displayMenu() ;
  ...
  try {
    switch (response.charAt(0))
      {
      case '1' :
      ...
```

code that includes calls of insert (which may throw QueueFullException) and first and remove (which may throw QueueEmptyException):

```
      ...
      default :
        System.out.println("invalid response") ;
        break ;
      } // end of switch
    } // end of try block
  catch (QueueFullException e)
    {
    System.out.println("no more room in the queue") ;
    }
  catch (QueueEmptyException e)
    {
    System.out.println("no elements in the queue") ;
    }

  if (continueLoop)
    {
    BasicIo.prompt("press RETURN to continue") ;
    response = Basicio.readString() ;
    }
  } // end of loop
```

We are now catching the two new exceptions rather than allowing them to be thrown out of our `main` method, so we no longer need to tell the Java system that we are throwing them (we could still throw an `IOException` of course):

```
public static void main(String[] args) throws IOException
```

In the normal course of events, when no exceptions are thrown, the program executes the statements of the try block, ignores the catch clauses, and proceeds to the `if` test at the end of the loop before proceeding in the normal way to the next iteration of the loop.

Suppose now we try to remove an element from an empty queue. The `remove` method will be abandoned when it reaches the `throw` statement. Since the exception was thrown inside the `try` block, the flow of control immediately proceeds to the appropriate exception handler, which will deal with it by printing an error message. It will ignore the other catch clause and proceed to the `if` statement and then the next iteration of the loop.

If any other exception is raised (such as an instance of the `IOException` class), no matching exception handler has been provided. The system will look for an enclosing try block, not find it, and the program will terminate with an error message.

A catch clause looks a bit like a method with a single formal argument of some class derived from `Exception` (and in this example, given the name `e`):

```
catch (QueueEmptyException e)
   {
   . . .
   }
```

We can refer to the exception inside the catch clause if we want. There is a `toString` method in the `Exception` class that is inherited by the derived classes and prints the exception name and any message associated with it. So we could write:

```
catch (QueueEmptyException e)
   {
   System.out.println("ERROR: " + e) ;
   }
```

This causes the `toString` method associated with the instance `e` to be called automatically (see section 13.4) to print a suitable error message.

We stated that a thrown exception was tested against each of the catch clauses in turn, to find the first one that matched. If we have thrown an instance of the `QueueEmptyException` class, the first catch clause it matches is:

```
catch (QueueEmptyException e)
   . . .
```

An alternative way of writing the this code might be:

```
while (continueLoop)
   {
   displayMenu() ;
   . . .
```

```
try {
   switch (response.charAt(0))
      {
      case '1' :
      . . .
```

code that includes calls of `insert` (which may throw `QueueFullException`) and `first` and `remove` (which may throw `QueueEmptyException`):

```
      . . .
      default :
         System.out.println("invalid response") ;
         break ;
      } // end of switch
   } // end of try block
catch (Exception e)
   {
   System.out.println("ERROR: " + e) ;
   }

if (continueLoop)
   {
   BasicIo.prompt("press RETURN to continue") ;
   response = BasicIo.readString() ;
   }
} // end of loop
```

Here we have provided only one catch clause:

```
catch (Exception e)
   . . .
```

But the `QueueEmptyException` class is derived from the `Exception` class, so (by polymorphism) a `QueueEmptyException` instance is also an `Exception` instance. So all the exceptions will be caught by this catch clause (including `IOException`).

15.4.1 *The finally Clause (optional)*

There is a slight problem if we have a lot of catch clauses:

```
try {
   SEQUENCE OF STATEMENTS WHERE WE WISH TO CATCH EXCEPTIONS
   }
catch (EXCEPTION-CLASS-1 variable name)
   {
   CODE TO DEAL WITH EXCEPTIONS OF THE SPECIFIED CLASS
   }
```

```
catch (EXCEPTION-CLASS-2 variable name)
   {
   CODE TO DEAL WITH EXCEPTIONS OF THE SPECIFIED CLASS
   }
catch (EXCEPTION-CLASS-3 variable name)
   {
   CODE TO DEAL WITH EXCEPTIONS OF THE SPECIFIED CLASS
   }
catch (EXCEPTION-CLASS-4 variable name)
   {
   CODE TO DEAL WITH EXCEPTIONS OF THE SPECIFIED CLASS
   }
```

If we have some tidying up to do after dealing with an individual exception, we would have to put it at the end of each of the catch clauses. To obviate this, Java provides a finally clause, which is always executed after *any* of the catch clauses have been executed (see Figure 15-5):

```
try {
   SEQUENCE OF STATEMENTS WHERE WE WISH TO CATCH EXCEPTIONS
   }
catch (EXCEPTION-CLASS-1 variable name)
   {
   CODE TO DEAL WITH EXCEPTIONS OF THE SPECIFIED CLASS
   }
catch (EXCEPTION-CLASS-2 variable name)
   {
   CODE TO DEAL WITH EXCEPTIONS OF THE SPECIFIED CLASS
   }
catch (EXCEPTION-CLASS-3 variable name)
   {
   CODE TO DEAL WITH EXCEPTIONS OF THE SPECIFIED CLASS
   }
catch (EXCEPTION-CLASS-4 variable name)
   {
   CODE TO DEAL WITH EXCEPTIONS OF THE SPECIFIED CLASS
   }
finally
   {
   CODE TO DO ANY TIDYING UP
   }
```

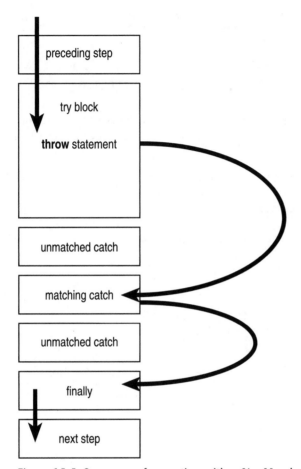

Figure 15-5: Sequence of execution with a `finally` clause.

In fact, the `finally` clause is executed however the `try` block is left, whether it leaves normally without throwing an exception or it throws an exception that is not caught by any of these `catch` clauses. So we can put in the `finally` clause any tidying-up code that we must guarantee to execute.

15.5   Key Points in Chapter 15

- If we have an unusual condition, we can *throw* an *exception* at the point where the condition is detected and *catch* it at a distant point in the program, where we can handle the condition.

- We define new exceptions by deriving them from the `Exception` class (or a class derived from it). We need to define a default constructor and a constructor with one `String` argument:

```
public class NewException extends Exception
    {
    public NewException()
        {
        } // end of constructor method

    public NewException(String message)
        {
        super(message) ;
        } // end of constructor method
    } // end of class NewException
```

- We throw an exception by setting up a new instance of the class and then using the keyword `throw`:

```
if (CONDITION)
    throw new NewException(" ... ") ;
    ...
```

- We can catch exceptions that are thrown in a sequence of statements (including those thrown by methods called from the sequence) with a `try` block:

```
try {
    SEQUENCE OF STATEMENTS WHICH MAY THROW EXCEPTIONS
    }
catch (EXCEPTION-CLASS-1 e)
    {
    HANDLER FOR EXCEPTION-CLASS-1
    }
catch (EXCEPTION-CLASS-2 e)
    {
    HANDLER FOR EXCEPTION-CLASS-2
    }
```

If no exceptions are thrown, the catch clauses are ignored. If an exception is thrown, the rest of the SEQUENCE OF STATEMENTS is abandoned and only the matching catch clause is executed. If none of the catch clauses match, the system searches for an enclosing try block. If no match occurs anywhere in the program, it will be abandoned with an error message.

■ If an exception is thrown by a method (or by a method that it calls) and the method does not handle the exception, it has to be mentioned in a throws clause in the method header:

```
public .... methodName( ... arguments ... ) throws NewException
```

15.6 Exercises

1. Rewrite the Person class so that an exception InvalidPersonAttribute is thrown if any of the set methods are passed an invalid argument (for example, a surname of length zero or a negative age).

   Rewrite the test harness program for the Person class (see section 4.8) so that it catches the InvalidPersonAttribute but not any IOExceptions.

   Rewrite the test harness further so that it also catches any IOExceptions.

2. Implement a stack of characters as an abstract data type in the class CharacterStack. The stack should be implemented as an array of characters, together with a count of how many elements are currently stored in the stack. It should have the following methods:

   ■ public void initialize() to initialize an empty stack.

   ■ public void push(char c) to push a character c on the top of the stack, throwing StackOverflowException if there is no room.

   ■ public char pop() to pop the top character off the stack and return it, throwing StackUnderflowException if the stack is empty.

   ■ public boolean isEmpty() to return whether or not the stack is empty.

   ■ public int size() to return the number of elements in the stack

   Write a driver program to allow the stack to be tested by a user from the terminal. The user should be able to specify the next method to call from a menu and then specify any arguments, and the program should print any return values for checking.

3. Use the CharacterStack class to implement a program to check an expression for matching brackets.

   The types of brackets it should recognize are round ('(' and ')'), square ('[' and ']') and curly ('{' and '}'). Thus {([])} and {(())[()()]} are valid expressions, while {(}) and () are not. The expression should be entered by the user as a string.

The algorithm for this program is as follows:

Starting with an empty stack and a string of characters, take each successive character in the string. If the character is an open bracket of some sort, push it on the stack. If it is a closing bracket of some sort and either the stack is empty or the character popped from the top of the stack is not an opening bracket of the same type, then the string is unbalanced. A balanced string will leave an empty stack when the string has been processed.

Graphics & the Abstract Window Toolkit

16.1 Graphical User Interfaces

So far in this book our programs have communicated with the user by reading and writing strings of characters. Typically, the program starts and then requires some input information. It prompts the user for a piece of data using the `BasicIo.prompt` method or some of the `System.out.print` methods. Then it reads in a value from the user using an appropriate method from the `BasicIo` class. It repeats this for each required piece of input data. Finally, it carries out some form of calculation and then outputs the results for the user, again using some of the `System.out.print` methods.

Nowadays many programs provide a different format for interacting with the user, a *Graphical User Interface* or *GUI*. The user is presented with one or more "windows" containing text, drawings, or diagrams of various types, or perhaps pictures or "images." The user communicates with the program by typing into designated areas of the display or by moving the mouse to a particular position and clicking the mouse button. This action is used to press buttons of various kinds on the screen, to scroll a window across a larger diagram or area of text, to indicate a particular location within a drawing at which some action or redrawing must take place, and so on. You have already seen a good example of this in the network browser introduced in the first chapter. The browser displays a page, and we can press various buttons to carry out actions (for example, to add the URL of the current page to our bookmark file), to scroll through the page if it is larger than the display area, and of course to click on a link in the page, which the browser interprets as a call to read the designated page from the Web and display it.

One of the problems in creating a Graphical User Interface in the past has been *platform independence*. Even if we write our program in a standard language like C, different operating systems (such as UNIX, Microsoft Windows, and the Macintosh operating system) have a different set of facilities for providing a GUI, with a different set of behaviors.

In this chapter, we describe how to build a Graphical User Interface for a program written in Java. Java provides a set of facilities called the *Abstract Window Toolkit*, or *AWT*, and this provides a standard set of facilities for building GUIs that is the same across all platforms. It does this by mapping the facilities provided by the AWT onto the facilities provided by the particular operating system on which the program is running.

There are significant differences between the Abstract Window Toolkit in the 1.0.2 version of Java and that in the 1.1 version; in this chapter we describe the 1.1 version and indicate in Appendix B the main differences in the 1.0.2 version. It is worthwhile, at this point, to talk a little about the changes between these two versions of Java. The first widely used version of Java was version 1.0.2, and this is the version described in most books published up to 1996. The current version of Java (Summer 1997) is referred to as 1.1, although there have been a series of minor releases such as 1.1.1, 1.1.2, and 1.1.3, which correct bugs in earlier versions but are otherwise not different from version 1.1. The "core" aspects of Java (such as the way the `if` and `for` control structures are used, or how inheritance works) have not changed between 1.0.2. and 1.1. What has changed is how some of the classes work, such as the Abstract Window Toolkit and some aspects of input/output (see Chapter 19). It is likely that future changes to Java will be similar in nature; there will be little or no change to the language itself, but there will be changes in the facilities provided by some of the classes.

There are more than 50 classes in the current version of the AWT. We will not therefore attempt to describe in detail in this chapter all the facilities available. To illustrate the general features of the facilities provided by Java, we will instead introduce a number of short programs that use the AWT to provide simple graphical interfaces. To find out more information, you can study the Java API documentation or read any of a number of books that describe the AWT in much more detail.

We write graphical interface programs in Java by deriving new classes from the classes provided in the Abstract Window Toolkit, so this is also a good introduction to the use of the inheritance features described in Chapters 12 to 14.

There is a significant difference between a program with a text interface, the type we have used up to now, and a graphical interface, the type to be discussed in this chapter. This difference relates to the range of events that the program has to be able to handle. When a program with a text interface is awaiting input from the user, the only thing that will happen is that the user will eventually type in some sequence of characters. The program has to interpret these characters, decide whether or not they are valid, and then take the appropriate action. In a graphical interface, on the other hand, there could be several different text areas, drawing areas, and buttons. The user could type into any one of the text areas, click on any part of a drawing, or press any one of the buttons.

Furthermore, the user could have several other windows on his or her screen that are connected to other programs. The user could move one of these windows over the top of the window connected to our Java program, partially or fully obscuring this window. Later the user could bring the Java window back to the front, and the system has to know how to redraw the parts of the window that have become visible again. The user could "resize" the Java window (that is, make it larger or smaller), and again the system has to know how to redraw the graphical interface at this new size.

A central feature of a graphical program is therefore an *event loop*. The program waits for some event to occur, and when it occurs, causes the appropriate action to be taken. If the window has become exposed after being hidden behind another window, or if the window has had its size changed by the user, a method will be called to redraw the window. If a button has been pressed, a suitable method will be called to deal with this event—presumably some calculation will be carried out, after which some part of the window may need to be redrawn. After the action appropriate to the event has been carried out, the program returns to waiting in the event loop. We say that such a program is *event driven*.

This event loop is inside the code that implements the AWT, and it does not appear explicitly as part of the code of our program. Our program normally does some initialization and setting up of the graphical components to be displayed and goes into the event loop inside the AWT. The rest of our program will be a number of short fragments (typically methods), each of which is called by the AWT event loop to deal with a certain type of event (for example, a button depression, or a mouse click at a particular location on a diagram).

There is a further feature of graphical programming that needs to be mentioned and that will be illustrated in the example programs that appear later in this chapter. As we will see, we are going to write a method which draws (or redraws) a portion of a window based on the current state of various program variables. In Java this method is usually called `paint`. When an event occurs, such as to press a button or move the mouse, the corresponding action should normally record details of the event and then request that the AWT carry out a redraw of the appropriate part of the screen at a suitable time. This request in Java is a call of the `repaint` method. So, for example, the method called as a result of clicking the mouse at a certain position should simply record the position and call `repaint`. This allows the action corresponding to an event to be fast so that the program can keep up with events as they occur. The redrawing of the parts of the window by the `paint` method, which is likely to be rather slower, can be carried out at a time scheduled by the AWT.

16.2   A Simple Program With a Graphical Interface

Our first simple graphical program is going to display a window like the one in Figure 16-1.

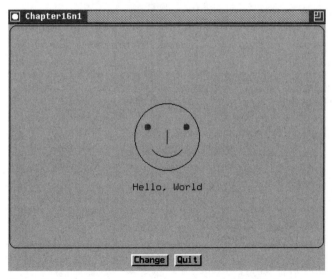

Figure 16-1: A first Java program with a graphical interface.

A smiling face is displayed. If we click on the Change button, it becomes a sad face, and if we click on Change again, it becomes happy again. We can leave the program by clicking on the Quit button. If you try running the program, you will see that if you cover this window with that from another program and then reveal it again, the face is redrawn. If you resize the window, you will see that the smiling face is redrawn in the new center of the area.

In fact we are going to start with a slightly simpler program as shown in Figure 16-2.

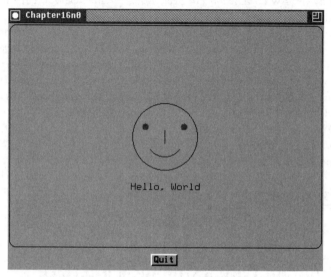

Figure 16-2: A simplified first graphical program.

This version does not have a Change button; rather boringly the face is always smiling. However, we have retained the Quit button so we can abandon the program when we wish. Here is the code for this program, which we explain in the next few sections; the program is in a file called Chapter16n0.java:

```java
import java.awt.* ;
import java.awt.event.* ;

public class Chapter16n0 extends Frame
                implements WindowListener, ActionListener
  {
  public Chapter16n0()
    {
    // set up basic window
    setTitle("Chapter16n0") ;
    setBackground(Color.green) ;
    setSize(500, 400) ;
    addWindowListener(this) ;
```

```
        // set up area for face
        Canvas c = new Canvas0() ;
        add("Center", c) ;

        // set up area with buttons
        Panel p = new Panel() ;
        p.setLayout(new FlowLayout()) ;
        Button quit = new Button("Quit") ;
        p.add(quit) ;
        quit.addActionListener(this) ;
        add("South", p) ;
        } // end of constructor method

    public static void main(String[] args)
        {
        Chapter16n0 f = new Chapter16n0() ;
        f.setVisible(true) ;
        } // end of method main

    public void actionPerformed(ActionEvent event)
        {
        // deal with "Quit" button
        dispose();
        System.exit(0);
        } // end of method actionPerformed

    public void windowClosing(WindowEvent event)
        {
        dispose() ;
        System.exit(0) ;
        } // end of method windowClosing

    public void windowOpened(WindowEvent event) {}
    public void windowIconified(WindowEvent event) {}
    public void windowDeiconified(WindowEvent event) {}
    public void windowClosed(WindowEvent event) {}
    public void windowActivated(WindowEvent event) {}
    public void windowDeactivated(WindowEvent event) {}
    } // end of class Chapter16n0


class Canvas0 extends Canvas
    {
    public void paint(Graphics g)
        {
```

```
// set up some dimensions for the drawing
Dimension d = getSize() ;
int cx = d.width / 2,
    cy = d.height /2,
    faceRadius = 50,
    noseLength = 20,
    mouthRadius = 30,
    mouthAngle = 50,
    eyeRadius = 5 ;

// draw the frame
g.setColor(Color.black) ;
g.drawRoundRect(2, 2, d.width - 5, d.height - 5, 20, 20) ;

// draw the face
g.setColor(Color.red) ;
g.drawOval(cx - faceRadius,
    cy - faceRadius,
    faceRadius * 2,
    faceRadius * 2) ;
g.setColor(Color.blue) ;
g.fillOval(cx - 30 - eyeRadius,
    cy - 20,
    eyeRadius * 2,
    eyeRadius * 2) ;
g.fillOval(cx + 30 - eyeRadius,
    cy - 20,
    eyeRadius * 2,
    eyeRadius * 2) ;
g.setColor(Color.red) ;
g.drawLine(cx, cy - (noseLength / 2), cx, cy + (noseLength / 2)) ;
g.drawArc(cx - mouthRadius,
    cy - mouthRadius,
    mouthRadius * 2,
    mouthRadius * 2,
    270 - mouthAngle,
    mouthAngle * 2) ;

// write the text
Font f1 = new Font("TimesRoman", Font.PLAIN, 14) ;
Font f2 = new Font("TimesRoman", Font.ITALIC, 14) ;
FontMetrics fm1 = g.getFontMetrics(f1) ;
FontMetrics fm2 = g.getFontMetrics(f2) ;
String s1 = "Hello, " ;
String s2 = "World" ;
int w1 = fm1.stringWidth(s1) ;
```

```
      int w2 = fm2.stringWidth(s2) ;
      g.setColor(Color.black) ;
      g.setFont(f1) ;
      int ctx = cx - ((w1 + w2) / 2) ;
      int cty = cy + faceRadius + 30 ;
      g.drawString(s1, ctx, cty) ;
      ctx += w1 ;
      g.setFont(f2) ;
      g.drawString(s2, ctx, cty) ;
      } // end of method paint
   } // end of class Canvas0
```

The Java class that implements an independent window on the screen is called Frame. Our version of Frame is going to contain an area upon which we will draw the smiley face—this is a version of another Java class, one that provides a drawing area or canvas, called Canvas. We have an area below the canvas that contains the Quit button (and later the Change button). So our program consists of two classes:

- A public class called Chapter16n0, which is derived from Frame. This provides the basic layout of the window, sets the program running in the first place, and specifies the action that should result if the Quit button (and later the Change button) is pressed.

- A class called Canvas0, which is derived from Canvas. This contains details of how to draw the smiley face and accompanying text.

The classes and methods for programming with the AWT are in two packages, java.awt and java.awt.event, so we import both of these.

16.3 Writing the Chapter16n0 Class

The class Chapter16n0 contains no instance fields, but it contains four methods:

- A constructor method, to specify the layout of the window.
- A main method, to set the program going.
- An actionPerformed method, to deal with pressing the Quit button.
- A windowClosing method, which is a necessary part of *any* graphics program, to ensure that we are able to kill off the program if it is not working properly. As we shall see, it is also necessary to have several more dummy methods to deal with other possible things that can happen to a window.

We deal with each of these methods in turn.

16.3.1   *The Constructor for the Chapter16n0 Class*

The constructor method `Chapter16n0` does the basic layout of our window.

First we specify a title to go in the title area at the top of our window using the `setTitle` method:

```
setTitle("Chapter16n0") ;
```

We have provided as title the string `Chapter16n0`, but we could of course have used something less boring. If we omit this step, a default title is displayed, such as the string `Untitled` or `*****`.

Then we set the background color for our window using the `setBackground` method:

```
setBackground(Color.green) ;
```

The argument to this method is an instance of the `Color` class. This class provides a number of color names as constants—we have used green (`Color.green`), but the full list is:

- black
- blue
- cyan
- darkGray
- gray
- green
- lightGray
- magenta
- orange
- pink
- red
- white
- yellow

It is in fact possible to construct other shades of color with the `Color` class, but it is beyond the scope of this book.

Next we specify the initial size of the window with the `setSize` method:

```
setSize(500, 400) ;
```

This takes two integer parameters, the horizontal width followed by the vertical height of the window. The units of these parameters are pixels. A *pixel*, or picture element, is the basic unit of resolution on the screen—it is the smallest addressable area on the screen, and it is the unit in which coordinates within the window are specified (from an origin in the top left-hand corner). You should not omit this step because the AWT needs to have some initial idea about the size of your window.

We discuss the call of the `addWindowListener` method later.

Now we can start to put the basic elements of the layout in our window. The main part of our window is going to be an area containing the smiley face. This will be derived from the class Canvas, and our derived class is going to be called Canvas0. We declare a local variable c of this type that refers to an object created with the constructor method Canvas0—more about the Canvas0 class and constructor method later.

```
Canvas c = new Canvas0() ;
```

We want the canvas to appear as the main item in our picture, with the button (or buttons) below it. If we wished, we could calculate the exact position of each item and tell the AWT to position the item at that point. But usually we want simply to arrange the items in specified relative positions and have the AWT work out the exact positioning (particularly as we cannot anticipate exactly how each platform may display the components, and we may later resize the window). To simplify the problem of layout, the AWT provides a number of what are called *layout managers* to do most of the work of positioning picture components within a larger "container" component. The default layout manager for classes derived from Frame is called the *border* layout manager.

We add a picture component to a container component with a version of the add method, one of whose arguments is the picture component to be added:

```
add("Center", c) ;
```

If we are using the border layout manager, the add method needs another argument to specify the positioning. This, the first argument, is one of the strings Center, North, South, East, or West to specify the relative position of the picture elements according to the diagram in Figure 16-3.

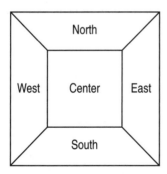

Figure 16-3: Positions in the border layout.

So the canvas c goes at the Center, and the group of buttons will go at South (i.e., at the bottom of the window). As you can see from this example, not all the positions in a border layout need to be filled.

Now we set up the Quit button. We are going to put the buttons on a panel, which is a general window component that can contain other components, so we declare a Panel instance p:

```
Panel p = new Panel() ;
```

We specify (with the setLayout method) that the panel should have another layout manager, the *flow* layout manager, which lays out components in a generally helpful way, filling up rows from left to right and then top to bottom.

```
p.setLayout(new FlowLayout()) ;
```

We then create a button, labeled Quit. We do this by creating an instance of the Button class, with the label as the argument to its constructor, and we add it to the panel p with the add method. Since the button is being added to the panel under the control of the flow layout manager, the only argument to the add method is the component being added.

```
Button quit = new Button("Quit") ;
p.add(quit) ;
```

We discuss the call of the addActionListener method later.

Finally we add the panel p to the class derived from Frame, requiring it to be positioned at the bottom of the window (i.e., South), as we have already mentioned:

```
add("South", p) ;
```

We have used the FlowLayout and BorderLayout managers in this example. There are a number of other layout managers, perhaps the most useful of which is the GridLayout manager. This allows a set of components to be laid out in a specified number of rows and columns. When we set up this manager, we specify the number of rows and columns:

```
p.setLayout(new GridLayout(2, 3)) ;                 // 2 rows, 3 columns
```

Then we add the components with the add method (with no additional arguments)—first the components of the first row, from left to right, then the components of the second row, and so on:

```
p.add(row0column0) ;
p.add(row0column1) ;
p.add(row0column2) ;
p.add(row1column0) ;
p.add(row1column1) ;
p.add(row1column2) ;
```

This would give the layout shown in Figure 16-4.

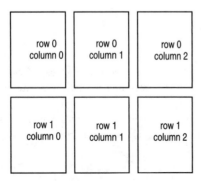

Figure 16-4: Using the GridLayout manager.

It is possible to be much more specific about how components are laid out (for instance, with a layout manager called `GridBagLayout`), but this is beyond the scope of this book. The three layout managers we have discussed will be sufficient for the tasks we want to carry out here. We can build up more complex layouts by using combinations of these three. For example, we could have a component with a `GridLayout` manager with two rows and a single column and add to it two components, each with a `GridLayout` manager with a single row and several columns, leading to a layout like the one shown in Figure 16-5.

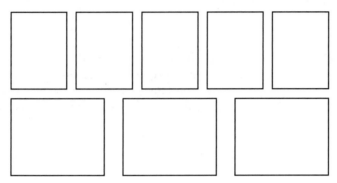

Figure 16-5: More complex use of the `GridLayout` manager.

16.3.2   *The main Method for the Chapter16n0 Class*

We move on now to the `main` method of our `Chapter16n0` class.

We first declare a local variable of type `Chapter16n0` and initialize it with the constructor method we have just described:

```
Chapter16n0 f = new Chapter16n0() ;
```

Then we call the method `setVisible`:

```
f.setVisible(true) ;
```

This displays the object on the screen and enters the AWT event loop, waiting for and then responding to events as they occur.

16.3.3   *The actionPerformed Method of the Chapter16n0 Class*

Next we have to specify what is to happen when we click on the Quit button. If we click on a button, the AWT system is going to call a method `actionPerformed`, which belongs to the `ActionListener` interface (in fact, it is the only method in this interface). We therefore first have to tell Java that our class `Chapter16n0` implements this interface:

```
public class Chapter16n0 extends Frame implements ActionListener
```

We need to tell the AWT which class contains the `actionPerformed` method for each button in our program. In our examples in this book, it will always be the class that contains the constructor that sets up the button in the first place. So we can use the keyword this as argument to the addActionListener method applied to the button when we have set it up:

```
quit.addActionListener(this) ;
```

We now have to write the actionPerformed method. This has a single argument, an ActionEvent, which gives details of what has happened:

```
public void actionPerformed(ActionEvent event)
  {
  ...
```

For the moment, we have only a single button. So, if this method has been called, we can assume that the Quit button must have been pressed. If so, we abandon the program by calling the System.exit method. Since this is a normal exit from the program, we give an argument value of zero. Before we do this we make sure we return all the system resources used by this object, using the method dispose:

```
// deal with "Quit" button
dispose();
System.exit(0);
} // end of method actionPerformed
```

16.3.4 The windowClosing Method of the Chapter16n0 Class

Finally, we need a windowClosing method to allow the user to abandon the program without having to click on the Quit button. You have to tell Java that you are implementing the WindowListener interface:

```
public class Chapter16n0 extends Frame
                implements WindowListener, ActionListener
```

You then have to specify that the windowClosing method is to be found in *this* class (Chapter16n0), so we insert in the constructor the statement:

```
addWindowListener(this) ;
```

The windowClosing method then simply abandons the program:

```
public void windowClosing(WindowEvent event)
  {
  dispose() ;
  System.exit(0) ;
  } // end of method windowClosing
```

Unfortunately, having promised to implement the interface WindowListener, we have to provide six other methods to deal with various things that can happen to a window. We provide dummy methods that do nothing:

```
public void windowOpened(WindowEvent event) {}
public void windowIconified(WindowEvent event) {}
public void windowDeiconified(WindowEvent event) {}
public void windowClosed(WindowEvent event) {}
public void windowActivated(WindowEvent event) {}
public void windowDeActivated(WindowEvent event) {}
```

You can simply copy the code we have provided into the class derived from Frame (that is, effectively, the main class) in each program you write.

This completes the discussion of the code for the class Chapter16n0. We now turn to the class Canvas0.

16.4 Writing the Canvas0 Class

The class Canvas0 contains no instance fields and only one method paint. We use the default constructor method for this class.

The paint method is called when the window is first displayed and whenever the AWT needs to redraw the canvas—after part or all the window has been hidden and then revealed again, when the window has been resized, and so on. Later, when we implement the Change button, we will tell the AWT that the canvas needs redrawing each time the button is pressed, and this will eventually result in this paint method being called.

In order to draw the canvas correctly, we need to know the current size of the area. This is provided with the getSize method, which returns an instance of the class Dimension. We extract the values of the instance variables width and depth from this object, and these are the current width and height of the canvas in pixels. From this we can calculate the center point of the canvas (cx, cy) and draw a line around the edge of the canvas.

The paint method has one argument, of type Graphics:

```
public void paint(Graphics g)
    {
    ...
```

When we draw lines, fill areas with color, write text characters, and so on, we call methods associated with this object. We have called this formal argument of the paint method g, so we call the method to draw a rectangle with rounded corners (drawRoundRect) with:

```
g.drawRoundRect( ... arguments ... ) ;
```

There is a large collection of methods to draw in various ways on the canvas. We list the most useful ones here, and we illustrate some of them in the code for our class Canvas0. Each one will draw using the current color, and we set this when required with the setColor method:

- drawLine draws a line in the current color (for example, the nose in the example program). The four arguments are, in order, the X- and Y-coordinates of the two ends of the line. These arguments are integers, and the units are pixels, with the origin of the coordinates (0, 0) at the top left-hand corner. So:

```
g.drawLine(10, 20, 30, 10);
```

would draw the line shown in Figure 16-6.

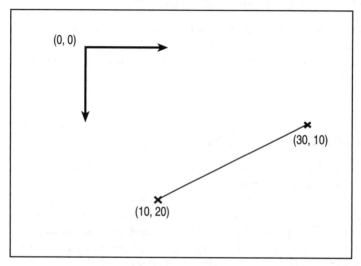

Figure 16-6: Using the drawLine method.

- drawRect draws a rectangle in the current color. The first two arguments are the X- and Y-coordinates of the top left-hand corner of the rectangle. The third and fourth arguments are the width and height (respectively) of the rectangle in pixels. If the third and fourth arguments are equal, then the rectangle will be a square. So:

```
g.drawRect(10, 5, 20, 15) ;
```

would draw the rectangle shown in Figure 16-7.

- drawRoundRect draws a rectangle in the current color with rounded corners—this is used in the example program to draw a line just inside the edge of the canvas. The first four arguments are the coordinates of the top left-hand corner, the width and the height, as for the drawRect method. The fifth and sixth arguments are the horizontal and vertical diameters of the arcs at the corners (in pixels).

- drawOval draws an oval in the current color. You need to imagine a rectangle inscribed around the oval that you want to draw, and you then specify the X- and Y-coordinates of the top left-hand corner and the width and the height of the bounding rectangle, just as with the drawRect method. So:

```
g.drawOval(10, 5, 30, 20) ;
```

would draw the oval shown in Figure 16-8.

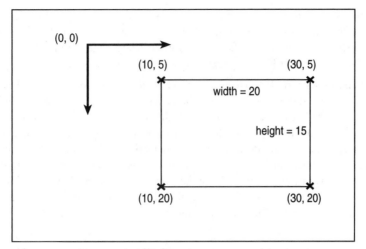

Figure 16-7: Using the drawRect method.

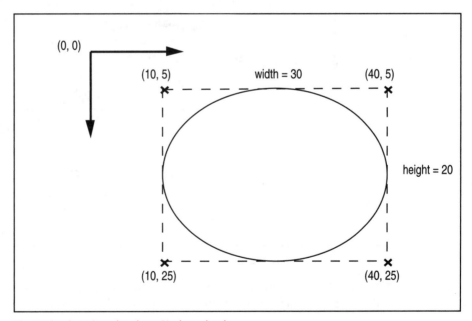

Figure 16-8: Using the drawOval method.

If the third and fourth arguments are equal, then the oval will be a circle.

- In some ways, defining the position by the top left-hand corner is not the most convenient procedure, but this is what most of these AWT methods use. In the code of the example program, you will see that in most cases the calculation works out the position of the top left-hand corner from the position of the center of the figure, and this is probably a more logical way of specifying a position. Notice generally how this code has been written to make clear how the positions, sizes, angles, and so on are specified in terms of the various basic dimensions that define the face.

■ drawArc draws part of a circle or oval. You have to specify the circle or oval by the top left-hand corner and the width and height of the bounding rectangle, just as with the drawOval method. The last two arguments (the fifth and sixth) specify which part of the arc to draw. The fifth argument specifies the angle at which to start, in degrees, with zero degrees being due east (as in the normal mathematical convention). The arc is drawn from this angle counterclockwise for the number of degrees specified by the sixth argument. This is shown in Figure 16-9. Note that the sixth argument is *not* the finish angle, as I thought when I started writing Java graphical programs—the finish angle would in fact be the sum of the fifth and sixth arguments.

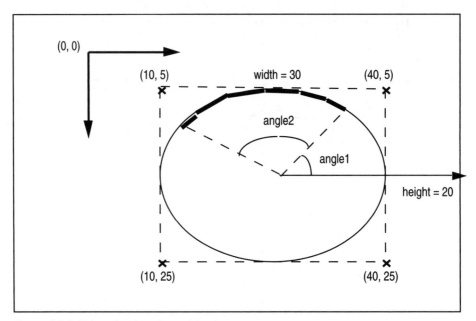

Figure 16-9: Using the drawArc method.

So we draw the smile on the smiley face in terms of the center of the canvas (cx, cy), the radius of the circle (mouthRadius) of which the smile is an arc, and a mouthAngle (50 degrees) with:

```
g.drawArc(cx - mouthRadius,
        cy - mouthRadius,
        mouthRadius * 2,
        mouthRadius * 2,
        270 - mouthAngle,
        mouthAngle * 2) ;
```

- There are methods `fillRect`, `fillRoundRect`, and `fillOval` that are variations (respectively) on `drawRect`, `drawRoundRect`, and `drawOval` (with the same set of arguments), and that fill the space enclosed by the drawing with the current color. The eyes in the example program are blue circles drawn with `fillOval`.

- There are methods `drawPolygon` and `fillPolygon` to draw an irregular figure between a number of points. The three arguments are an array of the X-coordinates of the points, an array of the Y-coordinates of the points, and a count of the number of points.

16.5 Writing Text on the Canvas

Having drawn the face, we want to write a piece of text just below it. To illustrate the features provided by the AWT for writing character strings, we are going to write `Hello` in a normal typeface and `World` in italics. The basic method is `drawString`, which writes the specified text (the first argument) at the specified position (the X- and Y-coordinates are the second and third arguments):

```
g.drawString("Happy Birthday", 100, 150) ;
```

The X-coordinate is the position of the left-hand edge of the first character, as you would expect. The Y-coordinate is the position of the *baseline* upon which most characters lie; some characters (for example *g* and *y*) may descend below the baseline. This is shown in Figure 16-10.

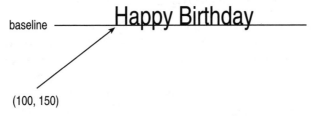

Figure 16-10: Using the `drawString` method.

The string is drawn in the current color and font. We are familiar with the concept of the current color, but we need to set the font with the `setFont` method, which requires an argument of type `Font`. We create instances of the `Font` class by calling a suitable constructor; for example:

```
Font f1 = new Font("TimesRoman", Font.PLAIN, 14) ;
```

The first argument is the name of the font—other commonly available font names are `"Helvetica"`, `"Courier"`, `"Dialog"`, and `"Symbol"`. There may be other fonts available on particular platforms, but this cannot be relied on.

The second parameter is the font style—this should be one of the constants:

`Font.PLAIN, Font.BOLD, or Font.ITALIC`

It is possible also to use the expression `Font.BOLD + Font.ITALIC` for this argument for a bold italic style of lettering if it is available for this font.

The third parameter is the point size required for the font. Typical sizes would be 8 for a small size, 12 for a medium size, and 36 or more for large sizes.

If we want to position a sequence of character strings, perhaps in varying fonts, Java expects us to specify where to position them, and for this we need to know how much room a particular sequence of characters in a particular font takes up. The class `FontMetrics` provides this information. We set up an instance of this class for a particular `Graphics` object and `Font`:

`FontMetrics fm1 = g.getFontMetrics(f1) ;`

and then we can find out the width of a particular character string in the specified font:

`int w1 = fm1.stringWidth("We want to know the space used by this String") ;`

In the example program we use string lengths obtained in this way to calculate the X-coordinate `ctx` for the beginning of the string so that it is centrally positioned in the window, and then we update this value to get the position of the next portion of the string.

16.6   Animating the Simple Graphics Program

We are now going to add the Change button to this program so that we can switch backward and forward between drawing a happy face and a sad face. We are also going to make another small change, by allowing the user to type in a name as a command-line parameter (see section 3.12); if a name is typed in, it is used instead of the word *World* in the greetings message.[*]

We find now that we have to be able to pass more information between the class derived from `Frame` (in this version of the program called `Chapter16n1`) and the class derived from `Canvas` (here called `Canvas1`). The `Chapter16n1` code needs to have a reference to the instance of the `Canvas1` class so that it can call for the face to be redrawn when the Change button has been pressed. We do this by making the variable referring to the canvas an instance variable of the `Chapter16n1` class rather than a local variable of its constructor. Since our `actionPerformed` method now needs to distinguish between a click on the Change button and a click on the Quit button, we similarly make the variables referring to the buttons into instance variables of the `Chapter16n1` class. The `Canvas1` code needs to have a reference to the instance of the `Chapter16n1` class so that it can access its instance fields as required. We do this by passing a suitable reference when we call the `Canvas1` constructor, which stores it away as an instance variable of the `Canvas1` class for later use.

---

[*] Listings for this and all other programs discussed in this chapter, as in other chapters, can be found on the associated Web site—see Appendix A.

The Chapter16n1 class now has five instance variables:

- A variable canvas, of type Canvas1, which refers to the instance we have created of this class so that we can require it to be repainted.

- Two variables change and quit, of type Button, for the two buttons.

- A String variable name, which will contain the word *World* or the name from the command-line parameter. The main method checks the command-line parameter (if any) and passes the appropriate String as the argument to the Chapter16n1 constructor method, which stores it in the variable name.

- A Boolean variable isSmiling to record whether the face should currently be smiling or not. We initialize this in the Chapter16n1 constructor method to true (we want to start off happy):

```
public class Chapter16n1 extends Frame
                implements WindowListener, ActionListener
   {
   Canvas1 canvas ;
   Button change, quit ;
   String name ;
   boolean isSmiling ;
   ...
```

The Canvas1 class now has a single instance variable parent, of type Chapter16n1, which refers to the instance we have created of this class:

```
class Canvas1 extends Canvas
   {
   Chapter16n1 parent ;
   ...
```

We now have a constructor method for the Canvas1 class, so we can pass this reference as an argument to be stored in the parent instance variable:

```
public Canvas1(Chapter16n1 f)
   {
   parent = f ;
   } // end of constructor method
```

We call this constructor from inside the Chapter16n1 constructor as follows:

```
canvas = new Canvas1(this) ;
```

The keyword this is a reference to the current instance of the Chapter16n1 class (see section 8.9). That is, we are passing to the constructor for the Canvas1 class a reference to the Chapter16n1 instance that is creating it so that it can be stored in parent.

In the Chapter16n1 constructor method, we have added the new Change button and registered that actionPerformed is to be called if it is clicked. We rely on the flow layout manager of the Panel it is in to position it correctly:

```
change = new Button("Change") ;
p.add(change) ;
change.addActionListener(this) ;
```

In the actionPerformed method, we need to test for which of the two buttons has been pressed. The ActionEvent instance passed as the method's argument contains a reference to the button pressed, and we can extract this with the getSource method:

```
if (event.getSource() == quit)
   ...
```

If the Change button has been pressed, we invert the value of the isSmiling variable. We then need to ensure that the canvas is redrawn by calling the repaint method associated with the canvas instance:

```
public void actionPerformed(ActionEvent event)
   {
   if (event.getSource() == quit)
      {
      dispose() ;
      System.exit(0) ;
      }
   else if (event.getSource() == change)
      {
      isSmiling = !isSmiling ;
      canvas.repaint() ;
      }
   } // end of method actionPerformed
```

The result of this is that the paint method of the Canvas1 class is called, and the whole of the canvas is redrawn.

The paint method is very similar to the original version. The method refers to the isSmiling variable in the Chapter16n1 class (using the notation parent.isSmiling). This establishes whether the mouth should be happy or sad, and paint redraws it accordingly, using the drawArc method:

```
if (parent.isSmiling)
   g.drawArc(cx - mouthRadius,
         cy - mouthRadius,
         mouthRadius * 2,
         mouthRadius * 2,
         270 - mouthAngle,
         mouthAngle * 2) ;
```

```
else
    g.drawArc(cx - mouthRadius,
        cy - mouthRadius + 50,
        mouthRadius * 2,
        mouthRadius * 2,
        90 - mouthAngle,
        mouthAngle * 2) ;
```

Similarly, the second part of the text to be displayed is at parent.name:

```
String s2 = parent.name ;
...
g.drawString(s2, ctx, cty) ;
```

16.7   Input of Character Strings in a Graphical Interface

In the previous program the only way the user could communicate with the program was to press one of the two buttons. Another desirable type of communication would be for the user to type a sequence of characters into a text field for the program to interpret. We illustrate this type of interaction with another sample program, Chapter16n2.java, shown in Figure 16-11. This makes use of the Temperature class introduced in Chapter 7.

Figure 16-11: A graphical interface with text input.

We can type a temperature in degrees Celsius in the text field labeled Celsius. If we now press the Convert to F button, the program uses the Temperature class (see section 8.5) to calculate the equivalent temperature in Fahrenheit and displays it in the text field labeled Fahrenheit. Similarly, we can type a temperature in degrees Fahrenheit in the field labeled Fahrenheit and have it converted to degrees Celsius in the other text area. We have to take care to check the validity of any string typed in. To make the program slightly more interesting, we draw a thermometer and display a mercury column showing the temperature.

16.7.1   Setting Up the Picture

As before, we have a class Chapter16n2 derived from Frame and a class Canvas2 derived from Canvas. In the Chapter16n2 class, we have seven instance variables:

- A variable temp1 of the Temperature class to provide the Celsius-to-Fahrenheit conversion.

- A variable canvas of the Canvas2 class, upon which we are going to draw the thermometer. This needs to be an instance rather than a local variable since we need to request that it be redrawn when the temperature changes.

- Two variables of the TextField class, called celsiusField and fahrField. The TextField class implements a small area into which the user can type a sequence of characters that the program can then extract and process in some way. We need to declare these two variables here so that we can call methods associated with them in the actionPerformed method.

- Three variables of the Button class (toF, toC, and quit) to allow the actionPerformed method to check which button has been pressed.

```
public class Chapter16n2 extends Frame
                              implements WindowListener,
ActionListener
   {
   Temperature temp1 ;
   TextField celsiusField,
           fahrField ;
   Canvas2 canvas ;
   Button toF, toC, quit ;
```

The constructor method Chapter16n2 looks very similar to that of the earlier programs:

```
public Chapter16n2()
   {
   temp1 = new Temperature() ;

   setTitle("Chapter16n2") ;
   setBackground(Color.green) ;
   setSize(400, 600) ;
   addWindowListener(this) ;

   canvas = new Canvas2(this) ;
   add("Center", canvas) ;
   ...
```

- We create an instance of the `Temperature` class for the variable `temp1` to refer to.

- We set up the window title, background color, and size, as before.

- We create an instance of the new class `Canvas2` upon which the thermometer will be drawn, and we position this in the center of the window (using the default border layout manager).

We now want a collection of graphical components at the bottom of the window, laid out as three lines of components. The first and second lines are rather similar—each requires:

- A text field in the middle into which we can type a temperature—this is an instance of the `TextField` class of graphical components. The constructor for this class takes two arguments: the initial string to appear in the text field (we set it to blank) and an integer specifying how wide the field should be in "columns"—it is best to make this one or two characters longer than the maximum number of characters you are expecting in this field (we have chosen 8).

- On the left, a character string to specify what type of temperature this is. We use an instance of the `Label` class of graphical components, whose only task is to display a character string. When we construct a `Label` instance, we pass the labeling string as the argument (in the first line it is "`Celsius`").

- A button to invoke the temperature conversion—this is an instance of the `Button` class, which we have met before. On the first line it has the label `Convert to F`.

We want to keep the three components of the first line together, so we put them in a panel p1 with a flow layout manager:

```
Panel p1 = new Panel() ;
p1.setLayout(new FlowLayout()) ;

p1.add(new Label("Celsius")) ;

celsiusField = new TextField("", 8) ;
p1.add(celsiusField) ;

toF = new Button("Convert to F") ;
p1.add(toF) ;
toF.addActionListener(this) ;
```

We do the same for the second line, in a panel p2:

```
Panel p2 = new Panel() ;
p2.setLayout(new FlowLayout()) ;

p2.add(new Label("Fahrenheit")) ;

fahrField = new TextField("", 8) ;
p2.add(fahrField) ;
```

```
toC = new Button("Convert to C") ;
p2.add(toC) ;
toC.addActionListener(this) ;
```

Finally, we set up a panel p3 containing just the Quit button:

```
Panel p3 = new Panel() ;
p3.setLayout(new FlowLayout()) ;
quit = new Button("Quit") ;
p3.add(quit) ;
quit.addActionListener(this) ;
```

We want these three panels to appear one above the other, so we declare a new panel p, specify that it should use the border layout manager, and then add the three panels p1, p2, and p3 using the border layout manager arguments North, Center, and South, respectively. Finally, we specify that the panel p shall appear South in the main window, as we did in the previous programs:

```
Panel p = new Panel() ;
p.setLayout(new BorderLayout()) ;
p.add("North", p1) ;
p.add("Center", p2) ;
p.add("South", p3) ;
add("South", p) ;
```

The overall situation is shown in Figure 16-12.

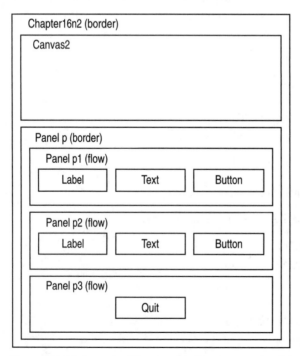

Figure 16-12: Layout of the graphical components of the Chapter16n2 program.

The `main` method simply creates an instance of the `Chapter16n2` class and calls the `setVisible` method to get things started:

```
public static void main(String[] args)
   {
   Chapter16n2 f = new Chapter16n2() ;
   f.setVisible(true) ;
   } // end of method main
```

The `windowClosing` method is exactly the same as before.

16.7.2   Getting a String from a TextField

The general structure of the `actionPerformed` method is similar to what we have met before. We test in sequence for the label of each button that could have been pressed and take action accordingly. We look in detail at the action to be taken if the `Convert to F` button is pressed; the action for `Convert to C` is similar. Here is the code:

```
...
else if (event.getSource() == toF)
   {
   String c1 = celsiusField.getText() ;

   double c2 = 0.0 ;
   boolean isValid ;
   try {
      c2 = Double.valueOf(c1).doubleValue() ;
      isValid = true ;
      }
   catch (NumberFormatException ex)
      {
      isValid = false ;
      }
   if (isValid)
      {
      temp1.setCelsius(c2) ;
      double f2 = temp1.getFahr() ;
      f2 = ((double) Math.round(f2 * 100)) / 100 ;
      String f1 = Double.toString(f2) ;
      fahrField.setText(f1) ;
      canvas.repaint() ;
      }
   else
      {
      celsiusField.setText("") ;
      }
   }
else ...
```

- We use the `getText` method to extract the string in the `Celsius` temperature field and store it in the `String` variable c1.

- Now we want to convert the string to a `double` value, which we do using the statement starting "c2 = . . . ". We explain how this mechanism works in section 19.4.2. Of course, if the characters we have typed into the field are not a valid `double` literal, this conversion will fail. We therefore arrange to catch any `NumberFormatException`. The Boolean variable `isValid` records whether or not the conversion succeeded. If it did, the result is in the `double` variable c2.

- If the input was valid, we convert it to Fahrenheit using the `Temperature` class, round it to two decimal places, convert it back to a `String`, and insert the result in the Fahrenheit text field with the `setText` method. Finally, we need to use the `repaint` method to request that the thermometer be redrawn with the new mercury level.

- If the input was invalid, we simply reset the Celsius text field to all blanks. We do not change the Fahrenheit text field, nor do we redraw the thermometer.

16.7.3 Drawing the Thermometer

We now consider the `Canvas2` class. It has a single instance variable to hold a reference to the parent `Chapter16n2` instance, just as in the previous program, and we set this from the argument passed to the `Canvas2` constructor method:

```
class Canvas2 extends Canvas
    {
    Chapter16n2 parent ;

    public Canvas2(Chapter16n2 f)
        {
        parent = f ;
        } // end of constructor method
    ...
```

We are not going to discuss in detail the code of the `paint` method, which draws the thermometer. It uses the methods that we have discussed earlier in this chapter, such as `setColor`, `drawLine`, `drawArc`, and `fillOval`. For example, we draw the mercury to the correct height in the tube with the code:

```
double tempC = parent.temp1.getCelsius() ;
int mercuryLength ;
if (tempC < - 11)
    mercuryLength = 0 ;
else if (tempC < 120)
    mercuryLength = (int) (30 + (2.6 * tempC)) ;
else
    mercuryLength = tubeLength ;
```

```
g.setColor(Color.red) ;
g.fillRect(cx - innerTubeRadius + 1,
        cy - bulbInnerRadius - mercuryLength,
        2 * innerTubeRadius,
        mercuryLength) ;
```

We extract the current temperature with the getCelsius method of the temp1 instance (of the Temperature class) of the parent instance (of the Chapter16n2 class). We then calculate how long the mercury should be and store it in mercuryLength. Finally, we draw a filled rectangle of a suitable color and size at a suitable position.

We mark the thermometer with some standard temperatures (32 and 212 degrees Fahrenheit, etc.), and we want to position the labels correctly. We set up a Font and a FontMetrics object as before, calculate a width w0 using the stringWidth method on the longest string, and calculate half the height of this font h0 using the getAscent method. This method gives the distance (in pixels) between the baseline (upon which all the characters rest, except those with descenders like lowercase *g* and *y*) and the top of the uppercase characters:

```
Font f1 = new Font("Helvetica", Font.BOLD, 14) ;
FontMetrics fm1 = g.getFontMetrics(f1) ;
int w0 = fm1.stringWidth("212F"),
    h0 = (fm1.getAscent() / 2) ;

g.drawString("100C",
    cx - 50 - w0,
    cy - bulbOuterRadius - tubeLength + 20 + h0) ;
```

There is a selection of other methods in the FontMetrics class for finding other details of the font dimensions; for example, getDescent gives the distance from the baseline to the bottom of characters with descenders like *g* and *y*.

16.8   Menus, Files & Images (optional)

In the programs presented so far in this chapter, all the pictures or diagrams we wanted to display have been drawn using the draw and fill methods supplied by the Abstract Window Toolkit. But there is another source of visual data to a Java program, pictures scanned into the computer and held in one of the standard formats for representing them, such as GIF or JPEG. Java provides as part of the AWT a number of methods for displaying such pictures, usually referred to as *images*. Most of the facilities for manipulating images, for example scaling and clipping, are beyond the scope of this book. But our final pair of programs in this chapter shows you how to display images with the facilities provided by Java. We take the opportunity in these programs to introduce you to a few slightly more complex parts of the AWT, which you may find useful in writing programs for yourself. We are going to introduce menus, file dialogs, and the handling of mouse events in these two programs.

In the first program, `Chapter16n4.java`, we allow the user to select a file that contains an image, and the program then attempts to display it in the center of the window, as shown in Figure 16-13. Rather than having all the buttons on permanent display, we attach them to a menu that is attached to a menu bar at the top of the window.

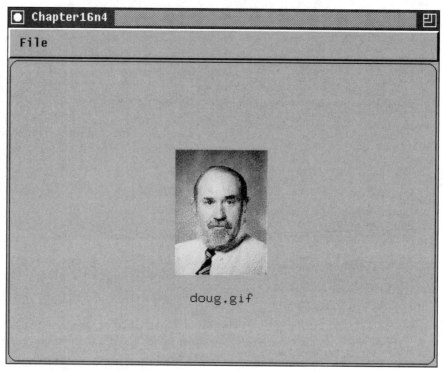

Figure 16-13: Displaying an image.

16.8.1   Setting Up Menus

We begin by setting up the menu system. We are going to set up a single menu containing two buttons, a Load button to select an image file to display and our old friend the Quit button. It seems to have become a tradition in GUI design that a menu of rather miscellaneous functions is called the File menu, and that is what we have done here. We need to declare instance variables (of type `MenuItem`) for the two menu buttons so that we can find out which one has been selected:

```
public class Chapter16n4 extends Frame
                implements WindowListener, ActionListener
    {
Canvas4 canvas ;
MenuItem load, quit ;
    ...
```

Here is the code in the constructor method for the `Chapter16n4` class. This code will set up the menu:

```
Menu menu = new Menu("File") ;
load = new MenuItem("Load") ;
menu.add(load) ;
load.addActionListener(this) ;
quit = new MenuItem("Quit") ;
menu.add(quit) ;
quit.addActionListener(this) ;
MenuBar menuBar = new MenuBar() ;
menuBar.add(menu) ;
setMenuBar(menuBar) ;
```

We create an object of type Menu, which will be labeled File in the menu bar. We then add the two menu buttons to it with suitable labels and register that we want to find out when either of them is selected. We then create a menu bar (an object of type MenuBar), add the menu to it, and use the setMenuBar method to add it to the Chapter16n4 instance that we are constructing. We can add a menu bar only to a class derived from Frame, so we cannot have menus attached to arbitrary panels.

We now need to be able to take action when one of the menu items is selected. We handle this in very much the same way we handled buttons in the earlier programs. We have an actionPerformed method in the Chapter16n4 class, and we check for which item was selected in the usual way:

```
public void actionPerformed(ActionEvent event)
   {
   if (event.getSource() == quit)
      {
      dispose();
      System.exit(0);
      }
   else if (event.getSource() == load)
      loadFile() ;
   } // end of method actionPerformed
```

There are a number of other useful features of menus. Suppose we declare the following instance variables:

```
public class Chapter16n4a extends Frame
       implements WindowListener, ActionListener, ItemListener
   {
   MenuItem buttonA1, buttonA2, buttonA3,
      buttonA4, buttonA5, buttonA6, buttonA7, quit,
      buttonB1p1, buttonB1p2, buttonB1p3,
      buttonB2p1, buttonB2p2, buttonB2p3, buttonB2p4 ;
   int noOfOptions = 7 ;
   CheckboxMenuItem[] options = new CheckboxMenuItem[noOfOptions] ;
   ...
```

Then we have the following piece of code in the constructor for `Chapter16n4a`:

```
Menu menuA = new Menu("MenuA") ;
buttonA1 = new MenuItem("Button A1") ;
menuA.add(buttonA1) ;
buttonA1.addActionListener(this) ;
buttonA2 = new MenuItem("Button A2") ;
menuA.add(buttonA2) ;
buttonA2.addActionListener(this) ;
buttonA3 = new MenuItem("Button A3") ;
menuA.add(buttonA3) ;
buttonA3.addActionListener(this) ;
menuA.addSeparator() ;
buttonA4 = new MenuItem("Button A4") ;
menuA.add(buttonA4) ;
buttonA4.addActionListener(this) ;
buttonA5 = new MenuItem("Button A5") ;
menuA.add(buttonA5) ;
buttonA5.addActionListener(this) ;
buttonA6 = new MenuItem("Button A6") ;
menuA.add(buttonA6) ;
buttonA6.addActionListener(this) ;
buttonA7 = new MenuItem("Button A7") ;
menuA.add(buttonA7) ;
buttonA7.addActionListener(this) ;
menuA.addSeparator() ;
quit = new MenuItem("Quit") ;
menuA.add(quit) ;
quit.addActionListener(this) ;

Menu menuB = new Menu("MenuB") ;
Menu menuB1 = new Menu("MenuB1") ;
buttonB1p1 = new MenuItem("Button B1.1") ;
menuB1.add(buttonB1p1) ;
buttonB1p1.addActionListener(this) ;
buttonB1p2 = new MenuItem("Button B1.2") ;
menuB1.add(buttonB1p2) ;
buttonB1p2.addActionListener(this) ;
buttonB1p3 = new MenuItem("Button B1.3") ;
menuB1.add(buttonB1p3) ;
buttonB1p3.addActionListener(this) ;
menuB.add(menuB1) ;
Menu menuB2 = new Menu("MenuB2") ;
buttonB2p1 = new MenuItem("Button B2.1") ;
menuB2.add(buttonB2p1) ;
buttonB2p1.addActionListener(this) ;
buttonB2p2 = new MenuItem("Button B2.2") ;
```

```
menuB2.add(buttonB2p2) ;
buttonB2p2.addActionListener(this) ;
buttonB2p3 = new MenuItem("Button B2.3") ;
menuB2.add(buttonB2p3) ;
buttonB2p3.addActionListener(this) ;
buttonB2p4 = new MenuItem("Button B2.4") ;
menuB2.add(buttonB2p4) ;
buttonB2p4.addActionListener(this) ;
menuB.add(menuB2) ;

Menu menuC = new Menu("MenuC") ;
options[0] = new CheckboxMenuItem("Monday") ;
options[1] = new CheckboxMenuItem("Tuesday") ;
options[2] = new CheckboxMenuItem("Wednesday") ;
options[3] = new CheckboxMenuItem("Thursday") ;
options[4] = new CheckboxMenuItem("Friday") ;
options[5] = new CheckboxMenuItem("Saturday") ;
options[6] = new CheckboxMenuItem("Sunday") ;
for (int i = 0 ; i < noOfOptions ; i++)
   {
   options[i].addItemListener(this) ;
   menuC.add(options[i]) ;
   }

MenuBar menuBar = new MenuBar() ;
menuBar.add(menuA) ;
menuBar.add(menuB) ;
menuBar.add(menuC) ;
setMenuBar(menuBar) ;
```

- In MenuA we have a large number of buttons, so we use the addSeparator method to put the buttons into three groups

- In MenuB we have two submenus, MenuB1 and MenuB2, each with its own set of buttons. If you click on the MenuB1 button, it brings up that submenu with its three buttons.

- In MenuC we have a number of "check boxes", each of which (independently) records an option as "checked" (on) or "unchecked" (off). Since we have a number of check boxes, we have declared an array of them, called a constructor method for each one, and then registered a listener for each and added them to a menu. Each time we click on one of these check boxes, it changes state (toggling between TRUE and FALSE) and the current state is indicated on the menu. The itemStateChanged method (of the ItemListener interface) is called every time the user clicks on one of the check boxes and it changes state:

```
public void itemStateChanged(ItemEvent event)
  {
  if (event.getSource() == options[0])
      System.out.println("the 'Monday' option was clicked") ;
  ...
```

The state of a check box starts out as FALSE. We can set it to a particular state with a setState method, and we can find out its state with a getState method.

16.8.2   Selecting a File

In the Chapter16n4 program the Load menu item called a method named loadFile to allow the user to select a file containing an image and then have this displayed. Here it is:

```
private void loadFile()     {
  FileDialog d = new FileDialog(this, "Load File", FileDialog.LOAD) ;
  d.setDirectory("... path name at which to start selection ...") ;
  d.setVisible(true) ;
  name = d.getFile() ;
  directory = d.getDirectory() ;
  canvas.repaint() ;
  } // end of method loadFile
```

We set up an instance of the class FileDialog. This requires three parameters:

- The owner of the dialog. This is the instance of the class Chapter16n4 with which this dialog is to be associated, so we can use the keyword this.

- A string to appear as the title for the window that is going to be popped up for the dialog—we have chosen Load File.

- One of two constants—FileDialog.LOAD if we are planning to read from the file (that is what we are doing here) or FileDialog.SAVE if we are planning to write to the file.

We then set an initial file directory from which the user can select the file and call the method setVisible, which displays the file dialog box. The system waits until the user selects a file and then clicks on a button to indicate that the dialog is complete.

At this point we extract the name of the selected file with the getFile method. If no file has been selected, a String of length zero is returned. Since the user can change the directory in the file dialog, you should extract this as well with the getDirectory method.

16.8.3   Displaying an Image

Having obtained the name of a file and a directory, we request that the canvas be repainted, attempting to display an image obtained from this file. Here is the paint method in the Canvas4 class:

```
public void paint(Graphics g)
   {
   Dimension d = getSize() ;
   int cx = d.width / 2,
      cy = d.height /2 ;
   // draw a line round the edge of the canvas
   g.setColor(Color.black) ;
   g.drawRoundRect(2, 2, d.width - 5, d.height - 5, 20, 20) ;

   if (parent.name != null)
      {
      String filename = parent.directory + parent.name ;
      Image image = Toolkit.getDefaultToolkit().getImage(filename) ;
      g.drawImage(image,
         cx - (image.getWidth(this) / 2),
         cy - (image.getHeight(this) / 2),
         this) ;

      // write the name of the file under the image
      Font f1 = new Font("TimesRoman", Font.PLAIN, 14) ;
      FontMetrics fm1 = g.getFontMetrics(f1) ;
      int w1 = fm1.stringWidth(parent.name) ;
      g.setColor(Color.black) ;
      g.setFont(f1) ;
      int ctx = cx - (w1 / 2) ;
      int cty = cy + (image.getHeight(this) / 2) + 30 ;
         g.drawString(parent.name, ctx, cty) ;
      }
   else
      {
      // write the message "No File" in the center of the canvas
      Font f1 = new Font("TimesRoman", Font.PLAIN, 14) ;
      ...
      }
   } // end of method paint
```

We set up the full name of the file fileName from the information saved by the loadFile method in the Chapter16n4 class. Then we read the file and construct an instance of the Image class with the statement:

```
Image image = Toolkit.getDefaultToolkit().getImage(filename) ;
```

Finally, we draw it with:

```
g.drawImage(image,
      cx - (image.getWidth(this) / 2),
      cy - (image.getHeight(this) / 2),
      this) ;
```

The first argument (of type Image) is the image we want to draw. The second and third arguments are the position at which it is to be drawn (the top left-hand corner, as usual); we have arranged for it to be displayed in the center of the canvas by calculating the coordinates of the center of the canvas (cx, cy), and finding out the dimensions of the image with the methods getWidth and getHeight. The fourth argument (of type ImageObserver) enables us to keep track of the progress of creating and drawing the image, checking that it is successful, and so on. Monitoring the processing of images is beyond the scope of this book—we simply set the fourth argument to this.

16.8.4 Tracking the Mouse

Finally, we are going to modify the program so that the image is positioned at the point where we last clicked the mouse. There are a number of methods to allow us to take action depending on various things that the user can do with the mouse. We select the mouseClicked method (of the MouseListener interface). We are interested only in mouse clicks within our canvas, so we specify that our class Canvas5 implements the MouseListener interface:

```
class Canvas5 extends Canvas implements MouseListener
    {
    ...
```

We need to register that this class is responsible for dealing with mouse clicks, so we add a statement to the constructor method:

```
public Canvas5(Chapter16n5 f)
    {
    parent = f ;
    addMouseListener(this) ;
    } // end of constructor method
```

Here is the method mouseClicked (in the Canvas5 class):

```
public void mouseClicked(MouseEvent event)
    {
    mx = event.getX() ;
    my = event.getY() ;
    repaint() ;
    }
```

The argument event contains the coordinates of the mouse click, and we extract these with the getX and getY methods. We store the information away in the instance variables (mx, my) in the Canvas5 class and call for the canvas to be redrawn (with repaint). In the paint method, we position the image at (mx, my) instead of (cx, cy) as we did before.

The `MouseListener` interface requires us to implement four other methods, which are dummies:

```
public void mousePressed(MouseEvent event) {}
public void mouseReleased(MouseEvent event) {}
public void mouseEntered(MouseEvent event) {}
public void mouseExited(MouseEvent event) {}
```

16.9   Key Points in Chapter 16

- A *Graphical User Interface* (GUI) is an increasingly popular way of interacting with a program. It presents a number of interaction elements to the end user, including windows (for text or graphics of various sorts), menus, buttons, text areas, and so on. The user interacts with these elements via mouse and keyboard.

- Java provides the platform-independent *Abstract Window Toolkit* (AWT), a standard set of facilities for building GUIs across all platforms. To write GUI programs in Java, we derive new classes from those provided in the AWT.

- A central feature of a GUI program is the *event loop*. The program waits for an event to occur and, depending on the event, carries out the appropriate action. Events that may occur include button clicks or window exposure/resizing. The event loop is within the AWT and does not appear in our program. We must provide the code for setting up the GUI elements and then for responding to events as they occur.

- A GUI application program has a class derived from `Frame`. The constructor for this class will set up the basic features of the display with the methods `setTitle`, `setBackground`, and `setSize`, and then it will put the picture elements in the window with the `add` method.

- The position of the elements inside a larger picture component is arranged by a layout manager such as `FlowLayout`, `BorderLayout` (the default for a `Frame`), and `GridLayout`.

- The `main` method in the class will call this constructor to set up an instance of the class and then call the `setVisible` method to display the window and start the program.

- There must be a `windowClosing` method in the class, to allow the program to be terminated if necessary. It can be in the standard form given in this chapter.

- Possible picture elements include buttons that can be pressed (the `Button` class), pieces of text to label parts of the window (the `Label` class), and areas where text can be typed in by the user (the `TextField`). There is also a `Panel`, which is simply a container for other picture elements and can be positioned inside another `Panel` or the `Frame`.

- A `Canvas` is a picture element on which we can draw lines, fill areas of color, write text, and so on. The drawing is done with a variety of methods, including `drawLine`, `drawRect`, `drawOval`, `fillRect`, and `fillOval`. We can set the color for these using the `setColor` method and the `Color` class.

- The coordinate system on the canvas is in units of pixels, starts at (0, 0) in the top left-hand corner, and extends downward and to the right.

- The drawing methods are specified in a paint method. Each of the methods is associated with a Graphics instance passed as the formal argument for the paint method. If the canvas needs redrawing, we call the repaint method.

- Text is written on a canvas with the drawString method. We can set up an instance of the Font class and then specify the font for a particular string with setFont. If we want to position a string carefully, we need to set up an instance of the FontMetrics class and then use the methods stringWidth, getAscent, and so on.

- An actionPerformed method (of the ActionListener interface) is called if a button is pressed. We have to register each button with a call of the addActionListener method. A reference to the button that has been pressed can be obtained by calling the getSource method applied to the ActionEvent argument of the actionPerformed method.

- We can extract the text typed into a TextField with the getText method and set it to a new value with setText.

16.10   Exercises

1. Write a GUI version of exercise 4.3. This should have four text fields and a "complete" button as shown in Figure 16-4.

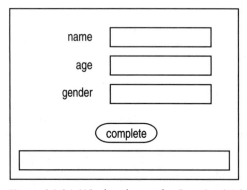

Figure 16-14: Window layout for Exercise 16.1.

The user types in a name (forename and surname) in the first field, an age in the second, and a gender in the third. When the "complete" button is pressed, the program should set the attributes of a Person instance with the data typed in (checking for missing or invalid values) and then display a message in the fourth field in the form:

```
this person is John Smith (21, male)
```

2. Write a new version of exercise 4.4, which draws on the screen the two `Card` instances selected. For example, if the four of clubs and the queen of diamonds have been selected, the program should display something like Figure 16-15. If you wish, you can try to draw and display symbols for the four suits.

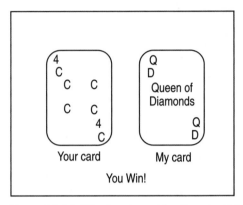

Figure 16-15: Window layout for Exercise 16.2.

3. Write a graphical program to display histograms of the characters in a text.

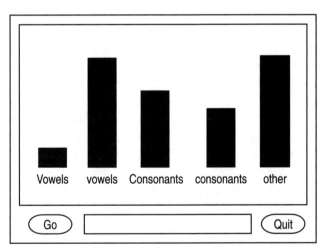

Figure 16-16: Window layout for Exercise 16.3.

a) Your program should display an area for displaying a histogram, two buttons (Go and Quit), and a text area, as shown in Figure 16-16. If a string of characters is typed in the text area and the Go button is pressed, your program should display a histogram showing:

- The number of capitalized vowels
- The number of lowercase vowels
- The number of capitalized consonants
- The number of lowercase consonants
- The number of other characters

The Quit button should allow the program to be abandoned, as usual.

b) Modify your program to display a scale up the left-hand side of the histogram to give an indication of the number of characters represented by each bar.

4. Read the Java API about the CheckboxGroup class. This provides a set of check boxes, only one of which can be "on" at a time. This is sometimes called a group of *radio buttons*, as it is like a car radio with buttons for preset stations, only one of which can be depressed at a time.

Change your solution to Exercise 16.1 so that the user specifies the gender attribute with a CheckboxGroup.

5. Write a program to draw a map of one floor of a building that you are familiar with. Label each room with a name.

Add a text field to your program. If a valid room name is typed into the field, draw a "stick" figure in the room specified.

Modify your program so that you can have several stick figures, each with its own name, in the same or different rooms. If the figures are in the same room, can you organize the program to arrange them without overlapping?

6. Write a class CountyMap (derived from Canvas) that draws and colors a map of a county and marks and labels selected locations in the county. It should have the following methods:

- public CountyMap(String filename). This constructor method reads a list of coordinates for the county map and locations from a file whose name is supplied as an argument.

- public void paint(Graphics g). This method displays the county map and location(s) in the usual way.

- public void addLocation(String location). This method adds the location to those to be displayed.

- public void clearLocations(). This method empties the list of locations to be displayed.

The file read by the constructor method contains, on separate lines:

- A count of points on the county boundary
- The X-coordinate (in pixels) of the first point on the county boundary
- The Y-coordinate (in pixels) of the first point on the county boundary
- The X-coordinate (in pixels) of the second point on the county boundary
- The Y-coordinate (in pixels) of the second point on the county boundary

... and so on

- A count of the locations in the county
- The name of the first location
- The X-coordinate (in pixels) of the first location
- The Y-coordinate (in pixels) of the first location
- The name of the second location
- The X-coordinate (in pixels) of the second location
- The Y-coordinate (in pixels) of the second location

... and so on

It will look like this:

```
37
253
25
238
25
...
22
Bodmin
193
115
Bude
238
45

...
```

Write a driver program to test this class.

Modify your program so that it reads in the coordinates in miles, or meters, or some other more display-independent units, and then converts them to pixels for a suitably sized picture.

7. Provide the Task Organizer program of Chapter 11 with a graphical interface.

PART 4

Advanced Java

CHAPTER 17

Linked Data Structures

17.1 Linear & Linked Data Structures

In Chapter 11, we introduced the idea of a priority queue. A priority queue is a *data structure* for holding and releasing information in priority order. Other typical data structures are:

- A *stack*, like a stack of plates in a cafeteria (see Figure 17-1). On a stack (or a FIFO [First In First Out] queue), items are removed in reverse order of insertion so that it is always the most recently added item that is the next one to be removed.

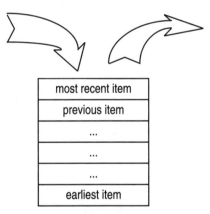

| most recent item |
| previous item |
| ... |
| ... |
| ... |
| earliest item |

Figure 17-1: A stack.

- A *tree*, like a tree to represent the relationships within a family (in Figure 17-2, we are showing only the descent through a single parent, not the marriages).

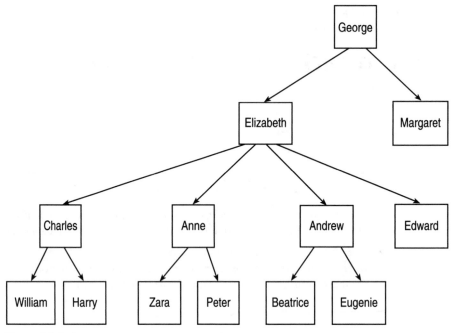

Figure 17-2: A tree.

In Chapter 11, we implemented the priority queue using an array (see Figure 17-3). An array is a *linear data structure*, where a sequence of elements is held in a contiguous array of store. We can calculate the position of any particular element by knowing the location of the store area and the index of the element we want to look at.

0	1	2	3	4	5	6	7
highest priority item	next item	...	...	...	last item		

Figure 17-3: Using an array to implement a priority queue.

There are a number of problems with holding data structures in an array:

- There are problems, or at least inefficiencies, in inserting or deleting elements in the middle of the array because adjacent elements need to be shuffled along to make room or to close a gap. In Java, we would normally be shuffling pointers to the elements rather than shuffling the elements themselves, but for a large structure, this could still be quite time-consuming.

- We have to decide some maximum expected size for the array when we declare it. If we choose too high a value, we are wasting space that might have been available to some other part of the program. If we choose too low a value, our program will run out of space or we have to declare a new larger array and move all the elements to this new array.

- It is difficult to implement some of the more complex types of data structure if we require that the elements are held contiguously in an array. For example, if we had a collection of elements that could be on two lists at the same time, it is not obvious how to arrange them in an array structure.

In fact the Java system provides a number of data structures, such as the Vector and the Stack, that get around these difficulties. We will look at these structures in Chapter 21, but in this chapter we look at an alternative way of constructing data structures—by using *linked* elements. In a linked data structure, each element of the structure may be located anywhere in the available computer store, and an element can hold an extra field, which gives a *reference* to the logical "next" element in the sequence. That is, the extra field contains the *address* of the next element, a pointer to the next element. So the priority queue in Figure 17-3 might look like Figure 17-4 as a linked data structure.

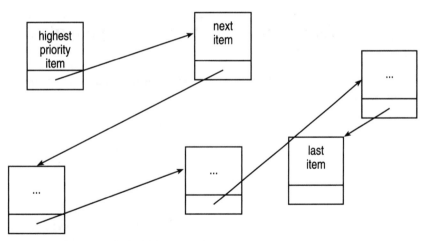

Figure 17-4: Using a linked list to implement a priority queue.

Generally, the ability to directly manipulate storage addresses in the computer can be dangerous. But Java restricts what manipulation it allows with references to objects in an attempt to ensure that these dangers are avoided.

You will recall that when we declare an variable of an object type, we are in fact setting up a location in the store of the computer capable of referring to an object of the specified type (see Figure 17-5).

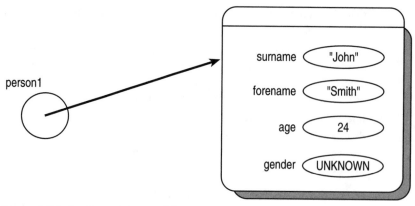

Figure 17-5: A reference to an object.

We can therefore create objects that have one (or more) attributes that act as a reference to another object of the same type. This will enable the first instance in the list to refer to the second as the "next" element in the data structure.

17.2 Implementing a Priority Queue Using a Linked Data Structure

We will illustrate the use of linked data structures by reimplementing the priority queue structure we introduced in Chapter 11 (see Figure 17-6).

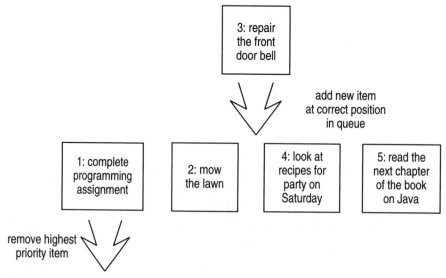

Figure 17-6: Manipulating a priority queue.

Each element in the queue is going to contain a priority (an int as before), the data to be held (a String as before), and a next attribute that refers to the next element in the queue (in priority order). The final element in the queue (the one with the lowest priority) has its next attribute set to the value null to show that there are no further elements in the queue. The definition for the QueueNode class that implements such elements, could look like this:

```
class QueueNode
  {
  int priority ;
  String data ;
  QueueNode next ;

  public QueueNode(int p, String d)
    {
    priority = p ;
    data = d ;
    next = null ;
    } // end of constructor method


  . . .
  } // end of class QueueNode
```

Notice that the definition of the class QueueNode refers to instances of the very class QueueNode that we are defining. Some programming languages have difficulties with this and require us to flag in some way that the class QueueNode contains a reference to the class QueueNode. This is not a problem in Java.

We have provided a constructor method with which we can set the priority and data attributes to specified values and that initializes the next variable to the default value of null. It is very important that we never have such a reference variable containing rubbish that might look like the address of a valid element. In fact, Java initializes such instance variables to null if they are not explicitly set to a value, but it is good practice to get into the habit of initializing reference values appropriately since other languages are not so forgiving.

One common source of problems in using linked structures is that a program might use a reference to one type of element as if it were a reference to a different type of element. Notice here that the attribute next can contain a reference only to an instance of the QueueNode class (or, of course, to an instance of a subclass of QueueNode). Any attempt to store a reference to another type of object in next, or to manipulate next as if it contained a reference to another type of object, will not be acceptable to the Java system.

Using the next attribute, we can insert a link from one queue element to the next (with a lower priority), and the next attribute of the last element (with the lowest priority) will contain a value of null. But we need to have a way of knowing which is the front element in the queue, the one with the highest priority. So we declare a variable firstPointer:

```
QueueNode firstPointer ;
```

and arrange that it contains a reference to the first element (see Figure 17-7). Note that the variable firstPointer contains a *reference* to the first element and not the first element itself.

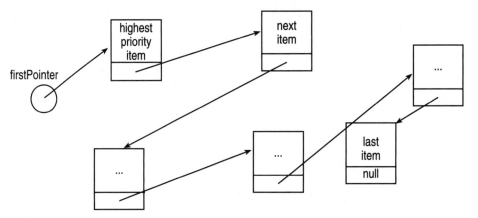

Figure 17-7: Identifying the head of the queue.

We need to have some way of creating new objects, putting appropriate values in the instance variables, and storing a reference to the instance in an appropriate place. If, for example, we want the first and only element in the queue to have the priority 5 and data Lancaster, we could write:

```
firstPointer = new QueueNode(5, "Lancaster") ;
```

The constructor method for the QueueNode class:

- Generates an instance of the QueueNode class.

- In this instance, sets the priority variable to 5 and the data variable to Lancaster.

- Sets the next variable to the value null to indicate that this is the final element in the queue.

- Passes back a reference to this instance, which we store in the variable firstPointer.

The result of this statement therefore appears as in Figure 17-8.

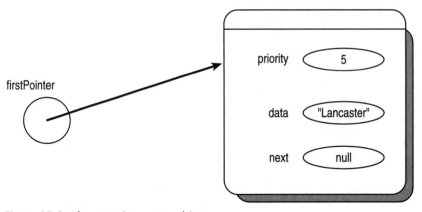

Figure 17-8: After creating a new object.

As usual, we can access the variables of an instance for which we have a reference by the notation instance name-dot-variable name. So, for example, we refer to the priority variable of this instance (with the value 5) with `firstPointer.priority` and to the next variable (with the value `null`) with `firstPointer.next`.

If we wanted to insert a second element in the queue, with priority 7 and data `Preston`, we could write:

```
firstPointer.next = new QueueNode(7, "Preston") ;
```

with the result shown in Figure 17-9.

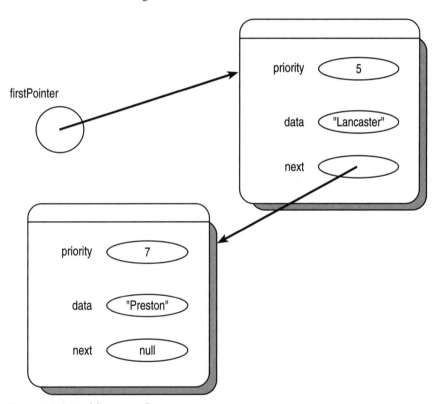

Figure 17-9: Building up a list.

Let us now look at the code for the `PriorityQueue` class with the linked data implementation. We have one instance variable, a reference to the first element:

```
public class PriorityQueue
    {
    private QueueNode firstPointer = null ;
    ...
```

It would probably be normal to have a second instance variable queueLength, which allows us to quickly find out the current length of the queue, and which must be updated each time we insert or remove an element. Instead, just to illustrate how it is done, we are going to recalculate the length each time it is required.

17.3 Methods for the PriorityQueue Class

We are going to have the same set of methods as before: a constructor method PriorityQueue, initialize, insert, first, remove, length, isFull, and isEmpty:

- The constructor and initialize methods simply set firstPointer to the value null. There are no queue elements to point to, so firstPointer must indicate this:

```
public PriorityQueue()
    {
    firstPointer = null ;
    } // end of constructor method

public void initialize()
    {
    firstPointer = null ;
    } // end of method initialize
```

- The isEmpty method is also easy. If firstPointer contains the value null, the queue is empty. Otherwise the queue contains at least one element:

```
public boolean isEmpty()
    {
    return firstPointer == null ;
    } // end of method isEmpty
```

- One of the advantages of linked data allocation is that we do not have to decide on an upper limit to the size of the data structure we can implement. Thus the queue can never be full (unless the program has completely run out of store space), so we have:

```
public boolean isFull()
    {
    return false ;
    } // end of method isFull
```

17.3.1   The length Method

Next let us look at the length method. We are writing this method rather than keeping track of the length of the queue as we go along in order to illustrate traversal of the linked data structure. Suppose that the queue appears as shown in Figure 17-10.

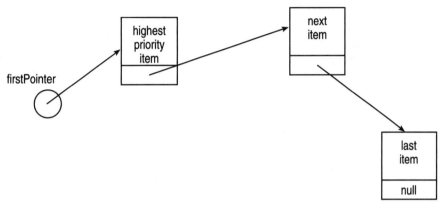

Figure 17-10: An example priority queue.

Under these circumstances, this method should return the value 3. Here is the code:

```
public int length()
  {
  int count = 0 ;
  for (QueueNode pointer = firstPointer ;
      pointer != null ;
      pointer = pointer.next)
    count++ ;
  return count ;
  } // end of method length
```

We initialize an integer count to zero, increment it by one for each element in the queue, and return its value as the result of the method.

We are going to traverse the whole linked data structure representing the queue, so we use the for loop. The INITIALIZATION section declares a variable of type QueueNode called pointer and initializes it to the contents of firstPointer. Thus this variable contains a reference to the first element of the queue (or the value null if the queue is empty) (see Figure 17-11).

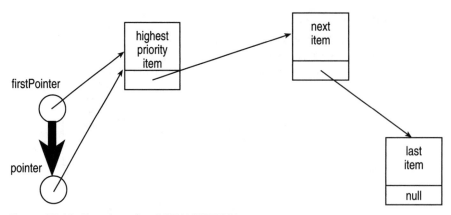

Figure 17-11: Situation after INITIALIZATION.

The MODIFICATION section moves `pointer` on to the next element with the statement `pointer = pointer.next` (see Figure 17-12).

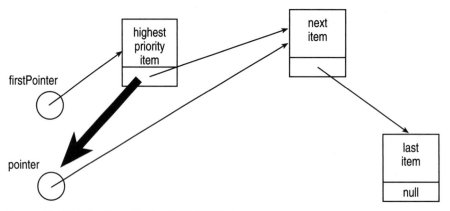

Figure 17-12: Situation after MODIFICATION.

The TESTING section checks that the variable `pointer` does not contain a value `null`, which marks the end of the queue.

In Chapter 5, we introduced rules of thumb for choosing between using the `for` and `while` statements. The more general statement said that we should use a `for` loop because we are expecting to scan through the *complete* data structure, even though (as here) we do not have the number of iterations (which is the number of elements) explicitly to hand. The INITIALIZATION, TESTING, and MODIFICATION sections—the three expressions in the `for` loop—implement a pointer control variable rather than the integer control variable we used in Chapter 5.

17.3.2   The first Method

The first method needs to return a priority (an int) and the data (a String). We can return an instance of the QueueElement class introduced in Chapter 11 since it encapsulates the priority and data attributes we need. Note the distinction between the QueueElement class from Chapter 11, containing a priority and a data string, and the QueueNode class introduced in section 17.2, which additionally contains a reference to another instance of the same type.

We need to return a copy of the priority and data values in the first element in the queue, pointed to by firstPointer. So we have:

```
public QueueElement first() throws QueueEmptyException
   {
   if (isEmpty())
     throw new QueueEmptyException() ;

   return new QueueElement(firstPointer.priority,
     firstPointer.data) ;
   } // end of method first
```

We must check that there *is* an element in the queue, and if not, throw the exception QueueEmptyException (we defined this exception class in Chapter 15). Remember that the compiler needs to be warned of the possibility that this exception will be thrown with the addition of the throws QueueEmptyException clause to the method header line.

We generate a new QueueElement instance and set its attributes from the first element in the queue (we are doing a deep copy, so the returned instance can be modified without affecting the values in the queue), and we return a reference to this instance.

17.3.3   The remove Method

Let us now consider the remove method. It looks like the following:

```
public QueueElement remove() throws QueueEmptyException
   {
   if (isEmpty())
     throw new QueueEmptyException() ;

   QueueElement temp = new QueueElement(firstPointer.priority,
                                        firstPointer.data) ;
   firstPointer = firstPointer.next ;
   return temp ;
   } // end of method remove
```

As usual, we check to ensure that the queue is not empty and that there *is* a first element to remove. We generate a new QueueElement object and set its attributes from the first element in the queue, and we store a reference to this object in the new local variable temp.

We must now remove the current first element from the queue so that the new first element will be what was previously the second element (let us for the moment assume that there is such a second element). The expression `firstPointer.next` is a reference to (that is, the address of) the element following the element referred to by `firstPointer`, and so is a reference to the second element. This is the reference that we now want to store in `firstPointer`. So we write:

`firstPointer = firstPointer.next ;`

Before this statement was executed, the situation appeared as in Figure 17-13.

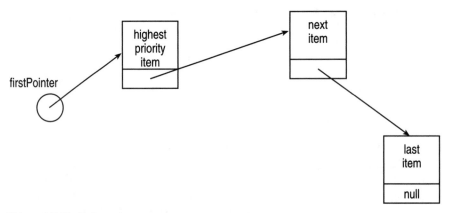

Figure 17-13: Before the statement.

Now it appears as shown in Figure 17-14.

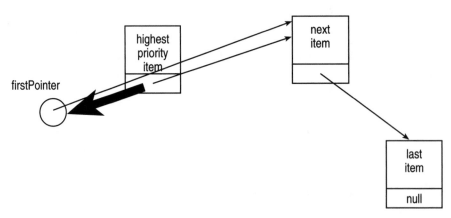

Figure 17-14: After the statement.

What happens to the area of storage that contains the original first element? Since no reference is made any longer to the instance by the program, a part of the Java system called the *garbage collector* will eventually recover the store area and make it available for further use in some other capacity by the program. The essential point is that we don't have to worry about it—it will be dealt with automatically.

Suppose now that there had been only one element in the queue. Then the next variable in the first (and only) element would have had the value null. The result of executing the statement:

```
firstPointer = firstPointer.next ;
```

would therefore have been to put the value null into firstPointer, indicating an empty queue, which is the correct result.

17.4   The insert Method

The insert method is a bit more complicated. It must work when we insert an element into an empty queue or when the element (according to its priority) should go at the beginning, somewhere in the middle, or at the end of the queue. Here is the code:

```
public void insert(QueueElement d)
   {
   boolean qStart = true ;
   QueueNode pointer = firstPointer,
      pointer1 = null ;

   while ((pointer != null) &&
         (pointer.priority <= d.getPriority()))
      {
      pointer1 = pointer ;
      qStart = false ;
      pointer = pointer.next ;
      }

   QueueNode newPointer = new QueueNode(d.getPriority(), d.getData()) ;
   newPointer.next = pointer ;
   if (qStart)
      firstPointer = newPointer ;
   else
      pointer1.next = newPointer ;
   } // end of method insert
```

Notice that we do not do any test to see if the queue is full as this is no longer a possibility.

We first need to find the right place to insert the new element in the queue, according to the priority of the element to be added. We are going to use a variable pointer of type QueueNode to work our way along the queue, looking for the right place. Since we do not know whether we are going to look through the whole queue or stop at some intermediate point, we use a while loop. The variable `pointer` starts off at the beginning of the queue, so its initial value is the reference to the first element in `firstPointer`. We scan down the loop until either:

(a) We have dropped off the end of the loop, which is signaled by the fact that `pointer` has the value `null`. Of course, if the queue is empty, this causes us to break out of the loop immediately without performing any iterations.

(b) The priority of the element to be inserted (which is `d.getPriority()`) is greater (numerically less) than the priority of the element pointed to by pointer (which is `pointer.priority`), so the new element should go in front of the element pointed to by `pointer`.

In each iteration, we need to move the variable `pointer` so it refers to the next element in the list. This is the effect of the statement:

```
pointer = pointer.next ;
```

This takes the reference to the next element (or `null` at the end of the list) held in the `next` attribute of the element referred to by `pointer` and stores it as the new value of `pointer`.

Unfortunately, when we come out of the loop the value of `pointer` doesn't quite give us the information we want. What we actually need is, in case (a), a reference to the last element in the queue and, in case (b), a reference to the element just before the one with a lower priority. In either case, *this* element is the one whose next attribute is to be modified to refer to the new element we are about to insert.

We therefore keep a second variable `pointer1`, which we set to hold a reference to the element just *before* the one referred to by `pointer`. Before we start, `pointer1` is initialized to `null`. In the loop body, we copy the current value of `pointer` into the variable `pointer1` just before we update `pointer` to refer to the next element for the next iteration. The effect is that (except at the beginning of the queue) `pointer1` always refers to the element just before the element referred to by `pointer` (see Figure 17-15).

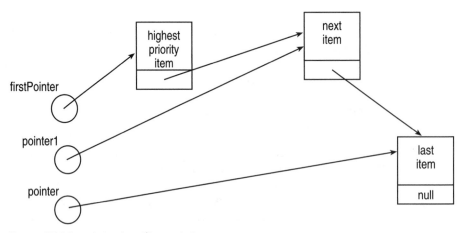

Figure 17-15: pointer1 trailing pointer.

If the scanning reaches the end of the queue (because all the elements have a higher priority than the one to be inserted), then `pointer` will have the value `null` and `pointer1` will refer to the last element in the queue (see Figure 17-16).

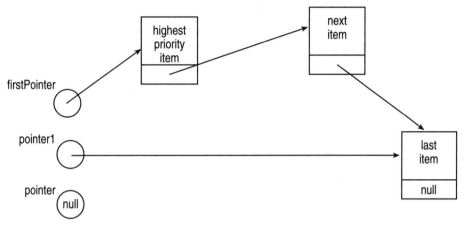

Figure 17-16: Reaching the end of the queue.

After we come out of the loop, we have `pointer1` referring to the element just before the one to be inserted. We generate a new `QueueNode` instance, set its attributes to the priority and data passed in the input argument, and put a reference to it (temporarily) into a variable `newPointer` (of type `QueueNode`) (see Figure 17-17):

```
QueueNode newPointer = new QueueNode(d.getPriority(), d.getData()) ;
```

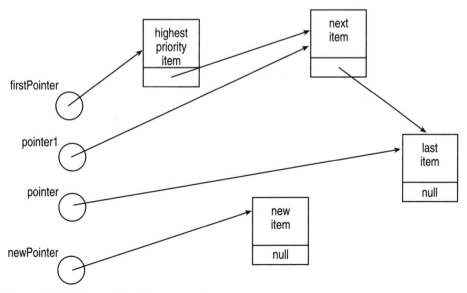

Figure 17-17: Generating the new node.

We want the next attribute of this new instance to refer to the next element in the queue, and (as a result of traversing the loop) a reference to this next element is in the variable pointer (see Figure 17-18). So we execute the statement:

```
newPointer.next = pointer ;
```

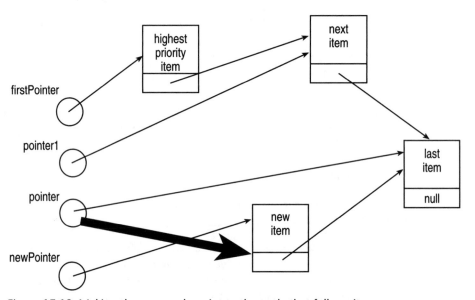

Figure 17-18: Making the new node point to the node that follows it.

If we were inserting a new *final* element, pointer would contain the value null, which is the correct value to insert as the value of the next attribute of the new element, which is currently pointed to by newPointer. So this statement still works correctly at the end of the queue.

Finally, we want to link the new element into the queue at the right place. Our first attempt at this might be the following statement (which will, in fact, require modification):

```
pointer1.next = newPointer ;
```

to insert a reference to the new element as the next attribute of the preceding element, the one referred to by pointer1 (see Figure 17-19).

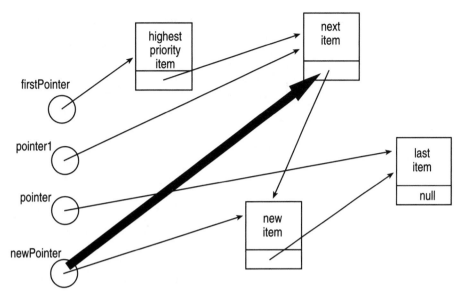

Figure 17-19: Making the prior node point to the new node.

There is a slight problem with this. If the new element is to be inserted as the *first* element in the queue (for instance, because its priority is higher than all elements currently in the queue), then there is no "preceding" element, and we need to put the reference to the new element directly in the firstPointer variable. The Boolean variable qStart keeps track of this; it is initialized to true and changed to false on the first iteration (and on all subsequent iterations) when pointer1 is given a usable value. If qStart has the value true, then no iterations of the loop took place and the variable firstPointer is to be updated. Otherwise, pointer1 has been given a value, which is a reference to the element whose next attribute is to be modified. So the correct version of this step is:

```
if (qStart)
    firstPointer = newPointer ;
else
    pointer1.next = newPointer ;
```

In fact, we could have done without the Boolean variable qStart. We could instead have written the preceding test:

```
if (pointer1 == null)
    firstPointer = newPointer ;
else
    pointer1.next = newPointer ;
```

When we return from the insert method, the queue now appears as shown in Figure 17-20.

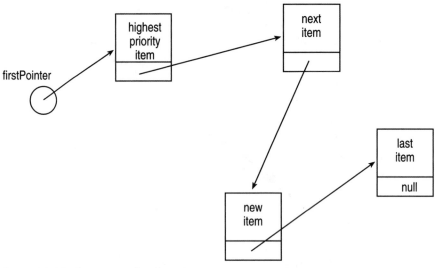

Figure 17-20: The queue after insertion.

We have argued that this code for insertion works correctly for the general case of insertion into the middle of a queue and also for the special cases of insertion into the beginning and the end of a queue. What about the special case of insertion into an empty queue?

In this case, the variable firstPointer will have the value null, so the initial value of pointer will also be null. We will exit from the loop without executing any iterations, and qStart will therefore have the value true. We generate a new element in the usual way, its next attribute receives the value null, and its reference goes into firstPointer. We arrive at the situation shown in Figure 17-21, which is the correct setup. So this special case also works.

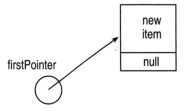

Figure 17-21: Insertion into an empty queue.

Finally, what happens if we insert several items with the same priority? The loop that scanned for the space in the queue for the new item used the test <= on the priorities. So a new item is put at the end of those elements in the queue with the same priority.

17.5   Deletion From a Linked Data Structure (optional)

You will have noticed that, while for the priority queue we have to be prepared to insert a new element at any point in the queue, we delete only from the front of the queue, which is particularly simple. If for some reason we wanted to be able to delete an element from an arbitrary place in the queue, we would have the same problem we have with insertion. That is, we have to know where the preceding element is so that we can modify the value held as its next attribute.

Suppose, for example, that we have the variable pointer referring to the element to be deleted and pointer1 referring to the preceding element. We would have to write:

```
pointer1.next = pointer.next ;
```

to copy the reference to the element that follows the one to be deleted into the next attribute of the element that precedes the one to be deleted. Before the deletion, we would have something like that shown in Figure 17-22. Afterward, it would appear as seen in Figure 17-23.

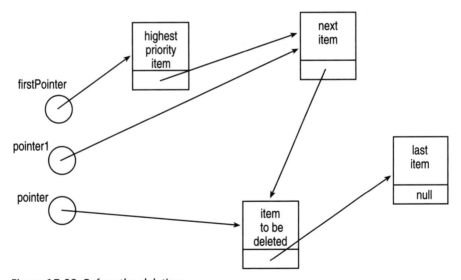

Figure 17-22: Before the deletion.

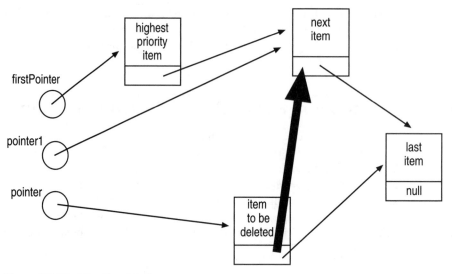

Figure 17-23: After the deletion.

After we returned from the `delete` method and the local variables `pointer` and `pointer1` have disappeared, the queue will appear as shown in Figure 17-24.

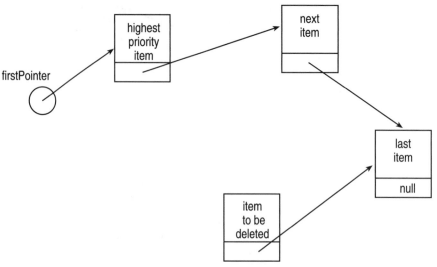

Figure 17-24: The final result.

Since there are now no references to the area of store associated with the element we have deleted from the queue, it will eventually be recovered by the garbage collector for reuse elsewhere in the program.

The code for deletion still works if the element being deleted is the last in the queue, in which case `pointer` contains the value `null`, which gets copied into the `next` attribute of the element preceding the one we are deleting. It does not work, however, if the element being deleted is the *first* element in the queue. We would again have to have some indication of this, either using a Boolean variable `qStart` as before, or perhaps ensuring that `pointer1` is set to contain the value `null` in this case:

```
if (pointer1 == null)
   firstPointer = pointer.next ;
else
   pointer1.next = pointer.next ;
```

We do not need to consider the case of an empty queue here, as we are assuming the `pointer` refers to an element in the queue to be deleted. Depending on how this reference has been obtained, it may of course be possible for `pointer` to contain the value `null` if there is no appropriate element to be deleted. We would then have to test for this special case.

17.6   Doubly Linked Lists (optional)

In the case of insertion into a priority queue, there is no particular problem in making sure that we establish a reference to the element preceding the insertion point, as we can do this while we are scanning through the queue looking for the appropriate place. But in some situations, we may be in the position of knowing the insertion point without knowing the identity of the preceding element, so we would have to find it by scanning from the beginning.

An alternative would be for each element to contain a reference to the preceding element as well as to the following element.

The declaration of a `QueueNode` for such a *doubly linked* list would look like this:

```
class QueueNode
   {
   int priority ;
   String data ;
   QueueNode previous,
      next ;

   public QueueNode(int p, String d)
      {
      priority p ;
      data d ;
      previous = null ;
      next = null ;
      } // end of constructor method
   } // end of class QueueNode
```

An example of such a list is shown in Figure 17-25.

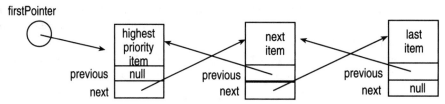

firstPointer

Figure 17-25: A doubly-linked list.

Suppose that we want to insert a new element in such a doubly linked queue. Let us suppose that `pointer` refers to the element before which we want to insert a new element, and `newPointer` refers to the new element we are about to insert (see Figure 17-26). There is no `pointer1` variable, as we can do without it.

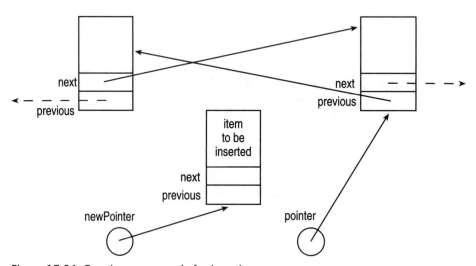

Figure 17-26: Creating a new node for insertion.

We need to update four pointer fields, the previous and next attributes of this new element, the next attribute of the preceding element, and the previous attribute of the following element. Here is a first attempt:

```
pointer.previous.next = newPointer ;          // step 1
newPointer.previous = pointer.previous ;      // step 2
newPointer.next = pointer ;                   // step 3
pointer.previous = newPointer ;               // step 4
```

The effect of each statement is shown in Figure 17-27.

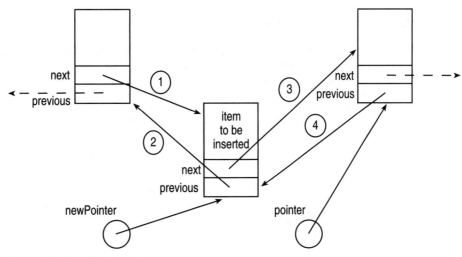

Figure 17-27: After insertion.

This code does not, of course, work properly at the beginning or end of the queue. In the first case, at the beginning of the queue, `pointer.previous` contains the value `null`, so we could rewrite the code:

```
if (pointer.previous == null)
    {
    firstPointer = newPointer ;
    newPointer.previous = null ;
    }
else
    {
    pointer.previous.next = newPointer ;
    newPointer.previous = pointer.previous ;
    }
newPointer.next = pointer ;
pointer.previous = newPointer ;
```

In the case of insertion at the end of the queue, we have said that `pointer` refers to the element after the place where we want to insert the new element and so presumably contains the value `null`, so we need some other way to locate the insertion position. In the spirit of this example, perhaps we should have a variable `lastPointer` to point to the last element in the queue, just as `firstPointer` points to the first element. We leave the details to the reader.

17.7   Using Linked Data Structures

As you will have gathered from the preceding discussion, you have to keep a clear head when writing code to manipulate linked data structures. There are a few well-known places where it is easy to write erroneous code:

- Sometimes it is possible to have a reference to some type of object, which the program manipulates as if it is a reference to a different type of object. Because Java is a strongly typed language, a variable that can hold a reference to one type of object cannot hold a reference to a different type of object, so the Java compiler is able to eliminate errors of this sort.

- It is easy to attempt to access an object through a variable that has not been initialized to a suitable value. The Java compiler makes an attempt to catch situations where this has happened, but it is important to get into the habit of initializing reference variables to the value `null` if there is no appropriate value at which to set it. It remains important not to attempt to access an object through a variable initialized to `null`, either by checking carefully to ensure that such situations cannot arise or by explicitly testing for this value before using the reference.

- There are some situations where it is particularly easy to manipulate pointers in the wrong way. One situation is when accessing the "edges" of the linked data structure. For example, in the priority queue code, we needed to be particularly careful when inserting at the beginning and end of the queue. Similarly, if we had a method to provide general deletion from the queue, we would have to be careful to make sure it worked at the beginning and end of the queue.

- We must also be particularly careful when dealing with an empty linked data structure. For example, with the priority queue, we need to ensure that inserting an element into an empty queue works correctly. Similarly, when we delete the last element from a queue, we need to check to ensure that it leaves an empty queue in the correct format for the next insertion.

Let us briefly consider the layout of the `PriorityQueue` code. We have four classes:

- `QueueElement`, containing the priority and data attributes
- `QueueEmptyException`
- `QueueNode`, essentially a `QueueElement` with an extra `next` attribute
- `PriorityQueue`

The first two are exactly the same as they are for the array implementation of the `PriorityQueue`, which we discussed in Chapter 11. We do not, of course, need the `QueueFullException` class, which we needed for the array implementation. These two classes are `public`, and the source code needs to be in two suitably named files, `QueueElement.java` and `QueueEmptyException.java` as before.

However, the classes `QueueNode` and `PriorityQueue` are closely connected. We have chosen to put the source code for both of these classes into the single file `PriorityQueue.java`. The class `PriorityQueue` is `public` as usual, but the code for the other class starts:

```
class QueueNode
  {
  ...
```

This class therefore has the default protection, which means that it is accessible from all classes in the package, which includes the code of the class `PriorityQueue`. The three instance variables in this class, `priority`, `data`, and `next`, all have the default protection, so that in the methods of `PriorityQueue` we can refer to the variables directly (as, for example, in `firstPointer.priority` and `pointer.next`) without needing to work through `set` and `get` methods. Indeed, the only method we have supplied for the `QueueNode` class is a constructor to set up appropriate initial values.

An alternative strategy could have been to make `QueueNode` inherit its `priority` and `data` attributes from `QueueElement` and add an additional `next` attribute:

```
class QueueNode extends QueueElement
  {
  QueueNode next ;

  public QueueNode(int p, String d)
    {
    super(p, d) ;
    next = null ;
    } // end of constructor method
  }
```

The constructor method for `QueueNode` calls the constructor method for `QueueElement` (using the `super` keyword) and then initializes the `next` attribute. We have to modify the code for the `PriorityQueue` class because we no longer have direct access to the `priority` and `data` attributes since they are private to the `QueueElement` class. The only way we can access them is via the `getPriority` and `getData` methods. An alternative would have been to declare them as `protected` in the `QueueElement` class, in which case we would still have had direct access.

We are going to look at another example of a linked data structure, a tree, in the next chapter.

17.8   Key Points in Chapter 17

- There are a number of well-known, very useful high-level data structures, such as queues, stacks, and trees. These high-level abstractions can be specified and used independently of their implementation; for example, we can define a Stack class with a set of operations and hide all details of implementation within the class. This is called an *abstract data type*.

- It is possible to implement these abstract data types using linear, static storage structures such as arrays. However, this approach can raise a number of problems, such as fixed maximum capacities and difficulties in rearranging the elements (for instance, to make room for an extra element).

- It is also possible to use dynamic storage structures such as a linked list. A member of such a list (an instance of a particular class) will contain such data as is necessary but also at least one reference attribute (called next, for example) to another instance of the same class.

- A linked list needs a variable (called firstPointer, for example) that points to the first member of the list. That first member's reference attribute will point to the next element of this list, and so on. The final element will have its reference attribute set to the value null.

- We can traverse a list by using a loop and following the value of the next attribute. A typical loop might look like this:

```
for (NodeClass pointer = firstPointer ;
    pointer != null ;
    pointer = pointer.next)
    . . .
```

  This algorithm can be used as the basis for printing, searching, or any general processing of the contents of the list.

- We can insert a new element anywhere in a list. We first use the constructor method to set up a new element, and then we insert the element by manipulating the pointers appropriately, having first scanned through the list looking for the correct position, if necessary.

- If we delete an element from a linked data structure, Java's garbage collector will return it to the available free store once there are no longer references to it.

- We must take care with linked structures (a) to ensure all pointer variables are suitably initialized (perhaps to null), (b) to ensure our algorithms work correctly at the "edges" of the structure, and (c) to ensure that they still work when the structure is empty.

17.9 Exercises

1. In exercise 15.2, you used an array to implement a stack of characters as an abstract data type in the class CharacterStack.

   Reimplement the CharacterStack class, this time using a linked list of elements. The only difference from the earlier abstract data type specification is that StackOverflowException will not be thrown by the push method.

   Test your package with the driver and parenthesis checker from exercises 15.2 and 15.3. You should not need to make any changes to them.

2. Add a method delete to the PriorityQueue class:

   `public void delete(int p)`

   a) This method should delete the first element in the queue with a priority equal to the value p.

   b) Rewrite the method so that it deletes *all* the elements in the queue with a priority equal to the value p. Check that it still works if all the elements in the queue have this priority.

3. Add a method merge to the PriorityQueue class:

   `public void merge(PriorityQueue q)`

   that takes all the elements in the queue q and inserts them in their correct positions in the queue to which the method is applied. Check what happens to the instance references in the queue q—should you be using a deep or a shallow copy?

4. Implement a normal (First-In-First-Out) queue of Strings as an abstract data type Queue. Use the same list of methods as for the PriorityQueue class, and use a linked implementation.

   Write a method append (not part of the Queue class):

   `public static Queue append(Queue q1, Queue q2)`

   that returns a Queue that consists of all the elements of q1 (in order) followed by all the elements of q2 (in order). The Queues q1 and q2 should be left unchanged, so the Queue you return should be a copy.

5. Along the lines discussed in section 17.6, reimplement the PriorityQueue class as a doubly linked list with instance variables firstPointer and lastPointer that refer to the first and last elements.

   Add a version of the delete method discussed in exercise 17.2.

   When you are scanning through the queue in insert and delete for the appropriate element, do not use a trailing pointer pointer1, as in the discussion in section 17.4. Instead, have the program work out the neighboring elements from the link variables provided.

6. Write a program that reads from the user the usual information (forename, surname, age, gender) for a sequence of instances of the Person class, and organize them into two linked lists, ordered by increasing surname and by increasing age. Then print the two lists in order.

7. A hotel receptionist needs to keep track of who is occupying which hotel room and whether they are in the room at present. Design a system that holds, for each occupied room:

   - The room number
   - A Person instance with details of the person occupying it
   - When the occupier checked in
   - Whether or not the occupier is currently in the room

   The receptionist needs to be able to ask who is occupying a room, or which room a person is occupying, since when, and whether they are currently in the room.

   Design a Register class that holds this information as linked lists of room information organized by room number and occupier's name so that the receptionist can search it by either attribute. The receptionist should be able to check a person into or out of a room and mark that the occupier is currently in the room or not.

8. The diagram shown in Figure 17-28 represents a grammar for a simple subset of English. It can be used as a grammar checker as follows:

Start in the state marked with the arrow (here state 1) and with the sentence to be checked. If there is no arc out of this state labeled with the next word of the sentence, the sentence is invalid (at least according to this simple grammar). If there is an arc labeled with the next word of the sentence, follow the arc to the new state. Repeat. When you reach the end of the sentence, interpret next word to be the word STOP. The sentence is valid according to this grammar if you arrive at the final state (marked with a double circle, here 10) at the end of the sentence.

Thus the sentence *the cat sat on the mat* would cause the program to visit states 1, 2, 3, 6, 7, 8, 9, 10, so it is a valid sentence.

Implement a grammar checker using this grammar. It should read in a sentence word by word from a file and match it to the grammar. If the sentence is valid, it should display the sentence and the phrase *is VALID*. If the sentence is not valid, it should display the valid words of the sentence, then the word *ERROR*, then the erroneous word.

Thus:

```
the cat sat on the mat
is VALID
```

and:

```
the big brown ERROR dog
```

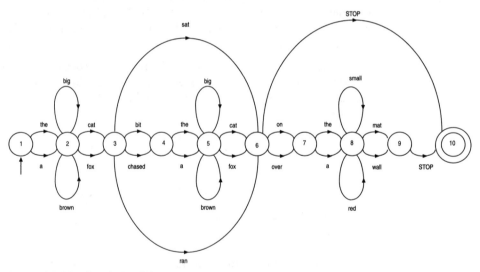

Figure 17-28 : Simple English grammar.

The class WordFile (derived from BasicFileIo and provided in the java.lancs package) provides a method readWord to read successive words from a file:

```
public String readWord()
```

to read the next word from the input file and return it, returning a null String if there are no more words.

The diagram represents a *finite-state machine*—a set of states, including a start state and one or more finish states, and a set of labeled arcs from one state to another; it is *deterministic*, as there is never a choice of which arc is the appropriate one to take. This type of grammar is called a *regular* grammar; it is too simple for English (or Java), but can be used to define things like time expressions (*ten to six, eleven forty-five*) or the format of Java identifiers or numbers.

Optional supplementary exercises:

a) Replace the arcs for individual words with arcs for parts of speech (determiner, adjective, noun, transitive verb, etc.) and a dictionary:

```
determiner :- the, a
adjective :- big, brown
noun :- cat, fox
transitive verb :- bit, chased
...
```

b) Provide a way to read the grammar in rather than building it into the program. If necessary, assume that there are never more than six arcs coming out of any state.

CHAPTER 18

Recursion & Binary Trees

18.1 An Introduction to Recursion

Suppose we have some task to carry out. We have already discussed the idea of "divide and conquer," where we split up a large task into a number of related subtasks that are easier to implement. It may be that some subtasks can be further subdivided until we reach a *base task* that cannot be further reduced but is solvable.

There are certain tasks that can be solved by using *recursive* algorithms. With recursion, when we try to subdivide the task, we find out that:

- The subtask is exactly the same as the task except that it operates on a reduced amount or value of data. The task is related to the subtask in some way. A typical recursive expression would involve:

  task(data) = expression relating to data + task(reduced data).

- There is a base task that operates on the simplest amount of data (for example, one item of data or the simplest value of that data—if we are processing a collection, then the simplest value is a single item; if we are processing a numeric value, then it is zero or one):

  task (simplest data) = fixed answer.

- Notice that the solution to the base task is trivial.

We basically apply the same task algorithm over and over again, reducing the data until we arrive at the base task. Recursion can be a complicated concept to grasp, but we will find that it often offers the simplest solution.

Thus, the strategy we have outlined defines a solution to a task in terms of the same task applied to reduced data, which "bottoms out" at a simple base task. This type of strategy is called *recursion*, and we are going to study its use in programming in this chapter. There is a well-known joke entry in a computer science glossary:

`recursion`: see recursion.

This would be *infinite* recursion, as we never make any progress with the task in hand (to define *recursion*). We must always have an alternative, nonrecursive path so that the recursion eventually stops.

Before we talk about recursion, we need to revisit how ordinary, nonrecursive methods call each other. An application program will start with a `main` method—let us suppose it calls `method1`, which then calls `method2`. When the Java system is executing the statement of `method2`, it needs to remember where in `method1` it came from (so that it can return there when `method2` has finished) and where in the `main` method it called `method1` (so it can return there when `method1` is finished). In principle, this chain of calls could be a long one. Not only must the Java system record where in the preceding method it should return to, there are other pieces of information about the method that must be remembered so that they can be reinstated when we return—for example the values of the formal arguments and the local variables. Whenever we leave a method, we return to the method we were previously executing, which means that the information is required in Last In First Out (LIFO) order. So the Java system stores the information about the current methods on a stack, called the *run-time stack* (see Figure 18-1).

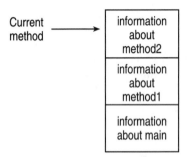

Figure 18-1: The run-time stack.

When we use recursion in programming, we have a method whose body contains one or more calls of the same method. A simple example would be a program to calculate the factorial of a supplied argument n. The *factorial* of a number is the product of all the values from 1 up to and including the number itself (it is defined only for nonnegative values of the argument). Thus the factorial of 6 is 6 x 5 x 4 x 3 x 2 x 1, or 720. We can give a recursive definition of the factorial function:

```
factorial(n) = 1                           if n = 0
               n * factorial(n - 1)        if n > 0
```

We can program this directly in Java. We have a `main` method to obtain a value for n from the user and to display the result, and we have a method `factorial`, which implements the definition directly. It tests for the nonrecursive *base case* (n having a value of zero) and deals with that. Otherwise it makes a recursive call to the `factorial` method and uses the result to calculate the answer to the original problem. Note that the recursive call deals with a smaller subtask, as it is solving the problem for a value of the argument one less than the original value. To be safe, the factorial method should probably check for a negative value of the argument and stop if it encounters it; otherwise we *could* have a case of infinite recursion.

Here is the code:

```
import java.lancs.* ;

public class Chapter18n1
  {
```

```
public static void main(String[] args) throws Exception
  {
  BasicIo.prompt("number? ") ;
  int n = BasicIo.readInteger() ;
  System.out.println("The factorial of " + n + " is " +
    factorial(n)) ;
  } // end of method main

private static int factorial(int n)
  {
  if (n == 0)
    return 1 ;
  else
    return n * factorial(n - 1) ;
  } // end of method factorial

} // end of class Chapter18n1
```

How does this work? Suppose the user typed 3 in response to the prompt. Then the `main` method makes a call `factorial(3)`. Each call of the `factorial` method effectively causes a new copy of the method to be created with its own copy of each argument (here n) and local variable (here there are none). These local copies are held in the run-time stack together with sufficient information for the program to "unwind" each recursive call back to where it came from. In fact, the information held is exactly the same as what Java holds for a nonrecursive method—it does not need to treat a recursive method as a special case. A diagram of this is shown in Figure 18-2.

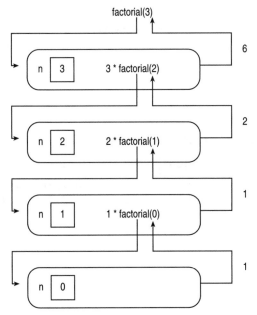

Figure 18-2: Recursive calls and unwinding.

The arrows down the left-hand side of Figure 18-2 represent successive recursive calls of the `factorial` method, with smaller and smaller values of the argument n. Eventually the base case (when the value of the argument is zero) is reached, at which time the method returns a value of 1. Then the recursion unwinds, following the arrows at the right-hand side of Figure 18-2, in each case returning a suitable value until the topmost (original) call of `factorial` returns a value of 6, which is output by the `main` method.

There is a cost to the use of recursion. As we have already pointed out, for each recursive call, the Java environment needs to keep a separate copy of all the arguments and local variables (in this case it is only the argument n) together with sufficient information to enable the "unwinding" of the recursion to take place successfully.

It so happens that with the factorial function there is also an iterative solution available, which is just as clear as the recursive solution:

```
private static int factorial(int n)
    {
    int result = 1 ;
    for (int i = 1 ; i <= n ; i++)
        result *= i ;
    return result ;
    } // end of method factorial
```

Before we enter the loop, we set the result to the base case when n is zero. Then in the loop, we simply multiply by successive values from 1 up to the value of the supplied argument (remember that a `*=` b means the same as a = a * b).

It is *always* possible to rewrite a recursive solution as an iterative solution. In some cases, this may be quite difficult since what we essentially have to do is to simulate the operation of the run-time stack (that is, implement the recursion winding and unwinding illustrated in Figure 18-2). As we have pointed out, there is an overhead in using recursion because the environment has to save and restore a certain amount of local information as we move from one copy to the next of the recursive method. But in some cases, it is so much easier to think of a solution to a programming problem in recursive terms that this is the most effective strategy for doing it.

18.2 Solving the Towers of Hanoi Problem

We now look at a different problem, for which we want to contrast the recursive and iterative solutions. This is the *Towers of Hanoi* problem (see Figure 18-3), which was invented as a puzzle in about 1883. You will find it on pages 57–58 in *Mathematical Puzzles and Diversions* by Martin Gardner (Penguin 1965).

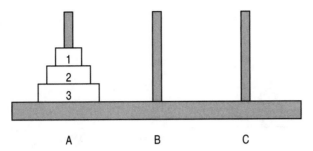

Figure 18-3: The Towers of Hanoi.

We have three pegs, here called A, B, and C. On one peg we have a number of disks; in this example there are three, although there were eight in the original puzzle. We start off with all the disks on peg A, with each disk smaller than the one it rests on. The problem is to move all the disks from peg A to peg B, making use of peg C if we wish, but there are two rules for moving the disks:

- We can move only one disk at a time.

- When we move a disk, it must start and finish resting on a larger disk (or, of course, on the stand).

Thus we could start by moving disk 1 from peg A to peg B. We could then move disk 2 from peg A to peg C. This is, in fact, the only reasonable move, as we could not move it to peg B (this is occupied by a smaller disk), and it doesn't make sense to move disk 1 from peg B back to peg A or on to peg C, as we would be wasting moves. We could then move disk 1 from peg B to peg C (on top of a larger disk). We have now successfully moved the top two disks from peg A to peg C, making use of peg B, and taking three moves (see Figure 18-4).

Figure 18-4: Starting the process.

We could now move disk 3 from peg A to peg B so it is in the correct final position (see Figure 18-5).

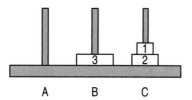

Figure 18-5: Disk 3 in the final position.

Now all we need to do is move disks 1 and 2 back from peg C to peg B and we are done. But in principle, we know how to move a stack of two disks from one peg to another because we have already done it (except that it was from peg A to peg C instead of peg C to B) (see Figure 18-6).

Figure 18-6: Completing the process.

So we can solve the problem for three disks, using 3 + 1 + 3, or 7 moves.

18.2.1 A Recursive Solution to the Towers of Hanoi Problem

The previous section suggests a recursive solution to the general problem with n disks:

```
public static void hanoi(int n, Peg fromPeg, Peg toPeg, Peg helpPeg)
    {
    if (n == 1)
        moveDisk(fromPeg, toPeg) ;
```

```
else
   {
   hanoi(n - 1, fromPeg, helpPeg, toPeg) ;
   moveDisk(fromPeg, toPeg) ;
   hanoi(n - 1, helpPeg, toPeg, fromPeg) ;
   }
} // end of method hanoi
```

If there is a stack of one disk to move (the base case), we can do that directly. If we need to move a stack of more than one disk from peg fromPeg to peg toPeg:

- We first have to move all but the bottom disk of the stack from fromPeg to the third peg helpPeg—this is a smaller problem, so we presumably know how to do this (recursively).

- Then we are free to move the bottom disk of the stack from fromPeg to toPeg.

- And finally, we move the remaining disks of the stack back from the helpPeg to toPeg, making use of our knowledge of the recursive procedure for moving a smaller number of pegs.

Whenever we are moving a stack of disks from one peg to another, we can make use of the third peg. It may have disks on it, but they will always be bigger than the ones we are moving, so they will not affect our strategy.

We would start the process going by writing something like:

```
hanoi(n, pegA, pegB, pegC) ;
```

and the result for the three disks would be a sequence of seven moves:

```
move disk from A to B
move disk from A to C
move disk from B to C
move disk from A to B
move disk from C to A
move disk from C to B
move disk from A to B
```

We have implemented the Peg objects as consisting simply of their names (A, B, and C), and our moveDisk method is:

```
public static void moveDisk(Peg fromPeg, Peg toPeg)
   {
   System.out.println("Move disk from " + fromPeg + " to " +
      toPeg) ;
   } // end of method moveDisk
```

If we want the program to print the number of each disk as we move it, we would have to keep track of where each disk was as the solution progresses, but we have not bothered to do this. Someone following the computer's instructions would be able to use the specification of the pegs involved to make the right move at each stage.

If we are going to get the computer to make the moves in the Tower of Hanoi problem, then this recursive solution is a good one. It is clear how it works (and that it works), and it is obvious how many moves are required. It is $2^n - 1$ moves for n disks (you can prove this using recursion!). So 1 disk requires 1 move, 2 disks require 3 moves, 3 disks require 7 moves, and so on. When the puzzle was invented in 1883, it was claimed that it was based on a real set of 3 pegs with 64 disks in the Great Temple of Benares, and the world would end when all the disks had been moved—the number of moves for 64 disks is about 18 followed by 18 zeroes, which gives us several thousand million years.

But if you try to carry out this strategy "by hand," you will find a major problem. You will have difficulty keeping track of where you are in the strategy; which move you are implementing for a particular stack of disks, inside the strategy for a bigger stack, inside the strategy for a bigger stack still, and so on. The recursive solution keeps (on the run-time stack in the computer) all this information about exactly where it has reached inside a sequence of nested strategies. Consequently, as we have seen in implementing the recursive solution, it doesn't really ever need to look at the pegs to see what disk is where because it knows this from its internal information. For a human being, it would be better not to keep all the information on our personal run-time stack (as it is pretty shallow) and instead make use of information about which disk is physically on which peg at any particular time.

18.2.2   An Iterative Solution to the Towers of Hanoi Problem

So we are led to consider an iterative solution to the Towers of Hanoi problem. Here it is:

```
public static void hanoi(int n, Peg fromPeg, Peg toPeg,
            Peg helpPeg)
    {
    if n is odd
        "cyclically" means fromPeg => toPeg => helpPeg => fromPeg ;
    else
        "cyclically" means fromPeg => helpPeg => toPeg => fromPeg ;

    while (true)
        {
        move the smallest disk one peg cyclically ;
        if (all the disks are on the toPeg)
            break ;
        make the only possible move not involving
            the smallest peg ;
        }
    } // end of method hanoi
```

This would be a sufficient algorithm for a human. It would be obvious from looking at the current situation of the pegs and disks which is the smallest disk and where it is, and what "the only possible move not involving the smallest peg" is. But we have to work a bit harder for an iterative computer solution.

We now have to reimplement the `Peg` objects to simulate the stack of disks that they contain at any time. We provide a method `noOfDisks` to tell us how many disks there are on a peg at any time and `top` to tell us the number of the uppermost disk on a peg (with a large number if the peg is empty). We have also added a public instance variable called `successor` to the `Peg` class so we can record what *cyclically* means. The iterative `hanoi` method in detail would now look something like this:

```
public static void hanoi(int n, Peg fromPeg, Peg toPeg, Peg helpPeg)
    {
    if (n % 2 == 1)
        {
        fromPeg.successor = toPeg ;
        toPeg.successor = helpPeg;
        helpPeg.successor = fromPeg;
        }
    else
        {
        fromPeg.successor = helpPeg ;
        helpPeg.successor = toPeg;
        toPeg.successor = fromPeg;
        }

    while (true)
        {
        Peg smallest = fromPeg ;
        if (toPeg.top() < smallest.top())
            smallest = toPeg ;
        if (helpPeg.top() < smallest.top())
            smallest = helpPeg ;
        Peg newSmallest = smallest.successor ;
        Peg otherPeg = newSmallest.successor ;

        moveDisk(smallest, newSmallest) ;
        if (toPeg.noOfDisks() == n)
            break ;
        if (smallest.top() < otherPeg.top())
            moveDisk(smallest, otherPeg) ;
        else
            moveDisk(otherPeg, smallest) ;
        }
    } // end of method hanoi
```

If you run this version, you will see that it generates exactly the same sequence of moves the recursive solution runs, although it is not obvious that it will do so. Although the iterative solution is probably the best for a human, it has a number of general disadvantages. It is certainly not obvious that carrying out this procedure will, in fact, move the stack of disks in the desired way. And it is not obvious how many moves are required.

So we see that there will be recursive and iterative solutions to a problem, and there may be particular advantages for each.

18.3   Binary Trees

In the previous chapter, we looked at some simple abstract data types and considered how to implement them using linked data structures, where one element contains a reference to one or more other elements. In this chapter, we consider how to implement *trees* using such linked data structures. As we will see, it is often useful to think in terms of recursive algorithms when we implement strategies for manipulating or traversing a tree.

To motivate our discussion, we consider the following problem. Let us suppose we have a very large text (let us say, hundreds of thousands of words long) and we want to make a list of all the words that occur in the text along with a count for each word of how many times it occurs. In principle, the program to do this is very simple:

```
set the list of words to empty
while there is another word in the text
   look the word up in the list
   if it is in the list
     add one to its count
   else
     make an entry in the list for this word and set its count to one
display the list of words and their associated counts
```

The problem is: what is the most efficient way to store our list of words? Here are some possibilities:

- We could keep the words and counts in an array. When we read the next text word, we need to see if it has occurred before. So we scan the array from the beginning. If we find the word in the array, we add 1 to the count and we are done with this text word. If we reach the end of the array, the word has not occurred before so we simply add it in the first free space at the end of the array.

  If the word is in the array, we search on average halfway through the array before finding it. If the word is not in the array, then we search all the way through the array to find that out. So in either case, we have an O(n) process—with twice as many words in the lexicon, we could expect to take twice as long to search.

- We have seen before that we can sometimes improve the situation by keeping the array in sorted order. If we did this, the searching could be done by binary search, which is an O(log n) process and clearly an improvement. But when we have to add in a new word, we have to shuffle around the array of words to make room for it, and this is still an O(n) process.

- A third possibility is to use what is called a *binary tree*.

A *tree* in computer science consists of a number of nodes or elements that are arranged like a family tree (one that shows descent from a common ancestor but not marriage)—see, for example, the inheritance hierarchy in section 13.3. Each element is joined by a line or *arc* to its parent element except that there is one element, the *root* element, that has no parent. The root is always drawn at the top of the page with the tree growing downward, like a family tree but unlike a botanical tree. The elements at the bottom of the tree, with no children, are called *leaves*.

In a general tree, an element may have any number of children, but in a *binary tree* it must have no more than a maximum of two children. Figure 18-7 shows an example of a binary tree, made out of the distinct words in the text, *now is the time for all good people to come to the aid of the party.*

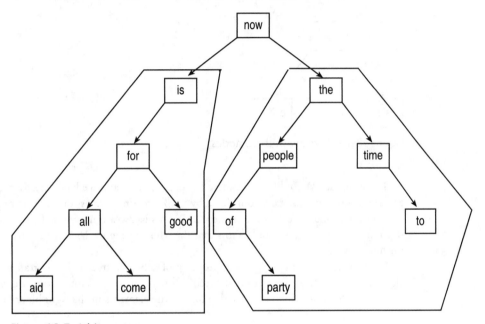

Figure 18-7: A binary tree.

A *subtree* is a connected portion of a tree that is itself a tree. Thus each of the sections enclosed in a line in the diagram is a subtree of the original tree. In fact, the two subtrees are called the *left* and *right subtrees* of the root node.

We can give a recursive definition of a binary tree:

- A *binary tree* is either empty.

- Or it consists of a root element, a left binary tree, and a right binary tree.

Consider the tree consisting just of the element *aid* (see Figure 18-8).

aid

Figure 18-8: A tree with a single node.

It could be considered as a root element, with empty left and right binary trees. So, considered by itself, it is a binary tree. Now consider the tree shown in Figure 18-9.

Figure 18-9: Another tree with a single node.

This is also a tree by the same argument. Now look at the tree in Figure 18-10.

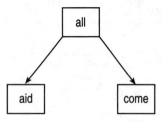

Figure 18-10: A tree with three nodes.

The element all could be considered a root element, and we have already proved that the aid and come elements, each considered by itself, are binary trees, so these are respectively the left and right binary trees of the element all. This is also a binary tree. By following through this type of argument, we could show that the whole of Figure 18-7 is a binary tree, rooted at the now element.

We have left out one important property of a binary tree. It is so arranged that all the elements in the left binary tree are ordered before (in this case, alphabetically earlier than) the element in the root, which is ordered before all the elements in the right binary tree.

18.3.1 Searching & Updating a Binary Tree

Here is how we use the binary tree to search for an element, the word "search", for instance. We start at the root and compare the item we are searching for with the item in that element.

- If we have a match, we have found the element we are looking for (in the problem under discussion, we would add 1 to the count of occurrences at this element).

- If the item we are searching for is ordered before the item in this element (i.e., it is alphabetically earlier), then we look at the root of the left binary subtree.

- If the item we are searching for is ordered after the item in this element (i.e., it is alphabetically later), then we look at the root of the right binary subtree.

- If the procedure requires us to look at a particular element that does not exist (i.e., that binary subtree is empty), then the item we are searching for is not in the tree. Furthermore, the correct place for this item in the tree is the point we have just reached.

To apply this procedure to the word search, we proceed as follows:

- We first compare search with now. It is alphabetically later, so we visit the right subtree (with root the).

- We next compare search with the. It is alphabetically earlier, so we visit the left subtree (with root people).

- We next compare search with people. It is alphabetically later, so we visit the right subtree (which is empty).

So the word search is not in the binary tree. If we wish to insert it in the tree, then we must create an element as the root of a new right binary subtree for the element containing people. It would look like Figure 18-11.

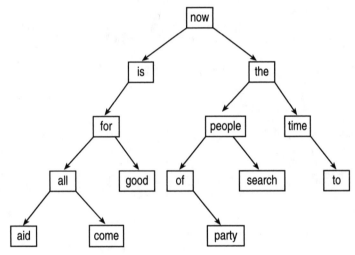

Figure 18-11: A tree with "search" added.

Now if we search for the word search, we would have the following:

- We first compare search with now. It is alphabetically later, so we visit the right subtree (with root the).

- We next compare search with the. It is alphabetically earlier, so we visit the left subtree (with root people).

- We next compare search with people. It is alphabetically later, so we visit the right subtree (with root search).

- We next compare search with search. And we have found the matching element.

A well-organized binary tree can be searched in time O(log n), as with binary search. But we can also insert a new element at the appropriate position in the tree, similarly in time O(log n). I specified that the binary tree should be "well organized," which means that the elements should be well spread out, as in the above example. Whether this is true depends on the order in which we introduce new elements in the tree. Suppose someone had perversely sorted the words in our text into reverse order before we read them in, so that the text reads `to time the people party of now is good for come all aid`. Now if we construct a binary tree in the same way as before, we arrive at the situation shown in Figure 18-12.

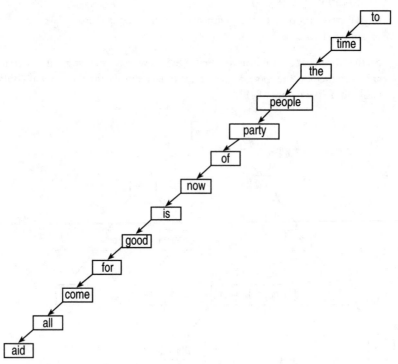

Figure 18-12: A very unbalanced binary tree.

If we try to search through, or insert into, such a binary tree, we are essentially doing linear search. So we are back at an O(n) algorithm.

There are mechanisms for taking an unbalanced binary tree (such as that shown in Figure 18-12) and making it more balanced or for reorganizing the tree as we go along so that it remains relatively balanced as we add new elements. More information is given on binary search trees in textbooks on the study of computer algorithms, such as Aho, Hopcroft, and Ulmann's *The Design and Analysis of Computer Algorithms* (Addison-Wesley 1974), Chapter 4, or *Data Structures and Algorithms: A First Course* by Iain T. Adamson (Springer 1996), Chapters 3 and 11. In our problem, we are going to ignore this issue, assuming that the words that occur in our text file are not in any particular order and that therefore our list of words is likely to end up reasonably balanced.

18.3.2 Writing the Code for the Binary Tree

We start by creating a class LexiconNode for an element of the lexicon; this needs to contain the word, the count of occurrences, and a pointer to each of the two subtrees, the left and the right. We are going to need a constructor for objects of this type. If we give the constructor a String argument that is the word, we can set the count to one and the pointers to the left and right subtrees initially to null:

```
class LexiconNode
    {
    String word ;
    int occurrenceCount ;
    LexiconNode left, right ;

    public LexiconNode(String s)
        {
        word = s ;
        occurrenceCount = 1 ;
        left = null ;
        right = null ;
        } // end of constructor method
    } // end of class LexiconNode
```

We next create a class Lexicon to represent our list of words. It is to have two instance variables, a pointer first to the root element of the tree and a count elementCount of how many elements there are in the tree (that is, how many distinct words there are in the tree), so that we can extract this information without having to recalculate it when required. The constructor and getElementCount methods are trivial and are shown in the following portion of the Lexicon class definition:

```
class Lexicon
    {
    LexiconNode first ;
    int elementCount ;

    public Lexicon()
        {
        first = null ;
        elementCount = 0 ;
        } // end of constructor method

    public int getElementCount()
        {
        return elementCount ;
        } // end of method getElementCount
    ...
```

18.3.3 Adding a Word Occurrence to the Lexicon

We are now going to write an add method to search for a specified word in the lexicon and take appropriate action—increment the count if the word is already in the lexicon, insert it with a count of 1 if not. We could write a recursive or an iterative version of this; we start with an iterative version. Here it is:

```java
public void add(String s)
    {
    if (first == null)
        {
        first = new LexiconNode(s) ;
        elementCount++ ;
        return ;
        }

    LexiconNode pointer = first ;
    while (true)
        {
        int result = s.compareTo(pointer.word) ;
        if (result == 0)
            {
            pointer.occurrenceCount++ ;
            return ;
            }
        else if (result < 0)
            {
            if (pointer.left == null)
                {
                pointer.left = new LexiconNode(s) ;
                elementCount++ ;
                return ;
                }
            else
                pointer = pointer.left ;
            }
        else // result > 0
            {
            if (pointer.right == null)
                {
                pointer.right = new LexiconNode(s) ;
                elementCount++ ;
                return ;
                }
            else
                pointer = pointer.right ;
            }
        }
    } // end of method add
```

We first check for the special case of the tree being completely empty. In this case we create an instance of the LexiconNode class containing the word we have read, and we insert it as the root element of the tree, pointed to by first.

Otherwise, we start scanning through the tree (iteratively) looking for the correct position for this word s. We have a LexiconNode variable called pointer, which points to the tree element that we are currently considering. We initialize it to point to the root element of the tree at first. Then we go around a loop until we have found or inserted the appropriate element.

We compare the word s for which we are searching against the word in the current element of the tree pointer.word. We use the compareTo method to compare them since we want a three-way comparison—equal, s earlier in the alphabetical ordering, s later in the alphabetical ordering. Make sure you check which way around you want this to work—the first version of this code had the test the wrong way around, and the lexicon was displayed in reverse alphabetical order.

If the element referred to by pointer is the same as the word s, we are almost done. We increment the count associated with this element, and then we have finished.

If the word s is alphabetically earlier than the element at position pointer, we need to explore its left subtree. If the left subtree is not empty, we can simply move our pointer to the root element of that subtree:

```
pointer = pointer.left ;
```

If the left subtree is empty, then we have nearly finished. We know that this word s is not in the tree, but it should be inserted as the root element of the left subtree of the element pointed to by pointer. So:

```
pointer.left = new LexiconNode(s) ;
```

We treat the third case, when the word s is alphabetically later that the element at position pointer, in a very similar way. Again the element referred to by pointer may or may not have a right subtree.

There are several ways to write a recursive version of the add method. One looks almost exactly the same as the iterative version. Here is another way to write it:

```
public void add(String s)
   {
   first = addToTree(first, s) ;
   } // end of method add

public LexiconNode addToTree(LexiconNode pointer, String s)
   {
   if (pointer == null)
      {
      elementCount++ ;
      return new LexiconNode(s) ;
      }
   else
      {
      int result = s.compareTo(pointer.word) ;
```

```
      if (result == 0)
        pointer.occurrenceCount++ ;
      else if (result < 0)
        pointer.left = addToTree(pointer.left, s) ;
      else // result > 0
        pointer.right = addToTree(pointer.right, s) ;
      return pointer ;
      }
  } // end of method addToTree
```

The add method simply calls the addToTree method at the root level with the word to be added.

Suppose we pass as the first argument of the addToTree method the address of the tree or subtree into which the word is added. The problem is that, if this (sub)tree is null, we have to set up a new LexiconNode containing the word and then put the reference to it somewhere. We cannot pass it back as an argument because it is the *value* of the reference to the LexiconNode that is passed to the method, and changing the formal argument would not change the actual argument. So we pass the reference to the new LexiconNode back as a return value to be stored in the appropriate place. If the first argument was not null, we pass back as return value the LexiconNode reference we were given.

18.3.4 *Outputting the Lexicon Information*

Finally, we need a display method for the Lexicon class to list in alphabetical order all the words and associated counts we have stored. This time we are going to do a recursive version because there is a natural recursive way of defining how to do this:

```
for any binary tree:
    display the left subtree
    display the root element
    display the right subtree
```

Incidentally, in the theory of binary trees, this is called an *inorder* traversal, because we visit the root element *in* between the visits to the left and right subtrees. There are also a *preorder* traversal, where we visit the root element *before* the left and right subtrees, and a *postorder* traversal, where we visit the root element *after* the left and right subtrees. They can both be defined recursively, in a similar way to inorder.

We write a private method displayLexiconElement to implement this recursive procedure:

```
private void displayLexiconElement(LexiconNode current)
    {
    if (current != null)
        {
        displayLexiconElement(current.left) ;
        System.out.println(current.word + "   " + current.occurrenceCount) ;
        displayLexiconElement(current.right) ;
        }
    } // end of method displayLexiconElement
```

and we call this from a public method `display`:

```
public void display()
    {
    displayLexiconElement(first) ;
    }
```

How would you write this as an iterative method? It is likely that you will have to use a stack to hold the various subtrees waiting to be dealt with, so to some extent you will be implementing a version of the run-time stack of the recursive version.

In the preceding recursive subroutines, we have examples of *direct* recursion where there is at least one explicit call of a method X in the body of the method X. It is also possible to have *indirect* or *mutual* recursion where, for example, method A might call method B and B might call A. As before, there must of course be some alternative course of action, otherwise we would have infinite recursion. In some programming languages, we have to warn the compiler of mutual recursion since it expects each method to be declared before it is called (and how can we have this, since one of A and B must precede the other?). But in Java, the compiler is clever enough to be able to deal with this situation without any requirement for an explicit warning from the programmer.

18.4 Key Points in Chapter 18

- *Recursion* involves describing the solution to a problem in terms of a simpler, smaller problem that is in some way related to the original problem.

- A recursive method thus typically contains one or more calls to itself with a "smaller" argument. When this argument is numeric, it may simply be the value of the argument less one. When it is a string or array or linked list, it may be the same structure with one less element.

- The recursive mechanism involves use of the run-time stack, which results in an overhead. However, the recursive solution to a problem may be more intuitive than an iterative one.

- A *binary tree* consists of a number of elements, each of which consists of some data and references to left and right subtrees (either or both of which may be null). There is a *root* element at the base of the tree. We can implement an element as an instance of a class that contains two instance variables of the same type as the class being defined.

- We can use a recursive method to traverse a binary tree in order to visit and process each of the elements in turn.

18.5   Exercises

1. The following are the Fibonacci numbers. The first two numbers are both 1, and each subsequent number is the sum of the preceding two numbers:

   1, 1, 2, 3, 5, 8, 13, 21, ...

   Write a recursive method to find the nth Fibonacci number for n specified in the argument. Write a program to test your method.

   Write an iterative method to perform the same calculation.

2. There is a function of two variables called Ackermann's function, which has a recursive definition:

ackermann(m, n) =	1	if m = 0
	2	if m = 1 and n = 0
	m + 2	if m > 1 and n = 0
	ackermann(ackermann	
	(m - 1, n), n-1)	otherwise

   Write a program to prompt the user for values of m and n and calculate the result. What is the value of ackermann(2, 1)? What about ackermann(4, 3)?

3. We want to be able to print out the contents of a string in reverse. Write a recursive method that:

   - Outputs the last character of the string.

   - Removes the last character.

   - Calls itself again with the shorter string.

4. Write a program to use the Lexicon class to print a list of all the distinct words in a large file of text. Make sure that your program is case insensitive; for example, you should treat the and The as the same word.

   The class WordFile (in java.lancs, derived from BasicFileIo) provides a method to read the next word from an input file and return it, returning null if there are no more words.

   In a sentence, the punctuation marks are usually written right next to the words, as in the (red) cat sat on the mat. Arrange your program so that, as far as possible, it eliminates these punctuation marks from the list of words.

5. Create a class SortedIntegerList, to hold a set of integers in sorted order. This class should provide the following services:

   - add, to add a new integer to the list—this should check that the value is not already in the list.

   - toString, to return the list of integers in sorted order.

   The SortedIntegerList should be implemented as a binary tree, but all details of the implementation should be hidden from the user.

   Write a suitable driver application program to test the class.

6. Add a method `delete` to the `SortedIntegerList` class to delete an element with a specified value.

   Hint: It is easy to delete an element from a binary tree if it has no dependent nodes (just delete it) or only one (replace the element to be deleted by its dependent node). If there are two dependent nodes, it is slightly more difficult. You have to look for the "next" element (or the "previous" element) in the inorder sequence, delete it from its current location, and insert it instead of the element to be deleted—this new element you have deleted must have no or one dependent node, so we know how to deal with this situation. See *Data Structures and Algorithms: A First Course* by Iain T. Adamson (Springer 1996), pages 68–71.

7. Here is a way to write a program to make a computer play a game of noughts-and-crosses (tic-tac-toe):

   a) Starting from the current position, generate all possible moves that the computer can make from this position—this leads to a number of new positions. For each of these positions, generate all possible moves by the opponent, leading to a further set of new positions. For each of these, generate all possible moves by the computer.

   Carry on like this until each position is a win for either the computer or the opponent or until there are no further possible moves and the game is a draw.

   b) This can be represented by a tree of possible positions, with the current position as the root element. This is sometimes called the *game tree* (see Figure 18-3).

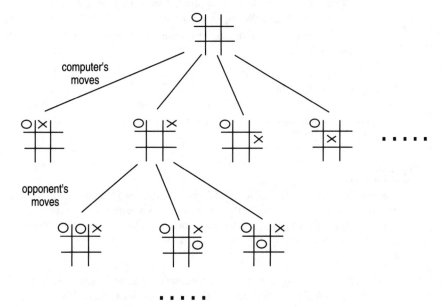

Figure 18-13: A game tree.

c) We mark each final position with a 1 if it is a win for the computer, a −1 if it is a win for the opponent, and 0 if it is a draw.

d) Suppose we have a position X where it is the computer's move, and all the positions we can reach by one move from X are marked with either a 1, a 0, or a −1. If any of these resulting positions is marked 1, we select one at random and write against X the number 1 and the selected move. If none of the resulting positions is marked 1, but some are marked 0, we select one at random and write against X the number 0 and the selected move. Otherwise, if all the resulting positions are marked −1, we select one at random and write against X the number −1 and the selected move. This implements the idea that the computer always chooses a winning move if there is one or plays to draw otherwise.

e) Suppose we have a position X where it is the opponent's move, and all the positions we can reach by one move from X are marked with either a 1, a 0, or a −1. If any of these resulting positions is marked −1, we select one at random and write against X the number −1 and the selected move. If none of the resulting positions is marked −1, but some are marked 0, we select one at random and write against X the number 0 and the selected move. Otherwise, if all the resulting positions are marked 1, we select one at random and write against X the number 1 and the selected move. This implements the idea that the opponent similarly always chooses a winning move if there is one or plays to draw otherwise.

f) We work back up the tree, applying this procedure (called *minimaxing*—can you see why?). Eventually we arrive at the root node. We make the move we have written against this element. This is the best move we can make (actually it may be one of the best moves).

Write a method that, given a position, returns the numerical value and the move assigned to the position by the above procedure.

Write a program, based on this method, that plays a game of noughts-and-crosses against a human opponent. The human and the computer should alternate for the first move.

Note

The numerical value returned for a position indicates the result if both players play as well as possible: 1 is a certain win for the computer, −1 is a certain win for the opponent, and 0 is a draw. Apply the method to the empty opening position. What does the resulting value tell you about the game of noughts-and-crosses?

8. In exercise 7, we suggested that you generate the tree and then traverse it, assigning values to the various elements. If you do this, you must visit all an element's dependent nodes before you can calculate the value for the element. So the traversal will look like this:

```
for the game tree:
```

```
visit the first subtree
visit the next subtree
...
visit the last subtree
visit the root element
```

This is a postorder traversal.

Actually we do not need to keep the whole of the tree. We just need to keep the path from the root to the element we are currently examining. The traversal looks like this.

For the current element:

- Visit the first subtree and remember the value and move.

- Visit the next subtree and remember the value and move if it is an improvement.

and so on

- Visit the last subtree and remember the value and move if it is an improvement.

- Pass back the value and the move that arrived at this element.

Although we generate and visit the whole tree, we do not actually need to set the tree up as a data structure. We need to keep only a stack representing the path from root to element. Rewrite your method to work this way.

9. Write a program to place eight chess queens on an 8 x 8 chessboard so that none of them can capture each other; i.e., no two of them must be on the same row, column, or diagonal line (see Figure 18-14).

Figure 18-14: A queen on a chessboard.

Hint 1

There must be exactly one queen on each row. So you could write a recursive procedure that tries to place a queen on each square of row i; if this is an acceptable position given the queens already placed in rows 1 .. $i-1$, call the same procedure again to consider positioning the queen everywhere in row $i+1$.

Hint 2

The obvious data structure for holding the proposed queen structure is a two-dimensional array representing the board and whether each square is occupied or not. A better data structure may be a one-dimensional array that specifies for each row which column the queen is in.

Optional Supplementary Problem:

Extend the program to make it display *all* possible positions for the eight queens, not just the first one encountered. Can you make it display only the distinct positions (i.e., eliminate all mirror image positions, etc.)?

CHAPTER 19

Input & Output in Java

19.1   Introduction

Any useful program must have some connection with the outside world. There are a very few, mostly trivial, programs that do not need any input to enable them to do their job (our first Java program, `Hello.java` was one), but usually a program needs some input from the outside world upon which to base its calculations. And any program is going to have to output its calculated results somehow; otherwise, what is the point of running it?

In the preceding chapters, we have met a number of ways by which a Java program can communicate with the outside world:

- In Chapter 1, we introduced the `System.out` object and its associated `print` and `println` methods to display at the user's terminal the results of the program's calculations. In this chapter, we explain exactly what sort of object this is and a number of related aspects.

- In Chapter 4, we provided a class called `BasicIo`, which contains a number of methods (for example, `readInteger`) to enable a program to read various different types of data (integers, strings, floating point numbers, etc.) when they are typed in by the user at the keyboard. In this chapter, we reveal the mechanism that underlies the methods of the class so that you can write code to enable your program to interact directly with the keyboard.

- In exercise 5.6, we introduced the `BasicFileIo` class, which enabled us to write programs that read data from, or write data to, files in the computer's filing system. Again, in this chapter we will be looking at the mechanisms used by this class that allow us to interact more directly with data in files.

- In Chapter 16, we met a completely different type of input/output system, provided by Java's AWT (Abstract Window Toolkit), which allows a program to draw various pictures, buttons, and text areas on the computer screen and receive input via the mouse and keyboard. Although in that chapter we only scratched the surface of the facilities provided by the AWT, we will not be pursuing that mechanism further here. You will need to read a more advanced book on the AWT for further information.

- For completeness, we need to mention one other method for the input of small quantities of data to a program, the command-line parameter mechanism introduced in section 3.12. This is a rather simple mechanism, and we have said all there is to say about it.

Thus, in this chapter we are going to look at the facilities that Java provides for simple input and output to the computer terminal or to the computer's file system. It turns out that this general mechanism can also be used in a number of other areas:

- If we have two or more programs running on a computer at the same time, we may wish to pass data to and fro from one to the other. The Java language allows us to specify a program as two or more independent subprograms, or *threads*, which can run on the computer conceptually at the same time. Java allows the communication between these threads to be provided by a form of input/output—the data output by one thread being the input to another thread. This type of mechanism is sometimes called a *pipe*; one program or thread feeds data into one end of the pipe, and another program or thread takes it out of the other end.

- Nowadays two communicating programs could be on two different computers connected by some form of communications link. Again, Java organizes the communication of data from our program to or from a program on another computer by the same overall input/output system. In particular, we can use Java's input/output system to obtain pages and other data from the World Wide Web. We give a brief example of such a program at the end of this chapter.

Many computer programming languages make a distinction between two types of input/output facility, which they see as quite distinct:

- One type of facility is for handling data in the form of (printable) characters, which are arranged in lines of text, with the lines of text possibly arranged in pages.

- A completely separate facility is then provided for handling data in the form of binary numbers.

As an example, let us consider how we might output the numerical value 1997:

- The first of the two types of input/output facilities would treat this as a series of characters representing the decimal digits of the number, as shown in Figure 19-1.

character 1	character 9	character 9	character 7

Figure 19-1: 1997 as a series of characters.

Exactly how much room this will take up would depend on the representation of characters the system is using. Stored using the popular ASCII character representation, each character would take up 1 (8-bit) byte. Stored using the Unicode character representation used in Java, each character may take up 2 8-bit bytes, since a much larger range of characters is represented. The number of units of storage taken up would, in this format, depend on the size of the number; the number 23 would require only 2 units, 19975 would require 5 units, and –23 would require 3 units (1 for the character representing the sign and 2 for the digits).

- An alternative way of holding the value 1997 is to use the way an integer is held inside the computer. It could be converted into a binary number, which is then held as a series of four bytes, as in Figure 19-2.

00000000	00000000	00000011	11001101

Figure 19-2: 1997 as a (4-byte) binary number.

If we hold a smaller number, or a negative number, or a larger number (as long as it is less than about two billion, and fits into a Java int), it will still take four bytes to hold the value. Furthermore, this type of format considerably reduces the amount of reformatting required, as compared with holding the number as a series of characters, since the format in which the number is held externally (on a file, for example) is almost exactly the same as the format in which it will be held internally in the store and registers of the computer.

As we have said, most programming languages provide two sets of facilities. One is a set of *character* file or *text* file facilities, for handling files consisting of lines consisting of characters. By extension, the computer keyboard and screen are treated as being of this type, as are streams of characters received over a communication line. Then there is a separate set of facilities, a set of *binary* file facilities, to handle data held in the underlying binary format.

Versions of Java up to and including 1.0.2 did not make the distinction in this way. The basic input/output facilities provided access to input or output data as a sequence of bytes of binary data, and some of the facilities were specialized to treat such a sequence of bytes as an encoding in some way of a sequence of characters making up a series of lines. In version 1.1 of Java, a further set of classes is provided, which are now the preferred method for handling the input and output of characters. In this chapter, we will be concentrating on the facilities that Java provides for handling data in the form of lines of (printable) characters, though we will mention briefly the facilities for handling data in binary form.

If we consider input/output between a program and a file, then there is another distinction to be made, between *sequential* access and *random* access to the file. With sequential access, we start at the beginning of the file and work our way, character by character or byte by byte, toward the end of the file. We could be reading data in from a file that previously exists, or we could be constructing a file from data calculated by the program. With random access, we can jump around the file, accessing one part and then another without visiting all the parts in between. It is feasible with random access to read part of the file and then change that part of the file without changing (or even reading) the other parts. Thus, if we have a file containing a set of bank accounts, it is feasible with random access to go to the part of the file corresponding to a particular bank account and read it into the computer, to change the data in some way (for example, to reflect a deposit or withdrawal), and then to write back the revised data without affecting the information held on anyone else's bank account.

With most other types of input/output (for example, piped to another program or read from the Web), the data *has* to be treated as sequential. Most of Java's i/o facilities therefore concentrate on providing sequential or *stream* access to data, but there are also facilities for handling random access to file data. In this chapter, we will similarly be concentrating on sequential access but will briefly mention random access in the appropriate place.

19.2   The Java Classes for Input & Output

The best way to explain the Java input/output facilities is first to present what is provided in version 1.0.2, since you still need to be familiar with some aspects of these facilities, and then to build on this knowledge in discussing the additional classes provided in version 1.1.

The basic classes provided by Java 1.0.2 for input and output (in the package `java.io`), illustrated in Figure 19-3, are:

- `InputStream` for input
- `OutputStream` for output

Figure 19-3: The basic Java 1.0.2 i/o facilities.

These are, in fact, *abstract* classes, and they specify the basic facilities provided by Java for input and output. The type of i/o provided is, as you can see from the names, stream i/o or what we have called sequential i/o. Thus the `InputStream` class considers input to be a stream or sequence of bytes of information, perhaps structured into lines of characters, or binary numbers, or whatever. Similarly, the `OutputStream` class considers output to be a stream of bytes, again perhaps derived from strings of characters or binary numbers inside the program creating it.

All the various different forms of i/o, such as to and from the user's terminal, or to and from a file, or through a pipe to another program, are provided by classes derived from these two basic classes, shown in Figure 19-4. The derived classes are arranged in such a way that they can be fitted together smoothly to provide exactly the facilities we need. The most important classes are `DataInputStream` for input, derived ultimately from `InputStream`, and `PrintStream` for output, derived ultimately from `OutputStream`.

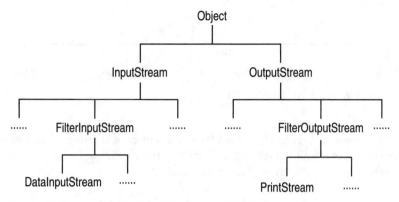

Figure 19-4: Input/output facilities in Java 1.0.2.

You will have noticed that these classes provide only sequential i/o, and do not provide the random access facilities mentioned earlier. For this, there is a separate class RandomAccessFile. This class is not derived from InputStream or OutputStream. However, to ensure commonality of facilities where possible, the class RandomAccessFile implements two interfaces called DataInput and DataOutput, as shown in Figure 19-5. The DataInput interface is also implemented by the class DataInputStream, and the DataOutput interface is implemented by a class called DataOutputStream, which is derived, like PrintStream, from OutputStream. More on this later.

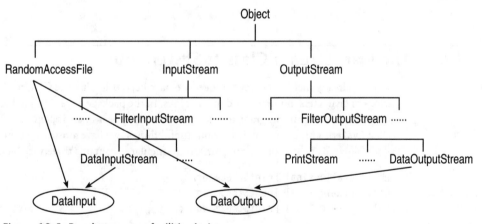

Figure 19-5: Random access facilities in Java.

As shown in Figure 19-6, version 1.1 of Java includes two new abstract classes, Reader and Writer, to provide (respectively) input and output of streams of characters.

Figure 19-6: The basic Java 1.1 i/o facilities.

As shown in Figure 19-7, the classes we will be discussing in this chapter, such as BufferedReader and PrintWriter, are derived from these classes (as are a number of other classes, which we will not need to refer to here).

Figure 19-7: Input/output facilities in Java 1.1.

19.3 The PrintStream Class & System.out

We have already met System.out; indeed we have been using it since Chapter 1 for displaying strings of characters, numbers, and other things. In the package java.lang (which, of course, is always available in our program and does not have to appear in an import statement) is a class called System. This class contains various useful things (we have already met the method exit, which allows us to abandon a program). In particular it contains three variables:

```
public static final PrintStream err ;
public static final InputStream in ;
public static final PrintStream out ;
```

So System.out is an instance of the PrintStream class, and it is usually connected to the user's display screen. Sending data to this stream makes it appear sequentially at the user's terminal.

The PrintStream class is derived ultimately from OutputStream (actually, it is derived from a class called FilterOutputStream, which is derived from OutputStream). The PrintStream class provides a set of methods that output values of various types in a suitable form, for example:

```
public void print(boolean b)
public void print(char c)
public void print(double d)
public void print(float f)
public void print(int i)
public void print(long l)
public void print(String s)
```

Each of these methods leaves the current output position immediately after the characters just displayed so that a further call of one of these methods would output a series of characters adjacent to the first call. This is illustrated in Figure 19-8.

Figure 19-8: Output—print followed by print(ln).

If we want to start a new line immediately after the characters output, we have an equivalent set of methods:

```
public void println(boolean b)
public void println(char c)
public void println(double d)
public void println(float f)
public void println(int i)
public void println(long l)
public void println(String s)
```

This is illustrated in Figure 19-9.

Figure 19-9: Output—println followed by print(ln).

There is also a method `println` with *no* argument which starts a new line without outputting any preceding value, as shown in Figure 19-10.

Figure 19-10: Output—using `println` with no arguments.

Normally, a line of characters is held in an internal buffer and not output until a new line is specified. However, the `flush` method outputs any characters currently in the buffer without waiting for a new line. So if we want to prompt the user to input a value, which is to appear on the same line as the prompt, we can write:

```
System.out.print("type the next value required ") ;
System.out.flush() ;
// read in the value
```

This is illustrated in Figure 19-11.

Figure 19-11: Output—use of the `flush` method.

We can use the concatenate operator + to put together a sequence of values to be printed out, as shown in Figure 19-12. Here we are attempting to concatenate the `String` `Today's date is` with the `Date` object `now`. In this type of situation, Java attempts to find a `toString` method for the required class, which should generate some form of `String` representation of the object. For the `Date` class, it finds one. If the class does not have a `toString` method, and neither do any of its ancestor classes, it will ultimately use the `toString` method of the `Object` class, and this returns a `String` that includes the class name.

Today's date is Thu Jun 12 16:44:46 GMT+01:00 1997

Date now = new Date() ;
             System.out.print("Today's date is " + now) ;

Figure 19-12: Output—use of the + operator.

Those `print` and `println` methods that output numeric values always output exactly as many characters as are required to represent the value specified. If we are trying to output a table of values, this is not quite what we want, as we need all the numerical values to appear in fields of the same width (with the positions of the decimal point, notional or otherwise, appearing in a vertical line one above the other). The `writeInteger` method in the `BasicIo` class has a second argument to specify the width in characters of the field in which the value of the first parameter is output.

19.3.1   *Output Redirection*

The `System.out` stream is usually connected to the user's screen. In some environments it is possible to *redirect* the output elsewhere. For example, if we have a Java program `Chapter19n1`, we can run it under the UNIX and Windows operating systems with output going to the screen:

```
java Chapter19n1
```

or we can run it with the output going to a file `xyz`:

```
java Chapter19n1 >xyz
```

No change is required to the program; everything output via the `System.out` stream is redirected to the file `xyz`. Sometimes this redirection causes problems because there are really two different types of data being output:

- The results of the program's calculations, which we presumably do want to be sent to the file (for subsequent printing or further processing).

- Messages to the user to do something, such as to input a value or take note of an error condition, which we would like *still* to come to the user's screen.

For this reason, the Java environment actually provides two `PrintStreams`, `System.out` and `System.err`. We should send any result data to `System.out` as before, and this will get redirected to a file if appropriate. However, prompts and error messages should be sent to `System.err`:

```
System.err.print("type in the next value ") ;
System.err.flush() ;
// read a value into x
System.out.println("the value of " + x + " squared is " + x * x) ;
```

If we run this with redirection, the prompt still comes to the user's screen, while the final line is redirected to the file.

19.4   The BufferedReader Class & System.in

We have already said that the System class contains a declaration of the variable in:

```
public static final InputStream in ;
```

Thus System.in is an instance of the InputStream class, and it is usually connected to the user's keyboard. Actually InputStream is an abstract class, so System.in must, in fact, be an instance of a concrete class derived from InputStream. It could be a BufferedInputStream, which is a class derived from InputStream with additional functionality.

In order to use this InputStream in a convenient way, we need to add further functionality. In particular, it is a stream of characters, so we are going to use the class BufferedReader, which is derived from the abstract Reader class. We construct an instance of a BufferedReader from the System.in stream with which we are provided, thus:

```
BufferedReader din = new BufferedReader(new InputStreamReader(System.in)) ;
```

This takes the System.in stream, "wraps" an InputStreamReader around it (to turn the bytes from the stream into characters), and then "wraps" a BufferedReader (which we have called din) around that, to provide a useful collection of methods.

The most useful method we have available as a result of this is one called readLine, which reads the next line of input from the keyboard (up to, but excluding, the keystroke that indicates the end of the line, Return or Enter) and returns this line as a String. Here is a piece of code that will read successive lines from the keyboard and display them (with println) until the user types in a line consisting of no characters:

```
BufferedReader din = new BufferedReader(new InputStreamReader(System.in)) ;
System.err.println("type in some lines, please") ;
while (true)
    {
    String line = din.readLine() ;
    if (line.length() == 0)
        break ;
    System.out.println("the line was **" + line + "**") ;
    }
System.out.println("**end of input**") ;
```

One small improvement might be that we would like to treat a line consisting only of spaces as if it was a line consisting of no characters and therefore terminating the loop. To do this, we could use the trim method from the String class (which deletes all leading and trailing spaces and tab characters):

```
BufferedReader din = new BufferedReader(new InputStreamReader(System.in)) ;
System.err.println("type in some lines, please") ;
while (true)
    {
    String line = din.readLine().trim() ;
    if (line.length() == 0)
        break ;
    System.out.println("the line was **" + line + "**") ;
    }
System.out.println("**end of input**") ;
```

19.4.1   Tokenizing an Input Line

Once we have read in a line of characters, we can process it. Usually a line can be expected to contain a succession of values or *tokens* (numbers, strings, etc.) separated by what is sometimes called *white space* (spaces or tab characters), such as in Figure 19-13.

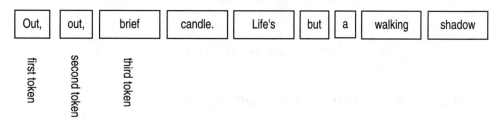

Figure 19-13: A line of characters divided into tokens.

We could of course write some code to do this, but Java provides a StringTokenizer class (in the java.util package) that does it for us. We first construct an instance of the StringTokenizer class from the line we have read in, and then we have available two methods:

- nextToken, to return a String that is the next token or sequence of characters between white space.

- hasMoreTokens, which tells us if there are any more tokens to process on this input line.

Here is some code to read a sequence of lines from the keyboard and display the successive tokens (using println):

```
BufferedReader din = new BufferedReader(new InputStreamReader(System.in)) ;
System.err.println("type in some more lines, please") ;
```

```
while (true)
  {
  String line = din.readLine().trim() ;
  if (line.length() == 0)
    break ;
  StringTokenizer st = new StringTokenizer(line) ;
  while (st.hasMoreTokens())
    System.out.println("the token was **" + st.nextToken() + "**") ;
  }
System.out.println("**end of input**") ;
```

Each line is read in, checked for an empty (or white-space-only) line, and then tokenized. As long as there are some more tokens on this line (indicated by the hasMoreTokens method), we can display the next token (provided by the nextToken method).

This version of the StringTokenizer assumes that the characters separating the tokens are one or more space or tab characters (or a new line character, if we had constructed a String containing such characters). Another constructor for the StringTokenizer class allows us, as a second argument, to specify a set of characters which are to be treated as separators. Suppose we wanted to tokenize a line where the individual tokens were separated by the vertical line character "|" ; we could write:

```
StringTokenizer st = new StringTokenizer(line, "|") ;
```

If we wanted to split the tokens with a space, comma, and period, we could write:

```
StringTokenizer st = new StringTokenizer(line, " ,.") ;
```

19.4.2 Converting Strings to Numeric Values

There is one further thing we will want to do, at least with some of the tokens. If the String we have read in represents a numerical value, we want that value rather than the character string.

For integers, Java provides us with the static method parseInt (in the Integer class), which takes a String as an argument and returns an int (there is a similar method for long). But for float and double, Java provides us only with a rather roundabout way of doing the conversion—we can convert the String to, say, a Double (that is the object-oriented "wrapper" version of double) using the static method Double.valueOf, and then we can extract the value and store it as a double with the doubleValue method. Here is an example:

```
BufferedReader din = new BufferedReader(new InputStreamReader(System.in)) ;
System.err.println("type an integer followed by a double") ;
String line = din.readLine().trim() ;
StringTokenizer st = new StringTokenizer(line) ;
int firstValue = Integer.parseInt(st.nextToken()) ;
System.out.println("the first value is " + firstValue) ;
double secondValue = Double.valueOf(st.nextToken()).doubleValue() ;
System.out.println("the second value is " + secondValue) ;
```

For simplicity, we have omitted the calling of the `hasMoreTokens` method, which would ensure that there is a value to convert.

You can see now why we hid this inside the `BasicIo` class when you were starting to program in Java!

What happens if we type in a string that cannot be converted to an appropriate number? We get a `NumberFormatException`. It would be better if we caught this exception, and told the user to try again. Here is a revision of the code to try to ensure that the user types in a sensible pair of values:

```
BufferedReader din = new BufferedReader(new InputStreamReader(System.in)) ;
System.err.println("type an integer followed by a double") ;
boolean invalidInput = false ;
int firstValue = 0 ;
double secondValue = 0.0 ;
do
   {
   String line = din.readLine() ;
   StringTokenizer st = new StringTokenizer(line) ;
   try {
      firstValue = Integer.parseInt(st.nextToken()) ;
      secondValue = Double.valueOf(st.nextToken()).doubleValue() ;
      invalidInput = !isInputOK(firstValue, secondValue) ;
      }
   catch (NumberFormatException e)
      {
      invalidInput = true ;
      }
   if (invalidInput)
      System.err.println("ERROR: retype both values") ;
   }
while (invalidInput) ;
System.out.println("the first value is " + firstValue) ;
System.out.println("the second value is " + secondValue) ;
```

As before, we read in a line, tokenize it, and try to extract the integer and double values from the characters read. If we succeed, we call a method we have provided called `isInputOK` to tell us whether or not the two values are acceptable—for example, that each value lies in a suitable range, and that the combination of the two values is also acceptable. On the basis of the (Boolean) value returned, we set the value of the Boolean variable `invalidInput`. If this has the value `true`, we print out an error message. In this example, the error message is particularly unhelpful; we should really have made the `isInputOK` method return much more information about what it doesn't like about the input values, and then we could construct a more helpful error message. We put all this code inside a loop (in this case a `do ... while` loop, where the test is at the end), and the code is repeated until the `invalidInput` variable is set to `false`, indicating that the values are now acceptable. We can then proceed to make use of the values we have read in.

We now want to trap the exceptions. We put the conversion of the strings to numerical values inside a `try` block, and we catch the exception `NumberFormatException`. If this exception occurs, we want to set the Boolean variable `invalidInput` to `true` so that we print the error message and repeat the loop at least one more time.*

Since the `isInputOK` method does not give us any information about *which* value is erroneous, we have simply required the user to type both values in again. It might be better:

- To read in the first value, convert that to a number (catching any exceptions), and test that it has a sensible value.

- And then to read in the second value on a new line, convert that to a number (catching any exceptions), and test that it has a sensible value (both considered by itself, and considered in combination with the first value).

In this way we would be able to print more precise error messages and require the user to retype only the minimum of information.

19.4.3   Redirection of Input

In the previous section, we discussed redirection of the `System.out` stream to a file. On some systems we can do the same for `System.in`. If we run our Java program with:

```
java Chapter19n1 <text.data
```

then `System.in` is connected to the file `text.data` rather than to the user's keyboard. If we make a `BufferedReader` from `System.in`, as we did earlier, we can use the `readLine` method to read successive lines of characters from this file, using exactly the same mechanism as if the lines came from the user's keyboard. What happens if the program reads past the last line in the file? In this case, the `readLine` method returns the value `null` rather than a `String`—we can test for this if we want:

```
BufferedReader din = new BufferedReader(new InputStreamReader(System.in)) ;
System.err.println("type in some more lines, please") ;
while (true)
    {
    String line = din.readLine() ;
    if (line == null)
        {
        System.err.println("fell off the end of the file") ;
        break ;
        }
```

---

* You may be wondering why we do not have to say `throws NumberFormatException` in the header line of the method containing this code. This exception is derived from the class `RuntimeException`, which contains exceptions likely to arrive in the normal course of running a Java program. Java does not require exceptions derived from `RuntimeException` to be put in the throws list.

```
      line = line.trim() ;
      if (line.length() == 0)
         break ;
      StringTokenizer st = new StringTokenizer(line) ;
      while (st.hasMoreTokens())
         System.out.println("the token was **" + st.nextToken() + "**") ;
      }
   System.out.println("**end of input**") ;
```

We have to check that the value returned is a `String` (rather than `null`) before we can apply the `trim` method to it. The prompt message will, of course, still be sent to the user's screen, even though we are reading in from a file. Input redirection is a useful mechanism if we want to be able to read in from *either* the keyboard or a file. If we know we want to read from a file, it is better to use the `FileReader` facilities, discussed in section 19.6.2.

19.5   Files & File Handling

We are now going to look at the facilities provided by Java to allow us to manipulate and, in particular, read data from and write data to files in the filing system on our computer. We could of course use the redirection features mentioned in the previous section if they are provided on our platform. Or we could use the facilities we have provided as the `BasicFileIo` class to allow simple access to file data. But to do serious work with the file system, we need to understand the facilities that Java provides.

We start with a brief reminder about the structure of the filing system on a computer; for more details refer to section 1.6. Useful information is held in *files* in the filing system, and files may be grouped together into *directories* (sometimes called *folders*). When we start to use the system, we will be placed at some position within this tree, the *current directory*, and there will be facilities for making some other directory the current directory. If we want to refer to a file in the current directory, we simply specify its name. Files in other directories are specified by a *path name* from the current directory or from the filing system's *root directory*.

Java provides a `File` class that allows us to manipulate files as a whole from within a Java program. We start by declaring a variable of this type, specifying the name of the file as an argument to the constructor:

```
File file1 = new File("text1.data") ;
```

This allows us to manipulate a file called `text1.data` in the current directory. There does not actually have to be a file of this name in the current directory—we can find out if there is one with the `exists` method:

```
BufferedReader din = new BufferedReader(new InputStreamReader(System.in)) ;
System.err.print("type a file name: ") ;
System.err.flush() ;
String fileName = din.readLine().trim() ;
```

```
File file1 = new File(fileName) ;
System.err.print("the file '" + fileName) ;
if (file1.exists())
   System.err.println("' exists") ;
else
   System.err.println("' does not exist") ;
```

Similarly, we can find out if we are allowed to read the file (with the `canRead` method) or write to it (with the `canWrite` method) and how long it is (in bytes) with the `length` method. We can find out whether the file is a directory with the `isDirectory` method; if it is, we can get a list of all the files in it with the `list` method, which returns an array of `String`s that are the filenames in the directory. We will see an example of `isDirectory` and `list` in section 19.6.2.

When we constructed the `File` instance, we specified the name of a file in the current directory. We could have specified a path name:

```
File file1 = new File("misc/letters/toBeth") ;
```

This assumes that the separator between directory names in the path is /, which is not true for all systems, for instance on the Windows operating system the above string would need to be written `misc\letters\toBeth`. The Java `File` class provides several constants specifying system-dependent values like this. In particular, it provides a `String` variable `separator`, which specifies the separator between directories in a path on the current platform, so we could write:

```
File file1 = new File("misc" + File.separator + "letters" + File.separator +
   "toBeth") ;
```

There are also `File` constructors with two arguments, the first specifying the directory (either a `File` that we have already constructed or a `String` that is the path name) and the second a `String` representing the name of the file.

Once we have constructed a `File` instance, we can manipulate the file in the filing system with which it is connected. We can:

- Delete the file with the `delete` method.
- Rename the file with the `renameTo` method.
- Create a directory with the `mkdir` method (and then presumably go on to create some files in this directory).

19.6   Reading & Writing Files

Of course, what we really want to do is read information from, or write information to, a file. For this, Java provides streams called `FileReader` and `FileWriter`, derived respectively from `Reader` and `Writer`, as shown in Figure 19-14. In order to make the data easy to manipulate, we usually want to add an extra layer of functionality on top of these types of streams.

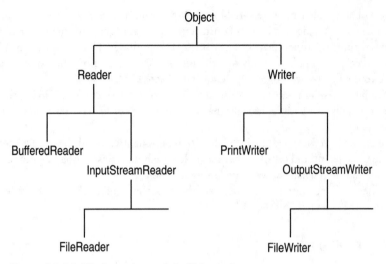

Figure 19-14: File input/output facilities in Java.

19.6.1   *Writing to a File*

We first consider output. We want to use the convenient facilities of a `PrintStream` for output of data, but in version 1.1 of Java, we in fact use a `PrintWriter`, which provides the same methods (`print`, `println`, and so on). We are going to manipulate a `FileWriter` using these facilities. Here is an example:

```
BufferedReader din = new BufferedReader(new InputStreamReader(System.in)) ;
System.err.print("type a file name: ") ;
System.err.flush() ;
String fileName = din.readLine().trim() ;
PrintWriter pout = new PrintWriter(new FileWriter(fileName)) ;

int noLines = 0 ;
while (true)
   {
   System.err.print("next line? ") ;
   System.err.flush() ;
   String line = din.readLine().trim() ;
   if (line.length() == 0)
      break ;
   noLines++ ;
   pout.println(noLines + ":" + line) ;
   }

pout.close() ;
System.err.println(noLines + " lines output to file '" + fileName + "'") ;
```

We obtain a filename (the variable `fileName`) from the user, and we create a `PrintWriter` instance `pout`. We do this by first constructing a `FileWriter` with the specified filename and then wrapping the functionality of a `PrintWriter` around it. This will create the file if it doesn't exist or set it to empty and ready to write into if it does exist. If we did not have permission to write to the file, we would get a `FileNotFoundException`.

We have used a `FileWriter` constructor that required a `String` specifying the filename (or more generally, the path name); another version of the constructor takes a `File` instance as an argument.

Since we have wrapped the `PrintWriter` functionality around the `FileWriter`, we can use all the usual `print` and `println` methods. Here each line consists of a line number, the character ":", and then whatever was typed in by the user.

When we have finished, we should use the `close` method to close the file, breaking the link between the program and the file.

19.6.2   Reading From a File

We now consider input, and we are going to look at the little program `Chapter19n4.java` to display the contents of any specified file. To make it a bit more interesting we have written a graphical user interface to this program, making use of the menu facilities introduced in the program `Chapter16n4.java` in Chapter 16. When the user selects the Load button on the menu, the method `loadFile` is called (as before). The full program is available on the Web site (see Appendix A), but `loadFile` looks like this:

```
private void loadFile()
    {
    FileDialog d = new FileDialog(this, "Load File", FileDialog.LOAD) ;
    d.setVisible(true) ;
    name = d.getFile() ;
    directory = d.getDirectory() ;
    try {
        File s = new File(directory, name) ;
        if (s.isDirectory())
            {
            String[] list = s.list() ;
            String t = "" ;
            for (int i = 0 ; i < list.length ; i++)
                t = t + list[i] + "\n" ;
            area.setText(t) ;
            }
        else // file is not a directory
            {
            FileReader s0 = new FileReader(s) ;
            BufferedReader s1 = new BufferedReader(s0) ;
            String t = "" ;
            while (true)
```

```
                        {
                        String line = s1.readLine() ;
                        if (line == null)
                           break ;
                        t = t + line + "\n" ;
                        }
                   s1.close() ;
                   area.setText(t) ;
                   }
             }
         catch(IOException e)
             {
             System.err.println("ERROR: " + e) ;
             }
         } // end of method loadFile
```

As before, the facilities provided by the FileDialog class allow us to have the user select the name of a file to read (and a directory). We then create an instance of the File class, given the directory and filenames supplied by the user (using a version of the File constructor which takes these as two separate String arguments) and find out if it is a directory or a normal file.

If it is a directory, we obtain a list of the names of the files contained in it with the list method. We are going to display this information with an instance of a class TextArea, which allows multiple lines of text to be displayed, scrolling through the text if necessary. We have declared area as an instance field of type TextArea in the class Chapter19n4 (which extends Frame, as usual for graphical interfaces). In the constructor for the Chapter19n4 class, we specify that the text area is to have 10 rows and 50 columns:

```
public class Chapter19n4 extends Frame implements ActionListener
    {
    TextArea area ;
    ...

    public Chapter19n4()
        {
        ...
        area = new TextArea(10, 50) ;
        add("Center", area) ;
        } // end of constructor method

    ...
```

Then when we want something displayed, we call the method setText, passing it the String we want to display (with \n characters where we want the new lines to start).

If the file is not a directory, we want to read its contents. This time, as an illustration, we first create a FileReader called s0, passing as argument to the constructor method the File instance s, which we have already set up. Then we wrap a BufferedReader called s1 around it to give us the functionality we need.

We read the data from the file using the `readLine` method provided as part of the `BufferedReader` facilities, and we create a suitable string to pass to the `setText` method of the `TextArea` instance. When there are no more lines to read, the `readLine` method returns the value `null` instead of a `String`. If the number of lines warrants it, the `TextArea` instance will allow us to scroll through the file.

If the file did not exist, or it was not readable, the exception `FileNotFoundException` would be thrown. We catch any `IOExceptions` that are thrown, and we simply output an error message.

Since we have wrapped a `BufferedReader` around the `FileReader`, all the usual `BufferedReader` facilities are available. Similarly, all the discussion of `StringTokenizers` in Section 19.4.1 still applies—we could have tokenized each line after reading it in if that had been what we wanted.

When we have finished reading the file, we remember to close it with the `close` method.

19.7   Binary Files (optional)

We have assumed that all the files we read and write consist of lines of characters. When we read, say, an integer from such a file, we read it as a series of printable characters. We then have to turn them somehow into the binary format in which such numbers are held in the store of the computer (of course, we don't have to do this ourselves; Java supplies methods to allow us to do it). But, as discussed in Section 19.1, we could store an `int` value in a file as four bytes in a format much closer to how it is held internally.

The streams `DataInputStream` and `DataOutputStream` provide methods for reading and writing data in this binary format. We could write a binary integer:

```
BufferedReader din = new BufferedReader(new InputStreamReader(System.in)) ;
System.err.print("type file to write to ") ;
System.err.flush() ;
String fileName = din.readLine().trim() ;
DataOutputStream dout = new DataOutputStream(new FileOutputStream(fileName)) ;

System.err.print("type integer to write ") ;
System.err.flush() ;
String number = din.readLine().trim() ;
int number1 = Integer.parseInt(number) ;

dout.writeInt(number1) ;
dout.close() ;
```

We construct a suitable `FileOutputStream` and wrap a `DataOutputStream` around it (just as we wrapped a `PrintWriter` around a `FileWriter`). Then we can write an `int` in binary format with the `writeInt` method. There are methods for writing all the other primitive data types; consult the documentation for the `DataOutputStream` class.

If we look at this file with a suitable program (not a normal editor, since that expects printable characters; on UNIX we can use the od program), we will see that four bytes have been written containing the binary value of the integer we have written.

We can read data back from the file in binary format in a similar way, using the readInt method of the DataInputStream class:

```
BufferedReader din = new BufferedReader(new InputStreamReader(System.in)) ;
System.err.print("type file to read from ") ;
System.err.flush() ;
String fileName = din.readLine().trim() ;
DataInputStream din1 = new DataInputStream(new FileInputStream(fileName)) ;

int number = din1.readInt() ;
System.err.println("the number was " + number) ;
din1.close() ;
```

19.8   Random Access Files (optional)

So far we have treated files in the filing system as streams of data; we can start at the beginning of an empty file and write data items one after another to the file. Or we can start at the beginning of the file and read our way through it from the beginning to the end (or as far as we want to read). When we open a file, we decide whether we are going to be reading from it or writing to it, opening a FileReader or a FileWriter as appropriate.

But we might need to be able to move around from one part of a file to another to modify the file selectively without visiting all the parts in between. If, for example, we imagine a file containing information about a lot of bank accounts, and we have to record a deposit or a withdrawal, we would want to go to the part of the file containing that account, read in the information about the account, change the balance, and write the information back to the appropriate part of the file without reading or affecting the other bank accounts in any way.

Java provides a class called RandomAccessFile that provides this type of access to the data. When we construct an instance of this class, we specify the file (as a String or a File) and a "mode," which is either r (we can only read the file with this instance) or rw (which means we can read or write to the file).

We can go to a particular position in the file with a method called seek. The position is specified as a number of bytes from the beginning of the file. If we specified the position as the length of the file, we could add new information at the end of the file.

When we have placed ourselves at the appropriate position in the file, we can then read or write information. As we have already mentioned, the RandomAccessFile class actually implements two interfaces, DataInput and DataOutput, which are also implemented by the classes DataInputStream and DataOutputStream. So, in fact, we have similar methods to those we have already seen—readInt, writeInt, and so on.

Random access files are discussed in more detail in Chapter 23.

19.9 Accessing Other Computers (optional)

Since an important feature of Java has been its use over networks of computers, the language provides a comprehensive range of facilities for communication between one computer and another. This is beyond the scope of this book, but we mention the basic features to whet your appetite.

The most basic facility provided by Java is a class `Socket` (in the package `java.net`). We can open a communication link by setting up a `Socket` and specifying the name of the computer and the port number on that computer we wish to connect to:

```
Socket s = new Socket(hostName, portNumber) ;
```

We can then construct a character reader or writer around this link (assuming it can be expected to transmit characters) and use the usual methods:

```
BufferedReader s1 = new BufferedReader(new
    InputStreamReader(s.getInputStream())) ;
String line = s1.readLine() ;
```

Java provides facilities for accessing the World Wide Web, and we finish this chapter with a simple example:

```
BufferedReader din = new BufferedReader(new InputStreamReader(System.in)) ;
System.err.print("URL? ") ;
System.err.flush() ;
String urlString = din.readLine().trim() ;

try {
   URL s = new URL(urlString) ;
   BufferedReader s1 = new BufferedReader(new
   InputStreamReader(s.openStream())) ;

   while (true)
      {
      String line = s1.readLine() ;
      if (line == null)
         break ;
      System.out.println(line) ;
      }
   }
catch(IOException e)
   {
   System.err.println("ERROR: " + e) ;
   }
```

We request a URL from the user; that is, an address on the Web, such as `http://www.lancs.ac.uk/`. We:

- Create an instance of the class `URL` (from the `java.net` package) using this `String`.

- Create an input stream to read from this location on the network with the `openStream` method.

- Wrap a `BufferedReader` around this input stream to allow us to use the usual facilities.

As before, we now have the usual range of `BufferedReader` methods. Here we use the `readLine` method to obtain successive text lines. We are assuming it *is* a text file, such as a normal Web page of information with interspersed HTML markers.

We need to catch any exceptions thrown by the process of making the connection. For example, if we type in rubbish at the user prompt, we are likely to get a `MalformedURLException`.

19.10   Key Points in Chapter 19

- Java provides a host of classes in the package `java.io` to support input to and output from an application. The main (abstract) classes are `InputStream`, `OutputStream`, `Reader`, and `Writer`, and a number of useful classes are derived from these fundamental classes.

- The `PrintStream` class is a concrete class that provides convenient output facilities; `System.out` is a `PrintStream` instance. This means that `print`, `println`, and `flush` (all of which we have used with `System.out`) are actually methods that belong to the `PrintStream` class.

- In some systems (i.e., UNIX and Windows), we can redirect `System.out` from the screen to a file using the > symbol. For example:

`java TestProgram >results`

places the output from the `TestProgram` application (everything that is written to `System.out`) in the file `results`.

- Another `PrintStream` instance that is available to us is `System.err`. Like `System.out`, `System.err` outputs to the screen, but when `System.out` is redirected, `System.err` still outputs to the screen. This is useful if the application needs to prompt the user—for example, for an item of input data.

- `System.in` is an instance of a concrete subclass of `InputStream`. To use `System.in` in a convenient way, we need to add functionality by wrapping it in an instance of the `BufferedReader` class:

`BufferedReader din = new BufferedReader(new InputStreamReader(System.in)) ;`

- `BufferedReader` provides a number of useful methods, such as `readLine`, which reads the entire next line as a `String`.

- It is often useful to be able to split up a line into recognizable tokens (and also to throw away any unwanted white space). Java provides the class `StringTokenizer` to support this:

```
StringTokenizer st = new StringTokenizer(line) ;
if (st.hasMoreTokens())
    String word = st.nextToken() ;
```

- Another version of the `StringTokenizer` constructor method allows us to choose the characters that separate the tokens.

- To handle the management of files, Java provides the `File` class with the following methods:
  - `exists`   Finds out if the file exists.
  - `canRead, canWrite`   Finds out if we can read from, write to the file.
  - `length`   Finds out how many bytes long the file is.
  - `isDirectory`   Finds out if the file is a directory.
  - `list`   Finds out what files a directory holds.
  - `delete`   Deletes a file.
  - `renameTo`   Renames a file.
  - `mkdir`   Creates a new directory.

- To read and write files, Java provides the classes `FileReader` and `FileWriter` respectively. As with `System.in`, it is often useful to wrap instances of these classes as instances of another class that provides additional functionality.

- For example, if we wrap up a `FileWriter` instance within a `PrintWriter` instance, we can use the `print` and `println` methods we are used to:

```
PrintWriter pout = new PrintWriter(new FileWriter(fileName)) ;
...
pout.println("I am writing to the file") ;
...
pout.close()
```

- Similarly, we can wrap a `FileReader` instance within a `BufferedReader` and provide the `readLine` method:

```
BufferedReader fin = new BufferedReader(new FileReader(fileName)) ;
...
String line = fin.readLine() ;
...
fin.close()
```

At the end of the file, `readLine` will return null.

- The `DataInputStream` and `DataOutputStream` classes (derived from `InputStream` and `OutputStream`) provide methods that allow us to read and write the basic Java types in binary—for example, we can use `readInt` and `writeInt` for `int` values.

■ In addition to reading and writing data sequentially (that is, starting at the beginning of the file and working through it, reading or writing data), sometimes we need to have random or direct access to a file. Java provides a `RandomAccessFile` class that provides this kind of access. In addition to the methods that `DataInputStream` and `DataOutputStream` provide, there is also a `seek` method, which allows us to change our position within the file as required.

19.11 Exercises

1. Write a program that reads a sentence typed in as a single line at the keyboard and outputs each word on a separate line. This program should not use any of the facilities of the `BasicIo` class and should use the `StringTokenizer` class to split the line into words. Words can be assumed to be sequences of non-white-space characters separated by white space.

2. Write a program that prompts the user to type in the path name of a file and then prints out the components of the path one per line. So, if the path name is `roger/Java/done/prog1`, it should output:

```
roger
Java
done
prog1
```

Modify the program so that it indicates whether the path is absolute (it starts with the file separator symbol) or not.

3. Rewrite your solution to exercise 16.6 (the `CountyMap` class) so that:

a) The argument to the constructor is a `BufferedReader` rather than a filename (so the driver program will open the appropriate file and wrap it up in a `BufferedReader` as the actual argument for the constructor method).

b) The X- and Y-coordinates of each point on the boundary, and the name, X- and Y-coordinates of each location, should now be held one per line in the file, as follows:

```
37
253,  25
238,  25
. . .
22
Bodmin, 193, 115
Bude,   238,  45
. . .
```

You should decide what ranges of X- and Y-coordinate values are appropriate, and your program should validate the input values accordingly.

4. Write a program that prompts the user for a filename and then outputs whether a file of that name exists in the current directory. If it does, it should also output:

   - Whether the file can be read from or written to.
   - How long the file is.
   - Whether it is a directory.

5. A file contains information about students on a computer programming course. The students have supplied a number of lines of information about themselves, and these have been collected together into a single file. Each student's information should commence with a line consisting only of the word DATA, followed by five lines containing, respectively, the surname, one or more forenames, the practical class number (in the range 10 to 20), the college (one of Bowland, Lonsdale, Cartmel, County, Furness, Fylde, Pendle, and Grizedale), and the name of the major course. Unfortunately, at the time the students typed in this information, they had not yet learned about the importance of accuracy in data input. You can therefore expect there to be a number of errors in the data supplied, and your program should do as much checking as possible, outputting information about any problems encountered.

   Your program should input a file of student information as described, and output a list of all students in alphabetical order of surname, a list of students in each practical class, and a list of students in each college.

   You should write a short report indicating what types of error your program would be unable to check for.

6. Write a program that reads a file of sales details and prints invoices for the sales. The first version of the program should expect the file to consist of several sets of sales details, one per customer, in the form:

```
SALE sales number
date in a suitable form
customer name and address in the form "name / first line of address /
    second line of address ...
number sold, item description, cost per item for the first item
    (separated by / characters)
number sold, item description, cost per item for the second item
    (separated by / characters)
number sold, item description, cost per item for the third item
    (separated by / characters)
...
END
```

Each sales invoice should look like this:

SALE by Java Industries Ltd

TODAY'S DATE: 5/4/97   DATE OF SALE: 2/3/97

customer name
customer address line 1
customer address line 2
customer address line 3

NUMBER	DESCRIPTION	ITEM COST	TOTAL COST	VAT
number of 1st item	description of 1st item	item cost of 1st item	total cost of 1st item	vat on of 1st item
number of 1st item	description of 1st item	item cost of 1st item	total cost of 1st item	vat on of 1st item
number of 1st item	description of 1st item	item cost of 1st item	total cost of 1st item	vat on of 1st item
...				
TOTAL		total of this column	total of this column	total of this column

PLEASE PAY: sum of total cost + VAT

TERMS: 30 DAYS

Today's date should be obtained from the Java system using the Date class. The user should be prompted for the VAT rate—it should lie in the range 5 to 25 percent.

Modify the program so that the sales information gives a code number for each customer and item sold. Details of customers (name and address) and items (description and cost) should be looked up in separate files using these code numbers.

Creating & Using Applets

20.1 Creating Applets

So far the Java programs we have written have been what are called *applications*. An application runs in a completely *stand-alone* fashion, and the user directly requests the system to start it by typing a command or clicking on an icon. Most programs in other languages are applications. Now we are going to look at how to write what the Java system calls applets. An *applet* is a program that can be downloaded across the World Wide Web and run as part of a page displayed by a browser such as Netscape Navigator or Microsoft Internet Explorer.

An applet program is derived from the class Applet in the package java.applet. The Applet class is derived from the Panel class, part of the Abstract Window Toolkit we explored in Chapter 16. So an applet is displayed as some sort of panel on the browser page, on which it puts appropriate data and through which it reacts to user input.

In Chapter 16, we wrote a program that drew a smiling face. The program had a Change button with which we could change the smiling face to a sad face (and then back again). With our first example of an applet, we will take the smiling face program and change it from an application program to an applet. Here is the code for the main part of the program, the class Chapter20n1:

```
import java.awt.* ;
import java.awt.event.* ;
import java.applet.* ;

public class Chapter20n1 extends Applet implements ActionListener
    {
    Canvas1 canvas ;
    Button change ;
    String welcomeName ;
    boolean isSmiling ;

    public void init()
       {
       setLayout(new BorderLayout()) ;
       welcomeName = "World" ;
       isSmiling = true ;
```

```
        setBackground(Color.green) ;

        canvas = new Canvas1(this) ;
        add("Center", canvas) ;

        Panel p = new Panel() ;
        p.setLayout(new FlowLayout()) ;
        change = new Button("Change") ;
        p.add(change) ;
        change.addActionListener(this) ;
        add("South", p) ;
        } // end of method init

    public void actionPerformed(ActionEvent event)
        {
        isSmiling = !isSmiling ;
        canvas.repaint() ;
        } // end of method actionPerformed
    } // end of class Chapter20n1

    ...Canvas1...
```

We start off with a class Chapter20n1 derived from Applet (we have to import the package java.applet to make this work, of course). This has, as before, four instance fields:

- canvas, a reference to an object of the class Canvas1, which we will create as part of this program. It will be almost exactly the same as the Canvas1 class we studied as part of the Chapter16n1.java program in Chapter 16. We need to be able to refer to this object because, as before, we need to be able to request that it be redrawn when the Change button is pressed.

- change, a reference to the Change button.

- welcomeName, a String variable to form part of the welcoming message we are going to write on the screen.

- isSmiling, a Boolean variable to remember the current state of the face.

In the program Chapter16n1.java, we had a constructor method for the class Chapter16n1, in which we laid out the components we wanted to display, and a main method, which called the constructor and set things going. In an applet, we instead write a single method called init, and this is called by the browser when the applet is being started. It contains all the initial instructions to lay out the panel that will be displayed, as follows:

- The class Chapter16n1 was derived from the Frame class, which has a default layout manager BorderLayout. We now have to set this explicitly since Applet is derived from the Panel class, which does not have a default layout manager:

  setLayout(new BorderLayout()) ;

- In the earlier program, we obtained a name for the welcoming message from a command-line parameter and passed it as an argument to the constructor. This route is not available for an applet, so for the present we will set `welcomeName` to a default string. Later we will see how an applet can be passed parameters.

- We initialize the value of `isSmiling` to `true` as before.

- We set the background color.

- In the earlier program, we set the title to appear at the top of the window, and we specified the initial size of the window. Both of these are set up in a different way for an applet, from outside the program.

- We then set up the canvas and the button exactly as before and registered that an action is to be performed when the button is pressed. Notice that we have provided only the Change button. We have a different mechanism for stopping an applet when we leave the page on which it is displayed.

- The `actionPerformed` method needs to deal with only the Change button now. It reverses the value of the `isSmiling` Boolean variable and requests that the canvas be repainted.

- We no longer need the `windowClosing` method or the other methods associated with the `WindowListener` interface.

- Our `Canvas1` class is very much as before. It contains a constructor method to store away the reference to the `Chapter20n1` instance for later use, and it contains a `paint` method. The latter draws the face on the canvas with a mouth shape indicated by the Boolean variable `parent.isSmiling` and writes a message including the string `parent.welcomeName`.

20.2   Using Applets

We compile our Java applet in the usual way:

```
javac Chapter20n1.java
```

to generate the code file `Chapter20n1.class`. How are we going to run it? Ultimately we are, of course, going to run it from a browser. For the moment, while we are still debugging the code of our applet, there is a simpler and rather more straightforward mechanism—using a program provided as part of the Java Development Kit called the *appletviewer*.

An applet is always invoked (even by the appletviewer) through an HTML page. We write a very simple such page and put it in a file called `Chapter20n1.html`:

```
<html>
<title>
This is my first Applet
</title>
<body bgcolor="ffffff">
<p>
```

```
Here is my first example of an applet,
written in the Java programming language,
to display a smiley face.
<center><p>
<applet code="Chapter20n1.class" width=500 height=400>
</applet></center>
<p>
If you click on the "Change" button,
it will change to a sad face;
if you click on it again,
it will change back to a happy face.
That's all it does.
<center><p>
<a href="http://www.lancs.ac.uk/">Click here when you've finished</a>
</center>
</body>
</html>
```

In a page of HTML, portions of text are enclosed in HTML *tags*. Thus the text `This is my first Applet` is enclosed between a "begin title" tag `<title>` and an "end title" tag `</title>`, indicating that the text is to be displayed in the browser's title area when this page is being viewed. HTML tags start with the character <, followed by the name of the tag, followed by the character >; end tags have the character / before the tag name. A tag may have one or more attributes in the format "attribute name = attribute value". For example the `bgcolor` (i.e., background color) attribute of the `body` tag (indicating what is to be displayed in the main browser window) is set to `ffffff` (i.e., white), and the `width` attribute of the `applet` tag is set to 500. For more details on HTML see *Using HTML: The Definitive Guide* by Bill Kennedy and Chuck Musciano (O'Reilly & Associates 1997).

Text enclosed in <a> ... </a> tags indicates a *link* to another page. If we click on text enclosed in this way (it will appear <u>underlined</u> when the text is displayed), the browser fetches the page indicated by the `href` attribute and displays it. So if we click on the text `Click here when you've finished`, the browser fetches a page from the Web site `www.lancs.ac.uk` (actually, Lancaster University's home page) and displays it. The value of the `href` attribute, the address of a place on the Web, is called a *URL* or *Uniform Resource Locator*. It has a standard format. The characters `http:` mean *hypertext transfer protocol*, indicating that the normal Web protocol is to be used for obtaining and displaying this new page. The next part indicates the name of a Web server computer, and there may be a third part, which indicates a particular file on the Web server.

The only part of this file that is really required at present are the two lines:

```
<applet code="Chapter20n1.class" width=500 height=400>
</applet>
```

since the appletviewer ignores all the rest (the browser won't be so cavalier). This HTML says that:

- An applet is to be run.
- Its code is to be found in the file Chapter20n1.class in the same directory as the HTML page.
- It is to be displayed in an area 500 pixels wide by 400 pixels high (this replaces the call of the setSize method we used in Chapter 16).

If we now give the command:

```
appletviewer Chapter20n1.html
```

the appletviewer will display the applet in a window (as shown in Figure 20-1) so that we can test whether all its features work.

Figure 20-1: Viewing our first applet with the appletviewer.

When we are reasonably satisfied that the applet is free from bugs, we can try running it in earnest. We start up a browser and point it to the file Chapter20n1.html. Alternatively, we could insert a reference to this file on another HTML page and reach it that way. If we do this, the browser will display our applet (as shown in Figure 20-2), and we can try out the button and see that it works. Unlike with the appletviewer, the browser deals properly with the other information that we put in the file Chapter20n1.html. In particular the <title> tag causes the string This is my first Applet to be displayed in the browser's title area.

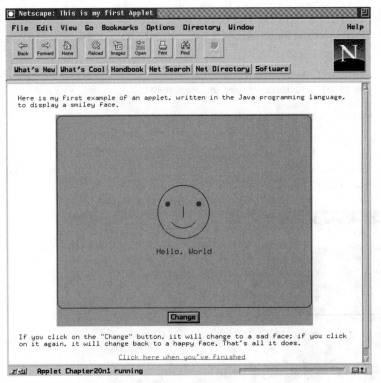

Figure 20-2: Viewing our first applet with a browser.

20.3   More About Applets

In the original smiley face program, we were able to pass a string to the program through a command-line parameter. We can do something similar with applets in that we can put parameters in the HTML page and have the applet read them when it starts up. Suppose we rewrite the HTML page with a `param` tag between the `<applet>` and the `</applet>` tags:

```
<applet code="Chapter20n1.class" width=500 height=400>
<param name="who" value="Roger">
</applet>
```

Now in the `init` method, we set up the `welcomeName` instance variable using the `getParameter` method, as follows:

```
welcomeName = getParameter("who") ;
if (welcomeName == null)
   welcomeName = "World" ;
```

The getParameter method searches for a parameter whose name field is who (it is sensitive to case) and returns the corresponding value field (as a String)—in this case it will return Roger. If it cannot find an appropriately named parameter, it returns the value null. We can have as many parameters as we want as long as they all have different name fields.

So far we have used only the init method for the Applet class. In fact, the Applet class provides four methods that we can override: init, start, stop, and destroy. Let us modify our applet again:

- We add as the first line of our init method the line:

```
System.err.println("call of 'init' method") ;
```

- We add three more methods:

```
public void start()
    {
    System.err.println("call of 'start' method") ;
    } // end of method start

public void stop()
    {
    System.err.println("call of 'stop' method") ;
    } // end of method stop

public void destroy()
    {
    System.err.println("call of 'destroy' method") ;
    } // end of method destroy
```

We now rerun our applet under the browser, but with the Java console window open, so we can see any messages sent to System.err by our applet. We will see that when the applet starts up, it calls init and then start. If the browser is not displaying the applet (the browser is iconified, or we have moved to a different page), then the stop method is called. When the applet is displayed again, the start method (but not the init method) is called. Finally, the destroy method is called when the browser stops.

Often we need to write only the init method. But if we are doing some extensive calculation (perhaps we are animating a display), we should stop when the page is not being displayed and start when the page is being displayed again—the stop and start methods allow us to do this.

20.4 A Useful Applet

We are now going to look at a simple but useful applet that displays a copy of any of the source code files for the programs described in this book as specified by the user of the applet. On the host computer, in the directory that holds the original copy of the HTML page (Chapter20n2.html) and this applet (Chapter20n2.class), we will store also:

- A copy of the source text file for each of the programs (for instance the files Chapter15n0.java and Chapter19n2.java).

- A list (the file `programList`) of all these text files, with an indication for each one of which chapter it belongs to (sorted into an appropriate order) in this format:

```
chap15/Chapter15n3.java
chap15/Chapter15n4.java
chap15/Chapter15n4a.java
chap15/Chapter15n5.java
chap15/Temperature.java
chap16/PriorityQueue.java
chap16/QueueElement.java
chap16/QueueEmptyException.java
chap17/Chapter17n1.java
chap17/Chapter17n2.java
chap17/Chapter17n3.java
chap17/Chapter17n4.java
```

When the HTML page and the associated applet are downloaded to the user's computer (the *client* computer) and the applet begins to run, it downloads the `programList` file and extracts the appropriate information for the user. When the user has selected a program to look at, the applet downloads that file and displays it. The mechanism is shown in Figure 20-3.

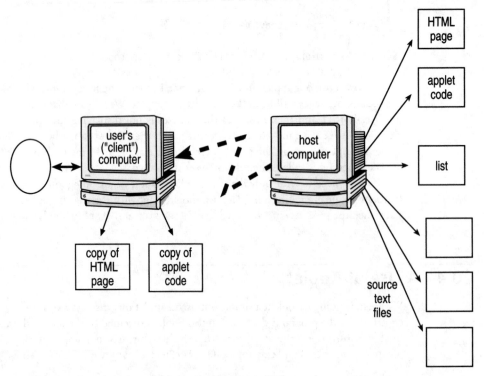

Figure 20-3: The mechanism of the `Chapter20n2` applet.

The user's view of the applet is shown in Figure 20-4.

Figure 20-4: The user's view of the Chapter20n2 applet.

There is a central area to display either a list of things that could be displayed or the text of the selected file (this is an instance of the TextArea class that we met in the previous chapter), a label at the top to indicate what we are looking at, and three buttons to allow the user to navigate through the information provided. We start with a list of chapters. When the user selects a chapter and presses the Chapter button, the applet lists all the programs in that chapter. When the user selects a particular program and presses the Program button, the applet displays the text of that program.

In some of the examples of using the Abstract Window Toolkit in Chapter 16, we would have put these buttons on a menu, allowing them to appear only when we need them. We cannot do that here. A Menu instance can be attached only to an instance of a class derived from Frame, and applets are derived from the Panel class rather than the Frame class. So we display the buttons along the bottom of the applet.

We do not give a full listing of the code for the program here because it is given in Appendix E. Notice the following points, however:

- This applet uses a lot of facilities provided by six different Java packages, so we need to import all these packages.

- In the class Chapter20n2 (derived from Applet), we have instance fields for all the AWT components we are going to need to manipulate during the course of the program—the label label at the top of the panel, the text area area in the middle, and the three buttons main, chap, and prog at the bottom.

- In the init method, we first read the file programList from the host computer and set up data structures containing the information—this is done in the private method readIndex, which we will look at shortly. We then specify details of the main panel and add the label, text area, and three buttons in the usual way.

We want the text to appear in the center of the label field, so we use a version of the Label constructor that allows us to specify this.

In this applet, we are going to ensure that the user can click on only the appropriate button or buttons at any particular time. For example, when the applet starts up, the user could press the Chapter button but not the Main Index or Program buttons. We therefore disable the first and third buttons with the setEnabled method with argument false; for completeness, we ensure that the Chapter button is enabled with the setEnabled method with argument true. When the applet is displayed, the disabled buttons will appear *grayed out* and will not react to the user.

20.4.1 *The readIndex Method*

In the readIndex method, the first thing we want to do is read the file programList file from the host computer.

The standard way to refer to the location of a piece of information on the Web is with a URL, or Uniform Resource Locator. Java therefore provides the URL class to model this important feature of the Web structure. The method getDocumentBase returns an instance of the URL class that refers to what is called the *document base*; that is, the location on the host computer where the HTML page and other documents can be found. In particular, this is the location of the programList file. There is also a getCodeBase method for returning a URL for the location of the applet code on the host computer if this location is different from that of the document base.

One form of the URL constructor method allows us to specify a URL as context and a String to represent a file within that context. The line:

```
URL index = new URL(getDocumentBase(), "programList") ;
```

uses this constructor to create a URL for the file programList within the context returned by the getDocumentBase method. That is, we construct a URL for the file programList in the same directory on the host computer as the original version of the HTML page that caused the applet to be started.

We can then create an instance of the BufferedReader class to read this file:

```
BufferedReader s1 = new BufferedReader(new
InputStreamReader(index.openStream())) ;
```

and then we can read the lines of the file with:

```
String line = s1.readLine() ;
```

until we reach a `null` line.

All sorts of things can go wrong with this process, and this would cause various exceptions to be thrown. For example, the URL that we are trying to set up may not make sense, in which case the `MalformedURLException` (derived from `IOException`) would be thrown. So we have to include this code in a `try` block. If an exception is caught, the program simply outputs an error message.

From the lines read in we create two data structures: an array called `progs`, which contains details of the individual entries in the list, and a `String` called `indexString`. The latter is a list of chapter names extracted from the first components of the lines (the part up to the / character). We have made use of the `StringTokenizer` class to chop up each line into the chapter name before the / character and the program name after. We also keep only one version of each chapter name, relying on the fact that the list is in alphabetical order. We use the `indexString` to set up the text area in the `init` method.

In this version of the program, we use arrays to hold the information about chapters and programs, and we have to decide on an upper limit to the array sizes—we have used the constant `maxNoOfProgs`, which we have set to 100. In the next chapter, we rewrite the applet using a Java class called `Vector`, which allows us to ignore the issue of how many programs there are to list.

20.4.2   *The actionPerformed Method*

We now look at the code of the `actionPerformed` method. The code consists of three sections corresponding to the three buttons. We are going to look in detail at the code corresponding to the Chapter button, which is the only one that is enabled when the applet starts up.

The program expects the user to have double-clicked on a particular line of the main index before pressing the Chapter button. The `TextArea` class provides two methods to enable the program to find out exactly which sequence of characters in the text the user selected. The `getSelectionStart` method tells us the position of the first character selected within the text string, and the `getSelectionEnd` method tells us the position of the last character selected within the text string.

The program uses these methods to obtain the position of the selected string of characters within `indexString`. It then uses information that was stored by the `readIndex` method in the array `progs` when `indexString` was set up to establish which line of the array was indicated and hence the name of the chapter selected. We leave it to you to follow through the code.

We chose to use a `TextArea` instance to display the list of chapter names and the `getSelectionStart` and `getSelectionEnd` methods to establish which one the user was interested in. In fact, Java provides a `List` class in the AWT to simplify this type of operation, and you could try looking at the API documentation and then modifying the program to use a `List`.

The program then goes through the original array progs looking for all program source text names belonging to this chapter. It makes a list of these names in an array progs1 and sets up a new text string indexString1 of the names to insert in the text area with the setText method. The contents of the label field at the top of the applet are changed to the chapter name using a setText method belonging to the Label class. Finally, the appropriate buttons are enabled or disabled.

If the Program button is pressed, then a sequence of actions takes place that is similar to the actions that take place when the Chapter button is pressed. We obtain the start and finish position of the selected text and establish which entry in the progs1 array corresponds to it and hence which program file has been specified.

We take this filename and construct a URL for this file in the context of the directory given by the getDocumentBase method:

```
URL t = new URL(getDocumentBase(), thisProg) ;
```

We then open this as a stream and wrap a BufferedReader around it:

```
BufferedReader s1 = new BufferedReader(new
                              InputStreamReader(t.openStream())) ;
```

Then we read in the lines of the file and display them:

```
while (true)
  {
  String line = s1.readLine() ;
  if (line == null)
    break ;
  ...
```

20.5   Security Aspects of Applets

A feature that we might like to add to the applet is a Save button so that we can save to a file on our local filing system the source code of any program we find interesting—but we cannot do this. While an applet is running in a browser, a *Security Manager* keeps track of anything the applet might try to do and disallows the things that are too dangerous (you can watch the error messages on the Java console in your browser). You should note that the appletviewer is not so careful; it will let your applet do things locally that the browser thinks are too dangerous to be done by an applet brought from another site and run on your computer.

An applet running in a browser cannot do either of the following:

■ It cannot read or write to a local file or in fact have any interaction with the local filing system. After all, it might corrupt some of our files, or it might take copies of interesting files and pass them back to the originating site.

- It cannot in general communicate with any other computer. This is a bit too restrictive. An applet is allowed to communicate with the site where it originated—in fact, we did that in the applet we have just looked at. But it cannot access any other computer. If it needs to access other parts of the Web, it will have to communicate with a program on the originating computer, which can then access the Web and pass back information as required.

There are a number of other restrictions, such as not being able to call the System.exit method, but these are the main ones.

20.6   Key Points in Chapter 20

- An *applet* is a Java program that can be downloaded across the World Wide Web and is executed as part of a Web page by a Java-aware browser.

- Applets are derived from the Applet class (in the java.applet package), and this class is in turn derived from the Panel class of the Abstract Window Toolkit. Applets are thus graphical in nature.

- When an applet is started up, the init method is called. This is similar to the constructor method for the class derived from Frame in an AWT program. The main differences are that we do not set the title or size of the window, there is no default layout manager, and we cannot use menus.

- Applets are compiled like ordinary Java applications but cannot be executed by the Java interpreter. They are always invoked via an HTML page, using the <applet> tag.

- To execute an applet, we can use a Java-aware browser, or during development and testing, we can use the *appletviewer* provided as part of the JDK.

- We can pass information from the HTML page to a running applet with the HTML <param> tag.

- We can obtain a URL for the directory containing the HTML page on the originating computer with the getDocumentBase method, and then we can read a file from that location as follows:

```
URL t = new URL(getDocumentBase(), fileName) ;
BufferedReader s1 = new BufferedReader(new
                InputStreamReader(t.openStream())) ;
while (true)
    {
    String line = s1.readLine() ;
    if (line == null)
        break ;
    ...
    }
```

- Because applets are executed locally on our machine, there are a number of security restrictions on what applets can do. The restrictions include *no* interaction with our local file system and *no* communication with other sites other than the applet's originating site.

20.7 Exercises

1. Take the program `Chapter16n2.java` (discussed in Chapter 16) to perform temperature conversion between Celsius and Fahrenheit and to display a thermometer and convert it to run as an applet.

2. Revise the task organizer, discussed in Chapter 11, to run as an applet.

3. Write a simple version of a Java applet that would allow a holiday-maker to access information about holiday accommodation over the World Wide Web. You will be supplied with a file `propertiesList` that contains details of the accommodation for one county in England (in fact, the data supplied will be for the county of Cornwall), and there will be one line per property—it will contain the location, the price, possibly an indication that the food is vegetarian (the characters `vegetarian`), the name of the property, and the contact telephone number (all separated by / characters). For example the file might begin:

```
Penzance / 145 / vegetarian / Queen's Hotel / 01736-12345
Newquay / 72 / Fistral Villas / 01434-65432
...
```

When the applet is running, it displays a map of the county in question. The user should be able to specify a location (such as `Penzance` or `Newquay`) or the word `any` (which matches any location), a range of prices (for example, 100 to 150), and whether or not they require vegetarian food. The applet should then search the list and display all the matching properties, indicating the location of the property or properties on the map.

A simple version might look like Figure 20-5.

Figure 20-5: A window layout for Exercise 20.3.

The task of writing this applet can be broken down into three main parts:

a) A class `PropertiesList` to handle the searching of the list of properties.

b) A class `CountyMap` to handle the drawing and displaying of the map.

c) A class `HolidayApplet` derived from the `Applet` class, which handles the overall graphical user interface and calls the methods of the other two classes. In particular, it calls the constructor methods of the other two classes, passing them instances of the `BufferedReader` class representing files of information on the host computer required by these classes. These `BufferedReader` classes should be set up using the `getDocumentBase` method.

The accessing of the `propertiesList` file should be done by the class `PropertiesList`, with the following methods:

- `public PropertiesList(BufferedReader din)`—This constructor method reads the properties list from the `BufferedReader` supplied as the argument.

- `public void searchProperties(String location, int lowerPrice, int upperPrice, boolean vegetarian)`—This method sets the arguments for searching the list for properties that match the user's specified location, price range, and vegetarian food requirements.

- `public boolean hasMoreProperties()`—This method indicates whether there are any more properties matching the current search requirements.

- `public PropertyDetails nextProperty()`—This returns the next property matching the current search requirements. It returns an instance of a class `PropertyDetails`, which should have the methods:

  ```
  public String getLocation()
  public String getName()
  public String getTelephone()
  ```

The drawing of the county map should be done by the class `CountyMap` (see Exercise 19.3).

CHAPTER 21

Other Features of Java

21.1 Vectors & Other Java Data Structures

In the `Chapter20n2` applet we studied in the last chapter, we needed to store various collections of information—details of the lines read in over the Web and how they are positioned in the text area. In that example, we used arrays of objects from a class called `ProgramDetails` to store the collections of information.

But as we know, there is a problem with arrays: we have to decide ahead of time how big the array should be, and we have to make sure we never attempt to exceed this limit. We did not bother to do this in the example program, as we knew that we had declared an array size that was going to be big enough (at least for the present), but this is extremely poor programming practice. Before adding an element to the array, we should have first checked that the current number of elements was less than the value `MAX_NO_OF_PROGRAMS`.

Furthermore, if the information had not been sorted into alphabetical order in the original file, we would have wanted to rearrange the elements in the array as we read them in, shuffling the elements around to get them into the correct order. We could alternatively have used a linked data structure, which does not have capacity restrictions and allows insertion into the middle of a list without rearranging the elements on either side.

21.1.1 The Vector Class

In Java there is another possibility. In the `java.util` package, there is a class called `Vector`, which provides us with what is essentially an array, but where we do not have to worry about capacity restrictions—it will simply reorganize itself to accommodate new elements. Furthermore, it provides methods for conveniently inserting elements in the middle of the `Vector` without the user having to worry about shuffling other elements to make room. Why have we not revealed the existence of the `Vector` data structure to you before so that you could avoid learning about arrays and linked lists? There are a couple of reasons:

- Many languages do not provide an equivalent of the `Vector` data structure, while they do have equivalents of arrays and (usually) the means to construct linked data structures. So to ensure that you have programming skills that transfer to other languages, you need to have studied these other features.

- There are some issues in the use of `Vector`s (and some of the other data structures provided by Java) that require you to know about the Java class hierarchy and how to cast objects from one type to another.

We start the new version of the `Chapter20n2` code by creating an instance `mainIndex` of the Vector type:

```
Vector mainIndex = new Vector() ;
```

We do not have to say anything about the expected maximum size of the `Vector`. If we wish, we could specify an initial size or an initial size and a size of *increment*; that is, how many new positions to allocate to the `Vector` each time the system makes it bigger. But if we do not specify these things, the `Vector` will organize them behind the scenes.

We can now add elements (of type `ProgramDetails`) to the `Vector` with the `addElement` method—this adds the element to the end of the `Vector`:

```
ProgramDetails newPD = new ProgramDetails(firstString, secondString,
   firstMarker, secondMarker) ;
mainIndex.addElement(newPD) ;
```

or:

```
mainIndex.addElement(new ProgramDetails(firstString, secondString,
   firstMarker, secondMarker)) ;
```

An example of the use of the `addElement` method is shown in Figure 21-1.

Figure 21-1: Using `addElement` on a `Vector`.

At any time, we can find the current size of a `Vector` with the method `size`. The elements stored in the `Vector` are numbered from zero to one less than the value returned by `size`. Some things we can do with a `Vector` are:

- We can add an element into the `Vector` at position i with the `insertElementAt` method (shuffling up the elements currently at i ... `size()`–1):

  ```
  mainIndex.insertElementAt(newPD, i) ;
  ```

This is illustrated in Figure 21-2.

Figure 21-2: Using `insertElement` on a `Vector`.

The second argument must be in the range zero to size. If it is equal to size, then the call of `insertElement` is equivalent to a call of `addElement`.

- We can change the element at a particular position with the `setElementAt` method, discarding the element that was previously there:

```
mainIndex.setElementAt(newPD, i) ;
```

This is illustrated in Figure 21-3.

Figure 21-3: Using `setElementAt` on a `Vector`.

The second argument must be in the range zero to one less than `size`.

- We can delete an element from the `Vector` with the `removeElementAt` method:

```
mainIndex.removeElementAt(i) ;
```

This is illustrated in Figure 21-4.

Figure 21-4: Using `removeElement` on a `Vector`.

- The argument must be in the range zero to one less than `size`. All elements with a higher index value will be shifted down.

At some point we want to look at an element in the `Vector`, say at position i, with the `elementAt` method:

```
ProgramDetails tempPD = mainIndex.elementAt(i) ;
```

This will not work. You will have spotted that when we set up the Vector in the first place, we did not specify that it was a Vector of ProgramDetails objects as we would if we had been declaring an array. In fact, a Vector is a Vector of Objects, and (using polymorphism) we can insert Objects of *any* type into a Vector. But when we want to extract an element, as we do in the statement above, we are trying to copy an instance of Object to a variable that holds references to objects of type ProgramDetails, and the Java compiler will not let us do this. We have to *cast* the object we get back from the Vector to the correct type:

```
ProgramDetails tempPD = (ProgramDetails) mainIndex.elementAt(i) ;
```

This means that when this statement is executed, a check will be made that the object returned from the Vector is from the class ProgramDetails. If it is, it can be assigned to the variable tempPD. But if it is not, a ClassCastException will be thrown.

You can see that this is not entirely satisfactory. If we have two Vectors for different types of objects, and by mistake we add an instance of one type to the Vector that is to hold instances of the other type, then we will not find out about it until we try to extract the element and get a ClassCastException. The compiler has nothing to say about it because all it knows about a Vector is that it is a Vector of Objects, so the extraction of an instance of *any* class is in principle perfectly legitimate. Similarly, adding the offending element to the Vector is acceptable since it is clearly an Object. There are several possible ways of dealing with this problem area:

- In some languages (for example, Ada and C++), there is an extra feature to deal with this problem: it is possible to specify, for example, what it means for a Vector to hold elements of type SOMETHING even though we have not defined exactly what that SOMETHING is. We can then write all the methods for the class Vector assuming that the elements are of this type; for example, the addElement method will take an argument of type SOME-THING, and elementAt returns an element of type SOMETHING. Then, at some later stage, we can say that we require a Vector, and at that point we have to specify what type the SOMETHING is (we might specify it earlier, but we certainly don't have to specify it when we first define what a Vector is). Then the compiler can check that any element being inserted into or extracted from the Vector is of the specified type. This feature (which is sometimes called *genericity*) is not available in Java.

- We could ensure that the ClassCastException does not occur by inserting program checks that an object taken from a Vector is the appropriate type and taking suitable action. This would make use of some of the features to be discussed briefly in section 21.3. But there are problems with this—the checking is still being done while the program is running rather than (much more safely and cheaply) while the program is being compiled; the programmer has to insert the tests explicitly; and it is not clear what the "suitable action" would be, except to stop with an error message.

- We could build a new derived class VectorOfProgramDetails and write versions of all the relevant methods that would have the Vector element as type ProgramDetails. But this is a lot of work, and it is work that in principle is redundant (except for security) because the code of the original Vector class contains all the relevant coding details.

- The final possibility is that we ensure, as programmers, that we are aware of this problem and are just very careful. But this is not entirely satisfactory. In fact, this is an area where the Java language does not really provide a fully satisfactory way of dealing with the problem of genericity.

In our new version of the `Chapter20n2` applet, we have searched through a `Vector` looking for entries for a particular chapter using a `for` loop:

```
for (int i = 0 ; i <mainIndex.size() ; i++)
    {
    ProgramDetails current = (ProgramDetails) mainIndex.elementAt(i) ;
    ...
```

In fact, the `Vector` class (like many of the data structures provided by Java) has a method called `elements` that returns an object that implements an interface called `Enumeration`. This interface specifies that there will be two methods, `hasMoreElements` and `nextElement`, that enable us to look at each element of the underlying data structure in turn. We could rewrite the above loop:

```
Enumeration e = mainIndex.elements() ;
while (e.hasMoreElements())
    {
    ProgramDetails current = (ProgramDetails) e.nextElement() ;
    ...
```

The enumeration returns an `Object`, so we have to cast it to the correct type, as before. This is rather like the `hasMoreTokens`/`nextToken` methods of the `StringTokenizer` class, except that with these methods, an object of a particular type (a `String`) was returned.

The `Vector` class also provides a selection of methods for searching a `Vector` for an element that matches an `Object` supplied as an argument.

We have already discussed and implemented versions of a stack, or last-in-first-out store, where the elements are held like a stack of plates in a cafeteria with access only to the top one. Java provides a `Stack` data structure, derived from `Vector`, that implements the usual "push" and "pop" methods. Note that it is a `Stack` of `Objects`.

21.1.2 The Hashtable Class

Another useful data structure is a `Hashtable`. Here we can store an element together with an associated key value and then recover the element by quoting its key value:

```
Hashtable t = new Hashtable() ;
t.put("shakespeare", new PersonDates(1564, 1616)) ;
t.put("austen", new PersonDates(1775, 1817)) ;
t.put("dickens", new PersonDates(1812, 1870)) ;
t.put("trollope", new PersonDates(1815, 1882)) ;
t.put("bronte", new PersonDates(1818, 1848)) ;
t.put("eliot", new PersonDates(1819, 1880)) ;
    ...
```

We declare a `Hashtable`—if we wished, we could have specified an initial capacity and a *load factor* (a number in the range 0.0 to 1.0, which specifies the point at which the system should make the `Hashtable` larger).

We use the `put` method to add an element (here an object of type `PersonDates`) and its key value (here a `String`) to the `Hashtable`. We cannot use *anything* as a key for a `Hashtable`; it has to be an instance of some class (such as a `String`), and not a basic data type like `int`. This is because the `Hashtable` applies two methods (`equals` and `hashcode`) to the key; as both of these methods are provided in the `Object` class, and every class inherits from `Object`, the `Hashtable` code can safely invoke these methods.

We have been a bit cavalier in that the `Hashtable` stores only one element with any particular key value. If we try to store a second element with this key value, it will indeed store it but will return the element previously stored with this key value (rather than `null`). We should therefore check the return value:

```
PersonDates result = (PersonDates) t.put("bronte",
                                          new PersonDates(1816, 1855)) ;
if (result != null)
   System.err.println("duplicate information") ;
```

We can extract information with the `get` method, quoting a key. We have to cast the object returned to the appropriate type, and the previous discussion about genericity applies here. A value `null` is returned if there is no entry for this key value:

```
BasicIo.prompt("type author's name ") ;
BufferedReader din = new BufferedReader(new InputStreamReader(System.in));
String name = din.readLine().trim() ;
PersonDates p = (PersonDates) t.get(name) ;
if (p == null)
   System.err.println("I have no information about " + name) ;
else
   System.err.println(name + " was born in " + p.getBirthDate() +
             " and died in " + p.getDeathDate()) ;
```

We can remove an element with a particular key from the hash table (with `remove`), and we can remove all the elements (with `clear`).

If we want to scan all the elements in a `Hashtable`, we can use the `Enumeration` interface, as with the `Vector`:

```
Enumeration hashElements = t.elements() ;
Enumeration hashKeys = t.keys() ;
while (hashKeys.hasMoreElements())
   {
   System.out.print(hashKeys.nextElement()) ;
   PersonDates p1 = (PersonDates) hashElements.nextElement() ;
   System.out.println(" was born in " + p1.getBirthDate()
             + " and died in " + p1.getDeathDate()) ;
   }
```

There is also a class called `Properties`, derived from `Hashtable`, where both the key and element are of type `String`. It also has additional methods to load a property list from a file (or more generally an `InputStream`) and output them to an `OutputStream`.

21.2   Strings & StringBuffers

So far, when we have wanted to handle strings of characters, we have used the `String` class, which is the standard way of manipulating strings in Java. As long as we want to treat a string as a single complete entity, or perhaps just inspect the individual characters (with the `charAt` method), the `String` class is perfectly adequate.

However, if we want to change individual characters of a `String`, we have a problem because the instances of the `String` class are immutable—that is, we cannot change them in any way. If, for example, we want to change the `i`th character of the `String` `s0` to an `X` character, we have to do something like:

```
s0 = s0.substring(0, i) + 'X' + s0.substring(i + 1) ;
```

We use the `substring` method and the concatenate operator to create a completely new `String`, and then the reference to this `String` is assigned to the variable `s0`. At some later stage, Java's garbage collector will realize that there is no reference to the original `String`, so its storage area will then be recovered.

This is obviously a fairly inconvenient mechanism for the programmer to use. It is also a fairly inefficient way for Java to manipulate strings of characters, since it has to create a completely new `String` and recover the old one even if only one character is changed.

So Java provides the `StringBuffer` class (in the `java.lang` package) for use if we are planning to do extensive modification to a string of characters.

- We start by using a `StringBuffer` constructor method to construct a `StringBuffer` instance out of a `String`. So, if `line` is a `String` (perhaps read in from a file), we generate a `StringBuffer` instance containing the same characters:

  ```
  StringBuffer line1 = new StringBuffer(line) ;
  ```

- We can find out the number of characters in the `StringBuffer` with the `length` method

  ```
  System.out.println("there are " + line1.length() + " characters") ;
  ```

- We can inspect individual characters in the `StringBuffer` with the `charAt` method, just as with a `String` (character numbering starts at zero):

  ```
  if (line1.charAt(5) == 'O')
      . . .
  ```

- Unlike with the `String` class, we can change the character at a particular position with the `setCharAt` method:

  ```
  line1.setCharAt(i, 'X') ;
  ```

- We can insert a character at a particular position (shuffling the rest of the characters up) or append a character at the end with the `insert` and `append` methods:

```
line1.insert(j, 'Y') ;
line1.append('Z') ;
```

- Finally, we can convert the `StringBuffer` instance back to a `String` with the `toString` method:

```
line = line1.toString() ;
```

21.3 Run-time Type Information (optional)

While a Java program is running, it keeps track of the type of all the objects that exist at any particular time. It is sometimes useful to be able to find out the class of an object so that the appropriate action can be taken. Suppose we have a method whose arguments could be an instance of any of a number of different classes (so we declare it as of type `Object`). We can use the operator `instanceof` (which returns a Boolean value) to test at run time to see what type the argument is:

```
public static void funnyMethod(Object x)
   {
   if (x instanceof String)
      {
      System.err.println("It was a String **" + x + "**") ;
      }
   else if (x instanceof Integer)
      {
      System.err.println("It was an Integer **" + x + "**") ;
      }
   else
      {
      System.err.println("It was something else **" + x + "**") ;
      }
   } // end of method funnyMethod
```

We are relying here on the fact that any object has or inherits a method `toString`, which the `println` method can call to obtain printable information from the object. Here is a `main` method to call `funnyMethod`:

```
public static void main(String[] args)
   {
   funnyMethod("Hello World") ;
   funnyMethod(new Integer(42)) ;
   funnyMethod(new Person()) ;
   } // end of method main
```

We could not have written funnyMethod(42) because this would pass an actual argument of type int, which (unlike Integer) is not derived from Object.

The class Object has a useful method getClass, which can tell us the class of an instance. It actually returns an instance of the class Class, which has a method getName, which returns the name of the class. So we could write in our funnyMethod:

```
...
else
    {
    System.err.println("It was a " + x.getClass().getName()
                + " **" + x + "**") ;
    }
} // end of method funnyMethod
```

These features of Java are quite useful to find out what type an instance might be when debugging a program. But it is extremely poor practice to make extensive use of them in programming because it is against the spirit of polymorphism and we are evading many of the type checks that the Java compiler helpfully provides for us.

21.4 Threads (optional)

If you watch carefully when your browser is loading a new page, you may see that when there is an image to be loaded, the rest of the page is displayed and the image appears a bit later, chunk by chunk. It looks as if what is happening is that the browser continues to look after its main task of displaying the main features of the page and delegates a separate task to another program, obtaining the image data from the host site and displaying it as it arrives. Similarly, if we request that something is printed, the browser will delegate this task to another program and in the meantime carry on as before, dealing with user input and so on.

This is a general and common feature of a modern computer system. We can have several separate "things" going on effectively at the same time. There are a number of different terms for these "things" that can be executing simultaneously—the terms *process* and *task* are often used, but the Java term for this is *thread*. When the browser needs to display an image, it starts up a separate thread, and then the main thread of the browser carries on as before to display the rest of the page (and if another image appears, another thread could be started up).

How the computer deals with having several threads around at the same time will depend on how the operating system is set up. The most likely scenario is that the computer will in fact execute only one of the threads at a time but will share out its attention to each thread in turn that all of them make reasonable progress with the tasks that have been delegated to them. In some systems, the computer simply executes a thread until it voluntarily decides it has done enough for the present (perhaps it has requested the next piece of data from a remote computer and is awaiting the result), at which point the computer chooses another thread to run for a bit. Of course, in this case, the threads have to be cooperative and voluntarily relinquish control from time to time. Other systems use *preemptive scheduling*, where each thread gets a share of the time available and then loses control to another thread whether or not it has reached a "natural break." Finally, some computer systems contain several processing units so that more than one thread can actually be executed at the same time.

Many modern programming languages provide some sort of mechanism to allow the programmer to specify that two or more tasks can be carried on at the same time and to specify how the several tasks can pass information to and fro between them. The fact that Java supports *multithreading* is one of the things that has generated great interest in the language. However, writing programs where the different parts can operate in parallel is a complex problem, as we have to ensure that the interactions between the several parts take place in a disciplined manner. The Java features for multithreading are therefore beyond the scope of this book.

In this section, we demonstrate a simple program that executes multiple threads, and we indicate one of the common pitfalls and how Java deals with it. For more information on multithreading in Java, see *Core Java* by Gary Cornell and Cay S. Horstmann (SunSoft Press 1996) or *Exploring Java* by Patrick Niemeyer and Joshua Peck (O'Reilly & Associates 1996).

We start with a program that does not have multiple threads. We have a class `ProcessString` with a single instance variable `originalString`. This variable is set to a suitable value from an argument passed to its constructor method when we declare an instance of the class:

```
class ProcessString
    {
    private String originalString ;

    public ProcessString(String string)
        {
        originalString = string ;
        } // end of constructor method

    OTHER METHODS

    } // end of class ProcessString
```

The class has a method `run` that consists mainly of a loop, which goes on forever. In this loop, we convert the "next" character of `originalString` to uppercase, display it on the screen, wait for a second, and repeat.

The waiting is done by calling a method `sleep` (in the `Thread` class) with one argument, the length of time, in milliseconds, to sleep. The `Thread` class is in the `java.lang` package, so we do not need any `import` statement for this. When the program has slept that period of time, it is awakened by an `InterruptedException`, so we put the call of the `sleep` method into a `try` block and catch the result; the corresponding `catch` does nothing, but it allows us to proceed around the loop:

```
public void run()
   {
   int offset = 0 ;
   while (true)
     {
     String s = originalString.substring(0, offset) +
          Character.toUpperCase(originalString.charAt(offset)) +
          originalString.substring(offset + 1) ;
     System.out.println("**" + s + "**") ;
     offset++ ;
     if (offset == originalString.length())
        offset = 0 ;
     try {
        Thread.sleep(1000) ;
        }
     catch (InterruptedException e)
        {
        }
     }
   } // end of method run
```

The main method (in a class Chapter21n4) simply sets up an instance of the ProcessString class with a suitable string and sets it going by calling its run method:

```
public class Chapter21n4
   {
   public static void main(String[] args)
     {
     ProcessString p1 = new ProcessString("lancaster") ;
     p1.run() ;
     } // end of method main
   } // end of class Chapter21n4
```

If we run this program, it will keep writing to the screen:

```
**Lancaster**
**lAncaster**
**laNcaster**
**lanCaster**
**lancAster**
**lancaSter**
**lancasTer**
**lancastEr**
**lancasteR**
**Lancaster**
**lAncaster**
```

until we stop it (with Ctrl+C or something similar). Figure 21-5 is a sketch of what is happening.

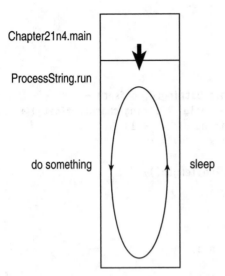

Figure 21-5: Executing `Chapter21n4`—a single thread.

Now we are going to make the `ProcessString` class run as a thread, separate from the `main` method (which we will modify to do something so we can see that multithreading is indeed taking place). If we want to treat a class as a thread, it must implement an interface called `Runnable`, which requires that we have a method (no arguments, no return value) called `run`. We have already done this, so we can rewrite the beginning of this class:

```
class ProcessString implements Runnable
    {
    private String originalString ;
    ...
```

Then we have to turn the class into a thread, which we do in the constructor method:

```
public ProcessString(String string)
    {
    originalString = string ;

    Thread thisThread = new Thread(this) ;
    thisThread.start() ;
    } // end of constructor method
```

This uses the `Thread` constructor to make a thread out of `this` instance of the class `ProcessString` and stores a reference to it in the variable `thisThread`. Then we set the thread going with a call of the method `start` belonging to the `Thread` class.

Back in the `main` method of the `Chapter21n4` class, we set up an instance of the `ProcessString` class as before. However, we no longer need to call its `run` method. When we call the constructor for `ProcessString`, it calls the `start` method, which eventually calls the `run` method (it knows there will be one because that is guaranteed by the fact that `ProcessString` implements the `Runnable` interface). All the `main` method has to do is carry on, doing something "useful." We simply wait in an infinite loop, displaying the message `Hello again` every five seconds:

```
public class Chapter21n4
   {
   public static void main(String[] args)
      {
      ProcessString p1 = new ProcessString("lancaster") ;

      while (true)
         {
         System.out.println("Hello again") ;
         try {
            Thread.sleep(5000) ;
            }
         catch (InterruptedException e)
            {
            }
         }
      } // end of method main
   } // end of class Chapter21n4
```

If we run this, we get something like the following:

```
Hello again
**Lancaster**
**lAncaster**
**laNcaster**
**lanCaster**
**lancAster**
Hello again
**lancaSter**
**lancasTer**
**lancastEr**
**lancasteR**
**Lancaster**
Hello again
**lAncaster**

...
```

until we stop it.

Figure 21-6 is a sketch of what is happening now.

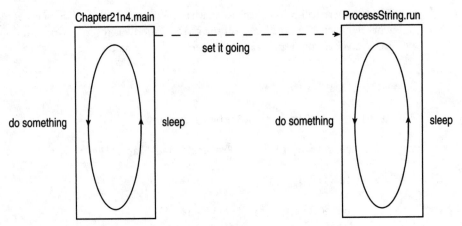

Figure 21-6: Executing `Chapter21n4`—two threads.

Now try changing the beginning of the `Chapter21n4` code to set up several separate `ProcessString` instances:

```
public class Chapter21n4
    {
    public static void main(String[] args)
        {
        ProcessString p1 = new ProcessString("lancaster") ;
        ProcessString p2 = new ProcessString("preston") ;
        ProcessString p3 = new ProcessString("kendal") ;

        while (true)
            {
            ...
```

If we compile and run this, we get:

```
Hello again
**Lancaster**
**Preston**
**Kendal**
**lAncaster**
**pReston**
**kEndal**
**laNcaster**
**prEston**
**keNdal**
**lanCaster**
**preSton**
**kenDal**
**lancAster**
```

```
**presTon**
**kendAl**
Hello again
**lancaSter**
```

and so on. The execution of the three `ProcessString` threads and the `main` thread are all inter-
leaved, as shown in Figure 21-7.

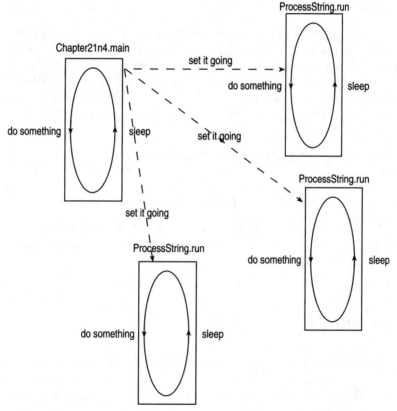

Figure 21-7: Executing `Chapter21n4`—four threads.

21.4.1   *Synchronizing Threads*

There is a problem with running several threads at the same time. In this simple program, each
thread was totally independent and did not need to interact with any other thread or with any
shared information. But a more serious use of threads might have a `run` method looking rather
like this:

```
public void run()
  {
  while (true)
    {
    chooseTaskFromCommonTable() ;
    doTheTask() ;
    go to sleep for a bit ;
    }
  } // end of method run
```

We imagine a common task table where all the threads look from time to time to choose the next task, remove the task from the table, and then do it. But suppose two threads both try to look at the task table at the same time. They might *both* choose the same task and *both* try to do it.

We need to make sure that, while one thread is in the chooseTaskFromCommonTable method, no other thread can get into it until the first one has finished choosing a task, removed it from the table, and left the method. To ensure orderly entry to such a method, Java provides the keyword synchronized:

```
synchronized void chooseTaskFromCommonTable()
  {
  ...
  } // end of method chooseTaskFromCommonTable
```

This tells the Java system that only one thread is allowed to be in the method at a time. Any other threads wanting to enter must form an orderly queue and enter one at a time, when the preceding thread has finished.

21.5   Key Points in Chapter 21

- A Vector is a dynamic data structure supplied by Java. It allows us to maintain a heterogeneous collection of objects. We can think of it as an array that can grow and shrink as required; it also allows insertion of elements at specified locations without the need to shuffle elements.

- When we extract an element from a Vector, it is a reference to an Object, and we must cast it to the appropriate class if we are to use that element correctly.

- If we wish to process the elements of a Vector sequentially, we can use the elements method to return an Enumeration instance. Subsequently, we can use the hasMoreElements and nextElement methods to process the elements (which again have to be cast to the correct class).

- A Stack class, derived from Vector, is available with additional "pop" and "push" methods.

- A Hashtable class is also available. We can store data elements with an associated key using put, and we can retrieve elements later using get and supplying the appropriate key. If we put two elements with the same key value, the first one is replaced by the second one.

- If we wish to manipulate a string of characters, we can convert it from a `String` to a `StringBuffer`. The methods `charAt` and `setCharAt` allow us to inspect and modify individual characters, and the `toString` method allows us to convert the `StringBuffer` back to a `String`.

- At run time, we can find out the class that an instance belongs to by using the `instanceof` operator.

- It is often the case that computer systems run separate "things" at apparently the same time. These "things" are commonly known as *processes* or *tasks*—the Java terminology is *threads*.

- It is possible to write a class that we can make into a thread so that we can arrange to have several parts of our program all running at the same time.

21.6 Exercises

1. We implemented our `PriorityQueue` class in Chapters 11 and 17 as a single queue, ordered by the priority (and within the priority, in a first-in-first-out manner). Assume there are only four priority levels (1 = Urgent, 2 = High, 3 = Medium, 4 = Low).

   Reimplement the `PriorityQueue` as four `Vectors`, one for each level of priority. Make sure the details of your implementation are completely hidden from the class user.

   Implement methods `deleteElement` and `changePriority` for this class. You can specify a queue element to be deleted or whose priority is to be changed by giving a version of the `String` held in the element. Your program should not require an exact match between the two `Strings`—it should be allowable matching `Strings` to differ at least in the number of spaces and the capitalization.

2. In exercise 15.2, you used an array to implement a stack of characters as a class `CharacterStack`. In exercise 17.1, you reimplemented it as a linked list.

   This time, implement it using the Java `Stack` class, still presenting the same `CharacterStack` methods to the outside world. Test it with your driver program.

3. A British postal code is a string of characters that generally corresponds to a particular range of houses on a particular street in a particular town. Many service firms nowadays, when receiving a telephone call, first ask the caller for their postal code. They look it up, confirm the street and town name with the caller, and then ask the caller for their house number, which can be checked against the range given by the postal code.

   Write an applet that, when started up, reads a file of information from the host computer where each line is in the form:

   `postal code / first house number / last house number / street / town`

   The applet should set up a `Hashtable` with this information and then display it for the user when he or she types in a postal code.

4. Write a Java program that *justifies* the text in a file so that it has smooth left and right margins. That is, the program should rearrange the text in the file so that all the lines (except possibly the last in each paragraph) are the same length.

The program should prompt the user for (a) the name of the file containing the text to be arranged, (b) the name of the file to contain the justified text, and (c) the required number of characters per line of text.

Paragraphs in the input file are marked by an empty line or one containing only spaces. No word in the input file should be longer than 20 characters, and the number of characters per line specified by the user should be in the range 40 to 100 characters, but your program should check both of these constraints.

No line in the output file should contain more than the specified number of characters. Normally there should be a single space between one word and the next on the line, but extra spaces should be added so that the line has the correct number of characters (unless it is the final line of a paragraph).

If the user specified 50 characters, and the input file began:

```
Introduction: Objects            and            Classes

Object orientation                        (or OO)
is a technique that has            pervaded
all aspects of computer science over the past decade or so.


Object-oriented ways of thinking have been applied to software system
design,          operating systems, programming languages and
database   systems, to name but a few areas            impacted by
this          recent technology. In this chapter, we will introduce
some of the basic concepts of object orientation.
```

the output file should begin like this:

```
Introduction: Objects and Classes

Object orientation  (or  OO) is a technique  that
has  pervaded all aspects of computer science over
the past decade or so.


Object-oriented ways of thinking have been applied
to  software  system  design,  operating  systems,
programming  languages  and database  systems,  to
name  but  a  few areas impacted  by  this  recent
technology.  In  this chapter, we  will  introduce
some of the basic concepts of object orientation.
```

PART 5

Object-Oriented Design

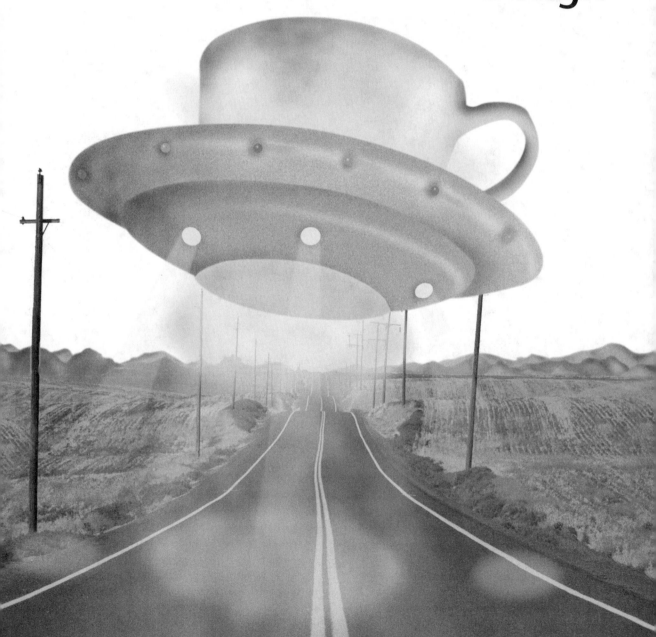

CHAPTER 22

Object-Oriented Design

22.1 Introduction

In this part of the book, we address issues of object-oriented design. Before concentrating on this particular aspect, we need to examine design in the wider context of software engineering and the software life cycle.

Ever since the identification of a software "crisis" in the late '60s, it was realized that a new engineering approach to the building of large-scale software systems was required. The increase of hardware power (both in speed and size) made it possible to envisage large and powerful software systems. However, it was as if someone capable of creating an artifact that allowed people to cross a small body of water (a wooden plank across a stream) was now being asked to build a bridge across a large body of water (the railway bridge over the river Forth) using the same techniques.

The problem, of course, is one of scale. Just as we would never expect a structural engineer to approach these two problems in the same way, it was clear programmers couldn't expect the same techniques that allow us to build programs with hundreds of lines of code to scale up to hundreds of thousands of lines. Thus the discipline of *software engineering* came to be.

To give a simple example of why such practices came into being, consider a large software system. Such systems have upwards of a quarter of a million lines of code. Typical examples include:

- Stock exchange trading system
- Production line control system
- Emergency command and control system
- Insurance proposal system
- Telephone switching systems (four million lines of code)
- Spreadsheets (half a million lines)

In terms of person years of effort needed to create it, it is clear that no one person (or even a small team of people) could hope to build it. It is also clear that no one person might be able to understand the detailed working of the system. The age-old problem-solving technique of "divide and conquer" comes into play. There will be an overall architectural design in place, but that in turn will be divided into subsystems. Subsystems in turn may be fragmented into a logical set of smaller subsystems. We continue this process until we arrive at a level of subsystems that a few people (a small group) will be able to fully design, implement, and test.

Each subsystem should present a "simple" and clearly defined interface to the other subsystems in order that we can construct the overall system from these building blocks.

22.2   The Software Life Cycle

Most introductory books on programming focus on the coding of rather small programs; we have in fact been in the position of the person placing a plank across a stream. The problems we have faced have not been overwhelmingly large; they have been well within the capability for one person to solve. In large-scale systems, it is easier to see that there are in fact a number of phases that the creation of a software artifact passes through. In our small problems, we have gone through all of these phases, but we may have done this so quickly that we scarcely noted their existence.

The collection of phases is known as the *software life cycle*. For the purposes of this book, we present one of the earliest and most simple—the *waterfall* model (as shown in Figure 22-1). The software process is generally more complicated than this model depicts; however, it does describe the broad phases that software development follows and is sufficient for our present needs.

The model consists of the following steps :

- Requirements
- Design
- Coding
- Testing
- Maintenance

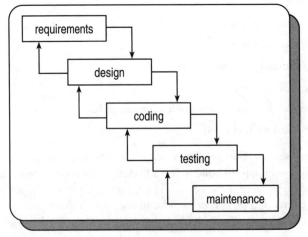

Figure 22-1: The waterfall life cycle.

Each of these steps is now examined in more detail.

22.2.1   Requirements

This phase is aimed at answering the "what" question; what problem is the system intended to address? This involves requirements *analysis* and *definition*. The services, constraints, and goals of the system are elicited from the system users. They are then defined in a form understandable by both users and developers. This software specification is passed on to the designers.

22.2.2   Design

Armed with a set of requirements for the system they have to build, the designers now face the "how" question; how will we build the system so that it behaves as specified by the requirements? It is this phase that we will concentrate on in this part of the book. The end result of this process will be a detailed design document.

22.2.3   Coding

Next, the design is passed on to a team of programmers and implementers whose job it is to realize the design in a working system. The act of programming has been the focus of much of this book, but it is important to realize that this part of the life cycle (in conjunction with design) only accounts for approximately 30 percent of the total costs.

22.2.4   Testing

Testing, although placed at this point in the life cycle, is something that we would expect to take place during the coding phase. The aim of modern software engineering is to approach the production of large software systems through the use (and reuse) of existing "black box" modules. We have already discussed how objects meet the requirements for such "black boxes" and shown how it is possible to write "driver" programs whose job is to exercise (and test) objects. This can be thought of as *unit testing*.

At this point, we would expect testing to refer to *system testing*; when we put together all the black boxes, does the complete system perform as expected? Did we get the design right? Does it meet all the requirements? Can the users understand and use it? Problems that arise at this point might be addressable by returning to coding: a fairly minor bug has been uncovered. It could be worse and reveal a problem with the system design, in which case the design would have to be reconsidered. Even worse, it could indicate an error in the requirements.

22.2.5   Maintenance

Strictly speaking, maintenance isn't really part of the life cycle in the same way the earlier phases are. This occurs after the system has been completed and delivered, and it typically requires twice the effort that development requires. Maintenance is intended to address any problems that arise in the everyday use of the system. Unfortunately, it may raise issues that can only be addressed by returning even to the earliest parts of the life cycle.

We may uncover bugs that even exhaustive testing failed to find; they may be fixable by programmers, or they may reveal deeper design flaws. Users may find the system does not perform as they expected, or it makes a simple task much more difficult than it should. This means there is a flaw in the requirements; either they were incomplete or just plain wrong. The requirements themselves may change due to external forces. If the application mirrors some real-world constraints, like the legal or financial system, and they undergo some changes (for example, a change in the tax laws, such as eligibility, tax rates, etc.), then the application must reflect those changes. The introduction of the application itself may cause changes in the way people work outside of the application; these changes may in turn have an impact on the application.

This concludes our "whistle-stop tour" of the life cycle; of necessity, it is (by its very nature) brief, and we refer you to a text called *Software Engineering* (Sommerville 95) for further details.

The difference between bridges and planks has been captured in the phrases *programming-in-the-large* and *programming-in-the-small*. To a great extent, we have been concentrating on the latter. While we cannot hope to cover "programming-in-the-large" in a book of this nature, we intend to give you an appreciation of what it means and to provide some examples of what we might call "programming-in-the-medium."

22.3   Design

It is clear that a full example of the design of a large-scale software system is beyond the scope of this book (or indeed, of just about any book). What then do we hope to achieve in this final part of the book? First, we will present a small example and develop it from an informal description through to a fully coded Java implementation. By applying some design techniques in-the-small, as it were, we hope to provide some appreciation of the techniques in general. Second, we believe you will find the techniques useful as your implementation experiences move from small programming problems to medium-scale programming projects that you may encounter in the rest of your training.

When facing these larger problems, it may even be required that you first prepare a specification (which is beyond the scope of this book) and a fully documented design. In this case, you should find the techniques and notations presented here to be of some use.

22.3.1   The Design Process

Broadly speaking, the design process is an iterative sequence of refinements, moving from an informal design outline toward a finished design. We can start with a broad outline of how we think the system can be realized and move through a number of refinements, including an informal design, a more formal design, and finally the completed design. At each step we are adding more details and refining our design, making it more and more formal.

Like the waterfall life cycle, this is an iterative process. As we start to think more deeply about our informal design and try to flesh it out by decomposing it into more detailed subdesigns, we may find our original intentions are too difficult to realize. We must therefore reconsider the earlier steps in our design and amend them accordingly.

22.3.2 Functional Design

Object-oriented design is a fairly recent development, achieving widespread adoption only in the late 1980s. Prior to its arrival, the most commonly used software design strategy was functional design. This strategy involves decomposing the design into functional components with system state information held in a shared data area. By comparison, in object-oriented design, system state is decentralized and each object manages its own state information.

Consider this crude comparison of the two approaches. In functional design, the data that is worked on by the components is passed between them; each component applies some transformation and passes the (transformed) data on to the next component for further processing. In object-oriented design, it is not data that is transmitted among the components, but commands (messages that are requests for services from the other components).

These design approaches are not in opposition; they are complementary. They will be applied when deemed most appropriate by the software engineer(s). It may be that for some systems, each approach will be applied to different subsystems when deemed suitable.

22.4   Object-Oriented Design (OOD)

As we have already seen, objects possess a number of very desirable features for software engineers. They are an implementation of the module concept, identified early on as an important "black-box building block" for complex software systems. They can be easily understood as individual, stand-alone entities. They are appropriate reusable components. For some systems, there may be obvious real-world entities that can be mapped onto system objects.

We discussed this in Chapter 2; the concept that everyday entities can be considered, and modeled, as objects (remember the CD player?).

Something worth considering is the relationship between OOD and OOP (object-oriented programming). They are, of course, related, but they are distinct. As Java programmers, we can exploit the fact that our design will consist of a set of class definitions and clearly defined relationships between the classes (be it inheritance or clientship), which we can readily map onto a language that is itself object oriented. However, there is absolutely nothing to prevent us from using OOD to produce a design that we can, albeit with probably more effort, realize in a non-OO programming language.

We can carry this argument a step earlier in the life cycle; there are now OO-requirement analysis techniques. The objects we identify in the requirements phase can naturally be carried forward into the design phase.

22.4.1   Capturing Our Design: A Design Notation

We will use and adapt a notation suggested in *The Object-Oriented Systems Life Cycle* (Henderson-Sellers and Edwards 1990), which we will refer to as H-S&E.

Figure 22-2: A single object/class.

H-S&E realize the importance of representing both single objects and class definitions and suggest that we can do both using the same notation. They refer to such generic capabilities as *O/C* (object/class). In Figure 22-2, we see a representation of a single object/class. At the top of the rounded rectangle, we give the O/C name. On the borders of the rectangle, we have the publicly available attribute(s) and method(s). Within the rectangle, we have the private attribute(s) and method(s). Attributes are contained in ovals, while methods are within rectangles.

There are two types of relationships between O/Cs that we are interested in. These are inheritance and clientship. We capture them in the notation as follows. Inheritance is represented by a thick arrow, pointing from superclass to subclass, starting and ending at the borders of the rounded rectangle.

Clientship is denoted by a circle within the body of an O/C, containing the start of a thin arrow pointing to the boundary of the server O/C.

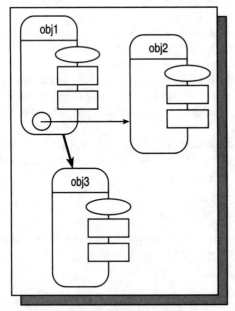

Figure 22-3: O/Cs and their relationships.

In Figure 22-3, we see that obj1 is the superclass of obj3, while obj2 is a server for obj1. An example we have seen earlier in the book is given in Figure 22-4, where we see Person is the superclass of Student, while OurDate is a server for Person.

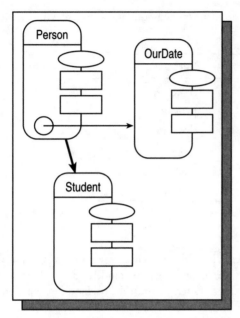

Figure 22-4: Person, Student, and OurDate represented as an H-S&E diagram.

22.4.2   Object Identification

Unfortunately, one of the hardest parts of OOD is also the very first step we must take, that of object identification. A number of approaches have been suggested, but there is really no single automatic process we can follow. Designers must use their skill and experience to help. This poses something of a catch-22 scenario for any text purporting to "teach" OOD.

Identification of objects includes the objects themselves, their attributes, their associated operations, and their interrelationships. One technique for generating a "first cut" is a grammatical approach (Robinson 1992, Booch 1986). We highlight nouns and verbs in the natural language description of what the system is to do. The nouns identify objects, and the verbs (actions) identify operations or object services. Other approaches to object identification can be found in Coad and Yourdon's OOA/OOD method (Coad and Yourdon 1991a, 1991b).

Of course, great care must be taken with the grammatical approach. We cannot assume nouns are always objects or verbs are always services. Also, the writer of the system description may assume knowledge is shared by the designer; if this is not the case, then important objects and services may be omitted.

As a simple worked example, consider the following text that describes part of the functionality of a personal organizer. *Nouns* are italicized, and **verbs** are in bold.

The *telephone directory organizer* **provides** *surnames*, the *user* **searches** for existing *phone numbers* by *surname*. The *organizer* **displays** the *information* regarding an *entry*, and the *user* **adds** new *entries*. Once an *entry* **has been displayed**, the *user* **can browse** forward or backward through the *entries*.

From this simple analysis, we can identify the nouns and verbs shown in Table 22-1.

Nouns	Verbs
telephone directory organizer	searches
user	provides
phone numbers	displays
surname	adds
(information regarding an) entry	browse
(new) entries	

Table 22-1: Nouns and verbs.

This is only the start of the process; it is a deceptively easy way of generating a "first cut." We must now weed out "false" objects, decide what is to be modeled as an object or an attribute, and decide what is and is not a method. Often we must fall back on our experience to help us make these decisions.

Trying to move from our initial identification of nouns and verbs, we can see that some nouns refer to attributes. For example, if we accept an *entry* as an object, then surely *surname* and *phone number* should be attributes of that object (see Table 22-2).

Candidate	objects	attributes	methods
	entry	phone number, surname	
	telephone directory organizer		search, display, add, browse
	user		
	entries		

Table 22-2: Candidate objects, attributes and methods.

The *user* appears in the description as users are the source of system commands. We do not need to formally model the user in our design.

We are by no means finished! For example, we have not defined all the methods required. We may also need to add more attributes; for example, for a directory entry, we will at least wish to add a forename. A set of initial classes are shown in Figure 22-5.

Figure 22-5: Initial classes.

There are other objects to define as well. We have begun to define a single entry; however, we will need to represent a collection of entries (as seen from our table of candidate objects). From our earlier experience of designing and using systems, we can visualize this collection as a database of directory entries. Just like database management systems, we will expect our collection to manage the addition, retrieval, and organization of entries.

It is this database that we will expect to provide most of the functionality of the directory organizer. When a user asks to search for an entry, we would expect this request to be passed on almost unchanged to the database; similarly, a request to add a new entry would be passed on unchanged. So, the add and search methods of the directory organizer should be handled by the database. However, the browse and display methods are more closely related to the user interface than to the database.

What is actually required is some means for the user interface to retrieve a "named" entry, which it then displays. Browsing will be achieved in the user interface by retrieving the next or previous entry (hence satisfying the "browse forward or backward" requirement). The actual service provided by the database (shown in Figure 22-6) will be getEntry.

Figure 22-6: The directory entry database.

Returning to our example, the telephone directory system (see Figure 22-7) is essentially intended to be an interactive one, driven by user commands.

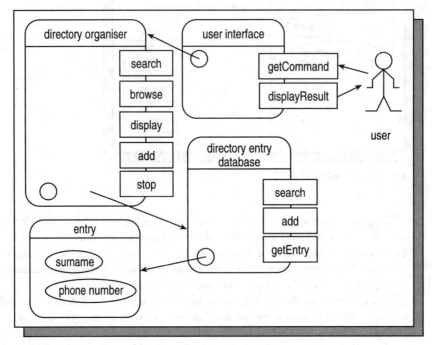

Figure 22-7: The system.

Note that we have added a new command, stop. Even though this was not mentioned in the original English specification, we clearly need some mechanism for terminating a session.

In the next chapter, we shall move toward implementation through the process of detailed design. Following this, we will discuss a possible implementation of the design. Finally, we present guidelines for a good object-oriented design.

22.5   Key Points in Chapter 22

- Software engineering came into being in response to the software crisis caused by the scaling up of computing power, which enabled more ambitious software systems to be developed.

- The software crisis can be summarized as the difference between *programming-in-the-small* and *programming-in-the-large*. Techniques for placing a plank over a stream (in-the-small) do not scale up to those for building a bridge over a river (in-the-large). Software engineering is intended to support developments in-the-large.

- The *software life cycle* describes the phases through which a software artifact passes during its creation. The *waterfall* model names requirements, design, coding, testing, and maintenance as those phases.

- The design process is an iterative sequence of refinements, starting from an informal design and adding more detail as we move toward a complete design.

- Prior to object-oriented design (OOD), the most common technique was *functional design*. In this approach, the design is decomposed into functional components that apply some transformation on data and pass on the (transformed) data to the next component for further processing.

- *Object-oriented design* is said to more closely model the real world. For example, there are everyday artifacts that can be considered, and modeled, as objects. Moreover, we can apply object orientation to the life cycle activities on either side of design—namely, requirements and coding. This means an object identified during the requirements phase can be tracked through design and coding.

- Identifying objects is the first step in OOD. One approach is to apply a simple grammatical analysis and identify nouns and verbs, where nouns are taken to be objects and verbs as methods. This is only a first cut, and the results should be treated with care. For example, some nouns may refer to attributes rather than objects.

- Our design can be captured and documented using a suitable notation.

22.6 Exercises

1. For the application that you wrote for exercise 17.7, produce an H-S&E diagram to document the final structure of your program.

2. The description of the telephone directory organizer has been extended as follows:
   "When it is no longer necessary to keep contact details of someone, we can delete his or her entry from the directory. We can also update entries in the following two ways :

   a) Someone's phone number changes

   b) Someone's surname changes"

   Carry out the noun and verb approach to identify candidate objects, attributes, and methods in this description. Extend the diagram in Figure 22-7 to show how our design can accommodate these additional requirements.

3. Here is an informal description of an information system based on a person's birthday:
   "The user provides the system with their date of birth. The system calculates the day that the person was born on and how long they have lived in months, weeks, and days and presents them with a line from the poem about days of birth."

   Apply the noun and verb approach to identify candidate objects, attributes, and methods in this description. Produce an initial H-S&E diagram to document your design.

4. Here is an informal description of a theater booking system:

"The theater booking system allows the booking office clerk to select information about a particular performance (specified by day and time—matinee or evening). The clerk can examine the status of a given seat (booked or unbooked) and change its status if required.

Customers may request single seats (row and seat number) or a range of seats (row start and end seat numbers). They may also ask the clerk to check by specification; that is, 'Have you a row of four adjacent seats?' or 'Have you a block of seats three by six?' For each seat booked, the name of the customer should be recorded as contact information. Seats are identified by a row (character) and a number.

The system should maintain persistent information regarding the status of seats for each performance. The system should be configurable for different seat layouts (we assume there is a single floor of seats)."

Apply the noun and verb approach to identify candidate objects, attributes, and methods in this description. Produce an initial H-S&E diagram to document your design.

22.7   References

Booch, G. 1986. Object-oriented development. *IEEE Transactions on Software Engineering* SE-12, No. 2 (February): 211–221.

Coad, P., and E. Yourdon. 1991a. *Object-oriented analysis.* 2nd ed. Englewood Cliffs, NJ: Yourdon Press, Prentice Hall.

———. 1991b. *Object-oriented design.* Englewood Cliffs, NJ: Yourdon Press, Prentice Hall.

Henderson-Sellers, B., and J. M. Edwards. 1990. The Object-Oriented Systems Life Cycle. *Communications of the ACM* 33, No. 9 (September): 142–159.

Robinson, P. J. 1992. *Hierarchic object-oriented design.* Englewood Cliffs, NJ: Prentice-Hall.

Sommerville, I. 1995. *Software engineering.* 5th ed. New York: Addison-Wesley.

CHAPTER 23

Case Study: Implementing the Personal Organizer (1)

23.1 Introduction

In this chapter, we move forward from the design stage into detailed implementation. Our problem is to implement the Java Personal Organizer (JPO), part of which is the telephone directory service we designed in the previous chapter. We intend to build a prototype application. A prototype is a system that exhibits most, if not all, of the functionality of the final application and allows implementers and users to experiment with the application. We will also provide a graphical user interface (GUI) for the prototype.

Initially, we could be said to be involved in detailed design; that is, we are exploring options as to how the prototype can actually be implemented. We are still addressing the "how" question, albeit at a much lower level. We still face a number of decisions based on how we will actually implement our design.

We begin by discussing the actual implementation of the telephone directory. We already know what the contents of a directory entry will look like; what we have to decide is how we will organize the directory, both on the filing system and in the program.

23.2 File Organization

Before continuing work on refining the design of our classes, we turn our attention to some lower-level details of how we will organize our data on the filing system. Our telephone directory (and the elements that it consists of) will have to be *persistent*. This means the information it contains must survive across executions of our application—no one would want to spend time inputting lots of telephone information, close down the application, and then start it up again at some later time only to find all the data has disappeared.

In order to save our data, we will use a number of files. The next thing to consider is how best to organize the structure of those files to support our application.

23.2.1 *Index Sequential Access*

If we examine a physical telephone directory, we will detect a standard organization. Each page consists of an alphabetized list of subscribers; at the top of each page is the name of the first subscriber on the page. The list of names from the tops of the pages is known as an *index*. This type of organization has been used in database management systems and is known as a *index sequential storage structure*. For further details on index structures, see chapter 5 of *Fundamentals of Database Systems* (Elmasri and Navathe 1994).

Here is a brief description of such a structure: We maintain two files, one for the index and one for the main file. The main file contains the actual data (in our case, the person's contact details), and the index file contains the index. We can consider the index and main files to consist of a sequence of *blocks*. A block normally consists of a number of bytes, where the number is a power of 2 (let's say 512).

The most common organization is one where both the main file and the index file are kept in sorted order. In our case, we will want to retrieve by surname, so we will keep our data in alphabetical order according to surname. An index entry will consist of a surname (where the surname is the first name in a main file block) and a pointer to a main file block (in our case, the number of the block). Consider the following, where we have decided an index block may contain three index entries (in practice, of course, we would expect it to hold a lot more) and a main file block can contain only two directory entries.

In database terminology, the main file consists of a sequence of *records*. A record is a collection of *fields* (or attributes) of interest. In this example, we can say that our directory entries are the records we are interested in, and they have three fields: surname, forename, and phone number.

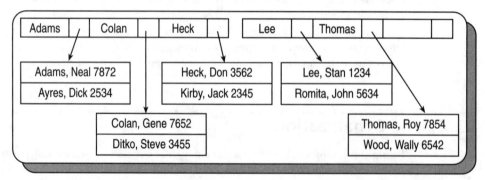

Figure 23-1: A sparse index.

Figure 23-1 shows an example of a sparse index; not every surname in the main file has a corresponding index entry. This situation is analogous to a real telephone directory; at the top of each page, we have the first surname to appear on that page. The name at the top of the page is the same as an index entry.

Given a surname, how do we find the matching details? The simplest algorithm would use a linear sequential search of the index entries.

If the search surname is:

- Equal to the current index surname
- Greater than the current index surname and less than the next index surname

then the matching entry, if it exists, should be present in the main file block pointed to by the current index pointer (see Figure 23-2).

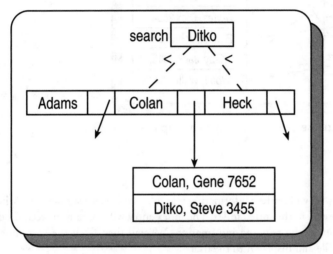

Figure 23-2: A sample search showing that Colan < Ditko < Heck.

Linear sequential searches are not so efficient when there is a large search space; we can take advantage of the sorted nature of the index and apply the binary search technique (see Chapter 9).

For our prototypical personal organizer, we have decided on a different organization. It is a simpler scheme; we do not need to consider the file as consisting of blocks, nor do we have to worry about keeping the main file in sorted order. This approach will be sufficient to get our prototype application up and running. Because of the "black box" nature of our design, this does not prohibit a move to a more complex organization at a later date should the demands on our application require it.

Our main file is going to act as a *heap*; this means new records are simply going to be added on at the end of the file as they arrive. Our main file is thus not going to be in sorted order. We will maintain the sorted order in our index, and we will have an index entry for every record in the main file. This is an example of a *dense* index (see Figure 23-3).

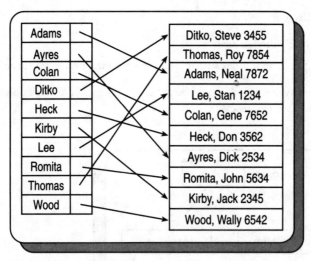

Figure 23-3: A dense index operating on a heap main file.

23.2.2 The Main File

The general way we will retrieve information is as follows: Given a surname, we will look up the corresponding entry in the sorted index. The index entry will contain the record number of the record that contains the required information. We will then fetch the corresponding record from the main file and display it to the user.

If the record doesn't exist, we will return a marker to indicate this condition (it may be in the form of a null record). If we have more than one record with the same surname, we will return the first occurrence.

Given a record number, how can we locate the corresponding record? The record number is the number of the record within the heap. We will number the record "slots" in the heap from 0 (zero) upward. We want to be able to transform this record number into a position within the main file and to directly read the requisite number of bytes from that position.

Java files have no inherent structure of their own. They are viewed, like files in the UNIX operating system, as unbounded byte streams. They consist of a sequence of bytes, addressed from zero. Any structure must be imposed by the application that uses the file. The first thing to do is to consider our detail records as fixed sized; that is to say, all records in the file have exactly the same size. The size of our record must now be calculated; our Entry class has three fields; two Strings and an int. We know that an int, on every Java platform, has four bytes. Strings are, in a sense, unbounded, so we have to decide how big we are going to make them as far as the stored record is concerned. We have decided to make our surname and forename 15 bytes long. This means a stored record will have (15*2) + 4 bytes, or 34 bytes.

In order to store the contents of a Java String in a file, we can first of all convert the String into an array of bytes. We do this using the String method, getBytes. We can then write the bytes directly to the file. We are using a RandomAccessFile in our example; we shall discuss this class shortly.

However, as we discussed earlier, we are imposing a fixed size record structure on our file. We must ensure that we write 15 bytes into the file, and not just the number of characters contained in the string. We need to :

- Convert the String into an intermediate array of bytes.

- Copy these bytes into an array of 15 bytes.

- Pad out the remaining, unused bytes (we will use the null byte as padding).

We implement this algorithm as a method, as shown below:

```
private byte[] process(String str)
    {
        int i;
        byte res[] = new byte[RECORD_STRING_SIZE];
        byte temp[] = str.getBytes();
        for (i = 0; i < str.length();i++)
                res[i] = temp[i];
        for (i = str.length(); i < RECORD_STRING_SIZE; i++)
                res[i] = '\0';
        return res;
    } // end of method "process"
```

NOTE ∎

The notation byte res[]=... is an alternative way of declaring an array of bytes. Alternatively, we could have written byte[] res=....

We can use this as follows when writing to a file:

```
String inString, outString;
RandomAccessFile file = new RandomAccessFile("file.dat", "rw");
static final int RECORD_STRING_SIZE = 15;

...

// declare and create a new byte array
byte b1[] = process(outString);
file.write(b1);
```

When we read bytes back from the file, we must first of all place them in a byte array. We can then use a String constructor that takes a byte array and converts it into a String:

```
// declare and create a new byte array
byte b1[] = new byte [RECORD_STRING_SIZE];
file.readFully(b1);
inString = new String (b1);
```

Unfortunately, our job is not quite finished. Consider how we will be using our filed data in our application. If we write the byte array that contains the five characters that make up the name "Smith", we also write 10 null characters (making up the 15 bytes of RECORD_STRING_SIZE). When we read back 15 bytes from the file and convert them back into inString, we will find we have the "Smith" characters but also 10 null characters.

In our experience, when printing inString, Java will only output as far as the first null character. Thus, inString appears to be correct. However, when comparing the value of inString with another (as we will do when looking for a match with a search key), the string "Smith" will not match with the contents of inString as it only has 5 characters while inString has 15.

To overcome this problem, we used the following steps. We convert inString into an array of characters. We then use our method sizeOf to count the number of non-null characters. Finally, we construct a new String from the array of characters using the size we have obtained. This will successfully convert "Smith" followed by 10 null characters into just "Smith", as we require:

```
char temp[] = inString.toCharArray();
size = sizeOf(temp, inString.length());
inString = new String(temp, 0, size);

private int sizeOf(char chArray[], int length)
    {
    int i = 0;
    while ((chArray[i] != 0) && (i < length))
        i++;
    return i;
    }
```

Our main file will contain a number of record slots, each 34 bytes long. Because we are using fixed sized records, this gives us a very simple way of calculating the start (byte) address of any record contained in the file:

```
bytePos = recordNumber * RECORD_SIZE ;
```

Finally, we require direct access to any record. What this means is that if we need record number 5, we do not want to have to start at the beginning of the file and sequentially read (and throw away!) the first 5 records (numbers 0 to 4) in order to get to the record we actually want. We want to be able to move directly to the start (byte) address of the record and to read in RECORD_SIZE bytes from that position.

As far as our internal representation is concerned, we will adopt a "one-record-at-a-time" approach. Whenever we need an entry from the file, we will read it into an Entry object.

23.2.3   The RandomAccessFile Class

Java provides a RandomAccessFile class that provides exactly the functionality we require. This class has the same capabilities as DataInputStream and DataOutputStream, plus the seek method, which allows us to dynamically change our current position in the file.

It is worth noting that `RandomAccessFile`, `DataInputStream`, and `DataOutputStream` share two Interfaces (`DataInput` and `DataOutput`). So while they are at different points on the inheritance hierarchy, the use of Interfaces guarantees that all three of the classes provide the same functionality (which is specified in the two interfaces).

To open a `RandomAccessFile`, we use a constructor as follows:

```
RandomAccessFile myInput = new
    RandomAccessFile("in.dat", "r");
```

The first parameter is the name of a file, and the second is an access mode specifier. We can open a `RandomAccessFile` for reading (as above, using "r") or for writing and reading (using "rw" as in our earlier example).

We can read and write arrays of `bytes` (among other things like `chars`, `doubles`, `floats`, etc.). In our example, we have used `readFully` instead of `read`. These methods are specified in the `DataInput` interface. The difference between these two methods are:

- `read()` reads data into an array of bytes, blocking until at least some data is available.

- `readFully()` reads data into an array of bytes, blocking until all the data is available.

Finally, the main reason we want to use `RandomAccessFiles` is the ability to randomly change our current position in the file. For this we use the `seek()` method. To use this, we provide a long parameter specifying the new location in the file we wish to read/write from/to, as follows:

```
myInput.seek((long) 100);
```

This would change our current position in the file to byte 100.

23.2.4 The Index

We now turn our attention to how we are going to represent and handle the index. We are going to make the following assumptions:

- We do not know in advance how big the index is going to become.

- However, we do know it will never be so big that we cannot store all of it in main memory.

An index element will be modeled by the `IndexElem` class, which contains two attributes: a key (in this case, the surname) and an integer (the number of the entry within the main file that contains full details on the person). For the moment, we assume distinct surnames.

The index will thus be a collection of `IndexElem` objects. Now we have to decide on the internal representation of the index.

An initial candidate might be a simple array of `IndexElems`; arrays have to be a fixed size in Java, so we would have to decide how big the array is going to be. However, in our assumptions earlier, we do not know how big the array might become. We could make an arbitrary decision and guess as to how big it would ever be and proceed from there. Alternatively, we could model the index as a linked list.

However, we know that Java provides a number of classes for dynamically growing (and shrinking) collections, so we might consider these instead. First of all, we turn to the `Vector` class.

23.2.5   Suitability of the Vector Class: Internal Representation of the Index

At first sight, the Vector class might seem ideal. It can store any objects and grows and contracts as required. Moreover, remember that the index must be maintained in sorted order. A new entry as it arrives cannot be simply appended to the end of the index in "heap" fashion. We must find out where it belongs in the index and insert it there. If we modeled the index as an array, we would have to shift along every subsequent entry in the array to make room for it. Using a linked list would remove this problem. So too does the Vector class; it will take care of all these details on our behalf.

However, we do not use the index only for storing information; we must be able to retrieve that data on request. In our application, we would provide a surname and expect to get a suitable index element in reply. How can we search the Vector for a surname?

The Vector class provides a contains method:

```
v . contains(searchKey)
```

This returns *true* if the searchKey can be found, *false* otherwise. A Vector is capable of handling heterogeneous collections; in our case, however, all the contents will be IndexElem instances. The searchKey must therefore be an IndexElem.

However, this means we can only find out if the Vector contains exactly the same object as the one we are now searching for. In most cases, the IndexElem we used to insert the information will not now be the same one we are using as the searchKey.

For example, consider the following fragment of Java code:

```
IndexElem ieOne = new IndexElem ("Jones", 2);
Vector index = new Vector();
index.addElement(ieOne);
IndexElem ieTwo = new IndexElem("Jones",  2);
boolean res = index.contains(ieTwo); // result will be
                                     // false
```

The reason the result is false is because while the Vector contains a reference to ieOne (which has state identical to that of ieTwo), it does not contain a reference to the actual instance ieTwo.

In other words, we do not want to base the result of contains on object references, but rather on the contents (or state) of the objects. This *content-based retrieval* is one of the prime functions of database systems.

Even here, we do not want to use all the state of the searchKey; we only know the surname, not the record number (that is the information we are after). The Vector class calls the equals method in order to decide if the searchKey is equal to an element it contains.

This inability to retrieve by key prohibits the direct use of the Vector class.

23.2.6   Suitability of the Hashtable Class: Internal Representation of the Index

Hashtables are an attempt to provide direct access to internal data structures. Based on the value of a key, the position of the data within the structure is calculated and the data stored there. Retrieval is by the same mechanism:

```
table.put ( key, data) ;
```

We can use the `put` method to add our (surname, record number) pairs to the `Hashtable`. We can get rid of our `IndexElem` class, as the hashtable has replaced it. Because our key is a `String`, an object class that is treated specially as part of the Java language, the correct `equals` method is called and we can indeed retrieve data from this structure. However, if our key was (say) `IndexElem`, we would have exactly the same problems as we faced with the `Vector` class and its use of `equals`.

However, what happens if our directory stored more than one person with the same name?

```
table.put ("Smith", 3);
table.put ("Smith", 54);
```

The second `put` call overrides the original data (3). The `put` method returns an `Object` result, which we can check for the above situation arising. However, the question remains, what to do about the situation?

Probably the largest objection to the use of a `hashtable` in our situation is the requirement for sorted order. We want the user to be able to browse backward and forward through the sorted data. We have already decided to realize the main file as a heap, so we look to the index mechanism to provide that sorted order. By its very nature, a `hashtable` does not keep data in sorted order. It "scatters" the data across its storage structure.

23.2.7 Using the Vector Class Indirectly

We return to the `Vector` class. As you recall, the `Vector` class was pretty good as far as inserting data was concerned; it was its ability to retrieve data that let us down. We can use clientship instead of direct use or inheritance. We can define an `Index` class that contains a `Vector` instance as one of its attributes. Requests to add data to the index can eventually be passed on to the `Vector`. Retrieval (or `contains`) can be implemented by the `Index` class as follows:

- Convert the `Vector` into an `Enumeration`.

- Scan the `Enumeration` for the appropriate `searchKey`; return *true* if found, *false* otherwise.

23.3 The Classes in Detail

In this section, in conjunction with our discussion on how we will organize the file structures, we will decide what further classes and services are required in order to support our `DirBase` (directory entry database) class.

`DirBase` is the main object for the telephone directory application. It hides from its clients all details of how the directory is actually implemented. The abstraction it presents is an alphabetically ordered sequence of directory entries.

DirBase	Attributes	Methods
		contains
		getEntry
		add
		open
		close

Table 23-1: `DirBase` attributes and methods.

We can define five major services (as shown in Table 23-1):

- **contains.** Given a surname, returns the number (position) of the first directory entry that contains that surname if it exists. Otherwise, it returns −1. This implements the "search" functionality seen in Figure 22-7.

- **getEntry.** Given the position of a directory entry, this returns that entry.

- **add.** Adds a directory entry to the ordered sequence.

- **open** and **close.** Opens and closes a directory entry database.

In this and subsequent tables, we have omitted the constructor method(s); they are implicit for each class we design.

`DirEntry` is the class that represents an entry (or a record) in the main file—it consists of the following attributes and methods shown in Table 23-2.

DirEntry	(Private) Attributes	Methods
	surname	getSurname
	forename	getForename
	phoneNumber	getPhoneNumber

Table 23-2: `DirEntry` attributes and methods.

According to our specification, we can see no need to be able to alter or individually change attributes of a directory entry. We have therefore not provided any mutator methods. It is only at construction time that attribute values can be provided. However, we will need selector methods (the user interface will want to be able to get hold of the individual attributes in order to present them to the user); these are listed below:

- **getSurname, getForename, getPhoneNumber.** Returns the corresponding attribute value.

`IndexElem` contains the attributes and methods shown in Table 23-3.

IndexElem	(Private) Attributes	Methods
	recordNumber	getNumber
	key	getKey
		equals

Table 23-3: `IndexElem` attributes and methods.

Like our `DirEntry`, we assume there is no need for mutator methods. However, we will need to be able to select the individual attributes:

- **getKey, getNumber.** Returns the corresponding attribute value.

When searching the contents of the index, we will need to be able to find out if an index element contains the surname we are looking for. We have chosen to override the `equals` method to do this:

- **equals.** If this index element contains the surname we are looking for, return `true`; `false` otherwise.

It is the `Index` that supports the ordered sequence abstraction (see Table 23-4).

Index	Attributes	Methods
		contains
		indexOf
		elementAt
		addElement

Table 23-4: Index attributes and methods.

- **contains.** Given a surname, this returns true if the surname is in the index, false otherwise.
- **indexOf.** Given a surname, this returns the position of the first such surname if present, −1 otherwise.
- **elementAt.** Given a position, this returns the index element at that position.
- **addElement.** Given an index element, this adds it to the index at the correct position (maintaining the sorted order).

We can see how the first three methods can be used in conjunction to ensure we access the index safely, that is, only retrieve valid index elements:

```
if (index.contains("Smith"))
    element = index.elementAt(index.indexOf("Smith"));
```

Or:

```
int pos = index.indexOf("Smith");
if (pos != -1)
    element = index.elementAt(pos);
```

This concludes our high-level design of the four classes that make up the functionality of the DirBase.

23.3.1   Filing System Considerations

We discussed earlier how we would organize the filing system for our index sequential structure. We have reached a point in our design where we consider the main file. We will identify the need for additional methods that we have not yet featured in our design thus far.

To reiterate, the main file will contain an unordered sequence of directory entries. The index contains a *record number* that relates to a position within the main file. Given a record number, we want to be able to retrieve the corresponding directory entry from the main file:

```
DirEntry dirEnt = new DirEntry();
dirEnt.read(recordNumber);
```

We will also need to be able to write a directory entry to the main file:

```
dirEnt.write(recordNumber);
```

It seems natural to associate these input/output methods with a DirEntry object. However, we will also require methods that open and close the underlying file. If we recall that we can think of a class as both a definition and a collection of all instances of a class, then we can associate the open and close methods with the DirEntry class; we make them static so that they belong to the class rather than to individual objects. They will be called by the open and close methods of DirBase.

We can now sketch our possible implementation of DirBase.getEntry:

```
indElem = index.elementAt(pos);
entryNum = indElem.getNumber();
dirEnt.read(entryNum);
```

We can also outline DirBase.contains:

```
contains("Smith") --

    int pos = index.indexOf("Smith");
    if (pos != -1)
        {
        IndexElem element = index.elementAt(pos);
        dirEnt.read(element.getNumber());
        }
```

The last method of DirBase to consider is add:

add("Smith", 1948) --

```
dirEnt = new DirEntry("Smith", 1948);
dirEnt.write(pos);
indElem = new IndexElem("Smith", pos);
index.addElement(indElem);
```

In Table 23-5, we consider the attributes and methods belonging to the DirEntry class.

DirEntry	(Private) Attributes	Methods
	surname	getSurname
	forename	getForename
	phoneNumber	getPhoneNumber
		read
		write
		(static) open
		(static) close

Table 23-5: DirEntry attributes and methods.

In a similar fashion, we must make the index elements persistent. They too will require a read and write method. However, responsibility for opening and closing the file that will contain the index elements rests with the Index class. We now list (see Table 23-6) the attributes and methods belonging to the IndexElem class.

IndexElem	(Private) Attributes	Methods
	recordNumber	getNumber
	key	getKey
		equals
		read
		write

Table 23-6 : IndexElem attributes and methods.

For the prototype, we assume we can hold all of the index in memory at run time. Unlike our directory entries, which we read/write individually as required, we need only read the whole index in when we begin and write it all out when we finish. We call these methods load and save. These methods will process the contents of the index, and for each index element, will call the appropriate `read` or `write` method belonging to the `IndexElem` class. The `Index` class will `open` and `close` the file as required. We now turn to the `Index` class and list the attributes and methods it contains.

Index	Attributes	Methods
		contains
		indexOf
		elementAt
		addElement
		load
		save
		open
		close

Table 23-7 : Index attributes and methods.

You may wonder why we have decided to have `load` as well as `open`, and `save` as well as `close`. This is because the operations of opening and closing the index file are fundamental operations; we may at a later date decide that the index may be too large to be loaded in all at once and move to an approach similar to that taken with the directory entries. Or we may offer the facility to periodically save the contents of the index even though we are not finished using it. We simply do not wish to tie up two distinct operations under one single method, although there would seem little harm in doing so in our prototype. We are, however, thinking about the flexibility of our design and subsequent implementation for future development and maintenance.

23.3.2 Clientship

Finally, in this section we describe the clientship relationships between our four new classes and also the `RandomAccessFile` class that we shall be using. We have summarised this information in Table 23-8.

	DirBase	Index	IndexElem	DirEntry	RandomAccessFile
DirBase	•	yes	yes	yes	no
Index	no	•	yes	no	yes
IndexElem	no	no	•	no	yes
DirEntry	no	no	no	•	yes
RandomAccessFile	no	no	no	no	•

Table 23-8: Clientship relationships.

We can capture our design in the diagram in Figure 23-4.

Figure 23-4: Our design.

23.4 Moving Toward Implementation

In the following sections, we look at the classes we have identified as part of the system and provide headers and descriptions of the services that instances of the classes will have to offer.

23.4.1 The DirBase Class

This class is shown graphically in Figure 23-5.

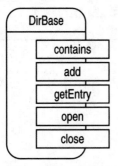

Figure 23-5: The DirBase class.

```
public int contains (String surname)
```

The abstraction presented to the DirBase client is an ordered sequence of entries. Given a surname, this returns the position of the first entry in the ordered sequence that contains that surname.

It returns -1 if the surname is not present in the system.

```
public DirEntry getEntry (int posNumber)
```

This method gets an entry back from the main file. The posNumber here refers to the entry's position in the sorted sequence of entries. Sequential calls of getEntry with an incrementing posNumber will thus see a stream of entries in sorted order.

```
public void add (String surname, String forename, int telNumber)
```

This method adds a new directory entry to the system.

```
public void open (String dbName)
```

This method opens the named directory database.

```
public void close()
```

This closes the current directory database.

23.4.2   The DirEntry Class

The DirEntry class (shown graphically in Figure 23-6) is intended to represent a directory entry. It possesses three private attributes: forename and surname to represent the person's names and phoneNumber to represent that person's phone number. Some of the methods of the class are intended to manipulate and manage these three attributes. They are as follows:

```
public String getSurname()
public String getForename()
public int getNumber()
```

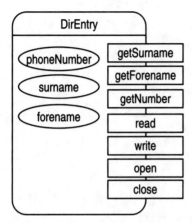

Figure 23-6: The `DirEntry` class.

These are the traditional `get` methods for the private attributes of the class.

The next two methods do not actually manipulate individual entries but are instead involved with the file in which entries will be stored.

```
static public boolean open (String filename)
```

This method opens a (random access) file. Part of the internal state of a `DirEntry` object is a random access file, which is set via this method. The method returns *true* if the file was successfully opened, *false* otherwise.

```
static public void close()
```

This method closes the (random access) file associated with the `DirEntry` object.

The last two methods are for reading and writing `DirEntry` information to and from the main file:

```
public void read(int recNum) throws IOException
public void write(int recNum) throws IOException
```

These interface routines calculate the start byte address of the entry in the file according to the parameter `recNum` and use the `RandomAccessFile.seek` method to make the start byte address our current position in the main file. They then handle the conversion of the internal attributes of `DirEntry` into a byte stream suitable for storage and loading from the file, and then they read or write from the calculated position.

Remember, here we take *record number* to refer to the entry's position within the main file. The *position number* in `DirBase` refers to the position of the index entry for the record within the sorted index.

23.4.3 The IndexElem Class

This class is shown graphically in Figure 23-7.

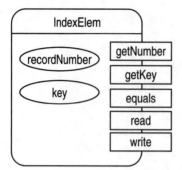

Figure 23-7: The `IndexElem` class.

```
public String getKey ()
public int getNumber ()
```

These are selector methods for the two attributes.

```
public Boolean equals (String key)
```

This returns *true* if the key associated with the calling object is equal to the key of the parameter, *false* otherwise.

The next two methods use the `elemNum` parameter to seek a position in the (random access) file before reading or writing an `IndexElem`:

```
public void read (RandomAccessFile file, int elemNum) throws IOException
public void write (RandomAccessFile file, int elemNum) throws IOException
```

23.4.4 The Index Class

This class is shown graphically in Figure 23-8.

Figure 23-8: The `Index` class.

```
public boolean contains (String searchKey)
```

If the String searchKey is contained within the Index, this method returns *true*, and *false* otherwise.

```
public int indexOf (String searchKey)
```

If the String searchKey is contained within the index, this method returns its position within, and −1 otherwise.

```
public IndexElem elementAt (int pos)
```

This method returns the index element residing at the given position.

```
public void addElement (IndexElem pie)
```

This method adds the index element pie to the index, maintaining its sorted order.
The next four methods relate to the persistent nature of the index.

```
public boolean open (String filename)
```

This method attempts to open the named file; it returns *true* if successful, *false* otherwise. The RandomAccessFile object is maintained as part of the internal state of the Index.

```
public void close()
```

This method closes the file.
As discussed earlier, in our initial prototype, we have decided to treat the index as a complete entity rather than individual blocks. This means that when our application starts up, we need to read all of the index file into the Index object. Similarly, when we shut down the application, we need to save the contents of the Index object in the index file. These next two methods are intended to take care of this problem:

```
public void save() throws IOException
public void load() throws IOException
```

23.5   Key Points in Chapter 23

- When designing a system that requires persistent data, the persistent data will normally be stored in a file. The use the application will make of this data influences how we choose to organize the layout of the file(s) involved.

- Our telephone directory application suggested the use of the *index sequential storage structure*. This involves two files, an index and a main file. Normally, the main file contains a sequence of records sorted by the field we will most commonly use for retrieval (i.e., surname). The index file contains a sequence of entries, again in sorted order. Each entry contains one search field (surname) and a pointer to the main file block that contains that surname in its first record.

- Care must be taken when converting `Strings` to byte arrays for storage in files and vice versa, as it is possible to end up with a `String` with trailing (invisible on printing) null bytes. This particularly causes problems when comparing `Strings`.

- `java.io` provides a `RandomAccessFile` class that supports random access to a file through the `seek` method that allows us to randomly change our location in the file.

- For our telephone directory application, we identified four classes: `DirBase`, `DirEntry`, `IndexElem`, and `Index`. The `Index` class uses a `Vector` instance as an attribute to support its operation.

- Filing system considerations caused us to make further design decisions and resulted in extending the design of our four classes to accommodate the need for persistency.

- Finally, we provided detailed method headers for each class.

23.6 Exercise

Continuing our work on the theater booking system, you should extend your design to take into account the persistent nature of the booking information. You may wish to consider using inheritance to add persistency to the classes you have already designed. This is discussed in section 24.5.

23.7 Reference

Elmasri, R., and S. B. Navathe. 1994. *Fundamentals of database systems.* 2nd ed. Redwood City, CA: Benjamin/Cummings.

CHAPTER 24

Case Study: Implementing the Personal Organizer (2)

24.1 Introduction

In this chapter, we continue the implementation process for the Java Personal Organizer (JPO). We present the source text for the four classes we have designed. We also discuss the process of testing the behavior of the classes through the provision of an application to set up an initial personal organizer from a text file and the provision of a text-based version of the final application. We can think of the latter as a kind of extended test harness for the classes involved.

We discuss and present the final, graphical version of the application. We then discuss the extensibility of our design and implementation.

24.2 Implementations of DirBase, Index, IndexElem & DirEntry

In these next four sections, we present and discuss the Java source code produced for each class following the design given in Section 23.4.

24.2.1 DirEntry Class Source & Commentary

The DirEntry class has the three attributes from the design and the associated get methods:

```
int phoneNumber;
String forename, surname;

// selector methods ..
public String getSurname()
  {
  return surname;
  }
```

```
public String getForename()
   {
   return forename;
   }

public int getNumber()
   {
   return phoneNumber;
   }
```

Next we have the constructor method:

```
public DirEntry (String fName, String sName, int number)
   {
   forename = fName;
   surname = sName;
   phoneNumber = number;
   }
```

Next we consider the main file methods. They are static, as they are associated with the class rather than individual objects:

```
static RandomAccessFile file;
public static boolean open(String fileName)
// tries to open the named file; returns "true" if
// successful,"false" otherwise
   {
   boolean res = true;
   try  {
      file = new RandomAccessFile(fileName, "rw");
      }
   catch (IOException e) {
      res = false;
      }
   return res;
   } // end of method "open"

public static void close()
// closes the currently opened file
   {
   try  {
      file.close();
      }
   catch (IOException e)
      {
      }

   } // end of method "close"
```

Next we provide the ability to read and write individual DirEntry objects. We begin by declaring some constants to represent the size (in bytes) of a dirEntry in the file. We have decided the largest string we will handle will have 15 characters (bytes). As a dirEntry is made up of two such strings (one for forename and one for surname) plus an integer (representing a phone number), we can calculate the total size of an entry:

```
// details of the number of bytes a "dirEntry" occupies
// on the filing system
private static final int RECORD_STRING_SIZE = 15;
private static final int RECORD_SIZE =
            (RECORD_STRING_SIZE * 2) + 4;
```

Now the read and write methods:

```
public void read(int recNum) throws IOException
// read a record from the specified RandomAccessFile
    {
    file.seek((long) recNum * RECORD_SIZE);
    phoneNumber = file.readInt();
    byte b1[] = new byte [RECORD_STRING_SIZE];
    file.readFully(b1);
    forename = new String (b1, 0);
    byte b2[] = new byte[RECORD_STRING_SIZE];
    file.readFully(b2);
    surname = new String (b2, 0);
    } // end of method "read"

private byte[] process(String str)
    {
      int i;
      byte res[] = new byte[RECORD_STRING_SIZE];
      byte temp[] = str.getBytes();
      for (i = 0; i < str.length();i++)
              res[i] = temp[i];
      for (i = str.length(); i < RECORD_STRING_SIZE; i++)
              res[i] = '\0';
      return res;
    } // end of method "process"

public void write(int recNum)
    throws IOException
    {
    file.seek((long) recNum * RECORD_SIZE);
    file.writeInt(phoneNumber);
    if (forename == null) throw new
       IOException("trying to output unset forename");
```

```
byte b1[] = process(forename);
file.write(b1);
if (surname == null) throw new
   IOException("trying to output unset surname");
byte b2[] = process(surname);
file.write(b2);
} // end of method "write"
```

We do not include the additional code discussed in section 23.2.2, which handles the additional null bytes that occur when we convert a byte array to a `String`. This is because we don't really need to as far as entries in our main file are concerned. All we ever do with these entries is display them, and `System.out.println` appears to stop printing characters in a `String` as soon as it reaches a null character. It is only of concern when we want to compare two `Strings`, as we do when searching the `Index` for a match, so we will see the code again in section 24.2.2.

Finally, we present a couple of additional methods. First, we override `toString`, often a useful thing to do:

```
public String toString()
   {
   return surname + ", " + forename + " " +
         phoneNumber + " ";
   }
```

Second, we provide a method that "clears" a `dirEntry` to a "null" entry. This operation is useful when we wish to return a `dirEntry` and we were unable to fetch one from the main file:

```
public void clear ()
// clear a "dirEntry" to appropriate "empty" values
   {
   forename = surname = null;
   phoneNumber = 0;
   } // end of "clear" method
```

The first line of this method sets both the `String` attribute references, `forename` and `surname`, to null.

24.2.2   IndexElem Class Source & Commentary

The IndexElem class has the two attributes identified in the design, plus associated constructors and selector methods:

```
String key;
int recordNumber;
// constructor methods ..

public IndexElem(String k, int rNum)
```

```
        {
        key = new String(k); // make a deep copy of the String
        recordNumber = rNum;
        }


    // selector methods ..
    public String getKey()
        {
        return key;
        }

    public int getNumber()
        {
        return recordNumber;
        }
```

Now we turn our attention to input and output of IndexElems. As with DirEntry, we begin by declaring some constants to represent the size of a String in a file and the size of a complete IndexElem.

```
    // input/output methods and constants

    static final int RECORD_STRING_SIZE = 15;
    static final int IE_SIZE = RECORD_STRING_SIZE + 4;
```

As we discussed previously, we have to take care about reading back Strings from a file because they are padded out with null characters when written. We present here again our sizeOf method and how it is used in our read method:

```
    private int sizeOf(char chArray[], int length)
        {
        int i = 0;
        while ((chArray[i] != 0) && (i < length))  i++;
        return i;
        }


    public void read(RandomAccessFile file, int recNum)
throws IOException
        {
        int size;
        file.seek((long)recNum * IE_SIZE);
        recordNumber = file.readInt();
        byte b1[] = new byte [RECORD_STRING_SIZE];
        file.readFully(b1);
        key = new String (b1, 0);
```

```
char temp[] = key.toCharArray();
size = sizeOf(temp, key.length());
key = new String(temp, 0, size);
} // end of method "read"

private byte[] process (String str)
  {
  // as seen earlier ..
  }

public void write(RandomAccessFile file, int recNum)
throws IOException
  {
  file.seek((long)recNum * IE_SIZE);
  file.writeInt(recordNumber);
  byte b1[] = new byte[RECORD_STRING_SIZE];
  if (key == null) throw new
    IOException("trying  to output an unset key");
  byte b1[] = process(key);
  file.write(b1);
  } // end of method "write"
```

Finally, an extra method, the ever useful toString override:

```
public String toString()
  {
  return key + " " + recordNumber;
  }
```

24.2.3   Index Class Source & Commentary

We begin with the attributes of the Index class:

```
Vector v;                     // the index's home in main memory
RandomAccessFile file;    // the index's home on the filing system
```

Our constructor initializes our Vector attribute.

```
public Index () // constructor
  {
  v = new Vector(10);
  }
```

While moving from our detailed design to implementation, we realized that we would need a method that returns how many elements our Index contains, so we provided a size method, as described next.

When a request is made to find out the size (the number of current elements in our index), we delegate this to our Vector attribute and return the result directly:

```
public int size()
// return the number of index elements in the index
    {
    return v.size();
    }
```

Similarly, when we need to return an element at a specific position, we delegate this to our Vector attribute. However, although Vectors are capable of storing any Object reference, we know that only IndexElems will be maintained in the Vector attribute of the Index class. This means we can safely cast the result of the Vector method to IndexElem:

```
public IndexElem elementAt(int pos)
// return the index element at the requested position
    {
    return (IndexElem) v.elementAt(pos);
    }
```

We move on to our two "search" methods, contains and indexOf. Both take a String searchKey parameter that will contain the surname that corresponds to the phone number we are after. They treat the contents of the Vector attribute as an Enumeration instance. We then loop through the contents of the Vector and test each one for equality with the search key. As soon as we find a match, we terminate the loop.

The contains method simply returns a Boolean result, "true" if the searchKey is in the index, "false" otherwise:

```
public boolean contains(String searchKey)
// given a search key, this method looks at each index   // element.
// if it finds the required key, it returns "true";
// "false" otherwise.
    {
    boolean res = false;
    Enumeration e = v.elements();
    IndexElem ie;
    while (e.hasMoreElements() && !res)
        {
        ie = (IndexElem)e.nextElement();
        res = searchKey.equals(ie.getKey());
        }
    return res;
    } // end of method "contains"
```

The indexOf method returns the actual position of the search key within the index and returns –1 if not found:

```
public int indexOf(String searchKey)
// given a search key, this method examines each index   // element.
// when it finds a match, it returns the position of the // element within
the index; 0 otherwise.
    {
```

```
boolean flag = false;
int res = -1, count = 0;
Enumeration e = v.elements();
IndexElem ie;
while (e.hasMoreElements() && !flag)
   {
   ie = (IndexElem)e.nextElement();
   flag = searchKey.equals(ie.getKey());
   if (flag) res = count;
   count++;
   }
return res;
} // end of method "indexOf"
```

Next, we come to the addElement method. This is probably the largest method in the Index class. This is because it is concerned with maintaining the sorted order of the Index; we can't simply just add the element directly to the Vector attribute:

```
public void addElement(IndexElem pie)
// this method adds an index element to the index,
// maintaining the sorted order
   {
   // find out where the element belongs
   boolean flag = false;
   int cres = 0, res = 0, count = 0;
   Enumeration e = v.elements();
   String add, current;
   IndexElem ie;

   // special case -- empty vector
   int vSize = v.size();
   if (vSize == 0)
      {
      v.addElement(pie);
      return;
      }

   add = pie.getKey();

   while (e.hasMoreElements() && !flag)
      {
      ie = (IndexElem)e.nextElement();
      current = ie.getKey();
```

```
        cres = add.compareTo(current);
        if (cres <= 0)
          {
          flag = true;
          res = count;
          }
        count++;
        }

    // if the new string is larger than the last element
    if (!flag) res = count;

    // at last we know where the new
    // index element belongs ..
    v.insertElementAt(pie, res);
    } // end of method "addElement"
```

We have two special cases to consider: First, is this the first element in the Vector? Second, is this larger than the last element in the Vector? In between, we must find out where within the current index the new element should be placed.

We start off with the simplest case; is the Vector currently empty? We can find out by using the Vector.size() method. If it is empty, we add the element and leave.

If it isn't, we must find out where it belongs. We extract the surname from the index element we are trying to add. As in our "search" methods, we treat the contents of the Vector attribute as an Enumeration instance and loop through. We compare the "add" String with the surname String from the current index element. As soon as we find a stored surname that is less than or equal to the "add" surname, we terminate the loop, as we have found out where to store the new index element.

As part of the scanning loop, we keep a count of which element we are looking at.

When the loop terminates because we have found a stored surname less than or equal to the surname to be added, res is set to the position where we should add the new element.

Having left the loop, we need to take into account the reason why the loop terminated. We terminate the loop because either:

- We have found a stored surname less than or equal to the surname being added, as we have described earlier.

- We have run out of index elements to look at without finding a suitable stored surname.

If it is the latter, then this means the surname to be added is greater than any of the stored surnames and should be added at the end of the Vector attribute. We can check this by examining the value of the flag boolean; if it is *false*, then we did not find a suitable surname, and we set the value of res to the value of count.

At this point in the method, then, res contains the position where the new element is to be added to the Vector attribute, regardless of whether it belongs somewhere within the Vector or at the end. We can finally add the element to the Vector.

We move on to the input/output methods by which we achieve the persistence of the Index. We start with the basic open and close methods, which simply open and close the underlying file used to store the Index:

```
// input/output methods; for the
// persistency of the index

public boolean open(String fileName)
  {
  boolean res = true;
  try {
    file = new RandomAccessFile(fileName, "rw");
    }
  catch (IOException e) {
    System.out.println("problem in Index.open");
    System.exit(0);
    res = false;
    }
  return res;
  } // end of "open"

public void close()
  {
  try {
    file.close();
    }
  catch (IOException e)
    {
    // not doing anything intelligent
    }
  } // end of "close"
```

Now we come to the load and save methods. As we have discussed, unlike the directory entries themselves (which are individually read and written as necessary), all of the elements contained in the index are loaded up when our application starts running; similarly, when the application terminates, all the elements are stored back in the file:

```
public void save() throws IOException
// saves the index elements in the file
  {
  Enumeration e = v.elements();
  IndexElem ie;
  int count = 0;

  file.seek((long)0);
```

```
while (e.hasMoreElements())
  {
  ie = (IndexElem)e.nextElement();
  ie.write(file, count);
  count++;
  }
} // end of method "save"
```

In method save, we begin by using the seek method associated with the RandomAccessFile class. We must make sure that we are at the start of the file before doing any "writes." This is because if we didn't, chances are we would be appending the index at the end of the file. If this is not the first time we've used the file, this would probably have the effect of placing the current version of the index after the old version.

Again, we treat the contents of the Vector attribute as an Enumeration instance and loop through them, writing each IndexElem individually:

```
public void load() throws IOException
// loads the index elements from the
// file into main memory
  {
  IndexElem ie = new IndexElem();
  boolean goon = true;
  int count = 0;

  file.seek((long)0);

  while (goon)
    {
    try  {
       ie.read(file, count);
       count++;
       }
    catch (IOException e)
       {
       goon = false;
       }
    if (goon)
       {
       v.addElement(ie);
       ie = new IndexElem();
       }
    }
} // end of method "load"
```

In method load, we again ensure that we are at the start of the file by using seek. We read in a new IndexElement from the file and add it directly to the Vector element. We don't need to make sure the index is in sorted order because we know it will always be saved in this order. We can use Vector.addElement instead of Index.addElement.

We control the loop that processes the file through the detection of an *end-of-file* exception. As long as this exception has not been raised, we add the IndexElement to the Vector attribute.

Finally, we again have an additional method to assist with debugging the Index class; it prints out the index elements in the index. We can therefore see at a glance if entries are being added in alphabetical order:

```
public void print()
// debugging method .. prints out all the index
// elements in the index
   {
   Enumeration e = v.elements();
   IndexElem ie;
   System.out.println("index contains ..");
   while (e.hasMoreElements())
      {
      ie = (IndexElem)e.nextElement();
      System.out.println(ie);
      }
   } // end of method "print"
```

24.2.4   *DirBase Class Source & Commentary*

The DirBase class contains a single attribute:

```
static Index index;
```

which represents the Index client.

Its constructor method takes a single String parameter that acts as the name of the directory entry database. Using the String concatenation operator, it adds a .ind extension to denote the index file and .dat to denote the main file. It passes requests on to the Index object and the DirEntry class to open up these files. It loads the Index object from the index file:

```
// constructor method ..

public DirBase(String dbName)
   {
   index = new Index();
   index.open(dbName + ".ind");
   try {
      index.load();
      }
   catch (IOException e)
      {
      // if we can't load the index, not much point
      // in continuing ..
```

```
        System.exit(0);
      }

    index.print();
    DirEntry.open(dbName + ".dat");
    } // end of constructor
```

The constructor therefore implicitly opens up the "database" (actually, the index and main files). We must have a matching close method:

```
public void close()
// close the database down ..
// delegates to the Index and DirEntry classes ..
    {
    try  {
        index.save();
        index.close();
        DirEntry.close();
        }
    catch (IOException e)
        {
        System.exit(0);
        }

    } // end of method "close"
```

We now present the add service. It does a fair bit of delegation. First of all it creates a new DirEntry instance using its parameters. It finds out where the end of the main file is by asking the index what size it currently is. This gives it the "next record slot" and it calls DirEntry.write accordingly. Having added the DirEntry to the end of the main file heap, it now creates a new IndexElem instance and adds that to the index (using Index.addElement to ensure sorted order is maintained):

```
public void add(String sname, String fname, int number)
// adds a directory entry triple to the system ..
    {
    // create a new "dirEntry"
    DirEntry rec = new DirEntry(fname, sname, number);

    // find out where the end of the main file is
    int nextRecSlot = index.size();

    try  {
        // write the new entry into the main file
        rec.write(nextRecSlot);
        }
    catch (IOException e)
```

```
        {
        System.err.println("DirBase.add " + e);
        System.exit(-1);
        }

    // create a new index element for the entry
    IndexElem ie = new IndexElem(sname, nextRecSlot);

    // add it to the index
    index.addElement(ie);

    } // end of method "add"
```

Now we come to the search (contains) and retrieve (getEntry) methods. The contains method takes a search key and, by delegation, uses Index.contains to find out if the search key is present in the index. If so, it uses Index.indexOf to get its position in the index; otherwise it returns −1:

```
public int contains (String surname)
// given a key surname, return it's position in the
// index if it is not present, return −1
    {
    int recNum = -1;
    if (index.contains(surname))
      {
      recNum = index.indexOf(surname);
      };
    return recNum;
    } // end of method "contains"
```

Once we have a position within the index, we can obtain the DirEntry indicated by the index entry. The getEntry method obtains the index element at that position, extracts the associated record number (the position of the directory entry in the main file), and used DirEntry.read to retrieve the entry from the file, which it returns as its result:

```
public DirEntry getEntry(int recNum)
// given a position in the index, return the record
// indicated by that index element
    {
    int  mainRecNum, position;
    DirEntry rec = new DirEntry();

    // get the relevant index element
    IndexElem ie = index.elementAt(recNum);

    // extract the main record number from
    // the index element
    mainRecNum = ie.getNum();
```

```
try {
   // read the directory entry
   rec.read(mainRecNum);
   }
catch (IOException e)
   {
   // make it into a "null" entry
   rec.clear();
   }
return rec;
} // end of method "getEntry"
```

Strictly speaking, this next find method could be implemented by the client because it really combines contains and getEntry. However, it was provided for client convenience:

```
public DirEntry find (String surname)
// this method combines "contains" and "getEntry" for
// the convenience of the client.
// given a key "surname", this returns the
// matching directory entry.
// If not found, returns a "null" entry.
   {
   int recNum = contains(surname);
   if (recNum == -1)
      {
      DirEntry empty = new DirEntry();
      empty.clear();
      return empty;
      }

   return (getEntry(recNum));
   } // end of method "find"
```

We now come to two debugging methods. One prints out the current state of the index by delegation, passing a "print" request on to the index. The second involves more implementation work as it reads through the main file, printing each directory entry individually. Arguably, this method should be part of the DirEntry class:

```
public void indexPrint()
// debugging method ..
   {
   index.print();
   }

public void mainPrint()
// debugging method ..
// sequentially read and display the contents of the
// main file, one record at a time.
```

```
{
int i = 0;
DirEntry rec = new DirEntry();
boolean goon = true;

while (goon)
  {
  try  {
     rec.read(i);
     }
  catch (IOException e)
     {
     // we expect "end-of-file" to occur, so
     // stop the loop when it does.
     goon = false;
     };
  if (goon) System.out.println(i+" "+ rec);
  i++;
  }

} // end of method "mainPrint"
```

Finally, we provide a size method so that clients can find out how many records are in the directory entry database. Again, this is implemented by delegation, to the Index instance:

```
public int size()
// return how many records are currently in the system
  {
  return index.size();
  }
```

24.3 Testing What We Have Done So Far

At this point, we want to test the various classes we have designed and implemented. In order to do this, we propose two programs. First, because it can be tedious to interactively enter lots of test data, we want to have an initialization (Init) program. It will read text from a file (through standard input) and then store the corresponding records in a DirBase. This will allow us to test the methods for:

- Opening and closing the index and main files
- Generally accessing the stored data
- Adding entries to the index (are they being kept in alphabetical order?)

The format of the data is:

```
surname forename phoneNumber
```

24.3.1 Using a StreamTokenizer

We can use a StreamTokenizer to help us process the data contained in the file. We have already met StringTokenizer earlier in this book (section 19.4.1); StreamTokenizer is similar except it operates on streams. It acts like a lexical analyzer on our input stream reader and breaks up the input into tokens. To use a StreamTokenizer (which can be found in the java.io package), we wrap an input stream reader inside an instance. Thereafter, we can use the method nextToken to return the next token in the stream. The result of nextToken is an int that represents the kind of token we have just processed; these are coded as class constants:

- TT_EOF—end of file
- TT_EOL—end of line
- TT_NUMBER—numeric value
- TT_WORD—text

The StreamTokenizer instance provides two public attributes, nval and sval. The nval attribute is a double and stores the numeric value if the result of nextToken was TT_NUMBER; sval is a String that contains the text if nextToken's result was TT_WORD. Notice that these attributes are public, so we can access them directly without using selector methods.

A general structure that we could apply to process a stream of input might be as follows:

```
StreamTokenizer stin = new StreamTokenizer(mySomeInputStreamReader);
boolean goon = true; int myNumber;

while (goon)
  {
  result = stin.nextToken();
  switch (result)
    {
    case TT_EOF : // finished processing!
      goon = false;
      break;
    case TT_EOL : // do something or just ignore it
      break;
    case TT_NUMBER :
      myNumber = (int) stin.nval;
      // process the value
      break;
    case TT_WORD :
      myText = new String(stin.sval); // deep copy
      // process the value
      break;
    default :
System.err.println("StreamTokenizer.nextToken produced strange result");
      break;
    }
  }
```

Anywhere we have a "simple fixed structured format" for input, a `StreamTokenizer` can prove very useful indeed. The design of `Init` is shown in Figure 24-1.

Figure 24-1: High-level design of Init.

```
// Init class (main program)
// ==========

import java.io.*;
import java.util.*;

class Init
    {
    public static void main(String[] args)  throws
         IOException
    {
    StreamTokenizer din = new StreamTokenizer(
            new InputStreamReader(System.in));
    int tok;
    String sName = new String();
    String fName = new String();
    int pNum = 0;
    boolean goon = true;
    DirBase db = new DirBase("telinfo");
```

We begin with a number of declarations. The declarations of most interest are those involving the `StreamTokenizer` and the `DirBase` classes. The `StreamTokenizer` constructor associates the stream with standard input (from the keyboard or redirected from a file). The `DirBase` constructor, which operates as an open method, takes the name of a directory entry database that we assume is currently empty.

```
while (goon)
  {
  tok = din.nextToken();
  if (tok != din.TT_EOF)
    {
    if (tok == din.TT_WORD)
      sName = din.sval;
    else {
      System.out.println("expected a surname");
      System.exit(0);
      }

    tok = din.nextToken();
    if (tok == din.TT_WORD)
      fName = din.sval;
    else {
      System.out.println("expected a forename");
      System.exit(0);
      }

    tok = din.nextToken();
    if (tok == din.TT_NUMBER)
      pNum = (int) din.nval;
    else {
      System.out.println("expected a phone number");
      System.exit(0);
      }

    if (tok != din.TT_EOF)
      db.add(sName, fName, pNum);
    } else goon = false;
  };
```

The while loop in the preceding code is the workhorse of the initialization application. As long as there are tokens left in the stream, we will keep going. In the body of the loop, we try to extract three tokens; one for the surname, one for the forename, and one for the telephone number. We attempt some error checking, in that we expect a word, followed by a word, followed by a number. If this order is broken, we print an error message and terminate the application.

If we arrive safely at the end of the loop body, we should have the components of a directory entry. We use DirBase.add to add this entry to the directory entry database.

```
System.out.println("index is ");
db.indexPrint();
db.close();
  }

} // end of Init class
```

Finally, we print out the state of the index contained within the `DirBase` class and close down the directory entry database.

Now that we have successfully implemented and tested our `DirBase` class (and by extension and delegation, the classes that support it) using our `Init` application, it would be possible to incorporate the `Init` functionality as a method within `DirBase`.

Note also that our design completely hides details of the `DirBase`-supporting classes (`Index`, `IndexElem`, and `DirEntry`) from clients of `DirBase`. We shall see in the next chapter that this is a desirable property of design.

24.3.2 Text-Based Interface—Intermediate Application & Testing

Our second "test" program is a complete implementation of the final functionality of the system. However, the interface is text based rather than graphical. The commands we want to support include some we have already identified, plus a couple for testing and for user assistance:

- **stop.** Closes down the application and asks the `DirBase` to ensure persistent data is saved and all associated files closed.

- **find <surname>.** Provided with a surname, uses the `DirBase` to find out if an entry with that surname exists. If it does, the entry is displayed on the screen.

- **add <surname, forename, number>.** Adds this entry to the `DirBase` .

- **help.** Prints out a list of commands supported by the application.

The next two commands are really only useful for testing and with small amounts of data. Imagine using them with a telephone directory with thousands of entries:

- **index print.** Prints out the current state of the index.

- **main print.** Prints out the current contents of the main file.

```
// Main class (main program)
// ==========

import java.io.*;
import java.util.*;
import java.lancs.*;

class Main
   {
   static DirBase dirBase;
```

We begin with two "interactive" methods. In order to make classes as reusable as possible, we have to be careful as to how much interaction they have with the end user. For example, if we were providing a class that may be used as part of an embedded system, there is little use in having extensive dialog with the user because:

- There may not be a direct user.
- The system may not be connected to a keyboard.

In our case, we have tried to limit direct interaction with DirBase and its supporting classes. This is partly because we knew we would have to provide a graphical interface, and here again, we expect most interaction to take place via graphical components such as windows, menus, buttons, and text fields rather than directly through the keyboard.

So that the keyboard user can access the find and add methods of DirBase, then, we provide a couple of "enveloping" interactive methods:

```
static void findInteractive() throws IOException
    {
    String sname;
    BasicIo.prompt("type surname : ");
    sname = BasicIo.readString();
    DirEntry rec = dirBase.find(sname);
    System.out.println(rec);
    }

static void addInteractive() throws IOException
    {
    String sname, fname;
    int number;
    BasicIo.prompt("Surname : ");
    sname = BasicIo.readString();
    BasicIo.prompt("Forename : ");
    fname = BasicIo.readString();
    BasicIo.prompt("Number : ");
    number = BasicIo.readInteger();
    dirBase.add(sname, fname, number);
    }
```

The next method is the workhorse of the text-based application. It reads in single-character commands from the end user and uses a switch statement to decide which action to take; often, as we would expect, this involves invoking a DirBase method:

```
static void interpCommands() throws IOException
    {
    String com;
    boolean goon = true;

    while (goon)
        {
        BasicIo.prompt(">> ");
        com = BasicIo.readString();

        switch (com.charAt(0))
            {
            case 's' : goon = false; break;
            case 'f' : findInteractive(); break;
            case 'a' : addInteractive(); break;
```

```
      case 'i' : dirBase.indexPrint(); break;
      case 'p' : dirBase.mainPrint(); break;
      case 'h' : listCommands(); break;
      default :
         System.out.println("Unknown command");
         break;
      };
   } /* end of command loop */


} // end of method "interpCommands"
```

Notice as an alternative to providing the two "interactive" methods, we could have included the code we needed as part of the appropriate case statement. However, as you can see in the preceding code, it is very simple to read and understand the case statement as it stands. By including the "interactive" methods code here, we may have complicated the overall switch statement.

Finally, we present the main method itself, and a simple method that will list the commands available to the end user:

```
private static void listCommands()
   {
   System.out.println("s : stop \n f : find \n a : add");
   System.out.println
      ("i : index print \n p : records print");
   System.out.println("h : help");
   }


public static void main(String[] args) throws IOException
   {
   dirBase = new DirBase("telinfo");
   interpCommands();
   dirBase.close();
   }


} // end of class Main
```

24.3.3 What Are We Testing?

We have written these two "intermediate" applications for the express purpose of testing the classes we have designed and implemented. We want to ensure that they operate as expected. We are looking for the following:

- When we open a DirBase, are the index and main files opened as expected?
- When we close a DirBase, are the index and main files closed correctly, with the expected information therein?

■ When we add a new directory entry to a `DirBase`, is the index updated correctly? Is the entry appended to the end of the main file as we expect?

When we are concerned with files, it is often helpful to have some way other than the application itself to examine the contents and layout of the files we are using. UNIX has a very useful `od` facility that allows us to view the contents of the file in various ways.

Issues of adding new entries focus on the sorted order of the index. Is it maintained? What we need to test are the boundary conditions—what happens when we add an entry:

■ To an empty `DirBase`?

■ That belongs at the end of the `DirBase`?

■ That belongs at the start of the `DirBase`?

■ That belongs in the middle of the `DirBase`?

We should test the system with a list of entries that are:

■ In random order.

■ In order.

■ In reverse order.

Finally, we must consider being able to find entries in the `DirBase`. Again, the emphasis is on boundaries. We should search for entries which we know:

■ Are at the start of the ordered list.

■ Are at the end of the ordered list.

■ Are in the middle of the ordered list.

■ Do not exist.

24.4   Graphical User Interface—The Final Prototype Application

Now that we are confident that the classes and files we have designed work as expected, we can turn our attention to providing a graphical user interface for our personal organizer. Most users now expect fairly sophisticated graphical interfaces and would reject an application that provided the kind of user interface our test harness has. Java's *AWT* classes at least ease the implementation problem of generating such a graphical interface. However, this does not help us handle the graphical design problems of such interfaces. Clearly, the AWT classes make it simpler to generate a slap-dash interface that is very graphical, but that interface may not be very useful.

The issues of graphical interface design are beyond the scope of this book; interested readers should refer to *Designing the User Interface* (Shneiderman 1992).

The GUI we designed can be described as follows. The main window displays a title for the general application and a number of buttons, one for each function of the JPO and a general

Done button to terminate the session. As we have only implemented one aspect of the personal organizer, we have only one button for the directory function.

The DirGui (directory interface) displays two buttons, one for New (interactively introduce new records to the system) and one for Done. For finding entries, we have a Find label and a blank text field. To initiate a search, the user types a value and terminates it by the Return key. An earlier design and implementation consisted of a Find button and a blank text field. However, using the system in practice showed that a user needed to undertake two separate actions to initiate a search: typing in the search key and then pressing a button. This felt unsatisfactory, and thus we switched to the current design/implementation.

The BrowseRecGui (browsing found records interface) has label and text field pairs, one for each Record attribute. It also has three buttons: the perennial Done button, plus a forward (>>) and backward (<<) button to support that mode of browsing.

The NewRecGui (new record interface) similarly has label and text field pairs, plus two buttons, Done and Enter. The latter causes the record, if fully specified, to be stored in the DirBase.

A sketch of the proposed interface is shown in Figure 24-2.

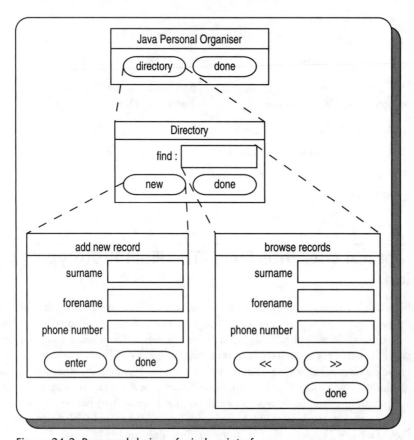

Figure 24-2: Proposed design of window interface.

Each window has a corresponding class of its own. This means we can map this quite readily onto the partial H-S&E diagram shown in Figure 24-3.

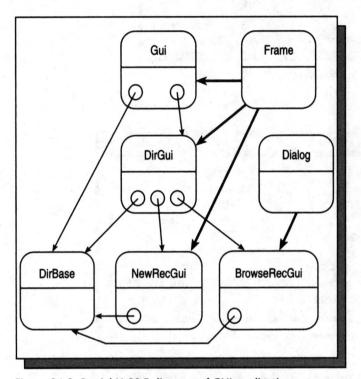

Figure 24-3: Partial H-S&E diagram of GUI application.

All of our GUI classes will have to communicate with the DirBase to search and retrieve records from it. They will also contain references to several AWT classes, including Buttons, Labels, and TextFields. As you can imagine, showing this in a diagram would lead to quite a clutter. When you examine the source for the application, you will also find a reference to the AlertDialog class that inherits from the AWT Dialog class.

Screendumps of the GUIs for the organizer and the directory, and the actions of browsing and adding, are shown in Figures 24-4 to 24-7.

Figure 24-4: The organizer.

Figure 24-5: The directory.

Figure 24-6: Browsing Records.

Figure 24-7: Adding a new Record.

24.4.1   *Testing the Graphical Interface*

We should repeat the set of tests that we carried out on the text-based version of our application. As you recall, those tests involved adding and locating entries at the boundaries and in the middle of our ordered list. The graphical interface gives us the additional ability to browse through the ordered list; we should, of course, ensure that this browsing presents the entries in the correct order.

24.5   Using Inheritance

In this example, we have used inheritance only in our GUI classes. We did not exploit the feature in our JPO classes. This is because (obviously!) either our design did not call for it or we were unable to use it. Once we had uncovered the unsuitability of using the Vector class directly, we could not introduce a new class Index that inherited directly from Vector. Instead, we had to use clientship to exploit those features of Vectors that were suitable.

Clearly, there will be cases where inheritance is more suitable; we have presented scenarios of inheritance in action earlier in the book. Let's stay with our JPO design for a moment and consider possible uses for inheritance if we were to evolve our design.

We quite deliberately named the DirEntry class to reflect the fact that we were treating the information contained within it as a classic example of a record in data processing. We were not modeling a person (as we have done so many times throughout this book), but a directory entry.

Consider, however, a computer dating agency. Its employees will also maintain a database of records about people, but when processing this data, they will often have to compare two people to gauge their suitability for each other. It will be more natural for the designers and programmers to think of people at this point rather than records. We can use inheritance to support this. We can design the class Person, which contains information regarding individuals. We can have a subclass PersistPerson, which contains the support for making Person information persistent (i.e., saving it between applications).

We have a clear division of concepts; on the one hand, we have the pure Person class, which can contain methods only about people. For example:

```
int compatible (Person p)
```

This could return a measure from 0 to 100 to show how compatible the calling Person object is with the parameter Person object.

On the other hand, we have the PersistPerson class (see Figure 24-8), which contains methods and management information about opening and closing the Person database and reading, writing, and retrieving information from that database. Because of polymorphism, everywhere we expect a Person instance, we can use a PersistPerson instance instead. Designers and developers of the Person class can exclusively think in terms of Person. Users and clients of the Person class, who are developing software in terms of PersistPerson, can quite happily use their PersistPerson instances with the Person class.

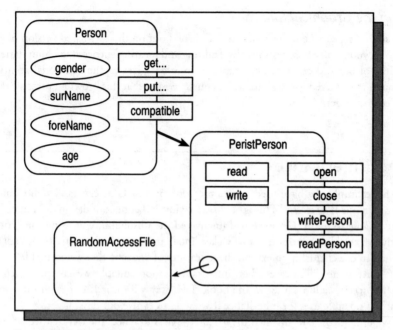

Figure 24-8: Extending the Person class through inheritance.

This separation of interests might be useful even for the JPO application. Now that the system is up and operational, it may occur to the users that they need to be able to delete entries! This does not appear in the requirements and so will probably send us back to the design phase. We hope we can "massage" our existing design so that it has minimal impact on the current implementation.

One possible approach is to add management information to a DirEntry; we can have a Boolean flag that tells us if the record is "in use" or has been "deleted." We can see there is a difference between this attribute and the existing three attributes; what we have at the moment can all be presented to the user and is truly part of the information we would expect to find in a telephone directory. The new attribute has to do with the management of the information on the filing system. Even here, it might be useful to think of a directory entry and of a persistent directory entry.

24.6   Key Points in Chapter 24

- The StreamTokenizer class, from the java.io package, is very useful as a lexical analyzer for simple, fixed-structure files.

- We propose the use of a text-based interface to act as a test application for the classes developed as the result of the design process.

- Where our application is "data intensive," it is often useful to pre-populate our database for test purposes. The populating application is also a useful test of our classes.

- It is useful to identify tests that exercise the boundary conditions of our application.

- When producing a GUI, the appearance and behavior of the GUI should also be designed and prototyped.

- While not graphically illustrated by the telephone directory example, inheritance is, of course, an important consideration during the design process.

24.7 Exercises

1. Show how the `contains` method of the `Index` class could be realized by using the `indexOf` method. Why could this be considered as a better implementation option?

2. You should now implement the birthday system, which you started designing in exercise 22.3. Note that there may be existing classes that you have written or are given in this book that you could use instead of writing brand-new ones.

    For the birthday system, you should provide a GUI interface that allows the user to input a date of birth and that presents the various items of information. It should also allow the user to easily provide different dates of birth as often as he or she wishes.

    You may want to produce a text-based interface to test your classes.

3. a) Write down a requirements statement for the diary component of the JPO. This should only be a short paragraph.

    b) Using the "noun-and-verb" approach, begin the design process by identifying possible objects, services, and attributes.

    c) Design a number of classes to support the diary component; produce H-S&E diagrams to illustrate your design and the interrelationships among the classes.

    d) Implement an "init"-style application to test your diary classes.

    e) Design a suitable GUI that will extend the existing JPO interface for the diary component.

    f) Finally, integrate your diary component software with the JPO.

4. Consider our suggested "computer dating" application.

    a) Implement a version of the `Person` class, ensuring that it contains the following attributes:

    - age
    - gender (male, female)
    - marital status (single, married, divorced, widowed)

    Include the following methods:

    - **eligible.** Returns `true` if the person can be legally married, `false` otherwise.

- **canMarry.** Returns `true` if the person can be legally married to the person provided as parameter to the method call, `false` otherwise.

Write a small test application.

b) Implement a subclass, `PersistentPerson`, that implements a "next free slot" file.

c) Write an `Init` application that creates a `PersistentPerson` file.

d) Write an application that examines the contents of a `PersistentPerson` file and generates:

- A list of all those who are not eligible (forename and surname).

- A list of all pairs of people who could marry each other (forename and surname).

5. For the theater booking system, you should provide a GUI interface for the clerk; this should include a two-dimensional display of the theater's seats and their status. You should have a set of panels that allow the clerk to:

- Book individual seats.

- Book a row of specified seats.

- Book a block of specified seats.

- Search for and display a row of required seats.

- Search for and display a block of required seats.

You may assume the representation of the theater (a collection of seats) can be held in main memory. You may assume there will not be a theater with more than 10 rows and 10 seats in each row.

When the clerk asks for information about a new performance (i.e., one for which no one has previously requested seats), the system should:

- Initialize the theater appropriately.

- Create the file that maintains the persistent representation of the theater.

The layout of a theater should be stored as characters in a file. This could be

```
XXXXXXXXXX
XXXXXXXXXX
-XXXXXXXX-
-XXXXXXXX-
--XXXXXX--
--XXXXXX--
---XXXX---
---XXXX---
----XX----
----XX----
```

You should assume seats are indicated by a row (letter) and a position within the row (number).

You may want to:

- Produce a text-based interface to test your classes.
- Provide an application that initializes the state of a performance from a text file.

CHAPTER 25

Criteria for a Good Object-Oriented Design

25.1 Introduction

In this chapter, we present a number of criteria that are drawn from several sources in the literature (Coad and Yourdon 1991a, 1991b; Korson and McGregor 1990) and are thought to be aspects of good design for a program. Some of the criteria have origins in pre-object work on the modular concept for software, but as you might expect, they are equally valid for objects.

25.2 Cohesion

Designs are made up of collections of pieces. For example, an object is a collection of attributes and methods. Cohesion addresses the degree to which the pieces actually belong together. In a good design, we are looking for *strong* cohesion. Issues of cohesion can be considered for classes, methods, and the inheritance structure.

When we define a class, we want the attributes and methods to be cohesive. We might expect classes to be naturally cohesive as they ideally model some real-world entity. There should be no redundant attributes or methods; they should all contribute to the responsibilities of an instance of the class.

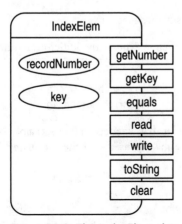

Figure 25-1: The IndexElem class.

In the example in Figure 25-1, every attribute and method is contributing to the responsibility of the class: to represent and maintain index elements. There are no redundant attributes; there are only the two required components of an index element. Two of the methods are selectors, one is a mutator (`clear`), and all are operating on the two attributes of the class. One method is the "standard" `toString`, and two more relate to the persistent nature of the index elements within a file.

The public methods should all be operators of the class. That is to say, they all operate on the (hidden) attributes of the class. There should be no redundant methods.

Similarly, methods should carry out one, and only one, function. We should avoid methods that do only part of a function or methods that do more than one thing. When methods do more than one thing, clients may not fully appreciate it, or they may misunderstand the general purpose of the method. We can say that the "unknown" other purpose is a "side effect" and may cause system behavior that the user will find confusing, to say the least.

Again, with reference to the `IndexElem` class, if we were to provide conventional mutators, we would intentionally provide a single `set` mutator. In other examples, we have had a `set` method for each attribute, and this is often acceptable. However, the way in which we will use index elements means that whenever we set up such an element, we will always set values for both the search key and the record number:

```
indElem.set("Sommerville", 3); // instruction set 1
```

```
indElem.setKey("Sommerville"); // instruction set 2
indElem.setRecordNumber(3);
```

The two sets of instructions in the preceding code are functionally equivalent, but the second set means we accomplish our aim in two steps. `setKey` and `setRecordNumber` are two distinct methods that contribute to our single aim.

Methods that accomplish more than one aim can be confusing. To start with a ludicrous example, consider our `Person` class. Imagine if the act of setting the value of a person's surname also incremented the person's age. If the user isn't aware of this, they could get a surprise when they access the person's age:

```
fred.setAge(5);
fred.setSurname("Jones");
System.out.println(fred.getAge()); // surprise for user
```

If we give the method a sensible name, the name exposes the ludicrous nature of what we have done:

```
fred.setSurnameAndIncrementAge("Jones");    // something wrong
                                            //  with our design
```

A more sensible example might be to consider that whenever a user sets a person's surname, we should clear the forename because we assume the user is in the process of changing the person's entire name:

```
myPerson.setSurname("Jones");
myPerson.setForename("Bill");    // OK
```

```
myPerson.setSurname("Smith");
myPerson.setForename("Jane");        // OK
```

There are a number of problems with this. What if Jane marries Bill? We just want to change her surname and leave her forename alone:

```
jane.setSurname("Smith");
jane.setForename("Jane");
// Jane marries Bill
jane.setSurname("Jones"); /* we've set the surname but lost
                             Jane's forename */
```

Even simpler, the action of setSurname assumes an ordering to the operations. We must set the surname before we set the forename:

```
bill.setForename("Bill");
bill.setSurname("Jones"); /* we've set the surname but lost
                             Bill's forename */
```

It seems pointless to insist on such an ordering.

We return to an earlier example, the Temperature class, which maintains two private attributes, celsius and fahr, and a link between them. When we set the celsius attribute, we make sure the fahrenheit attribute has the correct equivalent (and vice versa). Unless the user has a clear idea of what is actually going on—the class is intended to model a single temperature but maintain a dual representation of that temperature using two different scales—they might not understand what appears to be happening:

```
myTemperature.setFahr(34.2);
System.out.println(myTemperature.getFahr());
myTemperature.setCelsius(12.4);
System.out.println(myTemperature.getCelsius());
System.out.println(myTemperature.getFahr());
```

If they assume there are actually two distinct temperatures, they will be surprised to see that the second printing of the Fahrenheit information is different from the first. They might consider the alteration of the Fahrenheit value to be an unwanted (or at least, not understood) side effect of setting the Celsius value.

Perhaps a better design, which should lead to less confusion, would be to replace the two setFahr and setCelsius methods with a single set method:

```
myTemperature.set(34.2, Temperature.FAHRENHEIT);
myTemperature.set(12.4, Temperature.CELSIUS);
```

The class could contain two public constants, FAHRENHEIT and CELSIUS, which would allow users to specify the scale they are using. Similarly, we could have one get method:

```
myTemperature.get(Temperature.FAHRENHEIT);
myTemperature.get(Temperature.CELSIUS);
```

We use the constants to specify the scale in which we want the temperature returned.

A good guideline for ensuring cohesion of methods is to say that designers should be able to describe a method with a single imperative English sentence containing a single verb and a single direct object:

```
setCelsius : set the value of the celsius attribute to the value of the actual
parameter and set the fahrenheit attribute to the equivalent value.
```

This detailed description has already broken the guideline.

Here we see two verbs and two direct objects:

```
setSurnameAndIncrementAge : set the value of the surname attribute to the value
of the parameter, and increment the value of the age attribute.
```

When we link two classes via inheritance, we should also be asking whether these two classes should really be linked together, or more generally, how strong we consider that link to be. As we know, the inheritance mechanism captures the semantic concepts of generalization and specialization. When we make one class a subclass of another, we need to consider whether that subclass really is a specialization of its superclass. Have we accurately captured real-world semantics, or are we using inheritance as some kind of "useful trick"?

When we model an employee as a subclass of person, it appears to model the real-world situation if we consider the situation in terms of sets and subsets. The set of employees is a subset of all people. Similarly, if we consider the attributes and methods, everything a person has (surname, age, etc.), so too does an employee. And an employee has some additional attributes, such as salary and tax code.

It is a bit harder to defend our suggested use of `Person` and `PersistPerson` in section 24.5 as superclass and subclass. This certainly has very little to do with the real world and much more to do with aspects of software. `PersistPerson` has additional methods, but those methods relate to how we can load and save individual `Person` objects in a file; there is no equivalent real-world concept of a `PersistPerson`. The specialization here refers to how the object will be used in the computer system.

25.3 Coupling

An object-oriented program consists of an *object space*. Objects (clients) can call upon the methods of other objects (servers) in order to get their work done. Objects are naturally dependent upon each other and can be said to be interconnected. Coupling refers to the degree of interconnections.

If parts of a system are tightly coupled (strongly connected), then changes to one part of the system will have a "knock-on" effect on other parts. Ideally, when we change one part of the system, we want to limit the impact of that change on other parts of the system. We want to have weak coupling.

Another benefit of weak coupling is that if we want to understand what a particular object does (if we are trying to maintain the software), we shouldn't have to understand many other classes as well.

We can envisage the way objects interact as a process of message passing. To reduce object coupling, then, we need to reduce the number of messages sent and received by individual objects. Moreover, the amount of data sent as part of a message (the parameters to a method call) should also be kept to a minimum.

The inheritance structure is one place where *high* coupling is desirable, but only when used properly. If it is being used improperly, there are ways to avoid high inheritance coupling:

- Use a mechanism whereby a subclass can explicitly reject attributes from its superclass. This is not possible in Java.

- Use a subclass that is not using attributes of its superclass.

25.3.1 *The Law of Demeter*

As reported in "Surveying Current Research in Object-Oriented Design" in *Communications of the ACM* (Wilfs-Brock and Johnson 1990), the Demeter project (lead by Karl Lieberherr at Northeastern University) is developing CASE tools and their theoretical foundations to improve the productivity of object-oriented designers and programmers. They have produced a rule, the Law of Demeter, which minimizes coupling between classes.

The law states that one should not retrieve part of an object and then perform an operation on that part but should instead perform the operation on the original object, which can perform the operation by delegating it to the part.

In our JPO design, the DirBase contains a reference to an Index object. When we add a new telephone directory entry, the DirBase.add method delegates the process of adding a new index element to the Index object. Our design obeys the Law of Demeter, as shown in Figure 25-2.

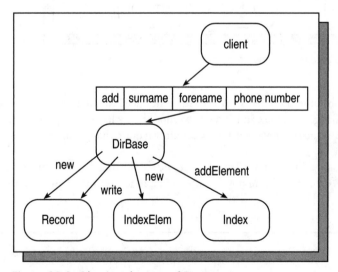

Figure 25-2: Obeying the Law of Demeter.

Here's how we might break the law:

- Add a new method to DirBase: getIndex.

- Use getIndex to obtain a reference to the DirBase Index object:

  myIndex = dirBase.getIndex();

- Now the client program has to create an appropriate index element (so we need previously hidden details on how to use the IndexElem class).

- Then we add the element (again, needing previously hidden details of the Index class).

The law enforces information hiding. If we do not follow the law, it means users can retrieve a subpart of an object and work on it directly (see Figure 25-3). If the structure of the subpart changes, it affects all clients (direct, or in this case, indirect) of the subpart. In a sense, the encapsulation we find so desirable in the object model has broken down. If we obey the law, the change to the subpart only affects direct clients. It shouldn't affect us.

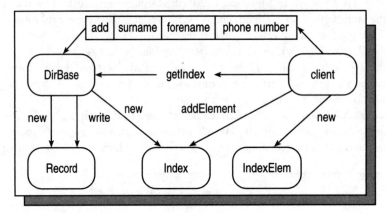

Figure 25-3: Breaking the Law of Demeter.

When we obey the law, clients of DirBase do not need to know anything about Index and IndexElem. Changes to Index and IndexElem should only have an impact on DirBase. When we break the law, such changes will almost certainly require changes to the clients of DirBase as well.

Our discussion at the end of Chapter 10 regarding the use of an OurDate instance to represent a Person's date of birth can now be interpreted in terms of the Law of Demeter.

25.4   Clarity

Clarity is obviously a good characteristic of any artifact we expect other people to use and understand. This can, of course, include our Java source code. What we say here briefly about design can equally be applied to our programming. We should use sensible names for our classes, attributes, and methods. They should be common names (nothing fancy), names that the users can be expected to understand. We should use consistency in naming; we have already seen this with our mutator and selector methods throughout this book (get... and set...).

We have also used capitalization in a careful and consistent way throughout the book. We have used it within names to indicate "visible spaces"; for example, get surname is written as getSurname. An alternative approach is to use underscore as a visible space, as in get_surname. The important thing is to pick a convention and stick with it.

Capitalization has been used to indicate the name of a class; the person class is written Person. This allows easy distinction between class names and instance/attribute/method names. Finally, we have used all capital letters as the names of constants, and it is here that we have also used underscores, as in MAX_STRING_LENGTH.

The names of classes should reflect their responsibilities. If we can't think of a good, simple name for the class we have designed, we should take a closer look at the design! The responsibility of a class should be derivable from its name (for example, DirBase, Index, and IndexElem seem pretty self-descriptive class names, although some might say they are too much of an abbreviation).

25.5 Extensibility of Our Design

A fairly good measure of the quality of our design is to consider how resilient it is to change. In this section, we consider extending our Java Personal Organizer in two ways to see how flexible our current design is and how well it will cope with the proposed alterations.

As far as personal organizers go, our JPO is simple; it only provides a telephone directory! There is plenty of room for extending the capabilities of the system. What we want to consider here is the robustness of our design process. How easy is it to extend the system, and how much disruption does it cause to the software we have already written?

25.5.1 Adding an E-Mail Attribute to a Directory Entry

Consider a minor change; we want our telephone directory to also handle a person's e-mail address. This may be a minor change, but it has repercussions to quite a few classes!

We have to extend our DirEntry class to have an additional attribute (eMail) and alter a number of associated methods (toString, read, and write to name but three). We will need to extend our constructor method(s) to cope and add a new getEmail method. Of course, these extensions can be realized using inheritance.

We have to extend our stored record to have an additional 15 (or more!) bytes to cope with the e-mail address. Notice that this presents problems that cannot be easily handled by inheritance. Our read/write methods, as they are currently implemented, need to know the overall size of an entry (be it index or directory) in the file in order to calculate the starting byte position of an entry from an entry number. We would require a fairly major reorganization of how this is achieved to cope with inheritance. This is because we require information to go from a subclass to a superclass (and this is opposite to the usual flow of information in inheritance schemes).

It would have to be the subclass's responsibility to work out the starting byte position and then call a version of the superclass's read method to read in the attributes it knows about from that start byte.

Our BrowseRecGui class will have to take account of the new attribute that it must now display.

25.5.2   *Adding a Diary Feature to the Personal Organizer*

A more major change is to add completely new functionality. Consider the addition of a diary feature. We can reuse some of our experience of designing and implementing the telephone directory.

We must decide upon what a diary entry looks like; it may be simply a `String` of some length, or we may require something a bit more structured; that is, "indexed" by time of day. Whatever we decide, we can treat a diary entry as a class (`DiaryEntry`) and as a fixed-size record for the file.

As far as the diary is concerned, we may decide that there are a maximum of 366 days in any year, and that we will maintain a file, one for each year, consisting of 366 `DiaryEntry` slots on the filing system. Given a date (day, month, and year) we can calculate which day of the year it is (`dayYear`) and this will be the number of the slot the corresponding `DiaryEntry` occupies within the file for that year. We can, as before, calculate the start (byte) address of the diary entry and read it into a `DiaryEntry` object.

However, if you are like us and do not have a dense diary, you may feel this is wasteful of filing system space. We can try to do something very similar to the telephone directory and use an index sequential storage structure. The diary file could again be a heap, and our index would be sorted according to day, month, and year.

However we choose to organize the diary, we could deliver a `DiaryBase` object for the system. This has minimal impact on the existing system; we need to provide a set of GUI interface classes and add a Diary button to the main menu, but otherwise little else has to change. In other words, we can apply our design experience in providing the Directory Entry Database to the task of building the Diary Entry Database.

25.6   Key Points in Chapter 25

- *Cohesion* is a measure of how well pieces of a design or implementation belong together. In a good design, we are looking for *strong* cohesion.

- *Coupling* is the degree of interconnection among pieces. We are aiming at *weak* coupling; the more an object can stand alone, the less likely that changes to that object will have a "knock-on" effect.

- The *Law of Demeter* provides a rule that, if adhered to, minimizes coupling.

- *Clarity* is a measure of how easily users can understand and employ an artifact. Naming, textual, and layout conventions can greatly assist clarity.

- *Extensibility* is how easily we can extend an existing design or application. Ease of extension is a sign of a good design.

25.7 Exercises

1. In exercise 20.3, we presented a problem regarding holiday accomodation. In essence, we had predesigned the application you were to build. We would like you to examine the structure and design of this application and assess it for quality.

2. In the telephone directory work, we placed the ability to browse in the user interface. This was not necessarily the right decision. If we had decided to test the browsing ability in the text-based interface, we would have duplicated the code. It may have been better to place support for browsing in the `DirBase` class. Decide on the service interfaces and additional state within `DirBase` to support the browsing activity and rewrite the `BrowseRecGif` method accordingly.

3. The need to delete and update directory entries has become pressing. Continue the design work from exercise 22.2, to produce an amended set of classes for the `DirBase` application. Implement and test these classes. Develop the `Init` and text-based test applications to handle the new functionality. Extend the Java Personal Organizer GUI classes to cope with the additional capabilities.

   A possible approach to handle deletion would be to add a new Boolean attribute, `inUse`. You may wish to use inheritance to distinguish between those attributes that truly belong to a directory entry and those to do with management of directory entries within the system. The `Init` application will have to ensure that `inUse` is set to *true* for each directory entry it sets up.

   The question now arises of what to do with the `DirEntry` slots in the file that are not in use. We can change our view of the `DirEntry` file from a heap to a "next free space" model. In other words, we want to reuse the "empty" slots. Note that if there are no empty slots, we return to using the file as a heap.

   You should make appropriate changes to the `add` functionality so that it searches for the "next empty slot" before falling back on the heap technique.

4. Select an applet you are familiar with from your exploration of the Web. Critique the software and, as far as possible, the design of the applet.

25.8 References

Coad, P., and E. Yourdon. 1991a. *Object-oriented analysis.* 2nd ed. Englewood Cliffs, NJ: Yourdon Press, Prentice Hall.

———. 1991b. *Object-oriented design.* Englewood Cliffs, NJ: Yourdon Press, Prentice Hall.

Korson, T., and J. D. McGregor. 1990. Understanding Object-Oriented: A Unifying Paradigm. *Communications of the ACM* 33, No. 9 (September): 40–60.

Wirfs-Brock, R. J., and R.E Johnson. 1990. Surveying Current Research In Object-Oriented Design. *Communications of the ACM* 33, No. 9 (September): 104–124.

Appendices

APPENDIX A

Getting Started With Java

The precise details of how to get started with Java will depend on your computer and the source of your Java environment. Here we list the main steps you will have to go through in order to be able to study the Java programming language—further up-to-date details will be available at the sources listed below:

- First, you need a development environment in which you can compile and execute Java programs. The standard one, the environment described in this book, is called the Java Development Kit (JDK) from Sun MicroSystems. It's possible to download it over the Web from the Sun Web site (http://java.sun.com/), which will give details of how to do so. This book describes a version of Java called 1.1. There is a "read me" document with all the JDK distributions; it is **strongly recommended** that you read this, as it provides details of the specifics of PATH and CLASSPATH settings required to get Java to run on your platform.

   The JDK supplies a command-line compiler (javac) and bytecode interpreter (java), along with a number of other utility programs (such as appletviewer and javadoc). There are also other more sophisticated environments for Java development, such as Symantec Café or Microsoft Visual J++.

- You need to be able to look at the extensive Java API, or documentation, of the standard classes. To do this, you need to have a browser, such as Netscape Navigator or Microsoft Internet Explorer. Make sure it is a *Java-aware* version (Netscape 2.0 or later, Explorer 3.X or later), and then you can use it to download and execute Java applets on the Web, although this is not necessary for looking at the Java API. The Gamelan site (http://www.gamelan.com/) is a good source of interesting applets.

- If you are using the JDK, you will, of course, need a suitable editor so that you can write and revise the source text of your Java programs.

- This book makes use of a number of specially written classes, such as the Person class in Chapter 3 and the BasicIo class, for providing simple keyboard input to a Java program. These are collected together as a package java.lancs, which can be downloaded from the Course Technology Web site at http://www.course.com. This site also contains the documentation on the classes and all of the example programs. Details of how to download and access these and how to adjust your CLASSPATH environment variable are available at this site.

APPENDIX B

Java 1.0.2

This book describes version 1.1 of Java, which was introduced in March 1997. The previous version of Java was 1.0.2. A number of changes were introduced in version 1.1, mostly to the classes provided in the standard API rather than to the language itself. The designers of the new version have arranged that, as far as possible, Java programs written for version 1.0.2 will still work under version 1.1. However, if you try to compile a 1.0.2 program, the compiler will generally complain if the program contains calls of methods that are no longer the preferred way of doing things, although it will attempt to produce a usable program. To obtain more details about the method calls to which the compiler objects, compile the program using the deprecation flag:

```
javac -deprecation filename.java
```

The main differences between versions 1.1 and 1.0.2 are discussed in this appendix. You should note that this is only a *partial* list of the differences.

B.1 Changes to the Abstract Window Toolkit (AWT)

A number of methods in the AWT have been renamed but still carry out essentially the same task. The ones referred to in this book are listed in Table B-1.

Version 1.1	Version 1.0.2
getSize()	Use size() to obtain the current size of the component (e.g., a Canvas).
setEnabled(false)	Use disable() to disable (gray-out) a Button.
setEnabled(true)	Use enable() to enable a Button so it can be pressed.
setSize(x, y)	Use resize(x, y) to specify the size of the main window.
setVisible(true)	Use show() to display the main window or a FileDialog.

Table B-1: Renamed methods.

The main AWT difference is how Java deals with events such as clicking on a button. In Java version 1.1, we implement an interface `ActionListener` to catch clicks on a `Button` instance:

```java
public class Chapter16n1 extends Frame implements ActionListener
    {
    ...
```

We register each `Button` instance:

```java
change.addActionListener(this) ;
```

and then we have an `actionPerformed` method:

```java
public void actionPerformed(ActionEvent event)
    {
    if (event.getSource() == change)
        {
        // code for the "Change" button
        }
    else if (event.getSource() == quit)
        {
        // code for the "Quit" button
        }
    } // end of method actionPerformed
```

There is no separate `ActionListener` interface in version 1.0.2. Instead, the AWT components such as `Frame` provide an `action` method, which we override to provide the behavior we want. So our class header becomes:

```java
public class Chapter16n1 extends Frame
    {
    ...
```

We do not require a call of the `addActionListener` method, since the `action` method is automatically called for all button depressions and similar actions. It looks like this:

```java
public boolean action(Event event, Object arg)
    {
    ...
    } // end of method action
```

For a button, the argument arg is a `String`, the label on the button, so we usually test that to decide which button has been pressed. We must, of course, make sure that each button has a different label, which is a good design principle anyway:

```java
if (arg.equals("Change"))
    {
    // code for "Change" button
    }
```

```
else if (arg.equals("Quit"))
   {
   // code for "Quit" button
   }
...
```

In version 1.1, the `actionPerformed` method is called only if we have registered it for a particular set of buttons. In version 1.0.2, several AWT components may have `action` methods. The system needs to know whether or not a particular `action` method has dealt with an event, and consequently, whether another `action` method needs to be tried. If our `action` method has dealt with the event, it should return TRUE; if not, it should return FALSE:

```
public boolean action(Event event, Object arg)
   {
   if (arg.equals("Change"))
      {
      // code for "Change" button
      return true ;
      }
   else if (arg.equals("Quit"))
      {
      // code for "Quit" button
      return true ;
      }
   return false ;
   } // end of method action
```

In version 1.1, we have to implement a `windowClosing` method (from the `WindowListener` interface) to ensure that our program can be killed off if necessary. In version 1.0.2, there is no `WindowListener` interface to implement and no call of the `addWindowListener` method. Instead, in the class extending `Frame` in each of our AWT programs, we should supply a `handleEvent` method, which looks like this:

```
public boolean handleEvent(Event event)
   {
   if (event.id == Event.WINDOW_DESTROY)
      {
      dispose() ;
      System.exit(0) ;
      }
   return super.handleEvent(event) ;
   } // end of method handleEvent
```

There is no `java.awt.event` package in version 1.0.2; we need only to import the `java.awt` package.

Selecting a menu item is treated in exactly the same way as clicking on a button. The `action` method is called, and we test the second argument for the label on the menu item:

```
...
else if (arg.equals("Load"))
  {
  loadFile() ;
  return true ;
  }
...
```

For tracking the mouse, there is no `MouseListener` interface, nor any call of the `addMouseListener` method in version 1.0.2. There are several ways of handling a mouse click. One is to override a method called `mouseUp` (provided in any class derived from `Component`, such as `Canvas`):

```
public boolean mouseUp(Event event, int x, int y)
  {
  mx = x ;
  my = y ;
  repaint() ;
  return true ;
  } // end of method mouseUp
```

B.2   Changes to the Input/Output System

In version 1.0.2, there are no character streams like the `Reader` and `Writer` classes and those derived from them. The equivalent of `BufferedReader` is the `DataInputStream` class, which provides a `readLine` method:

```
DataInputStream din = new DataInputStream(System.in) ;
String line = din.readLine() ;
...
```

We can then apply a `StringTokenizer` to `line`, as usual:

```
StringTokenizer st = new StringTokenizer(line, " ,.") ;
while (st.hasMoreTokens())
  ...
```

You can read or write files with the `FileInputStream` and `FileOutputStream` classes:

```
DataInputStream din = new DataInputStream(new FileInputStream("text.data")) ;
while (true)
  {
  String line = din.readLine() ;
  if (line == null)
    {
    System.out.println("dropped off the end of the file") ;
    ...
```

Output to a file can use the `PrintStream` class (there is no `PrintWriter` class):

```
PrintStream pout = new PrintStream(new FileOutputStream("results.data")) ;
pout.println("Hello again, world") ;
...
```

Input from a page of HTML tags and text on the World Wide Web can use the `DataInputStream` class:

```
URL index = new URL(getDocumentBase(), "programList") ;
DataInputStream s1 = new DataInputStream(index.openStream()) ;
while (true)
  {
  String line = s1.readLine() ;
  if (line == null)
    break ;
  ...
```

B.3   Changes to the Date Class

The handling of dates and times is simpler in version 1.0.2 (but treats less comprehensively the variations in how dates and times are represented in the different countries of the world). There are no `Calendar` and `GregorianCalendar` classes.

We can find out the current data and time with:

```
Date myDate = new Date() ;
```

We then have a group of methods to extract the various attributes directly from this instance: `getMinutes` (returns 0 to 59), `getHours` (returns 0 to 23), `getDate` (returns 1 to 31), `getMonth` (returns 0 to 11; note this), and `getYear` (returns the years since 1900, so in 1997 the value returned would be 97).

Keywords in Java

This appendix lists all of the keywords in Java, together with the numbers of the chapters where the main uses of the keyword are explained. These keywords are *reserved*—that is, you cannot use them as names of variables, methods, and so on.

abstract (14)	interface (14)
boolean (4, 6)	long (6)
break (4, 5)	native—not discussed in this book
byte (6)	new (3)
case (4)	null (3, 17)
catch (15)	package (3, 7)
char (6)	private (8)
class (3, 7)	protected (8)
continue (5)	public (3, 8)
default (4)	return (7)
do (5)	short (6)
double (6)	static (8)
else (4)	super (8)
extends (12)	switch (4)
false (4)	synchronized (21)
final (8)	this (8)
finally (15)	throw (15)
float (6)	throws (16)
for (5)	transient—not discussed in this book
if (4)	true (4)
implements (14)	try (15)
import (3, 7)	void (3, 7)
instanceof (21)	volatile—not discussed in this book
int (6)	while (5)

Note

A number of further keywords have been reserved for possible use in later versions of the language, and should therefore not be used—these include const and goto.

ASCII & Unicode Characters

Here we list the printable ASCII characters, the corresponding Unicode encoding (which is in hexadecimal, as explained in Section 6.6), and the decimal equivalent.

ASCII Characters	Unicode Encoding	Decimal Equivalent
space	\u0020	32
!	\u0021	33
"	\u0022	34
#	\u0023	35
$	\u0024	36
%	\u0025	37
&	\u0026	38
'	\u0027	39
(	\u0028	40
)	\u0029	41
*	\u002a	42
+	\u002b	43
,	\u002c	44
–	\u002d	45
.	\u002e	46
/	\u002f	47
0	\u0030	48
1	\u0031	49
2	\u0032	50
3	\u0033	51
4	\u0034	52
5	\u0035	53
6	\u0036	54
7	\u0037	55

ASCII Characters	Unicode Encoding	Decimal Equivalent
8	\u0038	56
9	\u0039	57
:	\u003a	58
;	\u003b	59
<	\u003c	60
=	\u003d	61
>	\u003e	62
?	\u003f	63
@	\u0040	64
A	\u0041	65
B	\u0042	66
C	\u0043	67
D	\u0044	68
E	\u0045	69
F	\u0046	70
G	\u0047	71
H	\u0048	72
I	\u0049	73
J	\u004a	74
K	\u004b	75
L	\u004c	76
M	\u004d	77
N	\u004e	78
O	\u004f	79
P	\u0050	80
Q	\u0051	81
R	\u0052	82
S	\u0053	83
T	\u0054	84
U	\u0055	85
V	\u0056	86
W	\u0057	87

ASCII Characters	Unicode Encoding	Decimal Equivalent
X	\u0058	88
Y	\u0059	89
Z	\u005a	90
[	\u005b	91
\	\u005c	92 (Note this character has to be written '\u005c\u005c')
]	\u005d	93
^	\u005e	94
_	\u005f	95
`	\u0060	96
a	\u0061	97
b	\u0062	98
c	\u0063	99
d	\u0064	100
e	\u0065	101
f	\u0066	102
g	\u0067	103
h	\u0068	104
i	\u0069	105
j	\u006a	106
k	\u006b	107
l	\u006c	108
m	\u006d	109
n	\u006e	110
o	\u006f	111
p	\u0070	112
q	\u0071	113
r	\u0072	114
s	\u0073	115
t	\u0074	116
u	\u0075	117
v	\u0076	118

ASCII Characters	Unicode Encoding	Decimal Equivalent
w	\u0077	119
x	\u0078	120
y	\u0079	121
z	\u007a	122
{	\u007b	123
|	\u007c	124
}	\u007d	125
~	\u007e	126

Program Listings

E.1   Person.java

This is the code of the Person class (see Chapters 7 and 8). You will notice that the comments in this code look a little different from the other listings in this book. This is because the comments are in a format that enables them to be extracted automatically by a program called javadoc which creates the documentation for the Person class that you've been accessing with a browser. Thus, the javadoc program knows that a line containing @param contains a description of one of the arguments of a method.

```java
package java.lancs ;

/**
 * Represents simple facts about a person
 * @author Roger Garside
 * @version Last Rewritten: 17th March 1997
 */

public class Person
    {
    // Person Class Constants

    /*
     * Constant - the upper limit for the age
     */
    private static final int UPPER_AGE = 150;

    /**
     * Constant - unknown gender
     */
    public static final int UNKNOWN = 99 ;

    /**
     * Constant - male gender
     */
    public static final int MALE = 1 ;
```

```
/**
 * Constant - female gender
 */
public static final int FEMALE = 2 ;


// Person Instance Variables

/*
 * the person's (single) forename
 */
private String forename ;

/*
 * the person's surname
 */
private String surname ;

/*
 * the person's age
 */
private int age ;

/*
 * the person's gender
 */
private int gender ;


// Person Constructor Methods

/**
 * Creates an instance of the Person class with default values
 * (forename = "NONE", surname = "NONE", age = 0, gender = UNKNOWN)
 */
public Person()
   {
   forename = "NONE" ;
   surname = "NONE" ;
   age = 0 ;
   gender = UNKNOWN ;
   } // end of constructor method
```

```java
/**
 * Creates an instance of the Person class with specified attribute
 * values
 * @param f forename of the person
 * @param s surname of the person
 * @param a age of the person
 * @param g gender of the person
 */
public Person(String f, String s, int a, int g)
    {
    if (f.length() < 1)
      {
      System.err.println("bad forename argument in constructor") ;
      System.exit(1) ;
      }
    forename = f ;
    if (s.length() < 1)
      {
      System.err.println("bad surname argument in constructor") ;
      System.exit(1) ;
      }
    surname = s ;
    if ((a < 0) || (a > UPPER_AGE))
      {
      System.err.println("bad age argument in constructor") ;
      System.exit(1) ;
      }
    age = a ;
    if ((g != MALE) && (g != FEMALE) && (g != UNKNOWN))
      {
      System.err.println("bad gender argument in constructor") ;
      System.exit(1) ;
      }
    gender = g ;
    } // end of constructor method


// Person Class Methods

/**
 * returns the upper limit for a valid age
 * @return the upper limit for a valid age
 */
public static int getUpperAgeLimit()
    {
    return UPPER_AGE ;
    } // end of method getUpperAgeLimit
```

```
// Person Instance Methods - Selectors

/**
 * returns the forename attribute of the person
 * @return the forename attribute of the person
 */
public String getForename()
   {
   return forename ;
   } // end of method getForename

/**
 * returns the surname attribute of the person
 * @return the surname attribute of the person
 */
public String getSurname()
   {
   return surname ;
   } // end of method getSurname

/**
 * returns the age attribute of the person
 * @return the age attribute of the person
 */
public int getAge()
   {
   return age ;
   } // end of method getAge

/**
 * returns the gender attribute of the person
 * @return the gender attribute of the person
 */
public int getGender()
   {
   return gender ;
   } // end of method getGender

/**
 * returns the gender attribute of the person as a String
 * @return the gender attribute of the person as a String
 */
public String getGenderString()
   {
   String x = "unknown" ;
   switch (gender)
```

```
      {
      case MALE :
         x = "male" ;
         break ;
      case FEMALE :
         x = "female" ;
         break ;
      case UNKNOWN :
         x = "unknown" ;
         break ;
      }
   return x ;
   } // end of method getGenderString


// Instance Methods - Mutators


/**
 * set the forename attribute of the person
 * @param f the forename of the person
 */
public void setForename(String f)
   {
   if (f.length() < 1)
      {
      System.err.println("bad forename argument in 'setForename'") ;
      System.exit(1) ;
      }
   forename = f ;
   } // end of method setForename

/**
 * set the surname atribute of the person
 * @param s the surname of the person
 */
public void setSurname(String s)
   {
   if (s.length() < 1)
      {
      System.err.println("bad surname argument in 'setSurname'") ;
      System.exit(1) ;
      }
   surname = s ;
   } // end of method setSurname
```

```
/**
 * set the age attribute of the person
 * @param a the age of the person
 */
public void setAge(int a)
   {
   if ((a < 0) || (a > UPPER_AGE))
      {
      System.err.println("bad age argument in 'setAge'") ;
      System.exit(1) ;
      }
   age = a ;
   } // end of method setAge


/**
 * set the gender atribute of the person
 * @param g the gender of the person
 */
public void setGender(int g)
   {
   if ((g != MALE) && (g != FEMALE) && (g != UNKNOWN))
      {
      System.err.println("bad gender argument in 'setGender'") ;
      System.exit(1) ;
      }
   gender = g ;
   } // end of method setGender



// Other Person Methods

/**
 * increase the age of the person by the specified amount
 * @param n the number of years by which the age attribute should
 *          be increased
 */
public void increaseAge(int n)
   {
   if ((n < 1) || (age + n > UPPER_AGE))
      {
      System.err.println("bad age in 'increaseAge'") ;
      System.exit(1) ;
      }
   age += n ;
   } // end of method increaseAge
```

```java
/**
 * set the full name of the person in one operation
 * @param f the forename of the person
 * @param s the surname of the person
 */
public void setFullName(String f, String s)
    {
    if ((f.length() < 1) || (s.length() < 1))
        {
        System.err.println("bad name arguments (s) in 'setFullName'") ;
        System.exit(1) ;
        }
    else
        {
        forename = f ;
        surname = s ;
        }
    } // end of method setFullName

/**
 * return the formal title of the person
 * @return the formal name of the person ('Mr' or 'Ms', initial,
 *          surname)
 */
public String formalTitle()
    {
    String s;

    if (gender == MALE)
        s = "Mr " ;
    else if (gender == FEMALE)
        s = "Ms " ;
    else
        s = "" ;
    return s + forename.charAt(0) + ". " + surname ;
    } // end of method formalTitle

/**
 * return a string representing the person
 * @return details of the person ('forename surname (age: gender)')
 */
public String toString()
    {
    return forename + ' ' + surname + " (" + age + ": " +
            getGenderString() + ')' ;
    } // end of method toString
```

```
/**
 * return a copy of the person
 * @return a copy of the Person instance
 */
public Person copy()
   {
   Person result = new Person() ;
   result.forename = new String(forename) ;
   result.surname = new String(surname) ;
   result.age = age ;
   result.gender = gender ;
   } // end of methoc copy
} // end of class Person
```

E.2 Chapter20n2.java

This is the applet to access copies of the programs used in this book (see Section 20.4).

```
/**
 *
 * applet to display demonstration Java program source code
 *
 * Written by: Roger Garside
 *
 * First Written: 2/Feb/97
 * Last Rewritten: 30/May/97
 *
 */

import java.util.* ;
import java.io.* ;
import java.awt.* ;
import java.awt.event.* ;
import java.net.* ;
import java.applet.* ;

public class Chapter20n2 extends Applet implements ActionListener
   {
   // picture elements
   private Label label ;
   private TextArea area ;
   private Button main, chap, prog ;
```

```java
private static final int maxNoOfProgs = 100 ;
// list of all programs available
private int noOfPrograms ;
private ProgramDetails[] progs = new ProgramDetails[maxNoOfProgs] ;
private String indexString ;
// list of programs for current chapter
private int noOfPrograms1 ;
private ProgramDetails[] progs1 = new ProgramDetails[maxNoOfProgs] ;
private String indexString1 ;

/**
 *
 * init
 *
 */

public void init()
    {
    readIndex() ;

    setLayout(new BorderLayout()) ;
    setBackground(Color.green) ;

    label = new Label("Main Index", Label.CENTER) ;
    add("North", label) ;

    // set up the text area
    area = new TextArea(20, 80) ;
    area.setText(indexString) ;
    add("Center", area) ;

    // set up the buttons
    Panel p = new Panel() ;
    p.setLayout(new FlowLayout()) ;
    main = new Button("Main Index") ;
    p.add(main) ;
    main.addActionListener(this) ;
    main.setEnabled(false) ;
    chap = new Button("Chapter") ;
    p.add(chap) ;
    chap.addActionListener(this) ;
    chap.setEnabled(true) ;
    prog = new Button("Program") ;
    p.add(prog) ;
```

```
            prog.addActionListener(this) ;
            prog.setEnabled(false) ;
            add("South", p) ;
            } // end of method init

/**
 *
 * readIndex
 *
 */

private void readIndex()
    {
    try {
        // access the file "programList"
        URL index = new URL(getDocumentBase(), "programList") ;
        BufferedReader s1 = new BufferedReader(new
            InputStreamReader(index.openStream())) ;

        // read the program list into the array "prog"
        //    and the chapter names into the string "indexString"
        noOfPrograms = 0 ;
        indexString = "" ;
        String previousFirst = "" ;
        while (true)
            {
            String line = s1.readLine() ;
            if (line == null)
                break ;
            StringTokenizer st = new StringTokenizer(line, "/") ;
            String first = st.nextToken() ;
            String second = st.nextToken() ;
            if (noOfPrograms >= maxNoOfProgs)
                System.err.println("too many programs") ;
            progs[noOfPrograms] = new ProgramDetails(first, second) ;
            if (!first.equals(previousFirst))
                {
                if (indexString.length() != 0)
                    indexString += '\n' ;
                progs[noOfPrograms].start = indexString.length() ;
                indexString += first ;
                progs[noOfPrograms].finish = indexString.length() ;
                }
            previousFirst = first ;
            noOfPrograms++ ;
            }
        }
```

```
      catch (IOException e)
        {
        System.err.println("ERROR: " + e) ;
        }
    } // end of method readIndex

/**
 *
 * actionPerformed
 *
 */

public void actionPerformed(ActionEvent event)
    {
    if (event.getSource() == main)
        {
        label.setText("Main Index") ;
        area.setText(indexString) ;
        main.setEnabled(false) ;
        chap.setEnabled(true) ;
        prog.setEnabled(false) ;
        }
    else if (event.getSource() == chap)
        {
        // get the line selected
        int start = area.getSelectionStart() ;
        int finish = area.getSelectionEnd() ;
        // look for the entry in the "prog" array
        int i = 0 ;
        while ((i < noOfPrograms) && (start > progs[i].finish))
            i++ ;
        if (i == noOfPrograms)
            System.err.println("no chapter selected") ;
        else
            {
            // extract a list of programs in this chapter into the
            //    array "prog1" and the string "indexString1"
            String thisChap = progs[i].first ;
            noOfPrograms1 = 0 ;
            indexString1 = "" ;
            for (int j = 0 ; j < noOfPrograms ; j++)
                if (progs[j].first.equals(thisChap))
                    {
```

```
                    progs1[noOfPrograms1] = new
                        ProgramDetails(thisChap, progs[j].second) ;
                    if (indexString1.length() != 0)
                        indexString1 += '\n' ;
                    progs1[noOfPrograms1].start = indexString1.length() ;
                    indexString1 += progs[j].second ;
                  progs1[noOfPrograms1].finish = indexString1.length() ;
                    noOfPrograms1++ ;
                    }
            label.setText(thisChap) ;
            area.setText(indexString1) ;
            main.setEnabled(true) ;
            chap.setEnabled(false) ;
            prog.setEnabled(true) ;
            }
        }
    else if (event.getSource() == prog)
        {
        // get the line selected
        int start = area.getSelectionStart() ;
        int finish = area.getSelectionEnd() ;
        // look for the entry in the "prog1" array
        int i = 0 ;
        while ((i < noOfPrograms1) && (start > progs1[i].finish))
            i++ ;
        if (i == noOfPrograms1)
            System.err.println("no program selected") ;
        else
            {
            // access the appropriate file of source text
            String thisProg = progs1[i].second ;
            try {
              URL t = new URL(getDocumentBase(), thisProg) ;
            BufferedReader s1 = new BufferedReader(new
              InputStreamReader(t.openStream())) ;
              // read the text into the string "textString"
              String textString = "" ;
              while (true)
                  {
                  String line = s1.readLine() ;
                  if (line == null)
                      break ;
                  if (textString.length() != 0)
                      textString += '\n' ;
                  textString += line ;
                  }
```

```
                    label.setText(thisProg) ;
                    area.setText(textString) ;
                    main.setEnabled(true) ;
                    chap.setEnabled(false) ;
                    prog.setEnabled(false) ;
                    }
                catch (IOException e1)
                    {
                    System.err.println("ERROR: " + e1) ;
                    }
                }
            }
        } // end of method actionPerformed

    } // end of class Chapter20n2

class ProgramDetails
    {
    String first, second ;
    int start, finish ;

    public ProgramDetails(String f, String s)
        {
        first = f ;
        second = s ;
        start = -1 ;
        finish = -1 ;
        } // end of constructor method
    } // end of class ProgramDetails
```

E.3   The GUI Source Code for the Java Personal Organizer

This section of code refers to the Java Personal Organizer discussed in Chapter 24.

E.3.1   The Gui Class

```
// Gui class (main program)
// =========

import java.awt.*;
import java.awt.event.*;
import java.io.*;
import java.util.*;
```

```java
public class Gui extends Frame implements WindowListener, ActionListener
  {

  // link to directory component
  static DirBase  dirBase;

  // application window components

  Button  dirButton, doneButton;
  DirGui  myDirGui;

  public Gui() // Constructor
    {
    super("Java Personal Organiser");
    setup();
    }

  // setup the window for the application
  public void setup()
    {
    setSize(300,60);
    setLayout(new GridLayout(1,2));

    dirButton = new Button("directory");
    doneButton = new Button("done");

    add(dirButton);
    add(doneButton);

    dirButton.addActionListener(this);
    doneButton.addActionListener(this);

    show();

    myDirGui = new DirGui(dirBase);
    } // end of method "setup"


  // Process actions

  public void actionPerformed (ActionEvent event)
    {
    if (event.getSource() == doneButton)
      {
      dirBase.close();
      // shutdown the program
      System.exit(0);
      }
```

```
        else if (event.getSource() == dirButton)
          {
          myDirGui.show();
          }
        } // end of method "actionPerformed"

    public static void main(String[] args) throws IOException
        {
        dirBase = new DirBase("telinfo");
        Gui myGui = new Gui();
        } // end of method "main"

    public void windowOpened(WindowEvent event) {}
    public void windowIconified(WindowEvent event) {}
    public void windowDeiconified(WindowEvent event) {}
    public void windowClosed(WindowEvent event) {}
    public void windowActivated(WindowEvent event) {}
    public void windowDeactivated(WindowEvent event) {}

    public void windowClosing(WindowEvent event)
        {
        dispose();
        System.exit(0);
        } // end of method "windowClosing"

    } // end of Gui
```

E.3.2   The DirGui Class

```
// DirGui class
// ============

import java.awt.*;
import java.awt.event.*;
import java.io.*;
import java.util.*;

public class DirGui extends Frame implements WindowListener, ActionListener
    {

    // link to directory component
    DirBase dirBase;

    // application window components
```

```
Button newButton, doneButton;
Label findLabel = new Label("Find : ");
TextField sNameField;
String sName;

BrowseRecGui myBrowseRecGui ;
NewRecGui myNewRecGui ;

public DirGui(DirBase db) // constructor
    {
    super("Telephone Directory");
    dirBase = db;
    setup();
    }

public void setup()
// setup the window for the application
    {
    setSize(300,100);
    setLayout(new GridLayout(2,2));

    sNameField = new TextField(10);
    newButton = new Button("new");
    doneButton = new Button("done");

    add(findLabel);
    add(sNameField);
    add(newButton);
    add(doneButton);

    sNameField.addActionListener(this);
    newButton.addActionListener(this);
    doneButton.addActionListener(this);

    myBrowseRecGui = new BrowseRecGui(this, dirBase);
    myNewRecGui = new NewRecGui(dirBase);
    } // end of method "setup"


public void actionPerformed (ActionEvent event)
    {
    DirEntry rec;
    int recNum;
```

```
      if (event.getSource() == doneButton)
        {
      setVisible(false);
        } else if (event.getSource() == newButton)
        {
      myNewRecGui.show();
        } else if (event.getSource() == sNameField)
        {
      sName = new String(sNameField.getText());
      System.out.println("request to find "+sName);
      recNum = dirBase.contains(sName);
      if (recNum != -1)
        {
        rec = dirBase.find(sName);
        System.out.println(rec);
        myBrowseRecGui.load(rec,recNum);
        myBrowseRecGui.show();
        } else {
        rec = new DirEntry();
        rec.clear();
        myBrowseRecGui.load(rec,-1);
        myBrowseRecGui.show();
        }
        }
    } // end of method "actionPerformed"


public void windowOpened(WindowEvent event) {}
public void windowIconified(WindowEvent event) {}
public void windowDeiconified(WindowEvent event) {}
public void windowClosed(WindowEvent event) {}
public void windowActivated(WindowEvent event) {}
public void windowDeactivated(WindowEvent event) {}

public void windowClosing(WindowEvent event)
    {
    dispose();
    } // end of method "windowClosing"

} // end of class DirGui
```

E.3.3 The BrowseRecGui Class

```java
// BrowseRecGui class
// ==================

import java.awt.*;
import java.awt.event.*;
import java.io.*;
import java.util.*;

class BrowseRecGui extends Dialog implements WindowListener, ActionListener
  {

  int recNum = 0;
  DirBase dirBase;

  // application window components

  Button  fwdButton, revButton, doneButton;
  TextField fName, sName, telNo;
  Label fNameLabel, sNameLabel, telNoLabel;

  public BrowseRecGui(Frame parent, DirBase db)    // constructor
    {
    super(parent, "Browse Entries", true);

    setSize(300,180);
    setLayout(new GridLayout(5,2));

    fName = new TextField(10);
    sName = new TextField(10);
    telNo = new TextField(10);

    fNameLabel = new Label ("First name");
    sNameLabel = new Label ("Surname");
    telNoLabel = new Label ("Telephone");

    add(sNameLabel);
    add(sName);
    add(fNameLabel);
    add(fName);
    add(telNoLabel);
    add(telNo);

    revButton = new Button("<<");
    fwdButton = new Button(">>");
```

```java
doneButton = new Button("done");
add(revButton);
add(fwdButton);
add(doneButton);

revButton.addActionListener(this);
fwdButton.addActionListener(this);
doneButton.addActionListener(this);
dirBase = db;
} // end of constructor


public void actionPerformed (ActionEvent event)
    {
    DirEntry rec = new DirEntry();
    if (event.getSource() == doneButton)
        {
        setVisible(false);
        }
    else if (event.getSource() == revButton)
        {
        if (recNum != -1)
            {
            recNum--;
            // implement wrapround
            if (recNum < 0)
                recNum = dirBase.size() - 1;
            rec = dirBase.getEntry(recNum);
            load(rec,recNum);
            }
        }
    else if (event.getSource() == fwdButton)
        {
        if (recNum != -1)
            {
            recNum++;
            // implement wrapround
            if (recNum > dirBase.size()-1)
                recNum = 0;
            rec = dirBase.getEntry(recNum);
            load(rec,recNum);
            }
        }
    } // end of method "actionPerformed"
```

```
          public void load(DirEntry rec, int rNum)
          // given a "dirEntry", this loads up the graphic display accordingly
             {
             fName.setText(rec.getForename());
             sName.setText(rec.getSurname());
             telNo.setText(Integer.toString(rec.getNumber()));
             recNum = rNum;
             };

          public void windowOpened(WindowEvent event) {}
          public void windowIconified(WindowEvent event) {}
          public void windowDeiconified(WindowEvent event) {}
          public void windowClosed(WindowEvent event) {}
          public void windowActivated(WindowEvent event) {}
          public void windowDeactivated(WindowEvent event) {}

          public void windowClosing(WindowEvent event)
             {
             dispose();
             } // end of method "windowClosing"

          } // end of class BrowseRecGui
```

E.3.4   The NewRecGui Class

```
          // NewRecGui class
          // ===============

          import java.awt.*;
          import java.awt.event.*;
          import java.io.*;
          import java.util.*;

          class NewRecGui extends Frame implements WindowListener, ActionListener
             {

             int recNum;
             DirBase dirBase;
             String fName, sName, telNoStr;

             // application window components

             Button  enterButton, doneButton;
             TextField fNameTf, sNameTf, telNoTf;
             Label fNameLabel, sNameLabel, telNoLabel;
```

```java
public NewRecGui(DirBase db)      // constructor
   {
   super("New Entries");

   setSize(300,180);
   setLayout(new GridLayout(4,2));

   fNameTf = new TextField(10);
   sNameTf = new TextField(10);
   telNoTf = new TextField(10);

   fNameLabel = new Label ("First name");
   sNameLabel = new Label ("Surname");
   telNoLabel = new Label ("Telephone");

   add(sNameLabel);
   add(sNameTf);
   add(fNameLabel);
   add(fNameTf);
   add(telNoLabel);
   add(telNoTf);

   enterButton = new Button("enter");
   doneButton = new Button("done");
   add(enterButton);
   add(doneButton);

   enterButton.addActionListener(this);
   doneButton.addActionListener(this);

   sNameTf.addActionListener(this);
   fNameTf.addActionListener(this);
   telNoTf.addActionListener(this);
   dirBase = db;
   } // end of constructor

public void actionPerformed (ActionEvent event)
   {

   if (event.getSource() == doneButton)
      {
      setVisible(false);
      }
   else if (event.getSource() == enterButton)
      {
      if ((sName == null) || (fName == null)
          || (telNoStr == null))
```

```
            {
            AlertDialog id = new AlertDialog(this,
                "Incomplete record specified");
            } else  {
            int telNo;
            telNo = Integer.parseInt(telNoStr);
            dirBase.add(sName,fName,telNo);
            sName = null;
            fName = null;
            telNoStr = null;
            sNameTf.setText(null);
            fNameTf.setText(null);
            telNoTf.setText(null);
            }
        }
    else if (event.getSource() == sNameTf)
        {
        sName = new String(sNameTf.getText());
        }
    else if (event.getSource() == fNameTf)
        {
        fName = new String(fNameTf.getText());
        }
    else if (event.getSource() == telNoTf)
        {
        telNoStr = new String(telNoTf.getText());
        }
    } // end of method "actionPerformed"

    public void windowOpened(WindowEvent event) {}
    public void windowIconified(WindowEvent event) {}
    public void windowDeiconified(WindowEvent event) {}
    public void windowClosed(WindowEvent event) {}
    public void windowActivated(WindowEvent event) {}
    public void windowDeactivated(WindowEvent event) {}

    public void windowClosing(WindowEvent event)
        {
        dispose();
        } // end of method "windowClosing"

} // end of class NewRecGui
```

E.3.5   The AlertDialog Class

```java
// AlertDialog class
// ================

import java.awt.*;
import java.awt.event.*;

public class AlertDialog extends Dialog implements WindowListener,
   ActionListener
   {
   protected Button button;
   protected Label label;

   public AlertDialog(Frame parent, String message)
      {
      super(parent,"ALERT",false);

      this.setLayout(new BorderLayout(15,15));

      label = new Label(message);
      this.add("Center",label);

      button = new Button("Okay");
      Panel p = new Panel();
      p.setLayout(new FlowLayout(FlowLayout.CENTER,15,15));
      p.add(button);

      button.addActionListener(this);
      this.add("South",p);

      this.pack();
      this.show();
      }

   public void actionPerformed (ActionEvent event)
      {
      if (event.getSource() == button)
         {
         this.setVisible(false);
         this.dispose();
         }
      } // end of method "actionPerformed"
```

```
        public void windowOpened(WindowEvent event) {}
        public void windowIconified(WindowEvent event) {}
        public void windowDeiconified(WindowEvent event) {}
        public void windowClosed(WindowEvent event) {}
        public void windowActivated(WindowEvent event) {}
        public void windowDeactivated(WindowEvent event) {}

        public void windowClosing(WindowEvent event)
          {
          dispose();
          } // end of method "windowClosing"

        } // end class "AlertDialog"
```

Index